Behaviour in Schools

Behaviour in Schools

3rd edition

Louise Porter
PhD, MA(Hons), MGiftedEd, DipEd, BA, BIntStuds

Open University Press

Open University Press
McGraw-Hill Education
McGraw-Hill House
Shoppenhangers Road
Maidenhead
Berkshire
England
SL6 2QL

email: enquiries@openup.co.uk
world wide web: www.openup.co.uk

and Two Penn Plaza, New York, NY 10121-2289, USA

First published in this third edition 2014

A catalogue record of this book is available from the British Library

ISBN-13: 978-0-335-26272-4
ISBN-10: 0-335-26272-4
eISBN: 978-0-335-26273-1

Library of Congress Cataloging-in-Publication Data
CIP data applied for

Typeset by Bookhouse, Sydney, Australia
Printed by Hang Tai Printing Company Limited, China

For Gerard
who truly, by now, is over it

Contents

PART THREE **The guidance approach**

Figures

Tables

Boxes

Overview

CHAPTER 1

The nature and causes of behavioural difficulties in schools

[Young people] with social, emotional, and behavioral challenges are still poorly understood and treated in a way that is completely at odds with what is now known about how they came to be challenging in the first place.[1]

In his theory of justice, the philosopher John Rawls called on each of us to invent our ideal economic system as if we had no knowledge of our eventual standing within it.[2] Behind a 'veil of ignorance' we *could* design a system of gross inequality – as long as we were willing to risk being on the bottom economic rung, of being one of the system's victims. Similarly, in this book I ask you to consider how you would design a school or classroom, if you did not know ahead of time whether you would be a teacher, a parent or a student and, if a student, whether you would be academically talented or, instead, someone experiencing learning impairments, family adversity, racial oppression and poverty. How *would* we design a system to treat disadvantaged students if there were a chance that we might be one of them?

As the first step towards answering that question, in this chapter, I outline some of the behavioural and emotional difficulties common in children and adolescents and examine their causes. This sets the scene in chapter 2 for a discussion of our aims for the education and discipline of students, in general, and for those with emotional or behavioural challenges, in particular.

Types of behavioural difficulties

Psychologists characterise emotional and behavioural difficulties as either internalising or externalising. *Internalising* behaviours are self-focused and are characterised by under-control. In lay language, they are typically referred to as emotional difficulties. Although the main person to suffer is the one experiencing the emotion, the issues are a problem for both teachers and parents, who routinely are concerned because of the children's anguish, because the behaviours are related to poor adjustment to school and because emotional difficulties can trigger disruptive behaviour.[3]

In contrast, externalising behaviours are directed against others. The overt forms include outbursts of aggression, impulsivity, disruptiveness and defiance.[4] A second class of externalising behaviours – covert actions – are surreptitious. These include relational bullying, telling lies, gossiping, playing mean tricks on others and, at older ages, vandalism and theft, for example.[5] These and the more overt behaviours, are typically referred to as *behavioural problems*. The resulting disruptive acts are considered to be a problem because they interfere with the rights or needs of surrounding people, or violate the rights of the children who are performing them – by, for example, earning them a negative reputation, or limiting their learning or social-emotional adjustment.

Almost all behaviours are functional at some time and in some contexts. A child assaulting and then escaping from a teacher is unacceptable, but the same act might be advisable when directed towards a would-be abductor. Many other behaviours are simply normal, given children's developmental capacities. Therefore, demanding though certain behaviours can be, they do not constitute a 'problem' unless they:

- are part of a constellation of difficult behaviours spanning oppositionality, negative mood and aggression
- are stable over time – that is, they persist beyond the age when they typically begin to decline
- are excessive in terms of frequency or intensity
- are aberrant regardless of age, for example head banging and biting oneself

- are evident in several settings
- are inappropriate in the context and
- impair children's social functioning or educational progress.[6]

Externalising behavioural problems

In the early childhood years, the behaviours that commonly concern parents and teachers are uncooperative behaviour (often termed noncompliance or defiance), high activity levels and aggression.[7] By school age, (as shown in a 2007 survey of teachers in 21 countries spanning 30,000 students), the most common externalising behavioural problems reported were inattentiveness and aggression; lesser concerns included absenteeism, tardiness and disputes between students.[8] Those behaviours that most impinge on school safety such as drug use, gangs, possession of weapons and abuse of teachers, while serious, occur at very low rates and reportedly are not increasing.[9] Violent behaviours, although rare and less frequent in schools than in homes, nevertheless are witnessed by large numbers and hence have an effect beyond traumatising their immediate targets.[10]

Cooperation

Children's cooperativeness increases over the preschool years.[11] With respect to prohibitions (such as not to touch forbidden items), 14-month-olds have been observed to comply 40 per cent of the time, rising to an average of 85 per cent cooperation by almost four years of age.[12] More challenging for young children are requests to persist at mundane tasks, such as packing away toys or sitting quietly during group activities. On these persistence tasks, 14-month-olds cooperate on 14 per cent of occasions, whereas by almost four years of age, children can do so around 30 per cent of the time.[13]

During the time frame of nine to 27 months, children become more negatively reactive in response to having their goals thwarted.[14] However, from 40 months onwards, they can communicate with language, increasingly can use self-talk to direct their own actions, and can direct their attention away from their own desires towards what is being asked of them.[15] Consequently, children with all three skills are better able to cooperate with adults' directives.

Meanwhile, a warm relationship with parents along with autonomy support increases children's willingness to cooperate with adults.[16] This was also shown in a preschool, where children followed 100 per cent of teachers' directives when the teachers' approval rates were high, with only 14 per cent of cooperation when their teachers were disapproving.[17]

Attention skills

A second difficulty that concerns teachers is children's distractibility. This can encompass any or all six forms of attention:

- *alertness*: maintaining an optimal level of arousal
- *focus*: the ability to focus on a task
- *selective attention*: the ability to filter out and ignore irrelevancies
- *alternating attention*: ability to change focus from one aspect of a task to another, and back again
- *divided or parallel attention*: ability to complete one task, while listening to instruction or planning the next activity

- *attention span (concentration)*: the ability to sustain attention.[18]

After their first birthday, children improve in their ability to focus, to resist distraction and to sustain attention.[19] Even so, half of all children aged from five to 10 years are variable, across time and settings, in their attention.[20] Inattentiveness in the early years of school depresses children's academic achievement in first grade[21] and subsequently. This comes about because the children miss out on learning some foundational skills, with the result that they achieve less well academically, particularly in reading skills.[22] This occurs, however, only in classrooms lacking in emotional support.[23] Warm relationships with their teachers motivate children to engage and persist, while structure will make it easier for them to learn – with a consequent improvement in their academic and literacy skills.[24]

Activity levels

The third behaviour that commonly concerns adults is children's overactivity. However, one large study found that at school entry, children with high activity levels achieved better than those who were passive.[25] Beyond school-entry age, though, rather than signalling curiosity and motivation, attention difficulties can indicate poor self-regulation skills.[26]

Trend is important: from three to five years of age, children's activity levels will typically decline and come under self-control so that these levels are appropriate for the situation. Absence of this trend – particularly in boys and when combined with low levels of fear – can lead to escalating behavioural and emotional problems throughout childhood.[27]

Aggression

The fourth behaviour of concern to adults is aggression. This gains perpetrators access to resources and status and, as such, serves a vital survival function; therefore, it is not surprising that aggression has a high incidence in our species. It first becomes apparent in infancy as a result of the emergence of anger, frustration, and an understanding of cause and effect. Infants' developing mobility permits more frequent peer interaction at the same time that their lack of language proficiency gives them few skills other than physical aggression for influencing their peers.

Reactive aggression occurs in retaliation against some real or imagined provocation or threat and arises from difficulties in regulating emotion, specifically anger and frustration.[28] Accordingly, this form is also known as defensive or 'hot-blooded' aggression.[29] In contrast, a second type of aggression is *proactive*. It is not provoked and hence it is also referred to as instrumental or 'cold-blooded' aggression.[30] It is directed towards obtaining desired goals, such as access to resources, or to secure or cement aggressors' social dominance.[31] By school age, children's frequent use of proactive aggression signals not that they are out of control of their emotions, but that they are failing to regulate their behaviour or impulses.[32]

Around 5 per cent of one-year-olds display high levels of aggression that continue to climb, peaking somewhere between 24 and 42 months of age. Following this, aggression begins a steady decline both in frequency and severity as children learn to manage their own emotional arousal.[33] With a few exceptions,[34] most studies report that this decline is most apparent for girls, with the result that, by 18 months of age, highly physically aggressive boys outnumber girls by a ratio of 5 to 1. This ratio persists throughout life.[35] One study found that 3.7 per cent of boys aged five to 12 years were frequently aggressive, compared with 2.3 per cent of five-year-old girls and just 0.5 per cent of 11-year-old girls.[36] A slower rate of decline (or even a slight increase) is seen in children whose mothers have emotional difficulties and in children with difficult temperaments who receive behaviourally and psychologically controlling parenting.[37]

In only 25 to 50 per cent of children does early aggressive behaviour persist one to three years later.[38] By school entry, the majority of children exhibit low to moderate levels of all forms of aggression that remain stable or decline steadily through the early and middle school years.[39] However, as many as 60 per cent of those three-year-olds who have *severe* antisocial behaviours maintain these high rates into the early school years and beyond.[40]

With respect to those displaying externalising problems in general, by the ages of nine to 13 years, four patterns have been found:[41]

- stable low rates (28 per cent) comprising proportionally more girls
- moderate but decreasing rates (53 per cent)
- moderate and increasing rates from adolescence and into middle adulthood[42]
- stable high rates (19 per cent).

The dual failure model of persistent aggression is that students rendered vulnerable by coercive parenting or family adversity experience academic failure.[43] Early-onset aggressors typically have attention difficulties, low reading ability and are weak at persistence, while those whose aggression emerges at school entry commonly have low language abilities.[44] These academic difficulties persist throughout the school years[45] but, on their own, lead to emotional difficulties, rather than to behavioural problems.[46]

Second, students with these risk factors then experience peer rejection.[47] For around one-third of students with moderate and increasing rates of aggression, peer rejection actually precedes the escalation.[48] By default, these isolated students associate with antisocial peers, who then cement their aggressive patterns. It is thus dual academic and social failure at school that leads to escalating oppositional and disruptive behaviours.[49]

Delinquency

As just outlined, there is no late-onset pattern of aggression but instead, for a minority, a continuation of early childhood aggression into adolescence and (sometimes) adulthood.[50] In contrast, delinquency follows two distinct patterns: early onset persistent antisocial behaviour; and a late-onset pattern that is limited to the adolescent years. (There is a third, less common, pattern of adult-onset offending seen mainly in females[51] but that is not relevant to our discussion of behaviour in schools.)

For both females and males and across ethnic groups, delinquency is linked to a lack of parental warmth and to coercive discipline.[52]

Early onset (life-course-persistent) delinquency. A core group of 'early starters' (with a ratio of 10 males to one female)

FIGURE 1.1 The dual failure model of antisocial behaviour

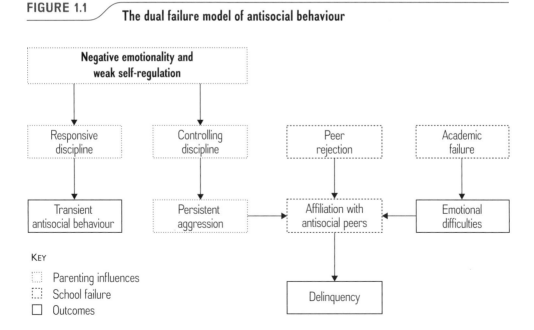

KEY
- Parenting influences
- School failure
- Outcomes

comprising 5 per cent of the population are extremely and consistently antisocial from their earliest years into adulthood, with a steep increase in antisocial behaviour between the ages of seven and 17 years, even as overt aggression declines (but from a high base).[53] By adulthood, as a group these early starters are responsible for 50 per cent of all crimes.[54] Although their behaviours vary across the lifespan, their antisocial quality is stable and is seen in all circumstances: 'Life-course-persistent antisocial persons lie at home, steal from shops, cheat at school, fight in bars, and embezzle at work'.[55]

The prognosis for this group of young people is bleak – comprising addiction, poor employment records, homelessness, unpaid debts, spouse and child abuse, drunk driving, violent assault, and imprisonment.[56] Their property crimes peak in the teen years and decline thereafter, whereas family violence shows a steady increase through adult life.[57]

The causes of life-course-persistent delinquency are cascading, with risks piling on top of each other, progressively closing off prosocial options. These children often start out life with irritable temperaments (either as a result of genetics or prenatal trauma), they are born to parents who lack the psychological resources to nurture them adequately, with maltreatment and neglect common.[58] (In one study, 84 per cent of incarcerated adolescent offenders had been abused by their parents, compared with almost none of the prosocial comparison group.[59]) As a result, these children do not acquire self-regulation skills.[60] They are subjected to coercive discipline, in response to which they become angry, distrustful of authority, aggressive, callous, unemotional, and less empathic towards others.[61]

Once in school they receive punitive discipline. Their early language-based and academic difficulties manifest in failure[62] and, ultimately, in alienation from school. Meanwhile, their antisocial behaviour provokes rejection by middle childhood, making only similarly disenchanted peers available for companionship.[63] Although their friendships are generally supportive, ongoing contact with very delinquent peers can add to the risk of antisocial behaviour.[64] This comes about because of positive reactions within delinquent groups towards rule-breaking talk, which gives members permission to act on that talk.[65]

By 18 years of age, the pattern is set.[66] The same personal qualities that got them into trouble when young (such as poor impulse control) cause repeated difficulties throughout their lives, while their failure to learn prosocial skills and their involvement in a delinquent lifestyle close off their alternatives.[67] Poor educational attainment, early parenthood, choice of an antisocial partner, imprisonment, or a poor work record, for example, eventually close off opportunities for association with prosocial peers and attainment of a conventional lifestyle.[68]

Late-onset (adolescence-limited) offending. A second delinquent pattern begins in adolescence, when around one-third of young people take up antisocial behaviour for the first time.[69] From the periphery, these transitory offenders observe that the rule-violating behaviours of lifespan delinquents give deviant youth access to adult status. Caught between their biological maturity and a lack of access to adult privileges, they temporarily mimic antisocial behaviours, particularly theft, vandalism and the use of alcohol and other drugs (while usually eschewing the physical violence that is more characteristic of life-course-persistent delinquents).[70] Although participating in antisocial behaviour in the company of their peers, these late-onset offenders typically observe school and family rules.[71]

By the age of 20, three-quarters of the late-onset delinquents will cease offending.[72] These individuals have participated in a group phenomenon; they are not psychologically deviant and most will have opportunities for a conventional life.[73] They have endured less social and familial disadvantage and less coercive parenting, with the result that they are less oppositional than are persistent offenders.[74] They have had more opportunities to learn self-regulation.[75] And they have abandoned their delinquent companions.[76] Consequently, as long as they have not left school early and they continue to receive parental support, their average intelligence and good school attainment gives them access to employment and to prosocial partners. Now that they are older, the autonomy of adulthood can be accessed legitimately, while adult privileges would be jeopardised by antisocial behaviour.[77] Accordingly, they desist.

Emotional (internalising) difficulties

In the absence of adversity or harsh discipline, throughout childhood and adolescence, externalising problems typically decline.[78] In contrast, emotional problems (particularly depression) tend to increase over time,[79] rising from around 14 per cent in childhood to 20 per cent in adolescence. It has been thought that

girls are more vulnerable to emotional difficulties, although it could be that boys' declining wellbeing simply starts later, in line with their later onset of puberty.[80] For both genders, there is a steady decrease in their emotional wellbeing through the high-school years.[81] Nevertheless, much of this is the result of family discord or is due to pre-existing emotional difficulties, not to the emergence of new problems associated with adolescence itself.[82] Moreover, adolescents' ultimate rate of emotional difficulties is the same as for adults and still means that 80 per cent of adolescents do not experience the emotional 'turmoil' for which this life stage is notorious.[83]

The exceptions might be that adolescents experience more intense and more frequent mood changes than children and adults, that their energy levels fluctuate more, and that they are more restless than at other life stages.[84] They also seem more self-conscious, anxious and, perhaps, depressed. Nevertheless, most adolescents make a successful transition into adulthood, acquiring greater self-regulation and a more realistic outlook on life.[85]

Any increased emotional maladjustment in the journey into adulthood is likely to be due to lifestyle factors (such as sleep deprivation)[86] and to the reduced support from teachers and denial of autonomy that young people experience within schools' authoritarian structures.[87] Internalising or emotional difficulties are also predicted by individuals' inability to shift their focus away from something upsetting, which makes them more reactive to negative events.[88] Academic success contributes to young people's resilience, while resilience contributes to academic success.[89]

Stress

Around one-third of adolescents are stressed, many chronically so, to the point that their health is at risk.[90] Stressed adolescents experience higher demands, less control and less social support than those who are not stressed.[91] As a result, they have low self-esteem, a performance orientation to learning (see chapter 16), poor eating habits, psychosomatic complaints and sleep deprivation.[92] Their poor emotional wellbeing also impairs their readiness to learn.[93] It seems that the more adolescents there are in the population at a given time, the more stressed they are, because of the extra competition for jobs and university places.[94]

Anxiety disorders

Anxiety disorders include anxiety, panic attacks, phobias, post-traumatic stress disorder, and obsessive-compulsive disorder. Around 16 per cent of individuals will have one of these anxiety conditions during their lifetime.[95] Estimates of their prevalence in adolescence vary greatly, from 5.8 to 17 per cent, with prevalence increasing with age.[96] Around one-third to one-half of episodes of anxiety remit spontaneously (sometimes, however, being replaced by other internalising conditions); without intervention, the remainder persist.[97]

The underlying emotion is fear, while the underlying thought is excessive worry.[98] While it is normal (and, indeed self-preserving) to have fear, those whose anxiety becomes immobilising are sending 'false alarm' signals:[99] they are over-reacting given the degree of threat, and are anticipating and worrying about events that may never happen. They might do this in general, or only in particular circumstances (such as examination anxiety).

Students whose families place them under pressure to succeed can have generalised anxiety and poor adjustment as a result. One study found that highly able young people were not immune to this pressure and that the children of migrant parents (in this case, Asians) were under most pressure to perform at school.[100]

Obsessive-compulsive disorder. Obsessions are persistent thoughts that constantly intrude on rational thinking and cause distress; compulsions are repeated actions taken in response to the obsessive thoughts, with the aim of reducing anxiety and restoring safety.[101] Fears are mostly about harm from contamination and illness, with ritualised washing and cleaning, straightening and checking being the most common compulsions.[102] Some ritualistic behaviour is normal and transient in early childhood, after which the typical age of onset is eight to 11 years, with boys outnumbering girls by 3:2.[103]

Panic disorders. In panic disorders, individuals acquire a fear or dread of their own physical sensations of arousal, and their behaviour (such as refusing to leave the house, as in severe agoraphobia) is an attempt to escape or avoid altogether these physical sensations.[104] Most sufferers (72 per cent) report an identifiable stressor around the time of the onset of the condition.[105] With repeated episodes, sufferers come to fear their own fear.[106] And they make 'catastrophic misappraisals' of their bodily sensations, believing that they are about to die or to lose all control of themselves.[107]

Social anxiety. Social anxiety is the fourth most prevalent emotional disturbance (after major depression, alcohol abuse and phobias), affecting approximately 12 per cent of individuals.[108] Those with generalised social fears have debilitating and overwhelming fear of interacting with others, which results in restricted relationships, reduced educational and occupational attainment and, commonly, other emotional disturbances.[109] Less broadly affected are those with specific performance fears, such as of eating in public or public speaking.[110] Social anxiety disorder is thought to arise from early noxious experiences in interacting with others: specifically, high rates of sexual, physical and emotional abuse, neglect, and victimisation by siblings and peers.[111]

Socially withdrawn and isolated children

There is good reason to be concerned about students who are disengaged socially. First, they are lonely. That is to say, they are aware of a lack of intimacy in their relationships and are sad about that.[112] Although everyone feels lonely on occasion, chronic loneliness is associated with maladjustment.[113] Lonely people experience their interactions as less positive, they have higher levels of stress (as measured by their cortisol levels), experience less restorative sleep and more degenerative changes with ageing, such as elevated blood pressure.[114]

At least 10 per cent of children in primary (elementary) school report feeling lonely most or all of the time, with those who are victimised experiencing even higher levels of loneliness.[115] Much of this is due to poor peer acceptance at school, a lack of friendships, and relational bullying

within friendships.[116] There are four groups of socially isolated students.

Anxious-solitary or 'shy' children react anxiously to challenging or novel social situations, such as entering new groups.[117] Heightened emotional sensitivity, excessive concern about what others think of them, and anticipation of social failure lead to inhibited and awkward social behaviour.[118]

If in early childhood their quests for parental support are rebuffed, they become primed to anticipate social rejection which, if manifested, results in their development of internalising problems.[119] Persistent social withdrawal is also a response to high levels of conflict in the setting, where the presence of dominant children causes tentative children to withdraw in self-protection.[120] In contrast, an inclusive norm reduces children's social withdrawal over time.[121] This indicates the need to intervene with the group rather than with withdrawn individuals.

Unsociability. A second group of isolated children are those described as unsociable.[122] Aloof from others, unsociable students have low levels of both approach and avoidance in social settings.[123] They are seen to be less approachable than purely shy children and are preferred less as companions, perhaps because (unlike shyness) their aloofness is seen to be intentional.[124] Nevertheless, unsociable children are socially competent when they do choose to engage with their peers and their friendship networks are as stable as more outgoing youths'.[125]

Unsociability differs from introversion. Although extroverts and introverts can be equally socially engaged, extroverts are energised by social contact whereas, after a time, introverts become fatigued and seek solitude.[126] Most introverts are as happy with their level of social engagement as are more outgoing children,[127] perhaps because although they may not have a breadth of relationships, they typically develop deep friendships. Their isolation is not a problem unless it causes peers to see them as aloof or unfriendly and hence leads to peer neglect or rejection.[128]

Rejected children. A third group of isolated children comprises those who are frequently aggressive. Among their peers, these children are the least popular, probably because their peers become victims of their anger, hostility, impulsivity and general lack of restraint.[129] Although they initially approach others often, their overtures are frequently rejected because their approaches are often disruptive or aggressive, with the result that, over time, they initiate less often and become increasingly isolated.[130]

Neglected children. Students with intellectual delays[131] and those who are sad or depressed[132] are commonly neglected or ignored by their classmates. It is not clear, however, whether depression inhibits socially competent behaviour and hence causes peer neglect; or if sadness is a result of social isolation or of other negative life events.[133]

Depression

This is the 'common cold' of mental illness in that virtually everyone has an encounter with at least minor depression at some time in his or her life, with the incidence highest in 15- to 25-year-olds and declining with age.[134] Community samples report rates of 2.5 per cent for adolescent males and 7 to 13 per cent for females although, in one study, the rate in at-risk adolescents was found to be around 10 per cent for both genders.[135] Although most (between 31 and 46 per cent) recover spontaneously, without adjustments to their thinking, they are vulnerable to relapses.[136]

Depression has three aspects:[137]

• Emotional despair in which the underlying emotion is sadness, often following bereavement (with grief often being mistaken for depression), conflicted relationships, role transitions and other stressful life events.

• Cognitive symptoms: rumination (recurrent gloomy thoughts), diminished ability to think or concentrate, and indecisiveness. Distorted patterns of thinking maintain individuals' negative views of themselves, their life and their future, and distinguish depression from sadness.

• Physical symptoms: the common pattern is slowing down; disturbed appetite with weight loss; insomnia or sleeping too much; fatigue and loss of energy. A lesser-known pattern is agitation, where individuals are anxious, restless and activated but not systematic in their approach and not seeing activities through.

The pharmacological explanation of depression is that it is a deficiency of serotonin. However, given that levels of neurotransmitters cannot be measured directly, this assumption is only conjecture. It is based on findings that medications that make more serotonin available alleviate depression. But this is akin to concluding that if aspirin relieves a headache, the headache must have been caused by a lack of aspirin. Instead, depleted serotonin may be the result, not the cause of depression; or anti-depressants may simply be masking the detrimental effects on mood of an imbalance of one of the nutrients needed to generate the neurotransmitters (see chapter 11).

Low self-efficacy makes individuals susceptible to depression if they experience a high number of negative life events.[138] Social self-efficacy is particularly potent during adolescence, not only assisting social problem solving but also enabling individuals to recruit social support, with numbers of friends declining with the onset of depression.[139] Bullying by peers causes victims to doubt the collective efficacy of teachers and peers to protect them, in turn lowering their own self-efficacy about their capacity to secure peer support.[140] Finally, controlling parenting is related to depressive symptoms in young people, whereas parental support reduces the likelihood of depression.[141]

Eating disorders

The two eating disorders are *anorexia nervosa* and *bulimia nervosa*. Both involve adherence to strict dietary regimes and sometimes purging through the abuse of laxatives, with bulimia distinguished by episodes of binge eating and self-induced vomiting.[142] Over time, individuals commonly migrate back and forth between the two conditions.[143]

In both conditions, individuals judge their self-worth largely or even exclusively on the criterion of weight, which results in dieting to lose weight. This is contrasted with simple weight dissatisfaction, which tends to lead to dieting until a specific goal weight is achieved.[144] Those with disordered eating mislabel other physical and emotional states as 'feeling fat' and overly scrutinise their bodies, intensely focusing on its alleged flaws.[145] They regard dieting as a positive strategy and, therefore, have little motivation to stop, even when demonstrably underweight and undernourished.[146] Ultimately, the starved body can breach a 'tipping point' where hormones and enzymes become so depleted that digestion is compromised and eating literally does cause nausea. In that case, any individual (however healthy emotionally) would find it difficult to recover physically.

One study in the US found that 11 per cent of nine-year-olds and 7 per cent of 10-year-olds score in the anorexic range on attitudes to eating and body image, with similar rates of body dissatisfaction across cultures.[147] Rates are higher for girls because their perception of their physical attractiveness systematically declines throughout the school years, whereas boys experience a lesser decline[148] (although boys may be catching up nowadays).

The eating disorders have been thought to be due to exercising *too much* control over food intake; however, it seems that they are a type of obsessive-compulsive disorder in which individuals exercise *too little* control over their obsessive thoughts about their weight and appearance.[149]

Drug abuse

Compared with other drugs, addiction to alcohol is relatively slow to develop, with physiological dependence achieved only after three to 15 years of heavy consumption, (compared with days in the case of heroin addiction, for example).[150] Psychological dependence – that is, reliance on alcohol to achieve emotional comfort – develops more quickly, however.

Notwithstanding the scourge of illicit drugs, alcohol is the main drug of choice among adolescents. During the first trimester of pregnancy, alcohol impairs brain development of the fetus, with fetal alcohol syndrome and the lesser syndrome of fetal alcohol effects accounting for around one per 100 live births.[151] During adolescence, brain cells – particularly in the frontal cortex and corpus callosum – continue to build myelin (the coating that speeds signal transmission).[152] This is known as white matter and, in the brains of binge drinkers, becomes less dense, in a dose-dependent manner.[153] Meanwhile, in mid to late adolescence, synaptic pruning occurs to make the brain more efficient, but preliminary evidence indicates that alcohol use inhibits healthy pruning of this grey matter.[154]

Even without damage to the brain, at the time of intoxication, the main social effects of intoxication are disinhibition – that is, people behave in ways they ordinarily would not. This contributes to elevated rates of aggression and risk-taking behaviours. Drug or alcohol intoxication contributes to 10 per cent of deaths, 73 per cent of violent crimes, half of all rapes, over half of domestic assaults, half of all car crashes and one-third of vehicular and pedestrian deaths.[155]

Self-harm

This refers not to the self-injury of people with profound sensory and intellectual disabilities but to people who cut, burn or otherwise injure themselves, the majority of whom are young women. They are no more likely than others to have been abused in childhood, although the subset of adolescents who self-harm following bullying have commonly been maltreated in childhood and have a family history of suicide; they may be depressed, have eating disorders, and have few adaptive strategies for coping with distress.[156] They are not suicidal: they want the pain – but not all feeling – to end.[157] The self-injury can become an obsession, signalling that self-regulation of both thought and emotion is impaired.

Those who harm themselves are commonly alienated from family and other supports. According to Selekman, three forces within the family contribute to invalidation of the young person's feelings and views: the mismanagement of anger, the silencing of women and corresponding lack of permission to express anger outwardly, and family secrets.[158] Why self-harm (as opposed to other symptoms) is the selected means for coping is perhaps due to the calming effect of endorphins that are released at the time of the injury and also to a contagion effect, where peers also engage in self-harming.[159]

Suicide

In people aged 15 to 24, suicide is the third leading cause of death.[160] Child abuse, social isolation, family stress, bereavement and previous suicide attempts are among the risk factors for suicide.[161] For males, one-third and, for females, one-half of lethal suicides have been preceded by prior non-lethal attempts.[162] In the US, the ease of access to guns in the home vastly increases the lethality of suicide attempts.[163]

Suicidal behaviour arises from learned maladaptive thoughts, emotion and behaviour in the face of everyday stressors such as a terminated relationship.[164] Suicidal adolescents have negative views of themselves and the future, and have great difficulty generating and implementing solutions to their problems and therefore see them as insoluble.[165] Suicide is their means to escape intolerable emotions.[166] It is, literally, a permanent solution to a temporary problem.

Being raped quadruples the risk of adolescents' suicide attempts, while those missing school for fear of being bullied are three times more likely to attempt suicide.[167] Gay or bisexual males and those questioning their sexual orientation are at elevated risk for suicide attempts.[168] For gay males, this translates to 45 per cent attempting suicide, compared with 8 per cent of heterosexual youth.[169] Their elevated risk is not the result of their sexual orientation as such, but of a lack of integration into the dominant culture and resulting lack of social support.[170]

Causes of behavioural difficulties

It takes many elements to derail children's emotional development. The process starts with the children's characteristics being met by dysfunctional parenting styles which, in turn, are exacerbated by family and social adversity.

Child characteristics

Other than being male (where the link is uncontested), three other child characteristics have been linked with children's difficult behaviour: their temperament, abilities and health status.

Temperament

Temperament is said to be a constitutionally based or innate behavioural style.[171] With respect to behavioural problems, the three most relevant facets are:

- *Emotionality and reactivity*: agreeable and positive versus irritable and negative. This element contributes to children's 'emotional temperature' as it were: that is, how readily and how hotly they react to events.[172]
- *Self-regulation*: control of attention, impulses and emotions.
- *Sociability*: extroverted and open to experience, versus withdrawn, socially fearful or inhibited.

When researchers gain reports of children's temperaments from the infants' mothers, studies have found that babies who are fussy and difficult later develop behavioural problems such as elevated rates of aggression and high activity levels.[173] However, when researchers measure the children's actual behaviours, this is not the case.[174] The infants do not start out with higher rates of behavioural difficulties; instead, mothers who are angry and who use restrictive control *produce* children with emotional and behavioural difficulties.[175] Parents possess negative attitudes to children even before their children are born, with mothers' parenting style having more to do with their own emotional state and their own childhood history of receiving nurturance, than with their child's temperament.[176]

The mechanism that produces emotional difficulties in children is that coercive and irritable parenting provokes negative emotions in the children; at the same time, parents are unresponsive to their children's needs and accordingly fail to soothe them, as a result of which the children do not learn skills for self-regulation.[177] Subsequently, children's behavioural difficulties persist because controlling and ineffective disciplinary styles become entrenched.[178]

Once these children enter school, they are typically met with the same controlling discipline that is problematic for them at home and which perpetuates their difficulties.

In short, on its own, temperament has little impact on children's trajectory of behavioural difficulties.[179] In the absence of negative parenting, there is no link between infants' emotionality and externalising behavioural difficulties.[180] While it is obvious that in later childhood and adolescence, parents adjust and respond to the characteristics and behaviour of their children, in early childhood at least, the main effects are from parent to child while, even in adolescence, improvements in parenting reliably produce improved adolescent functioning.[181]

Ability

A second quality of students assumed to affect their behaviour is their overall cognitive abilities and language skills.[182] School entrants' academic abilities at the time and their language skills during early childhood predict their academic trajectories, behavioural difficulties in school, and the quality of their relationships with their teachers and peers.[183] Low reading ability is also associated with behavioural problems. However, the relationship between academic failure and behavioural difficulties is weaker than first thought, having been based on teacher ratings – but teachers rate students with behavioural difficulties as being less competent academically than they actually are.[184] Nevertheless, for students with severe behavioural difficulties, the relationship with poor academic achievement seems strong.[185]

The core skill to have mastered by the end of the junior primary years is reading.[186] This is because, in the junior primary years, children are learning to read, whereas thereafter they are reading to learn. Therefore, if they cannot read proficiently by middle primary school, they have a distinct risk of failing across all subject areas. In turn, as academic tasks become more aversive, they are more likely to display behavioural difficulties. Accordingly, researchers have found that low phonological awareness at school entry predicts grade 5 disciplinary referrals (that is, six years later).[187] Students with initially low reading skills but who receive remediation display fewer behavioural difficulties over time, whereas those who start school with average abilities but who make minimal academic gains are the most likely to display both behavioural problems and academic difficulties six years later.[188]

Health

One often overlooked cause of emotional or behavioural problems is children's health. Physical illnesses such as thyroid, hormonal and metabolic disturbances are known to affect mental wellbeing directly.[189] For example, infrequent meals (for some children, longer than 90 minutes between food intake), an excess of high-carbohydrate foods or impaired pancreatic function can lead to hypoglycaemic episodes. Low blood sugars can cause the pre-frontal lobes of the brain to be deprived of sufficient fuel to function.[190] Hence, hypoglycaemia has been found to be the underlying cause of one-third of cases of attention deficit disorder.[191] Given that the brain has only three functions – thinking, feeling and behaving – hypoglycaemia and other health problems such as those listed in Box 1.1 can affect any or all of the brain's functions.

BOX 1.1   **Some health factors affecting nervous system functioning**

Allergies and intolerances

Allergies result when B cells of the immune system produce antibodies that attack partially digested proteins, whereas intolerance occurs when T cells produce an inflammatory response.[192]

- *Gluten.* After the gastrointestinal system, the second most commonly affected organ in celiac disease (an allergy to gluten) is the nervous system, producing both neurological symptoms[193] and emotional disturbance. Children with celiac disease are at increased risk of schizophrenia in adulthood; in reverse, as many as two-thirds of adults with schizophrenia manifest a gluten intolerance.[194]

Infections

The presence of viruses in the body causes the release of 'alarm molecules' known as cytokines that alert immune cells to the presence of a pathogen.[195] These cytokines cross the blood–brain barrier so that the immune cells within the brain can be triggered to protect the brain from damage. In turn, these immune cells in the brain release hydrogen peroxide to kill the pathogen, and nitric oxide to safeguard nearby cells by putting them into effective hibernation.[196] Nitric oxide is a toxic free radical that produces inflammation and affects both the development and function of the nervous system, damaging acetylcholine and GABA receptors in particular.[197]

- *Herpes viruses: herpes simplex* (cold sores), *herpes zoster* or chicken pox, Epstein-Barr virus and CMV. *Herpes simplex* has been found to migrate from the oesophagus to the enteric nervous system (nerves within the gut wall) and, from there, to neurones within the brain stem.[198]
- *Influenza.* There is an increased incidence of schizophrenia in children whose mothers contract the flu during the fifth to seventh months of pregnancy.[199] The cause appears not to be the flu virus itself, but that the antibodies produced by the mother in response to infection somehow alter the brain development in the fetus. Specifically, dopamine and glutamine receptors are implicated.[200]
- *Streptococci* infections can affect the nervous system.[201] For example, they can instigate obsessive-compulsive disorder in children, which is known as a PANDAS condition: a Pediatric Autoimmune Neuropsychiatric Disorder.[202]
- *Toxoplasma gondii.* Maternal infestation with this parasite in the first trimester of pregnancy can lead to severe neurological problems in the fetus; infection of the baby at birth has been linked to the development of schizophrenia later in life.[203] The parasite is neurotropic (capable of infecting nerve cells), affecting neurotransmitter production.[204]

Nutrient deficiencies

Nerve tissue is more sensitive than any other to nutrient deficiencies.[205] Even prenatal deficiencies can be devastating, with famine followed 20 years later by increased schizophrenia in the young adult population.[206]

- *Vitamins and minerals.* Brain function can be affected when individuals are deficient in any of the nutrients involved in neurotransmitter production: in particular, the vitamins B_2, B_3, B_6, and C; and the minerals calcium, copper, iron, folate, magnesium and zinc.[207] Zinc deficiency is especially common and is linked to depression and sleep disturbances through insufficient production of serotonin and, in turn, the sleep hormone, melatonin. A prenatal deficiency of zinc is highly suspect in children's emotional and behavioural problems.[208]
- *Essential fatty acids.* The human brain is around 60 per cent fat (by dry weight).[209] For optimal communication between brain cells and for optimal production of the neurotransmitter dopamine, cell membranes must contain adequate essential fatty acids (omega-3s in particular).[210] A deficiency of essential fatty acids, then, affects brain function. This is confirmed in studies finding high rates of depressive and bipolar disorders in geographic regions with a low intake of seafood (that is, diets low in essential fatty acids).[211]

Toxicity

Given that many toxins have an affinity for fat cells and that the brain is substantially comprised of fat cells, once the body is toxic, the brain will be affected.

- *Alcohol.* Prenatal exposure to high levels of alcohol (as found in maternal binge drinking) impairs children's intellectual and language skills, with learning, behavioural and social problems emerging by school age.[212]
- *Lead* interferes with the production of neurotransmitters and can produce a false neurotransmitter (ALA) that competes with the true neurotransmitter, GABA.[213] This inhibits the nervous system, preventing it from becoming over-active and hence lead poisoning contributes to attention deficits.[214]

Family stress

Family chaos or instability can also be detrimental to children.[215] Family adversity is associated with unpredictable displays and poor regulation of emotion, low positive affect and high negative affect within the family.[216] Adversity engenders high stress levels, making it difficult for parents to be responsive to their children. Both family adversity and coercive parenting foreshadow either the persistence of early childhood behavioural problems into middle childhood, or the emergence of problems in the early school years.[217]

Ongoing unresponsive and punitive parenting causes children to lack the skills needed for social competence, which manifests as peer difficulties throughout the school years and subsequent elevated risk of delinquency during adolescence.[218]

Nevertheless, when parents enduring adverse life circumstances can interact positively with their children despite the stress, their children adjust socially and behaviourally.[219] Even when their children have challenging behaviours in the preschool years, these tend to improve by school entry.[220]

Qualities of parents

Parents' personal characteristics before the birth of their child are strong predictors of their child-rearing practices and the child's temperament and behavioural dispositions.[221] The most significant include low maternal acceptance – that is, high levels of conflict between mother and child – drug use, and being criminal or antisocial.[222] Children with antisocial fathers are actually better adjusted and behave more cooperatively when their father is absent.[223] All other parental characteristics such as a mother's depression or mental illness, or being in her teens when her first child is born, seem to adversely affect children only if the circumstance disrupts responsive and supportive parenting.[224]

Abuse

Abuse and neglect produce early-onset aggression[225] and treble the likelihood of life-course-persistent aggression,[226] with over 40 per cent of children who are physically abused in the first five years of life going on to become reactively aggressive (compared with 15 per cent of children who are not abused).[227] As another measure, in one study, 84 per cent of incarcerated adolescent offenders had been abused by their parents, compared with almost none of the prosocial comparison group.[228]

Emotional abuse encompasses shouting, swearing or cursing at children, threatening to spank them, calling them names and threatening to kick them out of home.[229] One study found that over 88 per cent of young people aged under 17 years were exposed to such abuse in any one year.[230] And, whereas the frequency of the use of corporal punishment declines with age, verbal abuse increases with the children's ages.[231] As discussed in chapter 11, this psychological abuse is perpetrated not only by parents and other family acquaintances, but also by teachers. Fifteen per cent of students suffer repeated verbal abuse from their teachers from as early as their first year of school, persisting for many years through to adolescence.[232] Many of these students are also bullied by their peers,[233] perhaps because teacher abuse gives permission for peers to disrespect the targeted student also.

Box 1.3 lists some common signs and effects of abuse, which represent a cascade of neurological and emotional damage known as 'trauma spectrum disorders', and characterised by poor emotional regulation in maltreated children.[234] In turn, emotional dysregulation affects all aspects of abused children's competence: academic, social and behavioural.[235] In addition to emotional problems such as post-traumatic stress, depression, impulsiveness and

BOX 1.2   Statistics about child abuse[236]

Estimates of overall rates	4–11 per cent
Reported rates of physical, emotional abuse or neglect	16.5 per cent
Sexual abuse of girls	15–38 per cent
Sexual abuse of boys	7–16 per cent

aggression, children's social competence is the most impaired. Those who experience maltreatment from their parents develop expectations that others will be uncaring and, applying these expectations to peers, either anticipate hostile behaviour and act aggressively towards peers, or cope with their distress by constricting emotion and lacking empathy.

When child abuse occurs together with partner violence, the children have even more extreme emotional and behavioural difficulties and are slower to recover from stressful events.[237] In one study, the combination elevated by 500 per cent the risk of children's becoming aggressive victims of bullying (which risk is ordinarily 6 per cent).[238]

BOX 1.3   **Signs and effects of child abuse[239]**

Emotional adjustment

Child abuse activates the pituitary and adrenal glands, leading (among other things) to the production of excess cortisol, which makes children more reactive to stressors and less able to regulate their emotional reactions. Activation of the stress response leads to dominance of the sympathetic nervous system, which governs the flight–fight response (in contrast to the calming function of the parasympathetic nervous system). Irritability of the limbic system (the seat of emotions in the brain) and reduction in size of some parts of the pre-frontal cortex can produce deficits in self-awareness, self-regulation and perception of others, producing emotional symptoms such as the following.

- Maltreated children are hypervigilant for signs of potential threat.
- Neglected children in particular but abused children overall typically have lowered self-esteem. Parental criticism and insults cause them to see themselves as less worthy and to doubt that their peers will accept them.
- Many victims of child abuse display anxiety, depression, fearfulness, agitation and post-traumatic stress.
- Survivors of childhood abuse have a heightened risk of suicide.
- Most have low self-efficacy as a result of being unable to deflect the abuse.
- They demonstrate poor emotional coping. For example, they remain emotionally distressed for longer when observing unresolved conflict between others.

Social skills

Social skills are the most impaired by abuse and neglect, with maltreated children displaying fewer prosocial behaviours and more negative behaviour directed at peers and adults.

- They demonstrate poor social problem-solving strategies and conflict resolution skills. Their interactions are often unskilful.
- Abused children often display social anxiety. They may withdraw socially, interacting little with peers and being less responsive to friendly overtures from surrounding adults or children.

- Maltreated children have little understanding of their own or others' feelings. Their abilities to appreciate others' perspectives and to be empathic are impaired: they will be less likely to show concern or offer help to upset peers and will perhaps even delight in others' distress.
- They may not seek comfort from others when distressed themselves.
- They experience rejection from peers and adults.

Behaviour
Both maltreated and neglected children commonly have deficits in self-regulation that affect their regulation of both emotions and impulses.

- Abused children tend to vent rather than inhibit angry responses and other negative emotions.
- They are more disruptive in class, and cause peers more distress.
- The most common characteristic of chronically and severely abused children is aggression towards peers and adults.
- Over-excitability of neurones can lead to impulsivity and hyperactivity.
- In later life, abused children are more likely to be addicted to alcohol, nicotine and illicit drugs.

Relationships with adults
- Abused children are commonly hostile and uncooperative with adults, sometimes assaulting or threatening adults as a result of their experience that adults can be dangerous.
- They might 'freeze' in the presence of their abuser or be reluctant to accompany a particular adult, or adults in general. Alternatively, abused children can be highly dependent on adults.

Academic skills
Children's disorganised home environments, disrupted routines and inadequate supervision limit their ability to complete academic work at home or to be fully prepared for the school day. Long-term elevated cortisol levels contribute to delays in social, motor and cognitive skills. The mechanism may well be that childhood abuse is associated with a reduced size of the corpus callosum (the bundle of nerves connecting the two cerebral hemispheres), which causes diminished left-right integration, affecting all academic skills. There is also an indication that neurological changes impair working memory, attention and reasoning.

- Neglect results in a lack of stimulation that causes overall intellectual impairments and delayed language skills, particularly verbal expression.
- Neglected and physically abused children tend to perform at low levels academically. At younger ages, this is most pronounced for reading skills whereas, by late primary school, the disadvantage is across all subject areas. This may be because the stress response alters the thinking and memory centres of the brain, such as the hippocampus.
- Neglected children are often passive and helpless in their task orientation; give up easily; do not cope well with frustration; and are distractible, impulsive and lacking in initiative.
- Neglected children are more reliant on adult directions and have learned to rely on external consequences, being less intrinsically motivated.

- Physically abused children's reduced engagement in learning and their view of themselves as academically incompetent lead to declines in their school achievement, with the result that they are more likely to experience academic failure, be retained in a grade, have high levels of absenteeism and elevated rates of special education referrals.
- Children who have been neglected or physically abused are more likely to be suspended from school or drop out early.
- Children experiencing sexual abuse typically achieve reasonably well at school. This is remarkable given that their anxiety levels must make it difficult to concentrate on academic tasks.
- Sexually abused children often display knowledge of adult sexual behaviour that is in advance of their years or developmental level.

Physical signs

Because their immune system is compromised by chronic stress, many maltreated children suffer long-term somatic complaints.

- Children enduring physical abuse may have injuries such as bruises, welts, burns or fractures which have no convincing causal explanation.
- They might show little response to pain.
- Those suffering sexual abuse can have injuries or infections to the genital or anal areas, or throat.
- Many have sleep disturbances.
- Sexually abused girls experience earlier menarche, sexual debut and childbirth (18 months earlier than average) and commonly have problems with sexual intimacy.
- Alteration to the GABA receptors in the amygdala causes neurones to be over-excitable, which can trigger seizures.
- Prolonged stress increases the risk of obesity and type II diabetes, and accelerates the ageing and degeneration of brain cells in later life.

Poverty

Children are the most likely of any social group to be experiencing poverty (with the elderly being the next most probable group). In Australia, approximately 20 per cent of children live in poverty, with this figure considerably higher among Aboriginal children; the rate for the UK is 26 per cent, double that of a generation ago; the US rate falls between 20 and 30 per cent, with 8 per cent living in extreme poverty.[240] Even when family income is at double the poverty level, many families still experience economic hardship, which means that they lack sufficient income to cover living expenses, health and educational costs.[241]

Particularly when it is prolonged, poverty has a toxic effect on children across all domains, as listed in Box 1.4. Evidence of its developmental effects is found in the statistic that the rate of mild intellectual disability is eight times higher in the US than in Sweden, which Sameroff attributes to the superior levels of support available in Sweden to impoverished families.[242] Poverty during adolescence is also associated with earlier age of first childbirth and, thence, to harsh parenting and consequent behavioural problems in the next generation.[243]

As is the case for other forms of family adversity, poverty itself is not directly related to children's behavioural problems, such as aggression, but appears to exert its effect by disrupting responsive parenting.[244] This is not inevitable, however. On its own, socioeconomic level contributes only a 2 to 7 per cent increase in children's behavioural difficulties.[245] This is because, independent of family income levels, parents who have high self-efficacy are able to nurture their children and invest in them emotionally – and thereby avoid many of the deleterious effects that social disadvantage otherwise exerts on children.[246]

BOX 1.4   **Effects of poverty on children[247]**

- *Substandard accommodation.* Impoverished families are more likely to experience substandard and crowded housing, repeated change of residence, and limited social supports within a stressed or dangerous neighbourhood.
- *Health.* Children living in poverty are vulnerable to poor nutrition and elevated levels of stress hormones, both of which compromise their immune system. Consequently, they are more likely to experience fatigue, headaches, concentration difficulties and a range of illnesses. Restricted access to health care exacerbates these problems.
- *Development.* A lack of stimulation and poor health causes children growing up in poverty to display impaired cognitive and language skills by school entry. This has been measured as a loss of nine IQ points for children enduring persistent poverty, and four points for those experiencing transient hardship. These delays are enduring and difficult to alter subsequently.

    Harsh parenting that can arise from the stress of economic hardship lowers children's language comprehension skills relative to children whose parents use reasoning and negotiation in their discipline. Language impairments are found in 26 per cent of girls and 35 per cent of boys living in poverty. Low-quality childcare and under-resourced preschools and schools do not redress this inequity. Children's motor skills, however, are not affected.
- *Recreation.* Impoverished children and families have restricted access to leisure activities, for which costly sporting equipment will be unaffordable. In the resulting absence of recreational choice, they may become involved in antisocial behaviour.
- *Strained family relationships.* Financial strain is a direct source of stress for all family members, initiating conflict between them and leading to insensitive, unresponsive and harsh parenting; higher rates of parental conflict; and, commonly, a series of parental separations.
- *Emotional wellbeing.* Current (as opposed to previous) economic stress, family conflict and harsh parenting produce a deterioration in children's emotional adjustment. Impoverished children and

adolescents learn maladaptive coping strategies and fail to acquire emotional regulation skills, thus raising their propensity to anxiety and depression.

- *Antisocial behaviour.* Children's behaviour is especially susceptible to environmental influences. Harsh parenting fails to teach children socially competent problem solving, which exacerbates their aggression. The result is that between 20 and 30 per cent of disadvantaged children aged under five display behavioural difficulties such as aggression, which is around five times the rate of the general population. By the age of 10, 9.4 per cent continue to evidence severe behavioural problems, which is just under three times higher than usual. In adulthood, they display six times the rate of criminal behaviour.

Diverse family structures

It is not family *diversity* but *adversity* that affects children's adjustment. Single parenthood, for example, can be stressful for the adults, potentially reduce parental supervision and support for the children, and precludes one parent's acting as a check on the other's overly lax or controlling discipline.[248] Accordingly, single-parent families are sometimes accused of generating poorer educational outcomes and emotional adjustment for children.[249] However, children raised by stable single parents are as well adjusted as those in two-parent, contented families.[250] Any detrimental effects are due not to single parenthood, as such, but to the deepened poverty that commonly follows marital separation, ongoing parental conflict, and whether the parent subsequently experiences a sequence of disharmonious romantic relationships.[251] When these additional stressors can be avoided or managed, many young people in sole-parent families report that they enjoy a particularly close relationship with their parent.[252]

As for the effects on children of their parents' divorce, young people growing up within a stressed marriage experience poorer adjustment and greater disillusionment with relationships than those who grow up with a single parent who is less stressed.[253] At the time, parental separation produces small increases in the emotional and behavioural problems of young children in particular but, if these persist, they are not due to the parental separation but to other factors such as the acrimony, parenting problems and socioeconomic difficulties that preceded and contributed to the divorce.[254] Even then, differences in adjustment between children of divorced and intact families are small.[255]

Neighbourhoods

As children near middle childhood, they become increasingly exposed to their neighbourhood. Whereas non-delinquents make their friends at school, delinquents make their friends from outside of school.[256] The risk of association with delinquent peers is higher in impoverished neighbourhoods, doubling the risk of antisocial behaviour in children aged over 10 years.[257] Nevertheless, only extreme neighbourhood disadvantage is associated with behavioural difficulties in school-aged children, affecting mostly males who lack self-regulation, whereas students with high self-efficacy and high expectations for their future tend to resist the influence of antisocial individuals within their orbit.[258] And parents can insulate their sons and daughters from poor academic outcomes by taking an interest in their educational success and monitoring their friendships.[259]

School quality

Although school-based behavioural difficulties are often blamed on students' disadvantaging home lives, school settings which meet student needs for affiliation, competence and autonomy encourage students' bonding, engagement and academic achievement and successfully reduce every health risk except teen pregnancy.[260]

Nevertheless, although not a unanimous experience,[261] students' identification and satisfaction with school typically decline from 7th to 11th grades, particularly for males, for members of ethnic minorities, and for those from low socioeconomic groups.[262] In all likelihood, this estrangement comes about because of a growing mismatch between student needs and the opportunities and structures provided by school.[263] Specifically, high schools are typically larger than primary schools, with looser relationships with teachers at a time when young people continue to need support; are competitive at an age when young people are self-conscious; and are more controlling when youth need more autonomy.[264] All of these changes are in the opposite direction to what young people need and impair both adult and peer social support.[265]

BOX 1.5   **Qualities of effective schools[266]**

Safety
- How safe students feel from violence.
- Teacher commitment to clear and fair measures for responding to disciplinary problems.
- Low levels of drug and alcohol problems.

Autonomy
- *Structure*: how much teachers emphasise order for its own sake, versus supplying structure to enable students to achieve.
- *Self-regulation*: an emphasis on student self-regulation, rather than on the imposition of rewards and punishments, to maintain order.
- *Control*: working with students jointly to shape a productive and accepting setting.
- *Student decision making*: mechanisms for student input into decisions concerning their learning and school governance.

Belonging
- *Affiliation*: positive climate, sense of community, how well the students feel that they know each other, how willing they are to assist each other, how much they enjoy working together, the level

of interaction between student groups, and absence of gossip, particularly about peers' sexual behaviour.

- *Personal involvement with teachers*: reciprocal communication, the existence of pastoral care programs, the level of support or care students receive from teachers.
- *Competition*: the extent to which students compete with each other for grades and personal recognition in the classroom.
- *Acceptance of diversity*: as signalled by flexible dress codes, acceptance of the use of students' first language at school and inclusive practices across cultures, ability levels and genders.

Competence
- *Task orientation*: how much emphasis is placed on the content of tasks – getting them completed and being correct – compared with a focus on the learning process.
- *Engagement*: student active engagement in academic learning and extracurricular activities.
- *Innovation*: the extent to which teachers encourage student creativity and use innovative teaching practices.
- *Educational purpose or goals*: provision of explicit teaching for basic skills acquisition.
- *High expectations for student accomplishments*.

Organisational qualities
- Small classes with individual support.
- Purposeful leadership by the principal that also affords teachers professional autonomy.
- Effectiveness, visibility and accessibility of the principal.
- The availability of extracurricular activities.
- Facilities that are well maintained.
- Innovations driven from the bottom up, rather than imposed from the top down.
- Record keeping to monitor the effectiveness of teaching and disciplinary practices.
- Low levels of staff turnover.

Support for teachers
- High levels of teacher and collective self-efficacy.
- Collegial planning and exchange of ideas among staff.
- Ongoing professional development in topics salient to teachers.
- Preparation time to plan lessons.
- Support from the governing body.
- Minimal bureaucratic demands on teachers, while maintaining their accountability for student learning.

Community engagement
- Open door policy towards parents.
- Collaboration with and support for parents.

Young people display different behavioural difficulties at home from those seen in school. This indicates that it is not only child factors that are responsible for behaviours in the school setting.[267] Approximately 25 per cent of the variance in children's aggression is related to school factors.[268] Differences in achievement outcomes, attitude to school and – to a lesser extent – rates of absenteeism and other behavioural difficulties between schools are systematically related to schools' quality.[269] As an indicator of effects on academic achievement, in one study, the most effective schools improved (on a scale of 100 and with an average of 54 points) primary students' reading scores by 15 points beyond that predicted by their ability, whereas students in the least effective schools showed declines of 10 points.[270]

Culture

The school's culture represents its aspirational values, its goals and norms, the roles and relationships that exist between members of the school, and the history and traditions that distinguish it.[271] It is the atmosphere, climate, resources and social networks of the school.[272] It could be said to be the 'personality' of a school, or 'the way we do things around here'.[273] A setting where students feel secure, respected, nurtured and supported predicts students' satisfaction with and commitment to school.[274] Specifically, qualities of schools that affect students' engagement are students' connectedness to school; the academic support they receive; their trust in their teachers; school norms; student perceptions of their safety; and (to a lesser extent) school size and socioeconomic level; positive relationships with their teachers are also vital.[275]

Connectedness to school

With respect to connections to school, both teachers and students who experience their school as being supportive and caring become committed to the attitudes, values and skills promoted by the school.[276] From students' perspective, bonding has three aspects: a sense of social belonging, a commitment to academic work, and a commitment to the school as an institution.[277] School bonding has a pervasive influence on students' wellbeing and social skills and seems to be the determining factor in student achievement.[278] It reduces disruptiveness at school, aggression, risk-taking on the roads, drug use, likelihood to offend, and dropouts.[279] School bonding can be so powerful as to offset neighbourhood or community disadvantage,[280] as well as family adversity. In reverse, poor bonding to school, distant relationships with teachers, and a lack of striving for achievement all precede delinquency; and then delinquency contributes to poor bonding to school.[281]

Academic support

Students' satisfaction with school strongly predicts their engagement.[282] This satisfaction is based on a contract between teachers and students which upholds that students will invest expert teachers with moral authority and will consent to cooperate with them.[283] Ordinarily, even less capable teachers can secure the consent of students by exchanging the incentive of good grades for student cooperation.[284] However, those who are unable to experience success are more likely than successful students to withdraw from school psychologically and, ultimately, behaviourally by absenting themselves or dropping out. When students come to regard schooling and grades as irrelevant to their life chances, they do not value this trade.

Meanwhile, those whose needs, values and interests are excluded from the curriculum exclude themselves from engaging in something that accrues little of value for them.[285] Therefore, improving school quality can do much to advance student achievement and, thereby promote in students both a commitment to schooling and a sense of academic self-efficacy.[286]

Trust in teachers

Students' engagement at school is intimately linked to their trust in their school and their teachers.[287] Trust forms through experience interacting with others and is an assessment that the other party is open, honest, reliable, competent and benevolent.[288] Even alienated students who have been permanently suspended from school report that they want respectful relationships with their teachers.[289] Students expect teachers to treat them with respect and dignity, and to be neutral and impartial in their disciplinary responses (that is, they wish for procedural fairness).[290] When they experience their teachers as fair, they are likely to remain committed to the school, to education and to their own learning.[291]

Perceived injustices at the hands of teachers, and feelings of being 'picked on' rank highest in students' list of school-based problems that affect their emotional and behavioural adjustment at school.[292] Students from minority cultures commonly perceive unfair treatment in schools, which perception is borne out by disproportional disciplinary referrals of students from minority cultures and impoverished groups.[293] When teacher decisions seem arbitrary and without the best interests of the students in mind, the students see teacher authority as illegitimate. These disenchanted students give up hope of being respected, as a result of which they cease cooperating with their teachers and withdraw from participating in schooling.[294] In turn, young people who experience school authority as unfair and arbitrary transfer this attitude to social authorities such as the police, and are likely to display aggression and delinquent behaviour, both inside and outside of school.[295]

School size

Evidence about the optimal school size is still not clear. Findings are that students are more connected in smaller schools.[296] Accordingly, some research recommends a school size of between 600 and 1200 students at high school level, although school size might matter less in primary school where students have a one-to-one relationship with a single teacher.[297] Schools can also be too small: if there are fewer than 300 students, young people might not be able to locate like-minded peers for friendships.

In terms of the effect of school size on students' behaviour, larger schools have a greater number (but no higher rate) of behavioural difficulties; nevertheless, the increased number can overwhelm those administrators who are responsible for discipline.[298] Consequently, teachers may overlook incidents, knowing that administrators will not follow up because of their workload.[299] In that case, larger schools can be disadvantaged.

School socioeconomic level

A sense of community is impaired in impoverished schools; achievement levels (particularly in reading) are affected and both aggression and bullying occur there at higher rates.[300] Indeed, school poverty is more influential on student achievement than is family poverty, with the mechanism being detrimental effects on collective efficacy (see chapter 24) and teachers' lowered expectations of disadvantaged students.[301]

Even then, the community that a school serves accounts for only 1 to 6 per cent of the variance in school outcomes.[302] Schools that create a sense of community can offset the disadvantages of poverty in the student population.[303] Hence, a school is not doomed to high levels of behavioural difficulties or academic failure on the basis of its location or because of the demographics of its student population.[304] Moreover, whereas US studies report that impoverished schools uniformly produce poorer student outcomes, in New Zealand, for example, disadvantaged schools receive additional resources, as a result of which declines in student achievement, teacher morale and collective efficacy are not experienced.[305] And schools with high populations of impoverished students and with large class sizes have been found to have *fewer* office disciplinary referrals than more advantaged schools.[306] This counterintuitive finding may come about because teachers in these schools are accustomed to dealing with diversity of all types, including behavioural differences.

School norms

The demands of the school setting can lead to the emergence of new behavioural problems that students were not displaying prior to school entry.[307] Children in the same setting behave more like each other than the same child across settings.[308] This is because norms of the school and classroom contribute to behaviour, including physical aggression.[309]

Safety

Students perceive their school less positively when a high proportion of students with behavioural problems attend.[310] The provision of support and structure (in contrast to punishment) accounts for 8 to 50 per cent of the differences between schools in the rates of bullying and aggression, and students' sense of safety at school.[311]

Teacher factors

Students' relationship with their teachers is even more influential than aspects of the school, if only because there is probably more variation between teachers than between schools.[312] Different teachers have differing rates of behavioural difficulties in their classes.[313] Moreover, some students are disengaged and disaffected in some classes while being full participants in others.[314] This means that some teachers are more effective than others. This is not because successful teachers emphasise order and control, but because they engage students more and expect that they will succeed;[315] see fewer behaviours as a threat to their authority; can solve most disciplinary issues within their relationships; and encourage a cohesive group which accepts, includes and supports all its members. Thus, it seems that the personal style of the teacher has more influence on students' behaviour than do the characteristics of the students themselves.[316] Young people's adjustment *in the classroom* reflects their relationship to the teacher *in that classroom* (rather than to outside factors such as parenting).[317]

To quantify this effect, one study found that the student–teacher relationship accounted for 15 per cent of the variance in students' achievements.[318] Students with warm relationships with teachers achieve better at reading than those students with comparable ability whose relationships with their teacher are strained.[319] With respect to student behaviour, another study found that the quality of the relationship accounted for 11 per cent of the variance in behavioural difficulties and for 23 per cent of the variance in school suspensions.[320] That is, as relationship quality increased, teachers reported experiencing fewer behavioural difficulties in their students and less need to suspend students.[321] Students in classes with initial high levels of aggression tend to increase in aggressiveness over the school year.[322] However, the level of aggression of incoming students does not predict their end-of-year aggressiveness when their teacher is supportive.[323]

Emotional support

Teachers' responsiveness to students is more salient than individual students' temperaments, learning difficulties, behavioural difficulties or social adversity in predicting both their concurrent and future social and emotional adjustment and engagement in learning.[324] Even more than peer support, students' relationships with supportive teachers are vital in slowing the decline in academic engagement and interest through the high school years.[325]

Emotional support for students has four dimensions:

- the extent to which teachers develop warm and close relationships with students

- the teachers' efforts to minimise conflict between themselves and students and among the class
- teacher sensitivity and responsiveness to students' academic and emotional needs, including supporting their autonomy and
- regard for students' perspective and point of view.

Warm relationships with teachers benefit all students. However, across all age groups, students with learning or behavioural problems or from minority cultures benefit the most.[326] The quality of the relationship prevents these risk factors from being translated into poor academic, social and behavioural outcomes.[327] Vulnerable students who develop positive relationships with their teachers develop higher self-efficacy and expend more effort, and they display less disruptive and risky behaviour and more prosocial behaviour, including reduced aggression.[328] Students with internalising difficulties who receive teacher support show declining social difficulties over time.[329]

However, students who are distractible, disruptive or aggressive commonly experience conflict with their teachers, receiving four times more negative than positive teacher feedback and fewer positive responses to their constructive participation; these students also engage in more mutually angry exchanges with their teachers.[330] Negative exchanges occur more than 20 per cent of the time and positive exchanges in only 5 per cent of instances.[331] When these students do not comply with teacher requests, a chain of four negative interactions typically follows, in which the teacher is increasingly coercive and the student increasingly defiant.[332] The ongoing nature of this conflict with teachers contributes to the persistence of students' adjustment and behavioural difficulties in class.[333] Conflict is more likely with individual students when the class comprises many students with difficulties but, even then, it is most apparent when teaching quality is low.[334]

Structural support

Classroom organisation refers to proactive structuring of the classroom to ensure the productive use of time and materials; promotion of student engagement through varied and interesting teaching; and preventing and responding in a timely and minimalist manner to behavioural disruptions. Every researcher agrees and common sense tells us that clear instructions and well-structured activities and routines enable children to be successful learners.[335] Unsurprisingly, no one recommends chaos.

Whereas emotional support will help children to be more *willing* to cooperate with their teacher,[336] classroom organisation makes it *easier* for them to do so. Clearly structured teaching has a strong influence on children's academic and behavioural self-regulation, prosocial skills, work habits and engagement.[337]

Instructional support

Teacher effectiveness is the dominant factor affecting student progress.[338] While affecting students' behaviour directly, supportive relationships with their teachers improve students' *academic* performance only indirectly: by enticing students to engage with learning.[339] Once engaged, clear structure and high-quality instructional support assist students' acquisition of skills.[340] Instructional support reduces failure rates and produces academic gains, particularly in reading skills.[341] In turn, reading competence is vital for accessing academic curricula throughout schooling and ultimately predicts adult attainment.[342]

Elements of the classroom environment have consistently accounted for variation in learning outcomes over and above that predicted by the students' abilities.[343] Effective instruction is obviously important for all students, but is especially vital for those at risk of academic failure.[344] And, given the link between poor academic performance and disruptive behaviour, early identification and remediation of students' learning difficulties will also prevent future behavioural difficulties.[345] When early instruction maximises children's success and minimises failure, children find academic work more enjoyable, will engage more reliably and experience less anxiety, anger and boredom.[346]

Congruence between home and school

Phelan and her colleagues have proposed that the issue of students' alienation from school and consequent behavioural problems is not about the nature of their home lives, or about the nature of their school specifically, but about the ease with which young people can integrate the two settings. In that event, they propose the following four trajectories.[347]

The first is the group of students whose worlds of home and school share similar values, with this congruence – and the support that both settings provide – making it easy for students to achieve well in both places.

A second group live in two different worlds but nevertheless they can navigate between the two. However, these students – often from minority cultures – may not speak up or ask for help at school and, in schools with few other minority students, feel that they have to choose between hiding their identity, or devaluing aspects of their home and community culture.[348]

Third are those whose home and school are different worlds and border crossings between them are strained. These students are frustrated that they cannot understand academic material, while their parents want them to succeed but do not have the skills to support their children's learning or to advocate for them in schools. These students do not reject education unilaterally but worry about their future because they cannot see how they can succeed academically. They are often from families in economic hardship, and may be burdened with family care responsibilities and with paid employment which, when in excess of seven hours per week, interferes with schooling.[349]

Finally there are the troubled and alienated students for whom the values, beliefs and expectations are so discordant between home and school that they resist adopting the values of school. These students are failing but, contrary to the myth that they do not care, 80 per cent express discouragement and despair.[350] Although worried about their future, they have given up, alternating between self-blame and accusations that the system is unjust and stacked against them.[351] They cannot see a link between school learning and their life goals; and, with parents who lack the capacity to provide support,[352] they drift away – or, being punished at school, are discarded: they are not so much run aways from education, but throw-aways.

Conclusion

The conclusion is unequivocal: students' progress in school is more influenced by school quality than by their social backgrounds.[353] School quality accounts for between 20 and 25 per cent of the difference between schools in student progress, with family factors explaining only 5 per cent.[354] This tells us that, although disadvantaging home factors create the *potential* for negative academic outcomes, this risk will not eventuate when schools offer appropriate supports in the form of teacher involvement, effective teaching, high academic expectations and non-coercive discipline.[355]

Even students who are alienated from school express the desire to learn something meaningful and to make a success of their lives.[356] Student apathy and disrespect are not a sign that students do not want to learn, but that they do not want to learn within a hierarchical setting where they are denied due process and their views are disregarded.[357] Schools have an important developmental influence on young people.[358] While schools that are effective in promoting the progress of one group are equally effective for all student groups,[359] individuals who lack support from their families most need extra doses of support at school if they are to surmount their adverse start in life.[360] It is entirely within the power of schools and of teachers to create the conditions under which even disadvantaged students strive to learn.

CHAPTER 2

Styles of teaching and discipline

There is a time to admire the grace and persuasive power of an influential idea, and there is a time to fear its hold over us. The time to worry is when the idea is so widely shared that we no longer even notice it, when it is so deeply rooted that it feels to us like plain common sense. At the point when objections are not answered anymore because they are no longer even raised, we are not in control: we do not have the idea; it has us.[1]

Our disciplinary style must match our educational goals. Therefore, in the first part of this chapter, I discuss the purposes for education and for discipline. In the second part, I introduce the styles of discipline, only two of which are relevant in schools.

Purposes of education

Historically, education has had four purposes whose aims and methods often work counter to each other: induction of young people into the economy, ensuring the mobility of the advantaged few, equalising opportunities for all, and being a means of personal development.[2]

Economic

The economic purpose of schooling is to teach youth occupational skills needed within the economy. As essentially a preparation for the future, its means are control and standardisation. Its conformist curriculum transmits the dominant culture, social roles and norms; in so doing, it reinforces unequal power,[3] excludes 30 per cent of students, who drop out before completing high school, and stifles creativity.[4]

Taxpayers and employers are the main proponents of the economic purpose of schooling. These stakeholders require schooling not to be wasteful of resources and they prioritise subjects that seem most relevant to the economy. For them, the only justification for spending more or for teaching other disciplines would be to boost economic productivity. However, beyond teaching literacy, the education system has very little to do with economic prosperity:[5] a decline in test scores does not cause economic recessions, and economic recoveries have nothing to do with raising performance standards in schools, and certainly nothing to do with changing them relative to other countries' rankings.

Traditionally, the economic purpose dictates an academic curriculum that conveys conventional knowledge in a linear fashion; however Sir Ken Robinson and others argue persuasively that, in the coming century, the world will need students who can think laterally and who can harness their imagination, creativity and innovation in order to solve the emerging problems posed by a growing world population.[6] This, then, requires a broad curriculum of languages, sciences, the arts and physical skills. Moreover, rather than focusing only on rationality, logic and objectivity, it will need to foster students' intuition, emotion and spirit to inform their thinking skills and foster their wellbeing.

Competitive mobility

The role of competitive mobility (or *credentialism*) is to make winners. That is, the purpose of education is the pursuit of personal advantage.[7] The measures for achieving this include ability grouping, pull-out gifted programs, competitive testing, and capitalising on reputational differences between tertiary institutions. Competitive mobility *looks* meritocratic, with the brightest and most conscientious students coming out on top but, in fact, more depends on the social standing of students' parents than on personal ability. Although packaged as permitting social mobility for all who want to work for it, and although there is a *possibility* of upward mobility for less advantaged sectors of society, there is little actual *probability*.[8]

In addition to cementing social inequality, this function has a deleterious effect on individual students' learning styles. It encourages students to engage in education not to acquire useful knowledge and skills, but to exchange their credentials for something useful: a high-status job, social power, financial security and cultural prestige.[9] Hence, students learn to do what it takes to succeed. Their aim is to get the best credentials they can with the least amount of effort. What matters is not real learning, but 'surrogate learning': as long as tests are passed and credentials accumulated, the content is irrelevant.

Equity function

This role for education is opposite to competitive mobility: in the service of justice, it aims to reduce social inequalities so that all individuals have equal access to an appropriate education.[10] The second reason to promote equity is informed by enlightened self-interest: namely, to ensure that society does not lose the talent of those who currently cannot fully participate in the economy.

In the US at least (the only country for which I could obtain statistics), schools already do a decent job of minimising the achievement gap across cultures, with impoverished students in the first five years of schooling making greater academic gains than wealthy children.[11] However, over the summer holidays, reading scores of impoverished children go up by just 0.26 points in those same five years, whereas wealthy children's scores rise by 52.49 points.[12] The conclusion is that advantage accrues from the opportunities to which the privileged are exposed outside of school hours. If schools wished to promote equity, then, they would offer disadvantaged students the extracurricular activities (such as music lessons and tutoring) that the parents of privileged students already supply.

Personal development

The role of developmental education is to facilitate personal growth, the expression of talent and the pursuit of lifelong learning. The means is the satisfaction of young people's needs at the time. That is, the focus is on the present, with students' positive adjustment to adult roles more likely when they have been nurtured throughout childhood.

Styles of teaching

Our purposes for education inform our choice of teaching styles. The first is a top-down approach in which adults determine which skills and information are of value to young people and then set about teaching these. With a significant amount of teacher-directed instruction, curricula are largely originated by the teacher (although are not necessarily unresponsive to students' needs).

In contrast, a bottom-up approach is child-centred or child-referenced. In this approach, teachers follow rather than lead their students. Rather than attempting to instil a predetermined curriculum, this approach respects and responds reflectively to the skills and interests of students and their parents. Also known as a constructivist approach, this style sees students as inventive, enriched and vibrant human beings whose need to construct identities and generate understandings of the world is the starting point for, rather than an afterthought in, curriculum planning.[13]

Purposes of discipline in schools

The purposes of discipline must align with our purposes of education. The economic function employs controlling discipline, where students are taught obedience while teachers deposit knowledge into them.[14] Anything other than passivity is perceived as defiance and insubordination – that is, as a challenge to adult authority. Accordingly, this authority must be reinstated, not just to dissuade individual miscreants but as a symbolic 'message' to onlookers about who is in charge.[15] Today, blatant control of children's bodies and minds has been largely softened into a goal of ensuring that students 'internalise' controls and regulate themselves. Hence, textbooks outline how to teach students in ways that will secure their engagement and motivation.

In contrast, guidance believes that students behave disruptively when their needs are not being met; therefore, it aims to engage them actively in learning and to nurture their emotional and social well-being. Accordingly, in adopting the final two purposes of education (equity and personal development) guidance is interested not in how to *teach*, but in how young people *learn*.

Under controlling discipline, responding to student disruptiveness is considered a diversion from 'real' teaching. In contrast, guidance believes that education must, first and foremost, be about teaching young people to live together peaceably, for which they need to be taught skills for solving problems and considering others.[16]

The range of disciplinary styles

Fifty years ago, Diana Baumrind's seminal research detailed four distinct disciplinary styles, with a fifth style identified more recently. As illustrated in Figure 2.1, these approaches differ on the two dimensions of *control* and *structure* (or support) for young people. The five styles are: indulgent or permissive; disengaged or neglectful; authoritarian or controlling; a 'no-nonsense' style that is commonly employed in disadvantaged communities and an authoritative or guidance style.[17] In parents, these styles are stable and (with exceptions) commonly endure not only in individuals across time, but also across generations.[18]

Indulgent (permissive) style

Indulgent or permissive adults are warm towards children but lack structure. They have few expectations for children's behaviour and do not follow through on directives.[19] This chaotic style can arise either from adults' adverse circumstances or from their romantic notion of childhood as a time that should not be corrupted by adult interference. Children of permissive parents tend to lack impulse control and self-reliance and to have low self-efficacy.[20] Accordingly, this style of parenting is related to high levels of internalising (or emotional) problems in young children.[21] It is not recommended either in homes or in schools.

Disengaged (neglectful) style

Disengaged, neglectful or rejecting parents are under-involved with their children; inattentive; indifferent to them; minimally responsive; and emotionally detached.[22] These parents often convey negativism about their children and respond in kind to their children's disruptive behaviour, bickering with them and becoming aggressive in response to the children's uncooperativeness.[23] These adults are typically preoccupied with their own issues and fail to distinguish their needs from their children's. Their failure to monitor their children and to take an interest in the children's lives increases the risk of delinquency and academic under-achievement.[24] The children tend to be nonconforming, maladjusted, and dominating.[25]

This style can occur when parents have tried but have failed to curb their children's challenging behaviour and have now given up. The parents' disengagement commonly alternates with exasperation that may escalate into coercive and capricious restrictions and sanctions.[26] The damage done to children by parental neglect can thus be compounded by the deleterious effects of coercive discipline.

Authoritarian (controlling) style

Given that the *authoritarian* and *authoritative* labels are easily confused with each other, in place of the *authoritarian* label I will use the term *controlling discipline*. This title is apt because the method employs both psychological and behavioural controls. These operate from a dominance orientation, where adults think about their interactions with children in terms of 'Who is the boss?'[27] and expect obedience from children, without considering the children's perspective or concerns. These adults do not share decision making with children and they assume a stance of personal infallibility.[28]

The first method of this style, *psychological* (or *internal*) control is a conditionally approving attitude towards children in an effort to manipulate them into thinking, feeling and behaving in ways that adults approve of.[29] It aims to activate guilt, anxiety or shame so that, ultimately, children feel compelled to comply with adults' expectations.[30] It is applied to two different domains: young people's achievements and their personal lives.

Achievement-oriented psychological control involves contingently approving of children when they are successful.[31] It pressures children to excel academically or in other spheres such as music or sports,[32] requiring children to be who their parents demand. This can be achieved by approving of children when they meet expectations (conditional positive regard) or becoming inaccessible to them by withdrawing affection or contact when they displease us (conditional negative regard).[33]

For its part, privacy-violating psychological control blurs boundaries between the parent and child. It intrudes on young people's personal domains.[34] Enmeshed parents intrude upon young people's private domain in many covert ways, including the following:[35]

- constraining children's verbal and behavioural self-expression
- invalidating their feelings and perspective
- shaming children with personal attacks (such as comparing them to others, and ridiculing or embarrassing them in public)
- manipulating their thoughts and feelings by contingently ignoring them or withdrawing affection when they fail to comply
- inducing guilt on the basis that children should appreciate all the parents have done for them (when instead being cared for is a child's birthright)
- instilling anxiety at a failure to comply with parents' directives
- violating privacy.

Parents who intrude on their children's psychological or emotional life are experienced as warm and close (albeit enmeshed), whereas achievement-oriented parents are experienced by their children as cold and distant.[36] Psychological control has been robustly associated with emotional difficulties in adolescents, including lowered self-esteem and delinquency.[37]

The second controlling method – *behavioural* (or *external*) control – refers to adults' overt efforts to regulate children's behaviour.[38] It believes in the importance of clearly stated rules and regulations for children's behaviours.[39] Accordingly, it encompasses methods that employ rewards to increase the frequency of behaviours that adults approve, and punishment for those behaviours that we want to reduce. This controlling style of discipline was given the formal title of *behaviourism* in 1914.[40] Even before this, of course, it was part of folklore.

Behavioural and psychological controls are not entirely distinct, with most parents employing both forms. Nevertheless, behavioural control is aimed at securing compliance to external controls, whereas psychological control is aimed at manipulating children to suffer emotionally if they fail to comply.

'No-nonsense' style

A variant on controlling discipline has recently been described for impoverished disadvantaged groups, typically for cultural minorities.[41] It has been termed a *no-nonsense* style that resembles a 'tough love' approach that emphasises loyalty to authority and aims for obedience in children.[42] The behavioural controls that place restrictions on young people are considered to be a necessary response to dangerous environments and antisocial peers[43] or to be normative within a given culture or subculture. However, whereas *structure* protects young people from risk, *control* does not,[44] instead producing externalising problems in boys in particular[45] and rebellion in adolescents once they are able to escape adults' strictures. For disadvantaged youth, maternal responsiveness (in contrast to control) is even *more* influential in ensuring school engagement than it is for young people who experience fewer risk factors.[46] Meanwhile, psychological control is as disadvantageous for young people in adverse circumstances as it is for all others.[47]

Authoritative style (guidance)

In place of the *authoritative* title, to save mistaking it for the controlling or authoritarian style, I have adopted the term coined by Dan Gartrell: *guidance*.[48] Guidance is driven by an ethic of caring, in which teachers make an intellectual commitment to use their power in the service of young people.[49] As described by Rogers and Webb, more than affection or regard, caring anchors thoughtful educational and moral decision making.[50] It is about caring for ideas (everyone's), ourselves, each other, and the effects of our actions on others. It involves teachers trusting students' humanity and their ideas, and students trusting teachers because of their skill, tact and cultivation of a culture of growth in which everyone becomes more skilled.

Guidance believes that all people – regardless of distinguishing characteristics such as race, religion, gender or age – have an equal right to get their needs met. Accordingly, it prescribes that student needs not be an afterthought in planning curricula and disciplinary strategies, but be integral in framing these. This stance makes the other not an object whereby we do something *to* them but a subject:[51] we work *with* them. This form of power is used to affirm rather than disconfirm the other,[52] yet it is steadfast and dependable in its conviction that teachers will protect young people from the behavioural excesses of each other and from developing negative reputations, and will protect students from perceiving themselves as failures.

Instead of employing psychological controls, guidance teachers support students' autonomy, encouraging young people to take initiative, to solve problems with support and to express their individuality.[53] Rather than imposing behavioural controls, guidance provides structure that supports students' competence.[54] In place of rewards, it offers authentic acknowledgment of their achievements and considerate behaviour; and in place of punishment it teaches young people to manage their emotions and impulses so that they take account of the effects of their actions on others.

Theories of discipline in schools

In a previous iteration of this book, in the interests of appearing balanced, I included some approaches that proclaimed to be theories but which were merely an assortment of practices packaged together to fit the various authors' preconceptions. *Theories* offer hypotheses and then test these by gathering evidence. Therefore, I have excluded packaged models that lack comprehensive statements about the purposes of education or discipline and which lack evidential support. A theory

FIGURE 2.1   Styles of discipline

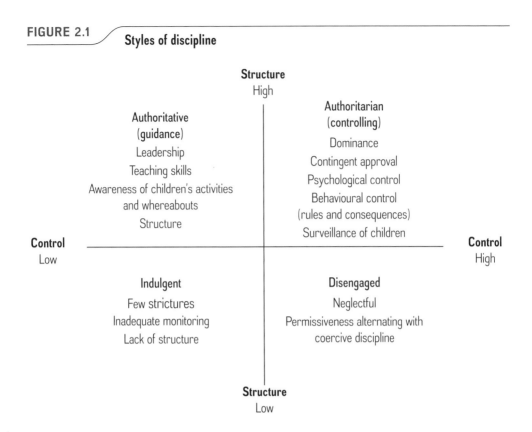

is only opinion if it is just a collection of untested hypotheses. Balance is not served by including ideas for which there is no evidence. Not all ideas are equally valid and, once evidence has amassed, presenting ideas that contradict the evidence does not promote balance: it is disingenuous.

One example of a model that is excluded in this new book is neo-Adlerian theory, popularised as *Systematic training for effective teaching* (or *parenting*).[55] Its authors claim that there are only four motivations – all of them negative – behind students' disruptive behaviour: to gain attention, seek revenge, exercise power or to withdraw from demands. Both a resounding lack of evidence and my own clinical experience tell me that there are more than four

reasons why children act disruptively. To name but a few triggers, I have seen the most intractable behavioural problems in children exposed to the *herpes simplex* ('cold sore') virus (see Box 1.1)...Children can act disruptively when they have a deficiency of the nutrients needed to convert amino acids into neurotransmitters,[56] or when they lack the essential fatty acids that ensure the quality of dopamine-producing neurones[57]...Individuals with a gluten intolerance can display a range of emotional disturbances including (in later life) the most severe of mental illnesses, schizophrenia[58]...Children can become impulsive when their blood sugar levels drop too low[59]...I have seen children have meltdowns in the aftermath of the death of a parent ... Children will explode when humiliated or shamed by a teacher ... They can behave poorly when they are just plain *lonely* ... They can have outbursts when they believe that they are academic failures ... And, as the substantial evidence reviewed in chapter 1 verifies, they can behave poorly when abused, neglected and exposed to violence. The claim that there are only four causes of human behaviour reminds me of the quip that there are only two types of people in the world: those who think there are two types of people in the world, and those who don't.[60]

Other models are really an assortment of teaching practices, such as Bill Rogers' work[61] and various packaged programs such as those reviewed elsewhere.[62] As exemplified by the neo-Adlerian model, many of these approaches lack a coherent theoretical base, with the result that some of their practices fall within the authoritarian camp and accordingly are mentioned in Part two of this book, while others are just good teaching practice or simple human communication skills and hence sit comfortably within the guidance approach.

This leaves only the five disciplinary styles just described. All have been extensively researched but, of course, no one recommends either the permissive or neglectful styles because of their deleterious effects on children. The 'no-nonsense' approach is really authoritarianism justified by the context and hence can be subsumed by controlling discipline. Hence, the only two theories to survive the cull are the authoritarian or controlling style (the rewards-and-punishment approach of behaviourism) and the guidance approach. I shall now examine the differences between these two styles.

Contrasting beliefs of control versus guidance

The fundamentally opposite theoretical stance of the two styles, from which all other differences pivot, is that behaviourism theorises that individuals' behaviour is governed by its external consequences, whereas guidance believes that all of our behaviour is an attempt to meet our (internal) needs. The corollary is that, under behaviourism, disruptive behaviour is regarded as being due to a lack of incentives to behave better; whereas under guidance the behaviour is assumed to be an inept attempt to meet needs.[63]

As for their practices, the core difference between the two styles is that, whereas behaviourism imposes consequences on students (either rewards or punishments), guidance uses no consequences but simply *teaches* young people how to behave thoughtfully. The idea that Kohn finds troubling (in the opening quote to this chapter) is the notion that individuals 'need' consequences in order to learn. Guidance recognises that some behaviours have *outcomes* (such as getting cold if you go outside on a chilly day), whereas *consequences* are contrived by adults to make children suffer for their choices. (Nevertheless, guidance practitioners may wisely decide to shield children even from natural consequences – say, when a child's asthma is exacerbated by cold.)

Status of adults versus children
Based on their contrasting views about the origins of behaviour, the first philosophical difference between the two styles is their assumption about the status of adults versus

STYLES OF TEACHING AND DISCIPLINE   41

children. This is a political issue – that is to say, it is about the distribution of power; in the case of schools, the distribution of power between teachers and students. By definition, authoritarian approaches assign power almost exclusively to teachers. Educationally, controlling discipline emphasises teacher-directed instruction on the grounds that, under the alternative constructivist approach, teachers would have too little control over what students learn.[64] In terms of disciplinary practices, the controlling approach assumes that teachers have the right – in fact, duty – to discipline students.

This power imbalance is reflected in the language used to discuss behavioural difficulties in schools. Terms such as *misbehaviour* and *unacceptable* or *inappropriate* behaviour do not make explicit that it is the teacher who is making these judgments and whose assessment is considered sacrosanct.[65] Moreover, the judgment defines the behaviour as a deficit within students, while overlooking the contributions of the environment to their behaviour. Meanwhile, our status as professionals ensures that these negative labels acquire the status of Truth and become irrefutable and, often, self-fulfilling.[66]

In contrast, guidance is based on the notion of power as the ability to act or produce an effect. Power, therefore, is unlimited, with plenty to go around.[67] Guidance believes that authoritarian control marginalises and silences young people:[68] their objections to their loss of autonomy are dismissed as merely self-serving, without considering that their protests might be righteous. Therefore, guidance practitioners gain their authority not from their use of coercion, but

from being expert, wise and connected to children.[69] Adults who employ guidance are leaders rather than bosses or, in the words of Banks, are like the orchestra conductor: the 'first among equals'.[70] In an orchestra, the conductor is obviously a highly skilled musician but is aware that he or she is not as capable on the flute as the first flautist, or on the piano as the pianist. The conductor has an overview of what the ensemble needs to achieve, notices when the musicians are struggling with a particular passage and offers extra guidance at those times but, on the whole, trusts the musicians to know their instrument. So it is with teachers. We have an overview of the tasks the group needs to achieve, can offer extra guidance when students are struggling, but on the whole trust young people to know their instrument: that is, to know their own minds. In the words again of Banks:

> The orchestra conductor faces individuals who are experts in their own instruments (their own lives) but also has some expertise to guide them as they play their life's music.[71]

Although leadership engenders two-way cooperation and consideration, nevertheless our relationship with students is asymmetrical. That is to say, it is our job to be their advocates or allies but it is not their job to look after us or meet our needs. Because of our extra life experience, we have to lead them. Nevertheless, our leadership position does not mean that we stop being people with them.[72]

From this description, it might seem that these two styles occupy opposite ends of a power continuum. Instead, the difference between them spans only from the political right (controlling approaches) to the centre

FIGURE 2.2 Relative power of teachers and students

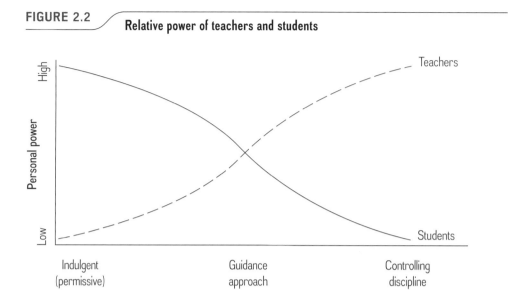

(occupied by guidance). On the extreme left is not guidance as is sometimes assumed, but a permissive approach, which no one advocates either in our homes or in our schools – see figure 2.2.

Beliefs about human nature

A second philosophical difference between the two styles of discipline is their view of human nature. Our species has a long history of distrusting our own nature, remnants of which remain in the language we use about children today. We continue to make statements that signify that we suspect children of evil intentions, such as:

- Children are 'attention seeking'.
- They are 'manipulative'.
- They do things deliberately – sometimes even to 'get at us'.
- We believe that we have to 'come down hard' on disruptive behaviours because, given children's evil tendencies, these will persist otherwise.

- We say that we have to be firm, have limits and set boundaries because 'if you give children an inch, they'll take a mile'.
- We must not give in to (or 'spoil') children because if we do, the children will have won and we will have lost.
- If we spare the rod, we will spoil the child.

If those kinds of statements were being made about different racial groups, as in, 'Asians are attention seeking' or 'Whites are manipulative', I hope that most of us would find them offensive and, accordingly, would dismiss the message and discredit the messenger. Yet we seldom question such stereotypes when they discriminate on the basis of age.

Guidance argues that these stereotypes about children are not even accurate. Examining some of the above statements more closely, first, everyone is 'attention seeking' if by this is meant that everyone wants to be acknowledged and affirmed by others. Second, if children cannot get their needs met by direct means, perhaps they will employ strategic measures. If this is manipulative, everyone is manipulative. By way of another example, you cannot spoil children by supplying what they need (or by sparing the use of the rod).[73]

While the previous lay descriptions of children could be dismissed as merely uninformed, statements by educational experts share the same distrust of children:

- 'Kids, when they are little, are – in a way – kind of nuts. They are not born reasonable and unselfish, they are born unreasonable and selfish'.[74]
- 'When students are not given the limits they need, they will act up in order to make the adults around them take notice'.[75]
- 'Children are not born good; they have to be disciplined, otherwise they are a threat to the rest of society'.[76]
- 'If students are given the freedom to do nothing, that is most likely what they will do'.[77]
- 'Noncompliant students are much more interested in doing what they want, when and how they want, rather than pleasing you'.[78]
- 'Children are not born human, they are made so'.[79]
- 'Today's youth is rotten to the core; it is evil, godless and lazy . . . It will never be able to preserve our culture'.[80]

The language of the last quote provides a hint about the longevity of our cultures' distrust of children: it was written on clay tablets 3000 years ago.[81] Guidance believes that these attitudes represent a sour view of human nature. It rejects what Miller terms this 'poisonous pedagogy'[82] and believes

instead that children are rational – that is (as is true for adults), their actions are intended to meet their needs.

A second accusation is that humans are competitive by nature. Contrary to a popular belief that 'real life' is competitive, cooperativeness is the natural stance of the human species. I review the evidence for this claim in chapter 10 but, in the meantime, our everyday experience confirms it. Despite the bad press that we give ourselves, on most days most of us experience almost everyone cooperating with us virtually all the time.

Third, in contrast to the picture given above of children's innate slothfulness, experience teaches us that children want to grow and learn, to surprise the adults in their lives, and to have us be proud for them.[83] Guidance sees that the existence of intrinsic motivation is proof that humans want to achieve something meaningful.[84] Accordingly, children do not need incentives to behave well, because they already want to be successful.[85] Given that every behaviour is an attempt to meet a need, thoughtless behaviour is not the result of a lack of incentives. Instead, it is a strategy for meeting a need, albeit sometimes an inept strategy. The response, then, is not to punish the attempt, but to teach children skills.[86]

Kohn notes that the qualities which we attribute to human nature are almost always the unsavoury ones, such as competitiveness or aggression, whereas we seldom blame 'human nature' for heroism or altruism.[87] Instead, we interpret heroic actions as evidence of the rare occasion when individuals triumph over their own base instincts. But everyday life is full of heroism: parents who attend a tedious job day after day to provide for their families; individuals who help each other in crisis; people who visit the elderly and infirm in hospitals; individuals who rescue others from natural disasters ... These acts of selflessness do not rate a mention on the nightly news or twitter precisely *because* they are so commonplace.

Beliefs about children's competence

Related to our beliefs about human nature is a belief about the relative competence (or incompetence) of children compared with adults. The philosopher John Locke saw children as bereft of useful knowledge, as 'blank slates', irrational and ignorant.[88] According to this view, children need shaping, training, controlling and schooling. This belief aligns with teacher-led instruction, which requires that teachers ensure orderly (that is, passive) behaviour so that students can absorb the information we impart.

In contrast, the guidance approach sees young people as skilled and trusts that they are innately driven to grow and become all they can.[89] It believes that, with support, children have the skills to solve the typical problems of childhood.

Beliefs about children's worth

The third aspect of our attitudes to childhood is a view about children's current worth, versus valuing them only for what they might become. Authoritarian views of children (usually espoused by politicians) proclaim that children and their education are worth investing in, because 'Children are our future'. This focus on the future leads to the concept of adults as gardeners: intervening at each stage of growth, taking deliberate control over the types of plants (children) that flourish, training and feeding them to 'maximise their potential'. Under this approach, the focus is not on children's present needs, but on how they will turn out in the future.

More perniciously, this perspective sees children as only *becoming* human. In

TABLE 2.1   Implications of beliefs about childhood

	Evil nature	Innocent nature
Children are incompetent or lacking in skills	Children are untrustworthy. Teaching is adult-directed. Discipline is controlling, authoritarian.	Children are vulnerable. Teaching is child-focused but adult-directed. Disciplinary styles are a mixture of control and guidance.
Children are competent and skilled	Children are blameworthy and culpable. They must take moral responsibility for their mistakes. Teaching is adult-directed. Discipline is autocratic.	Children are rational beings who, like all others, occasionally make mistakes. Teaching is child-centred. Discipline teaches skills rather than punishing children for their mistakes.

comparison with adults who are human *beings*, children are seen as being incomplete and therefore unworthy of respect until they have grown up.[90] This view gives rise to what Kohn calls the *Better get used to it* (BGUTI) syndrome, whereby we force children to learn in ways that are foreign to their nature, simply on the grounds that this is how they will be treated later – so they had *Better Get Used To It*.[91] This view is often expressed in the statement that 'He's *got* to learn', by which we mean that we are not interested in the student's present needs, but in the skills the student will require in future.

Guidance believes that children are people *now*, with current needs and rights that deserve recognition. The approach recognises that the future is an accumulation of 'nows' and that children's future wellbeing is built on their cumulative experience of having their needs met in successive moments.

Beliefs about children's behaviour

The inevitable outcome of seeing children as evil by nature is that we become judgmental when their behaviour inconveniences or harms others. We regard their actions through a moral lens that defines conforming and obedient behaviour as 'good' and children's having a mind of their own (disobedience) as 'bad'.

When we assume that a disruption is deliberate, we expect young people to be remorseful. Their lack of remorse is taken as a sign of wilfulness or wickedness and, therefore, they must be punished 'to teach them a lesson'. Thus, our negative attitudes towards children and their behaviour send us down the path of controlling discipline in an effort to make the children stop.[92]

But whereas controlling discipline adopts moralistic views about children's behavioural mistakes (using labels such as *inappropriate, misbehaviour, naughty* or *unacceptable*), this same form of discipline nevertheless understands and accepts that students will make academic or developmental errors. No teacher ever corrects a spelling error by sending a student to time-out; and no parent ever punishes toddlers for falling over when learning to walk. In other words, authoritarian discipline has distinct attitudes to behavioural versus developmental or academic errors – see Box 2.1.

In contrast, guidance believes that learning to behave thoughtfully is a developmental skill. Like learning the piano, it requires lessons and practice - and will, inescapably, entail mistakes. Guidance does not leave it at that, however. A grade 2 teacher would never declare that her students could not spell properly and hence her curriculum plan was to wait the year and hope they outgrew it. Instead, in the awareness that learning to spell is important, the teacher will teach it. And just as academic errors are inevitable, so too are behavioural mistakes. Although guidance will not punish students for lacking skill, neither will it accept thoughtless behaviour: instead, it will teach young people how to behave more considerately.

Causes of disruptive behaviour

Behaviourism believes that all behaviour (other than simple reflexes) is lawful, which is to say that it is controlled by its consequences.[93] This deterministic view of human behaviour states that positive consequences will reinforce behaviour (result in its increase) and negative consequences

FIGURE 2.3 Effects of beliefs about children

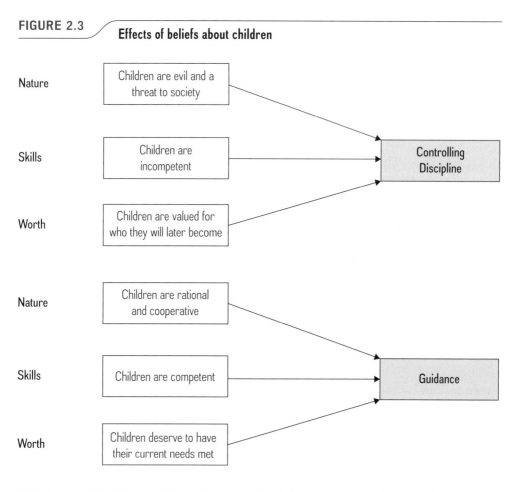

BOX 2.1 Authoritarian assumptions about behavioural versus academic mistakes

Behavioural mistakes	Academic mistakes
Children are trying to get things wrong: their errors are deliberate.	Children are trying to get things right: their errors are accidental.
Children should not explore limits: they should obey them.	Children need to explore in order to learn.
Children should not make behavioural mistakes: they should know better.	Mastery requires lessons and practice and will inevitably entail errors.
Children who have difficulties achieving behavioural expectations should be punished.	Children who have difficulties achieving developmental expectations need support.

will punish (result in a decrease) in the behaviour. Accordingly, students' disruptive behaviour is evidence either that they are not being sufficiently rewarded for better behaviour, or are being accidentally rewarded (say, with adult attention) for misbehaving. This belief sets the stage for using punishment so that the behaviour no longer 'works'. The pragmatic version of this belief is that children do well *if they want to* and, if they are not behaving well, they need incentives to do better.[94]

Guidance refutes this. It believes that every human behaviour is an attempt to meet our needs. On the basis of trust in human nature, Greene contends that people do well *if they can*.[95] His argument assumes that students with challenging behaviour are already motivated to do well, already know right from wrong, and have already been punished enough. If they are producing incompetent behaviour, this means that the task calls for skills that they lack. The response, then, is to teach the skills, not to punish children for not knowing them. If punishment were going to work, it would have by now.

Locus of causality

This debate is really about where we *locate* the source of our actions. Controlling discipline, by definition, has an external locus of causality: it believes that external consequences govern behaviour. The stance of the guidance approach, in contrast, reflects an internal locus of causality. It believes that our internal needs govern our actions. The following everyday examples exemplify this:

- If consequences dictated behaviour, no one (not the least teachers!) would enter low-paying professions when they would be better remunerated in, say, merchant banking.
- If consequences dictated behaviour, no one would perform voluntary work because it is unpaid. (Volunteers' motivation is not external rewards, but the internal satisfaction of knowing that they are making a contribution to others.)
- If consequences dictated our actions, our prisons would be empty.
- If consequences dictated behaviours, we would never have the conversation with a young child in which we rebuke, 'What did you do that for? Didn't you know you were going to get into trouble?' to which the child replies, 'Yes, I knew that. But, gee, it was worth it!'.

In other words, guidance believes that external consequences do not *make* us behave. Individuals might calculate the chances of being caught and factor in the aversiveness of any potential punishment but, if their need is compelling enough, they will take the risk and act to satisfy the need. If adults didn't mind the ethics of it, we could use cattle prods or tasers to punish misbehaviour – but there would still be a child somewhere someday who would declare, 'Don't care! Didn't hurt!'. In short, there is nothing we can do to *make* young people conform – but there is a lot we can do to nurture them so that they *want* to cooperate with us.

The concept of locus of causality also has deeper implications, posed by self-determination theory. This theory uses the term *locus of causality* to refer to the location of our *volition*. By this definition, we have an internal locus of causality when our behaviours are freely undertaken (autonomous), whereas we have an external locus of causality when we feel compelled by external forces to act in particular ways.[96] Using the term in this way honours that human beings have a fundamental need to be the authors of their own lives. This implies that, even if we *could* control behaviour from the outside, we *shouldn't*. To do so would violate Kant's 'categorical imperative' not to encroach on other people's autonomy.[97]

Goals

The main purpose of controlling discipline in schools is to establish, maintain or reinstate order so that students can be successful at learning. To that end, pragmatic behaviourists' overt goal is to ensure students' compliance[98] – although, to be fair, radical behaviourists recognise some dangers inherent in this.[99]

Guidance does not aim for compliance, on the grounds that obedience does not teach moral reasoning or guarantee prosocial behaviour. In support of this contention, various studies have documented that adult pedophiles molest children between 150 and 560 times before being caught, across as many as 380 victims.[100] When researchers asked prison inmates incarcerated for child sex offences how they got away with this high rate of abuse, the perpetrators unanimously answered that it was because children have been trained to obey adults.[101] In short, respecting authority (regardless of whether that respect is justified) and obeying rules (regardless of whether they are reasonable) can expose children to abuse because they do not learn that they can resist adults,

even those who manipulate them into abusive relationships.[102]

A second risk of seeking obedience is that the resulting compulsive compliance is unhealthy, with an excessive need to please and to obey adults having serious emotional consequences for children.[103] In their focus on conforming to what others expect of them, children lose sight of what they value and what excites their passion for learning.

Third, compliance can also endanger surrounding people when, for example, students collude with a dominant peer's directives to bully a vulnerable student. If the wannabes had the courage to stand up to their ringleader, he or she would not be brave enough to act alone – and the form of bullying known as mobbing would cease. In that one measure, rates of school bullying would halve.

Fourth, compliance can endanger whole communities when people obey authority figures' orders to harm others. The defence at every war crimes trial since the end of the Second World War has been that perpetrators of crimes against humanity were not responsible for their actions because they were 'only following orders' (see Box 2.2).

Therefore, guidance does not want young people to learn to follow orders. Instead, it wants them to learn to be considerate – that is, to consider the effects of their actions on other people.[104] It contends that we cannot teach this with rewards and punishments, because these focus students' minds on what happens *to them* when they act in a given way, when the essence of considerateness is to contemplate how the behaviour affects *others*.

BOX 2.2 A study of obedience[105]

In Milgram's research, subjects were told that they were conducting an experiment to discover how punishment affected individuals' learning. An accomplice (or confederate) (who was termed the 'learner') was to perform a memory task in an adjacent room while (allegedly) attached to electrodes. The experimenter instructed the research subjects to administer electric shocks of increasing severity whenever the learner made an error although, unbeknown to them, the shocks were simulated. Nevertheless, the learner would begin protesting once the 'shocks' reached moderate levels. If subjects became tense and sought reassurance from the researcher, using a series of four increasingly terse directives, they were instructed to continue nevertheless.

Whereas university psychology students predicted beforehand that 3 per cent of subjects would persist and deliver the electric shock marked 'danger', in fact all 40 subjects persisted to the point where the accomplice began to protest, while 26 (65 per cent) obeyed the experimenter to the end, proceeding to administer what they thought to be the most potent shock available. This was despite both their better judgment and obvious distress. Milgram explains these results in terms of people's willingness to overlook the suffering of others when given directives to do so by those in authority. He concludes in the words of Snow:

> More hideous crimes have been committed in the name of obedience than have ever been committed in the name of rebellion.[106]

The language of the two styles

It is important to be clear about the language employed by the two styles of discipline, because they will often use the same words and yet with different meanings. First, authoritarian theorists often talk of respect for authority, when they mean fear of authority. Respect has to do with mutual esteem:[107] I have never encountered one-way respect within any relationship – respect is always mutual, or the contempt is mutual.

Second, both theories talk of responsible thinking or responsible behaviour, but what the authoritarian theories typically mean is thinking and behaving compliantly. Canter defines compliance as the willing acquiescence to a request or demand.[108] However, research is clear that this is not 'responsible' in the sense of engaging moral reasoning skills and freely choosing the behaviour in accord with one's values.[109]

Third, controlling discipline often talks of developing a warm relationship with students, whereas guidance believes that any relationship that uses psychological controls might appear warm (indeed enmeshed) but such a relationship is not received positively. It is an oxymoron to talk of a benevolent dictatorship.

Fourth, behaviourists refer to *structure* but by this they mean restricting children's access to the material and emotional goods that the children need and inflicting punishment on them; guidance writers talk of structure as providing leadership characterised not by pressure or domination but by cooperation[110] and, with respect to teaching, as presenting organised lessons not so that students can conform but so that they experience self-efficacy.[111]

Fifth, behaviourists report that delinquency arises because of parents' inadequate monitoring of their sons' and daughters' activities.[112] However, monitoring can be carried out in a controlling fashion that entails intrusive surveillance and grilling young people about their activities and whereabouts which, given the lack of warmth in their relationship with parents, young people do not disclose spontaneously.[113] In contrast, under a guidance approach to monitoring, parents take an interest in the events in their sons' and daughters' lives and want to keep them safe which, in the context of a caring relationship, causes their sons and daughters to disclose voluntarily where they are and what they are doing.[114]

BOX 2.3   Comparisons between controlling discipline and guidance

Controlling discipline	Guidance
Power source	
Adult is a boss, with role, coercive and referent and reward power.	Adult is a wise leader with expert, referent and connective power.
Adults' beliefs	
Distrusts children.	Trusts that children are rational, want to cooperate with adults, and want to grow and surprise us.
Behavioural mistakes should not happen and should be punished.	Behavioural mistakes are inevitable and call for teaching more skilful behaviour.
Behavioural problems are due to faulty reward and punishment regimes.	Behavioural problems are a (sometimes inept) attempt by children to meet their needs.
Children's behaviour can be controlled by outsiders (an external locus of causality).	Children's behaviour is governed by their needs (an internal locus of causality).
Goals	
Aims for compliance and obedience.	Aims for considerate behaviour.
Methods	
Psychological control.	Responsive relationships that support young people's autonomy.
Behavioural control: rewards and punishments.	Teaches and supports children to manage their emotions and impulses.

A continuum of disciplinary responses

Behavioural management in schools is often reactive,[115] with the preponderance of school policies on discipline actually being punishment policies.[116] Their relative neglect of preventive measures will inevitably lead to frustration and failure because it is always more effective (and humane) to prevent difficulties than to correct them once they have arisen.[117] Crisis interventions alone cannot 'cure' the underlying reason for the crisis.[118]

This truth is recognised by both the controlling and guidance approaches and is signified by the triangle in Figure 2.4,

which illustrates that prevention must be the greater part of any discipline plan. However, as listed in Table 2.2, each theory places different strategies within each sector of this triangle (see also Figure 3.1 on page 63 and Figure 10.2 on page 140).

- The first component is primary or universal prevention procedures which focus on the larger environment and put in place protective mechanisms that safeguard all students and thus prevent behavioural difficulties on a school-wide basis.[119]
- While universal preventive measures will meet the needs of a majority of students, creating fewer disciplinary issues and thereby releasing resources to

FIGURE 2.4   Tiered model of discipline

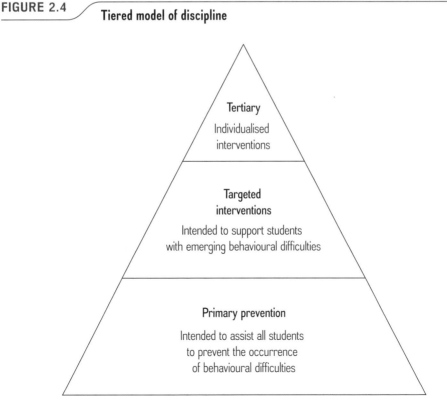

Tertiary
Individualised interventions

Targeted interventions
Intended to support students with emerging behavioural difficulties

Primary prevention
Intended to assist all students to prevent the occurrence of behavioural difficulties

TABLE 2.2   Tiers of interventions

Tier	Controlling discipline	Guidance
Primary *This tier encompasses a school-wide response relevant for all students.*	• Determine the rules and specify which behaviours signal their observance across all venues of the school. • Specify contingencies – that is the consequences that all students will consistently earn for infractions of the rules. • Teach these rules and consequences to all students.	• Build warm student–teacher relationships. • Meet students' needs, particularly for belonging, self-esteem and autonomy. • Adjust instruction so that students can be successful academically. • Identify and intervene early with students' learning difficulties.
Secondary *This tier encompasses targeted responses for students with emerging behavioural difficulties.*	• Refine reinforcement regimes for desired behaviours, either on an individual or class-wide basis. • Assess and remediate students' learning difficulties.	• Use communication skills and class meetings to resolve problems. • Provide increased personal support, such as mentoring. • Teach skills for self-regulation and problem solving.
Tertiary *This tier provides specialised interventions for young people with severe and chronic behavioural problems.*	• Conduct observations in classrooms and other venues to identify the particular antecedents and consequences that surround a given undesired behaviour. • Adjust these environmental events. • Insist on parental involvement.	• Use a solution-focused approach to look for and use what is working, rather than trying to identify and fix what is broken. • Collaborate with parents, consultants and other experts.

direct towards specific difficulties, they will not be sufficient for all.[120] Therefore, in addition to preventive measures, you will need to plan targeted strategies. These are focused or supportive interventions aimed at avoiding future disruptions by providing specific skills and supports to students who are experiencing academic failure or behavioural difficulties.[121]

• The tertiary and final level of practice is providing specialised interventions designed to prevent further deterioration of a problem.[122] These will encompass both immediate and longer-term actions.

Factors influencing teachers' choice of disciplinary style

The main influences on disciplinary styles are our beliefs about children's nature and their behaviour, and our goals of discipline. Our choices are also affected by our own self-efficacy; our focus; characteristics of the children; our social or (in the case of teachers) institutional context; our culture and religion.

Teachers' beliefs

Teachers' beliefs guide how they respond to their students' behaviours.[123]

- *The nature of the behaviour.* Adults who believe that the behaviour is not typical of other children of that age, that it is particularly reprehensible, or that it will negatively affect the student in future tend towards more severe and controlling forms of discipline.[124] In contrast, teachers are more willing to use guidance when they interpret unskilful behaviour as a reflection of the adversities under which students are functioning.
- *Beliefs about children's inherent nature (or disposition).* When teachers believe that a student behaves similarly across situations and over time, they tend to make negative inferences about the child's disposition and punish transgressions in an attempt to force him or her to change.
- *Inferences about children's skills and knowledge.* Adults assume that, as children grow older, they possess greater knowledge about appropriate behaviour and increased capacity to enact that knowledge and, therefore, are more responsible for their behaviour. However, teachers with authoritarian attitudes overestimate children's ability to guide their own emotions and impulses. Combined with a view of young people as evil, these unrealistic expectations cause teachers to see disruptive students as wilful, defiant

and culpable for their actions, which justifies their (the teachers') use of controlling discipline.[125] This tendency to interpret ambiguous child behaviour as having hostile intent is more common in teachers who themselves were abused as children.[126]

- *Assumptions about children's intentions.* Teachers who believe that children should have foreseen – and therefore must have intended – the outcomes of their actions or who think that children have hostile intent towards their teachers or others, feel threatened by children's behaviour and impose coercive measures in order to regain control.[127] In other words, when students are seen to be behaving in ways that are both intentional and controllable, teachers commonly react punitively.[128]

Teachers' goals

Teachers who believe that children should obey authority and who seek immediate compliance tend to use controlling discipline, whereas those who aim for children to develop autonomy and moral reasoning tend to use guidance methods.[129] Some of teachers' goals are imposed from above, however. Those who are under pressure from the school administration and higher authorities to control student outcomes (e.g. with national testing and benchmarks) are more likely to use authoritarian teaching and disciplinary methods with their students.[130] However, teachers' own beliefs can also affect this tendency. When they believe that their students are capable of exercising autonomy, teachers will provide more opportunities for them to do so than when teachers believe that students cannot regulate themselves.[131]

Teachers' self-efficacy

Self-efficacy refers to our beliefs about how effective we are at various tasks. Teachers with low professional efficacy are more likely to become overwhelmed by their work, stressed by disruptions,[132] and more concerned with promoting order than with meeting students' needs. They experience less job satisfaction and perceive colleagues, students and parents more negatively.[133]

Teachers with an external locus of causality blame students for their own frustrations. When this view is combined with low self-efficacy, teachers become angry when students are not compliant. Believing that teachers should be dominant, they activate coercive discipline to re-impose their authority.[134] In turn, coercive discipline causes students to behave more poorly, thus confirming the teachers' fears that the students are out of control.[135] As a result, teachers with low self-efficacy are likely to get into power struggles with noncompliant students in which they see themselves as victims and in a one-down position. The paradox is that teachers who believe that they have the least power impose the most controls on students.

In contrast, teachers who have high self-efficacy are prepared to engage in problem solving when experiencing conflict with students.[136] These teachers' positive methods cause students to become less distractible and more cooperative and responsible.[137]

Teachers' focus

Teachers who are willing to focus on children's needs rather than solely their own, can discern and respond to children's perspectives and are able to find ways to defuse rather than escalate conflict with students.[138]

Religion

Our religious heritage has a profound influence on both our theories about life and our disciplinary practices. Across the three monotheistic religions (Judaism, Christianity and Islam), adherents characterise their God as either nurturing or as authoritarian. The belief in a nurturing God directs adherents towards caring and supportive forms of discipline.[139] In contrast, regardless of the root religion, an authoritarian view of God has two basic beliefs that underpin controlling responses to children's behaviour: first, that human beings are inherently evil and, second, that God's love is conditional. These two beliefs imply that, to be loved, children must be worthy and, when they transgress, they must be punished. Ancient teachings and countless passages in the Old Testament advise:

- Folly is bound up in the heart of a boy, but the rod of discipline drives it far away.[140]
- Blows that wound cleanse away evil; beatings make clean the inner parts.[141]
- This son of ours is stubborn and rebellious. He will not obey us ... All the men of the town shall stone him to death.[142]

Although stoning was never really a serious option, in subsequent centuries, fundamentalist parenting advice nevertheless reflected these same themes:

> There is in all children ... a stubbornness ... which must ... be broken and beaten down.[143]

Modern writers echo these sentiments. For example:

Spanking is God's idea . . . The question we face as parents is this: do we love God enough to obey Him, and do we love our children enough to bring into their lives the correction of spanking when it is needed?[144]

Similarly, the modern day Christian fundamentalist James Dobson declares that unless we punish children, they will not learn appropriate moral (by which he means sexual) standards of behaviour, and will be 'damned in hell'. He advises parents that, when their child resists their directives: 'You had better take it out of him, and pain is a marvellous purifier'.[145] He offers the same advice to teachers, who he believes receive their authority from God[146] (although it is not clear how this applies to teachers who are pagan or atheist). Dobson asserts that, 'The shoulder muscle is a surprisingly useful source of minor pain; actually it was created expressly for school teachers'.[147] (And here we were thinking that the trapezius muscle was there to stabilise the arm!)

Childhood history

Teachers who themselves were punished during childhood think that controlling discipline is the natural order of things and, therefore, it is commonly their default method.[148] Part of this comes from their belief in controlling discipline, but also from an ignorance (from a lack of personal exposure combined with a lack of training) about alternatives.[149]

Teacher training

Few teachers receive training within their teacher preparation courses for responding to student behaviour and, in this drought of knowledge, their ability to reflect on their practices is impaired.[150] When they lack

a coherent theory, disciplinary methods are informed only by teachers' personal belief systems which, under pressure, can degenerate into a range of unprofessional responses to students' challenging behaviour.[151] A lack of knowledge condemns teachers to using the methods familiar to them from their own childhoods, which commonly ensures that controlling discipline is their default stance.[152]

Child characteristics

Teachers typically attribute behavioural difficulties to characteristics of the children themselves, rather than to the nature of their teaching.[153] Yet the evidence in chapter 1 led to the conclusion that children's difficult behaviour is a *product* of coercive discipline, not its cause. A related view is that a controlling style is necessary with younger children. If this were true, we would find that preschools were highly controlling and high schools were democratic. Instead, researchers have consistently found the opposite: that punitive responses are more common in upper than in the lower grades of primary school.[154] Compared with high schools, student–teacher interactions are warmer in the early years of school, teachers are more emotionally supportive and children have considerably more autonomy in the early childhood years.

In other words, 'pressures from below' do not account for teachers' use of controls; instead, 'pressure from above' and teachers' own personalities ('pressure from within') predict the use of controls.[155]

Social or institutional context

It is not the nature of the children, then, that causes increased authoritarianism, but the nature of institutions. Our social history documents a continual abuse of power,[156] sanctioned by our belief that children are the property of their parents to abuse at will,[157] and our certainty that their inherently evil nature must be repressed with rigorous discipline and regimentation. This history continues to cast its shadows on modern institutions designed to contain young people. Although the vast majority of teachers are genuinely concerned about their students and would prefer to craft humane relationships with them, the legacy of control imposes a hierarchical rather than caring structure within schools.[158]

Implicit theories

We each have theories, both explicit and implicit, about how the world works. In the case of the causes of behavioural problems in schools, as detailed in Table 2.3, there are basically two possibilities: either we think there is something wrong with the student or with external forces impinging on his or her behaviour. In turn, these two explanations vary according to whether

TABLE 2.3 Implicit theories about the causes of behavioural difficulties

Source of problem	Uncontrollable	Controllable
Internal Within the child	**Psychological deficits** Young people with severe behavioural problems are psychologically disturbed as a result of their inbuilt temperament. Given that educators are not therapists, teachers can do little to help these students, other than to refer them for counselling or other specialised supports and, meanwhile, suppress their behaviour so that others are not victimised by it.	**Guidance** Because of trauma or a lack of nurturing, young people with behavioural problems have not been taught certain vital skills (especially self-regulation and conflict resolution skills). Their behaviour is an expression of their distress and will abate when school meets their needs and teaches children problem-solving skills.
External Within the setting	**Sociocultural inequity** Children with behavioural problems lack adequate support from their disadvantaged and antisocial families and communities. Because schools cannot fix society, there is nothing teachers can do with these damaged and alienated students, except to contain their behaviour until they leave school so that others are not victimised by it.	**Behaviourism** Students with behavioural problems are being reinforced for their disruptive and antisocial behaviours. Therefore teachers have to adjust the environment so that it triggers fewer outbursts and alter the regime of rewards and punishments, so that students have incentives to desist.

or not we think the problem is within or outside our control.

Uncontrollable, internal explanations. One implicit theory blames students' behavioural difficulties on their internal characteristics such as genetics or temperament. This is a common view, with the teachers in one study blaming 30 per cent of student behaviour problems on the qualities of the children, with only 4 per cent attributing the problems to aspects of teaching.[159] Obviously, the personal qualities of students are unchangeable and therefore this view sees students' failure as inevitable.[160] This, in turn, can cause teachers to give up.

By blaming students' behaviour on their character flaws and conferring labels on students (e.g. *Oppositional defiance disorder)*,

this deficit model tells us nothing about the skills that the accused students lack and overlooks the institutionalised context or the relationship in which the opposition and defiance are occurring.[161]

Controllable, internal explanations. Like the previous explanation, this view also sees students' behaviour as being due to internal reasons such as emotional distress or a skill deficiency – but believes that students can surmount these problems. Under guidance, this view provides impetus for increasing school-based supports for troubled students. Under a deficit orientation, however, it incites practices where we do things *to* students including *observation* and *assessment*. Although our aim in using such language is to obey

FIGURE 2.5 Influences on teachers' disciplinary practices

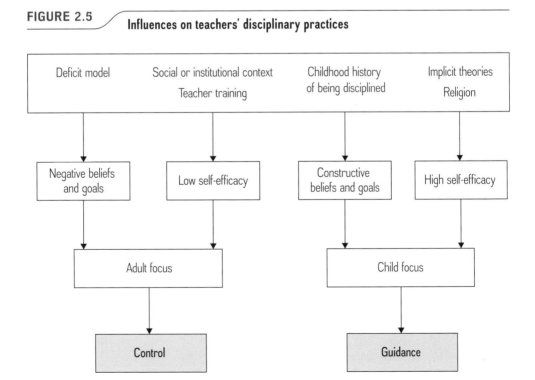

the scientific imperative to be 'objective', these top-down processes distance us from students' experience and overlook their frame of reference, typically resulting in a 'laundry list' of what is wrong with them that we then set about *treating*.[162]

Uncontrollable, external explanations. Instead of blaming students, this implicit theory blames their families and society for failing to provide the nurturing that young people need. Given that schools cannot fix society, this is a fatalistic view that causes us to give up on young people. This was found to be the dominant theory in the study just cited, in which teachers blamed 66 per cent of students' behavioural difficulties on home factors.[163]

Awareness of social inequity is a two-edged sword. On the one hand, it can sensitise teachers to students' adversity and signal students' heightened need for support; on the other hand, it can lead to a deficit discourse in which teachers use children's disadvantage or personal learning difficulties as an explanation for the students' academic failure that excuses teachers from teaching them.

Controllable, external explanations. The behaviourist perspective is that behaviour is controlled by features of the environment. Specifically, undesired behaviours are being reinforced and desired alternative behaviours are not being rewarded enough. This can be managed by adjusting the events preceding the behaviour so that these no longer trigger infractions, by increasing rewards for desirable behaviours, and by punishing undesired acts. In guidance hands, this view leads to holding optimistic expectations that all students can make progress and learn useful skills.

Conclusion

From this description and referring to Table 2.3, the two theories of discipline in schools (behaviourism and guidance) have one thing in common: a belief in controllability. Beyond that, they share little in the way of theory or practice. Controlling discipline believes in adults' unquestioned authority and that human behaviour is governed by its consequences; therefore, it enforces rules through the delivery of rewards and imposition of punishment.

In contrast, guidance believes that every behaviour is an attempt to meet a need. Accordingly, it sets about systematically meeting students' needs. Then, when a behaviour is inconsiderate or unskilled, the guidance response is to teach students the skills that they lack. It believes that if we punished children for lacking skills, we would be punishing them for *being* children because, by nature, children lack skills. That is why they have teachers.

PART TWO

Controlling discipline

CHAPTER 3

Overview of the controlling model

The social development of children is enhanced in environments in which there is predictability in the moment-to-moment interactions between adults and children and where it is clear to the child which behaviors are acceptable and which are not.[1]

The unit of study in behaviourist approaches is the environment – specifically, the events that trigger disruptions, and the consequences that follow them. That is, the unit of study is not the child. Therefore, behaviourism has little to say about the nature of children or about the aims for their education. Instead, it focuses on how to alter behaviour. The main purpose of doing so is to establish, maintain or reinstate order so that students can be successful at learning.

Variants of behaviourism

Behaviourism was an answer to Freud's psychoanalysis with its prolonged introspection and subjective judgments about the causes and cures for emotional distress. The circular Freudian theory contended that sexual desire was at the base of all human problems and that individuals' conviction that this was not so was simply proof of how suppressed their sexual drives really were. This theory endures because it cannot be disproven – but it quickly engendered rabid opposition from behaviourism. Formalised and given its title in 1914 by John Watson,[2] and subsequently popularised by B.F. Skinner,[3] centuries before this, folklore had long upheld the advice to reward behaviour that we want to increase and punish behaviours that we want to deter.

Pragmatic behaviourism

Purely pragmatic methods such as Canter's *Assertive discipline*[4] draw on meagre research either about teaching or about discipline. They employ rewards and punishments to encourage compliance and, if their methods do not succeed at suppressing disruptive behaviour, teachers are advised simply to apply more of the same class of intervention (that is, more consequences). In a unanimous display of hubris, these behaviourists do not require practitioners to evaluate the effects of their programs, nor even to consult students or their parents.[5] This non-scientific approach could be dubbed 'pop' behaviourism, as enacted on our televisions in the *Super nanny* programs. Although derided by serious researchers, of the three behaviourist variants, it is the style most employed in schools.

Radical (or pure) behaviourism

The second form, *radical behaviourism*, maintains that all behaviour (other than reflexes) occurs in response to environmental events, rather than being instigated by 'hypothetical' entities such as the mind or will.[6] Radical behaviourism relies on research findings that behaviour rates can be altered by changing the environment, specifically its triggers (or antecedents) and the consequences that follow a behaviour. This approach equates human behaviour to other natural phenomena, such as tides or gravity, which are subjected to the laws of nature and can be understood by observing their lawful relations to each other.[7] Unlike the pop version, it designs and monitors interventions on the basis of objective data about behaviours and their circumstances.[8] This branch includes three schools of thought that have emerged sequentially, but share many common elements.

Applied behaviour analysis (ABA) was originally known as behaviour modification. The term *applied* in its title means that the behaviours to be changed must have real-life (non-laboratory) applications for the recipients of programs.[9] The methods used have to be *behavioural* (that is, based on behaviourist laws) and *analytic*, which means being based on the analysis of data.[10] Its title emphasises that it is about more than modifying behaviour, but about

understanding the relationship between a behaviour and its environment.[11]

Positive behavioural support (PBS). These are structured programs built on ABA principles but packaged to be more holistic, collaborative and positive.[12] In this sense, *positive* means an emphasis on reinforcement rather than punishment. Although that is the intent of all versions of behaviourism, there is little evidence that teachers actually use reinforcement at anything like the levels needed for it to influence students' behaviour.[13] PBS programs are aimed at teaching students behavioural expectations, just as we teach academic subjects. A system that has achieved considerable coverage in the United States, known as *School-wide positive behavioural supports*, is designed to match the intensity of interventions to the severity of students' behavioural problems by having three tiers or levels of intervention.[14]

The chapters in this section detail each of these tiers, the first of which is the primary tier that addresses all students across the school with a school-wide system of rules and consequences that are explicitly taught to the students. Subsequently, when individual students do not respond to the school-wide measures, the rules are re-taught and social skills teaching is offered.[15] At this level, teachers might also provide remediation of students' learning difficulties and increase communication with their parents (or other caregivers). A check-in program might be used to monitor the student's compliance with expectations.

Finally, the third tier of interventions is directed to the few remaining students with chronic behavioural problems. It entails a systematic process for identifying which events reliably predict the occurrence or non-occurrence of the target behaviour.[16] This process is known as *Functional behaviour assessment* (described below).

Walker and colleagues use a dental care analogy to help explain these three levels. They suggest that Tier 1 approaches are like using fluoride in the town water supply to prevent dental decay; whereas Tier 2 interventions involve increasing dental checkups because of risk factors such as weakened enamel; while Tier 3 interventions are akin to filling cavities, inserting crowns and extracting teeth,

FIGURE 3.1   **Tiered model of positive behaviour support[17]**

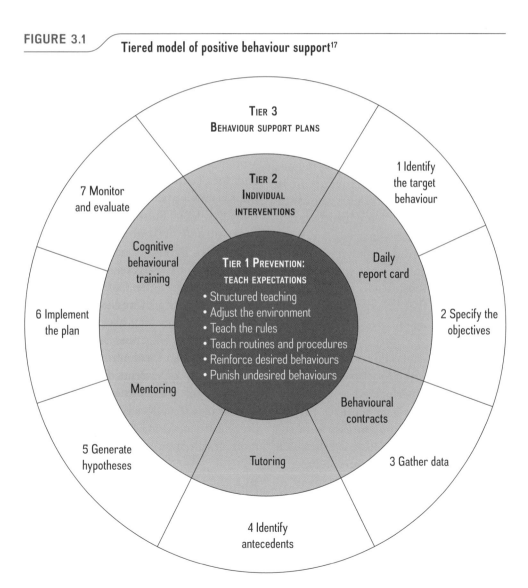

which would involve a team of specialists such as orthodontists and orthodontic surgeons.[18]

Functional behaviour assessment and *Functional behaviour analysis* (FBA). The basic premise of these twin approaches is that all behaviour serves a *function*: either to obtain a positive outcome, or to avoid a negative one.[19] In recognition that the same outward behaviour – such as calling out in class – can serve a different purpose for different individuals, functional behaviour *assessment* attempts to identify this function – that is, to discover how the behaviour pays off for the individual.[20] To perform this assessment, teachers gather data from interviews, review archival records of the student's previous behaviours, and observe actual events in order to generate hypotheses about the behaviour's function. Subsequently, teachers will select a consequence that reflects this function, instead of applying a general reinforcer or punishment to all similar behaviours. Advocates of functional assessments believe that this specific approach is more effective, although this is by no means proven.[21]

If the antecedents and consequences are difficult to discern, a functional behaviour *analysis* can be performed to refine the hypotheses.[22] Analysis achieves this by systematically manipulating each of the potential antecedents in turn and then each of the hypothesised reinforcers, in order to identify which is the active ingredient, as it were.[23] The difference between the two methods is that, in *assessment*, hypotheses are generated by data whereas, with *analysis*, hypotheses are generated and confirmed by experimentation.

Methodological behaviourism

The third behaviourist iteration is *methodological behaviourism*.[24] Whereas pure behaviourism enquires only into observable events, the methodological version acknowledges the role of thought processes and hence this approach embraces cognitive-behaviourism. To the extent that its methods are behaviourist, cognitive-behaviourism belongs under the umbrella of controlling discipline; to the extent that its methods are cognitive, they are just sound teaching practice.

Radical behaviourism agrees that people think and feel but does not believe that theories which include these unseen elements are parsimonious: that is, simple.[25] Moreover, it upholds that people will think and feel better when their behaviour improves.[26] It also believes that explanations that focus on students' biological or sociocultural deficits (such as 'learning disabilities' or 'emotional disturbances') can become excuses for teachers not to act, when more immediate events in the classroom are triggering the behaviours.[27] This provides hope that, because behaviour is controlled by the events surrounding it, teachers can alter those events and, thereby, help students to be successful.[28] Advocates claim that this offers students more options in their lives than does failure, and can also prevent the need for medication or other more drastic interventions.[29]

Behaviourist principles

The unit of study in all behaviourist approaches is the environment – specifically, the events that might trigger disruptions, and the rewards and punishments that follow them. Behaviourism is simply a technology for altering behaviour, which it achieves by observing certain basic principles.

Principle 1 Verifiability

The first behaviourist principle is that practitioners are interested only in descriptions of behaviour that can be verified through observation. This principle is in contrast with what behaviourists regard to be 'circular' definitions of problems, whereby children are said to behave poorly because they have a behavioural disorder and are diagnosed with this condition because they behave poorly. Instead, behaviourists focus only on which events occur, not in generating such untestable 'explanatory fictions'.[30]

By stating its goals in explicit, observable terms, applied behaviour analysis and its derivatives (PBS and FBA) make practitioners accountable for achieving those goals.[31] This accountability is the reason for amassing data to monitor and evaluate interventions. Monitoring and evaluation allow practitioners to adjust goals and interventions if progress towards the goals is inadequate.

Principle 2 Behaviour is controlled by its consequences

The second behaviourist principle is that all voluntary behaviour (as distinct from simple reflexes) is lawful, which means that there is an orderly or predictable relationship between actions and their consequences.[32] This determinist view of human behaviour states that positive consequences will reinforce behaviour (result in its increase) and negative consequences will punish (result in a decrease in) the behaviour. When consequences have no (or a neutral) effect, these are merely subsequent events.[33]

It is important to highlight that reinforcement and punishment are defined by their *effect* on a behaviour; whereas the more colloquial terms, rewards and punishers, are *things* which, regardless of the intent of their administrator, may or may not alter the rates of behaviour. If these consequences do not change behavioural rates, this means that what adults *thought* would be rewarding or punitive are not for this particular student in this setting at this time.[34]

Principle 3 Contingency

The third behaviourist principle is that, in order to influence behavioural rates, consequences must be delivered if, and only if, students display the target behaviours. You must deliver the consequence only when the behaviour occurs, and not when it is not displayed.

Principle 4 Least intrusive and restrictive methods

The next behaviourist principle is that any methods used must be the least intrusive and restrictive methods available. Intrusiveness (or invasiveness) is the extent to which interventions encroach on students' selves or rights, or interrupt the educational process; while restrictiveness refers to how much external control is imposed on students or the extent to which their freedom is curtailed.[35] The principle of least restrictive treatment states that methods must curtail individuals' freedom no more than is necessary to achieve desired behavioural changes.[36] Guided by this principle, the procedures used to alter behaviours must be socially and culturally appropriate.[37]

Therefore, teachers' first priority must be to prevent disruptive behaviour by changing the antecedents that occasion it, and by making natural conditions so highly reinforcing that students are motivated to behave appropriately.[38] Then, if a contrived intervention becomes necessary, reinforcement must be the first measure employed, with more restrictive methods applied only when reinforcement has failed.[39] Punishment should be reserved only for those behaviours – such as self-abuse – that cannot be suppressed in other ways and must always be accompanied by positive reinforcement to strengthen alternative, desired behaviours.

Principle 5 Plan for maintenance and generalisation

The fifth principle acknowledges that new behaviours have to be acquired, then performed fluently, then maintained over time and, finally, generalised or transferred to other settings and to other similar behaviours.[40] Maintenance and generalisation are important because teachers will not have time to implement permanent behaviour plans for individual students. However, pure behaviourists recognise that maintenance and generalisation are unlikely to occur spontaneously, not least because natural environments tend to respond more often to inappropriate than to appropriate behaviour and thereby strengthen the wrong behaviours.[41] Therefore, maintenance and generalisation have to be planned for within the program.[42]

Teach functional skills. The most assured means to promote generalisation is to teach only relevant, functional skills because these are most likely to attract natural reinforcement.

Employ natural settings, using naturally occurring reinforcers. Any behaviours that are reinforced by peers will be the most likely to be maintained.[43] Teachers can also teach students to recruit reinforcement by asking, 'How am I doing?' or 'Look at this! I did it!'.[44]

Ensure fluency. Ensure that students have mastered targeted skills fluently before ceasing training, because only reliably performed skills have a chance of being maintained. Teaching a sufficient range of exemplars will make maintenance more likely.[45]

Fade reinforcement gradually. You can also promote maintenance by fading reinforcers gradually, or by delaying the delivery of reinforcers. This makes it difficult for young people to detect the absence of reinforcement in the natural setting.[46] If a behaviour improves initially but then deteriorates, this may be because reinforcement has become too inconsistent and infrequent, and therefore will need increasing once more.[47]

Teach in multiple settings. Another method to promote generalisation is to simultaneously teach the behaviours across multiple settings, with a variety of teachers.[48] A related method is to teach to a level of fluency in the first setting, and then sequentially teach in each additional setting.[49]

Reinforce skill generalisation. Finally, reinforcing students for displaying the behaviour in other environments will also aid generalisation across settings.[50]

Establishing school-wide plans

Positive behaviour support programs have become popularised in the US under the banner of *School-wide Positive Behaviour Supports* (SWPBS). They represent a collaborative enterprise to respond to student behaviour in the three-tiered model mentioned earlier in this chapter and which is reflected here in chapters 6 to 8.

The steps for establishing a system of school-wide discipline are prescriptive, with the first step or phase being to assemble a leadership team of parents and teachers who represent various grade levels across the school, are respected by their colleagues and the principal, possess leadership skills, and are committed to behaviourist principles.[51] This group will meet at least monthly to review the needs of the school, devise an action plan and arrange staff development.[52]

In phase two, the leadership team secures the support of the wider school staff to use the necessary resources and to implement a behaviour support plan. This is the phase of converging on a shared vision.

In phase three, the team collects data about the nature and frequency of behavioural problems across the school and the consequences that these have earned students. The team might also choose to survey teachers and parents about what aspects of discipline are currently working and which need to be improved.

In the fourth phase, teachers will receive professional development to equip them to implement the behaviour plan fluently and skilfully.

Fifth, once the plan is in place, someone must be allocated the role of gathering data about behavioural infractions and the consequences meted out to students, so that the school staff are able to assess if the plan is working to reduce behavioural problems.

Ethics

Given that behaviourist interventions involve doing something *to* students in the form of administration of consequences, these interventions must be guided by ethical principles, the first of which is the imperative that teachers be fully qualified and that they implement behaviourist methods skilfully.[53]

Second, it is vital that the program is in the interests of the student, not merely for the convenience of teachers. The target behaviour must be a functional behaviour that improves students' or parents' quality of life.[54]

Third, teachers need to secure student and parental consent. This must be both informed and voluntary. *Informed* consent requires that you have considered a range of viable treatment options and have discussed these with students and their parents.[55] *Voluntary* consent implies that you cannot threaten students or their parents with any unfair consequences – such as school suspension – if they withheld consent to the program, and neither can you promise extravagant benefits of their participation.[56]

Fourth, you must have selected the least intrusive and restrictive interventions that are likely to be effective.[57] Your professional status may put parents or students under subtle pressure to consent, and therefore the onus is on you to ensure that what they are agreeing to represents best practice.[58]

Finally, as professionals we are accountable to students and parents to demonstrate that what we do is effective.[59] Therefore, we must gather data to monitor the effects of the intervention itself and to identify any unintended side effects.

Conclusion

On the assumption that students function best when they know what is expected of them, the behaviourist approach begins by establishing clear and consistent rules and monitoring students' compliance with these. Next it administers consequences: rewards for compliance and punishment for infractions. This external control is intended to teach students how to exercise control over themselves (although no specific approaches are recommended for transferring control to students).

Put this way, behaviourist principles are easy to understand: reward behaviour that you want to see repeated and punish behaviour when you want a student to desist. However, even advocates of behaviourism recognise that effective implementation is not so simple.[60] Its complexity is outlined in the upcoming chapters and reviewed in chapter 9.

Recommended further reading

Pragmatic behaviourism

Canter, L. (2010). *Assertive discipline: Positive behavior management for today's classroom*. (4th ed.) Bloomington, IN: Solution Tree.
Emmer, E.T. & Evertson, C.M. (2009). *Classroom management for middle and high school teachers*. (8th ed.) Upper Saddle River, NJ: Pearson.

Radical (pure) behaviourism

Alberto, P.A. & Troutman, A.C. (2013). *Applied behavior analysis for teachers*. (9th ed.) Boston, MA: Pearson.
Kearney, A.J. (2008). *Understanding applied behaviour analysis: An introduction to ABA for parents, teachers, and other professionals*. London: Jessica Kingsley.
Martin, G. & Pear, J. (2011). *Behavior modification: What it is and how to do it*. (9th ed.) Boston, MA: Pearson.
Shea, T.M. & Bauer, A.M. (2011). *Behavior management: A practical approach for educators*. (10th ed.) Boston, MA: Pearson.
Wheeler, J.J. & Richey, D.D. (2013). *Behavior management: Principles and practices of positive behavior supports*. (3rd ed.) Boston, MA: Pearson.

Methodological behaviourism

Kerr, M.M. & Nelson, C.M. (2010). *Strategies for addressing behavior problems in the classroom*. (6th ed.) Boston, MA: Pearson.
Zirpoli, T.J. (Ed.) (2012). *Behavior management: Positive applications for teachers*. (6th ed.) Boston, MA: Pearson.

For parents

Green, C. (2001). *Toddler taming: A guide to your child from one to four*. Sydney: Doubleday.
Phelan, T.W. (2003). *1–2–3–magic: Effective discipline for children 2–12*. (3rd ed.) Glen Ellyn, IL: ParentMagic Inc.
Sanders, M. (2004). *Every parent: A positive approach to children's behaviour*. Melbourne: Penguin.

Websites

Lee Canter's *Assertive discipline*: www.canter.net
99 ways to say 'Very good': www.careerlab.com/99ways.htm

CHAPTER 4

Strengthening appropriate behaviours

A large and convincing body of research suggests that reinforcing behaviors within natural environments is an effective and often necessary procedure to promote and maintain social behaviors.[1]

Behaviourist methods emphasise the use of reinforcement to strengthen appropriate behaviours. However, although reinforcement has been documented to improve on-task engagement and reduce disruptive behaviour,[2] the most portable form of reinforcement (that is, praise) is seldom used in classrooms. Some researchers have found rates in regular classrooms to be as low as one positive (praising) statement per hour, with children displaying aggressive behaviour patterns being praised as little as once every five hours.[3] Even then, only 5 per cent of teacher feedback is specific.[4] Meanwhile, increasing teachers' use of praise is difficult without ongoing feedback from consultants.[5]

Any reinforcers that do not occur naturally are known as contrived reinforcers.[6] The hope in delivering these is that they will be temporary (other than praise) until natural reinforcers take over.[7] Behaviourists distinguish reinforcers from bribes on the grounds that bribes aim to corrupt the recipients, whereas rewards are aimed at strengthening behaviours that benefit recipients.[8]

Teaching new behaviours

If the necessary positive skills are not within individual students' repertoire, you will need to teach these. The methods used are modelling (that is, demonstrating) a behaviour, using prompts, shaping, task analysis and chaining.

Modelling

Modelling is the process where someone's behaviour changes after observing someone else (the model) performing the behaviour and being reinforced for it.[9] It is especially useful for complex behaviours.[10] It works best when observers like the demonstrator and see themselves as similar in important ways to him or her.[11]

Prompts

Teachers can teach students how to perform a desired behaviour by giving *prompts* to help them complete a task. These can be verbal, gestural, or physical.[12] A system of least-to-most prompts involves a three-step approach of delivering progressively more intrusive prompts, beginning with a verbal reminder, modelling the behaviour, then physically guiding a student to perform it.[13] This last, however, has been found to escalate children's resistance.[14]

In a process called *fading*, prompts are gradually reduced until students can complete the task alone. A familiar example of this process is where a teacher writes a letter of the alphabet for a child to trace over, then guides the child's tracings with only dashes, then with dots, until the child is able to write the letter without any visual prompts at all.[15] Another example is where physical prompts are faded into shadowing,[16] when a teacher or aide remains nearby a child prone to aggression, as a reminder to desist.

In a second process known as *time delay*, the teacher pauses before prompting, giving students time to respond.[17]

Shaping

A third method for teaching a new skill is called shaping. This involves reinforcing suboptimal task performances and then requiring successive small improvements (or 'successive approximations') before you deliver reinforcement, until students are performing the skill at a desirable level.[18] In this way, the topography (physical performance), duration, latency or severity of a behaviour can be progressively improved.[19] For example, a teacher might use shaping for a student who presently leaves his seat every two minutes by requiring him to remain seated for three minutes before receiving a reward, then for four minutes . . . and so on until he can reliably stay seated for a duration of, say, 10 minutes.

Differential reinforcement of higher rates of behaviour (DRH) is a method for increasing the frequency of a desired behaviour. It involves reinforcing students for displaying a rare desirable behaviour more often. You would divide the session into intervals and reinforce at the end of each interval when the behaviour occurred at a predetermined level and then, over time, incrementally increase the number of behaviours needed to earn the reinforcer, until such time that the behaviour occurs at the desired rate.

An everyday version of shaping the latency of behaviours is known as *limited hold*.[20] This is where the reward is available only for a limited time, for example, if students are ready to start work within the count of 10.

With shaping, if the increments are too small, the procedure is inefficient and unnecessarily time-consuming but, if increments are too large, the student will not be able to achieve the next level and accordingly will not earn a reinforcer.[21] Moreover, students must have time to solidify achievement of each new level, without remaining on a plateau for too long. The teacher is unlikely to know beforehand how long each step will require, but instead will have to adjust the program as it proceeds, according to each student's response.[22]

Task analysis and reinforcement

Under this method, teachers break a long, complex or daunting task down into a series of steps or smaller tasks to be performed in a specific sequence.[23] Then the teacher delivers a reinforcer when students complete each element. Alternatively, successful completion of each discrete section can in itself be reinforcing.[24]

Chaining

When students cannot complete a task that comprises many steps, you can break it down or task analyse it into a series of small steps that they can achieve serially. With *forward chaining*, you reinforce students for completing the first step successfully, then for completing the first two steps, then the first three, and so on until they have learned the complete task.

But for some tasks (such as tying shoe laces), the first step might seem irrelevant or out of context. In that case, you can reinforce students for performing the final step, then the final two steps and so on, building up until they can complete the whole task. This is called *backward chaining*. Both approaches seem equally effective and children seem not to have a preference for one over the other.[25]

A variant is *total task presentation*, when the student has to perform all the steps in order to receive reinforcement.[26] This is used when the child has already mastered some of the steps.

The menu of reinforcers

Positive reinforcement involves the *presentation* of a consequence whenever the behaviour occurs, following which a desired behaviour occurs more often.[27] The range of positive reinforcers includes (from least to most intrusive) natural, social, activity, tangible, token, sensory and edible rewards. Although these are listed separately, inevitably the later reinforcers will be paired with social reinforcement such as praise, which will add to their effectiveness.

In contrast, negative reinforcement involves *removing something aversive* when the behaviour occurs, following which a behaviour is strengthened.[28] There are two types of natural negative reinforcement: *escape* from an aversive situation (say, by running out of the classroom), or *avoidance* of an aversive event before it occurs (say, by not having the equipment ready to do one's work).[29] When students are using avoidance or escape from academic tasks, teachers will need to give them a more appropriate way to make tasks more manageable for them, such as by asking for help or requesting a break.[30]

An example of a contrived negative reinforcer is when the teacher says that those who work well in class will get no homework that night. This removes the imperative to do homework (which students do not like) in an attempt to reward their diligence in class. (Note that negative reinforcement and punishment are opposites: negative reinforcement *increases* a *desirable* behaviour by withdrawing something *negative*, whereas punishment *decreases* an *undesirable* behaviour.)

Recall from chapter 3 that *Reinforcement is what reinforcement does*. That is, unless the consequence makes the behaviour more likely to recur, it is not a reinforcer, just a subsequent event.

Natural reinforcement

A formal intervention can sometimes be avoided by increasing the rate of natural reinforcers so that they occur at high enough levels for students to be able to connect their behaviour with its consequences.

Social reinforcement

Social reinforcement can maintain either disruptive or appropriate behaviour. Positive social reinforcers for *disruptive* acts can include recruiting teacher attention, gaining control, earning increased status with peers for defying adults, or being able to hang out with friends in the time-out area.[31] Given that social reinforcement can strengthen *in*appropriate behaviour, praise should exceed reprimands by a ratio of at least 4 to 1; otherwise the attention that accompanies reprimands can reinforce disruptiveness.[32]

Social reinforcement for appropriate behaviour typically entails verbal feedback (that is, praise) paired with social attention, proximity and approval.[33] This supportive feedback is driven by the slogan, *Catch them being good.*[34] All behaviourists agree that praise works best when it is specific.[35]

Caring touch can also be a social reinforcer, although may be unwise in educational settings beyond the early childhood years. Other social reinforcers include appointing a child as student of the day or leader of an activity, allowing the child to be first in a line or activity, calling or writing to students' parent(s) about their positive behaviour, or having a congratulatory visit from the principal.[36]

Activity reinforcement

To encourage students to complete activities that they do not like, teachers can reward them with the chance to do an activity that they prefer. This is Premack's principle,[37] also known as 'Grandma's law'.

Preferred activities may include free time, time spent with you, an opportunity to hand out materials to the other students, use of the computer, feeding the class pet, bringing a toy to school, listening to music, running errands, or reading a story.[38] Some naturalistic 'spirit lifters' – many of which could be defined as activity reinforcers – include playing music in the classroom, having dressing-up days, going for a walk, or attending special events such as fêtes or multicultural celebrations.[39] While many of these are all-or-none phenomena, others can be delivered in increments of time, such as having five extra minutes of free time for every 30-minute lesson that is free of disruptions.

There are some limitations to the use of activity reinforcers, however. First, scheduling problems may mean that the preferred activity cannot immediately follow the target behaviour, in which case the delay may render reinforcement ineffective, particularly for students with poor impulse control.[40] Second, some activities such as lunch time or music lessons should be available to students regardless of their performance in class.[41]

Tangible reinforcement

Tangible reinforcers are non-edible items that students value for their own sake. Inappropriate behaviour can be reinforced tangibly when it allows students to acquire equipment (e.g. by stealing it or snatching an item from a peer). When used to encourage positive behaviour, tangibles include stars, stamps, stickers, points, toys, magazines or awards such as certificates, badges and trophies.[42] Tangible reinforcers differ from tokens (to be discussed next) in that they are valued in themselves and are not traded in for any other reinforcer.

Issues with tangible reinforcement are that determining a reinforcer for each student separately can make using tangible reinforcers intrusive,[43] while the public delivery of a tangible reinforcer to some students but not to others could create differences in perceived status between peers.[44] The reinforcer also needs to be valued by students and yet inexpensive. Finally, tangibles can be subjected to satiation effects – that is, students can lose interest in attaining them.[45]

Token economies

Under a token economy system, teachers give students points or a portable and durable token (such as a poker chip) when they display target behaviours. Later, students can trade these tokens in for pre-negotiated backup reinforcers. It is most common for the exchange period to be scheduled at the end of each day or week – although, for students with developmental delays or impulse control problems, the first exchange session might need to be held in the middle of the first day.[46]

Although deceptively simple, token economies require detailed setting up. All share the same features:[47]

- the identification of specific target behaviours
- determination of the criteria for earning tokens
- development of a menu of backup reinforcers (items that tokens later purchase)
- determination of the costs of these various backup reinforcers
- procedures for exchanging tokens for the backup reinforcers

- establishment of a reliable recording system so that the system is perceived by students as being fair
- procedures for fading the use of the token economy.

The major advantage of token programs is that tokens can be exchanged for a variety of reinforcers, which avoids students tiring of a single reinforcer. A second benefit is that the symbolic reinforcer (the token) can be delivered immediately, although the actual reinforcer itself is delayed. This may be sufficient for some students; others may not be able to delay gratification until the backup reinforcer is delivered, however.

In addition to the work involved in establishing a token economy, one practical disadvantage is that the system is vulnerable to sabotage by theft, swapping, loss and counterfeiting.[48] A second disadvantage is that, as with activity reinforcers, you must be careful in your selection of backup reinforcers so that they have some value and students are willing to work for them, but are not so expensive that the system becomes too costly. A third disadvantage is that if you impose fines for misdemeanours, you could bankrupt students, negatively affecting their motivation to work within the system. For this reason, Zirpoli recommends that no student should ever have a zero balance at the time of token exchange.[49] Fourth, there can be a problem if students hoard the tokens and then consider that they have earned enough to buy all they want, and decide to stop working within the system.[50]

It is possible to have a token economy for only some of the students in your class, on the grounds that they need extra help and it is only fair that they receive this.[51]

Alternatively, everyone can receive tokens but for different behaviours.

Sensory reinforcers

Students with sensory integration difficulties (as found either alone or as part of the autism spectrum of disorders) will often engage in self-injurious behaviour because it increases their sensory stimulation or provides some sensory comfort.[52] To replace self-stimulation with a less dangerous or more appropriate form of stimulation, you can use an alternative sensory reinforcer which meets the same need for stimulation.[53]

Edible reinforcers

Food is a reinforcer for everyone because it satisfies a basic physiological need. However, edible reinforcers are unwise because their presence can be distracting,[54] teachers cannot take account of each student's food preferences and potential food intolerances, and there are nutritional concerns such as obesity and tooth decay.[55] Edible reinforcement is seldom necessary and only works when students are hungry (or, in behaviourist terms, are in a state of deprivation). Moreover, students can find them insulting or patronising.[56] Even more troubling would be teaching a link between food and emotional comfort, when eating should instead be a response to hunger.

Reinforcement schedules

Several properties of reinforcement can alter its effects on behaviour. One of these is the reinforcement *schedule*. This is a pattern for timing the delivery of reinforcers.[57] It refers to how often students have to display desired behaviour, or how much time must elapse, before they receive some reinforcement. In classroom settings (as opposed to research laboratories), it is not possible to be exact about schedules, but a few research results can be borne in mind.

The first of these is that, when behaviours are reinforced on each and every occasion (which is termed *continuous reinforcement*), students will learn them quickly. However, given that teachers will not see every instance of the behaviour, this might not be practicable in classrooms.[58] Also, behaviours that have been continuously reinforced are not maintained once reinforcement ceases because it is easy to detect its sudden cessation.[59] (It does not take many flickings of the light switch when a fuse has blown before you realise that the light no longer works.) Moreover, individuals can get satiated with (that is, tire of) the reinforcer. Continuous schedules are also a lot of work to administer.[60]

On the other hand, behaviours that are reinforced every now and then are slow to be acquired but are very resistant to extinction (as illustrated by gambling). This is termed *intermittent* reinforcement. This difference implies that high levels of reinforcement are needed when students are learning a new skill, while intermittent reinforcement is more appropriate for maintaining skills.[61] Teachers can therefore use continuous reinforcement at first and then gradually reduce the frequency of reinforcers (in a process known as *thinning*) until the reinforcement is intermittent.[62]

For discrete acts, you will reinforce students when they have displayed a specified number of target behaviours, such as completing a given number of maths equations. This is called a *ratio* schedule.

In contrast, for continuous behaviours (e.g. staying in their seats) you would reinforce students after a specified *time* period. This is called an *interval* schedule. Both can be difficult to administer within classrooms because ratio schedules require you to count all instances of a behaviour, while interval schedules require that you keep time records. This is especially demanding when each interval is brief, resulting in the need to reinforce as frequently as every 30 seconds, for example.

A third form is a *response-duration* schedule when as the teacher you would reinforce a student for persisting at an appropriate activity or for producing a desired behaviour for a given length of time (seconds or minutes, depending on the behaviour).[63] You would reinforce at the end of the specified time period for continuous production of an appropriate behaviour (such as staying seated), and restart the clock if there is a breach. As the student becomes more skilled, the interval is lengthened.

Reinforcement schedules need to match the students' ability to persevere and to delay gratification. Very young students and those with impulse control problems, for example, might require reinforcement every 10 to 15 minutes.[64] However, such a schedule will need to be thinned so that it eventually becomes similar to the rate of natural reinforcement, so that the behaviour will be maintained in natural settings.

Individual versus group reinforcement

Teachers can deliver rewards *independently* to one or a few individual students. In that case, all might have the same target behaviour (such as staying seated). This is a *standardised* criterion. Alternatively, different students might have different target behaviours, perhaps one student needing to raise her hand rather than calling out, another needing to get started on time, and a third needing to complete more work. This is the *individualised* criterion.

Instead of giving only certain targeted students a reward, teachers can institute a reward system that applies to everyone in the class.[65] Again (in the standardised criterion), it could be that each student has to produce the same target behaviour (such as raising a hand), or that different students have to produce different behaviours (individualised criteria). Each student's compliance will earn a reward for his or her entire group (rather than just for themselves). The aim of group reinforcement is to capitalise on peer pressure to correct a class-wide behavioural problem, to increase class unity and to create a feeling of belonging.[66]

A less desirable option is for an individual student to be responsible for earning a reward for the whole group. This 'hero' procedure can backfire, however, if the student fails to earn the reinforcer.[67] Peer pressure and scapegoating can be vicious. However, when an individual student's disruptions repeatedly penalise the whole group, that student can be placed on a personal incentive program (such as differential reinforcement) and the team given points when he or she reaches each interim goal.[68]

Principles for using reinforcement

The use of reinforcement must obey certain principles. Key among these is

TABLE 4.1   Variants on administration of reinforcement

	Individual (independent) reinforcement	Group (interdependent) reinforcement
Stardardised criteria (The same target behaviour for each student)	The target behaviour is the same for all students. Each individual who performs that target behaviour receives personal reinforcement. Example: Each student who raises a hand before answering receives 1 point.	The target behaviour is the same for all students. Each individual who performs that target behaviour earns reinforcement for the group. Example: Every time any member of the class raises a hand before calling out, that person's team receives a point. Once the group had x number of points, they get five extra minutes of recess time.
Individualised criteria (Different target behaviours for each student)	The target behaviour differs for each student. All individuals who peform their own specific target behaviour receive personal reinforcement. Example: Amy must complete 10 equations to earn five extra minutes of computer time; Mitch must complete 15 lines of writing to earn five extra minutes of free time.	The target behaviour differs for each student. All individuals who perform their own specific target behaviour earn reinforcement for the group. Example: Alyse must remain seated; Ethan must raise his hand; Sian must be ready to start work on time. If all achieve these behaviours, their group can have five extra minutes of recess time.

that it must be possible to administer the chosen reinforcers easily. Reinforcers must also be credible and of high quality and yet should not distract students from being engaged.[69] In addition, the following principles apply.[70]

Contingency. To be effective, reinforcement must be contingent on the desired behaviour – which is to say that it must be delivered if, and only if, students perform the target behaviour.

Immediacy. The time frame for delivery must take account of students' ages and abilities. In the early years of primary school, when students need more immediate reinforcement, the reward should be delivered within one day; students in middle and later primary classes (from grade 3 onwards) can delay gratification for longer, in which case the reward can be earned over a time frame of two days to a week; whereas, by high school, the incentive can be offered up to two weeks in advance. On the other hand, students with impulsive behaviour choose the most immediate reinforcer, even when it is less attractive,[71] which implies that for these students in particular, you will need to deliver a high-quality reinforcer *immediately* if it is to be more potent than competing reinforcers.

Frequency. Reinforce often at first, so that behaviour is learned quickly but gradually reduce reinforcement to natural levels so that the new behaviour is maintained.

Individualised. For reinforcers to be effective, they must be individually tailored to each student. This is because what serves as a reinforcer for one person might be neutral or even aversive to another.[72] You can base your selection on your knowledge of reinforcers that generally work and of those that have worked in the past, or by surveying students about their interests and preferences.[73] To gauge the latter, you can ask students to make a list of reinforcers that they would like to earn and select one of these, reserving the right to veto any item that you deem to be unsuitable or which might embarrass students (say, because it is delivered in public).

Value. The criteria for earning a reward need to be reasonable in that the amount of work required to earn it must be reflected in the value or size of the reinforcer.[74] For example, when behaviour allows students to escape the learning task altogether, your replacement reinforcer has to be both more powerful and reasonably immediate.[75]

Satiation. It will be important that the reinforcer is not over-used such that students tire of it or it loses its value as a reinforcer.

Teach students the contingencies. Tell students in advance exactly what behaviours you expect and which consequences will follow either their observance or noncompliance.

Natural reinforcement. Progress, maintenance and generalisation will be most easily assured if you employ reinforcers that are commonly and readily available in the natural environment.

Monitoring. You will need to record students' behaviours so that you can determine if they have earned a reinforcer. For this task you could use the board at the front of the classroom, marbles in a jar, or a marker on a chart. Once a reinforcement regime is in place, you will observe its effects and adjust it if it is not increasing the frequency of the desired behaviour.

Conclusion

Notwithstanding the advice that rewards must outnumber criticism and punishment in a ratio of 5:1, naturalistic observations in supervised common areas of schools find that the average rate of verbal reinforcement is once every 20 minutes.[76] Many teachers justify this low rate of reinforcement on the grounds that students should behave well naturally and should not expect nor receive special privileges for doing what they ought to be doing anyway.[77] In contrast, behaviourism relies on a body of research which concludes that students will behave more appropriately when teachers reinforce their desired behaviours. It believes that, just as we offer praise for learning a new academic skill, so too teachers need to praise students for achieving behavioural expectations.[78]

CHAPTER 5

Reducing inappropriate behaviours

If we consider problem behaviors as occurring in people, it is logical to try to change people. If we consider problem behaviors as occurring in contexts, it becomes logical to change the context. Behavior change occurs by changing environments, not trying to change people.[1]

The first priority in any behavioural intervention must be to reduce the causes of disruptive behaviour by changing the antecedents that occasion disruptions and by making natural conditions so highly reinforcing that students are motivated to behave appropriately.[2] Subsequently, if a contrived intervention becomes necessary, reinforcement must be the first measure employed and punishments administered only once reinforcement has failed.[3] Even then, punishment should be reserved only for those behaviours – such as self-abuse – that cannot be suppressed in other ways and must always be accompanied by positive reinforcement to strengthen alternative, desired behaviours.[4] In this way, corrective measures will help students identify what behaviour they should be producing.[5]

The menu of reductive measures

Lay use of the term *punishment* often refers to retribution against perpetrators and deterrent of onlookers but, in behaviourist terms, it simply means an aversive event that follows a behaviour and which causes the behaviour to reduce in frequency. Punitive methods can be ranked in order from the least to the most restrictive methods (which you might recall from chapter 3 refers to how much external control is imposed on students), as listed in Box 5.1. Movement along the hierarchy to a more aversive response must be based on data that the lesser intervention is not working.[6]

Just as is the case with reinforcement – which can entail either the delivery of something positive (positive reinforcement) or the removal of something aversive (negative reinforcement) – punishment can withdraw something positive (Type 2 punishment) or administer something aversive (Type 1 punishment).

Differential reinforcement

Differential reinforcement procedures involve reinforcing a positive behaviour while simultaneously withholding reinforcement of an undesirable target

---

BOX 5.1   **A hierarchy of reductive responses to undesired behaviours**

- Differential reinforcement
- Noncontingent reinforcement
- Stimulus satiation
- Withdrawal of positive stimuli (Type 2 punishment)
  - Extinction (terminating reinforcement)
  - Response-cost procedures
  - Time-out
  - Suspension
- Presentation of aversive stimuli (Type 1 punishment)
  - Verbal reprimands
  - Simple correction
  - Over-correction procedures
  - Restraint
  - Corporal punishment

---

behaviour.[7] Differential reinforcement is less aversive than other reductive methods because it employs reinforcement rather than punishment.[8] On the other hand, the fact that it is difficult to extinguish an undesired behaviour can reduce its effectiveness.[9] There are four main types of differential reinforcement aimed at reducing inappropriate behaviours.[10]

Differential reinforcement of lower rates of behaviour (DRL). Here the target behaviour might be desirable at low rates (such as recruiting teacher assistance), but is undesirable at high rates.[11] Therefore, in this method, you reinforce students when the behaviour occurs less frequently. You can reinforce after a full lesson if the behaviour has occurred less often than specified or, in a more gradual process, divide the lesson into smaller intervals and deliver a reinforcement at the end of each interval during which the student

displayed the behaviour at the permitted level.[12] Gradually, you would incrementally decrease the number of behaviours that you permit, or increase the length of the interval, until the behaviour occurs at a tolerable level.

This approach can take time to achieve results and relies on careful measurement of the frequency of the behaviour. It has the advantage that students continue to receive reinforcement, although your focus is on an undesirable behaviour rather than its positive alternatives.[13] It is ideal for innocuous behaviours such as calling out during class[14] and has been used with swearing,[15] but would be inappropriate for behaviours such as aggression, because that cannot be tolerated at any rate.

Differential reinforcement of incompatible behaviours (DRI). While ceasing reinforcement of the undesired behaviour, in this process, you reinforce incompatible behaviours such as staying seated when the target behaviour is out-of-seat behaviour. The behaviours are mutually exclusive in that performing one makes it physically impossible to display the other.[16] However, the incompatible behaviour may not serve the same function as the target behaviour; for this reason, DRA is often preferred.[17]

Differential reinforcement of alternative behaviours (DRA). With this method, you reinforce alternative (not opposite) behaviours such as putting up a hand rather than calling out. The alternative behaviour usually serves the same function as the undesired behaviour.[18]

DRI and DRA have the advantage of teaching students what *to* do, rather than what *not* to do, although reinforcement can be effective only if they perform the alternative behaviour often.[19] In real situations, it can be difficult to withhold all reinforcement of the undesired behaviour and always to reinforce its alternative, although perfect accuracy is not essential.[20]

Differential reinforcement of zero rates of behaviour (DRO). This is also known as differential reinforcement of the *omission* of behaviour. Under this method, you give students reinforcement for not displaying the target behaviour at all during a given time interval. The method can be used for self-injurious behaviours (such as head banging) and aggression, which cannot be permitted at all.[21] If the behaviour occurs at very high rates, the length of the interval will have to be very short at first so that the student can earn the reinforcer, and then lengthened incrementally as the behaviour improves.[22] When using this approach, it makes sense to use Reset-DRO, in which the timer is restarted if the behaviour is displayed.[23] Although this approach can achieve rapid results, it is less educational than the other methods because you do not teach any alternative, replacement behaviours.[24]

A complication of DRO is that, although the student might not produce the target behaviour at all – and thus is eligible to be reinforced – she or he might instead display another equally obnoxious act. In that event, practitioners need to use a second concurrent approach for responding to other undesirable behaviours.[25] For example, when instead of scratching at her eczema (which is the target behaviour), a student squirms under her desk and refuses to come out, rather than using DRO to reward zero rates of scratching, you might instead employ DRI, reinforcing her for using a fidget item instead of scratching at her skin sores.[26]

Noncontingent reinforcement

Under this method, the student receives a reinforcer (typically teacher attention) at the end of specified intervals, regardless of the behaviour that the student is producing at the time. Occasionally, the behaviour being performed when the reinforcement is delivered might happen to be an undesired one, but the reinforcer will coincide with it so infrequently that it will not be systematically strengthened.[27] Strictly speaking, this method is not reinforcement because no particular behaviour is being strengthened: the inappropriate behaviour is basically on extinction.[28]

Stimulus satiation

Stimulus satiation entails giving students so much of the antecedent to the behaviour that they tire of it. An example is giving dozens of pencils to a student who hoards these by taking them from classmates. The theory predicts that the student will eventually become overloaded with pencils and will no longer choose to steal them.[29]

Withdrawal of positive stimuli (Type 2 Punishment)

As its title implies, this method involves withdrawing something that students value when they perform an undesired behaviour, in the expectation that this will extinguish the behaviour. The three main types of this form of punishment are extinction, response-cost procedures and time-out. For any of these to work, there must be a high level of reinforcement in the natural situation, so that the punishing condition is noticeably less positive than the usual setting.

Extinction

Extinction withholds the precise reinforcer that is maintaining the target behaviour, in an effort to decrease its frequency.[30] When applied to undesired behaviours, it involves identifying and then withholding the particular reinforcer that is maintaining it at the same time as reinforcing an appropriate behaviour.[31]

The main application is when teacher attention is reinforcing students' disruptiveness. In that case, you would discontinue giving the disruptive behaviour your attention while ensuring that you reinforce alternative, more appropriate behaviours at other times.[32] In order that the student is aware that you are not paying attention, you can ostentatiously become involved with another student or read or write something busily.[33] You can also inform the student about the extinction in advance, for example: 'Each time you call out, I will not speak to you'.[34]

Extinction takes some time to work, particularly if the behaviour has been longstanding and has been reinforced only intermittently to date[35] (which will be the case for most behaviours). There are many instances where it will not be effective.

- It will not eliminate self-reinforcing behaviours such as rocking or thumb sucking by students with sensory integration difficulties.
- It will not eliminate behaviours that permit students to escape work demands.[36]
- When teachers are not in control of a social reward – such as when the behaviour permits students to interact with each other, or when clowning in class attracts the mirth or admiration of peers – teachers will not be able to withhold reinforcement because they are not the ones delivering it.

Moreover, there are some behaviours for which extinction is inappropriate.

- It cannot be used for self-injurious or violent acts because you cannot allow students to accumulate injuries while you wait for extinction to work.[37]
- Its slow effects mean that it will be unwise to use extinction for behaviours that may be contagious – that is, for behaviours that peers might copy.
- If the behaviour is escalating unacceptably, it will likely be inappropriate to attempt extinction.

In addition, four problems emerge with the use of extinction. First, it can be difficult to notice how your own actions might inadvertently be reinforcing a disruptive behaviour and therefore to apply extinction procedures to yourself. Second, it might not be possible to tolerate the behaviour while extinction takes effect and, meanwhile, in your exasperation you may accidentally reinforce it intermittently, which will prolong it further. Third, in what has been called an 'extinction burst', the undesired behaviours may initially increase before they get better, or frustrated students might display new antisocial behaviours such as aggression or agitation.[38] Finally, behaviour that has been extinguished in one setting is still likely to occur elsewhere. That is, gains made with extinction do not generalise readily.[39]

Response-cost procedures

With response-cost procedures, you systematically remove reinforcers when students act inappropriately. The consequence that is forfeited might be a privilege such as free time, or you could impose a penalty or fine such as the loss of points or tokens within a token economy system. The latter has the advantage that you can withdraw points at your discretion rather than, say, having physically to confiscate tokens.[40]

Although response-cost methods are generally more effective than administration of aversives (to be discussed next), they are vulnerable to a focus on negative behaviour, with the teacher overlooking the positive behaviours to be rewarded.[41] One practical difficulty with these approaches is establishing the magnitude of fines: if these are too severe and a day's gains can be wiped out with one misdeed, the students will resist the program or feel that they have 'nothing to lose' by further disruptions. Also, you cannot exact further

punishment from bankrupted students and hence would have no further influence over their behaviour. On the other hand, if fines are too lenient, they will have no punitive effect. For these reasons, under response-cost procedures, reinforcement for appropriate behaviour must far exceed fines for disruptiveness.[42]

Time-out (from positive reinforcement)

Sometimes we do not know what is reinforcing a given behaviour or, in a natural environment such as a classroom, there are so many potential reinforcers present that it is not possible to control them all.[43] In this case, rather than withdrawing reinforcers, we can ensure that the student no longer has access to them, either by removing reinforcement from the student, or by removing the student from reinforcement.[44] This procedure is known as *time-out from positive reinforcement*, or *time-out* for short.

Two factors are essential for time-out to be effective: first, the natural setting must be very reinforcing so that removal from it is indeed a punishment; second, reinforcement cannot be available in the time-out condition. This means that, while time-out cannot be punitive (e.g. by causing students embarrassment or anxiety), neither can it be positive: it must be neutral. The method works best with behaviours that are maintained by social or tangible reinforcers because these are the most easily withheld during time-out.[45] There are many types of time-out.[46]

Planned ignoring. The most naturalistic form of time-out is variously termed planned, deliberate or tactical ignoring. It involves paying the student no attention while the behaviour is occurring and instead lavishing attention on him or her when producing appropriate behaviour.[47] This is only advisable, however, for those behaviours where attention is the reinforcer, for mild behaviours that are not escalating, for those behaviours that are not contagious (such that other students start to produce them also), and for behaviours that are not being reinforced by peer amusement. Planned ignoring also needs to be paired with other strategies, such as reinforcing appropriate behaviour.[48] It is probably indistinguishable from extinction and therefore shares its shortcomings.[49]

Non-exclusionary time-out. This is where students remain where they are, but are deprived of access to any reinforcers such as attention, work materials, or the right to earn rewards such as points or tokens. You might, for example, direct disruptive individuals to place their heads in their folded arms on their desks.[50]

Exclusionary time-out. This involves physically placing students on the periphery of the group, from where they can observe their peers but are not permitted to participate.

Isolation time-out occurs when the teacher removes the student totally from the activity to a separate area within the classroom (such as the 'thinking chair') from where it is not possible for the student to view the ongoing activities.[51] This form and both non-exclusionary and exclusionary time-out may embarrass students in front of their classmates, engendering defiance and escalating disruptiveness.

Seclusionary time-out. This procedure confines students to a completely separate area for a specified and brief period of time.

The room must be of a reasonable size with adequate ventilation and lighting, should be free of objects with which students could hurt themselves and should allow you to monitor the student continuously. Your surveillance will be essential to ensure that students are both safe and not forgotten. To that end, you will have to determine an appropriate duration. On this issue, most advocates recommend a duration measured in minutes; any longer could justifiably be termed solitary confinement. Next, you will need to be able to prevent escapes. Although the most effective method to prevent escapes is to lock the student in the room,[52] this raises ethical objections.

Next, exiting criteria have to be established. Some writers recommend a fixed duration guided by the formula that its duration should not exceed one minute per year of the student's age, up to a maximum of 15 minutes.[53] This raises the issue of what to do if a student is still disrupting at the end of this period. Therefore, some recommend that students should not be allowed to exit until they cease all disruptive behaviour (including reactions of sadness or distress at having been placed in time-out). Under this criterion, timing starts only once the student settles down. However, this can prolong the isolation for too long and appears to make little difference to the effectiveness of the procedure anyway.[54] One effective strategy is to reinforce the first appropriate behaviour displayed once the student has returned to time in.[55]

Despite these practical demands on teachers, the removal of a troublesome student is a powerful reinforcer for them, thus giving rise to the potential for over-use.[56]

All forms of time-out have their practical difficulties. Most concerning is that it will result in a loss of instruction time,[57] which could further disadvantage students who have learning difficulties and could result in increased disruptiveness when they return to class. Practical difficulties include that it requires that a functional assessment be conducted to discover which reinforcer is maintaining the behaviour. This is because time-out in the form of ignoring will work only if the behaviour is being maintained by teacher attention; isolation time-out would be needed if peer attention were the reinforcer; and time-out should not be used at all for behaviours that are reinforced by avoidance of task demands. In that case, it will be ineffective or, worse still, time-out might reinforce disruptiveness because it allows the student to escape.[58] Such an assessment, however, is time consuming.

Suspension

Pure behaviourism recognises that suspension may not function as intended as a punishment, particularly for students whose behaviour allows them to avoid or escape from academic demands. Given the recidivism rate, it appears neither to be aversive to those on whom it is imposed, nor does it result in a reliable reduction in undesired behaviours. Nevertheless, pragmatic behaviourists continue to advocate its use, in which case it appears to be more retribution and an attempt to 'send a message' to onlookers about what teachers will and will not tolerate.

Presentation of aversive stimuli (Type 1 punishment)

The reductive measures discussed so far are known as Type 2 punishment, in which teachers remove something positive in an effort to decrease undesired student behaviours. In contrast, Type 1 punishment involves administering an aversive consequence, again with the same aim of reducing inappropriate behaviour.

Verbal reprimands

The first Type 1 punishment is the delivery of verbal reprimands in the form of brief, immediate feedback to students that their behaviour is unacceptable. As long as these are delivered in private and do not humiliate or embarrass students, reprimands can be very effective with mild behavioural difficulties but are less successful with more severe problems,[59] partly because being reprimanded can raise students' status among their peers.

Simple correction (restitution)

As the name implies, simple correction requires students simply to undo or correct the results of their behaviour, such as cleaning up a spill.[60] The restrictiveness of this approach depends on the extent to which students correct their behaviour willingly when asked. If no other punishment is delivered, it is one of the least restrictive (and intrusive) methods available.

Overcorrection

Overcorrection encompasses directed rehearsal and restitutional overcorrection. *Directed rehearsal* forces students to repeat a behaviour in an exaggeratedly correct form.[61] For example, if the class make a dash for the door when the bell rings, the teacher might require them all to sit back down and to vacate their desks in rows and walk to the door in an orderly fashion. The second form, *restitutional overcorrection,* requires the student to restore the environ-ment to a state that is better than before.[62] For example, if students have littered, the teacher will require them to pick up not only their own litter but also to clean up an entire area of the playground.

Both methods are time consuming and require the proximity of the teacher. Their intent is to be educational but there is little research supporting educational outcomes; instead the methods can readily deteriorate into being retaliatory.[63] They require the teacher to exercise moral or actual physical force to gain compliance and, if the students escalate their disruptions, not only will the methods be ineffective, but they can become aversive to both the students and teacher.[64]

Restraint

When students are injuring themselves, it can be necessary temporarily to restrict their movement.[65] However, if students are threatening others, potential victims would be better to leave the setting than to attempt to restrain a violent student. This crisis must be regarded as a failure of preventive measures and should trigger a re-evaluation of a behaviour program.

Physical (corporal) punishment

In many jurisdictions, the use of physical punishment by professionals (and, in some countries, by parents) is illegal. Even when it is permitted by law, there can be no moral justification for striking children. Not only is the method unethical, but also non-violent approaches are more effective.

Natural and logical consequences

Most of the pop or pragmatic behaviourists advocate the use of natural consequences

---

BOX 5.2 **Summary of consequences**

	Positive	Aversive
Administration of something	**Reinforcement**	**Type 1 punishment**
	Social (praise)	Reprimands
	Activity	Simple correction (restitution)
	Tangible	Over-correction
	Token	Restraint
	Edible	Physical (corporal) punishment
Removal of something	**Type 2 punishment**	**Negative reinforcement**
	Extinction	Avoidance
	Response cost	Escape
	Time-out	
	Suspension	

on the grounds that these are not punishment because they occur without adult intervention, (e.g. getting wet when you stand in the rain).[66] Although letting natural events take their course sounds reasonable, you cannot do so in dangerous situations, such as allowing children to run onto a road – the natural consequence of which can be injury. Not everything that is natural is benign. And using natural punishers is no guarantee of ethical practice: many things in life are natural (such as arsenic), but we still have a duty of care to protect children from exposure to them.

As an alternative, pragmatic behaviourists advise the use of *logical* consequences.[67] An exception is Nelsen and colleagues, who recant their early advice to use logical consequences, claiming (as do the advocates of guidance) that these are just a euphemism for punishment.[68] In contrast, advocates of logical consequences allege that these differ from punishment because, although arranged by the adult, they have a logical cause-and-effect link with the student's actions. For example, if a student draws on a wall, the logical consequence is to require the student to clean the wall. However, none of the pure behaviourists recommends that punishment be *illogical* and therefore this distinction does not hold up.

The second alleged difference between a logical consequence and a punishment is that when delivering logical consequences, the adult is objective about guiding students to take responsibility for their actions, with no disguised aim of forcing them to change their decision. According to the pragmatic behaviourists, experiencing the results of their choices teaches students that, while they can behave as they choose, they must still be responsible for their decisions.

(The exception is physical danger.) In this way, reality replaces the authority of the teacher.[69] Or, more colloquially, students have chosen to behave that way and hence have chosen the consequence, which means that the teacher is no longer 'the bad guy'.[70] However, pure behaviourists likewise believe that punishments should be delivered matter-of-factly, while the aim of having students 'take responsibility' is too fanciful for the purists on the grounds that it is unobservable.

A third supposed difference is that a logical consequence should be helpful, rather than hurtful by blaming or shaming students.[71] For example, apologising to a peer helps the aggrieved party to feel better; cleaning up a mess results in a clean space. In other words, logical consequences are also solutions. However, simple correction – which is one of the purists' punishments – equally fits this definition.

Finally, in contrast with punishments, consequences are supposed to focus on what will prevent future incidents, rather than making students pay for their past mistakes.[72] This is the difference between retribution and punishment, but not between logical consequences and punishment which, by definition, is an effort to decrease the behaviour in future.

In short, there *are* no differences between logical consequences and punishment. The term *consequence* more correctly refers to *any* event (either a reward or a punishment) that follows and changes the rate of a behaviour. Calling punishments *consequences* might make their administrators feel better and give them permission to 'punish with impunity',[73] but the term is just a euphemism for punishment,[74] or as Kohn frames it, is 'punishment lite'.[75]

Cautions for the use of punishment

In laboratory settings, studies have found that punishment works best to deter particular actions when it is fairly intense and is delivered both immediately (within seconds) and every time the inappropriate behaviour occurs; at the same time, any competing reinforcement (e.g. adult attention) must be eliminated.[76] These conditions are seldom achievable in schools, not least because teachers will not always witness students' actions, with the result that many are not detected and therefore cannot be punished.

Moreover, the very conditions that make punishment effective – particularly its intensity – are too severe to be justified for normal childhood behavioural mistakes and, moreover, are likely to provoke aggression, resistance and escape in punished students.[77] The alternative advice to teachers that consequences do not have to be severe because, 'It is the inevitability of the corrective action – not the severity – that makes it effective'[78] is theoretically incorrect: it is severity that makes punishment effective – but unethical.

The misuse of aversive methods has been a feature of institutions (including schools) since their inception. Punishment can be seductive because it negatively reinforces teachers: that is, it ends the aversive behaviour, which makes it more likely that teachers will use punishment again in future. Instead, it should be a last resort, applied only to those behaviours that have not been extinguished by lesser means.

Not only are the ethics of punishment troubling, but its effectiveness is weak. It can (unreliably) eliminate unwanted behaviour but, on its own, cannot teach replacement behaviours.[79] Moreover, punishment can accidentally reinforce the behaviour it is supposed to be extinguishing: for some students, watching a teacher lose control can be amusing.[80] Some punishers are not aversive to their recipients: for example, a student who wants to avoid school might welcome being suspended. Moreover, punishments lose their effectiveness if delivered too often.[81]

Third, punishment can have unwanted side effects, including that punitive teachers and school become aversive to students.[82] Students can lash out, become withdrawn, or seek to avoid or escape the setting.[83] Moreover, it is undesirable to teach young people to solve problems by using power over others,[84] while punishing antisocial behaviour may simply teach students to become more skilled at avoiding detection.[85]

Another shortcoming is that changes brought about by punishment seldom transfer to other settings (generalise) or are maintained.[86] If a behaviour is punished in one setting, it may increase in another where it is not being punished. This is termed *behavioural contrast*.[87] Unless practitioners can establish the function of the behaviour to be extinguished, simply suppressing it can result in its eventual return or replacement with another that is equally troubling or worse.[88]

Conclusion

Pragmatic behaviourists in general are more enthusiastic about the use of punishment than are pure behaviourists. In lay hands in particular, punishers (something noxious, unpleasant or aversive) are often substituted for punishment – that is, a consequence that diminishes the rate of behaviour. However, without stringent evaluation, practitioners cannot know whether the administration of a noxious event actually functions to reduce the target behaviour. Moreover, strict behaviourists are very clear that punishment should be used *only* as a very last resort and, then, *only* if reinforcement has failed to effect a behavioural change *and* if the target behaviour has a severe impact on the student's capacity to function adaptively.

Even with these caveats, the guidance writers dispute the assumption behind punishment that we have to make young people feel badly in order to motivate them to do better. In recognition of its negative effects and that it is better for students to learn from their mistakes than to pay for them, guidance advises teaching problem-solving skills, rather than imposing a punishment. This teaching can function only within a nurturing relationship, which guidance believes is damaged by the imposition of punishment.

CHAPTER 6

Classroom discipline

From 85% to 90% of students begin school having already learned the social skills necessary to become an effective learner . . . One way for schools to ensure that such behaviors become ingrained in a school's culture is through the development and systematic use of universal interventions.[1]

At the level of the classroom (Tier 1), the pragmatists dominate the purists. This is partly because behaviourist theory has nothing to say about thinking or emotions and hence takes little interest in how individuals learn. Nevertheless, all behaviourists agree that both discipline and instruction must be teacher-directed. Controlling approaches take for granted that the classroom belongs to teachers, who determine how they expect students to behave and express these expectations in the form of rules with predetermined consequences for their infraction. Pragmatic behaviourists believe that successful classrooms are those that are under firm teacher control.[2]

According to controlling discipline, adults possess the following three forms of power:[3]

- *Role power*: that is, status conferred by one's role as an adult and a teacher.
- *Reward power*: the power to control children's access to the material goods

and the emotional nurturance that they require.
- *Coercive power*: the ability to punish children to gain compliance.

The goal is 'responsible' behaviour, by which is meant '100 per cent compliance 100 per cent of the time'.[4] The purpose of this is not to accrue power for yourself but because compliance with your instructions will foster students' academic success.[5]

The aim of Tier 1 measures is to prevent having to intervene directly with individual students. Preventing disruptions is more humane than allowing students to get into trouble unnecessarily, and makes it likely that behavioural gains will be maintained.[6]

Elements of a classroom discipline plan

Tier 1 interventions aim to establish a culture that supports appropriate behaviour across all school settings.[7] This entails teaching both students and teachers the rules, expectations, policies and procedures that will enhance the smooth operation of the school.[8] This should prevent behavioural difficulties for as many as 89 per cent of primary school students; and just over 70 per cent of middle and high school students.[9]

Observation in classrooms has shown that, other than following through more reliably and seldom ignoring early disruptions, effective classroom managers are not necessarily any better at responding to disruptive behaviour than their less effective counterparts. Instead, they are better at preventing disruptions.[10] Ineffective teachers, on the other hand, seldom respond in a planned and predetermined way when their students disrupt.[11]

Therefore, teachers require a behaviour support plan, whose four elements are:[12]

- Instruction: maximise structure and predictability, actively engage students in instruction and ensure that the environment is conducive to student engagement.

- Institute rules: post, teach, monitor and reinforce expectations in the forms of rules and routines.
- Use a continuum of reinforcement to strengthen appropriate behaviour.
- Use a continuum of strategies to weaken inappropriate behaviour, including both off-task and disruptive behaviours.

These elements are illustrated in Figure 6.1. The purpose of a classroom discipline plan is to avoid the need for you to make hasty, ill-considered or emotionally charged responses to students' disruptions, resulting in inconsistent or arbitrary reactions.[13] A plan also enables you to secure support from parents and school administrators.

Instruction

Effective instruction requires teachers to prepare and deliver an effective and interesting curriculum. This not only maximises opportunities for students to be

FIGURE 6.1   Graded Tier 1 behaviourist responses

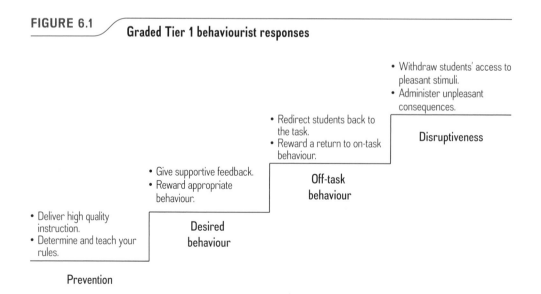

- Deliver high quality instruction.
- Determine and teach your rules.

Prevention

Desired behaviour

- Give supportive feedback.
- Reward appropriate behaviour.

Off-task behaviour

- Redirect students back to the task.
- Reward a return to on-task behaviour.

Disruptiveness

- Withdraw students' access to pleasant stimuli.
- Administer unpleasant consequences.

BOX 6.1   Tier 1 interventions[14]

- Write a school statement of purpose that expresses an explicit rationale for the discipline system, such as enabling students to learn.
- Establish a small number of positively stated school-wide expectations or rules.
- Define these expectations for each routine and setting of the school (e.g. classroom, playground, hallways, toilets, the school assembly hall).
- Develop scripted lessons to teach these, varying the lessons according to the ages of the students.
- Increase active supervision in all settings.
- Establish a continuum of strategies for rewarding appropriate behaviour.
- Establish a continuum of strategies for responding to inappropriate behaviour.
- Develop a staff reinforcement system to recognise staff for their effort in implementing the system.
- Develop an action plan for implementing the rules-and-sanctions steps.
- Develop a plan for collecting data on behavioural difficulties, in order to be able to evaluate whether the measures are having the desired effects.

successful but also prevents their behaving disruptively in order to avoid or escape tasks that they find aversive because they are unable to be successful at them.[15] In this way, a strong curriculum is necessary for maintaining order.

Many students with behavioural problems have learning difficulties and, therefore, it is important that teaching be tailored to their academic needs.[16] It will also be necessary to teach skills that students will need for school success, such as being ready to learn, completing and turning in homework and being on time.[17]

Effective teaching is aimed at ensuring that students stay engaged or 'on-task'. Students who are alert or restless will need to be actively engaged in learning, with frequent opportunities to respond to questions, either as a group in chorus or individually.[18] To that end, you can ask questions of the larger group, wait for a moment, and then call on individuals who do not appear to be engaged.[19] Alternatively, you can give each student a small whiteboard or laminated sheet of paper (or, these days, an electronic tablet) on which to write an answer to a group question and then hold that up for the teacher to read.[20] Tablets also allow students to write down a question before they forget it but without needing to interrupt, and to write an answer while they remember it even as other students are being called on.

Environment

Positive behaviour support upholds that, given that behaviours occur within specific contexts, it is not productive to blame disruptions on individual students and, in

---

BOX 6.2   **Modifications to instruction**[21]

- Match task difficulty to individuals' skill levels, attention span and favoured mode of output (for example, not requiring extensive handwriting by students with fine motor difficulties).
- Recruit students' active engagement by giving them ample opportunities to participate and respond during teacher-led instruction.
- Intersperse easy tasks among more challenging activities.
- Deliver clear instructions.
- Have predictable and manageable schedules and routines.
- Observe a brisk pace of instruction.
- Give students some choice about their activities, the materials and the sequence of completion of tasks.
- Alter schedules so that demanding tasks are not allocated late in the day.
- Institute breaks.
- Incorporate students' interests.

---

turn, to try to change them: instead, you need to adjust the contexts.[22] Environmental manipulations will include establishing a comfortable working environment, with adequate space and materials. Minimising crowding and distractions, and making sure that the classroom is orderly can all assist students to engage.[23] The layout needs to be planned to maximise students' access to the teacher, to peers and to resources and to minimise distractions.[24] Arranging desks in rows will promote on-task behaviour, in contrast with grouped desks which tend to encourage interaction.

Environments beyond the classroom need to be assessed also. Behaviourists advise minimising the amount of space that is difficult for teachers to supervise and improving scheduling to reduce student density in common areas such as hallways and the playground.[25] Staggered dismissal and lunch times can minimise traffic congestion in common areas.[26]

Establish and teach rules

Behaviourists base their interventions on establishing and teaching rules and the consequences for their violation. Teaching will provide a direct explanation of the rule and the rationale for it; demonstration and modelling of behaviours that signal its observance; activities or role plays for the students to practise the behaviours associated with observing the rules, and feedback about their behaviour.[27]

Most rules will be intended to ensure safety and courtesy.[28] Advice about the nature of these rules varies, with some writers recommending the following:[29]

- Be responsible.
- Be respectful.
- Be ready to learn.
- Be cooperative.
- Be honest.
- Be safe.

BOX 6.3   **Sample matrix of rules and routines[30]**

Classrooms	Toilets	School assembly hall
Be responsible	**Be responsible**	**Be responsible**
Keep work areas clean.	Keep area clean.	Treat furniture appropriately.
	Flush appropriately.	Leave area as you found it.
	Throw paper towels in the bins.	Enter and exit in an orderly manner.
		Take care of school property.
Be respectful	**Be respectful**	**Be respectful**
Keep hands, feet and objects to yourself.	Keep hands, feet and objects to yourself.	Keep hands, feet and objects to yourself.
Use a quiet voice.	Use a quiet voice.	Use a quiet voice.
Enter room quietly.	Allow others their privacy.	Stay seated until directed otherwise.
Be considerate of other people's belongings.	Wait your turn at the sink or fountain.	Respond to the speaker appropriately.
Use polite language.	Use polite language.	Use polite language.
		Treat speaker as a welcome guest.
Report all unsafe behaviour and vandalism.	Report all unsafe behaviour and vandalism.	Report all unsafe behaviour and vandalism.
Be ready to learn	**Be ready**	**Be ready**
Be on time.	Walk directly to the toilets.	Be prompt.
Be prepared.	Return to class immediately.	Sit in designated areas.
Do your best work at all times.		
Follow classroom procedures.		
Be cooperative	**Be cooperative**	**Be cooperative**
Be an active listener.	Do not disturb nearby classrooms.	Listen with eyes on the speaker.
Respond to quiet signal immediately.		Respond to quiet signal immediately.
Be honest		
Do your own work.		
Be safe	**Be safe**	**Be safe**
Use all equipment as intended.	Wash and dry hands.	Use all equipment as intended.

Others suggest: respect yourself, respect others, respect learning, respect property, respect the environment.[31] Regardless of their number and content, the rules need to be broad enough to include all desirable behaviour and be mutually exclusive.[32] Even so, because these rules are long-term, open to interpretation and are not readily observable, teachers must draw up a matrix of what observing these rules would look like, by listing behaviours relevant to each setting across the school. The advantage of these practical rules is that they are immediate, observable, and they apply throughout the school (see Box 6.3).

Although these matrices can be used for preschoolers, such a list is mostly as a guide and reminder for the teachers, given that such young children cannot read. Nevertheless, teachers can take photographs of children performing the target behaviours or use diagrams in addition to giving actual instruction in the behaviours through rehearsal and role play.[33]

Most behaviourists advise that, 'The teacher is the adult and knows what is acceptable and unacceptable behaviour'.[34] Nevertheless, some say that students can contribute to determining rules. Once the rules are in place, teachers must be careful to abide by them also.[35] Students are quick to notice when teachers violate their own rules by being disrespectful or ill-prepared themselves.

Lesson plans

After developing the matrices, the school team will develop lesson plans to teach students each behaviour in each setting. One such plan for preschoolers is detailed in Box 6.4.

Routines

Students find it easier to achieve expectations when they know what they are being asked to do and how they are to do it. Clear enunciation of procedures helps with this. Some of the routines for student use that teachers will need to teach include:[36]

- being prepared
- asking for assistance
- getting teacher attention
- solving problems.

Different routines will be needed during teacher-directed instruction, small group work, and individual seat work, as listed in Box 6.5. One way to signal a change of expectations is with a 'colour wheel'. This is a pinwheel coloured in thirds of different colours, each of which corresponds to a different instructional setting: seat work, free time, and direct instruction. The teacher teaches rules and procedures for each activity and, whenever the activity changes, the teacher indicates this by moving the wheel to the relevant section, thus signalling a new set of expectations.[37] It is likely that any method that clarifies and teaches expectations will be similarly effective.

Routines in other venues need to be specified as well, such as transitioning in hallways, use of the toilets, and entering and exiting common areas.[38]

Teach the plan

Behaviourists advocate teaching students not only academic content but also how to abide by rules and procedures.[39] The purpose of explicit teaching is to empower students to abide by your expectations. Appropriate behaviour, it is said, is taught, not caught.[40]

BOX 6.4 Sample preschool lesson plan for teaching children to walk indoors[41]

Rule: Be safe
Behaviour: Use walking feet

Instruction
1. Introduce the concept that a way to be safe indoors is to use walking feet.
2. Ask children, 'When do we need to use our walking feet?'. Discuss their answers.
3. Discuss why it is safer to walk rather than to run indoors.
4. Have the children trace a partner's feet on paper and cut these out, then make a trail for the children to follow while they practise walking.
5. Use pre-corrects every day that week before changing activities.
6. Remind the children to use walking feet.

Modelling and role play
1. Model walking ('Walking feet go 1 and 2 and 3 and 4 and 5').
2. Have students practise walking softly, loudly, quickly, slowly, forward and backward.
3. Play games such as Simon says or Follow the leader that entail different walks.
4. Have the children walk while balancing light books on their heads to practise walking softly.
5. Read story books and sing songs about the walks of different animals and have the children walk like an elephant, and like a duck and so on.

Follow up
1. Send a note home suggesting that parents ask the children about walking feet.
2. Review at the end of the week.
3. Pre-correct individual children who have difficulty using walking feet at particular times, such as when their parent arrives to collect them, or when it is time to go outside.

You will explain the rules and reasons for them, the supportive feedback that you will be using and the corrective actions and reasons for these, checking for students' understanding of each element. Younger children in particular will need opportunities to rehearse and practise these. Discussion and role play can help young children to learn the rules,[42] while older students have experienced rules already and therefore will need only a brief outline of each rule and its rationale.

You must also display lists or posters of these rules in prominent places in the room. After the initial teaching at the beginning of an academic year, you should offer booster training sessions over the next few months.

Supervision and monitoring

You must constantly monitor students' observance of rules and routines to ensure that you can respond to infractions in a timely manner.[43] This applies both to the

BOX 6.5 Necessary routines and procedures[44]

Beginning of the day or of a lesson
- Attendance check
- Updating students who were absent from the previous lesson
- Response to tardiness
- Students who need to leave the room
- Use of student materials and equipment
- Use of teacher materials

Managing students' work
- Distributing materials
- Collecting completed work
- Grading of work
- Handing back assignments

Procedures for seat work
- Talk among students
- Obtaining help
- Rules about leaving their seats
- Procedures for those who finish early

Procedures for group work
- Use of materials and supplies
- Assignment of students to groups
- Managing group or cooperative learning

Procedures during teacher-led instruction
- Student attention
- Student participation

Miscellaneous procedures
- Signals for quiet or that instruction is about to begin
- Responding to interruptions and visitors to the classroom
- Drills e.g. fire, earthquake
- Dismissal routines
- Completing paperwork and other administrative tasks
- Communicating with parents

classroom and to common areas of the school so that teachers are visibly present in locations where antisocial or disruptive behaviour can occur, while prohibiting students from congregating in areas where supervision is not practicable.[45]

Reinforcement

Teachers can be so busy monitoring inappropriate behaviour that they overlook positive behaviours, not least because these will be more normative. However, behaviourist philosophy advises that we 'Catch them being good'[46] and reinforce positive behaviours so that students are motivated to produce them again.

Verbal recognition (praise)

When students are displaying desired behaviours, you must offer supportive feedback to reinforce this. Verbal recognition involves naming the target student and offering sincere and specific praise that describes the appropriate behaviour. This must be simple, direct, personal, genuine, specific and descriptive. Older students may be embarrassed by public positive recognition; instead, therefore, it can be delivered in private, perhaps followed with a statement such as, 'You should be proud of yourself'.

Some behaviourists advise the delivery of four positive reinforcers for every correction or reprimand.[47] Others recommend a ratio of six to eight positive interactions with students to every negative one.[48]

Behavioural narration

When an individual is not following your directives, your supportive feedback can focus on those who are, using what Canter terms *behavioural narration*.[49] This involves identifying at least two students who are complying and naming both them and their appropriate behaviour. The aim of this method is to reinforce those who are complying while indirectly reminding others to do the same. For older students (who might resist being named as a 'goodie-goodie') Canter advises awarding extra points to the whole class for individuals' compliance, so that the whole group benefits.

With younger students, you can write on the board the names of those who meet expectations to see how many names can be accumulated, whereas for older students who might not want to be singled out, you can record anonymous points on the board and then reward the whole group when a specified total has amassed.

Tangible rewards

Tangible ways to recognise observance of the rules include positive notes or phone calls to parents, giving students awards, bestowing special privileges and giving students stamps, stars or stickers.[50]

Token reinforcement

Under a token economy system, you would give students points or a portable and durable token (such as a poker chip) when they display target behaviours. Later, they can trade these tokens in for pre-negotiated backup reinforcers. An example of a token economy is placing a marble in a jar whenever any student does something that you want to reinforce; then, once the number of marbles reaches a predetermined total, you reward the whole class.[51]

Positive peer reporting

Teachers cannot possibly see all instances of positive behaviour and, if they do not see them, they cannot reinforce them. Moreover, an emphasis on misbehaviour can teach students to focus similarly and to report the misdeeds of the classmates. This places the teacher in the position (having not seen the incident) of having to be detective, judge and jury and this, in turn, introduces the probability of mistaken judgments that then undermine students' confidence in receiving justice from teachers.[52]

To avoid these outcomes, teachers can enact a system of positive peer reporting, which is termed 'tootling'. In contrast to tattling about inappropriate behaviour, this system encourages students to report on displays of any prosocial or helping behaviours of their classmates.[53]

Targets. Variants include that a student is randomly selected as 'Star of the week'; or reports can focus on a single target student with disruptive behaviour; or all students in the class can be the target of tootling.[54] Reports can be made in public, or privately reported on index cards written throughout the day and placed in a feedback box.

Reinforcement. Each day, the teacher sets aside 10 minutes to recruit verbal reports, or to read out the written feedback. On receiving the report, the teacher praises both the reporter and the student named in the report. Alternatively, under a token economy, the reporter and the actor can both receive points or tokens to be traded in for a tangible or activity reinforcer.[55] It is also necessary to administer group rewards to maintain tootling at high levels.[56]

Another variant is that, at the end of a group learning activity, peers can provide a target student with positive comments about his or her behaviour and, in turn, that student is encouraged to report three positive comments to peers.[57]

Good behaviour game

In this 'game', all students in the group earn points whenever a class member observes a rule, and/or lose points when any individual student does not comply. This is termed an interdependent group contingency. One study in a preschool used the strategy to teach compliance to two rules: sitting on a personal mat on the floor, and having eyes on the teacher during a group story and song session.[58]

A variant on this is *Say–Do* correspondence training. In this intervention, teachers ask students for a commitment that they will comply with a given rule and then, after an activity session, the teacher asks each team (in a series of questions) to report whether they did or did not comply with each of the rules.[59] The teacher delivers small tangible reinforcers to each member of the winning team, medium-sized tangible reinforcers to all members of the team that wins most sessions throughout the day, and more substantial tangible reinforcers to winners of the week.

Responding to non-disruptive, off-task behaviour

Even when not interfering with others, when students are not paying attention, you cannot ignore this because doing so would be tantamount to saying that it is okay in your class for students to learn nothing.[60] Students' resulting lack of success would hurt themselves, while their off-task behaviour might grow into a disruption that interrupts teaching and learning for their peers.

However, imposing an immediate penalty is not the answer, because it will alienate students rather than return them to the task. Therefore, teachers should calmly redirect inattentive students back to the task. This can be done through directing a disapproving look towards the student; moving in close to him or her; naming the student while continuing with teaching; or praising those nearby students who are on-task. Once the student is back on task, teachers should praise this. If students need repeated reminders to remain on-task, you would move up the hierarchy of sanctions and implement a corrective action.

Reducing disruptive behaviours

Teachers will list behavioural disruptions in order of seriousness, with a series of punishments of increasing intensity and aversiveness, for example:[61]

- minor problems such as talking out of turn, tardiness, or being unprepared, are dealt with by the class teacher, unless they become chronic
- major problems such as fighting, defiance or insubordination, will be referred

to the principal or other administrator overseeing discipline and will incur consequences such as detention

- illegal acts such as vandalism or bringing weapons to school will be referred to the police or the governing body. The punishment for these acts is likely to be suspension or expulsion.

Teachers must be sure not to issue threats, ultimatums or warnings, because these might reward students' disruptiveness.[62] Instead, corrections must be delivered in a calm, matter-of-fact or businesslike manner, whereby you do not threaten but only remind students about the consequences if they continue to behave inappropriately. The teacher's response, in other words, has to be 'emotion free'.[63]

Pre-corrections

Pre-corrections are verbal reminders, prompts or opportunities for students to practise a rule prior to entering situations or before transitioning to new activities.[64]

Reprimands (error correction)

Teachers can respond to a first infraction with a reminder or 'desist'.[65] This will be delivered after moving in close to a disruptive student, because directives delivered from across the room will distract those who are on-task. This also avoids having the disruptive student challenge your authority to gain status with peers and ensures that your response does not excite peer sympathy for the student.[66]

Having moved in close physically, you concisely describe the inappropriate behaviour and exactly what students should be doing instead. These statements are also known as explicit reprimands[67] but Canter reminds teachers to deliver them from a stance of concern that the behaviour is not helpful to the student.[68] Next, Canter advises that you remind students of the corrective actions they have received so far and what will be the consequence if they continue to disrupt. If they defy your authority verbally or nonverbally, at the time be assertive (without getting angry) by repeating what you want them to do. With older students, it might be best if you conduct this conversation out of the room, away from the gaze of their peers because adolescents might front up to you in an effort not to lose face with their peers.[69]

Discrimination training

The same act (such as shouting) can be appropriate in one venue (e.g. at a sporting match) and inappropriate elsewhere (e.g. during school assembly). By providing cues and administering consequences differently in different circumstances, students will learn which behaviours are appropriate in various settings. In this way, they achieve some measure of self-control or learning. This procedure is very detailed when the person has a profound disability,[70] but for most students it is just a matter of saying something like, 'Your loud voice is fine on the playground, but not indoors'. In a similar vein, I taught my young daughter the difference between a restaurant (where patrons wanted a quiet atmosphere) and a café (where she could be more active).

Planned ignoring

It is important not to ignore minor disruptions, because these can escalate into more serious disruptions.[71] But neither should you give attention to those behaviours that are being reinforced by teacher attention.

Similarly, it is advisable to instruct students to ignore a peer who is off-task or whose behaviour is being reinforced by peer attention.[72]

Card system

Under this system, each student has a named pocket with three to five coloured cards (usually green, orange, red, blue and purple) with the outer card each morning showing green. For the first infraction, the green card is placed at the back to expose the orange card; a second infraction results in the red card being displayed; and so on, until a final infraction means that the student must leave the room for seclusionary time-out[73] (see chapter 5).

Debriefing

As a third step in a sequence of warnings and reminders followed by time-out, students report to a 'buddy teacher' or class assistant for debriefing before being permitted to return to their classroom.[74] The debrief involves giving students feedback about what they are doing incorrectly and what they should be doing instead. Students fill out a debriefing form that asks them to:[75]

• identify the inappropriate behaviour they displayed
• identify what they aimed to gain from behaving in that way (such as avoidance of work, or peer or teacher attention)
• reflect on whether the behaviour achieved that goal
• identify what they need to do when they go back to their classroom
• indicate whether they think they can do that.

Once he or she has filled out the form, the student waits for the teacher's assistant to check that the form has been filled out correctly, and then the student must return to the class and wait at the door until the teacher acknowledges his or her presence and invites the student back into the room.

Parent notification

For the fourth infraction on the same day (in primary school) or in the same lesson (in secondary school), you would contact a student's parents or have the student ring them him- or her-self. The final consequence (for the fifth violation) is being sent to the principal, with this having been planned in advance so that you know what support you will receive from the principal.

Re-teach the rules

If students repeatedly break a rule, teachers will need to re-teach the prerequisite skills, provide opportunities for students to practise these, test that students know the correct response, and reinforce them for displaying appropriate behaviour.[76]

Crisis plan

Teachers will need to have a crisis plan for those behaviours that are dangerous to the student performing them or to nearby students or teachers.[77] For severe infractions such as aggression, you should bypass the normal hierarchy of sanctions and instead send the student immediately to the principal. This is called the 'severe clause'.[78]

School-wide support

It is vital that teachers have support from school administrators, parents and consultants as needed. At the same time, although teachers need leeway to exercise professional discretion within their own classrooms, they must ensure that their responses are congruent with the purpose of the school and its rules and expectations.[79]

Guidelines for using corrective measures

Ethical guidelines for using punishments were listed in chapter 5. In addition, pragmatic behaviourists offer the following practical guidelines whose base recommendation is that the regime of rewards and punishment must be efficient and cost-effective, because the process of management cannot become more important than teaching.

• To avoid humiliation of students, keep track of infractions on a clipboard rather than on the more public black- or white-board.

• Corrective actions should not roll over into the next day. Each student must start each new day with a clean slate.

• Always follow a consequence with positive recognition when students return to appropriate behaviour.

• Misbehaviour that occurs outside the classroom comes under the school-wide discipline plan, which imposes its own sanctions. These are separate from your classroom system, with consequences imposed elsewhere not affecting the progression of corrective actions within the class.

• Students will need an 'Escape mechanism' that allows them to tell their story later, but not while a lesson is in progress.[80] This may mean that you allow them to write down what they want to say, which you can discuss together at a later time.

Conclusion

Tier 1 interventions target all students in the belief that prevention is cost-effective, is equitable in that it excludes no one from the benefits of the intervention, and that it capitalises on the superiority of prevention over intervening once problems have emerged.[81] These measures also ensure that problems of generalisation from an artificial setting to the classroom are avoided, because the program is based in the classroom.[82]

On occasions, however, individual students' behavioural problems may persist despite these broad-based measures. This signals the need to move to Tier 2 interventions, which are discussed in chapter 7.

CHAPTER 7

Targeted interventions

The secondary tier is designed to support a targeted group of students who have not responded to primary tier interventions, but whose behaviors do not pose a serious risk to themselves or others . . . Practices typically focus on intensifying the supports provided in the primary tier.[1]

The intention of secondary or Tier 2 interventions is to protect students from risk factors in their lives (such as family poverty) being translated into poor academic and behavioural adjustment at school.[2] It is estimated that these measures are relevant to approximately 15 per cent of primary and 29 per cent of high school students.[3] As described in the opening quote, the interventions aim to support individual students who have not responded to the primary measures of teaching the rules and applying universal consequences. Nevertheless, the behaviourist literature includes sparse mention of what constitutes this level of intervention.

Daily report card

One commonly used method is a daily behaviour report card, otherwise known as a check in–check out intervention.[4] This defines expected behaviour, which should be a discrete act (such as leaving the room without permission) whose occurrence can be readily observed. Next, the teacher specifies who will record whether students have displayed the target behaviour, and when and where the behaviour will be occurring. Subsequently, students check in with a teacher, a school psychologist or the principal regularly (e.g. at the end of each school day) for the adult to give them feedback about their progress.[5] These check-ins provide a venue for positive reinforcement, while carrying the card home is a means of one-way communication with parents so that they can also reinforce their child at home for behaviour displayed at school. The final element of the system is for all those involved in teaching the student, recording the behaviour, and giving feedback to meet regularly to monitor the success of the intervention.

Behavioural contracts

A contract is a way of writing down expectations for students, so that both the teacher and the students are clear about what they have to do to earn a reinforcer. The document will specify which behaviours you require, the timelines, what rewards will be delivered for success and which punishments will be administered for noncompliance, with a final clause giving students a right to renegotiate this agreement and to correct failure. These elements should all be negotiated with students.[6]

At first, the reinforcer will need to be delivered immediately and for successive approximations, rather than for perfect performances. The goal must be accomplishment, not obedience, and it must be fair – which is to say that the amount of effort needed by the student must be reflected in the quality of the reward.[7] As with all other interventions, teachers must monitor behavioural contracts to

---

BOX 7.1   **A sample behavioural contract**

This is an agreement between Alex (student) and Ms Teacher.
The agreement begins on (date) and ends on (date).

Alex agrees to:
- Be on time for school.
- When he does not understand a task, raise a hand and, when called on, ask for help.
- When he needs to move, raise a hand and ask to leave his seat.
- When moving about the room, he will not interrupt other students by talking to or touching them.

Ms Teacher agrees to:
- Check with Alex's parent if there is some reason that he is late.
- Respond as quickly as possible to Alex's raised hand.
- Allow Alex five minutes of extra computer time for each block of time (before recess, recess to lunch and lunch to bell time) that he is able to behave as agreed above.

Consequences:
- If Alex achieves expectations for one day, he can have 10 minutes' extra computer time the next day.
- If Alex achieves expectations on five successive days, he can have 30 minutes' extra computer time on Friday after lunch.
- If Alex does not achieve expectations on five consecutive days, his parents will be informed.

The agreement will be reviewed at the latest on (date) in a meeting between Alex and Ms Teacher. Alex or Ms Teacher can request a meeting sooner than this if they need to.

Signed:

Alex   _____   Alex's teacher   _____

Alex's parent   _____   School principal   _____

ensure that they are effective, and adjust the contract to meet current needs.[8]

By their nature, contracts are reciprocal in that each party does something. In light of this, a less structured contract, written here from the standpoint of the student could have the following elements:[9]

- I think I can . . . (perform a target behaviour)
- by . . . (date)
- If I do, I will be able to . . . (receive a particular reinforcer)
- Teacher will help by . . .

Remedial tutoring

In many cases, a behavioural problem masks a learning difficulty,[10] in which case teachers will need to offer remedial instruction. This will need to be designed on the basis of an educational assessment of students' learning skills and styles.

Mentoring

At-risk students can be paired with a senior student, a teacher with whom they have a warm relationship, or a member of the community who shares their interests and characteristics. Mentoring may be particularly effective with high school students, for whom the alternatives of daily report cards and social skills training are less likely to work.[11]

Peer support schemes

Peer support schemes can entail befriending schemes, mentoring schemes, conflict resolution schemes, or peer counselling programs.[12] Peer mediation trains (usually senior) students to help their peers to solve conflicts between them. In high school, peer mediation may be more successful than interventions by teachers, particularly given adolescents' belief that teachers should stay out of their conflicts.[13] However, many young people will lack the sophisticated skills needed; while the selection, training and supervision of mediators must be handled sensitively so that mediators are not exploited or undermined when antisocial peers denigrate them for colluding with the 'establishment'.[14]

Cognitive-behavioural training

For the purists, cognitive-behaviourism is an oxymoron because behaviourism believes that humans undergo and respond to environmental events, whereas cognitive theory upholds that humans are active agents of their experiences. Bandura argues that, if people acted only in response to environmental rewards and punishments, they would constantly shift direction; whereas cognitive theory recognises that individuals display self-direction in the face of competing influences.[15] Accordingly, cognitive methods assume a connection between thoughts (cognitions), feelings and behaviour.[16] When cognitive approaches are combined with behaviourist methods, the aim is to support students to control their own thinking and behaviour, without the need for adult oversight.[17] This is more efficient, avoids the need for communication and consistency between adults in various settings, and works even when adults are not available to supervise students.[18]

Methodological behaviourists have a broader aim of helping students to understand what they are doing and why they are doing it, and to judge if it is what they really want.[19] Hence, whereas ABA concentrates on what students do, cognitive theory focuses more on their thinking processes. And whereas ABA says that external control of students will give them the skills to control themselves (although it is not entirely clear how this transfer from outer to inner control would take place), cognitive theory systematically teaches self-regulatory skills.

Cognitive programs are of two types: training courses in social skills in general, or in specific skills such as problem solving or anger management;[20] and self-management programs for academic skills and classroom conduct.[21] A key set of skills for the latter interventions are the executive function skills – the skills that manage our own thinking and performance – which include inhibition of behaviour, self-regulation of emotions and attention, working memory, planning and self-monitoring.[22] As listed in Box 7.2, students can be in charge of 11 aspects

of these programs although, in practice, many of these components remain under the direction of teachers.[23]

Goal setting

Students perform better when they can set their own goals for their learning and behaviour, rather than having these imposed on them by their teachers.[24] These goals need to be specific, fairly immediate and challenging. To that end, you can guide students to set goals that are an improvement on their typical behaviour, but lower than their best performance (as no one can constantly achieve his or her best). Once students achieve one goal, they can be encouraged to raise their expectations, until both of you are satisfied with their performances.

Self-instruction

Self-instruction or self-talk is simply personal verbal prompts that we use to guide our own behaviour. When a task is

---

BOX 7.2   Components of self-management programs[25]

- selection of the target behaviour
- definition of the target behaviour
- selection of the primary (backup) reinforcer in token programs
- determining the performance criterion for the target behaviour
- prompts for the target behaviour
- observation of the target behaviour
- recoding the occurrence of the target behaviour
- evaluation to determine whether the performance goal has been met
- administration of secondary reinforcers (such as tokens or points)
- administration of primary (backup) reinforcers
- graphing or charting behaviour over time

new or challenging to us, we talk about it out loud to ourselves; then our self-talk becomes covert; and, finally, we no longer need to self-instruct because we have become competent at the task. You can teach these same steps using modelling, rehearsing and feedback – namely, in students' hearing you can complete an activity while commenting on the processes you are using; then have students complete the task accompanied by your commentary; then have them instruct themselves first out loud and then silently as they complete the activity.[26] Eventually they will learn to self-instruct quietly in their heads. (Out of embarrassment, adolescents will want to skip the step of talking out loud to themselves.)

However, students may already have their own personal way of structuring tasks which, although not what you might use, is successful for them. Therefore, when using this process, it pays to ask them how they are structuring the task so that you do not impose on them your own self-instructions that do not make sense to them. This can be especially crucial when you teach sequentially but students learn conceptually (see chapter 16).

Self-monitoring

Humans are always examining or monitoring their functioning.[27] Formalised monitoring has two aspects: first, students have to be aware of their own behaviour and, second, they need a system for recording it.[28] Students can choose to monitor either the presence or absence of the target behaviour, or they can monitor behaviours that are incompatible with it.[29] Specifically, they could note:

- the number of times they perform the target behaviour
- the rate of a behaviour
- the quality of their behaviour or of their work products
- their thinking processes.[30]

It is likely that students will be most successful when they are able to choose which aspect of their behaviour to monitor. Recording methods include simple tally sheets (perhaps with pictures for younger students) or counting devices. The sheet can be divided into intervals, with students recording whether they did or did not perform the target behaviour during each interval.

During self-recording training, you will need to use prompts to remind students to record their actions. Technology greatly assists this, with apps for various devices allowing teachers to set the device to vibrate at preset intervals to cue students to record what they are doing at the time.

The act of self-recording, itself, can produce a change in behaviour, particularly when students are focusing on successes rather than their failures.[31] Perhaps surprisingly, self-recording still works even if it is not accurate.[32] However, at the outset you can enhance students' accuracy by simultaneously recording their behaviour yourself and then rewarding them when their observations match your own.[33] Once they are clear about which behaviours they need to be taking note of, you will be able to fade this procedure to the point where students can record independently.

A less structured self-monitoring approach simply entails asking students whether they are complying with class rules at the time a violation begins: 'What are you doing? . . . What is the rule about that?'.

Self-evaluation (self-assessment)

In self-assessment, students compare their performance against a preset standard to determine whether they have met the criterion.[34] Given that this may be the most crucial phase of the self-management process, you will need to guide students to set appropriate performance standards. Some students may set themselves very lenient standards, while others either do not give themselves enough reinforcement, or are too demanding in their self-assessments.

Self-reinforcement

With self-reinforcement, the student chooses the reinforcer and delivers it following the target behaviour.[35] This is likely to produce better results than external reinforcers, particularly when students can select their own reinforcers. These can be administered both for improvement in the target behaviour and for the use of self-organisational strategies.

An alternative is that, once the student's records attest to a pre-specified level of achievement, the student can recruit teacher praise by reporting this success. At this juncture, you can reinforce meeting the criterion and also the act of self-recording itself.[36]

Academic survival skills

As well as focusing on skills for solving academic and other problems, you will need to teach certain students some practical skills which Rogers calls academic survival skills (as listed in Box 7.3). These can be construed as self-restraint skills. Rogers teaches these skills under the banner of his *Behaviour recovery* program.[37] In this program, you would withdraw individual students from the group for training sessions and begin by explaining in a relaxed and warm manner the behaviours that concern you, so that the students become clear about which of their actions are a problem and why. With young students in particular you can use a technique that Rogers calls mirroring, in which you briefly act out the behaviours of concern or use gestures or line drawings

---

BOX 7.3   **Self-restraint skills[38]**

- entering and leaving the classroom without violating the personal space of others
- settling down during group instruction so that teaching and learning are not disrupted
- getting teacher attention during instruction time (e.g. raising a hand)
- moving around the room at appropriate times and without disrupting others
- settling to a task
- maintaining focus on the task
- desisting from interrupting others during their work
- maintaining a 'partner voice' during work

depicting the troublesome behaviour. Then you can question the students about *what* (not why) they are depicted to be doing in the demonstration or picture. This needs to be a description of their actions, not a label such as 'being naughty'. If they cannot or will not answer, you can provide the description yourself. If such questioning would be too confronting, you could act out the behaviour of hypothetical students, leading into your demonstration with, 'Sometimes children do this when they get angry . . .' and subsequently posing the same questions about what they see while maintaining the ruse that this talk is hypothetical.

The next step is to demonstrate or depict in illustration an alternative, more appropriate, behaviour. Once again, you will ask the student to describe the actions now being depicted. These picture cues keep the behavioural plan concrete, immediate and specific and are a memory aid. There will be one picture cue (or one pair depicting both old and new behaviours) for each troublesome behaviour.

In the next phase of the program, young students in particular will need to rehearse the alternative behaviours. Initially you will demonstrate the new skill then talk them through all aspects of their performance of it. Meanwhile, you will offer encouraging feedback for their efforts. This can include a demonstration as well as verbal information about the improvements in their performance. During this phase, you can introduce students to privately understood cues and signals that you can deliver in the classroom to remind them to use their new behaviours in the regular setting. In subsequent training sessions, you would offer feedback and encourage self-reflection on how they have been performing in class.

Conclusion

Tier 2 interventions are directed at students with behavioural or academic problems (or both) with an aim to teach them specific skills that enable appropriate behaviour. At the same time, teachers will increase the intensity of the Tier 1 interventions to reinforce desired behaviour.

CHAPTER 8

Individualised interventions

[Tier 3] interventions are based on comprehensive assessments of the problem and the organization of strategies that incorporate information obtained from these assessments . . . To be maximally effective, prevention approaches and the interventions comprising them must be *directly linked* to and coordinated with each other within the context of a school site and its four systems of behavioral support (i.e., schoolwide, specific setting, classroom, and individual student).[1]

Tertiary-tier interventions are individualised multi-faceted programs designed to support students who have not responded to the earlier primary and secondary measures of teaching the rules and applying general consequences and teaching skills for performing those behaviours. It has been estimated that approximately 5 per cent of students will require this level of individualised programs.[2]

The intractability and complexity of the behavioural problems of students who have not responded to lesser measures means that this level of intervention requires a team-based approach whereby teachers, special education advisers, school psychologists, counsellors and other relevant specialists collaborate to devise and implement a comprehensive plan across the entire school.[3] The alternative of going it alone often leads, by default and

in desperation, to the use of punishments such as suspensions, which merely shift the problem elsewhere.[4]

Tertiary interventions must be do-able: the skills must be within the repertoire of both the students and of the teachers who deliver the interventions.[5] They must be congruent with the values of students and teachers; and teachers, students and parents must have the opportunity to contribute to the design of the behaviour support plans.[6]

Behaviour support plans

Positive behaviour support plans will gather data to generate hypotheses about the environmental events that occasion target behaviours and the consequences that follow them. Next, the team will devise a program for altering the behaviour. This plan will encompass:[7]

FIGURE 8.1   Steps of functional behaviour assessment and analysis

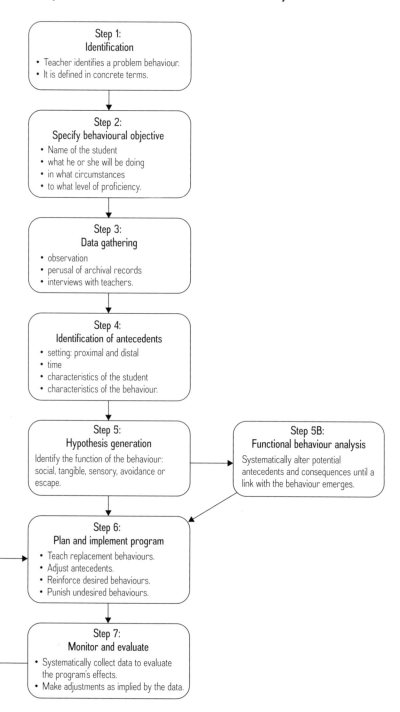

- an operational definition of the target behaviour
- strategies for altering the antecedents
- strategies for teaching appropriate behaviours
- strategies for reinforcing these desired behaviours
- methods for punishing undesired behaviours
- clear instructions about who does what, when, how and why
- instructions for handling crises
- statement about how the program's implementation and effectiveness will be monitored and evaluated and who will be responsible for this evaluation.

The steps involved in formulating a behavioural plan are listed in Figure 8.1. Park proposes the acronym *ERASE* for the components of a comprehensive functional behaviour assessment:[8]

E *Explain* what the target behaviour is, what precedes it and what follows it.
R *Reason*: explain what the student is getting or avoiding by displaying the behaviour.
A *Appropriate*: identify an appropriate behaviour that you want the student to be doing instead.
S *Support* and reinforce appropriate behaviour while weakening inappropriate behaviour.
E *Evaluate*: define the criterion for success and gather data to monitor progress towards that criterion.

Step 1 Identify the target behaviour

Just as teachers do not arbitrarily decide what to teach, so too they must not arbitrarily decide which behaviours to suppress or strengthen[9] (termed the *target* behaviour).

Some principles govern the choice of target behaviour. First, practitioners must define the target behaviour in specific, observable, unambiguous and measurable terms.[10] This ensures that everyone knows which behaviour we mean, and that observers can discriminate it from other behaviours. This means that the description cannot contain diagnostic terms (such as that a given student is 'aggressive') but instead spells out what that student does (such as hitting peers when provoked).

Second, although the main goal of pragmatic behaviourism is to ensure students' compliance,[11] those who have put more thought into it than this say that behavioural interventions must be in the best interests of students. That is to say, the target behaviour must be socially significant or relevant for students: it must teach skills that will enhance their quality of life and promote their welfare.[12] Sometimes, compliance will work counter to both of these aims and instead merely ensure the smooth functioning of the institution.[13]

Third, the behaviour must be severe enough to warrant an intervention.[14] We can check if an intervention is justified by asking if the potential target behaviour is dangerous to the student or others, is interfering with the student's academic progress or social inclusion, or is disrupting the student's relationships.[15]

Step 2 Specify the behavioural objective

Having identified which behaviour needs altering, you then specify in positive, precise, observable and measurable terms what modified form it will take as a result of successful intervention.[16]

A comprehensive objective will have the following components:[17]

- name of the student (or of the entire class)
- precisely what she or he will be doing when the desired behaviour is performed (the target behaviour)
- in which circumstances: which setting or instructional materials will be used
- the criteria for acceptability, focusing on accuracy or frequency (e.g. four out of five times; with 80 per cent accuracy), or latency (e.g. within 10 seconds of receiving an instruction).

This is called the *terminal* behaviour. The advice in formulating terminal behaviours or goals is to think small, keeping in mind that students with behavioural challenges cannot be expected to behave perfectly, nor better than students without difficulties.[18]

Step 3 Data gathering

In the third step, the teacher or consultant observes how often the student currently performs the target behaviour. There is no strict rule about how long to observe, other than that observers should ensure that they have captured enough examples to know what is typical.[19] Most writers assume that this will take 30 to 60 minutes per day over the course of several days to a week.[20] The observation method that you choose will depend on how much time you have available and, if the teacher is to be the observer, the system cannot be too complex to use alongside delivering instruction.

Depending on the type of target behaviour, the observer can focus on any or a combination of its following characteristics:[21]

- the *frequency* of the behaviour, which is the number of times it occurs
- its *rate*: the number of times the behaviour occurs within a specified time period
- the *duration* of each instance of the behaviour or the total duration, which is a sum total of time engaged in the behaviour during the observation period
- its *latency*, which refers to the amount of time it takes for a student to begin a task once instructed
- the *inter-response time*, which refers to the amount of time that elapses between instances of the target behaviour
- the *generality* of a behaviour – that is, whether it occurs only in certain settings or more generally across many settings and with different teachers
- the *intensity* or severity of the behaviour, such as with screaming or tantruming
- the *durability* of the problem, which refers to how long the student has been displaying the undesired behaviour
- the *accuracy* of a behaviour: for example, the number of items the student gets correct on a series of tests over time
- the *topography* of the behaviour: what it physically looks like
- the *location* of the behaviour: where it does and does not occur.

With *anecdotal* recording, observers simply record everything that they observe the student doing during the observation period.[22] Another method is for the observer to record every instance of the behaviour; this is termed frequency or *event* recording. This is well suited to discrete acts that can be counted, but is less suitable for continuous behaviours (such as tantrums) or behaviours that are difficult to count because they are so frequent (such as hand flicking in a person with autism). Once underway, the intervention will be deemed successful when an undesired behaviour occurs less often or a desired behaviour occurs more often.

A variant of event recording is called *controlled presentations*, when a teacher decides to give a student, say, ten opportunities to perform the target behaviour within a specified observation period, noting how many times that the student produces the behaviour on these trials.[23] This method can be suitable when there are time constraints on observations and has the advantage of making it possible to control the context.[24]

A third method is *interval* recording in which you divide an observation period (of, say, 15 minutes) into intervals (typically 5 to 15 seconds long), and note on a grid (with a plus or a minus sign) whether the behaviour did or did not occur at any time during the interval.[25] This method can be difficult to use at the same time as teaching, in which case a second person will be needed to act as observer.[26] Success of the subsequent intervention is demonstrated when an undesired behaviour occurs in fewer intervals, or an appropriate behaviour occurs in more intervals.

The fourth approach is *time sampling*. As with interval recording, the observation period is divided into intervals but, in this case, the period is longer (say, an hour) and usually the intervals are minutes rather than seconds long. Then the observer notes (again with a plus or a minus sign) whether the behaviour was occurring at the time that each interval ended,[27] cued by a timer that signals the end of each interval.

Two additional methods are *duration* recording, which measures how long a student engages in a particular continuous behaviour (such as a tantrum); and latency recording which documents how long it takes a student to begin an activity once instructed.[28]

In addition to making observations, team members will also peruse archival records of prior behavioural incidents and interview all teachers who work with the student.[29] They might also ask the student directly about the reasons for the behaviour.[30]

Step 4 Identification of antecedents

Observers will compare situations when the behaviour does versus does not occur, in order to discern features of the setting that govern the behaviour.[31] The events that precede the target behaviour are known as its *antecedents*, while the environment where it occurs is its *setting*. The behaviourist schools differ on the weight that they give antecedents: *Applied behaviour analysis* (ABA) takes stock of only the immediately preceding events; while methodological behaviourism will take account of the child's thoughts and feelings; *Positive behaviour support* (PBS) takes a wide view of potential triggers for behaviours including the student's social or family circumstances, for example; whereas *Functional behavioural assessment* (FBA) places more emphasis on the consequences of behaviours, because it contends that antecedents are important only inasmuch as they determine students' access to these consequences.[32] All, however, agree that the identification and subsequent manipulation of antecedents has many advantages: it can prevent behavioural problems, while

BOX 8.1

Antecedents that influence behaviours[33]

Identification of the antecedents and consequences that are salient for a given behaviour may be suggested by affirmative answers to any of the following questions.

Proximal setting
- Is the student more or less likely to display the behaviour when in a particular location in the classroom?
- Is the behaviour more likely in group or in individual settings?
- Is the behaviour more likely in large groups – that is, when the child is crowded?
- Does the behaviour occur only with certain teachers?
- Is the behaviour more likely when the student is seated?
- Is the behaviour more likely when the student is working near to particular peers?

Distal setting events
- Has a change in behaviour coincided with a significant event in the life of the student?

Instructional features
Is the behaviour more (or less) likely to occur:

- during certain academic or non-academic activities?
- in conditions of high or low stimulation?
- during activities with high or low structure?
- during verbal presentations?
- during visual presentations?
- with novel activities?
- during tasks that require passive versus active engagement?
- during seat work?
- for tasks that require writing, reading or mathematics output?
- during lessons that are difficult for the student?
- for tasks that offer students little choice?
- during particular routines?
- during transitions between activities?

Time
- Does the behaviour occur at certain times of the day? (This could indicate fatigue, hunger, or that medication has worn off.)
- Does the behaviour seldom occur at certain times of the day?

Characteristics of the student
- In the case of work avoidance or escape, could the behaviour be related to a skills deficit?
- Could the behaviour be a result of a medical condition, physical discomfort or side effects of medication?

Characteristics of the behaviour
- Does the behaviour occur as part of a chain of behaviours?
- Does the behaviour occur as a result of having another ongoing behaviour terminated?

changing antecedents can be simple (e.g. moving a student's desk) and can result in a swift, sizeable and enduring change in behaviour.[34]

Step 5 Hypothesis generation

Team members will analyse the data amassed from observations, interviews and behavioural records in order to generate a hypothesis about which antecedents trigger the behaviour and which reinforcers are maintaining it (as listed in Box 8.2). As mentioned in chapter 3, this step recognises that the same outward behaviour can serve a different function for different individuals, in which case the hypothesis attempts to identify how the target behaviour pays off for the student.[35]

Step 5b Functional behaviour analysis

With functional behaviour assessment, the team analyse the data collected to discern the links between a target behaviour and its antecedents and consequences. However, even when they are conducted by highly trained observers, approximately 25 per cent of functional assessments are unable to identify what is maintaining the behaviour.[36] Often, this is because an aberrant behaviour (such as head banging) has a sensory reinforcer, rather than the more observable social or tangible reinforcers.

When the team has been unable to discern the function of the behaviour, they can divert to perform a functional behaviour analysis. With this method, they test the various hypotheses by systematically altering each of the potential antecedents in turn (in what is known as a *structural* analysis) and then manipulating each potential reinforcer in turn (the *functional* analysis), until the factors maintaining the behaviour become apparent.[37] This can be very time consuming and is likely to be beyond the capacity of the classroom teacher and instead will be conducted by specialists.[38]

BOX 8.2 Functions of behaviour[39]

Sensory reinforcement
- for sensory stimulation: visual, auditory, smell, taste, touch, proprioceptive (information about our body position), and vestibular (balance mechanisms)
- to escape sensory overload

Social reinforcement
- to gain attention from adults or peers
- to escape from attention or social interaction (e.g. with shy or socially withdrawn students)

Tangible reinforcement
- to gain access to a tangible reinforcer: an object, activity or event

Avoidance or escape
- to escape from or avoid demanding or boring tasks

Functional behaviour assessment or analysis is not relevant for one-off or rare events, because there is no history of consequences to observe.[40] FBA also cannot be used for dangerous behaviours.[41] In that case, and in a departure from pure behaviourist principles, Nichols recommends *asking* the student why he or she performed the behaviour and then intervening to teach problem-solving or social skills that would correct the thinking that preceded the action.[42] The cognitive rationale for this is that any behaviourist diagnosis – say, that a student does something to get attention – implies that the student *wants* attention, in which case behaviourism is actually dealing with underlying thoughts and feelings.

This will yield a pathway from antecedent or setting event to the behaviour, as illustrated in Figure 8.2.

Step 6   Plan and implement the program

On the basis of an understanding of which events precede the behaviour and which are reinforcing it, you can now develop a plan to increase the frequency of a desired behaviour or reduce the occurrence of an undesired one. This will comprise four elements:

- teach desired behaviours if these are not already in the student's repertoire
- adjust the antecedents

- select relevant reinforcers and increase the frequency of their delivery for desired behaviours
- punish inappropriate behaviours, beginning with the least restrictive method first.

Teach replacement behaviours

For students to desist from disruptive behaviour, they will need to be able to perform positive replacement behaviours.[43] In this step, those devising the program will define this constructive behaviour so that it is observable. As detailed in chapter 6, teaching these desired behaviours might involve modelling, prompts, shaping, task analysis and chaining.

Adjust antecedents

The function of the behaviour might be to escape academic demands that exceed students' skill levels.[44] In that event, the team would recommend an academic assessment followed by adjustments to the curriculum or remedial tutoring as indicated.

Increase reinforcement for desired behaviours

Having ensured that students are capable of performing alternative desired behaviours, you will strengthen these by increasing the amount of reinforcement you deliver. You will also need to plan how to maintain the

---

FIGURE 8.2   **Problem behaviour pathway[45]**

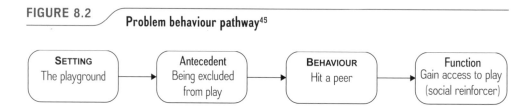

changes, for example, by fading contrived reinforcers.

Administer corrective measures

Once students' desired behaviours have been strengthened, any remaining undesirable actions can be reduced or weakened by punishment. Behaviourists advise the use of punishment on the grounds that consequences are imposed in the real world and classrooms should be no exception. Guidelines for the use of punishment are given in chapter 5. One principle specifically informed by FBA is that, if we intend to extinguish an undesired behaviour, we must replace it with one that fulfils the same function for the student.[46] For example, if the behaviour functions to allow a student to avoid or escape work demands, instead the teacher would teach that student how to ask for a break or to request an easier task.

Step 7   Monitor and evaluate the program

Once the plan is being implemented, observers will again need to record the behaviour (its frequency, intensity or other qualities as relevant, depending on the nature of the behaviour) in order to evaluate whether the intervention is working. This data collection is essential because intuitive judgments about improvement or lack thereof may be inaccurate owing to discouragement or biased perceptions. Of course, if those involved assess that the program is not working optimally, they will make adjustments as needed.

Home–school communication

Communicating with parents and teaching them skills for responding to their child's behaviours at home will be an integral part of Tier 3 interventions.[47]

Conclusion

Tier 3 interventions match the intensity of student problems with the intensity of the intervention. Behaviourists' lament that the measures would work if implemented properly[48] is commonly met with teacher reports that the programs' complexity and time demands are unworkable within schools. Teachers blame the model; behaviourists blame the execution. In chapter 9, I situate this debate within a critique of behaviourist methods in general.

CHAPTER 9

Critique of behaviourism

The most elaborate and empirically rigorous . . . measure is useless unless it can be applied by real practitioners to real problems of real people in the real world.[1]

A considerable body of research has demonstrated the effectiveness of the methods of applied behaviour analysis (ABA) and its disciples, positive behaviour support (PBS) and functional behavioural assessment (FBA).[2] There is evidence that controlling discipline can increase students' immediate compliance and modestly reduce their aggression, at least in the short term.[3] Controlling discipline has also been found to improve dysfunctional parenting styles and enhance parents' sense of competence.[4]

Effectiveness of specific elements

One meta-analytic study reported positive effects from many of the elements advised in chapters 3 to 8, namely: delivering well-structured teaching, posting and teaching rules, delivering specific and contingent praise, use of token economies, error correction, differential reinforcement, planned ignoring, response-cost procedures and time-out.[5] A sample of some specific studies on various elements follows.

Modelling. In one study, children observed brief videotapes of students being engaged on a task; as they watched, their teacher commented positively on the filmed children's behaviour, coaching the observers to perform similarly. This marginally increased the number of children who were on-task from two-thirds to three-quarters.[6] Some of the children also reported that the lesser noise in the classroom made it easier for them to complete their work.

Positive peer reporting. While it is clear that rewarding students for tootling increases the rate of positive reporting, there is little evidence that it improves the actual social behaviour of target students, the relationships within the class, or the class climate.[7] One study employed sweets (candy) as reinforcers to peers and the target child for reporting on the positive behaviours of others, and reduced disruptions by 10 episodes per day, which amounted to a 26 per cent decrease.[8] In another study, teachers and peers had improved attitudes towards previously rejected students, but did not increase their actual interactions with them.[9]

Daily report cards. A meta-analytic study found negligible results from the report card system over and above the specific behavioural contingencies already in place, with parental involvement a benefit only when parents contributed to all phases of design and implementation.[10] Students whose behaviour is negatively reinforced by escape seem not to benefit.[11] Teachers find it unmanageable to have to count the number of target behaviours during teaching, while simple tallies miss important aspects of the quality of the behaviour.[12]

Good behaviour game. One study found that the use of group contingencies to teach sitting on a mat and having eyes on the teacher dropped rule violations by six children from 50 per cent of the intervals to 15 per cent, with reinforcement working slightly better than response-cost measures.[13] The two teachers involved in the study preferred the reinforcement condition to the punitive one. A second study (of four preschoolers) resulted in improved compliance with instructions, although findings did not generalise across settings.[14] Another study in five kinder-garten classrooms found that 78 per cent of the kindergarten children wanted to continue with the game after its formal completion date.[15]

Response-cost procedures. One small study of ten children, in which they were fined tokens that were worth one minute of recess, produced immediate and substan-tial gains in on-task behaviour; moreover, these gains were maintained when the cost program was faded and replaced with natural reinforcement.[16]

Differential reinforcement of lower rates of behaviour. In one study, three children were permitted only a certain number of bids for teacher attention within a specified time period.[17] If they asked for attention less often than permitted, the teacher gave them a point for their team. This intervention reduced the children's excessive bids for attention, was seen by the teachers as being easy to use, and the children themselves enjoyed it. Each child returned to baseline levels once the intervention ceased, for which reason the teacher reported intending to continue it indefinitely.

Token economies. Evidence about the effectiveness of token economies is weak, partly because early supportive research would not meet modern standards for rigour. Token economies may be more effective at promoting task completion than at suppressing disruptive behaviour but, again, the studies are so flawed that even this tentative conclusion must be treated with caution.[18] In one study, 10 children who were rewarded with tokens that could be traded in for an extra minute of recess time showed significant gains in on-task behaviour but, once the reward schedule was thinned, these gains were not maintained for the five children with attention deficit disorders.[19]

Time-out. One study with four 3- and 4-year-olds (two of whom had autism) compared fixed-duration time-out with release-contingency time-out (when time-out is prolonged until the child stops crying, being aggressive or disruptive).

Both forms of time-out reduced the target behaviours, with the release-contingency method being no more effective than the fixed-duration method.[20]

Behavioural contracts. Contracts have been shown to increase on-task behaviour and task completion and to improve students' self-control.[21]

Self-management. On the whole, few elements of self-management programs (as listed in Box 7.2) are actually managed by students, with self-monitoring and self-evaluation being the minimum for benefits to accrue.[22] Across a range of difficulties and settings, programs that provide opportunities for the most student control are more effective, and produce gains that are better maintained than those where teachers are largely responsible for the program.[23]

Cognitive skills training. Advocates report that a skills training approach has greater potential than pure behaviourism to prevent recurrent disruptiveness.[24] As is true for pure behaviourist methods, however, much of the cognitive training in schools is performed by researchers, rather than by teachers; it is difficult to tease out which components of the training are effective; and few studies are rigorous enough to evaluate the training adequately.[25] Also, cognitive skill training is time consuming.[26]

With these limitations in mind, one research project found that cognitive training helped students who initially had reasonable self-regulation abilities to control their impulses, but was less successful with children who had more severe deficits.[27] In the case of aggression, this could be because children might choose to act aggressively not because they lack prosocial skills but because they value being powerful and expect aggression to achieve that for them.[28]

Meta-analytic studies of cognitive-behavioural interventions to teach social skills found that, compared with delivering no treatment, these approaches are effective across a range of conditions including behavioural disorders, disruptiveness, hyperactivity, school dropout, truancy and attention deficits.[29] Cognitive methods have also been effective with impulsivity, anxiety, depression; with improving targeted students' peer relationships; and at reducing aggression and antisocial behaviour, particularly in early adolescence.[30] They have been shown to improve the motivation and self-esteem of students with learning difficulties[31] and attention deficits, and can be useful in assisting teachers and parents to think less pejoratively about the children's behaviours.[32] Another study found that, while equally effective at the termination of the intervention, at follow-up, programs with cognitive components showed superior gains than purely behaviourist interventions.[33]

In meta-analytic studies, cognitive treatments have been found to be superior to no treatment but, when compared to alternative treatment methods, functional behaviour assessment and cognitive-behaviourism were found to be either equally effective or (marginally) *less* effective with conduct-disordered students than other methods.[34] Not surprisingly, the combination of family-based counselling and cognitive training for young people proved more effective than either one alone,[35] although some research has found no benefit from combined interventions.[36] Pure or radical behaviourists conclude that cognitive methods work, but do not know how[37] (because their paradigm does not encompass thought or emotion).

Outcomes of school-wide positive behaviour support

Evidence about the effectiveness of school-wide positive behaviour support programs is limited in that few studies ensure that the programs are implemented with fidelity.[38] In natural settings with the numbers of teachers, students and interactions involved, this would largely be impossible, but the lack of information does affect our confidence in the findings. The most common outcome measures for programs are office discipline referrals and suspensions. However, these sanctions represent the severe end of the spectrum of school-based behavioural problems, with few studies reporting data on the effect of the intervention on lesser infractions.[39]

These hesitations notwithstanding, one school-wide positive behaviour support intervention achieved a 40 per cent reduction in referrals to the school office for disciplinary infractions.[40] Another increased the numbers of students never referred for disciplinary problems from 76 per cent to 85 per cent.[41]

Another study employing a token economy reduced office discipline referrals in a school of 550 students from 1717 in one year, to 619 two years later, and after-school detentions declined from 845 to 21.[42] It is not clear how much of this improvement was due to the behaviour interventions, however, or to the fact that all teachers received training in remedial reading instruction, which was simultaneously delivered to all struggling readers.[43] In yet another school with 530 students, there were 2628 referrals to the office within one year – 1376 of these for the same 34 students.[44] After students were taught the rules, there was a 42 per cent reduction in referrals.

Much more modest results have been achieved in other studies,[45] with one that established, taught and reinforced universal rules actually producing an *increase* in office discipline referrals.[46] Another produced an increase in the first three months, followed ultimately by a decline.[47] This could mean either that teachers were more sensitised to infractions, or that rule breaking actually increased. Either way, it appears that Tier 1 aspects of the program are at best irrelevant and that any positive outcomes arise instead from Tier 2 improvements in remediating students' learning difficulties.

Another study employing the school-wide positive behavioural support produced a reduction in school suspensions from 77 in one year to 22 two years later, accompanied by a massive decline in disciplinary referrals to the school office from 608 annually to 46 two years later.[48] A second study produced an initial 20 per cent reduction in office discipline referrals and time-outs and a 57 per cent reduction in short-term suspensions, with expulsions unchanged.[49] However, rates returned to previous levels once punitive policies replaced reinforcement regimes and the remediation of students' learning difficulties.[50]

As for other outcome measures, school-wide positive behaviour support has achieved increased compliance and reductions in student aggression, with the numbers of students needing second-tier interventions declining from 15.8 per cent to 8.2 per cent.[51] A behaviourist early intervention program directed to school entrants with escalating antisocial behaviour produced improvements in their aggression and academic engagement, with gains maintained into the first and second grades of school.[52] Another program delivered at seven to nine years of age significantly reduced boys' delinquency and fostered their retention in the regular stream, with the gains of the program being maintained to just short of 15 years of age.[53]

One study focusing on teaching victims and bystanders not to reward a peer's aggression but instead to say 'Stop' or to walk away increased their performance of these responses, and reduced the aggressive behaviour of the six target students.[54] Another found that behaviourist programs were as effective in halving school-based aggression as were counselling or providing academic support.[55] Students who were most disadvantaged showed the greatest gains, while those in special education settings showed the least.[56] However, most of the interventions included in the meta-analysis were demonstration projects in which the researchers were directly involved in service delivery,[57] which makes it difficult to know whether schools can achieve the same improvements independently.

Another study in a special setting focusing on students with autism achieved a reduction in antisocial behaviour as seen in the virtual elimination of the use of physical restraint, which had been employed 122 times in the first 20 days of the school year and not at all in the last 20 days.[58]

Finally, an early childhood program labelled BEST in CLASS (Behavioural, Emotional, and Social Training: Competent Learners Achieving School Success) reduced children's behavioural problems and improved their social skills.[59] However, with this and other programs mentioned here, knowledge about the effective ingredients remains elusive.[60] We still do not have answers to the 'ultimate question' of 'What treatment, by *whom*, is most effective for *this* individual with *that* specific problem, under *which* set of circumstances?'.[61]

The conclusion is that behaviourist interventions are superior to the status quo (not quite 'doing nothing', but almost). However, when behaviourist interventions are compared with non-coercive interventions in schools, research has found not only that behaviourism is *less* effective, but that it also has undesirable outcomes. This research is detailed in chapter 20 but for now a single example will suffice: early childhood centres[62] and schools with punitive discipline have higher rates of delinquency and poorer attendance than those schools which use guidance.[63] Rutter found that:[64]

> in the long run good discipline is achieved by the majority of pupils wanting to participate in the educational process rather than doing so merely through fear of retribution.

Atypical programs

Aside from the research just mentioned, most behaviourist interventions are conducted with individuals with profound disabilities who are displaying atypical behaviours including pica and other feeding disorders; mouthing of objects; extreme noise sensitivity associated with Williams syndrome; social withdrawal; stereotypical behaviours and specific acts such as hand biting and flapping; self-injurious behaviours; and destructive behaviour.[65] Moreover, the programs are typically conducted in clinic settings or, when in classrooms, focus on only one or a handful of students rather than encompassing the entire class group.[66]

Some school-based research has demonstrated positive effects on reasonably typical problems such as students' getting started on tasks, improving reading fluency, the safe use of playground equipment, aggression, elopement (running away from the adult) and disruptiveness on the school bus.[67] Nevertheless, these interventions are usually implemented by researchers and academic psychologists, to whom teachers seldom have access.[68] This does little to allay doubts about the applicability of the methods in regular schools, particularly in high schools when reward-and-punishment regimes are less likely to be successful or practical given the organisational complexity of these settings.[69]

Generalisation and maintenance

Generalisation refers to the transfer of skills from one setting to another, while maintenance refers to the continuation of treatment effects over time. Given that few studies complete long-term follow-up, there remains minimal evidence that the gains in compliance achieved during intervention are maintained afterwards,[70] or that gains are transferred to other settings or to other teachers. This is true even when teachers specifically instruct students in skills for generalisation.[71] This lack of generalisation is a serious flaw, because teachers are unlikely to have the time to oversee permanent behavioural management programs.

Consumer satisfaction

School-wide positive behaviour support programs are typically well received by teachers: in addition to improvements in student behavioural problems, they have produced an improved collegial climate within the school.[72] Teachers also gain increased confidence in their ability to handle behavioural difficulties in their classrooms.[73] School staff in one study also reported feeling safer at school.[74] These improvements may be greater in early childhood and primary schools than in high schools, although there is too little long-term follow-up to be sure of this finding.[75]

In contrast, teachers often express distaste for ABA's philosophy,[76] while the high level of expertise needed to design interventions tends to exclude their input.[77] For these and perhaps additional reasons, teachers often refuse to enact behaviourist interventions.[78]

Whereas studies commonly ask teachers if they find the program effective and easy to use, few researchers have asked the recipients of the program – namely, the students themselves – for their views about its impact on their lives.[79] Non-behaviourists who *have* asked students about their satisfaction with school have found that students dislike teachers' rigid enforcement of rules and policies and protest that teachers are not interested in hearing their side of the story.[80] In one study, students reported preferring self-management to teacher control,[81] while in another study of students in grades 4 to 6, 80 per cent preferred non-behaviourist disciplinary strategies.[82] A third study found that students' sense of community was negatively affected by teachers' use of extrinsic rewards and by an emphasis on the teacher as the sole authority in the classroom.[83] Students are more anxious, angry and bored and accordingly less engaged in classes where they perceive that their teacher is punitive.[84] School connectedness is also lower in schools that impose suspensions on students, while students feel less safe in schools with harsh discipline policies.[85] Finally, children dislike school more when their classroom is highly structured and teacher-directed.[86]

Meanwhile, practitioners acknowledge that most behaviourist practice has been largely ineffective in involving and securing the support of the third consumer group, parents.[87]

Demands on teachers

As a result of school-wide positive behaviour support programs, studies find that administrators spend less time managing disciplinary issues, perhaps because teachers feel more confident of their ability to handle behavioural difficulties within their classrooms.[88] One study saved administrators 15.75 days per year of time on disciplinary processes, and students across the school amassed almost 80 extra days of instructional time.[89] Another study with a similar outcome measure achieved a decline from 41.2 lost days' instructional time to 21.2 days,[90] while a third reduced lost time by 659 hours per year in a middle school of 630 students.[91]

Time

Despite these findings, the amount of time needed to perform a functional analysis has often been criticised. One study found that 12 per cent of cases required three hours, with 13 per cent taking two hours, and 58 per cent concluded in under 90 minutes.[92] Nevertheless, this was only the hypothesis-generating element of the intervention, with interventionists also having to observe the students, interview teachers and scan records to gather the data on which to base their hypotheses.[93] An entire intervention can take an average of 58 days.[94] One study that involved consultants found that they spent on average just under 15 hours per student.[95]

In another study, over 13,000 observations were conducted and still the researchers had insufficient data to judge the function of the target behaviours.[96] This expenditure of time is particularly unjustifiable given that traditional ABA approaches seem equally, if not more effective, than the more detailed and rigorous FBA.[97] Furthermore, behaviourist assessment fails to ask the students themselves about the motivations for their actions, despite the fact that researchers have found that students can contribute more information about antecedents than can their teachers.[98]

Not only is assessment hugely time consuming but so too are behaviourist interventions. One study required 93 training sessions;[99] another took in excess of nine months merely to evaluate the differences between differential reinforcement and response-cost procedures in a preschool.[100] A third reported that it took up to six months from data collection to completed functional analysis before a behavioural plan could be implemented.[101]

Yet another study employed 10 volunteer observers to record the behaviour of five children.[102] Another functional analysis achieved behavioural improvements in three primary school children, but required 10 days each (of six hours per day) of observation in order to establish which consequences were reinforcing their behaviours, before implementing training in raising a hand and speaking in a quiet voice (dubbed social skills training), differential reinforcement of alternative behaviour, planned ignoring and time-out.[103] Even the authors questioned the feasibility for schools of this investment of time, while teachers find that it intolerably delays support for them and denies students timely treatment.[104]

With respect to school-wide positive behavioural support programs, teachers consistently report that the time demands for attendance at meetings is a huge deterrent.[105] Researchers and consultants commonly spend up to two years seeding the program, with ongoing coaching subsequently needed to support consistent implementation.[106] These considerable time demands on teachers in these first two years of planning and implementation, do reduce, however, once the program is under way.[107]

Complexity

Under behaviourist principles, consistency is essential. However, consistency is impossible in the busy classroom setting, because teachers simply cannot manage the dual roles of teaching at the same time as monitoring all student behaviours. They will not witness all events and accordingly cannot reinforce or punish reliably or immediately – yet the success of behaviourist approaches depends on their ability to do so.

Moreover, it is impracticable for teachers to select salient reinforcers for each student, decide on the magnitude of punishments, oversee trade-ins of tokens for tangible reinforcers, and provide a menu of reinforcers that are valued by students while still being inexpensive. Meanwhile, teachers also have to be able to manipulate highly technical program variables such as specific antecedents, the use of high- versus low-probability instructions and schedules of reinforcement.

With any reinforcement regime, there is a risk that, if one behaviour is targeted, other desired behaviours will reduce in frequency[108] and that students will tire of specific reinforcers. To overcome these threats, one group of researchers randomised all elements of a reward contingency: the target behaviour, the criterion required to earn the reward, and the reinforcer itself. The procedure was that at the end of a lesson, the teacher withdrew from a jar a piece of paper naming the target behaviour for that lesson (e.g. raising a hand before being called on); then from a second jar withdrew a piece of paper specifying the level to which it had to be performed by the students (e.g. no more than three infractions within a lesson); and then from the third jar withdrew the name of the reinforcer that the group would earn (e.g. an extra two minutes' free time at the end of the day).[109] Although the intervention reduced the incidence of disruptive behaviours, the teacher did not know ahead of time which behaviours would be targeted and therefore would have had to observe and record all the behaviours of all the students while simultaneously teaching the lesson.[110] While this method makes observation particularly onerous, the conclusion in general is that observation is unworkable without a specialist observer being permanently available.[111]

Functional behavioural *assessment* itself is complex, but performing an *analysis* by systematically altering a series of antecedents and consequences is beyond the capacity of most classroom teachers.[112] The proponents of FBA recognise that it requires a team approach but, even then, few team members would possess this expertise. Even avid behaviourists admit that skilful application of FBA is difficult in school settings, with some contending that it requires doctoral-level expertise – and yet observers with this level of training still can achieve low levels of agreement about the functions of a given target behaviour and the contingencies in operation.[113]

Poor practice is acknowledged to be unethical,[114] but it is highly improbable that teachers can apply the method accurately. Although researchers have been able to train teachers to understand the principles of FBA in a single three-hour training session,[115] such a low level of training is unlikely to translate into sophisticated classroom-based implementation. This is reflected in the fact that fewer than half of the published school-based interventions comprise a functional analysis and instead are simple behaviour modification.[116]

Further evidence of its impracticality is supplied by a study of behaviour plans submitted by 45 US schools, the majority of which plans did not record the antecedents or perceived function of behaviour.[117] The researchers observed that, without this information, it is difficult to design specific interventions. With the exception of programs overseen by university-based researchers, the majority of behaviour support plans are judged by experts to be inappropriate: 89 per cent of those developed by typical teachers and 35 per cent of those devised by behaviour specialists rely on punishment and fail to specify a plan for teaching replacement behaviours.[118] Others find that the interventions have little logical relationship to the antecedents and consequences of a behaviour.[119] Furthermore, few schools implement secondary- and tertiary-tier interventions within a school-wide positive behaviour support program: most employ only the primary measures of formulating, teaching and enforcing the rules.[120] Such a high rate of incompetent implementation and low rate of employment of advanced interventions implies that application is too difficult in regular settings.

Costs

In one study, the additional cost of a school-wide positive behaviour program was US$3000 annually (in 2000–2006 currency).[121] Some of this was spent on professional development and some on the tokens and backup reinforcers for the token economy system.

Critique of the behaviourist paradigm

The observation that an external event reliably follows a given behaviour does not prove that the behaviour is being caused by the event. This is a fundamental error in logic. It confuses motive with outcome.

Just because teacher attention follows a student's behaviour, this does not mean that this was the child's motive, even if the behaviour is repeated subsequently. An example might help: if a child learning to ride a bicycle falls off and receives a Band-aid, falling off the bike was not 'Band-aid seeking' behaviour but arose because of a lack of skill. The child, having received a Band-aid might fall off again, but that still does not mean that receipt of a Band-aid has reinforced falling off the bike. In confusing motive with outcome, behaviourism makes the very same unscientific inductions that it criticises in other methods.

The behaviourist paradigm cannot account for the fact that many behaviours are not necessarily rewarded in the immediate circumstances.[122] For example, children's aggression can be a learned response to witnessing domestic violence. Also, many behaviours are not learned by experiencing their consequences: I do not use heroin – not because I once experienced a negative consequence for doing so, but because I learned (from reading books) that it wasn't a good idea. Behaviourism has no satisfactory explanation for the thousands of things we know without direct experience.

Einstein is alleged to have said that theories should be as simple as possible, and no simpler. This raises a third criticism that the behaviourist paradigm is simplistic in its lack of interest in causes, attempting instead only to change the immediate behaviour.[123] I will argue in chapter 20 that this is both inhumane and ineffective in that satisfying an underlying unmet need would improve students' wellbeing *and* prevent a recurrence of the disruption.

Disadvantages of rewards

Given that it takes no interest in human thinking, the behaviourist paradigm fails to address the comprehensively researched question of the difference between internal and external motivation. Since his earliest research, Edward Deci found that external rewards in the form of payment caused intrinsic motivation to decline.[124] I review this evidence in chapter 16.

Second, rewards focus children's minds on what *they* will earn from their actions, rather than how these affect others. Therefore, rewards do not inspire considerateness, compassion or altruism.[125]

Third, rewards work counter to our intentions, in that delivering a reward for a given behaviour *decreases* the attractiveness of the behaviour and *increases* the attractiveness of the reward.[126] For example, when parents reward children with ice-cream for eating their vegetables, the children subsequently find vegetables *less* attractive and ice-cream *more* desirable.[127]

> Giving students rewards for learning does not teach them to like learning – but to like rewards.

Fourth, a compelling body of research focuses on the effects of rewards on children's self-esteem – which, of course, is not an issue that concerns behaviourists because it is unobservable. To be reviewed in more detail in chapter 12, the conclusion is that, when students receive praise or other rewards for their achievements, they develop an achievement-oriented self-esteem whereby they must keep proving their worth; whereas when their self-esteem is based on a non-contingent sense of their worthiness, their academic, emotional and behavioural adjustment are superior.

Observations in classrooms add another argument against the use of praise – namely, that it is typically administered so inaccurately that it cannot function as a reinforcer (that is, cannot possibly strengthen desired academic or behavioural skills).[128] Box 9.1 lists many common uses and misuses of praise within classrooms.

BOX 9.1 **Common uses (and misuses) of praise in classrooms[129]**

- Praise may be delivered as *recognition* for academic achievement. However, it is often given to low-ability students even when their work is incorrect; in which case, if it functioned as a reinforcer, it would be reinforcing poor-quality performances.
- Praise is often intended as a *reinforcement* for desirable behaviour. However, for this purpose it is a weak or even ineffectual reinforcer because it is typically delivered non-contingently or indiscriminately, may be accompanied by negative nonverbal behaviour that contradicts the positive verbal message, and occurs too rarely to be effective. It is particularly ineffective beyond the junior primary years, after which it is usually neutral or negative in its effects on student achievement and behaviour.
- Sometimes praise is a *spontaneous expression of surprise or admiration*. This is probably the most reinforcing for students, although teachers' surprise could communicate that the teacher believes the student is ordinarily incompetent.
- Praise may be used in an attempt to *offset earlier criticism*. To the extent that this has undertones of 'I told you that you could do better', praise may actually be punitive.
- Praise is sometimes used to *induce onlookers to emulate a praised student*. However, model students are seldom popular, in which case others will not choose to emulate them and may even reject them further. Praise delivered in public in this way is also likely to be detrimental for recipients, particularly for adolescents and those whose cultures shun having individuals singled out for accolade.
- Praise can be used *to set a positive tone* so that you do not feel that you are always nagging and issuing commands.
- Praise in the form of compliments is sometimes used to *make contact with alienated students*.
- Sometimes praise is given as a form of *student-elicited stroking*. Some students will approach teachers for praise but the awareness that they 'pulled' it may make any feedback less potent for them.
- Praise is sometimes used as a *transition ritual* in which teachers comment positively on students' work as a way to indicate that they have finished that task and can now move on to the next. Students are unlikely to attribute this sort of praise to anything special that they have done, in which case it will have little effect on their perceptions of themselves as learners.
- Finally, some praise is a *consolation prize* for the least able or most discouraged students. However, in a paradoxical effect, effusive praise for ordinary performances humiliates recipients and lowers their self-esteem because it communicates that adults believe that they can do no better.

Given that malpractice is so widespread, it is unlikely that so many teachers are incompetent, but instead that classroom settings make it difficult to administer praise accurately.

Disadvantages of punishment

The colloquial use of the term *punishment* disguises the fact that surprisingly little is known about its effective use in everyday settings.[130] Most research has focused in laboratories on rats, pigeons and monkeys being exposed to electric shocks, sprays of water, blasts of air, squirts of lemon juice, ammonia odour and physical restraint, none of which are applicable in classrooms.

The disadvantages of punishments centre on their limited ability to ensure even immediate compliance, their negative effects on children's emotional wellbeing, and the damage they cause to the teacher-student relationship. The presence of repeat offenders in detention and principals' offices is testament to the ineffectiveness of punishment. As Kohn asks, 'If punishment is so effective, how come I have to keep doing it?'[131]

BOX 9.2   **Pitfalls of tangible reinforcement**

At a seminar presentation when discussing the discouraging effects of reinforcement systems (star and sticker charts) on many children, a mother showed me a letter that her son, aged nine, had received the previous day from his teacher:

Dear Nathan
On the last day of term, the class is having a pizza party to celebrate the end of the school term. To be invited, you will need 72 points.

Mrs X

Two school terms into the academic year, Nathan had accrued the sum total of 6 points. Yet in the remaining two weeks of term, he was supposed to earn another 66 points. Recognising the impossibility of doing so, Nathan said to his mother, 'So I won't be going, will I, Mum?'

The inevitable happened and Nathan was sent to a different classroom during the class party, on the grounds that he had not earned enough points to be given access to the backup reinforcer (the party). (In fact, he was sent to the grade 1 class, adding to his humiliation.)

This illustrates that, while reward programs are ordinarily thought to be benign, they all necessarily involve withholding a reinforcer when adults deem that a child has failed to achieve their expectations. Thus, rewards are punitive: loss of a hoped-for reward feels like a punishment.

Furthermore, Nathan's exclusion is a clear message to his classmates that he is unacceptable and that it is permissible to exclude him. It also informs them about their own safety should they fail to meet expectations in future. Meanwhile, rather than being emboldened to try harder in future, there is a strong risk that Nathan will feel so disheartened at the unfairness of the system overall and the personal humiliation and injustice inherent in it that he will disengage from learning altogether.

Finally, punishment on its own cannot teach a desirable behaviour, but only suppress an undesired one.[132] It does not teach children the skills they need in order to behave well, such as self-regulation, flexibility, adaptability, problem solving, listening, or empathy for others.[133] Instead, the imposition of consequences teaches only that 'Might makes right'.[134] Its disadvantages far outweigh its advantages and, other than signalling who is in charge, it fails to produce any lasting behavioural improvements.[135] It spitefully seeks retribution or revenge against miscreants, rather than teaching them skills to prevent a recurrence.

Reprimands

Although behaviourists repudiate abuse, a licence to reprimand students can escalate into verbal abuse, by virtue not just of the content of teachers' statements, but also their public nature, which makes reprimands humiliating. As will be detailed in chapter 11, this is not a rare event, with 15 per cent of students suffering repeated verbal abuse from their teachers throughout their schooling.[136] As a result of abuse by teachers, victims are more likely to drop out of school, engage in high-risk behaviours such as alcohol and drug use and, if supported by similarly disenchanted peers, to become delinquent in adolescence.[137]

Time-out

Although some will contend that, of the various forms of punishment, time-out is reasonably mild, what is really being withdrawn from students during time-out is not teachers' attention, but their care and protection.[138] Children perceive this as a communication that they are unworthy.[139] At the time, it can lead to expressions of distress and protest that attract more punishment and, in the longer term, it leads to fear, anxiety, low and unstable self-esteem, avoidance of failure by evading challenge, truncated moral development, delinquency, poor emotional wellbeing, and difficulty forming relationships.[140] In group settings, time-out is even more problematic because it gives classmates similar permission to exclude peers of whom their teachers disapprove.

Suspension

The rationale for school suspension is to safeguard classmates' rights to learn and to protect them and their teachers from violence.[141] However, suspension does not

---

BOX 9.3   Pitfalls of using office referrals as a reductive measure

In the high school where I did my teaching practicum, the practice was to send the students to the principal whenever their behaviour got out of hand. Being a student teacher, the students were more carefree about what I overheard than they might have been with a permanent member of staff, and from their conversations I learned that the boys had a competition going to see who could get sent to the office most often. Within their peer group, emerging the winner was hotly contested, being a source of pride and status. It was little wonder that the 'punishment' of referring them to the principal was ineffective in restoring order.

contribute to a better learning environment for those who remain in class. Aside from the philosophical objection to deeming some students expendable in the interests of others, removing disaffected students simply results in new candidates emerging as the 'group barometer', whose disruptiveness signals their alienation from and dissatisfaction with school.[142]

Contrary to expectations, suspensions are most often imposed for relatively minor offences, such as absenteeism, failing to complete assignments, and the use of profanities.[143] Other than these minor offences, there are four identifiable groups of suspended students:[144]

- first offenders with no prior history of academic, attendance or behavioural problems
- disconnected students who are alienated from school, with poor attendance but average academic abilities
- troubled children and youth who have longstanding significant behavioural difficulties, with either chronic or acute family disruption such as child abuse or the recent death of a parent, who need emotional and family support rather than censure
- delinquents whose longstanding academic failure and behavioural problems were well known to the school, and for whom preventive efforts would have been advisable.

Given the disparate nature of the recipients of school suspension, its one-size-fits-all intervention is clearly inappropriate. School suspension does not reduce recidivism, truancy, school dropout rates or criminality but, indeed, exposes suspended students to a delinquent subculture.[145] It

does not fix the problem, but instead shifts it from the school to the community.[146] In the US, for example, 80 per cent of daytime burglaries are committed by suspended and excluded youth.[147]

The students most likely to be suspended are those with delayed academic skills.[148] The resulting loss in instruction time can only add to their academic difficulties.[149] This amounts to educational neglect, subtracting resources from disadvantaged youth to their educational, social and emotional detriment.[150] Rather than helping them to rise above their adverse circumstances, it traps them there. It essentially writes off the individual in order to send a message to the group.[151] That message is: 'Behave, or else'.

A study of 436 US schools (covering 60,000 students) that had implemented a *School-wide Positive Behaviour Support* program found that the rates of disciplinary referrals and suspensions of African-Americans were still double those of White students in primary schools, and almost four times as high in middle schools.[152] Referrals were mainly for 'defiance' and 'disrespect', which are categories that are highly subjective; whereas the same behaviour in cultural majority students is interpreted by their teachers as less of a threat.[153] That is, despite behaviourism's commitment to administering consequences consistently, there is bias in selecting which students will be disciplined and bias in determining the severity of the sanction delivered.[154]

The reactions of suspended students themselves are split. Although 20 per cent of suspended students reported that the punishment convinced them never again to act in a way that would earn a suspension, two-thirds reported that the suspension helped only a little or not at all.[155] In contrast, many suspended students are happy to escape.[156] Rather than being seen as a punishment, only 0.1 per cent of students in one research study reported finding the suspension embarrassing, with many instead seeing it as a chance to escape school.[157] For these students, being suspended is reinforcing.[158]

For others, suspension makes them angry.[159] They become less motivated and less invested in their education.[160] Many become less bonded to school; in turn, suspension may lead to broad social alienation.[161] Many suspended students subsequently drop out altogether, which suggests that suspension is in reality a tool for discarding these students: for 'push out'.[162]

For those who have been suspended repeatedly, the consequence is clearly not working, in which case something else needs to be tried.[163] Students who have been suspended report that their solutions would be to take classes that were more interesting and useful, to receive help to handle their emotions and solve problems, and being given someone to talk to.[164]

Physical (corporal) punishment

Corporal punishment is the use of force to cause pain (but not injury) to a child as a tool of discipline.[165] In the form of spanking (or smacking) with either a hand or an implement, it is still practised by the majority of parents. In the US (the only country for which I could obtain data), it is used by 93 per cent of parents of two- to four-year-olds; 58 per cent of parents whose children are aged five to nine years; and 40 per cent of parents of 13-year-olds.[166] Those who use corporal punishment do so 3.6 times a week, which amounts to a total of *187 times a year!*[167] In a recent early childhood study, teachers administered corporal punishment (on three- and four-year-olds) 15 times per day on average, with the range being from 15 to 65 times *in one day*.[168]

It is sobering to contemplate that, in democracies, there are restrictions on how prison guards can treat inmates (who have been *proven* guilty of antisocial behaviour) – and yet few countries limit the physical assault of innocents (children) by their parents, unless injury results.[169] And, whereas hitting an adult would constitute an illegal assault, in only a few countries is it illegal when children are the victims, with (at the time of writing) the most recent country to make it so being my homeland of New Zealand. It joins a group of minor nations, with the major Western powers conspicuous in their continued endorsement of this practice.[170]

Many episodes of child abuse (that is, injury to a child) are the result of an escalation of corporal punishment.[171] This risk alone implies that corporal punishment is unacceptable. Moreover, even without physical injury, there is considerable, consistent and robust evidence of its detrimental effects.[172]

Socially, corporal punishment increases children's aggression, particularly past the age of eight years. Although this could be because it is most often used in families whose other problems raise the risk of aggression, it is clear that violence against young people by their parents and in schools increases their perpetration of violence against both adults and peers, and elevates their likelihood of victimisation.[173]

Emotionally, when practised by parents and when accompanied by anger, corporal punishment (as distinct from child abuse) is associated with children's reduced mastery and lowered self-esteem that, in turn, contribute to elevated depressive symptoms in adulthood. Physical punishment also increases the lifetime risk of other psychiatric disorders, including anxiety and addictions. Children who are spanked are also more likely to develop an external locus of causality. At the time, children suffer emotional distress; perceive that they have been rejected; fear the loss of adult approval; and experience anger, humiliation at the loss of dignity, as well as guilt, shame and sadness.[174] Meanwhile, onlookers will subsequently fear their own safety, if they were to make a mistake.[175]

Behaviourally, physical punishment does not reduce antisocial behaviour in either homes or schools.[176] Indeed, it increases the severity of students' behavioural problems across time, raising the risk of behavioural problems at school entry by over 400 per cent.[177] These problems include reduced cooperation or compliance, escalating oppositional behaviour, and increased antisocial acts during childhood and adolescence and into adulthood.[178] Part of the mechanism is physical punishment's relationship to reduced moral reasoning.[179] In schools where corporal punishment has been discontinued, rates of behavioural difficulties have not risen subsequently while, in homes, a reduction in its use is followed by a lessening in children's antisocial behaviours.[180]

In terms of its *cognitive* effects, regardless of other parenting qualities, corporal punishment reduces two- to four-year-olds' IQ by an average of 5.5 points, with a 2-point loss at older ages.[181]

Although a few studies find differences in the effects of corporal punishment across cultures,[182] most research does not and indicates that children from disadvantaged groups or with difficult temperaments are most negatively affected by corporal punishment, even when the method is seen to be normative.[183] And, even where these detrimental effects cannot be demonstrated, no beneficial effects of physical punishment can be proven either.[184] The only 'positive' result ever found has been an unreliable increase in short-term compliance. However, this dubious achievement does not teach young people moral reasoning or encourage independent thinking.[185] Furthermore, where smacking achieves compliance, this is evidence that the children are amenable and therefore lesser methods would be equally effective.[186] In other words, physical punishment is unnecessary. Moreover, it teaches that violence is an acceptable means for handling anger and for controlling others, which method punished children then use on peers, siblings and parents.[187] Larzelere concludes that it is a training ground for violence, differing from child abuse in its effects only by degree.[188]

Corporal punishment in schools is institutional child abuse.[189] It is assault and, if it were perpetrated against an adult, would be subjected to criminal sanctions. And, when corporal punishment is perpetrated by someone powerful against someone who is defenceless, it is (by definition) bullying.[190] Given the findings about its lack of benefits and potential negative outcomes, it has no justification. It is in violation of the United Nations Convention on the Rights of the Child.[191] It is also discriminatory in that males and children from minority cultures are the most likely victims.[192]

Finally, physical punishment damages relationships between adults and children.[193] Yet it is particularly important to demonstrate compassion, empathy and constructive forms of discipline for those young people who have not been recipients of these methods at home. Especially when physical punishment is the only form of discipline that they know, it is the duty of schools to teach them a positive alternative.[194] Yet the rates of physical punishment already cited suggest that it is not used as a last resort, but as standard practice.[195] Our allegiance to physical and other forms of punishment arises from false either-or thinking that *either* we impose our will on children *or* they will become unmanageable. Perhaps its continued use is not because children don't know any other methods, but because adults don't.[196]

Conclusion

Positive behaviour support is perhaps misnamed: *proactive* behaviour support would be a more appropriate title because it emphasises teaching children how to comply with school rules in order to prevent infractions, but still employs punishment (which is aversive) when students violate teachers' expectations. Although behaviourist specialists emphasise positive methods, consistent evidence is that, in the hands of schools with their legacy of coercive approaches, the use of punishment outweighs positive reinforcement.[197] This indicates that, without high-level expertise, this approach cannot be well implemented in schools.[198]

Controlling discipline in schools has not helped teachers to feel less burdened nor has it assisted students to learn more or to behave better.[199] Schools in the US that use 'zero tolerance' policies are still less safe than those with more flexible disciplinary approaches.[200] Higher levels of disorder appear to result from restrictive efforts to police school premises.[201] Hence, the conclusion even from advocates of behavioural controls is that controlling discipline is effective for the 95 per cent of young people for whom lesser methods would work equally well, but is ineffective with the core 5 to 7 per cent of students with severe behavioural difficulties – that is, the students for whom teachers most need it to work.[202] These are the students who pose the majority of disciplinary problems in schools, the ones who are repeatedly sent to the principal's office – for whom we have to conclude that, if the method were going to work, it would have by now.

Guidance practitioners contend that the answer lies in seeing students and teachers as jointly invested in students' learning, which necessitates a sharing of power and responsibility. Education and discipline in schools cannot be things we do *to* students, but must evolve in interaction *with* students. Part three of this text, then, will describe classroom practices that abide by this philosophy.

Recommended further reading

Grolnick, W.S. (2003). *The psychology of parental control: How well-meant parenting backfires*. Mahwah, NJ: Lawrence Erlbaum.

Kohn, A. (1996). *Beyond discipline: From compliance to community*. Alexandria, VA: Association for Supervision and Curriculum Development.

——(1999). *Punished by rewards: The trouble with gold stars, incentive plans, As, praise and other bribes*. (2nd ed.) Boston, MA: Houghton Mifflin.

PART THREE

The guidance approach

CHAPTER 10

Overview of the guidance approach

> The focal point around which teaching should be organized is not the instrumental but the relational. Without this connection, a teacher may have the subject-matter knowledge and the technical ability to teach, but the opportunities for real learning will be scarce, because what the teacher does not have is the student.[1]

Although behaviourism dominated the 20th century, the model did not go uncontested. Shortly after it emerged, Carl Rogers founded humanist theory,[2] which believes that human behaviour is not controlled by its consequences, but is governed by our own needs. Rogers and subsequent writers have espoused a foundational conviction that all individuals – regardless of distinguishing characteristics such as age – have equal rights to have their needs satisfied. This philosophy forms the core of the guidance approach. Its later advocates were Tom Gordon with *Parent, Teacher* and *Leader effectiveness training*, his contemporary Haim Ginott and, more recently, writers such as Bill Glasser, Alfie Kohn, Dan Gartrell, Hart and Hodson, and myself.[3]

A model of teaching and learning

The principle that adults and children have equal rights to have their needs met amounts to a focus on the present, not the future. Rather than seeing education as a means of skilling up young people for the future, guidance believes that education is about engaging children in the present. As Sir Ken Robinson states, seeing education as a preparation for the future overlooks the fact that the first two decades of life are not a rehearsal: 'young people are living their lives now'.[4]

Guidance is built on the conviction that teaching must be responsive to children's natural efforts to make sense of their world; it must attend to their social, emotional and ethical development as well as to their cognitive and physical development; and it must occur in a setting where young people feel safe, where they can contribute and believe that they belong.[5] By this reasoning, teachers assume the responsibility of being a guiding force in the emotional lives of their students.[6] In addition to being a goal in its own right, research is also clear that students are more engaged in school when the school meets their needs.[7]

Under the guidance approach, the emphasis shifts from how to teach . . . to how children learn. Given that learning is a natural process, the next question is, what are the optimal conditions for learning to take place?[8]

Elements of the guidance approach

Guidance forms a coherent body of thinking and practice guided by some core beliefs. The model illustrated in Figure 10.1 informs the structure of this chapter.

An ethic of caring

The guidance approach is based on an ethic of caring. Occasionally, this will entail caring *for* students, although affection is spontaneous and cannot be imposed. More typically, therefore, professional caring will entail:[9]

• caring about students' wellbeing in a pastoral care sense by, for example, establishing respectful relationships with students, assisting them to navigate conflicts with their peers, and respecting their extracurricular obligations to their families

FIGURE 10.1 Elements of the guidance approach

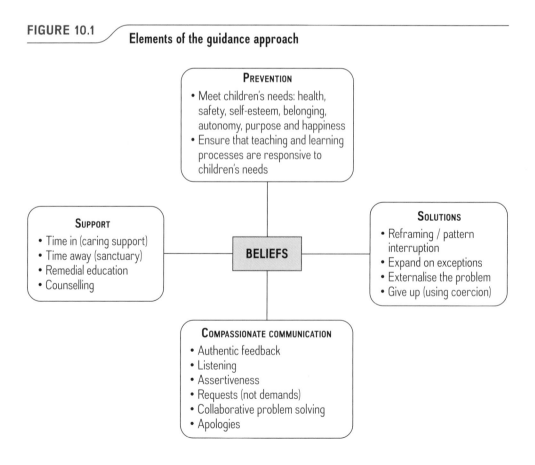

- recognising that students are in the care of their teachers and require your support and protection
- caring that certain children are struggling with adversity and offering support so that they can rise above the obstacles to their learning and wellbeing. This does not mean feeling sorry for disadvantaged children but providing support for them to transcend their circumstances.

Caring *about* and caring *that* rest on teachers' conscious attempt or moral commitment to be an exemplary person, whose personal relationship with students is reciprocal, with teachers eager to learn from students and willing to explore with them topics of interest.[10] It is a choice to place a premium on educational goals (in a broad sense that encompasses more than academic goals), over control.[11] It represents fidelity to teachers' moral obligation to ensure that students can succeed.[12] More than making students do what we deem to be good for them, it is instead responsive to students' needs.[13]

Students grant teachers authority because it is seen to be legitimate. Rather than being unilateral and based on institutional or 'role' power, teachers' power is a form of moral authority, in which students respect their teachers' leadership because they recognise that their teachers know their subject matter, are competent at teaching and are committed to helping them be successful in school and in life.[14] In short, students grant authority to teachers who care about them.

Nevertheless, a caring relationship between an adult and child is always asymmetrical: adults must care for the welfare of young people, but young people cannot be responsible for looking after adults. Therefore, a caring stance requires limits on the intimacy of teachers' relationships with students; the purpose of the relationship is the welfare of the students, not the wellbeing of the teacher. It is not teachers' job to be their students' friend, but to be their mentor, doing whatever it takes to empower students to engage in learning and be successful at school.[15]

Human needs

Needs are expressions of subjective longing.[16] They are distinguishable from mere desires on the grounds that: [17]

- they are relevant in diverse settings
- they are innate: we do not *learn* that we need to eat or to be loved, but are born requiring these
- they are universal – that is, they are found in every culture and across age groups
- their satisfaction is vital for our wellbeing
- they lead to *behaviour* designed to satisfy them, *thoughts* focused on meeting them, and *emotional* benefits from their satisfaction and, conversely, distress from their non-fulfilment.

In an adaptation of Maslow's model,[18] I have proposed a model (which is fashioned on a tree) that links the three emotional needs.[19] It is illustrated in Figure 10.2. As indicated by the upward arrow to the right of the tree trunk, like Maslow's this model is hierarchical, which means that the lower-level needs have to be satisfied before individuals can focus on meeting their higher needs. The main departure from

FIGURE 10.2   **A model of human needs**

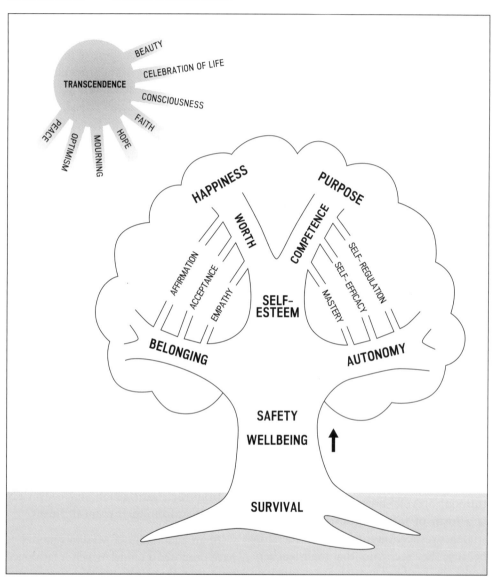

Maslow's model, however, is that this model recognises the human need for autonomy (to be described below.)

Box 10.1 lists these needs more comprehensively. Guidance theory upholds that all of our actions are an effort to satisfy these needs. If students are unable or not allowed to produce a skill (say, being assertive towards adults), the behaviour that they produce may be inept and may

BOX 10.1   Human needs

Survival
Air
Clothing
Food
Movement/exercise
Rest
Sexual expression
Shelter
Sleep
Touch
Water

Safety
Fairness
Justice
Order
Predictability
Privacy
Reliable care
Security
Stability
Support
Trust

Wellbeing
Awareness
Clarity
Comfort
Communion
Ease
Harmony
Health
Nurturance
Relaxation
Space

Belonging
Acceptance
Affection
Closeness
Communication
Community
Companionship
Compassion
Connection
Consideration
Cooperation
Empathy
Home
Inclusion
Intimacy
Love
Loyalty
Mutuality
Warmth

Self-esteem
Achievement
Affirmation
Appreciation
Competence
Equality
Independence
Learning
Mastery
Mattering
Presence
Respect
Stimulation
To be understood
Validation
Visibility (to see and be seen)

Autonomy
Choice
Creativity
Discovery
Effectiveness
Efficacy
Freedom
Integrity

Purpose
Authenticity
Challenge
Contribution
Fulfilment
Growth
Inspiration
Participation
Self-expression

Happiness
Celebration
Contentment
Enjoyment
Fun
Joy
Humour
Pleasure
Spontaneity

Transcendence
Beauty
Celebration of life
Consciousness
Faith
Hope
Mourning
Optimism
Peace

coincidentally inconvenience or distress others. In that event, we need to teach the skill, rather than punish them for not being able to employ it.

Survival

Taking each level of need in turn, the most basic human requirement – fundamental for all growth and therefore depicted in Figure 10.2 as the roots of the tree – is the biological need for physical survival: for food, shelter, warmth, clothing and sexual expression. These needs are known as the deprivation needs, because they become a paramount concern to people only when a paucity of material requirements threatens their survival. Once a (relatively low) threshold of material goods is attained, humans are freed to focus on satisfying their higher level needs.

Safety and wellbeing

At level two are the dual needs for emotional safety (or security) and wellbeing, depicted as the trunk of the tree in Figure 10.2. As we know from children reared in orphanages, it is not enough that they simply be fed and watered: children also need to feel assured that they will be nurtured and that adults will be sensitive to and alleviate their discomfort or pain.

Belonging

Belonging is the first of the three core emotional needs, which are depicted in Figure 10.2 as the tree's three main limbs. Belonging refers to the need to love and be loved, and to be connected to other people. Evidence for this need is compelling. We know that infants and parents from all cultures form loving bonds with each other; people are more satisfied in relationships characterised by mutual caring and frequent contact; and the development of new relationships (e.g. at weddings) elicits joy. In reverse, the dissolution of relationships (e.g. in divorce) creates distress; people think about and seek out relationships when they feel lonely; the prospect of rejection activates deep fears;[20] and a lack of connectedness leads to many negative outcomes such as higher rates of physical and emotional illness, suicide and delinquency.[21]

In schools, there is ample evidence of the imperative to belong. As described in chapter 1, a school that is experienced as a community enhances the emotional, social, ethical and intellectual development of all its members, improving teacher satisfaction and feelings of self-efficacy, and students' intrinsic motivation, achievement and interpersonal concern.[22] As for peer relationships, peer acceptance and supportive friendships protect students from maladjustment arising from family stress; help them to overcome reticence; feed the self-esteem of girls in particular; contribute to students' sense of wellbeing at school; deflect aggressive behaviour patterns; protect students from becoming targets or perpetrators of bullying; reduce the odds of grade retention throughout schooling; and improve students' attention, engagement and cooperation and thus achievement in school.[23]

For many people, belonging will also involve belonging to place, to a homeland. For children in particular, it also means having some wild places or, at least, places that seem wild to them.[24] And it requires a home: not just a building that shelters the body, but a place that serves an integrating function, where our needs (and some of our desires) can be met. A home provides comfort; connects us to our environment; houses our family; permits connection to outsiders because it allows people to find us; provides stability; forms part of our identity; is a place for securing our possessions; offers a private sanctuary; is a place where we can be informal; is a venue for daydreaming (it 'shelters the imagination') and is a place where we can become more skilful at activities that we value.[25] The nest is our refuge.[26]

Autonomy

Not to be confused with independence, self-centredness, or detachment from others, autonomy (the second emotional need in my model) is the capacity to steer our own course in life, to make choices for ourselves, to initiate action and to exercise volition. A synonym is self-determination. If it helps, think of adults who place a premium on autonomy as being 'control freaks' (although my daughter prefers the term, control *enthusiasts*). Its opposite is either helplessness, or experiencing pressure or coercion to be a certain kind of person.[27]

The requirement for autonomy is actually the earliest documented emotional need, having first been proposed by the German philosopher Immanuel Kant, who issued a 'categorical imperative' or moral absolute that humans must not use others as means to our own ends on the grounds that, by their nature, human beings have a fundamental requirement to be self-determining.[28]

Evidence that autonomy is vital comes from research that, across cultures (and even across species), when individuals feel out of control of their circumstances, they develop a syndrome known as learned helplessness.[29] This comprises cognitive impairments in the form of an external locus of causality and emotional and behavioural responses typical of depression.

A second body of evidence that this need is vital comes from self-determination theory, which has discovered that humans are more motivated when they are in command of their own activities.[30] Compared to individuals with external motivation, those with autonomy are better adjusted; have higher self-esteem and higher satisfaction both in general and in their schools and families; and experience less stress, depression and anxiety.[31] They are more engaged in schoolwork, enjoy it more, and behave more prosocially.[32]

Third, evidence (to be reviewed more fully in chapter 20) confirms that, when parents or teachers deny children's autonomy by employing psychological controls, young people's wellbeing suffers.[33] Children develop both emotional and behavioural difficulties: their overall self-esteem declines, they fail to develop appropriate self-regulation skills, are more aggressive, and possess less robust coping skills.[34]

This finding holds across cultures whenever adolescents experience their parents as intrusive and pressuring.[35] This 'universalism without uniformity'[36] occurs because autonomy is not an issue of independence versus interdependence (which does vary across cultures),[37] but an issue of being the initiator of our own actions. Psychological controls force the choice between being true to yourself, or being loyal to your parents (who want you to be otherwise); across cultures, this will universally pose an existential crisis.[38]

Self-esteem

Informed by humanist theory, guidance practitioners believe that human beings have a fundamental need to have a positive conception of themselves, to see themselves as both worthy and competent.[39] Allocating self-esteem the status of a need is warranted, in that it is found across all cultures, and gives rise to behaviours and thoughts designed to sustain our positive view of ourselves.[40] An unconditional, and hence secure self-esteem is related to healthy emotional adjustment, life satisfaction, and happiness.[41] In reverse, a contingent, fragile or unstable self-esteem is associated with many negative outcomes, including anxiety, loneliness, unwise risk taking, depression and delinquency.[42]

Self-esteem does not develop in a vacuum but instead feeds, and is nourished by, our interactions with others and from governing our own lives. Accordingly, in my model (in Figure 10.2) self-esteem is connected to belonging and autonomy.

Purpose

The two highest needs (happiness and purpose) – sometimes referred to as the 'luxury' needs – are depicted in Figure 10.2 as being among the tree's foliage.

The first of these is the need for our lives to stand for something, to have a purpose. Abraham Maslow referred to this as self-actualisation, which is the drive for long-term growth towards an ideal version of ourselves. Evidence for this need is less strong than for the lower needs, but existential dread asks the question, 'Is this all there is?', reflecting the malaise of having no purpose or feeling that life has no point.[43]

Happiness

Happiness is a subjective sense of life satisfaction or contentment with one's life.[44] For students, the quality of their relationships with their teachers is the most strongly related to their satisfaction with school.[45] In contrast, coercion makes people unhappy.[46] It is as simple as that: when we are forcing students to learn something, they will be miserable. This is enough reason not to do it. However, an additional instrumental reason is that happy students possess the emotional resources to engage with learning,[47] while those who are dissatisfied might express their feelings in the form of disruptive behaviour.

Transcendence

Unlike the other animals, humans have both a need and a capacity (in the form of imagination) to transcend everyday experience. We need opportunities to celebrate beauty and life itself, to live life consciously or deliberately, and to experience peace. We need optimism or faith in ourselves and others, and to have hope that we can set realistic goals, formulate a plan for their attainment and believe that, with persistence and effort, we can make them happen.[48]

Humans also need to be able to mourn over unmet needs so that we can heal old wounds. This mourning is not the same as seeking an apology from someone who has wronged us.[49] Seeking an apology and insisting that others feel remorseful implies that we are judging them to be in the wrong. This is an instance of *black-and-white* or *either-or* thinking ('I'm right; you're wrong'), which assertion we hope to prove by making others suffer and feel badly for their mistakes. For this reason, guidance does not encompass restorative justice,[50] whose first step is the perpetrator's admission of guilt and expression of regret. Although in the criminal justice system, this is preferable for both victim and perpetrator to a punishment that serves neither party, the actual issue for victims is not to induce remorse or to seek revenge – but to grieve for our unmet needs.[51] As for perpetrators, restitution needs to be offered willingly on a platform of self-worth that allows them to admit guilt or remorse for their *behaviour*, but not from having been shamed as a person.[52] Shaming young people for their actions as a tool of discipline teaches them that they are unworthy and threatens them with rejection; in response, they will either *move away* from others by withdrawing, hiding and silencing themselves; *move towards* others by becoming compulsively compliant in an effort to appease; or *move against* others by trying to gain power, being aggressive and shaming others in retaliation.[53] In contrast, guilt or remorse (given freely) can motivate restitution. As Brené Brown states, 'Recognizing we've *made a mistake* is far different from believing *we are a mistake*'.[54]

Beliefs

The core of guidance is its beliefs. An English playwright once said that a belief is not merely an idea that the mind possesses: *it is an idea that possesses the mind*.[55] The most fundamental belief that guidance challenges is the sour view of human nature that underpins pragmatic behaviourism.

Beliefs about human nature

Some believe that adults have to rely on rewards and punishments to discipline children because they are 'egocentric'. Piaget's concept of egocentrism has been mistaken for self-centredness (or an inability to empathise), when instead what he meant was that young children interpret others' feelings according to how they themselves feel at the time. That is, their interpretations *centre* on their own emotions (or *ego*). This is observable from as young as two days of age, when neonates cry in response to another infant's cries, reacting almost reflexively to others' distress as if it were their own (when they do not cry in response to an equally loud non-human sound).[56]

However, this egocentrism is overcome by the age of four. From a very young age, children who receive empathy can be roused by another's distress, will endeavour to interpret it, will express concern, and attempt to comfort others.[57] Babies as young as six months of age have been shown to look to a peer who is distressed, seek eye contact with the child's mother, look to their own parent, and lean, gesture towards or reach out to touch a distressed peer.[58] In their second year of life, infants can realise that another's misery is not their own, although they are still confused about the cause of someone else's distress and are uncertain how to help.[59] By three years of age, children are able to talk about emotions and therefore have a better idea about the likely cause of another's distress. Their attempts at consolation are more appropriate to the other's needs – for example, they may console a peer with, 'It's okay. Mummy will be back soon'. Finally, at four years of age, a child can ask another, 'What's the matter?' rather than assuming that what upsets her will have upset the other person. Their repertoire of helping behaviours has now expanded from a simple hug or pat to helping, sharing, offering verbal sympathy, protecting and defending victims and expressing anger towards the source of their playmates' distress.[60]

This natural development of empathy demonstrates that humans are not self-centred and selfish, as pragmatic behaviourists sometimes claim.[61] They can be *turned* that way by unresponsive parenting that fails to teach them about their own and others' feelings.[62] In contrast, they are empathic and likely to act on that by helping someone in distress when they receive parental nurturing.[63] The result is that, by 8 to 10 years of age, half of children spontaneously provide help to a distressed child; this figure rises to 90 per cent when it becomes clear to the children that they are allowed to leave the room in order to deliver help.[64] Research with adults has found helping response rates of between 85 and 100 per cent.[65] This makes sense, because altruism secures the survival of the species.[66] It is the human spirit to care for others. We do it constantly and everywhere: in our families, our communities, our schools, our hospitals and hospices. These instances of caring are not exceptions: they are human nature.

Cooperativeness

The second belief about human nature that guidance contests is the populist notion that 'real life' is competitive. This assertion reflects a bias on the part of competitive individuals who (wrongly) assume that others are as competitive as themselves.[67] They develop this perspective because their competitive behaviour pushes cooperative partners to become temporarily more competitive.[68] In turn, this confirms both their perceptions and combative behaviour.

Instead, cooperativeness is the natural stance of all human beings. This is because, as a species, our young are dependent for a prolonged childhood and we have few natural weapons (no claws, canine teeth or fast ground speed) to repel or evade predators. Accordingly, individuals' survival depends on the group's willingness to defend and protect each other.[69]

Evidence of human cooperativeness is everywhere. From as early as 10 weeks of age, babies mirror their caregivers' facial expressions. Among other things, this teaches us that children attempt to get in synchrony or harmony with adults.[70] As a species, we acquired language, agreeing within each tribe to symbolise objects and ideas by the same verbal label.

Throughout human history (the modern tragedy of the Commons notwithstanding) we have mostly shared natural resources to ensure our survival.[71] Across all cultures, cooperation is observed most particularly where resources are scarce.[72] This makes sense in that mutual interdependence assures survival.[73]

Although humans by nature strive for goals, our culture teaches us whether to strive *with* or to strive *against* others.[74] In humans, cooperativeness has been documented in young children[75] and across many indigenous cultures.[76] In contrast, Westerners have been accused of being competitive even when doing so is not in their interests.[77] However, it seems to be, first, that the apparent cultural variability is actually an urban–rural difference and, in turn, that city children are less cooperative simply because they are seldom exposed to cooperative activities. When they are shown the benefits of cooperation, they readily adopt it as a strategy.[78]

In light of this evidence, guidance trusts that children want to cooperate with adults. The question, then, is not: 'How do we get children to cooperate with us?' but, *'How do we ensure that we do not estrange children from us and damage their natural desire to please us?'*.[79] Part of the answer to this question lies in the quality of children's relationship with adults.[80] When cooperation is mutual, working together is reciprocal.[81]

Beliefs about causes of behaviour

With its internal locus of causality, guidance does not believe that individuals act as they do because of external rewards and punishments, but because they are attempting to meet their needs. My research discovered that the most commonly violated need is young people's need for autonomy.[82] Accordingly, it occupies the largest ring in Figure 10.3. When inquiring into the reasons for disruptions, this outer ring is the first to be considered.

Reactions to a denial of autonomy

Whereas the two emotional needs for belonging and autonomy have been comprehensively researched, it is only my own experience that tells me that people differ in the extent to which these needs contribute to their self-esteem. In my experience, the majority of children (perhaps 80 per cent) gain most of their self-esteem from belonging. They want us to like them and therefore behave well most of the time. When they do make a behavioural mistake, they are remorseful and want to make amends. Therefore, there is no need to punish them to 'teach them a lesson' because they have already learned from their mistake.

In contrast are the children (perhaps 20 per cent) whose self-esteem comes mainly from their need to be in command of their own lives. These spirited or non-conformist children are prepared to risk our displeasure to prove to us that we cannot make them do things. Spirited children have three mantras:

- You're not the boss of me!
- You can't make me.
- You can't stop me.

When we try to control these spirited children, they react against the loss of autonomy with deteriorating behaviour, as they resist, rebel, retaliate and, ultimately, escape from us (psychologically, if not physically). They simply become more unmanageable – perhaps even to the point of being labelled as having oppositional-defiance disorder. These spirited children can – and often do – deny adults the right to control them.[83]

> When we make children obey by force, threats, or punishment, we make them feel helpless. They can't stand feeling helpless, so they provoke another confrontation to prove that they still have some power.[84]

Very rapidly our controlling discipline degenerates into a 'dance' in which adult coercion is met with child defiance. As illustrated in Figure 10.4, this 'dance' begins when adults demand compliance, which the child resists ('You can't make me.'). In response, adults threaten a sanction, against which the child rebels ('You're not the boss of me!'). Faced with insubordination, the authoritarian adult then imposes a punishment, against which the child retaliates

FIGURE 10.3   Sources of children's behavioural difficulties

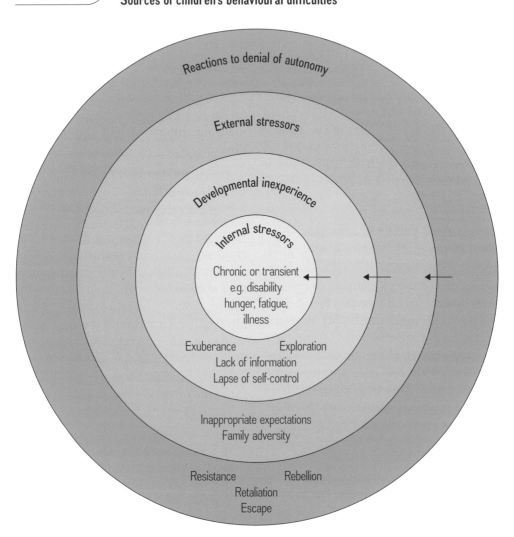

Reactions to denial of autonomy

External stressors

Developmental inexperience

Internal stressors

Chronic or transient
e.g. disability
hunger, fatigue,
illness

Exuberance   Exploration
Lack of information
Lapse of self-control

Inappropriate expectations
Family adversity

Resistance   Rebellion
Retaliation
Escape

(perhaps by hitting out: 'You can't stop me.'). Finally, in faith that punishment is the only option and will work if severe enough, the adult imposes a harsher punishment; and, in response, the child escapes by withdrawing, running away or hereafter refusing to heed adults in general or this adult in particular. In addition to my own observations, other researchers have also reported these recursive cycles of coercion and defiance.[85]

You could think of this 'dance' as being like a tennis rally, with the ball lobbing back and forth between yourself and a second player. On a hot summer's day, you are thirsty and want to end the match. You

FIGURE 10.4   The 'dance' of adult coercion and child defiance

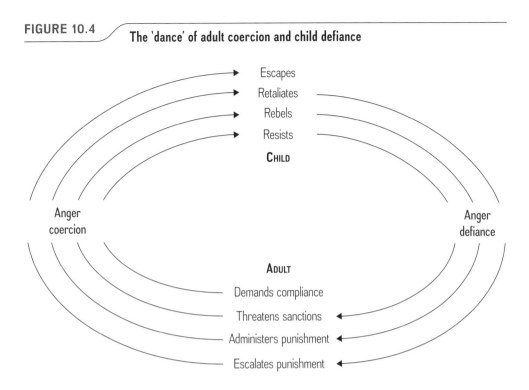

could try to talk your opponent into stopping the game (which is hard to do if she is winning!) – or, it would be more efficient to discard your racquet.[86] Similarly, when caught in a cycle of coercion and resistance, we could try to talk students into stopping – or we could cease being the force that they are opposing. In this instance, given that we are the adults, we are the ones who have to act like it and end the dance. We end it by ceasing coercive discipline.

External stressors

When you are sure – and are certain that the student is certain – that you are not using coercive discipline, working inwards on the model in Figure 10.3, your next hypothesis about the cause of a disruptive behaviour is that something in the environment is triggering stress that exceeds the student's coping capacity. The most proximal stressors will be the demands of the school setting; a more distal stressor is family adversity and, specifically, harsh or neglectful parenting[87] (see chapter 1).

Developmental inexperience

When these earlier hypotheses seem not to fit, the next possibility is that the student lacks the skill to produce a behaviour that meets his or her needs without negatively affecting others. For example, a young child might have hit out at another (which is unacceptable) in a (righteous) effort to retrieve something that her target took from her. These unskilled actions come about for a range of reasons.

Normal exuberance. Children will occasionally become elated and excited about simply being alive. This was nicely summarised in a US study of children's behavioural difficulties where the researchers concluded that 'kids do stuff'.[88] By this the researchers meant that, without malicious intent, some of children's rowdy behaviour might inadvertently inconvenience or irritate others. In the process of being active people, stuff happens.

Normal exploration. Just as children discover facts about their physical world, it is natural – and essential – that they explore their social world, to discover what adults stand for and what we won't stand. Rather than interviewing us to find this out, they will try out some behaviours and await our feedback. This will inevitably result in mistakes because they will not always be able to anticipate the effects of their actions.

Lack of information or skill. Very young children can behave disruptively because they do not yet know what is expected of them. This lack of information is uncommon after the age of three and a half years, however. At older ages, children typically know how they are expected to behave, but lack the skill to do so. Specific skills that commonly impair students' behaviour are listed in Box 16.6 (see page 256). A core skill deficit is low verbal ability, which interferes with young people's ability to self-talk and thereby to regulate their own behaviour.[89]

Lapse of self-control. Even more vital, however (as discussed in chapter 1), is the ability to regulate feelings and impulses. Past the age of three, most children have been taught how to share, take turns, or negotiate. Beyond that age, a failure to employ these kinds of skills, then, is seldom a lack of information – but a lapse of self-control. They know what they should be doing but cannot do it, because at this time they cannot regulate their emotions and impulses. This is normal: everyone 'loses it' at times.

This is even more common in children than in adults because babies *must* indulge and communicate everything they feel, so that they can receive what they need to survive. In newborns, experiencing and communicating emotions are inseparable.[90] Their survival demands that they tell their parents when they are tired, hungry, cold, in pain, frightened, sad, lonely . . . and so on. Children start to learn self-regulation from around the age of three and a half years, as they become able to employ language even when aroused and they refine their moral reasoning skills and empathy for others.[91] Nevertheless, at older ages they will still experience lapses of self-control that give rise to inconsiderate actions. (Even as adults we lose self-control: just consider how often we cheat on a diet, not because we lack information about the calories or fat content of a food, but because we lack self-control.)

Internal stressors
Finally in the model in Figure 10.3 (and signified by the inner circle), children's unskilled actions can come about because of internal stressors, including:

- transient conditions such as fatigue, hunger, or temporary illness
- disabilities, especially in language and sensory integration domains
- disorganised nervous systems (e.g. arising from food intolerances).

Goals

As detailed in chapter 2, guidance does not aim for students to do as they are told, because compliance places them at risk of abuse, exposes surrounding individuals to group bullying, and renders whole communities unsafe when others follow orders to harm them. Guidance does not want students to comply. Instead, it aims to teach them to be considerate of others – that is, to think about the effects of their actions on other people.[92] Considerateness has five aspects:

- self-awareness
- self-regulation of emotions and impulses
- empathy
- cooperation
- a sense of potency (self-efficacy, or agency).

Of these five skills, only three are left to outline.

Self-awareness. Understanding and being able to label their own emotions is a precursor to understanding others' perspective. Children also need to be aware of their actions and to adjust these according to group norms and feedback from others. They learn this when they receive responsive caring.

Self-regulation. Acquiring emotional regulation is the core task of the early to middle years of childhood. It affects all aspects of behaviour.[93] Unlike the behaviourist aim of teaching self-regulation so that students do not need to be policed by teachers, under guidance it is not merely an internalised form of self-control: its purpose is not only to protect surrounding individuals from children's outbursts – but, more important

still, it ensures that students will develop resilience in the form of an ability to manage their emotional reactions to the setbacks that they will inevitably encounter in life.

Self-regulation means that children can balance others' needs and values with their own and with the demands of the situation.[94] It means that children are aware of their own emotional states and can use that information to exercise choices about how they express their feelings.[95] This gives them a dimmer switch on their emotions, rather than only an on–off button, as it were,[96] in which their feelings are not so dysregulated that they are explosive, but neither do children have to repress or deny what they feel. This is not a question of having an optimal amount of self-control, but of having *choice*.[97]

Moreover, guidance does not expect that individuals will *always* consider others. Never considering oneself is just as thoughtless as never considering other people. Therefore, while guidance aims for considerate behaviour, it also recognises that people are most resilient when on occasion they can be spontaneous and express themselves.[98] Self-regulation needs to be flexibly adaptive to circumstances and to *balance* the rights of the individual with the rights of the many.[99]

Potency. Finally, guidance believes that we need young people to develop a sense of potency or self-efficacy, whereby they feel effective at running their own lives. We need them to learn that they can stay in command of what they feel and how they act, by staying in control of what they *think*.

In a stark contrast to behaviourism, guidance asserts that adults cannot teach considerate behaviour by administering consequences, because these focus children's minds on what *they* will earn from performing the behaviour: 'Will I get caught? . . . Will I get into trouble? . . . Will I have to go to time-out? . . . Will I be told that I'm a good girl? . . . Will I get a sticker, stamp, star, a student-of-the-day award?'. All of these questions contain the words *I* and *me*: 'What will happen to me when I perform this behaviour?'. However, the essence of considerateness is to think about how our behaviour affects *others*. Consequences cannot teach this, because they direct children's focus away from others, towards themselves.

Layered practices of the guidance approach

Like controlling discipline, guidance emphasises prevention. When students nevertheless display additional needs, it offers support and searches for solutions. Although these layers have the same tiered structure as behaviourism, the content of the levels is vastly different between the two approaches. This is illustrated in Figure 10.5 which you can compare to Figure 3.1 (see page 63). The following nine chapters detail these practices.

Prevention

Based on its beliefs, the first and most fundamental aspect of the guidance approach is its insistence that students' needs be met in schools. This is a pure aim of meeting these needs in their own right on the grounds that young people have the same rights as adults to be safe, fulfilled and happy. In terms of the topic of this book, however, there is an instrumental benefit that happy people are able to consider others, and contented students are able to learn.

In addition to meeting needs, the other main preventive measure is to avoid using coercive discipline and thereby triggering the dance of escalating adult coercion and child defiance. Specifically, guidance uses no rewards and no punishments, for the reasons detailed in Box 10.2.

BOX 10.2   Disadvantages of rewards and punishments[100]

When adults administer consequences, we are in control of children, regardless of whether our methods are aversive or appear to be benign or 'nice'. Naturally, given that they are inherently aversive, punishments have some particular disadvantages over and above those of rewards:

- Punishments can become addictive and escalate into abuse.
- Punishments can teach children to ignore adults who threaten but do not deliver punishment.
- Children can be shunned by their peers as a result of adults' discipline of them.
- Punishment can intimidate onlookers.

Shared disadvantages
The hidden intent of praise is to get students to do what we want them to do, and to manipulate onlookers into copying a praised peer. It imposes on students a certain way of being. In other

words, both rewards and punishments communicate to young people that our approval of them is conditional, which translates into conditional self-approval.

- Both punishments and rewards entail punishment. When students do not perform to our satisfaction, they will not receive a reward – which *feels* like a punishment. This shows that rewards and punishments are two sides of the same coin.
- Both are attempts to manipulate children into doing things our way. Kohn refers to rewards as 'sugar-coated control'.
- Given that the need to be self-determining is fundamental to all human beings, external control (including the delivery of rewards) will often excite reactive behavioural problems, such as resistance, rebellion and retaliation. This is particularly likely for spirited children.
- Consequences focus children's minds on what they will earn by their behaviour, rather than on the effects of their actions on others.

Limited effectiveness

- External controls reduce children's desire to cooperate and instead cause them to do so only if they expect to be rewarded for doing so.
- To have any effect on children's behaviour, rewards and punishments must be delivered immediately, frequently (consistently) and intensely. This is impractical.
- Rewards are addictive for adults (who need to deliver bigger and better rewards for these to have an effect) and for children (who find rewards hollow and therefore crave more and more reinforcement in place of genuine appreciation).
- When students are accustomed to having adults judge their actions for them, they do not learn to monitor their own behaviour: they notice neither their accomplishments nor their thoughtless acts.
- Consequences work mainly for those who are already cooperative and therefore do not need manipulation; for the remainder, their behaviour does not improve but instead can escalate as children resist outside controls.
- Coercion damages relationships.

Effects on recipients

Rewards such as praise can be seductive, in that children appear to like them, but praise is insulting and condescending in its dual implications that children were not considered worthy before they performed the behaviour, and that they cannot evaluate their actions for themselves.

- Controls undermine children's sense of safety and trust.
- Children's intrinsic motivation for learning declines.
- Onlookers who observe peers being rewarded for completing a task thereafter see the task as unattractive and are less likely to engage with it themselves.
- Children can become competitive with each other as they try to earn for themselves the limited rewards that are on offer.

- Conformist children will learn to comply but, in so doing, become submissive. In terms of their learning, they might avoid both taking intellectual risks and being creative in case they should fail.
- Peers can come to dislike students who receive frequent praise, either because it shows favouritism or because the least competent students receive the most praise, which seems unfair.
- The imposition of external controls can teach children to exercise control over peers (and adults) through verbal and physical aggression and bullying. Rewards and punishments teach children to manipulate others to make them do what they want.
- Rewards and punishments can discourage children and lower their self-esteem because their worth is linked to their achievements, rather than being unconditional.
- Praise and other rewards that are delivered for high achievement promote socially referenced perfectionism, whereby individuals feel that they have to be perfect in order to prove that they are worthy.

Compassionate communication

As illustrated in Figure 10.1, the third feature of guidance (after its beliefs and preventive measures) is that it uses compassionate communication to solve problems. In so doing, it works *with* students, rather than doing things *to* them. The use of communication skills avoids the need for rules. As seen in Part two, advocates of controlling discipline proclaim that rules are necessary to prevent disruptiveness and to give children the security of knowing what is expected of them and what is not allowed.[101] This idea is a hangover from the Victorian era, when rigid schedules were imposed on infants for the adults' convenience but were justified on the grounds of children's 'need' for routine. Children need guidance – but there is no evidence that they need regimentation, limits, boundaries or rules.

Guidance contends that the presence of rules instigates the need to police these, and that observance of rules does not ensure moral thinking.

- The presence of rules activates a rule-driven, rather than a value-governed, ethos while violating the educational aims of encouraging independent thinking.[102]
- While there may be a few children who act thoughtlessly, the presence of rules would not prevent this, because the perpetrators do not value the rules anyway. Intervention would not be made any easier or more effective by referring to the rule they have violated or the punishment it incurs.
- It is not possible to anticipate all infractions and generate rules for each potential conflict.
- Demanding conformity to rigid standards will alienate spirited children and lead to escalating behavioural difficulties.

The existence of rules is not why well-behaved students behave well: they do so because they *can*.[103] Meanwhile, those

FIGURE 10.5

Tiered model of guidance practices

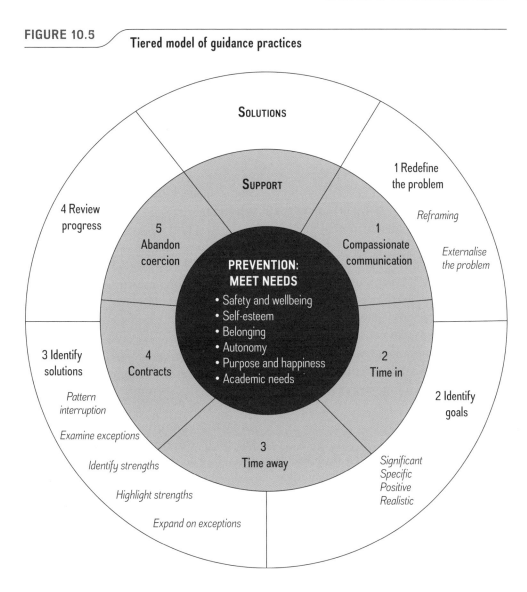

who are having difficulty regulating their emotions and impulses will not learn to do so by being punished for breaking the rules. Therefore, instead of imposing predetermined rules and sanctions for their infraction, the guidance approach advises that adults instigate problem-solving strategies, solving the issues within a personal rather than an institutional framework.

(The single exception will be those rare behaviours that are illegal, to which society – not institutional policy – dictates that there be a response.)

Without rules and without predetermined consequences for their infraction, consistency becomes unnecessary. Teachers still need (steadfastly) to insist that their own and others' rights be respected, but how they resolve conflicts can depend on the circumstances. This allows teachers to exercise both personal wisdom and professional discretion. Appropriate flexibility and avoidance of force will increase adults' influence because young people will be more willing to respect us when we have respected them.

Support

The main error that I see when individuals are adopting the guidance approach is that they believe that everything can be solved by talking. However, when students are in meltdown mode, it is necessary to wait until they are calm. To achieve that, guidance uses the only two strategies documented to work during episodes of high emotion: get some help from someone who cares about you (time in), or do something relaxing and soothing until you have calmed down (time away).[104]

Revealing solutions

Finding solutions to ongoing problems is the fifth element of guidance. The solution-focused approach gives us the choice to focus on what is working, instead of focusing on what is broken and trying to fix it. Accordingly, when looking for solutions, we will be like detectives, listening out for students' accounts of what is working in their lives so that we can guide them to apply these natural solutions to the problem at hand.[105]

Steps for resolving behavioural problems

Figure 10.6 illustrates the steps of the guidance approach.

Step 1 Prevention

Guidance emphasises prevention rather than intervention. This entails meeting students' needs, primarily for their own sake and also because students are more engaged when what we are asking them to do and how we are asking them to do it, meets their needs.

Step 2 Assess the effects of the behaviour

Fixed or rigid standards for judging students' behaviour do not reflect reality. First, with the exception of truly abnormal behaviours (such as self-injury and self-mutilation), virtually every behaviour is appropriate at certain times and places. Even violence can be valid, such as when a child is trying to foil an attempted abduction. Second, behaviours can have differing effects on different individuals: what troubles one person may not trouble another. And, third, the same behaviours can elicit differing reactions over time, depending on the emotional state of those involved and on the context (e.g. whether it is the first versus the tenth interruption in a series).

Therefore, what defines a given behaviour as a problem is not the act itself, but whether it happens to interfere with someone's needs. Accordingly, instead of judging behaviours by a fixed standard, we must instead assess them on the basis of either their observed or potential negative effects. This generates the first possible scenario, in which a behaviour may be irritating but is just normal childhood exuberance that does not interfere with anyone's ability to meet their needs. In that case, it is a non-problem that requires no response.

FIGURE 10.6   **Steps of the guidance approach**

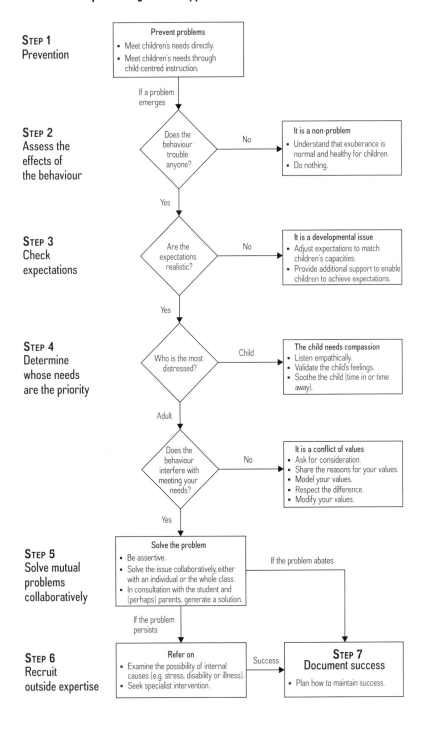

Step 3 Check expectations

It is vital to understand normal development, so that we do not ask students to achieve the impossible. This *understanding*, however, is not the same as patience. *Patience* implies that we are tolerating something that is unacceptable – and this is never appropriate. Understanding accepts children's natural limitations (while remaining optimistic, of course, about their potential for growth).

Step 4 Determine whose needs are the priority

Teachers will choose whose needs are a priority or, in Gordon's terms, who 'owns' the problem.[106] This is often interpreted as referring to who is most bothered by the behaviour which, in the case of disruptions will usually be the teacher. However, this is not what Gordon means. He means whose needs are least being met. In interactions between two adults, the person who is most distressed takes priority. But in interactions between an adult and a child, guidance recognises, first, that children's emotions are more intense and troubling to them than is the case for adults; second, children cannot defer gratification for as long as adults can; and, third, that it is the duty of adults to look after children, not vice versa. Therefore, in almost all circumstances, when students are acting disruptively (which tells us that their needs are unmet), although the behaviour may inconvenience us, we have to put aside our needs for the moment and attend to the students'. We need to listen.

If a behaviour is troubling but does not actually interfere with our ability to meet our needs (e.g. students' dress style), this is merely a conflict of values. In that event, although we can ask students to consider our values, we cannot impose our principles on them.

Step 5 Solve mutual problems collaboratively

A third scenario is when a behaviour has negative effects – or the risk or potential for these – for ourselves or students whom we have a duty to protect. The behaviour both troubles us *and* violates our needs, in which case we will use assertion. However, the behaviour signals that the student's needs are not being met either, which means that the problem is mutual. In that event, you will use collaborative problem solving once the student is calm enough to participate in this process. If collaborative problem solving does not resolve the difficulty, you will generate new solutions, based on solution-focused principles (see chapter 19).

Step 6 Recruit outside expertise

If our solutions fail, we may require external specialists, such as counsellors or remedial therapists to generate interventions that are beyond the mandate of teachers. These specialists might, for example, assess students' learning skills and styles, and design or deliver remedial education as required.

Step 7 Document success

Documents such as photos or letters telling positive stories about students can attest to their progress. The intent of these documents is to celebrate and congratulate, rather than to manipulate students into repeating their new behaviours. Rather than 'rewarding' students' progress, the documents are intended to punctuate it, to raise students' awareness of their successes.

FIGURE 10.7   Outcomes of need satisfaction

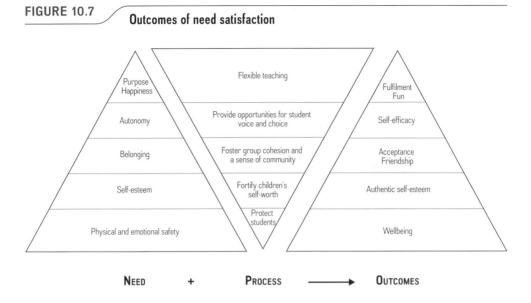

| NEED | + | PROCESS | → | OUTCOMES |

Conclusion

Guidance assumes that students do well when they can. It disputes the belief that individuals behave thoughtlessly because of the external contingencies, but instead upholds that disruptions occur when children lack a skilful way to satisfy their needs. Therefore, rather than doing things *to* students to change their behaviour, it works *with* them to teach them the skills they need. It does not punish them for not knowing a skill.

Behaviourists commonly claim that we are not doing students any favours by protecting them from the consequences of their actions. However, young people who are aggressive, for example, are already suffering natural consequences in the forms of peer neglect and rejection. By using guidance, adults are simply refusing to impose contrived or artificial consequences that fail to teach students the skills they require for meeting their needs. Every practice within the guidance approach pivots on the view that all behaviours are attempts to meet our needs. The coming chapters address how we can satisfy these needs for students in our schools.

Recommended further reading

Glasser, W. (1969). *Schools without failure.* New York: Harper and Row.

——(1998a). *The quality school: Managing students without coercion.* (rev. ed.) New York: Harper Perennial.

——(1998b). *The quality school teacher.* (rev. ed.) New York: HarperCollins.

Greene, R.W. (2008). *Lost at school.* New York: Scribner.

Kohn, A. (1996). *Beyond discipline: From compliance to community.* Alexandria, VA: Association for Supervision and Curriculum Development.

——(1999). *Punished by rewards: The trouble with gold stars, incentive plans, A's, praise and other bribes.* (2nd ed.) Boston, MA: Houghton Mifflin.

——(2011). *Feel-bad education: And other contrarian essays on children and schooling.* Boston, MA: Beacon.

Websites

Center for Nonviolent Communication: www.cnvc.org

Ross Greene's site: livesinthebalance.org

Alfie Kohn's site: alfiekohn.org

Louise Porter's site: www.louiseporter.com.au

CHAPTER 11

Meeting students' basic needs: Wellbeing and safety

There are many kinds of safety that are required for children to learn. At the most basic level, there is physical safety . . . [This] is not enough, however. Safety also means emotional safety – the safety to be yourself, to be vulnerable, to ask for help, and to be warmly supported . . . [W]hen people are not expending their energy trying to cover up or get by, afraid that someone will find out about their weakness or deficiency, they can learn easily.[1]

One of the reasons for being concerned about students' behaviour in schools is to ensure the physical and emotional safety of surrounding children and teachers. Schools must successfully reduce aggression and antisocial behaviour such as harassment and incivility in order to imbue the setting with a sense of safety.[2] However, guidance believes that punishment will not achieve this. It disproportionately targets the neediest students: young people who have been neglected or maltreated; are in foster care; are impoverished; have learning difficulties; belong to disadvantaged racial minorities, or are homeless. These are the very children who have few advocates within society or in schools.[3]

Instead of punishing young people for having difficulties coping with adversity, guidance provides them with additional support. This is the model employed in special education: when a child has a developmental disability (such as blindness), we adjust the setting to help the child function despite her impairment. So it is with social adversity: we adjust the setting to help the child function despite his challenges. When we nurture and offer kindness we demonstrate thoughtful behaviour, and we enact faith that adversity can be overcome.

The physical environment

The design, physical structure and organisation of a setting influence both attitudes and behaviour: 'Space does indeed speak'.[4] The first message that buildings can convey to those who use them is that they and the activities that go on there are valued. Therefore, the facilities must be well maintained, with good heating, cooling, ventilation and lighting, as well as being aesthetically pleasing. Improved aesthetic appeal in itself promotes student engagement.[5] Children, says Noddings, should not have to earn decent living and working conditions[6] – and neither, of course, should their teachers.

Second, the space communicates a welcome to students, families, teachers and visitors and signals their ownership of the space by reflecting their personal interests and requirements.[7] For example, the difference between noise and sound is the element of control; therefore, teachers and students need to be able to influence the noise level in the classroom or have ways to filter out sound, such as the use of earphones by students with auditory processing difficulties or attention deficits. Noisy environments also impair communication between the teacher and class and among the students, while seriously impeding listening by students with impaired hearing.[8] In noisy settings, because children who do not hear well are less responsive to language, teachers and peers converse with them less – and this lack of language stimulation in turn leads to language and cognitive delays.[9]

Third, physical arrangements convey to students and to teachers what they can do in that space. Not only does this refer to the activities but also children's control over their physical selves. Students need to be able to move freely and to have chairs that are comfortable and assist their engagement. For example, restless students can benefit from sitting on an inflated cushion that allows them to rock gently on their seats. As for comfort, adults would never countenance being told where and how they must sit and yet we take for granted teachers' rights to impose on students

prolonged sitting and even a particular posture.

Fourth, the physical layout allows instruction to flow smoothly – such as by keeping thoroughfares free of congestion, minimising distractions for students who find it difficult to concentrate, and allowing teachers to monitor and thus respond to students in a timely manner. Providing sufficient space also avoids a sense of crowding, which is especially vital for young children (e.g. when sitting on the floor for group story sessions) and for students with sensory integration difficulties. Dense settings also reduce social interaction and increase aggression and dissatisfaction.[10]

Fifth, the level of challenge, attractiveness and fun affects students' general behaviour (purposefulness, orderliness, persistence and involvement) and their attitudes towards the curriculum and to their peers. Students' feelings of autonomy, willingness to take risks and to persist are all responsive to physical design. Therefore, the design of the school and its classrooms should help students to feel safe, permit them to exercise choice, invite investigation, allow them to use ideas creatively and permit ready access to materials so that they can have control of their learning.[11]

Sixth, when students have easy access to materials within the classroom and to equipment in the playground, teachers can be less controlling and restrictive and the students more engaged.[12] Small groupings of desks and the use of natural barriers such as bookcases permit a certain degree of privacy for students, as well as designating certain areas for particular tasks. The opportunity to withdraw to a visually secluded space is an often-overlooked need and may be especially necessary for students on the autism spectrum and for introverts, who enjoy but eventually grow weary from constant interaction with others (in contrast with extroverts who are energised by social contact).

Finally, the decoration of the environment speaks volumes about the ownership of the space. If adults' posters adorn the walls of halls and classrooms, it is clear that the curriculum is not child-centred. Instead, when the students choose which of their products are displayed and when these displays demonstrate their creativity rather than conformity, students will feel ownership and pride in their space. Having said that, displays must not block the light (e.g. by being placed on windows) and may need to be minimised for students with attention deficits because a distracting environment can cause students to be less attentive to language.[13]

Students with chronic illnesses

Approximately 20 per cent of the student population have a chronic illness, with between 5 and 7 per cent experiencing severe health symptoms.[14] Meanwhile, common conditions such as asthma are likely to affect three or four students in every classroom.[15] These numbers mean that most medium to large schools will have affected students enrolled.[16]

Most chronic childhood illnesses do not have a direct permanent effect on the brain's capacity to learn, although fatigue and many conditions such as low blood sugar levels (e.g. associated with Type 1 diabetes mellitus) can temporarily

---

BOX 11.1   Modifications to the environment[17]

- Provide a comfortable setting in terms of lighting, temperature and noise levels.
- Provide adequate resources and ready access to these.
- Provide an environment where students feel safe and can exercise choice. This will invite investigation and permit the creative use of ideas.
- Provide areas where students can withdraw into solitude when needed.
- Keep traffic areas free of congestion.
- Ensure ease of supervision to facilitate a timely response to students.
- Offer plentiful opportunities for physical activity so that students can release pent-up energy and dispel stress.
- Provide some calming activities so that students' behaviour does not become disorganised.
- Enrich the environment so that it engages students' interests.
- Ensure that displays reflect children's cultures and genders as a celebration of diversity.
- Restrict the environment – giving students fewer distractions so that it is easier for them to function.
- Ensure the inclusion of students with atypical development by minimising obstacles to their participation.
- Keep group sizes within a comfortable range for the students.

impair students' cognitive functioning and emotional balance for the duration of the episode.[18] And some medical treatments such as radiotherapy or chemotherapy can themselves cause subtle learning difficulties, particularly in younger children.[19] Meanwhile, chronic illness has a well-documented effect on young people's school attendance and performance, increasing the risk of grade retention or dropping out of school.[20] Low teacher expectations can add to these students' risk of academic failure, while disrupted contact with peers can lead to social isolation, and a loss of trust in their own bodies can lead to low self-esteem.[21]

Children's relationships with adults can also be distorted by their experience of relating with medical personnel, which can cause them to direct their social interactions towards adults rather than to peers. Moreover, the requirements of their management can increase children's dependency on adults. To offset this tendency, you might have to assist their peer engagement. Meanwhile, their misunderstandings of their condition and its treatment, their early encounters with pain, and perhaps even the prospect of death, can lead to anxieties and fears that surpass those of healthy children, as seen in their elevated levels of the stress-related hormone, cortisol.[22] Without support to promote their coping and resilience, the children's anxiety and grief can lead to emotional adjustment difficulties.[23]

Teachers' knowledge affects both their confidence and the appropriateness of their interventions in support of unwell children academically, socially and emotionally.[24] However, few teachers receive training in health management while, in the early phases of an illness in particular, the diagnosis and prognosis may not be clear and hence appropriate management can be ambiguous. It will be vital to establish and maintain liaison with the student's parents and medical personnel (if appropriate) so that you have the information you need to manage the illness both long-term and in the event of medical crises.[25] A formal health care plan can ensure that responsibilities are clearly allocated, and that there are regular reviews of the plan in response to the child's changing needs.[26]

Given that they will have lost instruction time, students returning to school from a protracted absence are likely to need tutoring or other means to assist them to catch up academically.[27] It will also be important, however, to be aware that during convalescence, students may still lack the energy to do additional schoolwork, including homework. Physical exercise, extra-curricular activities and their school day will also need careful pacing.[28]

Food and nutrition

Of all the organs of the body, the brain is the most reliant on a fuel supply for its functioning. The brains of children under 10 years use between 40 and 50 per cent of available blood glucose, which is twice as much as adults' brains use.[29] Hunger or impaired pancreatic function can lead to episodic hypoglycaemia (low levels of glucose or sugars in the blood). Once there is insufficient food to fuel all of its functions, the brain directs blood flow away from the least vital brain centres to those that ensure survival. The result is that the pre-frontal lobes of the brain can be deprived of sufficient fuel to function.[30]

This area of the brain is responsible for self-control and executive functions such as planning and attention control. Accordingly, hypoglycaemia has been found to be the underlying cause of one-third of cases of attention deficit disorder.[31] Low blood sugar levels especially compromise brain function in younger children, given their brains' high need for fuel. Younger children in particular need to eat every 90 minutes to two hours, while the children most prone to hypoglycaemia need to have a bowl of (healthy) snack foods available at their desk as a constant food supply. We must give children access to food simply because they are hungry,[32] but also because hungry children cannot learn.

Further, our body has a backup plan for when we get hungry: it releases adrenaline to alert us that we need to eat. (This is what gives us the shakes at 3 pm when we have skipped lunch.) However, adrenaline – combined with under-functioning pre-frontal lobes arising from deprivation of fuel to that part of the brain – can cause children to have emotional meltdowns. I have long proclaimed that punishing children when their brain malfunctions will be roughly as effective as punishing them when their appendix malfunctions. Instead, guidance advocates providing physical support, in this case by giving a starving brain some food.

Moreover, children's nutrient intake, the ability of their digestive system to absorb nutrients and the capacity of their cells to assimilate these, affect the health and function of every cell in their body, including their brain cells. As seen in Figure 11.1, vital nutrients are needed to generate neurotransmitters, a lack of which will affect not only children's physical wellbeing but also their brain function. Given that the brain only thinks, feels and behaves, any or all three functions can be affected when brain cells lack adequate nutrition.

A key nutrient deficiency in any neurological condition is of the essential fatty acid, DHA (one of the omega-3 fats). This fat is vital for building membranes of nerve cells and hence is important for the transmission of signals between brain cells and for the production of dopamine.[33] A deficiency of DHA exacerbates dehydration and most adversely affects the function of the pre-frontal lobes,[34] where executive control is performed.

As mentioned in chapter 1, another common scenario is when children's nervous systems are being irritated by food intolerances or infections that have crossed the blood–brain barrier (such as the herpes viruses, see Box 1.1 page 17).[35] In my experience, affected children have a temperament like car alarms, firing uncontrollably in response to the smallest of triggers, and are seemingly unable to help their emotional outbursts.

Obesity

Between 1963 and 1980, obesity rates in the Western world rose by 98 per cent in children aged from 6 to 11 years and 64 per cent among adolescents.[36] Obesity disproportionately affects economically disadvantaged young people. Overweight status in babies seldom persists, but 25 per cent of preschoolers, 50 per cent of 6 to 10-year-olds, and 80 per cent of 10 to 14-year-olds who are obese remain that way into adulthood.[37] During puberty, males tend to lose 40 per cent of their body fat, whereas females gain 40 per cent, with the result that only 20 per cent of overweight

FIGURE 11.1   Nutrients needed to generate neurotransmitters[38]

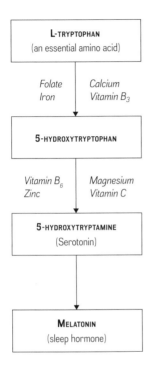

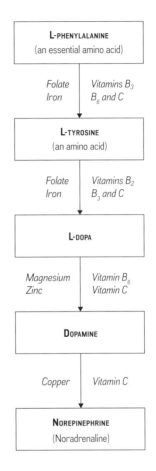

female adolescents will normalise their weight by adulthood, whereas 70 per cent of males do so.[39]

Obesity results in metabolic and hormonal disturbances, inflammatory illnesses, insulin resistance and diabetes, and an over-sensitised immune system.[40] Obesity is more than a mere cosmetic problem, and it ranks a close second to tobacco as the leading cause of preventable illness, disability and premature death – with a body mass index (BMI) above 32 reducing life expectancy by six to seven years.[41]

Health conditions that formerly emerged in adulthood are now commonly seen during childhood. More than half of the children who are obese show the early signs of cardiovascular and metabolic disorders (such as hypertension and insulin resistance); three-quarters have musculoskeletal complications; up to one-third have a fatty liver; and 20 to 58 per cent have attention deficits,[42] perhaps because of a preponderance of trans-fatty acids in the brain.

Furthermore, there is the psychological trauma of being overweight.[43] Obese

BOX 11.2   US obesity rates[44]

	1970s	2000
Preschool-aged children	5.0 per cent	10.4 per cent
6–11-year-olds	6.5	19.6
Adolescents	5.0	18.1
Adults	14.5	30.9

people experience more prejudice than with any other form of discrimination, including sexism, racism and religious-based prejudice. Obese children – and girls in particular – experience depressive symptoms and withdraw socially; have low self-esteem; have fewer friends; and are lonely, sad and nervous.[45] They are more likely in adulthood to be living in poverty and to not marry.[46]

Exercise

Children need plenty of physical exercise. However, one US study found that 92 per cent of primary students and 66 per cent of high school students did not have daily physical education classes.[47] Even for those who do attend classes, those with below-average physical prowess tend to watch on the sidelines,[48] with the result that even if they do attend classes, they are not active enough to benefit from them.

In addition to burning more fuel during physical activity and thus contributing to weight loss, exercise also raises the body's metabolic rate, making it more efficient at burning energy.[49] Aerobic exercise builds lean tissue, reduces inflammatory processes, and lowers the risk of both metabolic and cardiovascular disease, while anaerobic activities strengthen muscles and improve flexibility.[50]

Exercise also employs both sides of the body, which means that it also engages both sides of the brain. This will directly assist learning. Meanwhile, aerobic fitness (that is, oxygen supply to the brain) affects perception; verbal, mathematical and reading skills; and the executive functions of self-regulation and attention control.[51]

Sleep deprivation

Sufficient sleep is defined (not surprisingly) as the amount of sleep needed to permit optimal functioning by day. Sleep is not merely rest, but falling into a state of unawareness and unresponsiveness to the outside world. For unknown reasons, this is restorative, to the extent that deprivation of sleep results in death in around the same time that deprivation of food does.[52] It appears that REM sleep fulfils a 'housekeeping' role for the brain, maintaining optimal brain excitability.[53] Wakefulness activates synapses, whereas sleep promotes the survival, maturation and integration of new brain cells into existing circuitry, resulting in efficient cell functioning.[54]

Even small losses (one hour) of REM sleep adversely affect behaviour and almost all physiological processes and, with continued deprivation, can even compromise cell survivability.[55] One mechanism is an alteration of energy supply to brain cells; a second is increased levels of the stress hormone, noradrenaline (norepinephrine), in the brain.[56] To gain the restorative benefit from sleep, people need to remain continuously asleep for two hours to complete a cycle of REM and non-REM sleep.[57]

Over the past hundred years, the amount of children's sleep has declined by 75 minutes per day.[58] Adolescents in particular have half an hour's less sleep per night than they did 30 years ago. This is partly because, during adolescence, they begin to produce melatonin 90 minutes later than they did during childhood and therefore, even if they go to bed at a reasonable hour, they tend to lie awake.[59] At the age of 14, they tend to go to sleep just after 10 pm and at 11 pm at age 17.[60] To compensate for getting to sleep later, they need to sleep longer in the mornings but cannot, given their schedules, and therefore are constantly sleep deprived.[61] Their inability to get up on time also gives rise to conflict with their parents.[62]

Shorter sleep duration most commonly occurs on school days.[63] During school holidays, adolescents in particular wake later than they do during school terms; researchers assume that their holiday patterns reflect their natural circadian rhythm.[64] In other words, the early school start times deprive adolescents of up to two hours' sleep per day, which could be avoided if high school (and perhaps even middle school) started at 10 am.[65]

Given that humans lose muscle tone when they sleep, they need to feel safe in order to fall asleep. They are also highly dependent on the protection of the group,[66] which explains why adolescents who are being bullied at school commonly develop sleeping difficulties. Other common causes of sleep deprivation are media use; a diet with an excess of sugar, caffeine or alcohol; too little time for sleep; a sedentary lifestyle; poor sleep and waking rhythms (because we can seldom fall asleep within 15 hours of waking); and the use of certain medications.[67] Jet lag and shift work are other lifestyle causes, while parental disengagement can cause adolescents to spend excessive amounts of time in bed.[68] Children are often deprived of sleep in the early childhood years not because of their own body clock but because a busy household schedule makes adults unavailable to put them to bed until late in the evening.[69]

BOX 11.3 **Effects of sleep deprivation**[70]

Sleepiness
- Sixty per cent of high school students report that they are extremely sleepy by day, and 20 to 33 per cent of adolescents fall asleep in class once a week.
- Deprivation of total sleep time will lead to excessive daytime sleepiness, with consequent impairments of productivity, mood, social functioning and energy levels.

- A lack of sleep increases the risk of injuries and accidents. Elevated rates of traffic accidents arise because sleep deprivation causes declines in reaction time equivalent to having a blood alcohol level of .05 (mg per 100 mL of blood). Car crashes also occur when the driver falls asleep.
- Tired people have reduced motivation to perform tedious or routine tasks, although extra effort can sustain them during exciting tasks (such as attending a night club).

Emotional changes

Sleep deprivation has been associated with maladjustment in preschoolers and emotional difficulties in primary-aged children.

- Sleep deprivation increases moodiness, irritability and impatience; and leads to decreased tolerance for frustration, and to impaired emotional self-regulation. In turn, emotionality can cause increased conflict with adults.
- A relative lack of REM sleep increases aggression, irritability and confusion.
- Sleep deprivation can be caused by and can contribute to anxiety, particularly in middle childhood.
- Depression interferes with sleep; while a lack of sleep causes depression.

Alterations in attention and performance

Sleep deprivation has been associated with impaired intellectual functioning across the age range.

- It leads to the need to expend extra effort to do everyday tasks.
- Sleep deprivation leads to a two-year decline in academic performance (which is equivalent to that caused by lead poisoning).
- Tired children are inattentive, because sleep deprivation reduces the body's ability to extract glucose from the bloodstream, with the pre-frontal lobes becoming starved of adequate fuel to function. Hence, attention deficit symptoms are more frequent in children with sleep disorders.
- A lack of sleep makes it more difficult for children to generate solutions to problems, and it leads to memory impairment.
- Tasks involving planning – that is, which call on the use of the pre-frontal cortex – are the most impaired by tiredness.

Health effects

- Sleep deprivation is associated with poor health overall, including coronary heart disease, proneness to infections and diabetes – all presumably a result of inflammation.
- In children in particular, sleep deprivation leads to a dose-related increase in obesity. This occurs because sleep plays an important role in the regulation of hormones, including those that govern hunger, satiation, and blood sugar levels and because people eat more when they are awake for longer and exercise less because of fatigue.

Schools have three available measures to ensure that young people get enough sleep. First is not to allocate homework at all until the final two years of school, with realistic workloads in those final years so that students are not working on homework late into the evening (see chapter 16). Second, high schools could examine the possibility of a 10 am start time, to reflect adolescents' need to sleep in later in the mornings. Third, schools can help allay parents' concerns about their adolescents' 'hypersomnia', assuring them that it is both normative and temporary.

Child abuse in schools

Whereas teachers can do little to protect children from abuse at home (other than referring children to welfare agencies), they can ensure that schools are havens from verbal harassment. Information about abuse of children by their teachers comes from Canada, Israel, Poland and Zimbabwe.[71] These studies conclude that as many as 50 to 60 per cent of all students suffer psychological maltreatment from their teachers at least once during their schooling,[72] with 10 to 15 per cent of students suffering repeated verbal abuse from their teachers from as early as their first year of school and persisting many years through to adolescence.[73] One-quarter of these students are also bullied by their peers,[74] perhaps because the public nature of teacher abuse gives permission for peers to treat the targeted student with similar disrespect. Those most vulnerable to abuse by teachers are low-achieving boys who are socially and academically alienated, typically with attention difficulties and low motivation, whose rebellious and

disruptive behaviour feels to teachers like a threat to their control of the classroom.[75]

Defined by adult survivors as 'abuse of the spirit',[76] emotional abuse by teachers encompasses emotionally distancing, unsupportive and hostile practices including:[77]

- mockery, insults, humiliating and demeaning verbal put-downs about students' abilities, appearance or family
- discriminatory and prejudicial statements about and to students
- inconsistent and erratic behaviour
- screaming at students until they cry
- belittling students for becoming upset ('being silly') at teacher cruelty
- using threats of grade retention, suspension, failed grades, spot tests and contact with parents to control students
- imposing homework as a punishment
- allowing students to belittle their peers.

Although some of these practices are considered acceptable in certain cultures, their effects on children are uniformly negative. Human psychology is the same everywhere. Emotional abuse by teachers compromises the academic outcomes of students with mild learning difficulties who, with support rather than censure, might have remained engaged in learning.[78] It lowers victimised students' academic achievement and produces stress in students, with more serious cases leading to symptoms characteristic of post-traumatic stress syndrome, which affects 1 to 2 per cent of the student population.[79] Students can display a sudden onset of excessive worry about school, deterioration in self-esteem, somatic complaints (headaches and stomach aches), school avoidance, sleep disturbances and depression that correspond with a change of teacher.[80] These difficulties can be distinguished from 'school phobia' whose symptoms persist even with a change of teacher whereas, with teacher abuse, the symptoms abate when contact with the perpetrating teacher ceases.[81]

One coping strategy motivated by a desire to hide, is compulsive compliance and keeping one's head down to avoid being a target of teachers' vitriol[82] (while still, of course, having to witness it being directed at other students). These students

BOX 11.4   Actions during investigations of alleged abuse by teachers[83]

Immediately upon receipt of an allegation of abuse by a member of the school staff, the principal will need to take the following steps.

- Report the allegation to the child protection authorities. Document this call.
- Have the accused staff member leave the premises immediately. He or she cannot return to work until the allegation has been investigated. If the allegation is not credible, this will seem doubly unfair but is for the protection of all involved, including the accused.
- Recommend or assist the accused staff member to access a legal or industrial advocate.
- Contact your governing body.
- Obtain legal advice.
- Advise all embroiled in the investigation to cooperate in a matter-of-fact manner.
- To avoid innuendo, gossip and uncertainty as the news spreads on the school grapevine, write to all parents within hours of the allegation being raised, advising them that there has been an allegation of abuse by a member of staff (without divulging names). In order to check that there have been no other victims, this letter should advise parents to ask all their children if anything has happened lately that made them feel unsafe (with the wording being adjusted according to students' ages). Parents could also reflect on whether their children's behaviour has changed recently in any of the ways listed in Box 1.2 (see page 19), with a list of potential signs included with the letter.
- The principal will need to call a staff meeting where teachers can discuss the traumatic effects of the allegations on themselves and plan how to fill any staffing gap left by the suspended staff member.
- A counsellor will need to be appointed immediately to support the victimised child and parents, and to survey other students[84] with whom the accused teacher has had contact, in case there is more than one victim.
- In the longer term, the school can provide all teachers with staff development on issues such as child abuse, adversity and stress management.
- In the longer term, leadership will need to take steps to improve the school climate (which may have been negative in the first place and hence permitted abuse but will certainly have been damaged by the abuse allegations), and to improve collective efficacy.

appear to be coping, but commonly have emotional meltdowns at home, having held it together all day at school.[85] Opposite strategies, motivated by a desire to escape, include truancy and simulation of illness in order to stay at home while, in the long term, victims are more likely to drop out of school.[86] In the longer term, escape can also be sought through high-risk behaviours such as alcohol and drug use and, if supported by similarly disenchanted peers, delinquency in adolescence.[87] Oppositional and aggressive retaliation towards teachers is also common, with students reporting that the main reason that they are disruptive at school is because they want to get back at teachers who put them down, do not care about them, and disrespect them, their families or their culture.[88] However, this attracts sanctions against the young person, often imposed by the very teacher who is abusing them.[89]

In addition to abuse in schools, maltreatment is common in homes and in extra-curricular activities. It would be rare for students to disclose directly that they are being abused;[90] instead they may give vague hints or display some of the signs listed in Box 1.2 (see page 19). However the alarm is raised, it is vital that school administrators investigate – not to determine if abuse is actually occurring, but to establish if there is enough of a suspicion to request an investigation by child welfare specialists. A failure to act makes the administration accomplices.[91] Although there will commonly be ambiguity about what a student is reporting and although, from as early as preschool, children will tell lies to get out of trouble,[92] children do not tell lies that will get them *into* trouble. And disclosing abuse certainly attracts

trouble for the child. Hence, the default position of authorities must be to believe students who disclose abuse. Awareness rests on the recognition that child abuse occurs across all sectors of society. Hence the saying: *I wouldn't have seen it if I hadn't believed it.*

Supporting stressed students

Young people who are exposed to multiple genetic and environmental stressors are vulnerable to experiencing concurrent intellectual, social, emotional and behavioural adjustment problems as well as negative life events in the future.[93] Family adversity in the form of poverty, child abuse, marital conflict, domestic violence, parental drug use, mismanaged parental mental illness, neighbourhood stress and chaotic family life can all result in stress for children.[94] Moreover, parents' unavailability to empathise with their children and to teach self-regulation of emotion and impulses can result in emotional meltdowns and behavioural outbursts that get children into trouble at school.[95]

Prolonged and intense threat interferes with thinking.[96] At the time of a perceived threat, the body releases the stress hormones, adrenaline and cortisol, to equip the body either to fight the source of the threat, or to flee (which is known as the fight–flight response). However, positive experiences in school can compensate for or directly counter risks posed in other parts of students' lives, insulating them from detrimental outcomes.[97] When, for whatever reasons, students lack positive supports within their families, support from outsiders is particularly potent in inoculating them against maladjustment.[98]

BOX 11.5   Signs of stress in children and adolescents[99]

Young people living with adversity have difficulty regulating their emotions. Unlike typical children, they continue to display elevated rates of behavioural difficulties at school entry, while their emotional difficulties such as depression and anxiety increase through childhood. Specific manifestations of this include:

- *Hypervigilance*: scanning the setting to detect potential threats
- *Emotional problems*: distress, sadness, depression, anxiety, fearfulness and anger
- *Social problems*: social withdrawal, negative peer interaction, reactive or proactive aggression
- *Behavioural problems*: antisocial behaviour (e.g. damage to property) or becoming overly compliant
- *Academic problems*: fatigue, inattention or hyperactivity result in poor performance at school
- *Health*: increased health problems, disturbed sleeping patterns
- *Slow recovery* from stressful events.

School climate

Punitive disciplinary practices in schools contribute to students' perception that they are unsafe at school.[100] A lack of voice and due process make school toxic for many children, contributing to alienation; in contrast, school leadership that instils a sense of fairness and autonomy contributes to students' sense of wellbeing and safety.[101]

Teacher expectations

While we, as adults and teachers, can choose our own companions and activities that feed our self-esteem, children are at the mercy of the contexts in which we place them. This means that they rely on us to provide a setting where they feel emotionally safe about their ability to meet our expectations.[102] This requires that we check that our expectations are achievable. For example, we can (roughly) calculate young children's attention span for adult-led activities to be around 3 minutes times their age in years (up to a maximum of 20 minutes). If we exceed this, we invite disruptions[103] – not because individual children necessarily have impaired concentration, but because even when we are passionate, fascinating and engaging, we cannot triple the attention span of our audience.

Acceptance of mistakes

It is vital for young people's emotional safety and social inclusion that teachers respect all students' ideas, and not belittle or denigrate students who need extra help to understand a concept. Teachers must convey that it is not a failure when we try but do not succeed: it is a failure when we do not try. In this vein, I often tell young people that if you are not making mistakes, this means that you already knew the topic – and, if you already knew it, that is not called *learning*: it is called *practising*. Acceptance of mistakes is vital for students' engagement, for the quality of their relationship with their teacher, and to prevent disruptive behaviour.[104]

In contrast, individuals in competitive settings are more tense and anxious and they lose self-confidence.[105] When teachers chastise or punish failure, students become angry and anxious if convinced that they do not deserve their humiliation; in turn, they withdraw their engagement and this, in its turn, induces boredom.[106] An even more damaging outcome occurs when students are shamed – that is, they believe the implication that they are unworthy; this makes them try to appease adults in a desperate bid to regain approval; they will implode emotionally; or, if they blame others, they will explode.[107]

Time

Traditional schooling typically emphasises speed of intellectual processing, whereas accuracy rather than speed is more important in life. The pace of instruction must reflect students' need to engage deeply. Sometimes, students will master concepts quickly and will be craving to move on, whereas with other material, they need time to think. Hence, the typical schedule of 45- or 60-minute lessons in schools is the enemy of creativity and deep learning. One study found that teaching in 10-minute bursts followed by 10 minutes of physical activity improved students' learning over a longer lesson.[108] This is known as spaced learning.

Safe opportunities to engage

While students need opportunities to engage, their safety requires that, during teacher-directed instruction, they know that their teacher will not 'cold call' on them – that is, ask for their answer when their hand is not raised.[109] Soliciting students' answers can signal a preference for the more capable students by calling on them for the correct answer, or by not calling on weak students because they will not have the right answer.[110] When an answer is incorrect, teachers must respond not dishonestly but tactfully. Truth without tact is brutal. Teachers can comment, 'And what can we add to that idea? . . . Let's see if that stacks up against . . . I hear the passion; let's see if we can find some evidence . . .' Another option is to have students work in pairs to find an answer, so that their ignorance is not a cause for public humiliation, but instead is worked through privately before they come up with a response.[111]

Enhance students' resilience

It will be important for teachers to ensure that they do not scapegoat stressed students or respond to their provocative behaviour with controlling discipline – because that will only entrench these children's behavioural problems and may eventually result in their dropping out of school, with all its attendant antisocial sequelae.[112] Instead, teachers can enhance the resilience – that is, the ability to overcome adversity – of stressed students, first by providing high-quality teaching and any necessary early remedial tutoring to enable them to be successful.[113] In turn, success will foster their academic self-efficacy – that is, their belief in their ability to learn.

Second, young people enduring adversity will benefit from emotional support from peers and from adults in the school.[114] Schools are influential in shaping peer interactions and friendships. These relationships provide a buffer against stress reactions in young people and avoid associations with antisocial peer groups.

Third, teachers will need to convey to young people that they honour what these children are going through by engaging in respectful interactions with them and by giving them feedback that communicates your admiration for their 'courage under fire'.

Fourth, young people engaged in outside interests and prosocial activities are insulated against stress. These activities can be supported or directly organised by the school.

Fifth, there may be opportunities for teachers to guide young people to appraise challenges realistically and to employ coping skills. Coping does not mean feeling no symptoms when experiencing stressful conditions: it means using strategies to minimise the impact of the stress on your life, which can entail any of three responses.[115]

- *Problem-focused* action. As its title implies, this involves solving the problem that is provoking stress.
- *Emotion-focused* strategies involve adjusting our thinking to change our emotional reactions.
- *Behavioural adjustment* involves changing our behaviour so that we can adjust better to circumstances that we cannot change.

The most adaptive strategy depends on the nature of the stressor. In general, problem-focused strategies are effective when individuals can exert some control over a stressor, whereas emotional or behavioural adjustments are more suited to issues that they cannot change.[116] Disengagement can be useful in response

to acute, uncontrollable stressors, but less adaptive for ongoing or chronic stress.[117] The least effective strategies are emotional venting, engaging in wishful thinking, worrying, blaming themselves or attempting to ignore a problem.[118] Even so, as long as children do not rely on these ineffective coping mechanisms, it does not seem to matter how they cope but merely that they have a repertoire of positive responses from which to select.[119] Responding adaptively both gives them experience of being in command of their lives and stimulates supportive responses from others.[120]

Finally, the school can be a hub of services to disadvantaged families and the wider community, perhaps by inviting community health professionals to deliver some of their services within the school grounds. Given that those young people who are most at risk of poor adjustment are those experiencing ongoing, multiple stressors, any school program to support them will need to be both multifaceted and sustained; it will also need to begin early, in children's first years of school.[121]

Conclusion

We still treat students with challenging behaviour in ways that perpetuate how they came to be disruptive in the first place.[122] By school age, perhaps as many as 70 per cent of children who are experiencing behavioural problems have suffered abuse or neglect.[123] At home, their resulting emotional and behavioural disturbances are typically responded to with harsh discipline.[124] This injustice is compounded when distressed young people are met with more coercion at school.[125] This leads to the situation where, over time, many have been getting into trouble at school for so long that they have lost faith that adults care or will know how to help them.[126]

Therefore, to ensure that school discipline does not compound such injustices, it must not be repressive – that is, it cannot aim to correct and suppress troublesome behaviour, but instead must support the resilience of troubled students.[127]

Recommended further reading

Harris, R. (2007). *The happiness trap: Stop struggling, start living*. Wollombi, NSW: Exisle.

Seligman, M.E.P. (2011). *Flourish*. New York: Free Press.

CHAPTER 12

Meeting students' need for self-esteem: Worth and competence

We can't establish self-esteem as a learning objective and teach for it. Instead, we have to ask about the conditions under which self-esteem is nourished.[1]

Particularly in their compulsory school years, young people are captive in schools and are at the mercy of the contexts we create for them. Therefore, we must supply settings that safeguard their sense of worth.

The self-concept

Our self-concept is our description or perception of ourselves, an inventory of our qualities and achievements.[2] The list spans many aspects of human endeavour; hence, the self-concept is said to be multifaceted.[3] As illustrated in Figure 12.1, it comprises our physical prowess and appearance (which is the only element that persists across the lifespan), family, social status, emotional wellbeing, and academic abilities (further divided into verbal and mathematical skills).[4] Other less thoroughly researched but intuitively obvious domains include moral virtue (some might prefer to call this aspect spirituality) and creative–artistic talents.[5] There may well be more facets; and each domain can be subdivided further but, the more specific we get, the more the element resembles self-confidence rather than an overarching descriptor of who we are.

Self-esteem

In contrast to the self-concept – which reflects our thoughts – self-esteem is how we *feel* about ourselves.[6] It is the combination of two separate evaluations: about our competence and about our worth.[7]

Competence

Our evaluation of ourselves is achieved by comparing who we are (or who we think we are, which is not quite the same thing) with how we want to be. Mathematically, this can be expressed as:[8]

$$\text{Self-esteem} = \frac{\text{Perceived accomplishments}}{\text{Aspirations (or Ideals)}}$$

This formula yields different weightings for each domain, with the various domains eventually being organised hierarchically

FIGURE 12.1   The multi-faceted structure of the self-concept[9]

from those that are most to least important to us.[10] If we believe that we possess many qualities that matter to us, we will feel satisfaction, perhaps pride. In that case, our self-esteem can be drawn as illustrated in Figure 12.2. The circles have considerable overlap, signifying that we possess many of the qualities that we value. (The circles will never overlap completely; because once we achieve one of our aspirations, we will add a new goal; otherwise we would have nothing for which to strive in life.

There'd be no need to get out of bed in the morning.)

On the other hand, if we fail to achieve at something that we value highly, our self-esteem may suffer: we will feel badly about ourselves. We will judge that we have few of the qualities that we value. This can be drawn as illustrated in Figure 12.3.

Low self-esteem about our competence can come about, first, when we possess many skills and qualities that we value, but are not aware of these – that is, our

FIGURE 12.2   High self-competence[11]

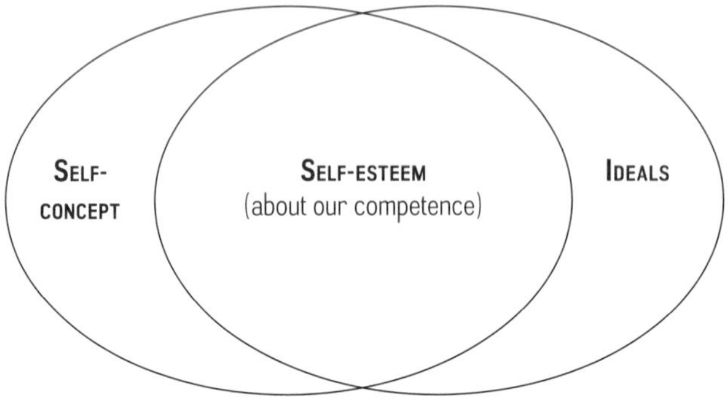

FIGURE 12.3   Low self-competence[12]

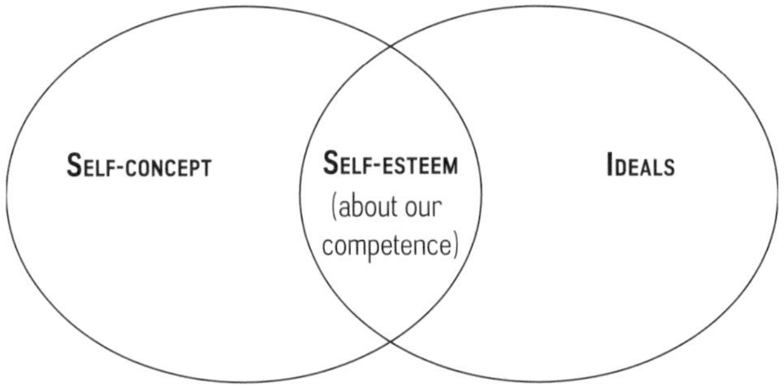

self-concept is impoverished. Alternatively, in a perfectionist pattern, our ideals can be so demanding that we cannot achieve our inflated expectations. Both are reasonably easy to fix, using one of four solutions. The first is to devalue that domain.[13] For example, I am a poor swimmer – but I don't care. I don't care because the statistics are on my side: namely, adults who don't swim, don't drown. (It's hard to drown on dry land, right?) Students experiencing ongoing failure at school use this solution: they decide not to care about scholastic pursuits. This solution involves changing our ideals.

A second solution is to channel ourselves into something that we *are* good at. Again, what we have done here is change our ideals so that we can measure up to a different set of aspirations. Some students who are rejected by their peers use this solution: they decide that, 'If I can't be likeable, I'll be powerful', and they escalate their aggression.

These self-defence mechanisms mean that we are protected from suffering too dreadfully over our failures. But we also have a third option: if we want to feel better about our skills, we can learn new skills!

A similar route is to work hard enough so that we do not fail at a skill on which our self-esteem is staked.[14]

Fourth, we can take an objective inventory of our skills, perhaps seeking feedback from others who can help us to notice the skills and qualities that we might be overlooking or taking for granted. This expands our self-concept.

Worth

The second aspect of our self-esteem is our worth. This equates to global liking, respect and acceptance of ourselves.[15] These feelings are crystallising from as early as 27 to 36 months of age.[16] As illustrated in Figure 10.2 (see page 140), they are acquired in concert with belonging: through experiencing that the people who are important to us accept us, understand us (offer us empathy) and affirm us for who we are.[17] In other words, whereas our esteem about our competence is *earned*, our esteem about our worth is *given*. It is our birthright: it has no prerequisites.[18] When it is given unconditionally, we experience wellbeing and happiness.[19]

In contrast, a problem arises when our worth is conditional. I suspect that our evaluation of our worth doesn't work the same way as our evaluation of our competence. It is not as calculated; it has a much more subliminal and emotive (some might say 'unconscious') quality. This means that, when we feel unworthy, we do not have the same solutions available to us that we have when we feel badly about our competence: we cannot 'not care' (certainly not convincingly); we cannot find another channel for measuring our worth (certainly not easily in childhood, other than premature orientation to peers and alienation from

disapproving parents); and the only route for *earning* a sense of worth is by proving it – and the only way to prove it is to through achievement. This quest for achievement, in turn, will take on a compulsive quality because it is not underpinned by certitude about our worth.

Types of self-esteem

Given these two dimensions of self-esteem – competence and worth – there are four types of self-esteem, as illustrated in Figure 12.4.

Low self-esteem

Approximately 7 per cent of people have consistently low self-esteem, although during adolescence this figure might climb to 13 per cent.[20] This group (represented in the third quadrant of Figure 12.4) has low, unstable or confused evaluations of both their competence and their worth, feeling not only ambivalent about themselves but also about life in general.[21] Academically, they are primed to react negatively to any hint of failure and, therefore, will choose safe goals, give up on challenging tasks and display deteriorating performances when in doubt about their skills.[22] Compared with people who have high self-esteem, children with low self-esteem are at increased risk for a range of future emotional problems (such as depression even under benign conditions), poorer physical health, early school leaving, worse economic prospects, and lower life satisfaction.[23] Socially, although they have negative attitudes towards others, these attitudes do not necessarily translate into hostile actions.[24] Nevertheless, being extremely sensitive to rejection, they may unwittingly sabotage

FIGURE 12.4   Types of self-esteem[25]

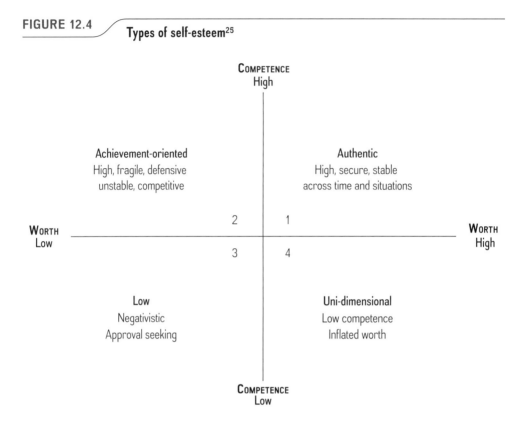

relationships, or they may suppress their own feelings and needs in an effort to gain others' approval.[26] Accordingly, they may remain victims because they believe that they do not deserve to stand up against their oppression.

A second group with low self-worth attempt to disguise their self-doubts with displays of conceit, arrogance, intolerance, criticism and a lack of empathy.[27] These tactics are commonly aversive to peers. Accordingly, this group is often labelled as narcissistic (especially in popular literature) because they appear to exaggerate their own importance.[28] However, I believe that this label is mistaken: their self-esteem is not in fact inflated but *low*,

while the feeling behind their obnoxious behaviours is a fear of being ordinary.[29] In essence, the feeling is one of shame at not being enough (not good enough, not clever enough, not athletic enough, not good looking enough . . . or any imposed standard).[30] The common temptation of outsiders is to 'take them down a peg' but, in reality, they are already 'down' – and kicking them while they are there will not help.

What causes a low self-esteem to be stable is that, any time these people start to feel better about their *skills*, their persistent reservations about their *worth* drag down their esteem. These deep doubts arise from early and repeated invalidating messages. Insidious parental criticism and withholding of approval cause children to see themselves as unwelcome and unworthy.[31] This sense is more resistant to change than a sense of incompetence because, unless we truly *experience* being valued, it will take a lot of work to convince ourselves that we are worthy.

Uni-dimensional self-esteem

When we focus on one element of our self-concept to the exclusion of others, we will have an inflated self-esteem because it notes the highs but overlooks the lows. The main group for whom this applies are those whose self-esteem is based on the possession of *power.* This group (located in the fourth quadrant of Figure 12.4) sees the world in terms of winners and losers and will do what it takes to win. They value dominance and use power to secure others' admiration.[32] Accordingly, they are frequently aggressive and bully others. But, with their worth reliant on winning, it is stable only as long as they can *keep* winning. This fragility of their self-esteem is verified by their proneness to depression.[33]

My conjecture is that, nevertheless, emphasising dominance and consequently having higher worth than competence is just a form of 'armour' against a hostile world. Brené Brown reports that, at the core of the discrepancy between worth and competence is a fear of being vulnerable, learned from admonitions to 'Man up' and from being the recipient of parental bullying, aggression and violence, commonly from an early age. This conclusion is supported by findings that, when these children do detect an unflattering evaluation, they commonly over-react, sometimes using aggression (particularly in the case of boys).[34]

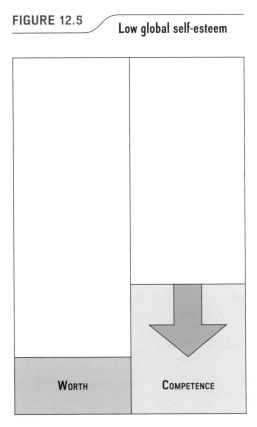

FIGURE 12.5 — Low global self-esteem

Unlike those with uniformly low self-esteem (who focus *too much* on any feedback, particularly about their worth), this group attends mostly to feedback about their agency or power and accordingly fails to question their inflated opinions of their overall social competence in particular.[35]

A second, rarer, group with a uni-dimensional self-esteem are those who emphasise ability. These individuals have often been the smartest person in the room until they reach university or adulthood. This is not healthy for anyone and can cause them to be contemptuous of any who seem less able than them. No doubt they have learned this by being pressured to be clever and accordingly feel compelled to live up to inflated expectations; the unfortunate part is that they impose these same standards on others and mistakenly equate a difference in competence with a difference in worth.

I speculate that there is a third group that comprises bigots, who emphasise race, gender or religion and assume their superiority relative to outsiders. A lack of focus on counter-examples of the skills and laudable qualities of outsiders, and a blind belief in the superiority of insiders, mean that this group is not amenable to changing its prejudicial views.

Occasionally, however, being impervious to negative feedback can be beneficial. This applies to children whose peers dislike

them, but they do not know it. For example, many students with attention deficits are unaware of their social ineptness.[36] Their ignorance of their peers' disdain emboldens them to remain socially engaged. Although their self-esteem will be fragile because, while interacting, they can be exposed at any time to negative feedback from others, nevertheless, over time, the practice they get means that they do gain in skilfulness and acceptance, while declining in aggression.[37]

Achievement-oriented self-esteem

Individuals who doubt their worth and who, therefore, believe that they must *earn* self-esteem through high achievement occupy the second quadrant in Figure 12.4. Their self-esteem is not backed by a strong sense of innate worth but instead is tied to the opinions of others. Necessarily, then, it will be fragile because fortune is fickle: the next rejection or failure is just around the corner. Therefore, this form of self-esteem is unstable because it requires constant validation.[38] In an effort to prove their competence (which is the same thing, in their eyes, as affirming their worth), they feel compelled to succeed, even being willing to cheat given that the stakes are so high.[39]

Having an achievement-oriented self-esteem has emotional, academic and social effects. Emotionally, these individuals experience maladaptive emotions and poor coping when challenged.[40] They are highly anxious, depressive and stressed, and experience shame or denial following failure and engage in self-enhancement following success.[41] Their socially prescribed perfectionism causes them to treat themselves harshly when they perceive that they have performed below expectations.[42] Compared

FIGURE 12.6   Uni-dimensional self-esteem

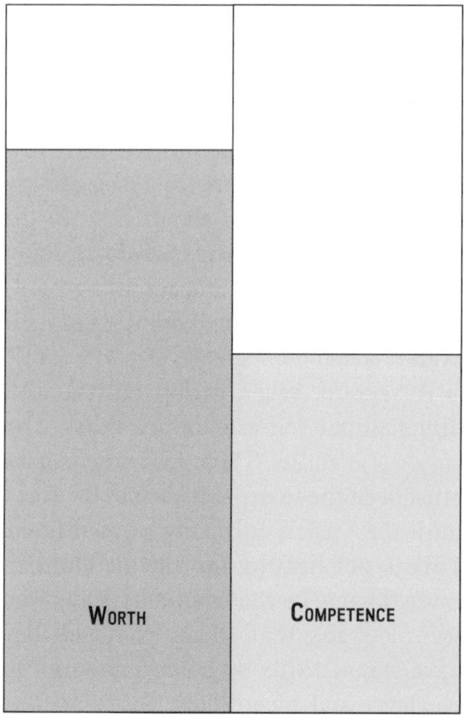

WORTH   COMPETENCE

to those whose self-esteem is grounded in their worth, they have less purpose in life and exercise less autonomy.[43]

Academically, they adopt performance goals (which means that they seek to outdo or out-perform others to prove their superiority);[44] they avoid tasks where failure is a possibility; when challenged, they give up in an attempt to save face; they procrastinate; and they choke under pressure.[45] Their focus on others' approval sabotages their results, producing lower grades in school compared to those whose self-esteem is supplied by both their competence and their worth.[46]

Socially, these individuals are devastated by social disapproval[47] and accordingly are more willing to change their behaviour to be accepted by their peers.[48] Being susceptible to peer pressure, this form of self-esteem amplifies antisocial tendencies.[49] In adolescence, this group has retained a 'looking-glass' orientation typical of early childhood which upholds, 'If others approve of me, I will like myself'.[50]

Achievement-oriented self-esteem is learned when controlling parents demand rather than encourage high standards[51] and when they induce guilt in their children or withdraw their love when their children perform below expectations; it also comes from competing for school awards.[52] As a result of this contingent feedback, these children become preoccupied with others' opinions of them and equate failure with rejection.[53] Given that rejection is devastating to humans, failure must be avoided at all costs.

Authentic high self-esteem

An authentic high self-esteem (illustrated in the first quadrant in Figure 12.4) is

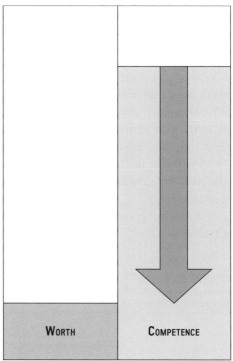

FIGURE 12.7   Achievement-oriented self-esteem

WORTH   COMPETENCE

secure and genuine. This is because it is balanced: it is made up of roughly equal proportions of worth and competence. As a result, these individuals' self-worth is well anchored, without the need for constant validation and without the compulsion to prove themselves by outdoing others.[54] They feel competent to take achievement risks, and worthy enough to sustain a failure.[55] Failure – even in highly salient domains – will not imperil their overall self-esteem, because their sense of worth is not reliant on their achievements. Accordingly, although (as indicated by the double-headed arrow in Figure 12.8), there is some minor fluctuation in their esteem about their competence (in response to successes or failures), on the whole they will use failure as a guide to future action.[56] This is because 'true high self-esteem is not "earned", nor can it be taken away'.[57] It is neither undeserved nor inflated because it has developed naturally.[58]

Whereas in infancy, our sense of worth arises from receiving approval or validation from others, individuals with an authentic self-esteem mature into adopting the stance, 'If I like myself, others will like me too'.[59] That is, they are relatively independent of the judgments of others.[60]

Not obsessing about their evaluations of themselves, they are open to experience, are resilient and trust their instincts.[61] An authentic self-esteem, then, provides a sense of direction in life: it is an 'internal compass' that propels us towards actualising the best version of ourselves.[62] It is associated with self-referenced perfectionism, intrinsic motivation and prosocial behaviours.[63] Compared to those with an achievement-oriented self-esteem, these individuals have higher school grades, and more positive attitudes and adjustment to school.[64]

Educational implications of self-esteem

There are two reasons for teachers to take an interest in students' self-esteem. First, people with an authentic self-esteem are happier than individuals whose self-esteem is low or is contingent on their successes.[65] And children have the right to feel happy.[66] Second, although our esteem about our competence is grounded in the past, our sense of worth shapes how confidently we approach future tasks and thereby contributes to scholastic achievement.[67] Students who believe in their capabilities are more interested in academic work and are willing to surmount challenge.

The above description of the four types of self-esteem is testament to the vital importance of ensuring that students do not acquire a contingent self-esteem. A low self-esteem is resistant to change, while an achievement-oriented self-esteem is a charlatan, masquerading as high self-esteem but lacking a deep sense of worth to support a healthy interchange with the world. It will suffice in benign conditions, but lacks the substance to withstand life's storms.

FIGURE 12.8   Authentic high self-esteem

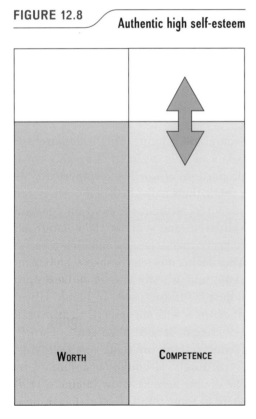

WORTH   COMPETENCE

Promoting an authentic self-esteem

A sense of competence is achieved in concert with autonomy: through exercising choice, feeling efficacious and accomplishing meaningful tasks. These routes are the subject of chapter 14. The topic here is that, for self-esteem to be truly authentic, children need to acquire a non-contingent, unquestioning belief in their worth. Referring back to Figure 10.2 (see page 140) and as already summarised here, feelings of worth are achieved in concert with belonging, specifically by:

- being accepted and valued by others
- receiving empathy – that is, validation of our feelings and perspective
- receiving affirming feedback.

Acceptance

According to guidance theorists, students will feel worthy when we convey a genuine acceptance of them, allowing them to feel, think, talk and act as they are. Your acceptance is communicated by your tone of voice, by listening to young people, by honouring their emotions, appreciating their uniqueness, respecting their outside interests, enjoying your job and having a sense of humour.[68] Acceptance also encompasses affirming students' families and cultures. This involves not only communicating interpersonal respect, but also ensuring that curricula include stories and presentations from community leaders of diverse cultural groups, so that young people from all cultures see themselves as being a part of something that is valued.[69] Only when school values diverse cultures will the individual members of those cultures value education.

Empathy

As illustrated in Figure 10.2 (see page 140), the second quality that feeds children's self-esteem about their worth is receiving empathy. Empathy has been aptly described as emotional resonance with others.[70] It is the ability to appreciate how others feel and to respond in a caring way to alleviate their distress.[71] It requires both the cognitive ability to see the world from other perspectives and the emotional sensitivity to appreciate others' feelings (see chapter 17). This requires that we understand that children's feelings are a signal about their needs and, although we might not approve of the disruptive behaviours that these might trigger, we can understand *that* children feel as they do. When we validate even negative feelings, we teach children that all emotions are valid – indeed, that *they* are valid.

Affirmation

In his earliest research, veteran researcher Edward Deci discovered that individuals thrive and become more motivated when they receive external feedback about their performances.[72] However, Deci soon discovered that feedback has two elements – a controlling aspect and an informative element – and that these two facets had opposite effects.[73] Information inspires a greater investment in a task,[74] whereas control leads to a decline in intrinsic motivation and in achievement, because it shifts the learner's locus of causality from internal to external.[75]

Subsequent research has verified that receiving praise for being successful leads to negative responses to failure, partly because (in terms of the topic of this chapter) it promotes an achievement-oriented self-esteem, whereby we feel worthy only if we are successful. Therefore, teachers must give students affirming feedback about their achievements, without linking these to any measure of their worth.

All theorists agree that this feedback must convey specific *information* about students' achievements and the skills and qualities they exercised to attain them. In this way, students will learn about who they are: their self-concept will expand. In contrast with behaviourists, however, guidance practitioners uphold that this feedback must not judge students. Even positive judgments (such as '*Good girl/boy; You're clever; Good work'*) convey to students that we approve of them when they meet our standards. In young-child speak, if they are good for getting things right, this means that they would be bad if they got them wrong. In this way, judgmental feedback makes their worth contingent on meeting others' standards. In short, it will promote an achievement-oriented self-esteem.

An extensive body of research has detailed the following negative outcomes of judgmental feedback.[76]

- Praise of the person imposes an obligation to continue to act in a praiseworthy manner. Anxious about their ability to attain this ideal, children's cognitions, affect and behaviour all mimic helplessness, with consequent reduction in their engagement and work quality.
- Person praise orients children to define their self-esteem according to their achievements (not their worth) and,

therefore, leads to more negative affect and helpless reactions to errors.

- Praise for high ability promotes in children a fixed rather than an incremental view of ability, and produces a performance-avoidant orientation whereby students choose safe tasks and avoid challenge, do not persist and experience less task enjoyment and declining performance.
- Meanwhile, those students who seldom earn rewards also develop performance-avoidant goals which will similarly disadvantage them academically and emotionally while increasing their behavioural disruptiveness.
- The delivery of praise or other rewards for achievement reduces children's intrinsic motivation for the task. It leads to less enjoyment of the activity, reduced conceptual learning and weaker persistence. This has consistently been found to be particularly true for children; for females; within controlling interpersonal climates; and for those whose relatively poorer performances result in their not earning an equivalent reward to their peers.
- Rewarding students implies to them that the task is noxious: otherwise, they would not need to be bribed to do it. When, for example, adults reward children (say, with ice-cream) for eating their vegetables, children come to dislike vegetables more. Similarly, rewarding students for learning makes the task *less* not *more* attractive.

Guidance practitioners attribute these negative outcomes to the contingent nature of praise. It uses students' competence or their compliance as a measure of their *worth.* These combined negative effects give rise to the following principle:

> When you want students to develop an authentic high self-esteem, do not praise them.

Given that a low or achievement-oriented self-esteem has negative emotional, social and academic outcomes, it is vital to ensure that students are not preoccupied with comparative judgments about their skills and, consequently, caught up in debating their personal worth.[77] To that end, the guidance approach uses no rewards – be these praise, tangible rewards such as stars, stickers or merit certificates, token rewards, or social rewards such as grades or student-of-the-day awards.

Yet students *do* need feedback that describes to them – or asks them to reflect on – what they have achieved and what their next goal might be. Elsewhere, I have termed this 'acknowledgment'.[78] The distinctions between the two are given in Box 12.1, with tips for delivering acknowledgment given in Box 12.3.

Informative feedback will be particularly beneficial when it gives students specific information about their strategy use or about their own progress over time. In contrast to judgmental feedback, acknowledgment helps students feel both competent *and* worthy, enhances their intrinsic motivation,[79] promotes a mastery rather than a performance orientation to learning (see chapter 16), and fosters an incremental rather than fixed view of ability.[80] It also ensures that students do not come to rely on external judgments of their effort, but instead trust their own wisdom and self-evaluation.[81]

Hence, guidance practitioners believe:

> When you want students to develop an authentic high self-esteem, acknowledge and celebrate (but do not praise) their efforts and successes.

Minimise competition

In order to protect students' self-esteem, it will be vital that your feedback does not compare them to each other. In competitive

---

BOX 12.1   Distinctions between praise and acknowledgment[82]

Praise	Acknowledgment
Approves of work that meets adults' standards.	Guides students to evaluate their own achievements.
Judges others or their efforts.	Gives our opinion.
Prescribes what others must do to earn our respect.	Describes qualities which others display that we already respect.
Is delivered in public as a way to manipulate students into repeating a desired behaviour or to incite others to copy a praised student.	Is a personal event that does not show students up in public or compare them to each other, but instead shares in the celebration of their achievement.

BOX 12.2   **Benefits of acknowledgment**

- Acknowledgment gives students information about who they are and what they are capable of being: it *expands their self-concept*.
- It *does not imply doubt about their worth* or link their worth to their ability to satisfy our expectations.
- Because it is *authentic*, it is credible, meaningful and, therefore, successful at low doses.
- It does not undermine *intrinsic motivation*.
- It promotes *mastery* rather than performance achievement goals.
- It encourages *self-referenced perfectionism*, rather than socially prescribed perfectionism.

settings, success is measured not as an increased level of knowledge or skill, but as besting others. This emphasis on social comparison generates differences in perceptions of individuals' abilities, with winning adding to students' prestige.[83] Ability becomes salient, with status differentials developing between classmates.[84] This competitive climate is damaging to all, but most especially to those who already feel incompetent.[85] Rather than motivating them to do better next time, it induces anxiety for many – and this emotion, while noxious in itself, also impairs learning.[86]

Competition is also detrimental for students with an achievement-oriented self-esteem, because failure challenges their competence and, thereby (in their eyes), also their worth. Even when they win, it might not promote their self-esteem because winning is relative to the performance of one's rivals and hence can be attributed to luck.[87]

In contrast, cooperative settings minimise status differentials such that students' *worth* is not dependent on their achievements.[88] Although social comparison is inevitable as a way of measuring oneself against a standard, seeing oneself as better than or deficient compared to others is not inevitable. A difference in competence does not have to mean a difference in *worth*.

Imposing a competitive climate on children is an ethical issue. Very few adults would persist at a game at which they constantly lost; yet we impose losing on some students every day of their school lives – and still expect them to remain engaged and hopeful.[89] It is not surprising that so many become disaffected; it is more surprising that so few become seriously disruptive out of discouragement.[90]

Conclusion

In addition to the effects of rewards on students' motivation and learning, a fundamental criticism of praise and rewards in general is that these convey to students that they are valued not for who they are, but for what they do.[91] This conditional acceptance will produce a low or achievement-oriented self-esteem, resentment of adults, and reduced motivation.[92] Individuals who seek rewards as evidence that they have out-performed others or to prove their worth become competitive and,

BOX 12.3   **Tips for acknowledging students' achievements**[93]

- Ask students how they feel about what they have achieved:
    Are you pleased?
    What do you think of *that*?
    Are you happy with that?
- When students are saying or giving nonverbal messages that they are pleased, reflect that:
    You look delighted!
    You seem very proud of yourself.
    You look very pleased.
- When appropriate, add your opinion (but not a judgment):
    Well, I agree with you!
    I agree that you can be very pleased with yourself.
    I think it's special too.
- Give information or feedback in the form of I–verb:
    I admire . . .
    I respect . . .
    I value . . .
    I'm impressed that . . .
    I appreciate . . .
- Intend to congratulate, not manipulate:
    Congratulations!
    Hey! You did it!
    Wow! Look at that!
- Express appreciation:
    Thank you!
    I'm grateful that . . .
    I appreciate that because . . .
- Focus on the process, not the product:
    I admire that you tried something new.
    I'm impressed that you had another go.
    Looks like you really worked at that.
- Verify students' own assessment that they have achieved something worthwhile, highlight their successes so that they notice these, and expand on what they have achieved:
    I agree that it's quite an achievement.
    Did you know you could do that?
    And not only have you finished it, but you worked on it for ages.
- Use natural manners, without patronising. For example, in response to a student's thanks:
    You're welcome!
    It's a pleasure.
    I hope you enjoy it.

if they cannot win, grow despondent or disengaged.[94]

Therefore, the shared conclusion of guidance practitioners and many educational researchers is that, while it is essential that students receive feedback about their performances, specific informative feedback will supply the information that promotes their engagement, without detrimental effects on their self-esteem arising from judgments.[95] Naturally, behaviourists disagree with this summation, largely because they interpret abandoning evaluative feedback as meaning the elimination of all feedback.[96] They claim that when students are discouraged, are failing, or are finding tasks uninteresting, difficult, tedious or complex, these students will need extrinsic reinforcers to motivate them to engage and persist, after which their success will cause intrinsic satisfaction to take over.[97] The guidance view merely reiterates that, for discouraged students, informative feedback would be equally effective – and less risky.

Recommended further reading

Brown, B. (2010). *The gifts of imperfection*. Center City, MN: Hazelden.

Kohn, A. (1992). *No contest: The case against competition*. Boston, MA: Houghton Mifflin.

CHAPTER 13

Meeting students' social needs: Affiliation and connection

Classroom groups organized so that students feel liked and respected are more likely to have youngsters acting in ways that warrant the liking and respect of others.[1]

The purpose of meeting students' social needs is that the human species is inherently social and requires relationships with others; an instrumental gain is that support from teachers and peers changes students' social and academic perceptions of themselves which, in turn, promotes their academic engagement.[2] Within a supportive setting students feel safe to participate and to take intellectual risks because they know that they will receive help if they need it and that their worth will not be diminished if they fail.[3] A second instrumental gain is that an accepting social context has a powerful influence on behaviour, increasing prosocial and reducing antisocial behaviour.[4] Given the importance of the need to belong, we cannot leave to chance that this need will be met during breaks at school, but instead must actively foster a sense of cohesion and acceptance within classrooms.

Classroom climate

The term *climate* refers to the learning atmosphere, attitudes, beliefs, values and norms of a setting.[5] It is the extent to which students and teachers share mutual warmth, respect and enjoyment between and among each other.[6] More than being mere subject matter specialists, teachers can shape the social climate, establishing norms for the interactions that occur in the classroom and in the wider school.[7]

Group cohesion

Communities can be defined by proximity, shared participation in various functions, security and mutuality, order and by integration of the individual into a whole; communities can also refer to communities of mind, where members share common interests and passions.[8] This connectedness is forged within a stable group whose

FIGURE 13.1

Aspects of classroom belonging[9]

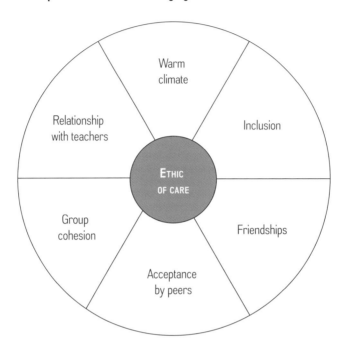

members know each other, where there are opportunities for social interaction, and where aggression is rare.[10]

Class groupings must not only support high levels of attainment in members but must also provide social and emotional support for individuals, such that groups:[11]

- promote in members a sense of belonging by welcoming everyone into full membership of the group
- allow members to experience influence, which is the perception of making a difference to others
- promote the expectation that their needs will be met by participating in the group
- foster identification with the group by sharing a common history and experiences

- ensure self-renewal, which is the capacity of the group to negotiate and adjust its processes to meet changing group or individual needs.

When groups are both cohesive and supportive, their members experience less stress, greater engagement, reduced competitiveness, fewer disruptive behaviours, and lower rates of aggression.[12] Young people who have difficulties with self-regulation are less likely to develop behavioural problems in cohesive settings, partly because there is less friction to arouse negative feelings in them and partly because group support enables them to employ self-regulation skills.[13] In turn, they will behave less disruptively.

Relationships with teachers

Support from teachers fulfils different functions for young people than does support from their peers.[14] Students' relationships with their teachers are the strongest influence on their engagement and interest in learning, academic self-esteem, and their sense of belonging in their class and their school.[15] While problems with peers and friends are disturbing, adolescents rate their interactional problems with teachers as more difficult to handle.[16] When students perceive that their teachers do not like them, over time, these students show increasing loneliness and declining grades.[17]

In contrast, positive relationships with teachers have been defined as the degree to which students feel respected, supported and valued by their teachers.[18] When asked, students define good teachers as possessing personal qualities such as charisma, kindness, humour, patience, fairness and enthusiasm.[19] Throughout the primary years of schooling and beyond, students attach considerable importance to the support they receive from their teachers, with teachers remaining prominent figures in the students' emotional and academic lives, supplementing the personal and emotional support provided by their parents and peers.[20] This support comes in four forms:[21]

- *emotional*: perceptions of trust, care and empathy, which implies teachers' interest in student wellbeing beyond their academic progress
- *instructional support*: provision of tangible assistance with learning, such that teachers are willing to promote understanding of academic material by the whole class and by individuals
- *appraisal support*: providing feedback that gives students information about what they have achieved and what their next goal might be
- *informational*: the provision of guidance, advice or information that can provide solutions to problems.

Of these, the most vital are emotional and instructional support.[22] Warm relationships and low levels of conflict with their teachers are powerful at preventing risk factors in students' lives being translated into poor academic outcomes and behavioural difficulties.[23] Students' engagement, achievement levels and conduct all improve when they are cared for by emotionally supportive, responsive teachers with whom they experience minimal conflict.[24] Students' connectedness with sensitive teachers is even more influential for those who are aggressive,[25] are less capable of self-regulation,[26] for boys,[27] and for children with devalued minority status.[28]

Although teachers cannot like all students equally, it is vital that their personal preferences are not displayed in the form of negative interactions with troublesome students.[29] Young people who are distractible, who disrupt group processes or who are aggressive commonly experience adult rejection, receiving four times more negative than positive teacher feedback, and fewer positive responses to their constructive participation; they also engage in more mutually angry exchanges with their teachers.[30] Many of these students receive controlling discipline at home and then are met with more coercion at school, which only entrenches their difficulties, causing their antisocial behaviours to persist and prosocial acts to decline.[31]

Peer relationships

Young people's freedom within the classroom to interact with their peers is strongly linked to their enjoyment and academic motivation and engagement.[32] Students' social acceptance and friendships are a major source of their pleasure in their educational settings.[33] Those with warm adult support are more likely to develop mutual harmonious friendships and receive high levels of peer support, in all likelihood because these students receive empathy and thereby learn how to give it and because, with warm support, they learn how to regulate their own emotions, which helps them to accommodate to others.[34]

Acceptance

Peer acceptance is a group phenomenon, signalling that the group as a whole values each member's place within it. Belonging in the group is more than simply fitting in. Fitting in involves becoming who we need to be for the group to accept us, whereas belonging is about being accepted for who we are.[35] Teachers lead this acceptance: their warm relationships and low levels of conflict with students shapes the students' relationships with their peers.[36] Positive teacher comments actively help to recruit peer support for excluded children.[37] When young people see their teachers being supportive of disruptive peers, they perceive the peers as both more competent and more likeable.[38] This is particularly so with aggression, which is the most susceptible to teacher influence,

with peers being more tolerant of aggressive children when their teachers are; in turn, this reduces perpetrators' aggression and general emotional and behavioural problems over time.[39]

In contrast, teachers' repeated reprimands of students with demanding behaviours signals to onlookers that these children are less worthy of their friendship.[40] Although children's poor social skills and behavioural problems (particularly aggression and bullying) can cause peers to reject them, rejection itself has a strong influence on subsequent maladjustment.[41] Being socially isolated leads over time to declining academic participation and achievement; increased levels of reticence; lowered self-esteem; depression; social anxiety; and escalating antisocial behaviour and reactive aggression.[42] These effects are pervasive but have been found particularly for students who are predisposed towards aggression or are already vulnerable for other reasons.[43] Rejection is so powerful that it is manifested physically, with excluded students having higher cortisol levels at school compared to children who have friends, and higher than children who, although victimised, have some social support.[44]

Friendship

Whereas cohesiveness and acceptance are characteristics of *groups*, friendship is a voluntary, ongoing bond between individuals who have a mutual preference for each other and who share emotional warmth. Although different in this way, cohesiveness and friendships reciprocally affect each other in that friendships are more likely to develop in cohesive classrooms while, in reverse, classrooms are more likely to be cohesive when every member has at least one close friend.[45]

Despite the fact that peers can make unique and powerful contributions to children's development in many domains, adults often regard peer influence with suspicion. Yet throughout childhood and adolescence, friendships provide young people with a context for skill acquisition, supply emotional and cognitive resources, and are models for their future relationships. The benefits of having friends (as listed in Box 13.2) are found across cultures and are particularly valuable for students whose home life is strained, when peers can provide the support that parents cannot, thereby helping young people to function positively in school. In contrast, sustained friendlessness alters children's beliefs in their own worthiness. Emotionally, this leads to difficulties such as depression and loneliness. Socially, friendlessness leads to pessimistic and distrustful expectations of peers.[46] Academically, it exacerbates students' attention difficulties, producing lowered school achievement and increased dropping out of school.[47]

Young people's healthy adjustment does not require a large number of friends, but instead friendships that are of high quality.[48] These will be relationships that affirm their self-esteem, are low in conflict, and are intimate.[49] Compared with their interactions with less preferred playmates, children interact more with reciprocal

BOX 13.1   **Qualities of teachers[50]**

Qualities that convey care	Qualities that convey a lack of care
Emotional support	*Emotional*
• asks students how they are	• has a lack of interest in students' names, interests, emotional concerns or health
• asks students about their lives	• uses an aversive tone of voice
• invests in students' interests	• calls students names
• promotes a positive emotional climate	• violates students' privacy (e.g. by sharing confidences)
• uses humour	• threatens students with failure or disciplinary action
• shows respect for students	• favours students on the basis of ability, race, gender or behaviour
• respects students' privacy	• discriminates against students for their reputation, appearance or personality.
• provides fun activities	
• treats all students similarly	
• is real, honest	
• displays a kind disposition	
• keeps promises	
• advocates for students	
• helps students solve personal problems	
• employs cooperative rather than competitive learning.	

Qualities that convey care	Qualities that convey a lack of care
Instructional support	*Instructional*
• maintains high expectations for students' success	• is insufficiently interested in students' understanding of academic content
• attempts to alleviate students' academic concerns	• requires students to learn independently
• checks for students' understanding	• shows no concern if students find material difficult
• matches teaching to learning styles	• offers classwork that is unrelated to learning objective (it's 'busy work')
• provides additional academic assistance	• relies on a single mode of instruction
• is accessible to students	• imposes a workload that is overwhelming and uneven
• uses diverse teaching strategies	• ignores students' questions
• monitors that students are completing their work	• provides a limited or shaming response to students' questions
• helps students prepare for tests and complete projects	• is unavailable to answer questions.
• helps students improve their grades	
• ensures a manageable workload	
• provides sufficient time for students to produce work	
• encourages and answers students' questions.	
Appraisal support	*Appraisal*
• has high performance expectations	• praises in an automatic and insincere way
• communicates to students and parents about student achievements	• has a strict approach to grading
• provides constructive feedback	• shows no leniency in grading policies
• offers encouragement	• distributes positive feedback unequally.
• does not converge on correct answers but explores ideas.	
Behaviour management	*Behaviour management*
• takes time to identify what happened	• sets firm expectations, rules and limits
• delivers consequences fairly	• enforces overly strict or senseless rules
• attempts to solve a problem rather than punishes automatically.	• issues repeated reminders of rules
	• punishes the wrong student
	• punishes automatically on the basis of assumptions rather than of information
	• behaves hypocritically.

friends, are less likely to over-react and vent their feelings inappropriately, are more conciliatory when in conflict, and are less vengeful or passive in resolving disputes.[51] Girls report more social support from their friendships than boys experience.[52] However, girls' more intimate groupings can be less stable than boys' larger groups and conflict with a best friend could take a greater toll on girls' adjustment.[53]

Young children's friends are the people they play with most. These playmates become familiar and predictable. Later, by four years of age, in a phenomenon known as homophily, children start to select friends who match their developmental skills (particularly language abilities), their activity levels, gender, social class and temperament.[54] This is the beginning of true reciprocal friendship.

However, in middle childhood, the pressures of the group start to dictate children's choice of friends. Now the model is rather like the stock exchange: that is, it is safe to invest in friends who will raise your status within the group, and risky to associate with peers whom the group does not respect. This can break the heart of six- and seven-year-olds whose former close friends now abandon them. It can even be that the children remain best friends on a playdate or at the weekend – but then that same

---

BOX 13.2   **Benefits of friendship[55]**

Academic benefits
- Friendships enhance young people's engagement with and wellbeing at school.
- They provide practice at using language skills.

Social skills
- Friendships provide a venue for developing and practising social skills.
- They teach reciprocity, cooperation and collaboration.
- They give children experience at problem solving.
- Friendships teach adolescents about intimacy, loyalty and self-disclosure.
- They teach empathy, compassion and altruism.
- They support young people's developing sexuality.

Emotional support
- Within friendships, children learn self-regulation.
- Friendships supply reassurance.
- They promote a healthy self-esteem.
- Support from friends enhances children's confidence in stressful situations.
- Friendships avoid loneliness.
- They provide fun.
- They prevent victimisation from bullying, which is particularly vital for children who are maltreated at home.
- Friendships foster individuals' happiness.

Informational support
- Friendships allow young people to exchange skills and information that they do not readily acquire from adults.
- Friends offer practical and emotional support by giving information, advice and counsel.
- Friends provide assistance with school work.

friend shuns them at school where others are watching.

Measures to enhance belonging

In order to meet students' need for connection, the guidance approach aims to create a caring school community whose members know, care about and support each other, enjoying a shared commitment and sense of purpose.[56]

Eliminate competition

As seen in chapter 12, competitive settings threaten students' self-esteem; here the focus is their effects on peer relationships. Competition causes students to regard each other as rivals[57] and contributes to hostility and ill feeling towards one's peers.[58] It corrodes the cooperative climate of a classroom, weakening group cohesion and producing increased aggression and disruptive behaviour.[59]

The emphasis in Western schooling on academic excellence not only belittles the importance of skills in other domains but also emphasises individual achievement at the expense of others. As Kohn observes, 'Competitiveness cannibalises cooperation'.[60] It increases rivalry between group members; reduces empathy for others and makes altruism less likely.[61] In competitive settings, students criticise each other to diminish their peers so that they can emerge the winner[62] and make self-aggrandising statements that enhance themselves at others' expense (such as, 'Look how many I've done!').[63] Unlike the common experience in Western classrooms, many cultures repudiate the glee of a child who can answer a teacher's question correctly to the humiliation of the classmate who cannot.[64]

In contrast, in cooperative settings, children have been found to comment favourably on others' efforts.[65] Consequently, those in cooperative settings have more reason to feel accepted and supported.[66]

Interracial tensions are more pronounced in high-achieving schools that have a competitive climate.[67] Largely because there are typically few minority students in these schools, members of devalued cultures experience a higher social cost for achieving well at school: that is, they are less well accepted by their cultural peers.[68]

Teachers who promote an academic hierarchy by valuing the more academically able students contribute to alienation of students who are less able and behaviourally poorly adjusted,[69] plus their neglect and rejection by peers.[70] Even able students are not immune from these effects. They have reported that competition scapegoats them and promotes jealousy from classmates.[71] Thus, competition can actually lower the social inclusion and achievement even of those students who consistently excel.[72]

Conduct regular class meetings

Gathering together regularly allows students to see themselves as a group and thereby to develop a sense of community.[73] Meetings are an excellent venue for airing issues that concern members of the class. These will be most effective when conducted daily in primary school and twice weekly in high school.[74] It is crucial that meetings do not become an exercise in control where you impose your views on the students, but instead support them in generating their own ideas and solutions, even running the meeting themselves.[75] Therefore, you will need to give your opinions sparingly and these should carry equal weight with students' views.

Students will generate most of the topics for the meetings, with communication skills used in an atmosphere of cooperation and orderliness to achieve win–win (or non-punitive) solutions. For whole-group issues such as deciding on an excursion, voting is appropriate, unless this would leave a disgruntled minority, in which case finding a consensus is more useful.[76] Reaching a consensus is a more sophisticated task than mere voting because it requires students to fashion creative solutions to accommodate all people's points of view.[77]

Meetings do not always run smoothly, especially when first instigated and particularly when students have little experience with exercising autonomy. In that case, you can use the meetings themselves to solve initial problems such as students' acting out, outrageous suggestions or resistance.[78] You can help to share talk time evenly by giving all students a certain number of tokens, one of which must be surrendered each time they have a turn at speaking,[79] and help to have one person talking at a time by passing a stick to the speaker, who is then the only person allowed to talk.

Problem-solving meetings. These attempt to solve issues that concern any student, teacher or parent. The need to resolve conflict and tension is not an indication of malfunction in the group or of individual deficiencies, but is a reality in any social grouping. The process of solving problems in the group is a real-life application of skills. To avoid scapegoating students whose behaviour is the subject of a complaint, you can ask the complainant, 'How is that a problem for you?' so that the focus is on fixing the effects of the behaviour, not blaming the actor.

Educational-diagnostic meetings are related to what the class is studying. In these meetings, students will discuss the rationale for curricular content and classroom procedures to determine whether these are effective in producing in the students a living, working understanding of the concepts being taught.

Open-ended meetings allow the students to discuss any issue that is relevant to their lives, including any dissatisfactions with school. Meetings can be a place for sharing news; deciding anything from how to arrange the classroom to how to raise funds for a charity; or jointly planning field trips or other class activities.[80]

Class size

Structural variables such as teacher education, number of students in the class, and teacher–student ratios, while important, are less influential than is the quality of the relationship between students and their teacher.[81] Nevertheless, children naturally congregate in groups whose size numbers one more than their birthdays. When we exceed this comfortable number, many children will find it difficult to participate. Teachers can limit the numbers of children by offering small-group experiences throughout the day, so that personal interaction can occur. This has been linked to improved academic engagement and subsequent achievement.[82]

Class sizes of under 20 students have been found to be especially beneficial for young students and for those who are disadvantaged, particularly assisting them to acquire reading and mathematics skills.[83] The benefits occur because in smaller classes, teachers better get to know students and interact more often and more positively with them, and the students are more supportive of each other.[84] Academically, students tend to be more engaged and less disruptive, perhaps because a cohesive group has a norm of cooperation.[85] When disruptions do occur, teachers' proximity means that they can more readily intervene because there are fewer students to oversee, and they can be more lenient because the contagion effect is less strong in a smaller group, allowing teachers to be more proactive and less reactive in their responses.[86]

Teachers are more likely to use controlling discipline with larger classes, but this method – not the numbers of children – engenders the disciplinary problems that teachers are attempting to solve.[87] My own research found that controlling discipline is *least* effective with larger numbers because the teacher cannot be everywhere and see everything that is going on whereas, under the guidance approach, this level of monitoring and intervention is unnecessary because the children are self-regulated (the occasional lapse notwithstanding).[88]

Offer group-based learning

Teacher-directed learning places the teacher in centre stage as the expert who is active and transmits knowledge to largely passive students. Any conversation, when it occurs, involves only the teacher and one student answering a content-related question. The teacher's language is typically directive, comprising statements and closed questions, and the delivery of collective discipline.[89] In contrast, group-based learning is a structure whereby students coach each other.[90] The teacher becomes 'the guide on the side, not the sage on the stage'.[91] In this looser structure, the teacher's language is more personal, while the students' is more spontaneous and creative.[92] Importantly, in the group setting, talk is more than a way of sharing thoughts: it represents a social mode of thinking.[93]

Adolescents have the opportunity for only 12 momentary interactions with peers per day, with less popular students having even fewer.[94] Small-group learning offers opportunities for more frequent and higher-quality engagement and conversation that connects group members and allows them to experience themselves as part of a community.[95] In smaller groupings, diffident students can be more outspoken, which can embolden them to speak out more often in the larger group setting as well.[96]

Group-based learning can entail student *collaboration* on a mutual activity;[97] *complementary learning*, in which each student researches one aspect of the topic and then combines what they have each discovered;[98] and *cooperative learning*, which requires students to work together to achieve a common goal that typically is structured by the teacher in such a way that the group can achieve if, and only if, each and every member is successful and participates fully.[99]

Cooperative learning teams must overcome tendencies for free-loaders who will not contribute, the disempowerment of students who cannot contribute, the emergence of fixed hierarchical roles, the surfacing of a kind of 'group think' where dissent is discouraged, and increased pref-erence towards one's own group members and the exclusion of those from other groups.[100] It is important that the most able students do not become domineering, but neither should all of their learning time be given over to teaching others. This 'Robin Hood' method is criticised in gifted education circles for robbing time from able learners, when they have as much right as other students to be progressing.[101]

When group interaction is skilful, however, both low- and high-achievers develop high collective efficacy, and it is this feature that produces academic and social benefits and feelings of satisfac-tion with the process.[102] For the group processes to be of high quality, teachers need to teach social skills including explaining, reasoning, evaluating ideas, providing constructive feedback in response to others' ideas and resolving conflict amicably.[103] In collaboration with students, teachers must establish norms for student engagement.[104] They need to monitor the groups so that they can intervene when students do not know how to proceed, at which point teachers will need to give content-related help by asking students to explain their think-ing, evaluating the group's ideas and questioning their thinking rather than issuing directives.[105] Teachers will also need to give process-oriented help when the group members are having problems communicating with each other and when individuals are dominating the group.[106]

A controversy about cooperative learn-ing is the recommendation by its advocates to reward students both for participating and for the group product.[107] However, guidance practitioners believe that this undoes much of the advantage of coopera-tive learning, in particular the social effects and the benefits for intrinsic motivation.[108] Guidance theorists contend that external rewards are unnecessary when the task truly requires interdependence and is inherently interesting to students.[109]

Cooperative learning is best used for open-ended, conceptual tasks with ill-structured solutions – that is, those requiring higher-level thinking skills, divergent or creative thinking and prob-lem solving, whereas lower-level thinking tasks such as the acquisition of facts and converging on one right answer are more amenable to individual effort.[110] Academically, cooperative learning appears to have greater benefits for disad-vantaged students and for junior primary students compared with those in the later primary grades.[111] Socially, students in cooperative groups engage in more help-ful and supportive conversation, whereas those in individual work tend to interrupt and distract their peers.[112] Cooperative learning (in contrast with competitive structures) encourages greater feelings of safety, support and acceptance by others and improved empathy, with students who work together also more likely to develop friendships across cultures, with students with disabilities, and with members of the other sex.[113]

Mentors

Ensuring that young people spend at least some of every day with a homeroom teacher will help them to have a greater connection to school.[114] An alternative is to allocate them a mentor from within the school or wider community from whom they can receive support and – as discussed in chapter 15 – encouragement to pursue their passions.

Looping

Looping is the retention of the same teacher with an intact class for a number of consecutive years. This practice maintains group stability and avoids the disruption to friendships that occurs when student groupings are rearranged each year.[115] When teachers know that they will be working with students for an extended time, they are committed to developing relationships with them, can establish meaningful relationships with their parents, and can gain a deep awareness of students' learning history, strengths and weaknesses.

Peer tutoring

In peer tutoring, one child with some expertise instructs a peer with lesser knowledge. The relationship is less unequal than between a student and adult teacher and, compared with being instructed by an adult, the novice may be more willing to ask questions and express ideas, in which case the interaction would be more mutual.[116] Peer tutoring can improve the participation of the learner and enhance the academic self-esteem and competence of both learner and tutor.[117] Cross-age tutoring and buddy systems (with an age difference of at least three years between the older and younger student) can overcome the status imbalance of peer tutoring, because the inequalities are inherent in the age difference between tutor and learner rather than in their abilities. Cross-age tutoring and the less structured cross-age grouping for non-academic classes have both been shown to lead to improved social interactions across the school, including

a decrease in stereotypes about and put-downs of students.[118]

Inclusion

Sexual minorities. Just over 7 per cent of males and 5 per cent of females report (not necessarily exclusive) romantic attraction to the same sex,[119] with additional numbers being trans-gender. Many of these young people report being lonely at school and absenting themselves out of fear for their safety.[120] However, it seems that maladjustment is not a result of their sexual orientation as such but comes about if they are bullied and lack family support.[121] Bisexual youth commonly have least family support.[122]

Those who have disclosed their same-sex orientation tend to be able to receive support from other gay or lesbian youth, whereas those who are still questioning their sexual orientation seem most isolated and report higher levels of teasing.[123] Meanwhile, whereas students from a cultural minority usually have parents from the same culture who repudiate racist bullying, sexual minority students usually have heterosexual parents, whose support they might jeopardise by disclosing their sexual orientation.[124]

Gay and lesbian support groups or gay-straight alliances within the school can challenge heterosexist bias. The latter have been shown to improve the relationships of gay, lesbian and bisexual adolescents with the broader peer group and enhance their feelings of safety at school, their self-pride and their sense of belonging to school.[125] A school policy that speaks out against homophobia will also need backing with everyday responses from teachers, such as intervening when students use homophobic slurs.[126] In high school, the incidence of these has been reported to be *26 times* per day, with teachers responding only 3 per cent of the time.[127] The author of that study asks us to contemplate if teachers would be so idle if a student referred to another by the ugly term 'nigger', for example.[128]

Cultural minorities. Over one-third of cultural minority students report repeated distressing school-based incidents of discrimination, spanning verbal and physical assaults and racist comments.[129] Some internalise the hostility and yield to hopelessness; others separate themselves from the mainstream; and others attempt to hide who they are in an effort to fit in.[130] Discrimination can push low-status cultural members towards an anti-school ethos and towards retaliatory contempt for the group whose members exclude and bully them.[131]

While by the age of six to seven years, children normatively have a preference for friends of their own ethnicity, this preference crystallises into prejudice only when individuals have low self-esteem and low status within their group; when prejudice is normative in their group; when there is competition between groups for access to resources; or when the dominant group feels threatened.[132] Stereotypes allow individuals to exaggerate within-group similarities and highlight between-group differences, while a lack of contact fails to challenge these assumptions.[133] In contrast, in the absence of threat, children prefer their in-group but do not dislike or denigrate the out-group.[134] They do not equate difference with deficiency. Indeed, when their group excludes or bullies others on ethnic grounds, seven- to 10-year-olds

like their in-group less than when it is inclusive.[135]

An ethos of pluralism has a strong effect on the academic engagement of young people from minority cultures.[136] They will experience their teachers as caring when teachers validate their language and cultural identity.[137] Particularly in the face of the traditional silencing of minorities, when you are a member of the majority culture, you will need to listen to students, their families and cultural leaders to find out how to make learning culturally and socially meaningful and relevant for these students.[138] Among other measures, this will entail prohibiting gender, racial or heterosexist discrimination within your classroom and school, and respecting the knowledge that students bring from home and their use of dialects and home languages.[139] Meanwhile, an anti-bias curriculum must not perpetuate stereotypes through a 'tourist curriculum' that focuses on other cultures' exotic customs, but must critique social inequalities and recognise how the various cultural groups that make up a society have contributed to how it has been shaped as a collective.[140] This points to the need to promote pluralism (in contrast with assimilationism) so that students from minority cultures feel that they can preserve their own cultural heritage at the same time as acquiring the knowledge and skills that are necessary for success in the majority culture.[141] Minority students' pride in their own community can be mirrored by pride in their community of learners.[142]

Australian Aboriginal students are accustomed to more equal relationships with adults than are typically found in schools.[143] And, whereas Anglo children will know to monitor the teacher, Aboriginal children might orient to their peers. Authoritarian teachers might interpret these culturally normative behaviours as defiance that warrants reprimands,[144] whereas a guidance practitioner will both accept and encourage autonomy in all children. Other manifestations of including students from minority cultures include:[145]

- spaces that display multicultural materials, not just maps of the world or stereotypical photos of festivals, but art and poetry and books that will allow students to know their own history, artefacts and culture
- spaces that encourage interaction
- discussion of race and individuals' feelings about being victims of racism, and insisting that taunts or supposed jokes about a person's characteristics are not funny or permissible
- greeting children in their home language and expressing admiration for children's bilingualism
- asking parents to teach you their family's and culture's norms
- having a visible presence of minority culture members at all levels within the school and inviting community leaders and elders into the school to teach about their culture and its traditions
- providing support for learners whose first language is other than English
- giving instructions in unambiguous language: 'I'd like you to sit at your desk now' rather than, 'You need to sit down' (when the child needs no such thing; otherwise she would already be doing it).

Whereas multicultural curricula achieve very little immediate change in attitudes and behaviours,[146] inclusive day-to-day conversations and practices within your classroom will communicate more effectively than any other means that you honour diversity. Equality cannot just be a 50-minute lesson once a week. At the same time, fair treatment does not mean equal treatment. Instead, *fair* means that, in this classroom and in this school, everyone gets what he or she needs.[147]

Conclusion

The reality that people learn from those they care about is expunged from most educational policy.[148] A lack of caring support from teachers and peer rejection are linked to escalating behavioural problems in students; therefore our responses must involve leading the group's acceptance of troubled students and ensuring their full inclusion in the social life of the classroom. This will support their academic and behavioural adjustment but, more than this, it will meet their needs for connection and belonging.

Recommended further reading

Elman, N.M. & Kennedy-Moore, E. (2003). *The unwritten rules of friendship.* New York: Little Brown.

Kohn, A. (1992). *No contest: The case against competition.* Boston, MA: Houghton Mifflin.

Sapon-Shevin, M. (1999). *Because we can change the world: A practical guide to building cooperative, inclusive classroom communities.* Boston, MA: Allyn & Bacon.

Thompson, M., Cohen, L.J. & Grace, C.O'N. (2002). *Mom, they're teasing me: Helping your child solve social problems.* New York: Ballantine.

Thompson, M. & Grace, C.O'N. (2001). *Best friends, worst enemies.* New York: Ballantine.

Wiseman, R. (2002). *Queen bees and wannabes: Helping your daughter survive cliques, gossip, boyfriends and other realities of adolescence.* London: Piatkus.

CHAPTER 14

Meeting students' need for autonomy: Voice and choice

We need young adults who can think and act creatively, who value human life, are able to make discerning decisions, and know how to communicate and negotiate rather than fight. It is our responsibility as guardians of these values to establish learning environments that foster freedom and responsibility.[1]

As detailed in chapter 10, the 'auto' in autonomy is not to be confused with independence: it means being self-driven, self-governing or self-determining. It is the difference between being the origin of one's own actions, or a pawn that is controlled externally.[2] Its opposites are either feeling helpless, or being controlled by others; its opposite is not independence. Autonomy is about intentionality, having volition, or choice. It is the need to be in command of our own lives, to be the initiator of our own actions. It does not imply self-centredness or detachment from others but instead refers to the exercise of choice or volition.[3]

Like the two other emotional needs, autonomy is valued for its own sake, in that its satisfaction improves individuals' wellbeing. Individuals who perceive that they can control their lives are less inclined to risky behaviour such as drug and alcohol use.[4] At the same time as promoting young people's self-esteem about their competence, autonomy in schools also has the benefit of fostering student engagement.[5] Autonomous learning has been associated with curiosity, persistence, striving for conceptual understanding, a preference for challenge and a sense of enjoyment and vitality.[6] Support for students' autonomy predicts their adoption of mastery goals and deep processing which, over time, predict increases in grades compared to those who lack this orientation.[7] Self-regulated learners are also more likely to remain lifelong learners[8] and students whose autonomy is supported at school are less likely to form an intention to drop out.[9]

In contrast, in terms of their wellbeing, students whose autonomy needs are not met tend to be anxious, angry and bored, and they report avoiding, ignoring or faking their schoolwork.[10] As for educational outcomes, students will not think for themselves or be motivated to learn in an environment that attempts to control them.[11] Psychological and behavioural controls are associated with reduced self-regulated learning and academic achievement in students.[12] When students lack opportunities to exercise autonomy, there follows a decline in their intrinsic motivation.[13] Self-determination theory upholds that this loss of autonomy is directly responsible for students' subsequent reduced engagement in schooling.[14] Students who are initially low in personal autonomy show the most gains in achievement within an autonomy-supportive classroom, compared to those who were already self-driven.[15]

Of the two emotional needs (belonging and autonomy) that feed self-esteem, autonomy is the greatest need for that subgroup of individuals who are nonconformist (or 'spirited') – that is, those who pose the greater proportion of disciplinary problems in schools. Authoritarian reactions to their difficulties will only exacerbate their disruptiveness.[16]

A continuum of relative autonomy

A continuum of relative autonomy has been outlined by self-determination theory (illustrated in Figure 14.1), with the levels distinguished by how much choice they afford the learner.[17]

- *External regulation*, where students engage in a task simply because of its outcomes, notably to earn external rewards or to avoid punishment. Students may perform extrinsically

motivated tasks with disinterest, resistance or even resentment.
- *Introjected regulation*, whereby students feel pressured to earn social approval or to avoid guilt or anxiety. They have an achievement-oriented self-esteem.
- *Identified regulation*, where individuals consciously choose a particular behaviour because it has acquired personal significance for them.
- *Integrated regulation*, where individuals internalise or integrate a consistent set of values into their self-concept. In this case, the task is carried out willingly because they inwardly accept the value of the task. Nevertheless, the task is still instrumental in achieving something else.
- *Intrinsic motivation*, where individuals freely choose to engage because the task is inherently satisfying or enjoyable – that is, it meets their needs and is not instrumental in achieving any other goal. Intrinsic motivation reflects our species' natural inclination to make sense of the world around us.

Taking each type of motivation in turn, external rewards attempt to incite learning through external incentives or pressure. However, when students' learning is governed by the promise of grades or other rewards, they engage in the task not for its own sake, but because engagement is instrumental in earning them a reward.[18] Compared to those with intrinsic motivation, these extrinsically motivated students show less initiative and curiosity, avoid challenge and learn less, particularly on complex conceptual tasks.[19] External rewards can promote rote learning, but they also result in more decay or loss of memory for facts learned in this way, compared

FIGURE 14.1   **Locus of regulation**

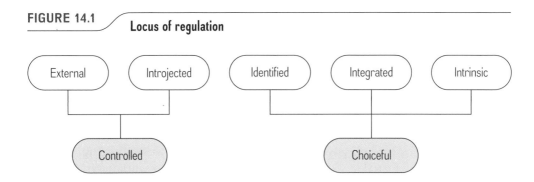

with when learning is self-regulated and motivation is intrinsic.[20]

If students feel compelled to live up to adults' expectations, this *introjected* motivation can have debilitating effects on their emotional adjustment, engagement, effort and achievement. Tasks can lose the value that they once had. For example, students in primary school tend to value academic tasks but then, from early adolescence onwards, their sense of value declines. This deterioration is linked to the tasks and school setting no longer meeting students' needs in general, but particularly their autonomy needs.[21]

At the other end of the continuum (see Figure 14.1) is intrinsic regulation, where we choose to engage in an activity for its inherent pleasure.[22] Adults with intrinsic aspirations have more vitality, less depression, fewer physical health problems and are more self-actualised (that is, have a sense of purpose) than those whose goals are for wealth, fame or impression management.[23] Accordingly, researchers have concluded that attainment of extrinsic goals is less nutritive than achieving something we value in itself.[24]

Intrinsic motivation is the pinnacle: it is related to mastery goals, creativity and high-quality learning.[25] Nevertheless,

over time, even a behaviour that has been extrinsically motivated can become integrated into one's values and then is perceived as being autonomous.[26] For example, students might initially work hard at school in order to please their parents, but then come personally to value learning.[27] To the extent that adults support their autonomy and students believe that they can meet expectations, this originally external motivation can become integrated into students' personal goals and accordingly result in improved engagement in school.[28] Integration is more likely to occur under conditions that support autonomy, rather than under external control, however.[29]

That is, the fundamental factor is volition. Autonomy connotes an inner endorsement of our own actions, the sense that they emanate from ourselves, rather than being pressured from without. I might, for example, do housework (which I don't enjoy) for the pleasure of having a clean home; or I might do housework because I worry about what my visitors will think of me if I don't.[30] Both motivations are instrumental, but the first is freely chosen, whereas the second is controlled or compulsive.

Autonomy supportive measures

Support for students' autonomy is intimately connected to being student-centred because it respects others' need to be the author of their own decisions: it starts from their perspective, acknowledges their feelings and needs, presents salient information and opportunities for self-governance, and minimises external pressure and controls.[31] This autonomy support is about granting students influence over the use of their time and activities, and offering choice and opportunities for participation. Encouragement of their thinking and problem solving, and resisting imposing controls will foster a mastery motivational climate (see chapter 16) that promotes student initiative and optimises student effort.[32]

Box 14.1 lists some behaviours that have been identified as supporting students' autonomy, which essentially are aimed at nurturing students' inner resources. This is in contrast with autonomy suppressing or controlling behaviours, which pressure

BOX 14.1   Autonomy-supporting and -suppressing teacher behaviours[33]

Autonomy-supporting	Autonomy-suppressing
Procedural	
Gives students choice over seating arrangements.	Directs seating.
Gives students choice about due dates.	Imposes rigid deadlines.
Organisational	
Uses informational feedback.	Uses evaluative feedback.
Uses formative feedback.	Uses summative feedback.
Cognitive	
Teacher listens.	Teacher monopolises talk.
Asks what students want.	Directs students.
Gives students time to work in their own way.	Exhibits solutions or answers 'to save time'.
Offers hints.	Supplies solutions.
Values creative thinking.	Focuses on correct answers.
Values conceptual understanding.	Focuses on memorisation.
Responds to students' questions.	Dismisses questions.
Provides rationales.	Teaches facts in isolation.

students towards a certain way of thinking and acting.[34]

Autonomy involves freedom *from* unnecessary constraints, and freedom *to* express oneself. Core ingredients of self-expression are:[35]

- a licence to exercise choice
- self-efficacy (the belief in one's abilities) and agency (the ability to initiate actions and see them through to a successful conclusion)
- freedom from external controls in favour of self-regulation
- mastery of skills that are worth knowing.

That is, although choice is part of autonomy, autonomy is more than the exercise of choice. Some intentional behaviours are initiated and regulated by choice, whereas others are pressured or coerced.[36]

Choice

For students to enact their preferences, they will need environmental supports.[37] The first of these is choice. Students, however, do not want or expect complete freedom, but ask for the freedom to exercise meaningful choices about both what and how they learn.[38] This increases their engagement and amount of their learning, while reducing disruptive behaviour.[39] It also improves their creativity and subsequent voluntary engagement.[40] It is important to be clear, however, that fake choice is no choice at all. Despite the claims of the pragmatic behaviourists, it is deceptive to pretend that 'My way or the highway' edicts offer students choice.[41] These unequal choices disguise the threat of punishment as a 'choice' that the student is making.[42] For example, 'You have chosen to be kept in because you did not behave' – as if a student *would* voluntarily

choose to be excluded from interaction and to be humiliated in front of his or her peers. Critics retort that the only choice on offer here is, 'Behave or else!'.[43]

> In this smoke and mirrors game, the children are 'causing' everything to happen and the teachers are the puppets of the children's choices. The only ones who are not taking responsibility for their actions are the adults.[44]

Instead, true choices have equally valued options and are guided by children's interests, not by the desire to avoid humiliation, to protect self-esteem or to minimise effort.[45] Choice is real only when the various alternatives offer authentic opportunities for students to select between personally meaningful options.[46] Indeed, children learn to make good choices by making choices, not by following directions.[47]

But self-determination theory (which informs this aspect of guidance) sees choice as even deeper than the mere act of selecting between two options.[48] Choice has three levels:[49]

- *organisational*: whether to work independently or collaboratively; or the choices of work partner, where to sit, due dates for assignments
- *procedural* decisions about the mode or style in which products of learning would be presented (as a PowerPoint, on a chart, as a play, for example); choosing between a range of study topics
- *cognitive*: where students are the initiators of their own academic pursuits.

In conditions of organisational or procedural choice, students will typically still take limited responsibility for their conceptual learning.[50] In contrast, teachers who support students' cognitive autonomy regard themselves as co-investigators, assuming a co-learner's role by asking students how they arrived at particular solutions; express admiration for the variety of ideas that students generate; allow students time to complete their thinking processes so that they can defend their approach; compare and contrast ideas; and ask students to repeat their process out loud so they can re-evaluate their ideas – all amounting to allowing students choice in *how* to think, as well as *what* to think.

When students are taking intellectual risks in this way, they might not need or even benefit from organisational choice but, indeed, might need a clear structure within which to function.[51] Accordingly, autonomy supportive measures do not imply a laissez-faire (or 'anything goes') approach. Instead, providing structure and clear instructions allows students to understand tasks and, hence, to feel in control of what they are doing.[52] Under these conditions, students report being less bored, less confused, and less interested in doing something else.[53] They are more motivated and, hence, achieve better. In contrast, structure without autonomy support does not engender self-regulated learning.[54]

At a wider level, students' participation in learning will be fostered by engaging them in decisions about the organisation of their school.[55] Opportunities to exert influence foster not only students' individual autonomy but also a sense of a community within the school.[56]

Self-efficacy

Self-efficacy is our belief in our ability to achieve a particular task in a particular setting. As such (unlike self-concept), it has nothing to do with social comparison.[57] Either I can leap that fence, or I cannot. We can feel efficacious in the following various domains:[58]

- *metacognitive* efficacy: the ability to manage our own thinking, control our thought processes, and achieve our academic goals
- *social* efficacy: the ability to influence others, to gain support from others, to gain companionship, to resist peer pressures, and to meet social expectations
- *ability to run our lives*. This form of self-efficacy answers the question, 'How effective, competent or powerful am I in my life?'.

Self-efficacy is a *belief*: the sense of oneself as a causal agent,[59] someone who can form intent; while its close relative, agency, refers to the production of a required *behaviour* in order to bring about an intended outcome. When students believe that they are responsible for the outcomes of their actions (that is, when they have high self-efficacy), they have a greater incentive to invest effort in tasks and to strive for success and are more persistent and more reflective learners.[60] Self-efficacy contributes to students' willingness to take academic risks, to persist, and to master skills; and it contributes to their intrinsic motivation.[61] Having felt empowered in the past to surmount obstacles and achieve success, individuals with high self-efficacy expect that they will be able to do so again and thus are willing to confront challenges and persist at tasks. They approach challenges as something to be mastered rather than as threats to be avoided.[62]

In contrast, individuals with low self-efficacy for the task at hand maintain a self-diagnostic focus whereby they dwell on their deficiencies, rather than focusing on how to perform the task successfully; anticipating the worst outcomes, they avoid challenge and, when they do experience failure or setbacks, their faith in their abilities is slow to recover because they lack belief that they can do anything about failure.[63]

Our sense of self-efficacy results, first, from judgments that we make about our previous success or failure at tasks similar to the present one. Second, our self-efficacy is open to social persuasion. Someone can tell us that we can do it and, as long as we are successful, our self-efficacy is enhanced.[64] Failure, of course, will be disconfirming. For this reason, self-efficacy is less stable over time than self-concept, which is based on our cumulative history of successes and failures. Because it is less stable, educators will therefore have more influence on students' self-efficacy, compared with their self-esteem. Teachers can enhance students' self-efficacy for a given task by:[65]

- pointing out how the current task is similar to another one that the student has previously mastered
- breaking complex tasks into smaller, achievable steps
- giving students feedback about their progress along the way (formative feedback), rather than only at the completion of the task (summative feedback)
- expressing confidence that they can do it
- teaching them to attribute their successes to the strategy they used (rather than to dumb luck) – see below
- prompting students to reflect on their own progress and satisfaction with it.

Emotional support from teachers and peers, and encouragement to be less preoccupied with social comparison are related to students' academic self-efficacy.[66] The main means to achieve this will be to deliver informative feedback (acknowledgment) rather than judgmental feedback (see chapter 12). We must cherish effort over certitude.

Causal attributions

Our self-efficacy is reliant on the way that we explain our previous successes and failures. When we have succeeded previously – and particularly when we have failed – we will have generated explanations (or 'attributions') about the cause of these failures and successes. These attributions have four properties:[67]

- where we locate the cause of events: whether we believe them to be due to internal versus external forces;
- whether we see these forces as durable (e.g. personal traits such as ability) or temporary events (e.g. lack of effort);
- whether the causes are pervasive (e.g. inability at maths) or specific (e.g. not understanding fractions); and
- how controllable we believe events to be.

When students blame their failures on permanent, pervasive and uncontrollable aspects (such as fixed ability), they are less likely to attempt to manage their own actions because they feel powerless to affect what happens to them anyway. When these maladaptive attributions lead to a lack of engagement and effort and to poor self-regulatory skills, failure can become habitual and is entrenched. In its extreme form, this pattern has been called learned helplessness.[68]

Instead, in order for students to feel efficacious, they need to explain outcomes as being due to something that is internal, temporary, specific and controllable – namely, strategy use.[69] Therefore, teacher feedback needs to focus on the processes students employ, rather than on the outcomes of their learning, so that students recognise the link between effort and outcome.

You can correct students' maladaptive attributions by coaching them to define failure as:

- *temporary* rather than permanent;
- *specific* to the event rather than as a sign of a general or all-pervasive failing on their part;
- in terms of their *actions*, not personality.[70]

Specifically, when you hear students blame their personality for failings (e.g. when they say 'I'm hopeless at this') or when they assume that the problem is permanent ('I'll never be able to do it'), you can affirm their disappointment but then gently correct their statements with something like: 'You're right: It hasn't worked out ... What could you do to fix it?'. Your aim is to teach them to convert self-defeating talk into helpful self-statements.[71]

It does not pay, however, to comment favourably that students were successful because they 'worked hard'. This is because children commonly believe that you have to put in effort only if you have no talent. Of course, this is patently untrue, as evidenced by elite athletes. However, when students find that they have to put in effort or are admonished by adults to 'try harder', they read this as meaning that they lack ability and are likely to give up.[72]

Accomplishment

Glasser contends that, of the three emotional needs, it is least easy for young people in schools to satisfy their need for personal power: not only power over their own bodies (when they can talk, or where and how they sit, for example), but also to experience the power of mastering content that is worth knowing.[73] Real and meaningful success is the most reliable route to a high self-esteem about our competence. Students will not be deceived by the achievement of easy tasks.[74] I cover this vital topic in chapter 16.

Conclusion

Being denied choice is aversive to human beings. For the recipient, there is no such thing as a 'benevolent dictatorship'. Students' protests at its denial are typically termed 'defiance' and constitute the main reason for disciplinary referrals in middle schools.[75] However, the need for autonomy is fundamental to humans; therefore, it should not be met with a punitive response. Although behaviourists acknowledge that controlling discipline denies students freedom of choice, they argue that, if we do not restrict students' choice to fail, their options as adults will be restricted for them.[76] They claim that behaviourism expands students' options and personal freedom[77] – in other words, that the ends justify the means.

Guidance practitioners agree that we must protect young people from behaviours that will disadvantage them and which are inconsiderate of others – but contend that the same ends can be achieved by less damaging means. They assert that you cannot teach people to be humane by using inhumane methods, and you cannot teach people to be self-governing by controlling them externally. The means, they say, are as important as the ends. And the ends (self-regulated individuals) can be achieved without violating students' autonomy. Guidance believes that giving students rewards for learning does not teach them to like learning, but to like rewards. External consequences can teach students to adopt adults' standards for their accomplishments – but this contrived motivation is not intrinsic. That is to say, it is not freely chosen, joyful or selected in the pursuit of skilfulness.[78]

Behaviourists counter that rewards do *not* violate students' autonomy because young people can choose (by their behaviour) whether or not to earn the reward.[79] The guidance rebuttal is that knowing how to get the environment to reward you represents an internal locus of *control* but, given that outsiders rather than yourself impose the reinforcement regime, this does not represent an internal locus of *volition*.[80]

CHAPTER 15

Meeting students' 'luxury' needs:
Purpose and happiness

The purpose of life is a life of purpose.[1]

The final two human needs (pictured in Figure 10.2) are sometimes called the 'luxury' needs because we can focus on them only when the lower-level needs have been satisfied. Indeed, the lower needs provide the engine for our pursuit of purpose and happiness, with our self-esteem (-worth) impelling us to do something significant or worthwhile with our lives.[2]

These two needs for purpose and happiness are partners: the theory of positive psychology says that humans are happiest when we are pursuing goals in life that are meaningful to us.[3] Hence, purpose and joy go hand in hand, with neither being sufficient without the other. The extent to which we achieve our purpose governs our satisfaction or happiness, whereas a purposeless life breeds resentfulness, listlessness and resignation.[4]

Purpose

Purpose gives direction to our lives.[5] It reflects our need to fulfil our mission in life, to live out our life script, or to follow our own 'true north'. It is based on a capacity that we share with no other species: an innate propensity for growth. This capacity is seen in intrinsic motivation, in young children's tendency to explore spontaneously, in curiosity, and in our drive to pursue activities that provide us with satisfaction.[6]

Pursuing a purpose in life entails *meaning*, in the sense of engaging in something meaningful *to us*. This points to the first aspect of purposefulness: namely, that we will not be happy when our goals are imposed on us from the outside.[7] We cannot be fulfilled by doing our duty and sacrificing ourselves to live out others' version of who we should be.[8] When we adopt others' expectations, we develop a 'rat-race' mentality where we are just on a treadmill, deferring happiness to some time in the future: after we get good grades, get into a good university, get a good job, get a promotion . . . and so on.[9] There is no joy in postponing being true to our own goals. Instead, each of us finds joy and will apply ourselves to ideas and skills that we care about.

Second, having a purpose entails *meaning to* – that is, being intentional in a pursuit.[10] Human beings do not find ourselves: we create ourselves – and pursuing our purpose will inevitably bring satisfaction and, indeed, happiness. When we pursue a significant goal with resolution, we achieve coherence or a harmony of purpose that unifies our life and gives it significance.[11] Like a magnetic field, it attracts our spiritual or 'psychic energy' and becomes a theme upon which all other goals depend.[12] It is like a compass setting that helps us steer our way through life, acting like a rudder that prevents us from losing our bearings.[13]

Linda Silverman, a specialist in giftedness, referred to this as a sense of having 'sealed orders' and that our life's work is an effort to discover what those orders are. Given our collective nature as a species, the goals that will be valuable to us are ones that focus on growth, connection and contribution,[14] such as those listed in Box 15.1.

BOX 15.1 **Identifying your passions**[15]

Discover your goals by examining which of the following self-growth values are important to you:

- *physical self-care and health*: taking care of our body through exercise and diet, either to live healthily to an older age or to be around for others
- *spirituality*: being inspired by the mysteries of life and a belief in something larger than ourselves
- *creativity*: in any discipline, such as the arts or music, writing, cooking, homemaking or gardening, for example
- *leisure and play*: recreation absorbs us in our senses and in the activity for its own sake, allowing us to express a playful part of ourselves
- *work and career*: this can be paid employment, volunteering or homemaking that is personally rewarding
- *personal growth and education*: this entails developing ourselves as a human being, learning new skills and confronting new challenges
- *self-kindness and compassion*: showing acceptance of ourselves, our feelings, memories and old wounds.

Imagine that you can take all of the values that are important to you in a boat to a deserted island. Now, imagine that during the journey the boat starts taking on water, weighed down by the load. You have to throw one of your values overboard. Which one would you toss away?

Now imagine that the boat continues to take on water because the load is still too much. Which value would you discard this time?

Repeat this until you are left with one. Which one is it? Why did you choose it? *This* is your passion.

Happiness

Happiness is not just a permanent good mood, or the experience of transient pleasurable sensations, such as watching a fireworks spectacle. Hedonism without regard for meaning will not satisfy us: mere pleasure does not produce psychological growth.[16] Neither is happiness the outcome of material success. And happiness is not selfish: we cannot be happy when we reduce other people's capacity to express their core selves.[17]

Instead, happiness is the experience of joy, contentment or wellbeing in response to a life that is well lived or is satisfying.[18] Happiness and joy come from within ourselves, rather than from our external circumstances; they come from appreciating or being grateful for the ordinary, rather than from seeking extraordinary delights.[19] They are the outcome of a meaningful answer to the question, 'How should I live?'.[20] The drive for purpose (whose achievement engenders happiness) means that it is not merely pleasure that motivates learning, but gratification – that is, our sense of accomplishment when an activity calls on our strengths to rise to an occasion.[21] Also known as *flow*, gratification marks psychological growth.[22] We experience ourselves as doing what we are meant to be doing. This fills us with energy, whereas activities that we dislike quickly drain us.[23]

Implications for education

Noddings believes that happiness is the ultimate goal of education. Given, however, this conception of happiness as the fulfilment of all of our needs,[24] an emphasis on happiness is really an injunction to meet all of students' needs.

Multiple intelligences

The first educational implication of the higher or (dismissively) 'luxury' needs is that there are more ways to be fulfilled than in the core academic disciplines of reading, writing, mathematics, logic and analysis: that is, in the skills highly prized in school.[25] People are propelled to excel in a pursuit in which their passion meets their natural aptitudes, which Sir Ken Robinson terms their *Element*.[26] Yet education exalts intellectual skills above all other abilities.[27] Even within academic skills, there is a hierarchy of status, with many schools neglecting the arts, theatre and dance, for example, because these are valued less than science and mathematics.[28] As a result, many students feel uninspired, with their imaginations not captured by the narrow range of disciplines to which they are exposed. Those whose skills are discounted become disaffected about learning, while skills that are never discovered are squandered.[29]

Adults who see intelligence as a fixed entity, bestowed upon us at birth, and who believe that it spans only logical and academic endeavours narrow the scope of self-fulfilment for themselves and the individuals they teach.[30] Instead, our abilities and capacities are like a fingerprint (that is, unique), they are dynamic (like a dance, swaying to the rhythm of life), and malleable (which means that we will become more skilled when we put in effort).[31] This idea that human intelligence is diverse and multi-faceted was formalised in Howard Gardner's conception of multiple 'intelligences', which he sees as potentials that can be activated in many adaptive ways by individuals and cultures. His original list comprised seven of these intelligences; he subsequently added an eighth.[32]

- *Linguistic* intelligence involves sensitivity to language in spoken, written or signed forms and the ability to use language to accomplish goals.
- *Logical-mathematical* skills entail analytic and systematic problem-solving skills, including scientific investigation and the ability to recognise patterns and manipulate objects or symbols.
- *Musical* intelligence involves skills in discriminating sounds, performing, composing and appreciating music and the ability to express or gain meaning from ideas or emotions in music.
- *Bodily-kinaesthetic* skills comprise the physical coordination skills necessary for using one's body.
- *Spatial* skills involve being able to interpret information in two or three dimensions, such as when appreciating art, reading maps or completing jigsaw puzzles.
- *Interpersonal* intelligence refers to the capacity to understand the intentions, motivations and desires of other people, and enacting this social awareness and knowledge to produce effective social behaviour.
- *Intrapersonal* skills involve the capacity to understand yourself and to use this emotional perceptiveness to inform your thinking, and to make choices that will promote personal growth.
- *Naturalistic intelligence*: This is the eighth and most recent intelligence to be identified by Gardner, described as expertise in recognising and classifying

species and being attuned to the natural environment. However, I see the first aspect as classification, which is an applied aspect of language skills; and the second as part of interpersonal intelligence, albeit a communion with nonhuman species.

Having reviewed the evidence across disciplines, Gardner believes that each of these skill areas has its own characteristic cognitive style and that individuals' abilities are unevenly distributed across them.[33] Although research supports him on this,[34] nevertheless, the title is perhaps misleading, reflecting various disciplines (in a broad sense) rather than 'intelligences'. Because of this confusion, some have inferred from Gardner's list that everyone is gifted (that is, highly intelligent) in one or other of these domains. This is arithmetically absurd: everyone cannot be above average. Nevertheless, the list does remind us that intelligence is much richer than what is exposed by IQ tests, that there are more ways to be capable than in academics, and that teachers have an obligation to provide students with opportunities to pursue their preferences or strengths in any domain, so that they can flourish. That is, instead of asking how intelligent our young people are, our teaching needs to focus on *how they are intelligent*.[35]

Encourage creativity

Eminent creativity is the production and implementation of an idea or *product* that is original and valued within its field.[36] However, creative achievement capable of earning social acclaim is generally beyond the capabilities of school students; hence the term will be used here in its *everyday*

BOX 15.2   The daring greatly manifesto[37]

To our teachers

We want to show up, we want to learn, and we want to inspire.

We are hardwired for connection, curiosity, and engagement.

We crave purpose, and we have a deep desire to create and contribute.

We want to take risks, embrace our vulnerabilities, and be courageous.

When you no longer see us and no longer encourage our daring, or when you only see what we produce or how we perform – we disengage and turn away from the very things that the world needs from us: our talent, our ideas, our passion.

What we ask is that you engage with us, show up beside us, and learn from us. Above all else, we ask that you let yourself be seen and be courageous. Dare greatly with us.

Your students

---

sense of using creative *processes* to make fresh connections and yield something that is novel for that individual. Creativity in this everyday sense is applied imagination.[38] Because all human beings are born with curiosity and imagination, they are born with an ability to be creative.[39]

Fostering creativity is important for students personally because it will meet their diverse needs, encourage their engagement in learning and release the 'best they have to offer'; it is also important socially because the issues that will arise in the lifetimes of current students will require novel solutions generated from imagination, creativity and innovation.[40] When instead we prioritise only logical thinking in schools and marginalise creativity, we stifle the very skills in students that the world will need in future.

As with intelligence, creativity can be in any domain, not just in the arts. Even scientific hypotheses are often generated by intuition before being tested by logic.[41] Far from being an undisciplined process, divergent thinking involves many of the same problem-solving skills inherent in convergent learning. As illustrated in Figure 15.1, it goes through the following recursive phases, all of which require time for elaborate investigation.[42]

- *Fact finding.* Creativity is not freedom from constraints: ideas must be referenced to the times, the culture, current knowledge, conventions of a field and technical ability within a given medium.
- *Problem identification.* Sometimes it is not the answers we generate, but the questions that we ask, that matter. Problem identification (also referred to as a discovery orientation), involves discretion or judgment about what is worth devoting one's efforts to. Specific skills include detecting missing information, asking perceptive questions, isolating key aspects of a problem, analysis and

reframing problems, for example. At this phase, it will be important that teachers value creativity and encourage students to believe in their own creative skills so that students are emboldened to find and explore questions that they care about.

- *Generation of ideas.* In this phase, divergent thinking calls for fluency (the production of *many* ideas), flexibility (the production of *alternative* ideas), originality (the production of *unique* ideas) and elaborated thinking (the ability to *embellish* an idea). Ideas cannot emerge in a vacuum but often require a dynamic group of individuals

with disparate interests to collaborate to openly play with ideas, to fail together and to recover together from their mistakes. In addition to structuring collaborative learning, then, teaching in this phase will also involve asking open-ended questions to explore possibilities that encourage generative thought.

- *Evaluation of ideas.* In this phase, ideas are tried out to see if they work, rejected if they do not, and refined if they show promise. This involves judgment, critical thinking, analysis, synthesis, exploration of ambiguities, planning, making inferences, prioritising, recognising relevance, cause-and-effect thinking, persistence,

FIGURE 15.1   **Phases of creativity[43]**

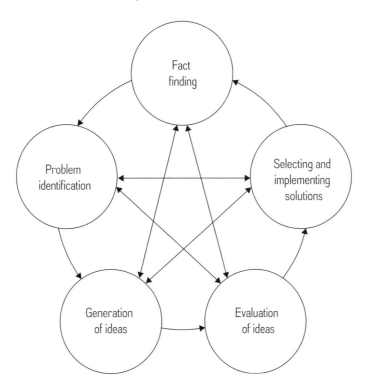

avoiding premature closure, and resilience. In this phase, it is particularly important that students treat failures as information about what does not work, which informs what will.

- *Selecting and implementing solutions.* This may involve *analogical* thinking, which is the willingness to borrow ideas from one context and adapt them to another and *transformational* thinking, which is the ability to put something to a new use.[44]

Like intelligence, creativity is not only a function of individuals' abilities but requires a conducive environment. Creativity grows when it is exercised. Teaching for creativity will involve helping students to discover their own creative strengths and then to develop these. For creativity to flourish, both the school as a whole and individual teachers need to give students – and teachers – the freedom to take risks; to develop their natural talents and passions; to know that there are no right answers and no stupid questions; and to value playfulness, irreverence, the lively and the surprising.[45] As a teacher, you will demonstrate this by not placing a premium on getting things right and by not pretending to know all the answers or to have all the ideas yourself.[46] It also requires that assessment of creative thinking should focus less on the product and more on the process, in contrast to a political emphasis on national testing and benchmarks, where converging on the correct answer is paramount.

Teachers will need to foster openness to new ideas and experiences, having tolerance of ambiguity, and being willing to explore and to seek alternatives. Welcoming the independence, risk-taking, energy, curiosity and unconventionality of students also means accepting the occasionally troublesome characteristics of nonconformity, resistance to external authority, low interest in details, and restlessness that accompany the more positive traits.[47] Suppressing these would engender conformity and common sense, which (among others) are blocks to creativity, as listed in Box 15.3.

Creativity thrives on intrinsic motivation; here again is another reason to avoid external rewards for achievement.[48] When students enjoy learning for its own sake and have autonomy about what they are learning, they will feel ownership and therefore will be more willing to engage in extended exploration and experimentation.[49]

Finally, creativity – previously considered a general capacity in the same way that intelligence has commonly been – might after all be domain-specific: individuals will use different creative skills in different disciplines.[50] This implies that creativity cannot be taught out of context, but must be fostered within children's particular talent domains.[51] That is, children require a medium – such as dance, art materials, a musical instrument, algebra equations, language and so on – to manipulate and control.

Fun

Humans – and the very young in particular – need fun. Although in childhood, fun is justifiably an end in itself, throughout life enjoyment also signals safety and, therefore, opportunities for growth. Play undoes stress and broadens our intellectual, physical and social resources, building up reserves that we can draw on when under stress.[52] As a result, people who have fun are happier,

BOX 15.3   Blocks to creativity[53]

Perceptual blocks
- There is only one right answer.
- That's not logical.
- Be practical.
- Avoid ambiguity.
- That's not my area.
- I'm not creative.

Conformity pressures
- Follow the rules.
- To err is wrong.
- Play is frivolous.
- Don't be foolish.
- Be sensible.
- Don't rock the boat.

Institutional blocks
- It won't work.
- It's not in the budget.
- We've never done that before.
- The parents will object.
- We already have enough to do.
- It's not in the curriculum.
- It's against regulations.

more productive, healthier, more altruistic and more resilient.[54] In short, fun causes much better commerce with the world.[55] Therefore, for young children especially, teachers must heighten the appeal inherent in tasks by embellishing these with fantasy.[56]

Guide students to find their passion

Many believe that life is linear and that, if you study a particular course and pass all the tests, 'your life will fall neatly into place'.[57] This is simply not true: Sir Ken Robinson documents that many people who have found their purpose in life have done so through unconventional routes – and yet schools seldom expose students to activities other than academics. Instead, teachers can expose students to domains that they might not have encountered, by arranging excursions to performances or workplaces that might spark a passion in students; or teachers can organise extra-curricular activities where groups who share the same passion can band together. These 'tribes', says Robinson, can validate each other's interests and inspire each member to excel.[58]

Careers counselling can also guide students to find their element. Here, though, rather than trying to fit students into a narrow list of occupations, we need to discover who students are and what they are most drawn to doing, either within a general discipline (such as the arts) or within a specific aspect of it (such as drawing, painting, or sculpture). The world needs people who have come alive; therefore, rather than asking what the world needs, we should ask students what makes them come alive, and advise them to go do that.[59]

Students also need mentors to open doors for them and get involved in their growth.[60] Robinson advises that this role involves that teachers *recognise* the skills of individual students, *encourage* students so that they come to believe that it is possible to express themselves through their talent, *facilitate* their acquisition of skills through advice and apprenticeship, and *stretch* them past their self-doubts and self-imposed limits.[61] This is where fostering students' healthy self-esteem is vital: students need to believe that they deserve to pursue their passions. It is also where self-efficacy is crucial: students need to believe that they can make it happen. An effective mentor will refuse to give up on students and will not allow them to give up on themselves.[62] We need to let students see that their fears and doubts can travel with them, like passengers on a bus; tolerating the jibes, obstacles and challenges will prove worth it when the bus is headed in the right direction. The alternative is not to take command of the bus, but this will condemn them to being listless passengers on a road to nowhere.[63]

Conclusion

Whereas wellbeing is parents' top priority for their children, typically it is a low priority for their teachers.[64] Human wellbeing depends on gratification of all the needs in Figure 10.2 (see page 140); it particularly

---

BOX 15.4 **An activity to identify your element[65]**

Imagine that you are a colleague who is writing a reference for yourself to someone who is interested in supporting your future plans. You might begin with '(Your name') is interested in . . .' Then mention your interests, skills, aspirations, what you feel you have to learn, and what you would like to experience next. Describe your personal qualities and achievements that you value the most, and the opportunities you would like to have in the future.

BOX 15.5 **The tombstone technique[66]**

Imagine that you are writing an epitaph for your tombstone. Write a single sentence that captures what your life is about. This does not have to be true for you yet, but can be something that you want to make true. *This* is your purpose in life.

BOX 15.6 **Life review[67]**

For adults, divide your life into five- (or 10-) year segments; for children, make each segment a few years only. On the left-hand side of a divided page, for each era, list five incidents where you felt good about yourself; on the right-hand side list five incidents where you were disappointed in yourself.

Regrets and satisfactions about the past signal what matters to you. Hence, the themes in each column will point to what you are trying to be, to learn, and to do in your life.

depends on doing something meaningful, accomplishing something that matters to us. This demonstrates the importance of making sure that the curriculum does not condemn students to being less than they are.[68] Given our higher needs for purpose and happiness, the aim of education must be for individuals to be inspired to continue learning and growing through life.[69] This is an end in itself. But, instrumentally, happy people are more altruistic, productive, helpful, likeable, creative, resilient, friendly and healthy.[70] They are both inspired and inspirational.[71]

The goal is to create a place where students, teachers and parents want to be. *This* – not 'zero tolerance' measures – will assure their wellbeing. Aggression, student apathy and alienation are not the problem: they are the *symptom*. Happy people don't behave that way: 'Happy people are rarely mean, violent, or cruel'.[72] Guidance believes that it is not that disruptive students are being 'reinforced' for poor behaviour, but simply that they are *distressed*. It is surprising that this self-evident statement is seen to be radical.

While we cannot permit thoughtless behaviour that results from students' distress, neither can we punish young people for *being* distressed. Instead, we need to look for a solution, not a culprit. This is the focus of the next four chapters.

Recommended further reading

Ben-Shahar, T. (2007). *Happier*. Boston, MA: McGraw Hill.

Csikszentmihalyi, M. (1990). *Flow: The psychology of optimal experience*. New York: Harper Perennial.

McKay, M., Forsyth, J.P. & Eifert, G.H. (2010). *Your life on purpose: How to find what matters and create the life you want*. Oakland, CA: New Harbinger.

Noddings, N. (2003). *Happiness and education*. Cambridge, UK: Cambridge University Press.

Robinson, K. & Aronica, L. (2009). *The element: How finding your passion changes everything*. New York: Penguin.

——(2013). *Finding your element: How to discover your talents and passions and transform your life*. New York: Viking.

Seligman, M.E.P. (2011). *Flourish: A visionary new understanding of happiness and well-being*. New York: Free Press.

CHAPTER 16

Facilitating learning: Mastery and accomplishment

When tasks are meaningful to students, when students have authority over their learning, and when mistakes are considered as part of the learning process, [this] would encourage students to display more on-task behaviours and would arouse less anxiety, and therefore less disruptive behaviour.[1]

The guidance approach believes that 'People, not curriculum, are the desired outcomes of schooling'.[2] Therefore, education cannot confine itself to academic aims alone, but must attend to the human needs of its recipients.[3] Guidance believes that the heart of education is the relationship between students and teachers because, without this, teaching might be occurring but education will not be happening.[4] Given that learning is a choice, students will make the choice only when they feel connected to their teachers.[5] Therefore, meeting students' needs is a valued end in itself – but it also serves the purpose that students will be engaged in learning when what we are asking them to do and how we are asking them to do it, meets their needs.

Whereas education usually places a priority on academic skills, the reason to address the basic and emotional needs before discussing students' learning needs is that research shows that an improved school culture needs to be in place before students can be enticed into learning.[6] Academic work cannot proceed until young people feel safe, valued and secure.[7] Even if the research did not tell us this, it makes sense that students will be more willing to listen to our teaching if we have first listened to them.

Therefore, instead of asking, 'How can we make students conform to our expectations?', guidance asks, *'How can we provide what students need so that they can learn?'*.[8] In order to answer that question, we must recognise that, rather than being a type of orderly cognitive, left-brain activity, meaningful learning involves both thinking and feeling.[9]

The teacher as facilitator

Guidance adopts a constructivist approach to teaching. This shifts the educational emphasis away from telling students what

BOX 16.1 Characteristics of two styles of instruction[10]

Teacher-directed	Student-centred
Correct answers are primary.	Questions are primary.
The curriculum is the focus of teaching.	The student is the focus of teaching.
Breadth of subject matter.	Depth of subject matter.
Rote memorisation.	Conceptual understanding.
Assumes child incompetence.	Assumes child skill.
Demands student obedience.	Supports students' autonomy.

they should know and how they should behave, towards listening and responding to the richness of their present lives. It capitalises on 'teachable moments', when students' behaviour, interests or questions demonstrate that they are particularly receptive to learning.[11] It is distinguished from teacher-led instruction as listed in Box 16.1, with the disadvantages of teacher directedness listed in Box 16.2.

A model of teaching

Chapters 11–15 have been building towards the model of teaching illustrated in Figure 16.1, which is an amalgam of research into effective teaching. In a deep commitment to justice,[12] it focuses on meeting students' needs (as listed in Box 16.3), guided by the acronym TARGET:[13]

- *Tasks* (curricula) are meaningful, challenging and interesting and individualised without differences in ability being highlighted.
- *Authority* for choices, structures and rules is shared between the teacher and students.

- *Recognition* is available to all students and is based on processes such as effort, persistence, creativity, problem solving and resilience, rather than on outcomes.
- *Grouping* is not by ability but is heterogeneous and inclusive.
- *Evaluation* is criterion-referenced and is not made public, with grades and test scores interpreted in terms of students' own improvement rather than comparing students to each other.
- *Time* use is flexible, with students given time to work quickly on familiar material, and more slowly on new concepts so that they can marshal their thoughts and delve deeply into content that is their passion.

As illustrated in Figure 16.1, these essentially egalitarian practices nurture students by fostering a healthy self-esteem; a sense of personal self-efficacy and agency; connectedness to their teachers, peers and the school as a whole; a sense of autonomy or self-governance; and the desire to master skills. Together, these personal qualities contribute to students' emotional commitment to learning and behavioural

BOX 16.2 Disadvantages of a preponderance of teacher-directed instruction[14]

- Excessive teacher-directed learning generates a negative climate that diminishes students' pleasure in and motivation for learning, particularly for boys.
- Students become more dependent on teacher directives and approval.
- Students are more compliant in the presence of adults, but less self-regulated in their absence.
- Students are more anxious, displaying twice as much stress, with disadvantaged students (who may have higher life-stress levels overall) being particularly vulnerable.
- Academically, students receiving high levels of teacher instruction achieve less well than do students with many opportunities to engage in self-directed learning.
- When teachers structure tasks for them, students engage in and practise less planning, improvisation and brainstorming.
- Young children engage in less imaginative play and less complex interactions with peers and objects when teachers direct their activity.
- During self-directed social play, students display more persistence, sophisticated thinking and emotions than during teacher-led pretend play.
- The developmental inappropriateness of rote drill to teach young children basic literacy and numeracy causes the children to dislike these activities.
- In the years prior to school, children in constructivist settings show improved academic and verbal achievement and motivation, and increased self-reliance compared with those receiving high levels of teacher-directed instruction.
- Young children in constructivist classes also enjoy their educational experiences more.
- Students in teacher-directed settings display increased behavioural difficulties.
- Teacher-directed instruction also tends to create a competitive social hierarchy, whereas being in a child-centred setting teaches students empathy and reduces peer rejection.

engagement in academic activities, both of which are the precursors to achievement. In a feedback mechanism depicted by the arrows in Figure 16.1, students' engagement then feeds their emotional wellbeing.[15]

Of this model's many elements, given that the remainder are covered elsewhere, only four need explication here: teachers' egalitarian values with respect to ability; relevant curricula; structural support; and teachers' goal structure. I will describe these aspects here before turning to the

more significant model – namely, the model of learning.

Egalitarian values

The model of teaching (in Figure 16.1) is informed throughout by egalitarian values, which refers to teachers' acceptance of young people regardless of their ability or other characteristics. This ethical stance feeds into the quality of relationships within the classroom. Egalitarian practices convey respect to students, optimistic expectations about their capacity to make progress, care for them personally and for their success, opportunities to make substantial choices about their learning, and time to learn concepts deeply rather than acquiring disconnected facts. The focus is on developing students' absolute competence, rather than having them prove it in relative terms.[16] Accordingly, teachers with an egalitarian stance are effective with classes that have a wide range of ability.[17]

In contrast, teacher-directed learning in combination with a controlling discipline style commonly emphasises single correct answers and values students who conform to teachers' edicts and expectations and who are academically able[18] (but not gifted).[19] This sets up an academic hierarchy favouring the more able students.[20] These teachers display an emphasis on ability both in the quality and quantity of their interactions with students.[21] Ability-oriented teachers typically assign the same tasks for everyone, use ability grouping, deliver evaluative and public feedback to students, show preference for the high-ability students, and have rigid time structures.[22] They typically interact less frequently with the

---

BOX 16.3   **Young people's needs in schools**[23]

Safety: Acceptance of mistakes, respect for the diverse abilities and characteristics of students
Wellbeing: For a comfortable environment
Self-esteem: To feel worthy and competent
- *Acceptance*: To feel accepted and included in the learning setting
- *Empathy*: To receive emotional and instructional support when in need
- *Affirmation*: To experience success and receive authentic feedback about one's progress
Connectedness: Opportunities for interpersonal involvement with others through collaboration with peers and a warm relationship with teachers
- *Warm relationships with teachers*: Receiving emotional, instrumental and informational support from teachers
- *Warm relationships with peers*: Being accepted and befriended by peers
- *Inclusion*: Welcoming of diverse interests, abilities, characteristics and cultures of students and their families
Autonomy: Opportunities to direct their own learning content and processes
- *Choice*: to be included in organisational and procedural decisions about their learning
- *Self-efficacy*: To believe that they can achieve desired outcomes
- *Accomplishment*: To be exposed to challenging and meaningful curricula and time to integrate learning and to develop deep understandings
Purpose: Ability to be creative, original and express who they are and who they want to be
Happiness: To find a passion for learning – that is, to fall in love with what they are doing and how they do it.

FIGURE 16.1 A model of teaching

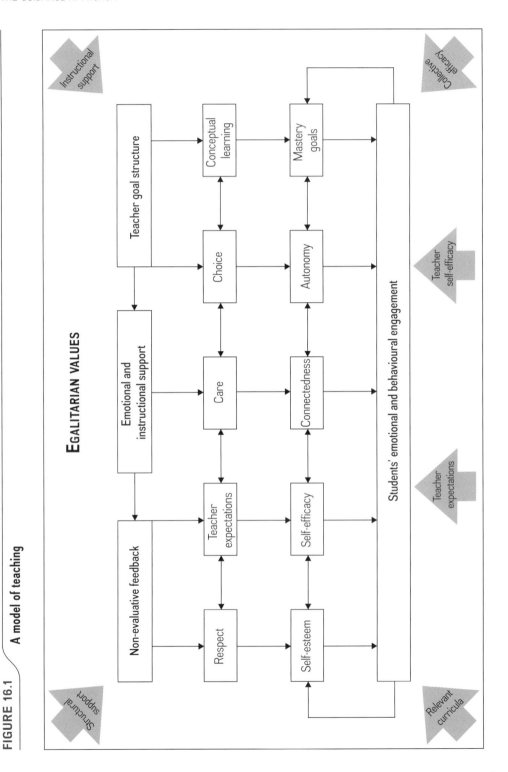

less capable students, call on them less often, wait less time for them to answer, give them the answers rather than hints, do not supply extra time for them to formulate their thoughts, seat them further away from the teacher, and praise substandard responses from them, which can be seen as patronising.[24] In classes where ability differences are salient to teaching, 15 per cent of the resulting disparity between low and high achievers can be attributed to teacher preference towards the more able learners.[25]

Structural support

Guidance assumes that young people are fundamentally inclined to explore, discover and make sense of the world around them.[26] The existence of intrinsic motivation is proof of this. However, some information is abstract and needs an adult to facilitate students' grasp of it. Therefore, teaching will include adult-led instruction. Preschool-aged children from disadvantaged backgrounds with some learning delays have been found to gain more literacy and numeracy skills when exposed to individualised teacher-led instruction than when engaging only in free play.[27] Nevertheless, the facilitator empowers students to be in command of their own learning and behaviour, giving them practice at exercising initiative, learning cooperatively and communicating accurately.[28] This style of leadership is not to be confused with a laissez-faire style in which, despite having legitimate power, the leader fails to exercise it and instead allows group members to act as they wish.[29] This style is undesirable because individuals and groups become stressed and disorganised under this type of leadership.

Relevant curricula

Curricula must represent an appropriate use of students' and teachers' time.[30] As Martin Seligman states, 'If it is not worth doing, it is not worth doing well'.[31] There are three issues with curriculum relevance:[32]

- *what* we are asking students to learn;
- *how* we are asking them to learn it; and
- *why* they are having to learn it.

Whatever we teach, we must be able to provide a coherent answer to why we are doing so. The answer cannot be that it is preparation for a test or for next year's topics, or to benefit society by teaching skills needed by the economy. In a totalitarian state, political aims are to be expected; in a democracy, the aims should be focused more on individuals.[33] Therefore, Newmann and colleagues propose that teaching will be authentic when it allows students to construct knowledge; engage in disciplined inquiry (that is, to challenge and critique ideas in order to arrive at a deep understanding); and has real-world applications – that is, is of value beyond indicating success at school.[34] Teaching that is meaningful, therefore, will engage students in higher-order thinking, allow them to arrive at complex understandings, engage them in substantial conversations about the subject matter, and connect what they are learning to personal experiences or real-world issues.[35]

According to Glasser, the only content that is indispensable to an education is learning to read, write, do arithmetic (but not higher mathematics because that is not useful in everyday life); how to research information, and to speak in public.[36] For the rest, we should ask:[37]

- Would it be worth knowing as an adult?
- Would the adult be better off for having learned it in childhood (as opposed to later in life)? Is it relevant to young people at this time in their lives?
- Would engaging in it during childhood help the child at the time and help the future adult to be happier? That is, we need to be concerned about the quality of both the present experience, and its likely contribution to the person's future happiness.

One basic recommendation is that curricula emphasise depth rather than breadth, so that students can master worthwhile content to a level of competence that empowers them.[38] Achieving deep knowledge would involve providing opportunities for experimentation and reflection, rather than transmitting information: knowledge that is discovered is more meaningful than knowledge that is conveyed. Therefore, teachers would refuse to require students to memorise facts because this involves no thinking and generates 'throwaway information' that students forget almost as quickly as they learn.[39]

Teachers' goal structure

As illustrated in Figure 16.1, a fundamental quality of teachers is their achievement goals. The four types of achievement goals are illustrated in Figure 16.2. With mastery goals, the learner strives to gain new skills, competencies and deep understanding whereas, with performance goals, the aim is to outdo others, to win. Each broad goal is also broken into an approach mentality in which the goal is to surmount challenge, or an avoidant mentality where the goal is to avoid failure (or being seen to fail).

Students' choice between mastery versus performance-approach goals is sensitive to the learning environment in general[40] and teachers' goal structure in particular. Teachers with high self-efficacy[41] and who believe that ability is malleable tend to model mastery goals. These mastery-oriented teachers foster more active engagement of students, tolerate their higher activity levels[42] and minimise competitiveness between students. These teachers focus on meeting the social and emotional needs of students, and foster respect and warm relationships with and among students.[43] They provide varied opportunities for students to demonstrate their competence, adapt learning materials to the students' level of understanding, provide opportunities for students to take responsibility for their own learning, and highlight how what students are learning is of value in their lives.[44]

In contrast, teachers who view ability as fixed tend to promote performance goals. Performance-oriented teachers use praise and other rewards that evaluate students' performances compared to each other. This comparative feedback is often delivered in public, and correct answers are valued over effort and learning.[45] As a result of praise for correct answers, students can become less willing to use higher-order skills such as inquiry.[46]

Mastery goals are more common in primary school, when teaching tends to emphasise overcoming challenges.[47] Further up the schooling system, the emphasis becomes ability and comparative assessment – that is, outperforming others.[48] In response to teachers' performance orientation, students increasingly adopt performance goals also.[49] Teachers' emphasis on performance goals seems especially detrimental to those students with an avoidant (in contrast to an approach) orientation.[50] Students' goals also emerge from competing for school awards.[51] Accordingly, whereas infants and young children naturally have mastery goals, these are often supplanted by performance goals because the feedback children receive implies that their worth is contingent on being successful.[52] In such a setting, students are likely to strive to

outdo others in order to demonstrate not only their superior competence but, more insidiously, their *worth*.[53] When a task is framed in performance terms, even mastery-oriented students come to focus on the external contingencies rather than their own intrinsic motivation.[54]

A classroom performance goal structure tends to produce more disruptive behaviours in students, occasions cheating, and engenders a negative attitude to school.[55] When students are trying to impress their

FIGURE 16.2

Types of achievement goals

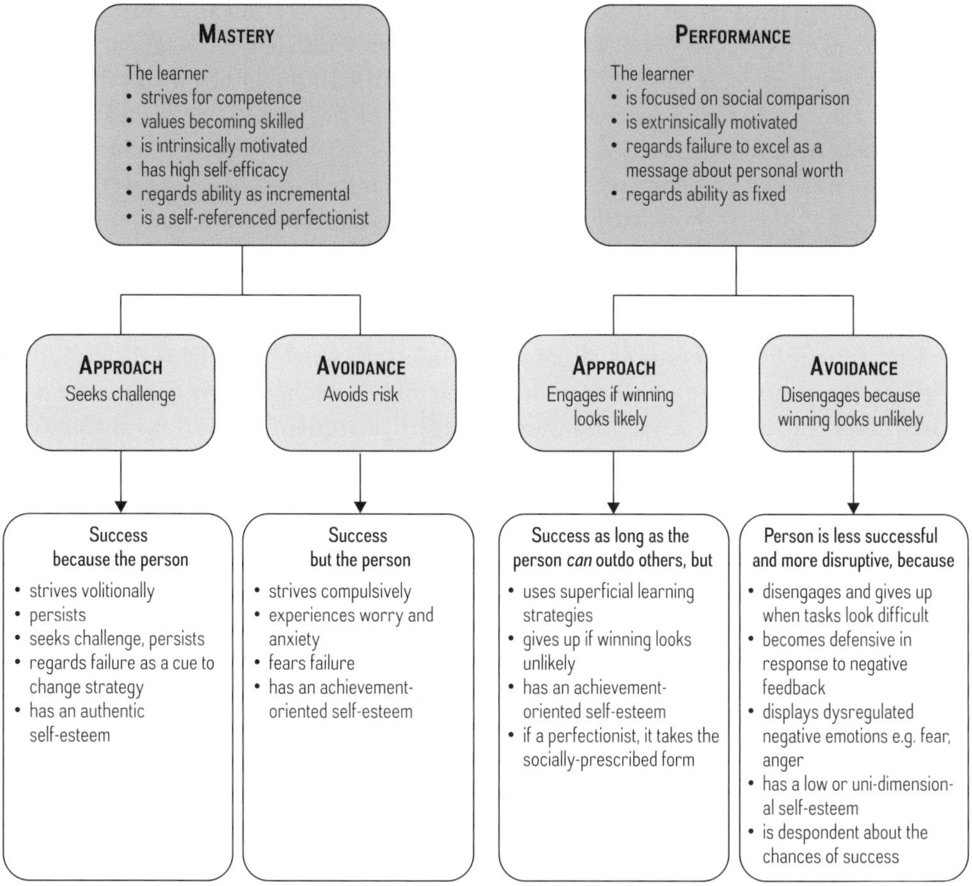

MASTERY

The learner
• strives for competence
• values becoming skilled
• is intrinsically motivated
• has high self-efficacy
• regards ability as incremental
• is a self-referenced perfectionist

PERFORMANCE

The learner
• is focused on social comparison
• is extrinsically motivated
• regards failure to excel as a message about personal worth
• regards ability as fixed

APPROACH
Seeks challenge

AVOIDANCE
Avoids risk

APPROACH
Engages if winning looks likely

AVOIDANCE
Disengages because winning looks unlikely

Success because the person
• strives volitionally
• persists
• seeks challenge, persists
• regards failure as a cue to change strategy
• has an authentic self-esteem

Success but the person
• strives compulsively
• experiences worry and anxiety
• fears failure
• has an achievement-oriented self-esteem

Success as long as the person *can* outdo others, but
• uses superficial learning strategies
• gives up if winning looks unlikely
• has an achievement-oriented self-esteem
• if a perfectionist, it takes the socially-prescribed form

Person is less successful and more disruptive, because
• disengages and gives up when tasks look difficult
• becomes defensive in response to negative feedback
• displays dysregulated negative emotions e.g. fear, anger
• has a low or uni-dimensional self-esteem
• is despondent about the chances of success

teacher or outdo their peers, they are typically less engaged and instead apply effort-minimising strategies.[56] They avoid or fake their way through lessons and employ self-handicapping behaviours such as procrastinating and not seeking help.[57]

Finally, the peer group also fosters individual students' goal orientations. Highly achieving students pursue academic goals, whereas low-achieving students are less willing to conform to the school's achievement norms.[58]

Teacher expectations

Given the asymmetrical power within the teacher–student relationship, teacher expectations have a great influence on students' own expectations about their ability to be successful at school.[59] Students whose teachers hold high expectations for all students make larger academic gains and show enhanced academic self-esteem, compared to students whose teachers have low expectations.[60]

Many studies report that teachers commonly have lower expectations of students from minority cultures, although this effect appears to be small[61] and has detrimental effects on student attainment only if teachers overlook contradictory evidence of the students' capabilities.[62] Low expectations of students' capabilities can become a self-fulfilling prophecy, particularly in classrooms where teachers emphasise ability differences.[63] Subtly, low teacher expectations are communicated to students who, over time, come to perceive themselves as less capable.[64]

A second expectation is called a sustaining expectation whereby teachers anticipate that students' past behavioural patterns will persist.[65] Both self-fulfilling and sustained expectations of students' low performances can result in teachers assigning less challenging tasks to students who they believe have low ability. In contrast, positive self-fulfilling prophecies are powerful at stimulating improved performances from less able students in particular.[66]

Teachers need to regard ability as malleable, so that they hold optimistic expectations for students' success. Naturally, their expectations cannot deny the reality of students' skill levels but can communicate through authentic feedback that everyone can make progress. Rather than having a normative view that every student can achieve normally, this is a realistic expectation that every student can learn. This view can be communicated powerfully through the maxim that 'Good enough is not good enough'. In one study, students reported that a teacher's insistence that they do something well and not settle for less communicated to them that their teacher cared about their success.[67] Brophy recommends setting goals in terms of floors, not ceilings, so that individuals can soar to whatever heights their abilities permit.[68] Teachers with this stance will regard a student's failure as a signal to redouble their efforts to reach the student, rather than a remit to give up or to refer the student for remedial placement.[69]

A model of learning

The existence of intrinsic motivation is evidence that human beings are driven to learn and to master their world.[70] Guidance trusts this drive. Like the orchestra conductor who trusts the musicians to know their instrument, teachers trust students to know *their* instrument: their own

FIGURE 16.3   A model of learning

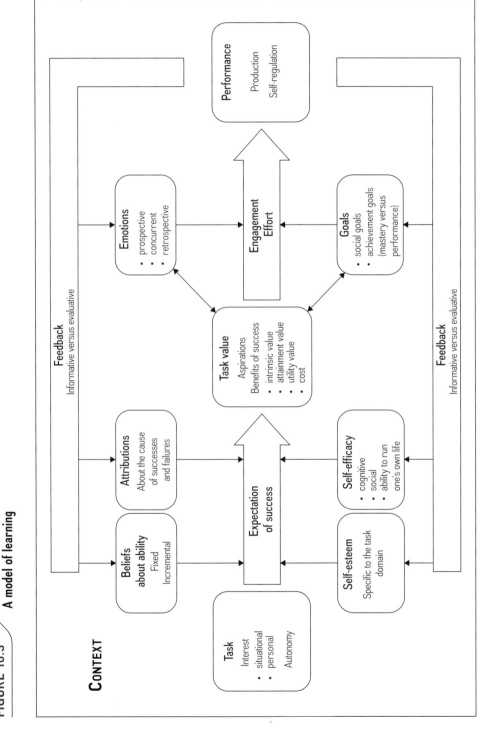

mind.[71] Whereas the model in Figure 16.1 is a model of teaching, guidance is more interested in how students learn. To that end, Figure 16.3 presents a model of learning. It illustrates that motivation – or a lack of it – is not an inherent part of students' personality, but depends on the task and social setting. In other words, motivation is not an individual trait but a response of the individual to the environment (or climate).

Although the model is linear, it is not as cleanly sequential as the model implies: for example, emotions will intervene at all stages.[72] Moreover, although cognitions and emotions are illustrated separately to enable discussion of them, they are intricately intertwined.[73]

Context

The model adopts an *outside-in* perspective on motivation which upholds that motivation and engagement are situated within the setting. The context entices engagement, empowers or constrains thinking and excites positive and negative emotions.[74] The school climate not only has indirect effects on students' achievement by fostering a sense of being supported, but it also has direct effects through affirming feedback from teachers and peers.[75] As seen in chapter 12, supportive settings embolden students to take intellectual risks – and therefore they will learn more – because they know that they will not be ridiculed for their mistakes.[76] In contrast, settings that are competitive and critical make students risk-averse.

Task

Motivation refers to individuals' willingness to invest time, effort and skills into the tasks at hand. It answers the question, 'Why am I doing this task?'. It governs the direction, intensity and quality of engagement.[77] Given that no human being is unmotivated (we are all motivated to meet our needs), when we say that individual students are not motivated by a particular activity, all we are saying is that *this* activity, at *this* time, presented in *this* way, is not meeting their needs. Their apathy does not mean they have lost their drive to learn, but that there is no way to motivate anyone to do something that is futile.[78]

Interest

Interest is a psychological state combining thoughts and feelings that emerges from and is sustained through interaction.[79] It has two elements: *catch* and *hold*, otherwise known as:[80]

- *situational interest* ('catch'), which is roused by features of the task or setting, such as novelty, vividness and comprehensibility
- *personal interest* ('hold'), which within each domain is relatively stable and which itself has two components:
  - emotional interest, which is often captured by narratives
  - cognitive interest, or the arousal of curiosity through incongruity or surprise.

While it is comparatively easy to catch someone's interest, it is a lot more difficult to hold or sustain it.[81] The model in Figure 16.4 illustrates four phases of interest development over time.[82] The first phase is the 'catch' phase where situational features excite temporary positive emotion (interest) in students. Incongruous or surprising information, identification with a character, or personal relevance will invite examination of the content; while group work, activity and the use of computers or electronic tablets will invite engagement in the process.[83] You can also 'catch' students' interest by incorporating your own passions into your teaching so that, rather than explaining your vision to students, you invite them to stand beside you and see it for themselves.

In the second phase, interest is maintained by the meaningfulness of the tasks. While gimmicks may spark the desire to investigate a topic more deeply, interest will only be sustained when the topic is meaningful and learners are actively involved.[84] To that end, teachers will need to make real problems the subject matter of lessons.[85] You might begin with asking students what issues confront them, or by posing questions that they will need to deal with later in life. Project-based learning, cooperative group work and paired learning can all be important processes for sustaining interest.[86]

In the third phase, our individual interest is emerging and we identify ourselves in some way with an idea or activity, as a result of which we allow ourselves to become absorbed in it.[87] We now have some knowledge that will energise our learning and we will put in effort to assuage our curiosity.[88]

In the fourth phase, individual interest is well developed, and depth and precision are valued. This enables individuals to sustain long-term constructive and creative projects in their interest domain, which has become integrated into their identity and is personally meaningful.[89]

Deep investigation might arouse interest, particularly when students can initiate their own investigations and conceptual thinking.[90] But teachers cannot wait around until students express an interest because individuals first need exposure to a content domain before interest can be sparked: people need a knowledge base to act on.[91] Nevertheless, teachers can use students' interests as a bridge to new material that is being introduced. For example:

- When teaching about the electoral system, instead of studying the political system in the abstract, teachers can use students' interest in the latest *Idol* series to have them elect their favourite performer.[92]

- To teach students mathematics, the class might choose to bake pizzas. For the dough, they will need wheat, which they have to plant. Given the average yield, they can calculate how many plants they will need, how many rows . . . and so on. The process of gardening can also teach about water conservation and climate warming, with teamwork and allocation of tasks all part of the learning experience.

- To teach weights and measures, a class with active members could go outdoors and build a see-saw, with each student in turn standing on one end and the group counting the number of bricks needed on the other end for balance. Back in the classroom, the results (in bricks) could be plotted on a graph.

- Adolescents could learn about research by studying how much sleep the class members get each night (a topic that is dear to their hearts).

- A child who loves computer games can gain in literacy skills by reading the instructions for the games.

FIGURE 16.4 Development of interest

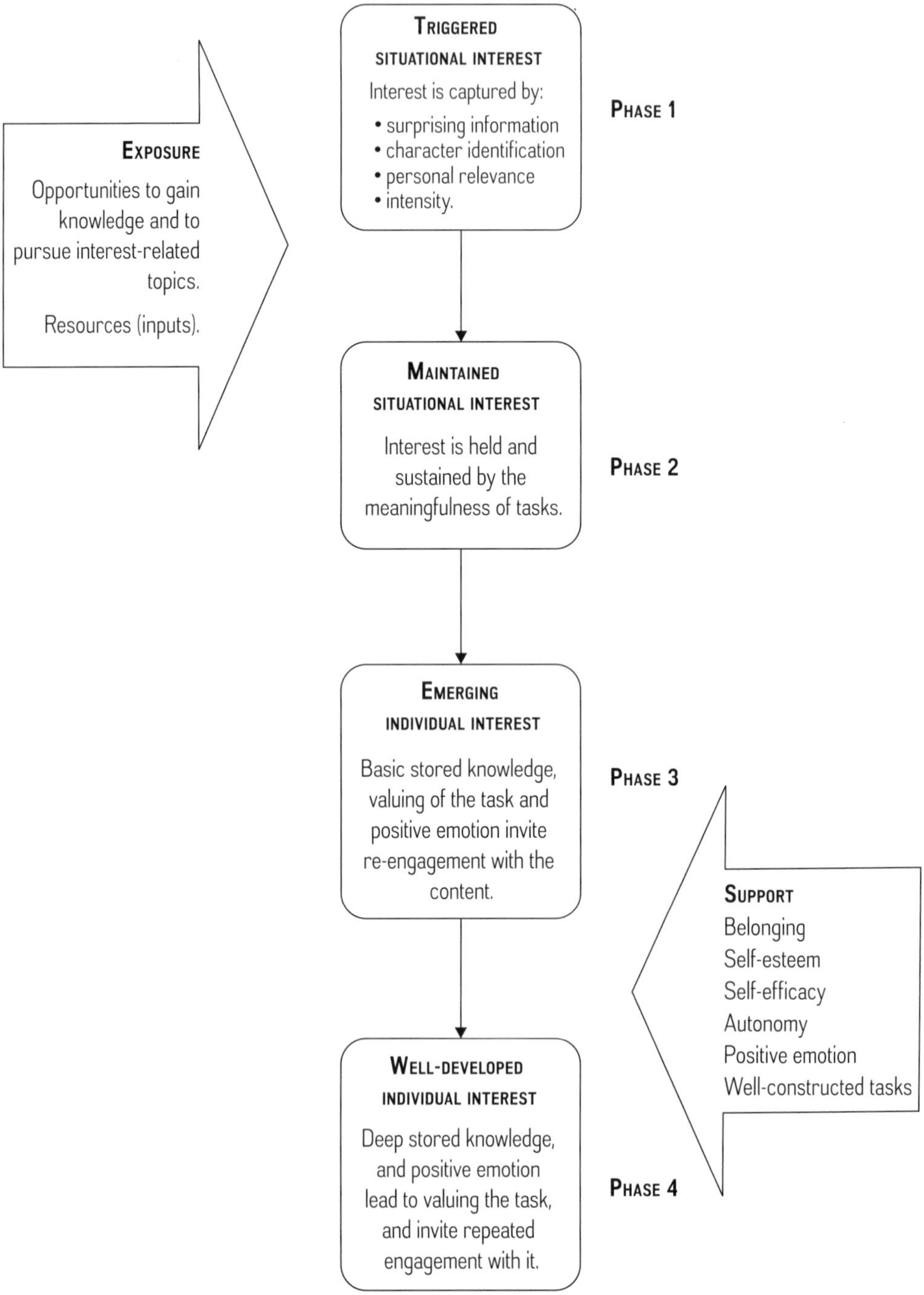

EXPOSURE

Opportunities to gain knowledge and to pursue interest-related topics.

Resources (inputs).

TRIGGERED SITUATIONAL INTEREST

Interest is captured by:
• surprising information
• character identification
• personal relevance
• intensity.

PHASE 1

MAINTAINED SITUATIONAL INTEREST

Interest is held and sustained by the meaningfulness of tasks.

PHASE 2

EMERGING INDIVIDUAL INTEREST

Basic stored knowledge, valuing of the task and positive emotion invite re-engagement with the content.

PHASE 3

SUPPORT
Belonging
Self-esteem
Self-efficacy
Autonomy
Positive emotion
Well-constructed tasks

WELL-DEVELOPED INDIVIDUAL INTEREST

Deep stored knowledge, and positive emotion lead to valuing the task, and invite repeated engagement with it.

PHASE 4

- For beginning readers, I especially like reading dominos. These are a series of cards, half of which contain the beginning of a statement and half contain the ending. For example a pair might read, 'My teachers like to' . . . 'read in the evenings' and another pair might be, 'Elephants in the zoo' . . . 'eat all day'. When young children put the wrong endings on the stem, they can find the results hilarious: 'My teachers like to . . . eat all day' and 'Elephants in the zoo . . . read in the evenings'.
- A child who is vitally interested in a particular sport can use its data to learn about statistics.

In infants and young children, interest is inspired mainly by emotions such as curiosity; whereas, at older ages, stored knowledge and values combine with positive emotions to create interest. Hence, with young children, the main way to attract their interest is to engender positive feelings about learning.[93]

In the early phases of interest development, teachers may need to provide young children with questions for them to answer but, in the later phases, it is important that students be encouraged to ask their own questions so that they can connect their knowledge to something of personal meaning to themselves.[94] Meaningfulness gives a reason to be interested, while support maintains the self-efficacy needed to act on that interest.[95] Even so, it will not be possible for all students within a class to pursue their own individual topic; instead, a teacher can ask each of them to select from a menu of five or six topics for which the teacher can amass rich resources.[96]

The role of middle school is to tempt students with subject matter that, once exposed, might ignite their passions.[97] This introductory material should not be subjected to testing but should depend on informal learning.[98] When, however, it becomes clear that a topic does not interest students, they need to move on to one that does because to expend equal effort on everything is a road to mediocrity.[99]

Autonomy

Returning to the model for learning as shown in Figure 16.3, the second aspect of the task that will affect students' motivation is their control over their learning. Although I detailed this in chapter 15, the thing to keep in mind here is that, according to self-determination theory, the key aspect is an internal locus of *volition* – that is, the sense that tasks are freely chosen. Motivation and engagement will be highest when students believe that they have freely chosen an activity (in contrast with being rewarded for participating).[100]

Beliefs about ability

The next factor in Figure 16.3 to influence learning is students' beliefs about ability. These are of two types. The first, a fixed view, sees ability as a 'thing' or entity, of which one possesses either a little or a lot. Those with this fixed view believe that ability comes naturally and, therefore, when they experience the need to put in effort, this is evidence that they lack ability.[101] Failure is demoralising because it is proof of a lack of ability.[102] Therefore, they avoid challenge and are more interested in looking clever than in learning.[103]

In contrast, an incremental or growth mindset upholds that ability improves with effort.[104] Individuals with this mindset believe that:

> Effort surpasses talent when talent makes no effort.[105]

Adults teach children these beliefs about ability. When we praise young people for their ability, we teach a fixed view of ability.[106] After being praised for being clever, it is too humiliating to admit mistakes, so students become defensive or evasive. Instead, when we give students information about the outcomes of the strategies that they used, they learn that they can change failure into success by changing strategies.[107] Not surprisingly, over time, students with a growth mindset pull ahead academically of those with a fixed view of ability.[108]

Attributions

Attributions are our explanations for our successes and failures. These influence our willingness to engage with a task. As discussed in chapter 14, the most adaptive attributions – the ones that will encourage students to engage and persist – will explain success as being due to temporary, internal, specific and controllable events.[109] When explaining a failure, of these four features, the most important is *stability*: that is, students need to interpret failure as something temporary.[110] In combination with seeing ability as incremental (not fixed), students with a temporary attribution about their failures will feel empowered in future to change outcomes by changing strategies.

Self-esteem

Referring back to Figure 16.3, the next influence on learners is their self-esteem.

The more capable that students believe themselves to be, the more challenging the goals they will set for themselves.[111] In absolute terms, children's sense of how able they are will increase with age but, if they use comparative measures, their self-esteem will decline if they come to believe that they are less able than their classmates.

Self-efficacy

Self-efficacy is the next influence on learning (see Figure 16.3). It is our estimation of our ability to achieve a particular task. As detailed in chapter 14, it affects students' engagement, degree of effort, and persistence.[112] It also avoids adverse emotions in that those who believe in their ability to make a success of a task are less debilitated by stress and anxiety.[113] Obviously, students' level of self-efficacy will differ across subject domains but their metacognitive self-efficacy allows them to regulate their learning in general. This improves performance.[114]

Expectation of success

As shown in Figure 16.3, these previous elements affect students' expectation that they can be successful. Students need optimal (not too high or too low) levels of challenge so that they anticipate success and therefore feel confident that they can meet demands. When they believe that the task is too difficult for them, they can experience anxiety (fear of failure), worrisome thoughts, and physical symptoms of stress.[115] This stress syndrome will reduce students' motivation to invest energy in the tasks, compromise their learning and show itself in processes such as procrastination (avoidance) and attempts to escape task demands.[116] In contrast, students who experience less pressure to excel report enjoying tasks more and experiencing less tension while completing them.[117]

Task value

Anticipating success is important, but students also need to value the outcome. In addition to the context (or climate) already mentioned, we now have detailed three elements of motivation,[118] depicted in the following formula:[119]

> Motivation = expectation of success
> × anticipated benefits of success
> × the emotional climate

Young people will value tasks (that is, find them relevant) and aspire to be successful at them when they anticipate that success will benefit them now or in the future.[120] Individuals will appraise the value of a task in one of four ways.[121]

- *Intrinsic value.* The task is intrinsically interesting and enjoyable. Here, the focus is not on the outcome, but on the process or pleasure of engaging with the task.
- *Attainment value.* Individuals see the task as important when success at it is central to their self-esteem.
- *Utility value.* The task is considered to be important if it benefits our future plans, such as career or other personal goals. In that event, the activity is a means to an end.
- *Cost.* This refers to what we have to give up to do the task, how much effort is involved, and its emotional cost.

Motivation and engagement will be highest when students believe that their achievement will meet their personal needs.[122] Intrinsic value may be most important in early childhood and the early years of schooling, when children may not yet appraise the attainment value or utility of outcomes.[123] Subsequently, however, there is a trend of declining academic task valuing over the school years.[124] This is commonly attributed to a lack of emotional support for learning and to a focus on comparative evaluation, which causes students to disengage from tasks and domains where they do not achieve well.[125]

As illustrated in Figure 16.3 (page 233) by the double-headed arrows, task value affects achievement goals and, in reverse, achievement goals might cause us to either devalue or enhance the value of tasks. Because students will not always be able to discern the utility of a given task, teachers should explain how it will help students to meet their goals, detailing why, when, where and how they could use the information now or in the future.[126]

Goals

Students will engage in tasks for social or academic reasons. Those who pursue both social and achievement goals tend to achieve well.[127] These goals are not necessarily conscious but may be implicit.[128]

Social goals

Students' social goals might include being part of a group, having friends, having fun and achieving socially valued outcomes.[129] Students who see their classroom as socially supportive are more likely to value both their integration into the group and academic success.[130]

Achievement goals

Figure 16.2 illustrated the four types of achievement goals. Another way of

FIGURE 16.5

Structure of achievement goals

GOAL
Competence

Mastery-approach
- is intrinsically motivated
- seeks competence and embraces challenge
- has high self-efficacy
- regards ability as incremental

Mastery-avoidance
- is intrinsically motivated
- seeks competence but avoids risk
- fears failure
- has low self-efficacy
- regards ability as fixed

FEAR OF FAILURE
Low

FEAR OF FAILURE
High

Performance-approach
- is externally motivated
- gives up if winning looks unlikely
- has an achievement-oriented self-esteem
- regards ability as fixed

Performance-avoidance
- avoids challenge
- seeks competence but avoids risk
- fears failure
- has low or uni-dimensional self-esteem
- regards ability as fixed

GOAL
Competitive

thinking about these goals is illustrated in Figure 16.5, showing a structure where the goal for competence versus competition is orthogonal to high versus low fear of failure. This locates one goal in each quadrant.

Mastery goals. The aim of students with mastery-approach goals is to learn new skills, acquire deep understanding and to gain in competence. They personally value what they learn and, therefore, when given the choice, will choose challenging tasks that extend their skills.[131] Central to mastery goals is the belief that ability is incremental and improves with effort.[132] Individuals then measure their progress against their previous performances (rather

than in comparison to others).[133] If they encounter a difficulty, because they feel hopeful about their chances of success, they are likely to persist effectively, using obstacles as a cue to change strategies.[134] This often produces improved performance in the face of setbacks.[135] Students are intrinsically motivated and therefore generally have a strong work ethic: they are organised and thorough in their study habits.[136]

Although primarily self-referenced in their assessment of their performances, students with mastery goals might also want to get good grades,[137] not because of their comparative nature, but because grades give students feedback about their command of the content.[138] Or high grades could have the utilitarian purpose of gaining student access to university or a good job (which reflects neither mastery nor performance goals).[139]

Those with mastery-avoidant goals share this intrinsic desire for mastery, but this goal is accompanied by a fear of not meeting their own standards of excellence and a desire to avoid mistakes or, later in a successful career, not wanting to lose one's edge.[140] This need to avoid incompetence and mediocrity can be seen in disorganised studying, worry, anxiety[141] and a compulsive attention to detail. It may be that the maladaptive nature of mastery-avoidant goals hinges on their compulsive quality, whereas mastery-approach goals are autonomous, volitional or freely chosen.

Both of the mastery goals are associated with a functional form of perfectionism known as *self-referenced* perfectionism, where individuals strive for high achievement because of the satisfaction of becoming skilled.[142] This style of perfectionism is perhaps misnamed, because these people strive for *excellence*, not perfection. Driven to achieve, they nevertheless are compassionate towards their imperfections.

Performance goals. Students with performance goals believe that learning is a means of achieving recognition and rewards.[143] Success is equated with being able to out-perform others. On this basis, rather than focusing on effort, students with performance orientations are anxious to prove their ability.[144] Underlying this goal is an achievement-oriented self-esteem, in which they doubt their worth and therefore have to keep proving it by demonstrating their superiority over others. They must avoid failure because failing would prove

that they are not good enough; the underlying drive is to avoid shame (the belief that they are unworthy of acceptance and belonging).[145] The defining features of performance goals, then, are social comparison and impression management.[146]

Beneath performance goals are many purposes, not all of them competitive: some students want to do well to please their parents or to avoid shaming them; some want to prove themselves to peers who have been disparaging their abilities; some want to be role models for their younger siblings;[147] still others want to do well to debunk negative stereotypes about the abilities of their cultural group or gender.[148] A final group want to do well because they enjoy competition. Nevertheless, competitiveness detracts from intrinsic motivation.[149]

A *performance-approach* orientation is associated with high engagement and achievement[150] and hence can be successful inasmuch as students with this goal will approach challenges when they anticipate earning accolades for doing so. However, when their confidence is shaken and they perceive that they cannot win, their engagement, effort and performance decline, accompanied by an increase in negative emotional reactions.[151] They develop helpless reactions to failure and give up when challenged.[152] Meanwhile, their relationships are jeopardised by their obsession with beating others.

In what has been called the 'big-fish-little-pond' effect, gifted learners who have a performance orientation – those who seek to *be* the best rather than to *do* their best – commonly suffer increased anxiety and reduced self-esteem when placed within a very able peer group, where they cannot outdo their classmates.[153] This decline in self-esteem does not occur in those with mastery achievement goals.[154]

A performance orientation is associated with socially prescribed perfectionism where students feel that their success is a measure of their worth. They consequently avoid tasks where failure is a possibility. They are highly anxious and depressive; have low self-esteem; and treat themselves harshly when they perceive that they have performed below expectations.[155] They have an 'all-or-nothing' mindset, in which they believe that there is no middle ground between failing and perfection, and that only perfect performances will earn them the approval and affirmation they need.[156] This form of perfectionism involves compulsive striving to avoid the shame of failure and the rejection that they anticipate this would attract from others.[157]

A second type of a performance achievement goal (although less well researched)[158] is an *avoidant* goal. Those with this type of goal avoid being seen to be inferior compared to others. When past experience tells them that they are unlikely to outdo others, they will choose safe tasks and avoid challenge.[159] They lack persistence, and experience both less enjoyment of learning and declining achievement over time.[160] When combined with low self-efficacy and an achievement-oriented self-esteem, this goal is associated with low achievement, becoming off-task, being disruptive in class and self-handicapping.[161] This last is the use of planned strategies such as not practising or not studying before a test, procrastinating, being hung over for an exam, and not getting enough sleep prior to a test.[162] Incapacitated or with too little time left to prepare deeply,

those using self-handicapping strategies generally use surface-level studying techniques and poorer self-regulation; they are also more anxious and likely to choke under pressure, all of which can impair their performance.[163] Nevertheless, they will be able to explain the failure to others by ascribing it to a lack of effort, although this does not truly protect their self-esteem.[164]

The distinction is not quite as clear-cut as I have painted it here, however: most people will adopt different goals across school subjects, at different developmental stages, over time and according to the learning task (e.g. reading versus preparing for a test).[165]

Emotions

Next to influence our motivation and performance is emotion (see Figure 16.3). Although we all know what emotions are, formally they are defined as physiological states that are generated by what we think about events, as a result of which we may be mobilised to act. Our feelings can change rapidly and will be experienced at varying levels of intensity which, in turn, affects how strongly or weakly we are activated to do something about them. As we experience emotions, we will typically become aware of them and then have a second-order or meta-ability to reflect on and to choose either to indulge or to regulate what we are feeling.[166] Regulation refers to processes of adjusting the type and intensity of our emotions and how we express them.

Emotions are not merely the side effects of learning but fundamentally drive motivation and engagement.[167] They govern our wellbeing, satisfaction and happiness.[168]

They attune us to how well we are doing and cause us to focus on particular aspects of tasks.[169] The angled double-headed arrow between task value and emotions in Figure 16.3 indicates that all prior elements in the model influence how students feel about the tasks they are being asked to do: specifically, the emotional climate – that is, their sense of support from their teacher and peers; interest and degree of control over tasks; students' beliefs about ability; their attributions about their prior successes and failures; their academic self-esteem and self-efficacy; and the extent to which they value the task.[170] Of these, the most crucial aspects are students' perception of control and their subjective assessment of the value of the task and its outcomes.[171] The fact that the angled arrow is doubled-headed also signals that emotions can enhance or detract from the personal value of tasks.

Three kinds of emotions accompany learning tasks:[172]

- *Prospective* or *anticipatory* emotions are those that occur before individuals undertake a task. These include hope versus hopelessness, and anxiety.
- *Concurrent* emotions are experienced during the task, and include happiness, enjoyment, boredom, frustration, annoyance and anger.
- *Retrospective* emotions are experienced when the person reflects afterwards on an activity. These emotions might include satisfaction, joy, pride, relief, disappointment, sadness, or shame.

These emotions will be most intense when success at the task matters to us: that is, it is salient to our self-esteem.[173] As well as being distressing, the aversive emotions in particular can distract students from tasks and use up working memory space which will impair their performance, while positive emotions such as enjoyment can facilitate engagement.[174]

One emotion of particular concern in school is boredom. This is more than the mere lack of interest, which is emotionally neutral and does not cause any emotional pain. Instead, boredom comprises low-intensity unpleasant emotions such as dissatisfaction, emptiness and impatience. These feelings come about because human beings are programmed to maintain optimal levels of arousal,[175] whereas boredom arises when we are experiencing under-arousal. Dissatisfaction distinguishes boredom from feeling relaxed, the distinction arising from a craving for more stimulation.[176]

This physiological state then leads to additional *emotions* such as frustration, hostility and anger; *cognitive* distortions such as a sense of time standing still; *expressive* components such as sleepiness, yawning and slack posture; *behavioural* aspects of restlessness, distractibility, daydreaming, aggression, diversionary activities, absenteeism and (in the long term) early school dropout; and *motivational* aspects of withdrawing effort and an impetus to escape.[177] If students are unable to escape, boredom is intensified.[178] It de-energises effort and, accordingly, can be a serious barrier to students' engagement in school[179] and might trigger disruptiveness. Boredom leads to shallow processing of information and exerts a negative effect on achievement.[180]

A certain amount of boredom is inevitable. (You might be feeling it right now: sorry.) However, students typically feel boredom during 32 per cent of schoolwork, and 23 per cent at other times. Boredom during homework rises to 44 per cent.[181] (By the way, that same figure was measured in undergraduate psychology and education courses.)[182]

Boredom can be the result of a lack of either internal or external stimulation. In school, it is mainly felt during passive, teacher-directed activities where there is little interaction, when the content is abstract rather than skills-based, and where students do not understand the material; whereas at home it is typically caused by 'having nothing to do'.[183] Specifically, the main causes are monotony, repetitiveness and tedium; a sense that the task seems meaningless (that is, irrelevant to the satisfaction of needs); and low control over tasks.[184] Intrinsic value (but not utility value) protects against boredom.[185] Students with low academic self-esteem and self-efficacy relate it to being over-challenged; whereas gifted learners experience it most when challenge is low.[186] Liking the teacher protects against boredom and resulting disengagement: that is, even when these precursors are present, if students like their teacher, they are often willing to engage anyway.[187]

The opposite of boredom is not interest, but the experience of 'flow' or being in our element.[188] This is when our energies ('attention') are focused on achievable and meaningful goals that are under our control.[189] In these circumstances, doing is its own reward.[190]

Engagement

The next element to consider in the model of learning (see Figure 16.3) is engagement. Motivation is necessary but not sufficient for learning to take place: in order to learn from instruction, students must be actively involved or *engaged* with it. Although often seen to be a quality of individuals, engagement depends first and foremost on the setting, on students' emotional connectedness with others and the support and resources that they receive.[191] In short, engagement demands a fit between the person and the environment.[192]

In the short term, engagement predicts students' achievement, as seen in grades and test scores while, in the long term, it predicts patterns of persistence, retention in school, and academic resilience.[193] It also protects against aggression.[194] Engagement is also reciprocal: the more that students participate in school, the more successful they become; this, in turn, encourages them to remain engaged.[195] Once engaged, they receive more support from teachers, which further supports their continued participation.

Engagement has three aspects: *emotional*, *behavioural* and *cognitive*.

Emotional engagement refers to a commitment arising from an interest in, enjoyment of and a positive attitude to learning.[196] It encompasses feeling hopeful about the chances of success versus helpless; calm versus anxious; and not being bored.[197] It is fed by self-efficacy (a belief that one can be successful) and mastery achievement goals, and by valuing the knowledge and skills one will gain.

Behavioural engagement. In turn, this positive attitude to the work propels students to engage *behaviourally*, by focusing, putting in effort, persisting, and attending (in the dual senses of paying attention and in contrast to being absent or truanting).[198] In the longer term, the end result of a gradual alienation from the enterprise of academic learning is dropping out of school.[199]

BOX 16.4   **Indicators of engagement and disaffection[200]**

Engagement	Disaffection
Emotion	
Curiosity	Resistance
Enjoyment	Frustration and anger
Enthusiasm	Worry and anxiety
Interest	Boredom
Happiness	Anger
Pride	Shame
Satisfaction	Emptiness
Vitality, zest	Fatigue
Behaviour	
Absorbed	Disruptive
Attempts	Avoidant
Attentive	Distracted
Effort	Passive
Initiative	Helpless
Involvement	Withdrawn
Persistence	Giving up

Cognitive engagement involves the use of study skills and metacognitive skills to regulate one's learning.[201] There are three approaches to learning.

- *Deep-level* studying, where students intend to extract meaning and to understand the material.[202] These students are willing to engage with challenging tasks, examine debates and weigh up the evidence, all aimed at establishing links between the new material and their existing knowledge base. This is usually associated with mastery goals, intrinsic motivation, curiosity and high self-efficacy, although not always with excelling at examinations.[203]

- *Surface-level* learning occurs when students intend to extract superficial details from the material, learning key facts but in unconnected ways. When employed as students' dominant style, it is usually associated with a fear of failure, or performance-avoidant achievement goals. High challenge incites surface-level learning in those who have low self-efficacy; subsequently, the poorer results they attain from using this approach then entrench their low self-efficacy.[204]

- *Strategic* learning occurs when students intend to maximise the benefits with the minimum of effort. This is associated with a competitive setting and extrinsic motivation.[205] Students adopting this approach are determined to do well and focus mainly on getting good grades, but are interested in doing 'just enough' rather than doing their best.[206] Sometimes, they may prefer to master the material but are constrained by an overloaded curriculum which forces them to be strategic about how much of it they learn.[207]

Surface learning is not necessarily an inferior learning style: for example, students might scan large tracts of information in an effort to see the big picture without becoming bogged down in details.[208] Indeed, the ability to employ the two styles as needed reflects good metacognitive skills.[209] Although students' self-efficacy, self-esteem, anxiety levels and other traits affect their choice of study approach, their choice is also shaped by the nature of assessments. For example, students usually study at a deeper level for open-ended tasks such as projects or essays and at a superficial level for short-answer and multiple-choice tests.[210] Finally, students' study approach is also shaped by sources of feedback. Extrinsic rewards tend to encourage a surface or strategic approach, with more literal and factual learning, whereas intrinsic goals result in improved conceptual integration of material.[211]

Performance

All of the previous cognitive and emotional factors contribute to the quality of task performance (see Figure 16.3). This entails not only producing a skill, but also regulating our skill use. This requires us to plan, monitor and regulate our thinking, emotions and behaviour in the service of our goals.[212] In particular and as would be expected, high self-efficacy and mastery goal orientations are associated with higher self-regulation, whereas low self-efficacy and performance-avoidant goals are associated with weak self-regulation during learning tasks.[213]

Feedback

Finally in the model of learning in Figure 16.3 (page 233) our own reflections and feedback from others have powerful effects on our learning habits, affecting our subsequent motivation to commit, challenge or reform our goals[214] and to engage in similar tasks in future. Using comparative (or norm-referenced) measures such as grades as an evaluative symbol is meant to motivate students, providing both comparative feedback about their ranking in the class and earning them the consequences of good grades, such as potential entry into a preferred tertiary course.[215]

In contrast, descriptive or criterion-referenced feedback can help students to become less preoccupied with comparing their performances with their peers' and instead to use their own progress as the index of their achievement.[216] This will directly influence their engagement and behaviour in the classroom and contribute indirectly to a more robust self-esteem.[217] Feedback that focuses on the strategies or processes that students used will ensure that ability (as evidenced by the products of their learning)[218] does not become salient in the classroom, corrupting relationships and fostering in students an achievement-oriented self-esteem.

Assessment

To a significant extent, assessment practices shape students' learning by signalling what is valued; while, in reverse, assessment methods are an outcome of the curriculum.[219] Therefore, improving the quality of assessment tasks will enrich the quality of teaching.[220] Authentic assessment emphasises the quality rather than the quantity of students' learning.[221] It focuses on conceptual and higher-order learning, to encourage students to think about what they are learning, not about how well they are doing.[222]

Assessment practices must satisfy the following criteria:

- *Comprehensive.* Assessment should collect data from multiple sources in order to generate a comprehensive picture of students' particular strengths and relatively weaker achievements. Our best assessment instrument is knowing individual students well.[223] To that end, assessment should be an ongoing process, rather than a one-off event.[224] This formative, in contrast to summative, assessment should also allow students to revise and then improve on their performance. Glasser defends this suggestion with the observation that there is no point assessing students' skills if we are not going to give them a chance to improve them.[225]

- *Efficient.* Comprehensiveness must be balanced with pragmatism in that assessment must be an appropriate use of teachers' time.
- *Valid.* The first use of this term implies that assessment should measure something meaningful. A second use refers to the purposes to which assessment information is put.[226] For example, assessment results are often used to determine eligibility for higher education and yet school attainment has very little power to predict achievement in either tertiary education or in the work force; hence this is an invalid use of the results.
- *Reliable.* Assessment results should be an accurate reflection of students' learning.
- *Equitable.* Assessment methods must be fair, which means that they should not disadvantage any cultural groups or either gender.[227] This criterion also implies that test scores should not be manipulated to conform to a bell curve.[228]

Authentic assessment

Critics accuse conventional assessment of focusing on the reproduction of discrete facts and the performance of routine computational procedures that are often 'trivial, contrived and meaningless' and, in turn, breed low student engagement.[229] In contrast, authentic assessment involves students deeply both in terms of intellectual complexity and intrinsic interest, and evaluates skills that have value beyond the assessment itself.[230] Authentic assessment also requires that students be involved in establishing the criteria for evaluation and will engage in self-evaluation to increase their commitment and ownership of their learning.[231]

Grades

Testing is the main measure of accountability for schools. However, tests are mainly about efficiency rather than effectiveness[232] and are a poor way for students to demonstrate what they know. They are seldom rich and, by discouraging higher-order thinking, they deny students more relevant ways to understand ideas, while being professionally unfulfilling for teachers.[233]

Public honour rolls, classes for high achievers, rewards for superior performance and public accolades for achievements all contribute to a decline in young people's academic motivation and emotional well-being over time.[234] They link students' self-worth to their grades[235] and, therefore, even those who are successful know that they have to keep on the treadmill to maintain their status, while those who already feel incompetent are not emboldened to try harder, but are more likely instead to give up. Those with the poorest academic and emotional adjustment and who therefore need most support, are the ones least likely to receive it.[236] Accordingly, these students are likely to feel alienated from school and to withdraw either psychologically or physically by absenting themselves.[237]

Superficial learning. Grades distort the curriculum, with only those things that can be counted being measured. The resulting focus on discrete facts reduces curricular relevance and leads to the use of strategic rather than deep learning habits.[238] Furthermore, if teachers are clear about what will be assessed, students will study that and no more. The practice of coercing students through tests to memorise irrelevant information discourages independent thinking and causes students to cheat, not because they lack ethics but because they lack time to master the workload and because they realise that, 'there is no virtue in learning nonsense'.[239]

The result is that students do not go to school to learn; the successful students go to get good grades as a stepping stone to a university course.[240] These highly able students learn to play the game, rather than learn how to learn.[241] Even more importantly, enforcing memorisation of isolated facts causes many students to detest the subject matter, which 'is worse than just not knowing it'.[242] It would be better for young people to emerge from the education system ignorant than hating to learn.

Closed-book examinations are based, says Glasser, on the fallacy that 'knowledge remembered is better than knowledge looked up'[243] when in fact rote learning is suitable for a relatively small range of material. Given the decay of facts in memory, and given that it is now possible to google facts on our mobile (cell) phones, there is even less need nowadays for students to learn facts by rote.[244]

Competitiveness. The bell curve imposes an artificial shortage of grades which generates competition amongst the ambitious students.[245] Their competitiveness is a driving force in their relationships with friends, with peers resenting others who do well, causing able students either to hide their skills or risk becoming isolated.[246]

Hierarchies based on ability. The repeated nature of the contests (graded tests) means that hierarchies are developed within the classroom, with the academically able students attaining elevated status, with the least able students eliminated from the running altogether.[247]

Performance achievement goals. Grades encourage performance achievement goals, with over half of the group in one study who received grades reporting performance goals, compared with just over 7 per cent of those who received feedback in the form of descriptive comments.[248] Grading leads to avoidance of risk and to reduced interest in learning, particularly for students with low self-efficacy.[249] This combination can lead to failure avoidance but, more insidiously, to failure acceptance.[250]

In an attempt to avoid challenge and potential failure, extrinsic rewards for learning (including grades and other accolades) cause students to choose easy tasks.[251] This also manifests as students' selection into easier subjects, in which higher grades are easier to come by, even when the subjects may not be of interest or use to them.[252]

Conformity. Under grading systems, creative individuals do less well than those who conform.[253] In the pursuit of good grades, high achievers must compromise their individuality, their health, their happiness and their personal style.[254] Their focus on being evaluated means that they produce work that their teacher will reward, rather than work which satisfies themselves.[255] Feeling obliged to choose between conformity and authenticity, high achievers become chameleons, changing from class to class as they conform to the various teachers' expectations and, in so doing, falsifying and disguising themselves.[256]

Stress. In the pressure to succeed, ambitious students' focus is on their future (getting into a good university), while their present needs do not matter and their individual accomplishments lack meaning. To them,

worrying about a test is equivalent to worrying about their future.[257] If teachers are vague about what will be in the test, these students become especially overwhelmed and stressed; in turn, their anxiety can impair their achievement.[258]

Superficial feedback. Normative evaluations are often perceived as an attempt to control, rather than as any genuine means of providing feedback about mastery.[259] And because grades are summative, they give very little information about the skills that contributed to their allocation.[260] Yet students crave meaningful feedback, preferring their teachers to emphasise learning, rather than ability and evaluation.[261]

Authoritarian. Grades are an application of top-down teaching in that they are almost always awarded by teachers, with both students' own assessments and group processes overlooked. In the guise of legitimacy, grading systems help enhance teacher power and provide a tool for imposing conformity.[262]

Unfairness. While grades are supposed to be an objective measure of students' progress, it is hard to make any finer distinction than pass–fail. Attempts to do so are subjective, inaccurate, unfair, unreliable and phoney.[263] Grades are not a good indicator of success at anything other than school work, and there is no recognition of late maturing, with few second chances for late bloomers to redeem a poor school record: school failure can damn one to failure for life.

Effects on teachers. The irony is that teachers suffer from the same trap as their students: burdened by too much work, with too little time to compose meaningful assessments, too little personal contact with their students and colleagues, and experiencing high demands from administrators.[264] Setting and marking assignments use time that could be spent on facilitating more authentic learning. In short, no one benefits from the system – and yet it endures.

On the basis of these criticisms of comparative assessment, the core recommendation for implementing authentic assessment is that it should be descriptive (or criterion-referenced), whereby students are graded according to how well they master specified criteria, rather than relative to each other.[265]

Ultimately, only students' own judgment about their grasp of useful skills (that is, self-evaluation of a relevant curriculum) will motivate them to invest continued effort in academic work. Students' narratives about their learning, compilations of their work into portfolios, exhibitions and presentations all encourage students to extract deeper meaning than from test scores.[266] When, however, testing and grades are imposed on teachers, this can become just one more problem for the students and you to solve jointly. As a group, you might elect to implement the following measures:

- Students could nominate when they believe they have mastered the content and therefore are ready to take a test.[267]
- Students might choose to submit questions that they think should be included in a test.
- Tests should be open book and examine students' skills rather than their memorisation of facts.
- Those who achieve well on a test could proceed to new material; those who did not would be given the opportunity

to practise further until they have mastered the content.
- Teachers could supplement normative test results with students' own self-evaluations.
- Teachers can also supplement formal assessment with specific feedback so that students can identify what they have achieved and what their next goal might be.

These measures safeguard society's need for an accountable education system, while still promoting students' growth. Research has shown that, just as authentic assessment improves students' higher-order skills, it also improves their memorisation of factual knowledge because it has been connected to meaningful content.[268] One substantial study found that it increased individual students' performances from the 30th to the 60th percentile ranking.[269]

Individualisation

The educational aim of guiding students to fall in love with what they are doing is the rationale for differentiation. It is unjust to provide the same curriculum to students who have differing needs.[270] Individualisation also implies that what we are asking students to take an interest in, reflects their lives.

Activity levels

With boys' language skills (on average) being below girls' throughout the school years, boys tend to be less engaged by talk and more in need of physical activity during their school day. Schools need to honour boys' and young children's need for activity and build this into teaching processes.

Atypical learners

Students whose abilities render them outliers (those with disabilities or with advanced or gifted learning) will need individualised education plans, not because they are any more deserving of these than other students, but because they have the same right as all others to have their needs met.[271] Given the need for reading skills to access the rest of the curriculum, assessment and remediation (as necessary) of literacy and language skills will be a priority for many students with behavioural difficulties in schools.

Learning modes and styles

Young children almost universally learn physically but, by the age of five, are proficient with both verbal and visual input.[272] While most tasks employ the range,[273] some individuals, are more capable in one mode than the other. I suspect that their preference (visual versus auditory) is inbuilt, with the sons and daughters of website designers, television producers, beauticians, architects and builders all likely to be visual, as are their parents. In bygone eras, many visual learners would convert to learning by listening, because the only source of information about the outside world came via radio. Today, however, visual learners have little impetus to convert to listening, given that they can now access so much information in the visual mode.

Their favoured modality may, in turn, incline learners towards a preferred processing style. Individuals who are strong listeners typically process information sequentially, because language is sequential. In contrast, visual learners usually (but not always) develop into conceptual learners, because images appear as a whole (like viewing a painting in an art gallery). There may also be cultural differences, with non-sequential learners more common in certain cultural groups.[274]

Figure 16.6 illustrates the various learning styles (with the percentage in each quadrant being estimates only):

- *Verbal-sequential style.* These learners are capable listeners and are good at sequencing. This likely represents the majority of the population.
- *Visual-conceptual style.* These learners are strong at visualising and learn concepts as a whole. They are inattentive to verbal instruction. Accordingly, I receive many referrals of these learners for a presumed attention deficit disorder. (Most literature calls this a 'visual-spatial' style, but that label overlooks those who learn concepts verbally.)
- *Verbal-conceptual style.* These learners have excellent verbal skills but nevertheless learn conceptually or intuitively. These students' strong verbal abilities cause adults to expect strong sequential and logical abilities, but these skills are surprisingly deficient. The students are distractible during sequential tasks and appear not to be 'applying themselves' to these activities, particularly compared to how intuitive and quick they are at other tasks. Accordingly, these students are often described as being very capable 'when they want to be'.
- *Visual-analytical style.* These learners are attentive to visual detail and are able to analyse patterns. In contrast, they may be inattentive to language, appearing to be disengaged from most academic subjects, given their premium on verbal skills.

Most individuals will fit the balanced profile and practice is running ahead of the research, such that the statistics in Figure 16.6 are estimates only – but what we think we know so far about conceptual learners can be accessed on my website. The main point to be made here is that distractible students need a comprehensive assessment in case their inattentiveness is associated

BOX 16.5

Adjusting instruction for conceptual learners

Students with sequential weaknesses can benefit from the following adjustments to teaching and learning processes:

- Supplement verbal instructions with written prompts.
- Give instructions in visual language. Rather than: 'Get your book from the shelf' try, 'Picture the bookcase . . . Can you see where your book is? . . . Okay, get it.'
- With younger children, limit a directive to only two steps.
- Sometimes visual young children have a fixed picture that they need, say, to complete a task, but this conflicts with your imperative that they move on to something else. In such situations, do not force them to abandon their picture entirely but just set it aside temporarily. You might instruct them to 'change channels' in their head – just as they change channels on the TV – to shift attention to a different picture, knowing that they can return to their own picture at another time.
- To help conceptual children to appreciate their skills, when giving feedback, it is important to highlight not their results but the processes that they used to attain these.
- Conceptual learners typically *can* perform sequences but, being so proficient at conceptual learning, prefer to do things in their favourite mode. If we forced them to learn sequentially, this would be like asking them to drive a car in reverse for an entire journey: the car can do it, but it is not efficient. We do not want to take away their more efficient style, but to supplement it with enhanced sequencing abilities that they could employ when those skills would produce more success. Therefore, it can help to cue conceptual learners to perform the sequence of steps for problem solving. The first step is to remind them to pause . . . then ask, 'Where will you start? What will you do first?' . . . . 'Is it working?' . . . 'What will you do next?' . . . 'Is that working?' . . . 'Are you finished?'.
- Give them the bigger picture first before asking them to apply themselves to details: they can learn only when the task has some meaning for them. Otherwise it is like asking them to do a jigsaw puzzle without the picture on the box as a guide: they can become overwhelmed by all the pieces.
- Explain the rationale for a task or explain it as being a small part of becoming competent at bigger skills.
- Give them extra time to devote to their conceptual learning. This means giving them less homework so that they are not so busy that they do not have time to learn anything meaningful; reducing the number of structured extra-curricular activities; and giving extra time in class and in tests for them to think in the sequential ways that do not come naturally to them.

FIGURE 16.6   Learning styles

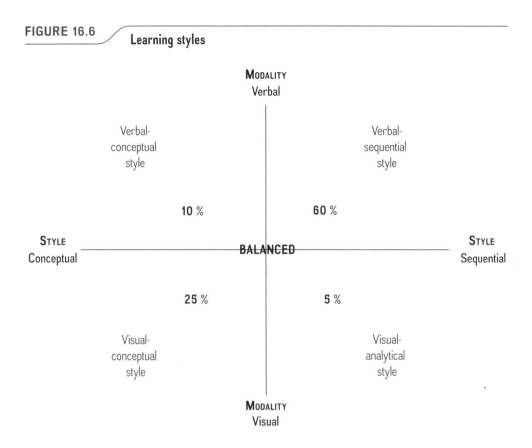

with a learning style that is not catered for routinely in the classroom. Without adjustments such as those listed in Box 16.5, they are likely to be less engaged in schoolwork and to under-achieve both at school and in their adult occupations.[275] Coincidentally, an advantage of catering for visual and verbal-conceptual learners is that the adjustments are likely to assist the engagement of boys in general.[276]

Higher-order thinking

Lower-order thinking requires the routine application of prior knowledge, whereas higher-order thinking transforms information and ideas, using synthesis, analysis, explanation, hypothesising, predicting, problem solving, interpreting and concluding.[277] The main reason for an emphasis on higher-order thinking is to teach students how to learn so that they become producers of ideas rather than mere consumers of information.[278] An integrated curriculum and many measures already discussed here (such as linking learning with students' interests, authentic assessment, collaborative learning, class discussions and a de-emphasis on correct answers) all facilitate higher-order thinking. The guidance approach will also assist students to understand how they learn by raising their awareness of higher-order skills such as:[279]

- stating and defending a point of view
- looking for links between different ideas, topics and subjects
- examining the evidence for opinions
- noting contradictions in one's own or in others' points of view
- considering alternatives
- challenging accepted answers provided in texts or by teachers.

The aim is to foster critical thinking. This can be applied to any subject matter; it does not have to be a separate course, but it does have to be applied to issues that are salient in students' lives.[280]

Adaptive skills

Guidance believes that students do well when they can.[281] The corollary of this view is that disruptive behaviour occurs when students lack skills for adaptive social, emotional and behavioural functioning,[282] such as those listed in Box 16.6. This philosophical stance is supported by research linking learning difficulties with behavioural problems in schools (as reviewed in chapter 1).

Students who struggle to adapt – otherwise known as rigid (or 'black-and-white') thinkers – attempt to apply concrete rules to ambiguous situations. They cannot see the big picture. Having a preference for predictability, they consequently do less well during transitions from one activity to another, when routines are altered, during unstructured activities such as play times, and when experiencing frustration and disappointment.[283] Once adults know which situations and which lagging skills are troublesome for children, we can teach the necessary skills proactively in order to

prevent meltdowns that arise when young people become overwhelmed.[284]

Problem-solving skills

One key skill which students need for academic and behavioural success is problem solving. Given that problems are inevitable in the course of living, human adjustment relies on the ability to identify and then solve difficulties. The benefit of using communication skills to solve problems (see chapter 17) is that students gain everyday practice at applying these skills to situations that matter to them. And the students with the most problems get the most practice!

In addition, structured teaching can prompt students to examine what has to be done, scan a range of behavioural options and select the option that they think will be most successful. To achieve this, they need to be capable of paying attention, pacing themselves, persisting, and noting feedback, among other skills. Most fundamental of all will be their ability to use self-talk to guide their problem solving. The following explicit steps may be written or drawn on cue cards as reminders.[285]

1. Pause.
2. Ask: 'What is the problem?'.
3. Ask: 'What do I want?'.
4. Ask: 'Is what I'm doing helpful to me?'.
5. If not, plan solutions: 'What else could I do?'. It can be helpful at this point for students to generate a number of potential solutions so that subsequently they do not become frustrated if their first one does not work out.
6. Choose what to do and do it.
7. Evaluate the results. (Go back to step 4).
8. Self-reinforce.

FIGURE 16.7

Prompts for problem solving

Stuck?

Stop.
Breathe.

Plan

What do I need
to get started?

Have a go

Put it together.

Check

Is it working?

Keep going

What's next?

I have sometimes simplified these steps into laminated bookmarks for students to place in each of their books. I designed the one pictured in Figure 16.7 for a younger child who wanted to become a mechanic, although the bookmarks can be stylised to suit any student's interests and age.

Homework

Work allocated by teachers for completion after hours has many facets. Its effects depend on whether it is graded, whether it is compulsory, and the flexibility of deadlines; in addition, the amount, purpose and individualisation of homework tasks influence its effects.[286]

Effects of the amount of homework. One study of Australian Year 12 students found that the students were completing an average of 37 hours of homework per week (with the range being from 10 to 65 hours).[287] This was on top of a full week of class-based work – and it coincided with teacher expectations. In terms of the effects on students' performance, differences in attainment mainly depend on how much of the allocated homework students complete, rather than how much their teachers actually allocate. Those conscientious students who complete most or all of the allocated homework do better academically, but this may not be due to their homework completion as such,[288] but to the fact that these students are more engaged during class time as well. Also, the most relevant homework assignments are set by the best teachers,[289] who usually also have the most able students; these students would do well regardless of homework completion, because of their abilities and the quality of instruction they receive.

The second finding is that, although in the senior years of high school, completing homework improves student achievement, even at this level, more than 1 to 2 hours per night is detrimental.[290]

Third, the amount of time spent on homework is a poor indicator of its effects

BOX 16.6 — **Adaptive functioning skills**[291]

Changing mindset (flexibility versus 'black-and-white' thinking)
- handling transitions
- deviating from routine
- handling unpredictability, ambiguity, uncertainty, novelty
- taking into account situational factors that would indicate a need to adjust a plan of action

Working memory
- reflecting on multiple ideas simultaneously
- considering a range of solutions to a problem

Attention skills
- sustaining focus (concentration)
- persisting with challenging tasks

Language skills
- expressing concerns, needs or thoughts in words
- understanding what is being said (verbal-sequential processing)
- speaking up when one does not understand
- expressing disagreement
- use of self-talk to govern one's own behaviour

Sequential skills
- having a sense of time
- setting goals
- planning a strategy before starting work
- considering the outcomes of actions
- performing tasks in a logical sequence of steps

Self-regulation
- regulation of emotions
- inhibition of impulses
- ensuring that irritability, anxiety, stress and other forms of heightened arousal do not interfere with problem solving
- self-soothing emotionally
- effortful control of attention
- self-instruction (self-talk)
- ability to delay gratification (as appropriate)

Self-awareness
- recognising one's own emotions
- understanding the reasons for feeling as one does
- verbalising and coping with anxiety, sadness, anger and frustration
- noticing one's own strengths
- activating hope and optimism

Perspective taking (reading social cues)
- interpretation of others' intentions without bias
- listening to and empathising with others
- attending to and interpreting social cues and nuances
- accommodating others' point of view
- monitoring how one's own behaviour affects others
- appreciating how one is coming across to others
- heeding feedback from self and others
- working collaboratively
- employing problem-solving skills

because the least able students take longer than more able students to complete the same homework tasks, some of the extra time being due to their lack of understanding and some to being off-task.[292]

Purpose. Teachers set students work to do at home for a range of reasons:

- *Academic* purposes: to give students practice and opportunities to consolidate content they have learned in class; to prompt the elaborations of ideas covered in class; to transfer knowledge into other situations; to help prepare students for upcoming tests or units of work.
- *Self-regulation* goals: to foster self-discipline, motivation and personal responsibility.
- *Parental involvement*: because parents seem to expect it, or as a way to involve parents and to keep them informed about what their daughter or son is doing at school.
- *Punishment* for being off-task during lesson time.

With respect to the first goal, the effects of homework on academic outcomes differ according to the type of task that is allocated. The majority of homework involves drill and practice assignments, which are associated with declines in homework effort and achievement.[293] The effects also differ by grade level, with senior high school students' achievement levels higher when they study after hours; with only small gains in the early high school years and none in primary school.[294] The effects also differ according to subject area, with students' effort being selective across various school subjects.[295] The conclusion

is that homework completion appears to slightly improve students' grades, but not their achievement scores.[296] The effect on grades comes about because teachers feel more positively about and give higher grades to students who complete their homework.[297]

Meanwhile, homework has significant emotional costs. Many students report that it is the chief source of stress in their lives and it is a common source of concern for young people attending medical practitioners.[298] The Year 12 students in the Australian study just mentioned reported being stressed by the sheer volume of what they had to learn, the timing and spacing of assignments, lack of time for study, and not being certain about what was important to study.[299] Emotional effects included stress, tension and anxiety; fatigue and inertia; confusion and bewilderment; and depression and dejection.[300]

With respect to the second goal of fostering self-regulation, this has not been researched.[301] It stands to reason, however, that when teachers and parents are enforcing the homework; when the work contributes to grades; and when teachers or parents punish its non-completion then, by definition, this is not self-discipline. Indeed, high levels of teacher control are associated with students' negative emotions about homework and poorer achievement, while grading imposes superficial or strategic study skills and raises temptations to copy another's work.[302] One conceptual learner complained to me that the amount of work and imposed superficiality were frustrating: 'I'm so busy doing homework that I don't have time to learn anything!'.[303]

With respect to the third purpose of involving parents, research is clear that parental 'help' is sometimes intrusive and does not help, but instead pressures the student.[304] The phenomenon of 'homework hysteria' is familiar to many. This occurs with the discovery that a child is ill prepared for an upcoming assignment or test, when it is a toss-up who is the more hysterical: the parent . . . or the child.

Individualisation. Homework that involves practice or preparation can be more challenging than same-day recall tasks; on the other hand, high challenge leads to the poorer engagement of students who lack self-efficacy.[305] Choice (in the sense of selecting between two tasks) seems to affect student interest in homework tasks, while high-quality tasks that are individually tailored for students' abilities and interests promote student engagement and effort.[306] However, individualisation is rare and, in all likelihood, unmanageable for teachers.[307]

Given the very limited academic benefits, the onerous workload for teachers and considerable emotional costs for young people (as detailed in Box 16.7), many guidance practitioners believe that teachers should not assign compulsory homework. Based on another instance of *either–or* thinking, teachers often assume that *either* they allocate homework *or* students will be self-indulgent and unproductive.[308] My own (perhaps strident) stance is that teachers have no business dictating how students spend their personal time. Nevertheless, in the following instances you might invite students to complete some home-based activities voluntarily:

- if the work can only be done at home and is not just an extension of class work

– such as when students need to watch a particular TV program or interview relatives
- if students chose not to apply themselves to their work during the school day, thus electing to complete it in their own time
- if students choose to revise and practise in order to improve their skills by completing extra work at home.[309]

Even then, this voluntary work is an opportunity to try things out and therefore should not be graded.[310] Freed from policing and marking the unnecessary homework of their entire class group, teachers could assess the needs of the handful of students with learning difficulties, plan individual remedial homework activities for them, and deliver specific and personalised feedback that would help them to improve their skills.

Conclusion

When teachers become mired in students' complex behavioural problems, it is easy to lose sight of their core obligation to do whatever it takes to teach young people intellectual processes and knowledge that will be useful to them in life.[311] When what we are asking students to do and how we are asking them to do it meets students' needs and empowers meaningful accomplishments, we will have fulfilled our duty to them. In turn, they will perceive that success is not only possible but probable – and will return the courtesy of doing their duty by us.

Research has shown that schools with the most supportive learning environments are also the schools that cultivate and practise egalitarian values.[312] In tune with this, guidance recognises that when

BOX 16.7

Disadvantages of compulsory homework[313]

Reduction of student motivation and achievement

- Compulsory homework reduces the quality of students' lives: it does not meet their needs.
- Homework is irrelevant, especially until the most senior years of high school.
- Students have no choice about doing homework, which makes them unmotivated.
- Homework allows students to make the same mistakes over and over when studying at home without teacher supervision.
- Most homework is more easily and better done at school.

Contribution to student dropout and burnout (stress)

- Homework is excessive and tedious and causes students to detest school and learning.
- Homework eats into relaxation time, which would offset stress.
- Homework truncates students' abilities to engage in extra-curricular activities, when they would enjoy themselves and learn something useful.
- Bright students who are conscientious about doing homework have no time left to pursue other recreational activities; less able students do not do the homework but because this defines them as failures, they do little else either. Thus, both groups of students are denied other learning and pleasurable activities. And by adulthood, they have not developed ways to enjoy their leisure time.

Exacerbation of inequity among students

- Students from privileged homes have the facilities for quiet study whereas students from disadvantaged homes have not, leading to a widening of the differences between their academic achievement

levels. Students who have family or work responsibilities in the evenings are unable to complete the work, as a result of which they are seen by their teachers to be lacking commitment.

- Just as it contributes to social status differences between students, homework highlights differences in their academic status, given that the academically able students complete their homework, while the remainder are defined as disruptive.
- Parents for whom English is not a first language or those with little formal education cannot assist their children, which can be humiliating for them[314] and undermine their role as family leaders.

Interference with high-quality teaching

- Assigning and reviewing homework costs teachers time.
- Homework must be graded, with all the disadvantages of grading.
- Failure to do homework is often punished, with all its disadvantages.
- To avoid arguments, teachers (and parents) accept low quality homework, which sends the message that it is acceptable to do poor work.

Contribution to antagonistic relationships with young people

- Compulsory homework leads to conflict between students and teachers.
- Voluntary homework that involved talking to adults could help bring parents and children together, whereas compulsory homework creates antagonism between them, as parents frequently believe that it is their role to ensure that their children complete their homework.

students' behaviour is still a problem by school age, their families and society have let them down. It is our duty to ensure that we do not let them down too. Although we must steadfastly insist on considerate behaviour, this does not imply the need for external controls. These contradict the aims of guidance: we cannot teach students to be bold intellectually but then oblige them to conform behaviourally.[315]

Recommended further reading

Good, T.L. & Brophy, J.E. (2008). *Looking in classrooms*. (10th ed.) Boston, MA: Pearson.

Greene, R.W. (2008). *Lost at school*. New York: Scribner.

Jones, V.F. & Jones, L.S. (2013). *Comprehensive classroom management: Creating communities of support and solving problems*. (10th ed.) Boston, MA: Pearson.

Kohn, A. (1999). *The schools our children deserve: Moving beyond traditional classrooms and 'tougher standards'*. Boston, MA: Houghton Mifflin.

——(2000). *What to look for in a classroom . . . and other essays*. San Francisco, CA: Jossey-Bass.

——(2004). *What does it mean to be well educated?* Boston, MA: Beacon Press.

——(2006). *The homework myth: Why our kids get too much of a bad thing*. Cambridge, MA: Da Capo Press.

——(2011). *Feel-bad education: And other contrarian essays on children and schooling*. Boston, MA: Beacon.

Conceptual learners

Golon, A.S. (2004). *Raising topsy-turvy kids: Successfully parenting your visual-spatial child*. Denver, CO: DeLeon.

——(2008). *Visual-spatial learners*. Waco, TX: Prufrock Press.

——(n.d.) *If you could see the way I think: A handbook for visual-spatial kids*. www.visual-learners.com

——(n.d.) *The visual-spatial classroom: Differentiation strategies that engaged every learner!* www.visual-learners.com

Maxwell, B. & Punch, C. (2012). *Picture it!: Teaching visual-spatial learners*. CreateSpace Independent Publishing Platform.

Silverman, L.K. (2002). *Upside-down brilliance: The visual-spatial learner*. Denver, CO: DeLeon.

Websites

www.gifteddevelopment.com
www.louiseporter.com.au
www.starjump.com.au
www.VisualSpatial.org

CHAPTER 17

Compassionate communication

'Real' listening requires courage, generosity and patience on our part . . . It requires courage, because if we seriously entertain another's ideas it makes us vulnerable as we move out of our own comfort zone and see another point of view that could challenge our own or reveal it as flawed. Listening requires our generosity, because it is something we do for another person even when the message is less than welcome or is unattractive to us. Finally, listening requires patience because we need to suspend our own thoughts, questions and judgements and make sure we have understood the message before responding to it.[1]

A core component of a caring community is for teachers to relate to students with acceptance, respect, empathy, compassion, humanity and as a real person, rather than hiding behind our role or professional façade.[2] Compassion, says Brené Brown, 'is not a relationship between the healer and the wounded. It's a relationship between equals'.[3] The quality of this relationship is valuable in itself but also, in terms of our topic here, it helps students to engage in learning and to regulate their own behaviour.[4] Teachers who know their students can often deflect a mounting confrontation.[5]

For some of the reasons listed in Box 17.1, the emotional climate of secondary schools is often arid and one of distancing from feelings.[6] Emotions are often ignored, being attended to only when they threaten to intrude upon teaching.[7] In contrast, guidance practitioners are willing to support students not as compassionate exceptions but in everyday interactions so that students' voices can be heard.[8] Teachers' capacity to use emotions well, shape the climate of the classroom and the support students can provide to each other.

In one study asking students how they sensed that their teachers cared about and were willing to nurture and support them, the students reported that it was through talk.[9] This talk was reciprocal, giving both students and teachers experience at speaking but also of listening and hearing. That is, talk is the currency of caring, with each conversation being a brick that builds and shapes teachers' relationship with students.[10] The guidance approach believes that teachers must listen to young people even when their behaviour is disruptive because this behaviour merely signals that students' needs are unmet.[11] However, while compassionate listening notices the other's feelings, it treats these as the messenger, not the message. The *message* is that they have an unmet need. Moreover, rather than focusing on the fact that the need is not being met, we recognise that the need is important to the student, and then move on to identifying what *will* satisfy it.

Compassion, however, also involves boundaries, which means that we can hold others accountable (without blame or shame) when their actions infringe on us.[12] We do this by being assertive and engaging in collaborative problem solving to resolve a behaviour. In reverse, boundaries remind us that teaching is not a licence to share with students our unfulfilled needs or to become involved in students' lives: we must be friendly without attempting to be students' friend. We must remember that the primary purpose of our relationships with students is not for our own personal satisfaction but as an avenue to student growth.[13] For that purpose only, we can allow students to get to know us by being assertive about both our positive

and negative reactions to events that are important to us, while using natural events to tell them about who we are, what we stand for and will not stand, and what we will and will not be asking them to do.[14]

Naturally, teachers – whose role is already demanding – cannot be expected to be counsellors, social workers, psychologists or psychiatrists. But teaching in essence is professionalised communication. Therefore, we *can* ask teachers to be skilled at communicating: it is their core business. And, because we are all human, we each know the qualities of communication that we appreciate, and those that shut us down. That is, we already have a wellspring of knowledge about compassionate communication.[15]

An understanding of emotions

Whereas babies' survival *demands* that they indulge and communicate everything they feel in order they receive the care that they require, adults' wellbeing requires

---

BOX 17.1

Constraints on empathy between teachers and their students[16]

- *Power differentials* (or the hierarchical status of teachers) distort the communication between them and students.
- *Goals*: teachers' purposes can be at odds with those of students or their parents.
- *Professionalism* can cause teachers to adopt a formal professional role that distances them from students and their parents.
- *Physical geography* in the form of fragmented, infrequent and episodic encounters with students means that students and teachers are disconnected, and teachers lack personal knowledge about their students.
- *Cultural differences* can render students and teachers who are from different cultural or socioeconomic backgrounds alien to each other, contributing to misreads of each other's emotional communication.

instead that we can filter and regulate our emotions so that our feelings enrich our lives, rather than block us from achieving our goals.[17] Acquiring this self-regulation is the most important task of childhood.[18] Given that this ability is not hard-wired into humans and that children's feelings are more intense than are adults', acquiring self-regulation will take considerable practice, and inevitably will entail many mistakes in the form of lapses (or 'meltdowns').

Acquiring self-regulation begins in infancy,[19] with children's ability to regulate emotions continuing to undergo important changes into middle childhood. By school entry, most children can already manage their emotions effectively most of the time.[20] Children increasingly become less emotionally intense and less expressive of all emotions, particularly anger, up till 10 years of age.[21] However, students whose parents fail to nurture them will be less able to regulate their feelings. If

in addition children happen to have hot temperaments, they are at risk of venting their feelings in ways that others consider to be inappropriate.[22] This can manifest as behavioural problems. Therefore, you will need to teach these students skills for self-regulation. To do this, you will need to:

- ensure that you do not blame, shame or humiliate students for their feelings or resulting behaviour
- express your own emotions appropriately to demonstrate to students how to do so
- help students to recognise and understand their own feelings by labelling these for them
- listen to students and reflect their feelings so that they expand their understanding of their emotions
- help students who are emotionally overwhelmed to feel safe, by giving support while they calm down. This will teach them that they can remain in command

---

BOX 17.2 — **Key points about feelings[23]**

- Difficult feelings are a necessary part of life and of struggling to live your values.
- What you feel now is exactly what you should be feeling, given your history and whatever you are doing or not doing.
- Feelings simply are: they do not need to be judged.
- Feelings have a natural life span: they do not have to be fixed or controlled, because they will go away by themselves.
- Difficult feelings are your allies: they alert you to your unmet needs.
- Difficult emotions teach you what matters enough in your life to hurt for.
- Feelings cannot harm you. If your feelings are clouds and your mind is the sky, once the clouds disperse, the sky is the same as it always was.
- Accepting that pain is inevitable gives you the freedom to do what matters and dignifies the effort you put in to living your life.

of the intensity and duration of their feelings, and therefore find them less distressing.

To be able to defuse emotion, we need some emotional literacy skills. To that end, it is useful to know the difference between thoughts and feelings.

Thoughts versus emotions

Feelings involve physical sensations (such as a chemical release in the brain and changes to our heart rate, blood pressure and so on). However, we could not interpret and understand the meaning of these physiological changes without *thinking* about the external events that might be stimulating them. The thoughts we choose to entertain about events determine both the type and intensity of the emotion that we experience.

Pleasurable feelings tell us that our needs are being met. These feelings signal that we are safe and, therefore, that we have an opportunity for growth.[24] In contrast, the unpleasant or negative feelings serve the vital survival function of signalling when we need something that we are not receiving. The purpose of unpleasant emotions is hinted by the very word e*motion*: these feelings mobilise us to take action to meet our needs.[25] For example, fear tells us that we need to take action to make ourselves feel safe again.

Our understanding of our feelings can get muddled when we mistake thoughts for feelings. One way to tell the difference is that we can non-verbally demonstrate feelings (such as being excited, happy or sad), whereas we cannot act out our thoughts. Another way is to identify the three types of 'fake' emotions. The first of these is *judgmental thinking*. This uses words such as '*should ... ought to ... should not*' to demand that we or others act in particular ways. The sequence begins when we experience an original feeling – such as hurt or fear – and then we generate demanding language; this, in turn, intensifies our original feeling. Ellis termed this *catastrophising*.[26] With our feelings inflamed, we then see threats that do not exist, underestimate our ability to cope, and exaggerate the consequences of not coping. The outcome is that our feelings become more difficult to resolve. In comparison, thoughts that accurately express our desires are less likely to provoke exaggerated emotions and they make it easier for us to focus on what we need. We may still have unpleasant emotions such as sadness, regret, sorrow, annoyance or frustration, but these are healthy in that they are realistic and are more likely to propel us towards solutions.

A second type of fake emotions is *thoughts in disguise*.[27] These are *I-feel* statements that are followed by words such as *that, as if,* or *like*:

I feel *that* I'm being asked to do too much.

I feel *as if* I'm the only one willing to go the extra mile.

I feel *like* I'm under pressure.

We can tell that these are thoughts, because they would make just as much sense if they were stated in these ways:

I *believe* that I'm being asked to do too much.

I *consider* that I'm the only one willing to go the extra mile.

I *am* under pressure.

When we give these statements the status of feelings, we believe that we are justified to act on them and to make others suffer for 'causing' them. Instead, we must realise that these are only thoughts, which we have chosen to invite in and entertain.

The third type of thinking that generates excessive or fake emotion is when we focus

---

BOX 17.3   **Comparison between judgmental and compassionate styles[28]**

Judgment	Compassion
Denies choice	*Acknowledges choice*
I have to, I must. I can't.	I choose to, I want to, I can.
There's only one way to meet needs.	There are many ways to meet needs.
Perceives scarcity	*Perceives abundance*
There's not enough to go around.	I am enough; you are enough.
We can't meet everyone's needs.	We can meet everyone's needs.
Life is competitive.	Life is a cooperative venture.
It's you or me.	It's you and me together.
Evaluates and judges	*Observes and expresses*
You're too . . .	Here's what happened . . .
He's mean; she's rude.	I see, I hear, I remember.
Ranks	*Celebrates*
Your behaviour earns you a place in my ranking system.	Expresses gratitude or acknowledges that your behaviour has created joy for me.
Blames others/Blames self	*Takes responsibility for my own feelings and needs*
I feel . . . because you . . .	I feel . . . because I need . . .
Makes demands	*Asks for what I would like*
You have to . . .	Here's what I'd like . . .
If you don't . . .	If you're willing . . .
Listens selectively	*Listens compassionately*
Suggests, lectures, advises, argues, fixes, analyses.	Are you feeling . . . because you need . . . ?

on how others 'should' be treating us. These thoughts place us in the role of victim and give power to others by placing them in the role of the enemy or our oppressor. Victim language includes words such as: *attacked, betrayed, excluded, intimidated, let down, manipulated, persecuted, taken for granted, used* and so on. This victim language implies that we believe that other people are to blame for how we feel: their behaviour 'makes' us feel as we do. When we believe this, we tend to demand that they stop it; believe that they deserve to be punished for how they are acting; and exaggerate the consequences if they do not desist. Instead, how we *feel* about others' actions depends on what we *think* about these.

Managing our emotions, then, (particularly, in our case, about students' disruptive behaviour) requires not only that we manage our thinking but also that we resist judging students or their behaviour, but instead silently empathise with ourselves so that we can identify what our emotion is telling us about which need of ours is not being met. We might feel intimidated by a behaviour, in which case our need for safety is unsatisfied; annoyance might signal that our need for a sense of order and control (autonomy) is being thwarted; while anger will signal an original need, plus the presence of judgmental thinking that is inflaming our emotions.

Listening

When we want to validate students and what they are feeling, we will need to listen to them. Listening to young people requires, first, that they are not so upset that they are not ready yet to talk, and for our part, that:[29]

- We have an *attitude* of acceptance towards children as people and are willing to allow them to be themselves and to feel as they do.
- We have the *intention* to empower children's own problem solving, rather than instruct, compel, advise, or solve children's problems for them. When something children are experiencing causes us pain, we will need to deal with those feelings – but later.[30]
- We use *skills* for decoding or interpreting what children are telling us.
- We have skills to reflect the thoughts, feelings and meaning behind what children tell us and to correct misunderstandings when they occur.

Even when students' behaviour is a problem for us, we will listen, rather than talk. If this fails, it is seldom because we have listened too much and more commonly because we have done most of the talking.[31]

Listening skill 1: Attention
Attending comprises the following cluster of skills:[32]

- Define your availability: if you cannot talk then, make a commitment to meet up later.
- Create a suitable space, with privacy and minimal distractions.
- Be present: don't just do something, *stand there*.[33]
- Tune in and attend to the most immediate needs first, connecting to what is alive for the student in the moment.
- Maintain a posture of involvement and appropriate eye contact, communicating

nonverbally that you are attending by approximating the child's tone of voice, gestures or facial expression.

Listening skill 2: Empathy

Empathy is a validation of what another person is feeling.[34] Whereas sympathy is being in touch with our own feelings in response to someone else, empathy is being connected to their experiences. Teachers will need to use empathic listening when young people are talking or behaving in ways that signal that they have a problem. This is easier to do when others display distress or sadness, but empathy is also needed when young people are acting in ways that inconvenience us. Even disruptive behaviour is an attempt to meet a need, while its intensity is a communication about how important that need is to the person performing the behaviour.

BOX 17.4 **Steps for giving empathy[35]**

Inner processing

Step 1. Be present. Focus on the other person's needs. At the moment, it is not about you. Connect with what is alive in the child at the moment.

Step 2. Form a careful, tentative impression of what the student is experiencing and needing.

Give empathy outwards

Step 3. Stay with the child. Use minimal encouragers and reflection to gain a deeper understanding of the needs, values and feelings that the child is expressing. (Some tips are given in Boxes 17.5 and 17.6.) Verify if your guess is accurate. The message here is that you want to be sure that you understand what the child needs. Even when your guess is slightly off target, it will still be helpful because it demonstrates an ethic of care and helps children to think through and understand their emotions.

Step 4. Check. Keep reflecting your impression of what they feel and need, until they give off a sense of relief and are quietened. These two signs mean that they have received the empathy they require. Once the relief is felt, check with the child, 'Is there more that you'd like to say?' Shift your attention away slowly. Move on only once you are sure that the child is finished.

Step 5. Empathise with the child's post-empathic request. When individuals are upset, they want to know that they have been understood. To signal your understanding, you can ask, 'Would you like to hear how I feel about what you said?'.

Occasionally, children will want some advice. However, our almost reflexive impulse to solve children's problems for them means that we will be too quick to give advice. Therefore, Rosenberg recommends that we should never give advice to children unless they request it in writing, with a lawyer's signature![36]

Listening skill 3: Decoding

Behaviour is children's loudest form of communication. To support and teach children, we need to abandon a behaviourist focus on *what* they are doing and instead care about *why*. Or, more specifically, on the understandings that all behaviour is an attempt to meet a need, and that needs are always legitimate, we must discover what need children are trying to satisfy by their actions.[37]

Note, however, that asking students *why* never works, because a request for insight will only confuse young people. (Besides, we already know *why*: their behaviour was an attempt to meet a need!) Instead, we will ask them *What* questions. Once we know what need inspired the behaviour, it will be easier to find a solution. The following questions will have to be adjusted to the circumstances and the age of the students, but will always be delivered in an enquiring tone (rather than an outraged '*What* do you think you're doing?').

- In what way did you hope that would help?
- What did you have in mind when you did that?
- What do you need right now?
- What can I do to help you?
- What is your objection to / problem with (doing what has been asked)?
- What can you do right now to feel better?
- I'm worried about you. Do I need to be?
- I'm feeling concerned for my safety while you're this angry. Do I need to be worried?

BOX 17.5

Examples of colloquial expressions of needs[38]

Need	Expression
Acceptance	You'd like people to accept you just as you are?
Autonomy	You'd like some choice about what you do?
Belonging	You want to be part of the group?
Consistency, order	You want to be able to count on things happening when you need them to?
Contribution	You'd like to be able to help/share?
Ease	You need this to be easier for you?
Inclusion	You want to be part of what's happening?
Mourning	You need to show how sad you're feeling?
Purpose	You want something worthwhile to do?
Security	You need to know that you're going to be okay?
Self-esteem	You want to feel good about yourself?
Validation	You want to be heard about how special/hard this is for you?

Listening skill 4: Reflection

Listening entails being reflective, in two senses. First, like a mirror, we will reflect what the other person feels and needs; and, second, listening requires us to be in a reflective, contemplative frame of mind that accepts others and 'lets them be'.[39] Rosenberg likens this to surfing – trying to go with the energy of the wave, of the moment.[40] When reflecting, we must always focus on the child's own experience, rather than on the actions of others. For example, instead of saying, 'Samantha is mean, isn't she?', reflect what the upset child *needs*: 'Sounds like you want Samantha to let you play because you need to be part of the fun'.

Roadblocks to communication

Tom Gordon identified that sometimes when we believe that we are listening, we are actually responding in ways that block communication and discourage others from talking with us. He called these mistaken listening responses *Roadblocks to communication*.[41] Most of our errors with listening come about with good intentions, in that we falsely believe that in order to be helpful we have to know all the answers, come up with the solutions ourselves, make the other person feel better, or be right.[42]

When we act on these false beliefs, we cause the problem to escalate in three vital

---

BOX 17.6 **Tips for reflection**[43]

- Listen for the thoughts, feelings and meaning behind what the child is saying.
- Encourage the other person to continue talking, using silence and minimal encouragers ('Mmm . . . Uh-huh . . . Okay . . . And . . . ?')
- Reflect the need underlying the feeling: 'Because of . . . you need . . .'
- Sum up what the other person said, translating it into your own words, making it clearer and more real.
- Check that you have understood and interpreted the speaker's meaning accurately.
- Reassure the speaker that he or she is being heard, that you 'get it'.
- When the speaker is expressing mixed feelings or separate ideas, include them all: 'You feel . . . and you also feel . . . (because you need . . .)'
- Vary your reflective statements. Do not use the same phrase, e.g. 'What I hear you saying is . . .' or 'So you need . . .'. With repeated formulaic responses, your listening can be perceived as a maddening word game.
- Ask very few questions – especially ones that call for a yes/no answer – because questions will direct, rather than follow, what the children say, and can make speakers feel that they are being subjected to an inquisition instead of being listened to.
- Avoid attempts to diagnose or interpret what the child is feeling, because interpretations are intellectual tools that distance us from being present and prevent us from offering emotional connection (empathy).

BOX 17.7   Useful reflective phrases[44]

When you think you understand the other person accurately, you might use reflective statements that start with:
- It seems that you need . . .
- It sounds like you feel . . .
- Are you feeling . . . because you need . . . ?
- From your point of view . . .
- You're feeling . . . (name the emotion)
- You believe . . .
- You mean that . . .
- In other words . . .

When you are not certain that you understand the other person accurately, use your ignorance constructively, trying reflective statements that start with:
- Let's see if I understand; you feel . . .
- I get the impression that you need . . .
- Is that what you mean?
- I'm sorry. I'm lost. Tell me again.
- Do you feel . . . ?
- Maybe I've misunderstood, but it seems . . .
- Is it possible that . . .
- Maybe it seems to you that . . .
- Maybe you need . . .
- Perhaps you're feeling . . .
- You seem to be feeling . . .
- It appears that you need . . .
- What I think you're saying is . . .

ways. First, the disruption can grow when young people who feel misunderstood become out of control of their emotions. Second, we convey subtle negative evaluations buried in our impatient or intolerant responses. Children will resent these messages and may act out in protest. Third, by communicating that we do not understand, children are left with their original feelings, plus the sense that they have no support. The resulting fear, shame or alarm will add to the strength of the original emotion.

Putting up barriers to communication sends the messages:

- I don't validate you ('Don't be silly').
- I won't validate you ('I don't care . . .').
- I want you to be someone else ('Your brother is so clever at this . . .').

- I want you to feel differently ('Don't worry').
- I want you to be different ('If you worked harder, you wouldn't have to panic over tests').
- I know better than you what you need.

The roadblocks convey a desire to change or influence others. They disrespect others by telling them what they are and are not experiencing and feeling.[45] In turn, children experience this lack of listening as threatening, manipulative, frustrating or condescending. As a result, they may avoid disclosing to us anything personal. Importantly, the roadblocks miss an opportunity to help someone in need so that they can grow in the direction that they choose.

BOX 17.8   **Communication roadblocks[46]**

We use these responses with the intention of communicating that we are listening but they in fact make it less likely that others will talk about anything significant.

Judging/Inducing shame
Judgmental responses can have devastating effects on children's self-esteem. They make children afraid of getting things wrong and of being reprimanded. Judgments all involve using labels that are inaccurate, hurtful, partial (in the sense of overlooking positive examples that contradict the label) and can be self-fulfilling. Judging others incites conflict with them, and gives outsiders the power to tell us who we are.

- *Criticising, blaming, name calling, ridiculing and making fun of children* all communicate to them that they are unloved, unworthy, stupid or 'no good'. Alternatively, criticism provokes 'answering back' in retaliation.
  Examples include:
  – You people are such slobs! Look at this mess!
  – Don't be ridiculous.
  – You must have done something to start it.
- *Emotional blackmail or martyrdom* tries to blame and induce guilt in others for how we feel. It overwhelms children with responsibility for things over which they have no control and therefore they feel powerless; alternatively, they reject the implication of fault and, with it, the person who is blameful.
  Examples include:
  – Look how angry you've got me!
  – It makes me sad when you do that.
  – How could you put me to so much work?
- *Praising or agreeing* with children is patronising, manipulates children into behaving the way we want and creates anxiety and the anticipation of criticism should they in future fail to meet our standards.

Examples include:
- You're *such* a good child that I know you'll do the right thing.
- You're so clever. I know you'll figure it out.

- *Diagnosing, analysing or interpreting* can be threatening and frustrating, causing children to feel trapped, exposed, misunderstood or disbelieved. Children will be afraid to say anything in case it is turned around and used against them.

  Examples include:
  - Maybe you're just still upset over what he said to you yesterday.
  - Perhaps you're jealous that she was playing with someone else?

Sending solutions (fixing)

Solving problems can *be* a problem because it does not resolve the original difficulty and limits the other person's growth and confidence.

- *Ordering, directing* or *demanding* are solutions backed by coercion. They demonstrate that you do not accept or respect individual children, suggesting that their judgment is unsound and that you do not care about their objections.

  Examples include:
  - Do it now – *or else!*
  - I don't want to have to tell you *again*!

- *Threatening, warning* or *delivering negative prophecies* will make children feel unaccepted, scared and meek; or, alternatively, resentful to such an extent that they are prepared to try us out to see if we will carry out our threat. Threats and ultimatums also remind children that they are not living up to our expectations.

  Examples include:
  - If I have to talk to you children about this again, I'll send you both to the principal.
  - You'll never pass your exams if you keep this up.
  - Be careful! You'll fall!

- *Preaching* or *moralising* are an attempt to 'put a halo' around our advice, giving it moral authority. This generates feelings of guilt, communicates the belief that children do not know right from wrong, and causes them either to retreat or to become defensive, with reactions such as, 'Who says I have to?' or 'You shouldn't either'.

  Examples include:
  - You ought to know better.
  - That wasn't very nice. How would you like it if someone did that to you?
  - What you have to understand is that other people have rights too.

- *Interrogating, probing, questioning* or *grilling* cause children to withhold information for fear that what they say will get them into trouble or result in being told what to do. Therefore, they learn to reply to interrogations with half-truths or lies, or without disclosing anything significant. If they are not sure where we are going with our questions, they feel intimidated and scared. They lose sight of the original problem.

Examples include:
- What's making you so upset, do you think?
- How long has this been going on?
- Are you sure that's what she meant?

• *Giving advice* makes children dependent, preventing them from thinking through their problems and considering different ways to solve them, and devalues the problem-solving skills they already possess. (Bolton calls it an 'interfere-iority complex'.)

Examples include:
- How about you do . . . ?
- I think you should try . . .
- What if you did . . . ?

Avoidance

When we avoid children's feelings, they receive the message that it is not alright to feel upset. It implies that their problems are not real or important, and stops children from being open about their concerns. When avoidance is used often with young people, they learn not to tell us about what matters to them in their lives.

• *Distracting, diverting, trivialising, story telling, one-upping and 'me-too'isms* suggest that if something is too hard, we should avoid it.

Examples include:
- Try thinking of something cheerful so you feel better.
- I had that happen to me when I was your age.
- Don't worry. Be happy.
- You think you've had a bad day? Try mine!

• *Persuasion, education or logical argument* can generate more conflict, or cause children to switch off and stop listening to us. It sends the message: 'Don't feel: think'.

Examples include:
- You know you'll be less stressed once this test is over with.
- Next time, do a mind map first so that you can get started on time.
- Give it a try. It will probably be more fun than you think.

• *Reassuring, sympathising, commiserating* or *consoling* cause children to feel misunderstood and alone – that is, feeling unsupported adds a second layer of emotion to the original feeling.

Examples include:
- Cheer up!
- I know you'll feel better tomorrow.
- That's really too bad. You poor thing.
- At least it could be worse.

Assertiveness

No specific behaviour will have the same effects on each outsider: any given action may interfere with meeting the needs of one person, whereas another is unaffected. Neither will actions have the same effects across time. A behaviour that did not interfere with our ability to meet our needs yesterday may provoke problems for us today. Moreover, our reactions can depend on our emotional state: when we are unwell, tired, worried, stressed or overwhelmed, we are less able to tolerate particular behaviours and more likely to need extra consideration. Our reactions can also be a product of the environment, context or timing: loud noise indoors will disturb us more than when it is outside, or a behaviour may bother us more when it is the tenth disruption compared with when it is only the second.

Children cannot know that their actions will have a negative effect on us now, when the same behaviour might not have bothered us previously. Because people are not mindreaders, if we do not tell them what we need, the chances are that they will not know.[47] Therefore, we need to be assertive, employing I-messages. These are in contrast with You-messages that tell students about themselves, with this difference distinguishing assertion from aggression – see Box 17.9.

Assertiveness is based on some core principles. First, it assumes that (regardless of age or other distinguishing characteristics) we each have the same rights to have our needs fulfilled and are happier when we can do so.[48] Therefore, while aggression is unfair to others, not listening to our own needs is just as inconsiderate as

not listening to others.[49] Second, we are each responsible for our own feelings and actions: the only behaviour we can change is our own.[50] Third, assertiveness is reciprocal, giving both adults and children permission to assert and defend their needs, with the result that respect and consideration are mutual.

The key benefits of assertiveness are that it provides predictability for others and respects their right to know where they stand with us. (In the language of behaviourism, it provides 'boundaries' or 'limits'.) Being assertive also communicates to others that you respect that they can handle what you tell them, while the opportunity to solve the problem protects the relationship because we do not become resentful.

I-messages

The usual three-part assertive message of: 'When you (do x), I feel (whatever) because . . .' is seldom effective, because it is dangerously close to blaming others for our feelings, as a result of which it produces defensiveness in listeners. In young children, this will manifest as a swagger or an eye roll while, in older children, you might even get a verbal response such as, 'Well, I'm sorry, but you've mistaken me for someone who cares!'. These responses are the inevitable outcome of using the 'you' part of the message.

Instead, the intent of I-messages is not manipulation or control, but honest communication. I-messages are authentic and describe our inner reality: they do not contain evaluations, judgments or opinions of others. There are four types: declarative, positive, preventive and problem solving.

BOX 17.9

A comparison of submission, aggression and assertion[51]

Submission	Aggression	Assertion
Your behaviour		
Do not express wants and feelings, or express them in a self-deprecating way.	Express wants, ideas and feelings at the expense of others.	Express wants, ideas and feelings in direct and appropriate ways.
Your intent		
To please, avoid conflict or rejection.	To dominate, humiliate or punish others.	To communicate.
Your feelings		
Anxious, disappointed with yourself, often angry and resentful, hurt and powerless.	Self-righteous, superior, sometimes embarrassed later.	Confident, feel good about yourself, both at the time and later.
Your response to anger		
Deny, repress, bottle up anger, or express it indirectly.	Explosive, blame others for your feelings, deny self-responsibility.	Accept anger; take responsibility for identifying the unmet need behind it.
Others' feelings about themselves		
Guilty or superior.	Humiliated, hurt.	Respected, valued.
Others' feelings about you		
Irritation, pity, disgust, confusion about your needs.	Angry, vengeful, feel justified at the prospect of 'getting even'.	Usually respect (although sometimes annoyance).
Outcomes		
Do not get what you want, anger builds up.	Often get what you want at the expense of others.	Often get what you need.
Payoff		
Avoids unpleasant conflict, tension and confrontation.	Aggressor vents anger; feels in control of others.	Feels good; respected by self and others; relationships are improved.

Declarative I-messages

This first type of I-message has no agenda. It just expresses your thoughts, feelings, values, opinions and ideas in the here and now. Declarative I-messages foster mutual understanding. Examples include:

- I like that song.
- I feel discouraged that this is taking so long.
- I don't enjoy musicals.

Positive I-messages

This type of I-message simply describes your positive feelings about students, with no intent to 'reward' or manipulate them, but just to appreciate them for who they are:[52]

- I'm enjoying doing this topic with you all.
- I like listening to you playing your music.
- I admire you.

Preventive I-messages

Preventive I-messages can prepare students for situations where they have experienced problems in the past, with the aim of preventing a recurrence. These messages can also flag a future need so that you create an opportunity for students to cooperate or change in ways that will fulfil your needs. For example:

- I'll need 10 minutes to get this paperwork done before the end of the afternoon.
- I will need some time with Ethan now to give him some pointers so he can get started.
- I'd like us to think about how we can organise next term's excursion.

Problem-solving I-messages

The fourth type of assertive message is the problem-solving I-message. This type is relevant when other people's actions are interfering with meeting our own needs. When we express that this is happening, it is important that we are clear that they are not responsible for looking after us and that neither they nor their behaviour are causing our feelings. These are a result of our thoughts or interpretations of events.

When we deliver a problem-solving assertive statement, we need to be ready to switch back to listening before repeating the message. Hence, this type of message has three parts.

Part 1: Assertion. My preferred formula for problem-solving I-messages is empathic assertion. This has four parts, with the examples given based on the scenario that students are having difficulty taking turns with the computer.

- *Self-empathy*: silently in your head, identify what you feel and what need this emotion signals . . . and *breathe*.
- *Empathy for the other*: 'I understand . . .' (that you all really enjoy the computer and need it for your research).
- *Statement of need*: 'Although I need . . . (things to be fair and for you all to solve this quietly so that everyone else can concentrate on what they're doing).
- *Solution building*: 'So what can we do so that you can all get what you need, without getting cross and disturbing the rest of us?' (The students might volunteer to write up a roster, to use a timer, or to listen to each person's arguments for needing priority access. You can guide them to select one solution that works for them while, of course, having the right of veto over any that would not also work for you or for their classmates.)

Part 2: Changing gears to listen. Even when you do not intend to accuse or blame other people, listeners can sometimes react as though you have. Regardless of your intent, they will react according to what they *think* you said and meant. Their responses can include:

- defensiveness: 'So? . . . Who cares . . . So what?'
- hostility: 'And I care because? . . . Tough . . . Boy, you're in a bad mood!'
- questioning (e.g. whether you had to do this kind of thing at their age)
- debating: 'Why do I have to?'
- becoming hurt and tearful or using a quivering voice
- withdrawing, avoiding eye contact
- becoming silent.

You do not have to worry when they become upset, as long as you are willing to change gears and *listen* compassionately to their reaction. Their responses simply signal that they now fear that their own needs will not be met.

Part 3: Recycling. Because listeners' feelings block their ability to understand your point of view, after their feelings are resolved through listening to their reactions, you will need to repeat your assertive message, clarifying your statement and checking that they have understood it. The key is persistence, and engaging in a repeated rhythm of asserting then reflecting the listener's response.[53]

Teaching students to be assertive

We need to be clear with students that the right to be assertive is mutual. This means that we must listen to them when they tell us about their needs, and that we must follow up when they have been assertive with a peer but their peer has not desisted. Our own use of I-messages will teach students how to disclose their feelings without upsetting others. Naturally, as with any complex skill, there will be times when children will get it wrong, perhaps using aggression instead of assertion. On these occasions, as for every other error, we need to understand that mistakes are inevitable, reflect the children's feeling or the underlying need, and support them to regain emotional control.

Making requests

There will be dozens of times every day when you ask students to do something. Being assertive means issuing requests, whereas demands attempt to control others by threatening, bossing, manipulating or shaming them. Particularly when students' behaviour troubles or inconveniences us, demands result from thinking that they 'make' us feel as we do. On this basis, we demand that they change. We can tell from our reaction whether we are issuing a demand: if we try to make the other person feel guilty for not complying or if we attempt to force compliance, we were making a demand.

Demands attract either submission or rebellion, as people feel forced into doing what we want because otherwise we can make their life miserable by blaming or punishing them.[54] The more that listeners hear demands, the less they will want to be around us and the more controlled they feel. In contrast, requests take the form:

- 'I understand that . . .
- and I feel . . . (Disclosure of feelings is optional and may even be ill advised

in relationships between an adult and child.)

- because I need/value/hope . . .
- therefore, would you be willing to . . .'

Again, we can tell if we are making a true request by noting our reaction to the other person's non-compliance. When we are willing to listen to, understand and accommodate their objections, we have made a request.

When we hear a 'No' to our request, we need to listen for the 'Yes' that is behind it. That is, when students are saying 'No' to one thing, they are affirming a 'Yes' to a different strategy for meeting a need. For

---

BOX 17.10

Differences between demands and requests[55]

Demands	Requests
Aims	
Our objective is to change others' behaviour.	We want others to consider us willingly out of compassion for our needs.
We want to meet our needs.	We want to find a strategy that meets both people's needs.
Our thinking	
Demands contain judgmental thoughts of others and assume that we are justified to demand compliance: ('*She should . . . He's supposed to . . . I have a right . . . I deserve . . .*').	Contain observations of others' actions that allow us to see them as human beings who are attempting to meet their needs and to make life enjoyable and satisfying.
Our responses	
We react to noncompliance with outrage and an attempt to punish in order to secure compliance.	We respect others' needs and are willing to listen to their objections empathically.
Our expressions	
Do this right now, or else!	I'd like us to find a solution that works for everyone.
Don't make me ask you again!	I'd like to hear how this sounds to you.
Just do as you're told!	I'm wondering what you need right now.
Don't talk back to *me*!	Would you be willing to . . . ?
How many *times* do I have to tell you?	Can you explain why doing it is a problem for you?
I don't care what you think.	Please help me understand what you have in mind.

example, they might refuse to sit down when asked because they need to move around (not because they are being defiant). Once we know the need, we might be able to discover a way that they can meet that need while still behaving in ways that consider others.

Sometimes, even when we are clear that we are making a request, listeners hear a demand. This is particularly likely when we have more power than they do, as is the case between teachers and students. With older children and adolescents, we can undo this by asking for their advice:[56]

- Would you be willing to tell me how I could say what I want so it wouldn't sound like I didn't care about what you'd like?
- How could I tell you what I want so that it didn't sound like I was bossing you around?

Collaborative problem solving

Collaborative problem solving is useful when both we and our students are bothered or inconvenienced by a behaviour. It is also needed for chronic, repeated problems that assertiveness has not resolved. Collaborative problem solving combines the skills of listening to others and asserting our own needs, and adds a structure for jointly generating solutions. It is essential when a solution will require a change in the student's behaviour.

As with the other communication skills, the people involved need to be motivated to solve the problem, and both parties need to be calm: you cannot reason with people while they are being unreasonable. In contrast with controlling discipline, which imposes solutions on

students, guidance trusts young people to know their own minds and to be able to generate workable solutions. When we recruit students' ideas about what they think will work, we increase the chances of finding relevant and vibrant solutions, not just because two heads are better than one, but because the students' contribution makes them more willing to put the solution into action.

Guidance also takes account of the differences in power between adults and children so that attempts at resolution do not put students at a disadvantage.[57] Within this context, our goals with collaboration are, first, to solve a challenging behaviour in a mutually satisfactory manner so that the solutions arrived at are durable.[58] The aim is not to find a compromise – in which no one's needs are met – but to find a strategy that honours and meets everyone's needs.[59] The second goal is to teach children the skills they lack, including taking another's perspective, listening to others, expressing their own needs, managing their own emotions and solving problems. Rather than teaching these skills in specific lessons, collaborative problem solving allows students to learn and practise the skills in real-life situations that concern them.[60]

Using the anagram SOLVED,[61] the basic steps for problem solving are:[62]

S *Specify the problem.* Use I-messages to disclose your needs and listen empathically to the student's expression of his or her needs: 'I wonder if there is a way to help you when you get frustrated, so that you don't have to bolt out of the classroom?'.

O Invite the student to contribute to generating *options* for solving the problem: 'What are your ideas?' Brainstorm all possibilities and listen to all suggestions.

L Consider the *likely outcomes* of these options.

V Choose the solution that seems *viable* (or, for younger children, the *very best one*) – that is, one that is realistic (which means that it is achievable by the child and in the circumstances) and mutually satisfactory. This stage recognises that the solution is not predetermined. When you hear acquiescence but are uneasy about the student's commitment, you can say, 'I'm feeling uneasy with your 'Okay'. Can you reassure me that you're happy with what we've decided?' or 'I'd like you to take a moment to check that you're happy to do what we've agreed'.

E *Enact* it and *evaluate* how it is working.

D *Do it again: re-negotiate.* If subsequently the solution fails, this simply signals that the previous plan did not capture the original problem, or the solution was too ambitious. You will need to repeat the process to generate a different strategy until one is found that those involved *can* achieve and which works to meet both their needs.

Collaborative problem solving can go wrong when, instead of stating their concern, adults attempt to impose a solution. This can result in 'duelling solutions'[63] that, in turn, can result in meeting halfway. However, this is rarely an ideal solution. Instead, durable solutions will typically entail one of three options: giving the student some help; giving a little in your expectations; or doing things differently.[64]

Problem solving between students

When students are in dispute with each other and appear to be unable to resolve it themselves, the following steps can be useful:

BOX 17.11 Differences between listening and assertiveness

When a child is upset	When I am upset
I am a listener.	I am the sender.
I am a counsellor.	I am an influencer.
I want to help the child.	I want to help myself.
I am interested in the child's needs.	I am primarily interested in my own needs.
I am a sounding board.	I want to sound off.
I help the child to find his or her own solution.	I need to find a solution myself.
I can accept the child's solution: I do not need to be satisfied.	I must be satisfied with the solution.
I am more passive.	I am activated.

- *Discover what the conflict is about* by asking: 'What's going on?' (in an enquiring tone that seeks information in order to help, not in an accusatory tone that seeks information in order to blame someone).
- *Restate the problem*: 'I can see your problem. There are two of you and there is only one bat'.
- *Guide the children to find their own solution*: 'What can you do?' Suggest solutions if the students are too young to generate their own (which is typically not necessary once they are of school age).
- *Ask them to choose and commit to a solution* that satisfies them both.
- *Invite them to seek further help if needed*: 'If you have any more trouble, come and ask me for more help'. (This last step may be unnecessary with older children and adolescents.)

Conflicts of values

While most conflicts between adults and children will be over behaviours that interfere with each person's ability to meet his or her needs, some will be about differing values. Unlike needs, values are *learned* and, if someone else does not abide by our values, this has no tangible effect on us. Gordon gives the example that if you declared to your neighbour that you didn't like her car and she should buy a different one, she is not likely to be willing to do as you say, on the grounds that it's none of your business because her choice of vehicle does not affect you.[65]

Because conflicts over values do not interfere with meeting our needs, any fear in us that our needs will not be met is misplaced. Instead, values conflicts are about autonomy – that is, about being self-governing and choosing our personal behaviour for ourselves. Young people accept that adults have the right to insist that they behave in morally principled ways but, from a surprisingly young age, children resent adults' attempts to make them conform to conventional or non-moral rules, or to restrict their personal choices (such as their choice of clothes).[66] This is because they recognise that these personal behaviours do not detract from other people's ability to live their lives.

As adults, it is our duty to teach children values that we believe will help them to live their lives both now and in the future. However, our duty is to teach them *how* to think morally, not *what* to think. Just as we filtered our own parents' values, young people will be selective about which of ours that they adopt. This is how societies make progress. Therefore, while we can model and teach our values, we cannot impose them on others.

Managing anger

Given the closeness of their relationship, primary school teachers experience more anger with their students than do high school teachers.[67] Teachers report that a common trigger into anger is when students whom they are trying to help are not responding to their efforts, or when students show their teachers up in front of the class or defy their authority.[68] In my experience, however, a large part of this anger is at ourselves for not knowing what to do about the behaviour, rather than at the student as such.

Anger occurs in three phases. First, we need something that we are not receiving. This gives rise to a feeling – say, of hurt

BOX 17.12 Responding to conflicts of values[69]

Assertiveness is not applicable to conflicts of values, because there is no tangible effect on us if children do not abide by our values. Their non-observance does not stop us from breathing the air we need to stay alive. Using power to make children comply or threatening to use power to insist that they abide by our values will only incite rebellion and generate problems of enforcement.[70]

Instead, we can:

- Ask for consideration of our values (e.g. not to use certain swear words in our company). When our relationship is empathic, children may voluntarily observe these standards out of courtesy, even when they have no obligation to do so.
- Share with students our life's lessons that cause us to be concerned about their behaviour. (This is suitable only for recently emerging difficulties; it will not work if delivered as a repeated lecture.)
- Model our own values in the hopes that students will come to cherish them also.
- Respect that young people's values differ from our own and decide not to turn the difference into a point of contention.
- Listen to the students' reasons for their beliefs and, when persuaded, change our own attitudes accordingly.

– that motivates us to do something to satisfy our needs. In this way, our original feelings are our allies, alerting us to the fact that our needs are not being met. We can think of them as being like the car's dashboard light that signals when its engine is overheating, or an alarm clock waking us up to what we need.[71]

Second, we fear that our needs will not be met. This heightens our arousal level.

Third, in this inflamed state of mind, we may judge others to be in the wrong, and demand that others *should* supply what we need. When they do not, we blame them for 'making' us angry. In other words, anger is stirred up by a diversion into judgmental thinking that adds to the intensity and unpleasantness of our original feeling.[72] This is illustrated in Figure 17.2 in which anger is depicted as the part of the iceberg that is visible above water level, with the bulk of the feeling below the surface.

Anger = a feeling about an unmet need
   + fear that the need will not be met
   + demanding thinking

At the end of this unhelpful sequence of mistaken thinking, we are likely to speak or behave in a way that will virtually guarantee that we will not get what we want – or that, if we do, it will not be given willingly.[73] Instead, rather than judging the student (for acting in that way) or ourselves (for not knowing what to do about it), we can connect empathically with our own and with the student's needs.

Being compassionate and empathic will require us to create some space for processing. This means that the basic steps for dealing with anger are:[74]

FIGURE 17.1   **Pathways for selecting a communication skill**

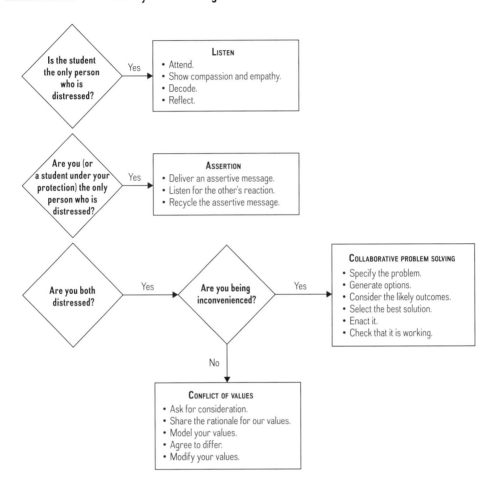

1. *Stop*. Take a few deep breaths. Take some time to connect with yourself.
2. *Identify your unmet need* that gives rise to your first feeling.
3. *Identify the judgmental thoughts* that are causing your anger. Listen out specifically for the words *should, shouldn't, ought, must* or *must not*.
4. *Reconnect with your intention or purpose*. Decide what you want to achieve right now for yourself and for your relationship with the student.
5. *Express your feelings* and unfulfilled need. (Again, expressing feelings is optional within a professional relationship and, at times, may even be unwise.)
6. *Request what the other person can do to meet your needs*, using language that avoids judgments and criticism.

These steps are based on the recognition that, like us, the student with whom we are angry is simply trying to meet a need. The conflict is not because our needs are

FIGURE 17.2 The anger iceberg

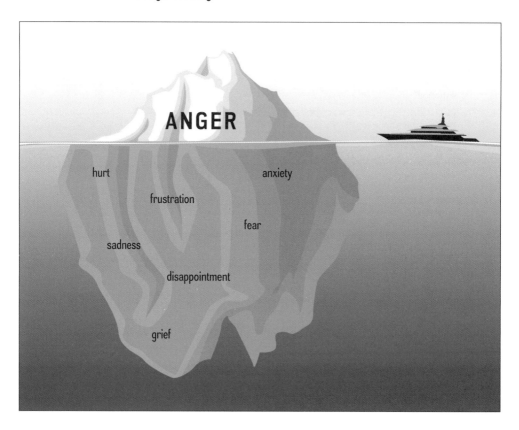

in opposition, but because the strategies they are using to meet their needs interfere with our ability to meet ours. Once we can identify the underlying need, we will be able to generate alternative strategies for meeting it. In this way, we have not achieved a compromise but a solution that suits both people involved.

Apologies

Rosenberg says seeking an apology and insisting that others feel remorseful implies that we are judging them to be in the wrong, when all they were doing was attempting to meet their needs (albeit unskilfully sometimes). We are addicted, he says, to making others suffer and feel badly for their misdeeds.[75] Instead, when our needs have not been met, the appropriate response is to mourn this, rather than to seek revenge.[76] When we are in touch with an unmet need, we will feel sadness, but not depression or anger.

When students have said something hurtful to us, we must take care not to take it personally. It is not their job to look after us but ours to look after them. Therefore, we cannot seek an apology. If one is offered, it is a credit to the young person, given the power differential between teachers and students. It is also a signal of the health of the relationship, given that students find it impossible to offer a sincere apology to adults who exercise control over them.

When students have hurt a peer, our first step will be to empathise in the perpetrator's hearing with the victim's physical and emotional pain, and apologise on the perpetrator's behalf. If we attempted to force an apology from perpetrators, they may refuse, lie by saying they are sorry when they are not, or offer an apology grudgingly – upon which we have to demand, 'Now say it like you mean it!'. If during the process of comforting the victim, the perpetrator offers an apology willingly, that will be heartfelt.

When we recognise that we have failed to meet someone else's needs, we can feel sad, but not guilty or ashamed. Depression, anger, guilt and shame are blameful. Nevertheless, when we have wronged students, we will gain their respect if we can find the courage to acknowledge this – both to ourselves and to them. They already know that we have wronged them; they don't yet know if we are heroic enough to admit it.

Conclusion

Advocates of a controlling approach believe that only consequences will make children accountable for their actions. In this usage, *accountable* means seeking retribution for children's misdemeanours. In contrast, guidance aims to teach young people skills so that the misdeed is not repeated. Under this approach, students become *accountable* for participating in finding solutions and for taking others' concerns into account.[77]

One benefit is that, because students choose willingly to cooperate with teachers who consider them, teachers feel 'in control', without having to exercise power over students or enforce their compliance. Meanwhile, victims and onlookers do not need perpetrators to suffer for their actions: they need them to develop skills that will prevent a recurrence.[78]

The communication skills detailed here are not just to build better relationships with children – although that is a laudable end in itself – but also because, when students experience receiving empathy and being listened to, they learn how to return those courtesies; teachers also gain the information that we need to assist with solving the problem that triggered the disruptive behaviour; and, by engaging young people in the process of problem solving, not only do we ensure a better quality solution but we are simultaneously teaching students self-regulation and problem-solving skills, a weakness in which is a core reason for their challenging behaviour in the first place.

Recommended further reading

Bolton, R. (1987). *People skills.* Sydney: Simon & Schuster.

Faber, A. & Mazlish, E. (1999). *How to talk so kids will listen and listen so kids will talk.* New York: Avon.

Faber, A., Mazlish, E., Nyberg, L. & Templeton, R.A. (1995). *How to talk so kids can learn at home and in school.* New York: Fireside.

Gordon, T. (1974). *Teacher effectiveness training.* New York: Peter H. Wyden.

Hart, S. & Hodson, V.K. (2004). *The compassionate classroom: Relationship based teaching and learning.* Encinitas, CA: Puddle Dancer Press.

Rosenberg, M.B. (2003). *Nonviolent communication: A language of life.* (2nd ed.) Encinitas, CA: Puddle Dancer Press.

——(2005). *The surprising purpose of anger: Beyond anger management: Finding the gift.* Encinitas, CA: Puddle Dancer Press.

Websites

Cate Crombie: www.metacommunicate.com

Center for Nonviolent Communication: www.cnvc.org

CHAPTER 18

Providing support

When a person is drowning that is not the time to
give swimming lessons.[1]

During crises, such as when children are in danger, talk will not do the work we need it to do to keep them safe. (A lecture that 'Force equals mass times acceleration' will not keep a child from running onto a busy road!) Talk also does not work when students already know what we are telling them. At those times when they already know how they should be behaving, another sermon on the topic will be fruitless.

We can discover if they know what they should be doing, by asking ourselves two questions:

- How many times have I told this student about this particular behaviour?
- How many times would I have to tell this student where I had hidden some chocolate?

If the number in answer to the first question exceeds the number in answer to the second, we know that they know how they should be behaving, because the second question is a measure of their memory capacity. Given that most children have been told directly or have overheard a peer being told about most prosocial behaviours by the age of three years, this means that after that age, the behaviour is unlikely to be due to a lack of knowledge – but instead, to a lapse of self-control. In that event, we need to support children to regain control.

Similarly, when students are in emotional meltdown (drowning in emotion, as it were), they need support to calm down. You cannot reason with people while they are being unreasonable and therefore the communication skills outlined in chapter 17 will not be helpful – yet.

As far as we can tell, humans are the only species that have feelings *about* our feelings: we can panic over the intensity of our emotions. This is particularly likely the younger we are. Very young children lack words to explain what they are feeling and why and, because they have less experience at resolving emotion, can worry that they might not be able to calm down without help. Even adults can panic about the intensity of our feelings: for example, when we are in grief over the loss through death of or desertion by someone we love, we can be so intensely sad that we panic that we are going crazy. Given this tendency to panic over extreme emotion:

Children need our compassion the most when they appear to 'deserve' it the least.[2]

Rationale for support

Support is provided to students with disruptive behaviour on the reasoning that:

- Children do well if they can.
- A given student is not doing well.
- This is evidence that it is difficult for this student (although you may not know why that is the case).
- Given that it is clearly more difficult for this student than for others, you will offer extra support.

Many of us believe that we have to have the solutions to other people's problems (especially children's). However, we are not the ones experiencing the problem. Given that people know more about themselves than outsiders ever will, students can teach us what they need. By asking them for their ideas about what they think will work for them, we increase the chances of finding solutions. We can do this through collaborative problem solving or by inviting students to act as our consultant, asking questions such as, 'When I work with another student with this kind of problem, what do you think I should do to help him/her?'.[3]

Responding to emotional meltdowns

Given that our survival as infants demanded that we communicate all feelings, it is inevitable in people of all ages that there will be lapses of self-control. (You might recall your own lapses when on a diet!) Although some spontaneity in life is desirable, when children feel overwhelmed by their feelings or are indulging inconsiderate impulses, we need to teach them how to calm themselves, providing a safety net for them while they do so.

Lapses in appropriate self-control could be termed emotional meltdowns. Four common patterns are the following.[4]

- *Protesting tantrums*: thrashing about, screaming, crying, spitting, self-harm (e.g. head banging). Beyond the age of three, these are uncommon.
- *Whingeing or whining*: the passive version of the protesting tantrum, involving sulking, whining, nagging and complaining over a disappointment. By three and a half years of age, children can use language when distressed and can concentrate for longer and therefore this meltdown has a greater duration than the active protest. Although the decibels are lower, the dynamic is the same: the student cannot overcome the disappointment or frustration of the moment.
- *Aggression*: name calling, hitting others, biting (after the age of 18 months), bossing others, refusing to share or take turns, bullying and exclusion. Aggression takes two forms:
  - *reactive* aggression, in which children lose control of themselves in reaction to a trespass on their rights. In this case, they are out of control of their feelings (principally anger).
  - *proactive* aggression, in which they hurt another not in response to a provocation, but simply because they *can*. In this event, they are out of control of their impulses or ideas.
- *Uncooperativeness*: not being able to overcome their distaste for a (reasonable)

directive and therefore refusing to follow it on the grounds that they 'don't feel like it'.

All these behaviours signal that children are feeling something unpleasant and cannot get past that emotion to get on with what needs to be done. Emotion (not reason) is driving their actions. The guidance approach considers their resulting behaviours to be 'cues and clues' that they are out of control emotionally. It is clear that, while we do not have to tolerate (or be *patient* with) the resulting inconsiderate behaviour, we do have to *understand* that children are still learning self-control. If we punished them for lacking self-regulation skills, we would be punishing them for *being* children. Instead, we must look for a solution, not a culprit.[5]

Our reasoning, again, is that we know that they know how they should be behaving, but are experiencing a temporary lapse of self-control. In that event, we do not have to re-teach what they already know – but, instead, teach and support them to get back in control. The only two methods that humans have for doing so are to receive some support from someone we care about, or do something that soothes us.[6]

Time in

Therefore, the first method is to bring children in close physically or emotionally, so that we give them support to calm down and ensure that they do not become alarmed by the intensity of their feelings. In broad terms, this can mean staying with them until they have fully resolved their feelings. This is usually only necessary for those aged under four years (because children this young find it difficult to calm down without support), and when children's feelings have frightened them into hysteria. Staying with them can mean sitting beside them, sitting them next to you while you continue your teaching, or having them shadow you while you perform your regular duties. All along, you will be saying that you're there for them until they feel better. If you are called elsewhere, you can pass them over to another teacher for that person to keep them company.

For older students, time in will seldom involve being physically close, but perhaps standing near them and saying, 'You look like you're having a tough day. Anything I can do to help?' or 'Some days it's not easy being you, is it?' or 'I can see you're upset. Can you get on with things anyway, or do you need some time before you get down to work?'.

If the students escape (which is less common when they are clear that you are not coercing but in fact protecting them), do not chase them: you will look ridiculous. Instead, wait until they return into your orbit and draw them in close to you again then, even if they are already calm.

The object of time in is for you to be students' safety net when their own feelings are out of their control. This must be nurturing and should never be accompanied by a discussion about their wrongdoing: they already know this anyway, so there would be no point. Instead, you will chat with them about their lives or a shared interest, for example.

You cannot use time in if students are thrashing about violently and risk injuring themselves or you. Instead you will use the next approach (time away) and then follow up with time in.

Time away (sanctuary)

When help is not available from someone who cares about us, humans' second strategy for soothing their stress is to do something visual (such as watching TV); something auditory (such as listening to music); or something physical (such as exercising or having a rest). What none of us has ever thought to do when we need to calm down, is to sit ourselves on a chair in the laundry facing the wall. This reflects the difference between time-out and time away: with time-*out*, the message is that it is naughty/ unacceptable/ inappropriate to get out of control of feelings, and you are to be punished for doing so; with time *away*, the message is that everyone gets upset sometimes and that, when no one is available to help them, they will find comfort by going off somewhere pleasant and doing a favourite activity ('chilling out') until they feel better.

The use of time in and time away is based on early liberal principles that individuals' freedom can be curtailed if their actions could harm others.[7] Accordingly, when students are harming themselves or others, you are justified to *insist* that they remain with you (in time in) or in time away until they are back in control of themselves. But, unlike coercive force whose aim is to enforce compliance[8] ('Do it because I said so'), the aim of protective force is to:

- protect students from injury
- protect individuals from injustice
- provide a safety net for young people whose feelings are scaring them
- protect students from developing a negative reputation and being rejected

---

BOX 18.1

Tips for responding to meltdowns[9]

- For protesting tantrums, listen and reflect children's feelings, using a 'broken record' technique of repeating similar consoling statements, without debating the reasons for the child's protests: 'I understand that you're angry . . . I'm sorry you're feeling so upset . . . I'll be here for you until you feel better'.
- When young children are regularly whingeing (or whining), ask them if they can find their 'happy voice' or if they can ask again happily. If they cannot, they need soothing.
- For social meltdowns (aggression), in the presence of the aggressor, empathise with and soothe the victim, apologise on behalf of the aggressor and, when the victim is mollified, turn to the aggressor and say, 'I wouldn't let them hurt you and I cannot let you hurt them'. Insist that the perpetrator remain in your company but separate from peers until she or he 'feels better and you know that the other children will be safe'.
- When students are not cooperating with a reasonable request, on occasion you can allow them to have a 'slack attack' and not perform tasks that they object to. Or you can ask what their objection is. For repeated refusals, announce, 'I'll wait'. The students already know what is required of them and why, in which case this announcement just gives them time to get in touch with their own reasons for completing the task.

by peers as a result of their antisocial behaviour.

Moreover, whereas under controlling discipline, coercive force is common, under guidance protective force is reserved only for emergencies and hence is used rarely.

Contracts (or deals)

As used by controlling discipline, contracts can cement an agreement about young people's behaviour. But authoritarian contracts about students' behaviour usually list what students must do and detail what will happen to them if they do not. Instead, under the guidance approach, contracts will have two parts. Part one specifies – in negotiation with young people – how you need them to behave. You would check that they agree that these expectations are reasonable. (With aggression, for example, your rationale would be, 'I wouldn't let the others hurt you and I cannot let you hurt them'.)

Part two of the contract is guided by the sequence of reasoning given earlier: students behave well when they can; this student is not behaving well; this means that she or he cannot. (Often, we will not know *why*, only *that* the student is having difficulties.) In that event, the student needs extra help. Therefore, the second part of the contract will list the *help* you will give (not the rewards you will supply). This help might be in the form of a secret signal that you arrange to use as a reminder to calm down; it could be provision of a chill-out space to which a student could withdraw when feeling overwhelmed; it could be that she is given a card to put onto your desk when she needs to leave the room to go to

the counsellor's office for a chat. I don't know what will help a given student until I ask. And if the help doesn't help, we will need to find something else that will.

This is the same approach that we use for students with additional educational needs – for example, we do not try to change a student with a vision impairment by demanding, 'Use your eyes!'. Instead we adjust the environment (e.g. lighting, size of print, and distance from the teacher) to enable students with impaired vision to circumvent their impairment. Similarly, when individuals have difficulties considering others, we need to adjust the demands and supports we provide to make it easier for them to circumvent their difficulties so that they can function successfully.

Abandon coercion

When students are displaying ongoing chronic behavioural difficulties, adults in the grips of authoritarian beliefs will often proclaim that they have 'tried everything' to get a behaviour to stop. This statement means that they have tried every *consequence*. This, however, is not the same as having tried *everything*. Guidance advises that, typically, the one thing we have not tried is abandoning coercion.

'Giving up' is based on recognition that the vast majority of chronic behavioural problems in children aged over four years are reactive – that is, the children are protesting at being denied self-determination.[10] Therefore, this approach abandons trying to 'make' students change their behaviour. Reserved mainly as a last resort for students who are repeatedly aggressive, it entails the following steps.

- Tell the student that you – and everyone else who has been involved (and you name each adult individually: parents, former teachers, current teachers, the principal, counsellor) – have tried everything you can think of to make the behaviour stop. You realise that this is not working, so are giving up.
- Explain that the behaviour still has to stop. Therefore, someone has to think of a way for it to stop. (Given that everyone you have just named has run out of ideas, the clear implication is that the student will have to be the one to figure out what to do to solve it.)
- Remove aggressors from the group setting. They might, for example, sit outside the principal's office. Here, however, they are not to be treated as if they are 'in trouble': adults will be friendly, kindly and supportive, and will not talk about the troublesome behaviour but instead chat about whatever interests the student. The student can help clerical staff to staple and collate papers, can run messages around the school, complete school work, read, eat and generally have a pleasant time (although computer games are probably unwise, as these will be too much of a distraction). Nevertheless, the adults steadfastly insist on separation until the student 'thinks of a way to keep everyone else safe'. The student remains separated from peers (but not from adults) for as long as it takes – hours, days or even weeks – for him or her to figure out a plan for ending the behaviour.
- Once aggressors declare that they have a solution and will stop the behaviour, congratulate them but advise that the difference between a goal and a dream is that a goal has a plan.[11] The rationale here is that resolutions made in haste are broken in haste. (Recall your own New Year's resolutions.) Hence, adults need to put the brakes on students' enthusiasm, to give them all the time they need not only to come up with a plan, but also to develop commitment to it. Therefore, students will need to stay with adults until they have been able to develop a plan. As with all other contracts or deals, this plan will ultimately have two parts: how they will manage their impulses and emotions so that they can resist the temptation to lash out at others, plus what supports you will provide to help them do this.
- Once you are satisfied that there is a viable plan, allow them to return to the group. If they become aggressive shortly thereafter, this simply means that they need longer to think how to manage their behaviour. You will insist that they return to the company of the adults. After this second withdrawal period, you will need to re-negotiate the contract, making sure that it is not too ambitious.
- To convince them that you have ceased all coercion, it can help to give the 'I'm-not-your-enemy' speech which can be any variant on, 'Excuse me. I'm not the enemy. I am here to help you become the kind of person you want to be' or 'I'm not your enemy. I'm here to help you enjoy your time at school, and keep you and everyone else safe'.

A word of caution: this method does not work when adopted from a behaviourist stance of trying to make the perpetrator stop. When applied to aggression, the method honours that humans are a social species and, therefore, that when you cannot be sociable, you cannot be social (that is, have access to the group). Although perilously close to a consequence, I see this as a natural outcome of being unwilling to keep others safe. The method works because it employs protective force, aimed not at coercing compliance, but instead at ensuring that the student's peers are safe from injury and that the aggressor is protected from developing a negative reputation. Therefore, you will need to emphasise its inherent justice ('I wouldn't let them hurt you, and I cannot let you hurt them') lest students mistake it for controlling discipline.

Conditions needed for change

Giving up coercion rests on the belief that the person performing the behaviour has to be the one accountable for making it stop. It recognises that change requires four conditions:

- *discomfort*: this motivates action
- *information about alternatives*: this informs change
- *self-efficacy*: the belief that we can make those alternatives a reality – this empowers change
- *self-esteem*: the conviction that we deserve better sparks the courage to make changes.

However, when students have been aggressive for some time, everyone around them is distressed by their behaviour – but they are not. Because they value aggression, they can be doing very nicely. The intent of giving up using coercion is to communicate that, while we will not punish them or try to make them change their behaviour, we are willing to do all we can to keep everyone safe at school. At heart, this is an attitude, not a technique.[12] It is an application of protective force (which supplies the discomfort); at the same time as implying that we believe they have other options (which informs change); that we trust that they can change (promotes self-efficacy); and that they *deserve* to the given the time needed to resolve the problem (supporting their self-esteem).

Monitor effectiveness

Once a solution is in place, you will need to check that it is working. To establish if you need to move to the next level, your decision process could follow the steps in Figure 18.1. You might also refer to Figure 10.3 (see page 148) to guide you about where the source of an ongoing problem might lie.

Consistency

Life is inconsistent. *People* are inconsistent.[13] The reason that behaviourism deplores inconsistency is that rewards and punishments are so ineffective that they have to be delivered for each and every instance of a behaviour. In contrast, guidance recognises that the more practice you get, the more quickly you will learn something. Therefore, the more often we can support students to regain control of their feelings, the more quickly they will learn it. You could take students for daily swimming lessons and they will become competent in two weeks; or, if you took them once a month, they would still learn

FIGURE 18.1   **Evaluating solution effectiveness**

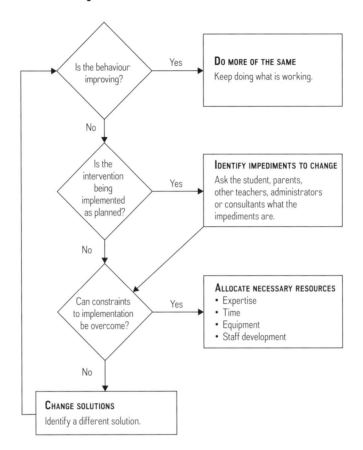

to swim – but it would take longer. This tells us that, while consistency is not necessary, repeated practice helps.

Although abandoning the notion of consistency, you will nevertheless be *steadfast* in your resolution that students will act thoughtfully. But how you respond to any given instance of thoughtlessness will be a matter of your own wise judgment and what the circumstances at the time will permit.

The corollary of this message is that all teachers do not have to respond to students in the same way – to 'gang up'

on the student.[14] If some use controlling discipline and some use guidance, students will not be confused. They will simply have poor relationships with the former, and warm (and cooperative) relationships with the latter. As I say to parents when one is controlling and the other favours guidance: they will not have parenting problems; they'll have marital problems. The same is true within staff teams: inconsistency will not confuse students, but it *will* impair team functioning.

The second corollary is that parents do not have to be using the same methods at home that we do at school. Students' behaviour at school is largely triggered by events there and, again, they can learn at school to manage their emotions, even if at home they are not supported to do so. The more practice they get, the quicker they will learn it. It would be better if they had practice in most places but, if they do not get practice at home they will still learn it at school: it will just take longer.

Conclusion

Behaviourists believe that time in and time away are rewards for inappropriate behaviour. Guidance believes that it is not about rewarding or punishing – but about *teaching*, in this case teaching how to recover from intense emotion. Getting help from someone who cares about us or doing something relaxing until we feel better, are indeed the only two strategies that our species has for calming down.[15] Supporting students while they find their own solutions and while they locate their reasons for employing them is considerably easier than having to find the solutions yourself. It is liberating.

Recommended further reading

Greene, R.W. (2010). *The explosive child*. New York: Harper.

CHAPTER 19

Revealing solutions

*There is nothing wrong with you that what's right
with you couldn't fix.*[1]

Teachers will be readily able to use some of the methods to be described in this chapter; whereas (as is true for the advanced behaviourist methods), others might be more relevant for school counsellors or other specialists.

A solution-focused approach

My discipline of psychology has given us a model that looks for problems and tries to fix what causes them. However, even if we could identify the cause, sometimes it cannot be fixed, perhaps because it occurred in the past, or because we do not have the technology (e.g. to fix 'central auditory processing disorder'). At other times, as outsiders we do not have enough information about what is happening in children's lives to be able to identify the cause and then solve the problem; or, even if we have the information, we cannot access sufficiently qualified professionals to do the work.

Solution-focused ideas offer a second option. Instead of focusing on what is not working and trying to fix it, we can focus on what *is* working and try to use it. Accordingly, our task is not to assess problems, but to listen out for individuals' accounts of what is working.[2] Like a detective, we use persistent questioning and listening to reveal the natural solutions that those involved are already using.[3] Respondents' answers (rather than our own assumptions) will provoke our next question.

Principles of a solution-focused approach

Just as the orchestra conductor trusts the musicians to know their instrument,[4] guidance trusts young people to know their own minds. From this fundamental principle of a solution-focused approach, all others flow.

Principle 1. People know more about themselves than outsiders ever will. This means that when people have problems, they are more familiar with those problems than outsiders can ever be.[5] They are the experts on how the problem affects their lives and, often unbeknownst to themselves, are the experts on how they can change it.

BOX 19.1

Comparisons between problem solving and solution building[6]

Problem solving	Solution building
Attempts to understand what is going wrong and how to fix it.	Focuses on what is working and how to use it.
Focuses on weaknesses and deficits.	Focuses on strengths and resources.
Examines instances of problems.	Examines exceptions to difficulties.
Asks why people do things.	Asks how people do things.
Focuses on the past.	Emphasises future possibilities.
Sees people as sick.	Sees people as stuck.
Regards people as flawed.	Sees people as capable.
The adviser aims to diagnose.	The adviser aims to uncover solutions.
The adviser is responsible for providing a solution.	The person experiencing the problem is the source of its solution.
The adviser is the expert.	The individual with the problem is the expert.
The client follows the expert's lead.	The adviser follows the client's lead.
The adviser tells.	The adviser asks and listens.
The adviser is certain.	The adviser is curious.
The adviser takes credit for progress.	Individuals take credit for their own progress.

Principle 2. Individuals have reasons for their behaviour – namely, it is meeting a need; if it weren't, the behaviour would stop.

Principle 3. Problems signal that people are stuck, not sick. People persist with ineffective responses in the hopes that these will work eventually. This is not because they are foolish or illogical, but because they have too much faith.

Principle 4. The person is not the problem: *the problem is the problem.*[7] Our focus has to be on solving the difficulty, not finding who is to blame for it. We will look for a solution, not a culprit.

Principle 5. All individuals, no matter how stuck, are doing *something* to prevent their problems deteriorating. Instead, therefore, of focusing on aspects of their lives that are not working, we need to direct our focus onto those things that *are* working.

Principle 6. All environments, no matter how bleak, provide some resources to support individuals to be effective in their lives. Even families enduring adversity draw on internal resources and external supports to assist them to function.

Principle 7. The problem is not with the individuals involved, but with the way they are interacting. Put another way, the problem is not the dancers: *it's the dance*. When students' behavioural difficulties are chronic, a repeated cycle (or 'dance') of adult coercion and child defiance develops, as illustrated in Figure 10.4 (see page 149). Given that this cycle is circular, the search for an initial cause is both fruitless and unnecessary, because there *is* no beginning or end in a circle. As the starting point does not matter, the place to intervene in this repetitive cycle is with the adult, because we are the ones with most power and because no one can make anyone else change. We can influence only ourselves.

Principle 8. Finally, solution-focused theory accepts that small changes can make a big difference.[8] Just as when we drop a pebble into a pond, changes have a ripple effect, resonating from the point of change to many other aspects of life.

Define the problem

Sometimes within the culture of a school 'everybody knows' what the problem is. Gossip in the staff room, months if not years of history, and a series of formal interventions with the student, parents and counsellors all tell us what the problem is. But if that view were helpful, the problem would have been solved by now. Therefore, through questions such as those listed in Box 19.2, we have to start with a fresh slate by specifying:[9]

- Who?
- Is doing what?
- How does that constitute a problem?
- To whom does it become a problem?

When asking about the problem, we have to listen out for absolutist words and

FIGURE 19.1   **Steps for revealing solutions**

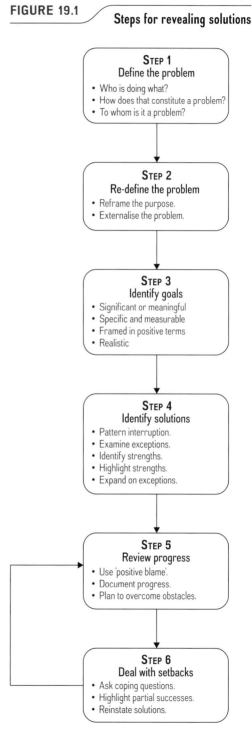

STEP 1
Define the problem
- Who is doing what?
- How does that constitute a problem?
- To whom is it a problem?

STEP 2
Re-define the problem
- Reframe the purpose.
- Externalise the problem.

STEP 3
Identify goals
- Significant or meaningful
- Specific and measurable
- Framed in positive terms
- Realistic

STEP 4
Identify solutions
- Pattern interruption.
- Examine exceptions.
- Identify strengths.
- Highlight strengths.
- Expand on exceptions.

STEP 5
Review progress
- Use 'positive blame'.
- Document progress.
- Plan to overcome obstacles.

STEP 6
Deal with setbacks
- Ask coping questions.
- Highlight partial successes.
- Reinstate solutions.

BOX 19.2   **Questions that elicit descriptions of the problem[10]**

- Can you describe a recent example of the problem?
- If I were a fly on the wall, what would I see?
- What happens first? What happens next? Then what?
- How often does this happen?
- Who is usually involved?
- What are they doing or saying?
- What stops it?
- In what ways is it a problem? For you? For others (e.g. their teacher)?

---

phrases such as *always, nobody, never,* or *all the time*. These cause us to feel stuck and to lose hope that things can change: they leave us despondent. Therefore, when we are listening to descriptions of the problem, we need to translate hopeless language into words that imply the possibility of change. As illustrated in Box 19.3, we do this by:

- converting language from present to past tense
- translating words such as *always, never* etc. into partial statements
- highlighting the subjectivity of the claim.[11]

Re-define the problem

Two things have to happen for an everyday difficulty to become a problem. First, the difficulty has to be mishandled (that is, the solution did not work) and, second, when it does not work, people apply more of the same solution.[12] In other words, recurring problems are a sign that people are stuck.[13] Solution-focused theory takes little interest in how they got stuck in the first place, but focuses instead on how solutions can

be developed.[14] As such, it has a future orientation, rather than an interest in the past.[15] It also recognises Einstein's wisdom that you cannot solve a problem with the same kind of thinking that created the problem.

When the solution has not been working, it is time to change solutions. This will pivot on changing our understanding of the problem. So far, our explanation for it will have been one of two types:

- students are misbehaving deliberately (which is a common explanation when they show no remorse), or
- they cannot help themselves.

There would be nothing wrong with these explanations – if they worked. But the problem is persisting, which means that the explanation on which we have been basing our solution is not helpful. Therefore, the first option for changing chronic behavioural problems is to change explanations.

Deliberate behaviour: reframe its purpose

There are many maps of any given country, but some are more useful for a particular

BOX 19.3   **Changing language**

Complaint	Translation
Change of tense	
He's always in trouble.	He's been in trouble a lot.
Things will never change.	Up to now, things have stayed the same.
I just have a depressive type of personality; I can't do anything about that.	So far, you haven't found a way to change your depressive thinking.
Partial statements	
Nothing ever goes right for me.	Right now it seems like nothing ever goes right for you.
She never behaves herself.	Sometimes it feels to you like she misbehaves all the time.
Highlighting subjectivity	
I can't do anything right.	You really believe that you can't do anything right.
He'll never amount to anything.	Because of the difficulties he's having at the moment, it seems to you that he won't amount to anything.

purpose. If we wanted to pan for gold, for example, we might consult a geophysical map of mineral deposits; if we wanted to go mountaineering, we would need an elevation map; if we wanted to plan a road trip, we would need a road map. Similarly, when we want people to change, we need a map to help them plot how to get from where they are now, to where they want to be.

To achieve this, we need a way of looking at or thinking about the problem that suggests how it can be solved. But some descriptions, 'maps' or understandings of people's behaviour are not especially useful at suggesting how it can change. Explanations that focus on the past, on people's personality (which is relatively fixed), or on their limitations tend to imply that they can*not* change. To initiate change, we need instead to adopt a point of view that suggests that change is possible. If our present map does not achieve this, it just means that we're using the wrong map for our purpose.

Family therapists call this *reframing*. This title alludes to the fact that an old picture can take on a new lease on life when we put it into a fresh frame. On the grounds that a positive explanation is just as likely to be true as a negative one, and that change is less likely when people feel blamed or criticised, any theory aimed at encouraging change should be positive and generate hope that things

BOX 19.4

An example of reframing

A boy (I'll call him Martin) in his last year of primary school was repeatedly in trouble at school for aggression. In one incident, he had thrown a chisel during woodwork class and was banned from attending that class again. He'd thrown chairs at teachers, used sticks as weapons, and had violent outbursts at least twice a week for the past four years. Usually when he got upset, a teacher could calm him down but occasionally even this did not work, and his mother would be called in. She lived near the school and was not working outside of home, so could come down, which she was called on to do at least once a week.

The school's explanation for Martin's behaviour was that he was emotionally disturbed. They arrived at this explanation because they knew that, when he was aged six and his younger brother was aged four, his mother discovered that his father had been sexually abusing both boys. She threw the father out of the house, never to be seen again. A few months later, the strain told on her and she had what she described as a 'nervous breakdown' and was briefly hospitalised.

Although the school's explanation was sympathetic (indeed charitable, in the face of flying chisels!), it was not helping. Therefore, the explanation had to change. The alternative to 'He can't help it (because he is damaged)' is 'He is doing it (semi-)deliberately, because it works'. But what could it be gaining for Martin, given the obvious costs in terms of escalating peer and teacher disapproval?

The reframe

The new view of the problem turned on my observations that, when fathers leave the family, the eldest son is told that 'He is the man of the house now' and that he has to 'Look after his mother, now that his father is gone'. (Apparently, being female is so disabling that even a 30-year-old woman needs looking after by a six-year-old boy.) I would have laid odds that someone had told Martin this at the time that his father left.

Once his mother had a nervous breakdown, he had proof positive that she needed help. But, when you are a school student and are not allowed to leave the school grounds, how can you look after your mother?

You've guessed it: you behave in such a way that she has to attend the school, where you can check up on her.

So our reframe was that Martin was not damaged goods, but that he was being a loyal son. However, now that he was entering adolescence and did not have a father to teach him how to be an honourable man, he would need to devote all his energies to looking after his own growth. Besides, his mother was now truly back on track.

So I invited his mother to thank Martin for giving up his childhood to look after her, and to give him permission to start looking after himself. She also expressed her faith that she knew that he could become an honourable man, because he had been such a loyal and honourable son. Meanwhile, his teachers gained new respect for him and did not need to fear that he was fragile or had an emotional disturbance.

can improve.[16] Therefore, when we have been thinking that a student's behaviour is deliberate (often an attempt to 'get at us'), in light of Principle 2 that *every behaviour is an attempt to meet a need*, our task is to discover what *positive* need the behaviour might be serving.

Once we have reframed the behaviour's purpose, we might simply be able to let go of old (usually punitive) solutions that are not working. This might be enough to end the problem. Or we could guide the student to find a different strategy for meeting the same need, one that does not disrupt other people.

Helplessness: Externalise the problem

The second explanation for chronic behavioural problems is that students cannot help it, because of past abuses, their family circumstances, or a disability. I imagine that, like me, you've heard a 10-year-old proclaim, 'I can't help it. I've got ADD'. Now, this is all very well, but – again – the problem is persisting, which means that this explanation and the solutions it engenders, are not helping. In that event, we can externalise the problem. By this method, we avoid locating blame *within* children by giving their behaviour a name and speaking about it as if it were external to them. This reverses the internalising logic of guilt, embarrassment and shame.[17]

This method rests on the knowledge that the words that surround us and which others use to describe us get mapped onto our psyches, or are internalised. Moreover, they are totalising: they take over in such

---

BOX 19.5 **A simple reframe**

I saw the parents of a three-year-old who had consulted a psychiatrist over the child's tantrums. These were certainly ferocious but no different in kind from any other young children's. The psychiatrist had conferred a diagnosis of *Emotional disturbance*. The problem with this is that, given the child's young age, the only people to blame for disturbing her emotions were the parents – and yet they were now supposed to be the ones to fix it. The result was that they were walking around their daughter like they were on eggshells, unable to insist that she get a grip on her feelings, because she was allegedly too damaged to be able to do so. They were stuck, disempowered by their guilt and by the belief that only professionals could help.

I told the parents that I had a different opinion from the psychiatrist and, given that they were the ones who knew the child best, only they could decide which one of us was right.

I told them that I thought she was being a brat.

Their response was, 'Oh, you think so? Well, we know what to do about that!' and went off to teach her to take charge of her outbursts (using time in and time away).

Although I have done this rarely because the label of *brat* is pejorative, changing the descriptor normalised the child's behaviour and acquitted the parents of culpability, liberating them to resume leadership of the family. The reframe, while negative, had a positive effect by reversing the deficit logic of the psychiatric diagnosis.

a way that no other view of the child can penetrate: they acquire the status of 'truth' and become irrefutable. Despite the fact that labels reflect only *some* of the characteristics of individuals, the descriptions come to dominate outsiders' and recipients' own concept of their *whole* self and, furthermore, highlight their deficits rather than their competencies. Externalising, then, puts the problem back where it belongs: outside of us.[18] The method can be particularly useful when the problem seems to have a life of its own, or when children report feeling helpless to control it. The steps are as follows.

Step 1. In discussion with students, give the problem a name. Use their language to label the problem, or have them select from a list of potential labels that you generate, such as:

- outbursts of anger might be labelled as *Temper, Trouble, Agitation* or *Rage*
- sadness might be labelled as *Misery*
- for those with learning difficulties, it could be that *Squirmies, Rushing* or *Guessing* make them unsuccessful.[19]

You can also just refer to the problem as *It*, or *The Depression*. Naming the problem is also very useful when interaction patterns are blocking solutions. I have already demonstrated this once (in chapter 10) by calling the cycle of child defiance and adult coercion a 'dance'. Other interaction patterns can be named using questions such as:[20]

- How much say does *Racism* have in your relationships here at school?
- How much has *Secrecy* ruled over you and prevented you from getting help (say, from sexual abuse, or bullying)?

Step 2. Investigate the problem's strategies and pattern of entry.[21] Ask students what strategies the problem uses to get them off course, or into trouble (as relevant):

- When does it make an appearance?
- When is it most likely to strike and catch you off guard?
- Does it sneak up on you, or burst onto you?
- Does it boss you around?

Step 3. Gauge their motivation. Once you know how The Problem manipulates them, gauge their motivation for change by asking questions such as:

- How do you feel being bossed around by *Trouble*?
- Are you happy about that?
- Are you happy being in the passenger's seat in your life, or would you prefer to be the driver?[22]
- Do you want to do something about it?

Step 4. Examine the Allies. Sometimes, Problems have Allies that team up with them and cause further oppression, such as *Self-doubt* or *Self-criticism*.[23] In that case, you can ask if the Ally insults them and, if so, does it whisper or shout at them?

Step 5. Gauge their feelings about the problem. Once you know the tactics that the Problem and its Allies use, you can again gauge how motivated the students are to tame, conquer, subdue, overcome or overpower them. You can ask or comment:

- What have you *ever done* to deserve being spoken to like that?
- You wouldn't let anyone else say such nasty things to you, and you must not say them to yourself either.

Although I dislike the language, young people find that it makes sense when I ask them who their enemy is. They can usually name someone in their class; let's call that person Jamie. Then I ask 'If Jamie said that you were stupid, what would you say back?'. They can usually produce some counter-attack. The next step is to guide them to use that same counter-attack when they are saying it to themselves. Abuse is still abuse, even when it is self-abuse.

Step 6. Teach students to disbelieve the thoughts that the Problem has them believe about themselves. *Acceptance and Commitment Therapy* (ACT) believes that we were designed to be pessimistic, that worry kept our distant ancestors alive in dangerous environments. Unlike cognitive theory, it believes that we cannot gain control of our thinking by suppressing or challenging it. When we try, first, we find that we can't do it; second, we criticise ourselves for not being able to do it; and, third, we then obsess about our inability to do it – and the thought becomes more rather than less intrusive.[24]

ACT likens our mind to the sky, with our thoughts and feelings being the storm clouds that appear now and again. Once these clouds (our thoughts and feelings) pass, the sky (our mind) is the same as it always was. In other words, we do not need to fear or fight our own thinking or emotions. Instead, we can defuse them by treating the words and images in our heads as mere stories. Like music playing in the background, we can choose to pay attention to these stories if they help us – or, if they are particularly unhelpful, we can refuse to take them so seriously. We can do this with one of the following options.[25]

- Set the thought to music (Jingle Bells or the Muppet song, for example) and sing the thought to yourself.
- Repeat the thought in a humorous voice (e.g. Homer Simpson's or Yoda's).
- Preface the thought with 'I'm thinking that . . . I'm stupid'. This calls into question the truth of the statement, as illustrated by: 'I'm thinking that . . . I'm a banana'. It reminds us that, just because we think something, that does not make it true.
- When you detect the thought, tell yourself, 'Meh, that's the *I'm stupid* story again'. Maybe followed by 'BOR-ing . . . Heard it before . . . Whatever . . . Tell me when you've got something new'.

Identify goals

Under the ubiquitous controlling model, students have been told what they should be doing and, when they do not do it, are punished. As a result, as seen in chapter 10, they and the adults get caught in a dance in which the student is angry and defiant, and the adults are angry and coercive. Seldom have the students themselves been asked what they want.

Asking them about their goals is guided by principle number 1 (*People know more about themselves than outsiders ever will*) and is a significant departure from this coercive dance. Some potential questions are listed in Box 19.6. The answers to these questions will uncover what is important in life to the students, what they value and how they would like to live. This is their goal. However, to provide a clear direction for change, their goals must have the following qualities.[26] They must be:

- *Significant* or meaningful to those having to make changes so that they are motivated to do so. Their goal will allow them to answer: 'What do you want your life to stand for?'.
- *Specific* and measurable so that improvement can be recognised.
- Framed in *positive* terms that state what students want to happen in their lives. When they declare, for example, that they want a given behaviour to stop, this negative goal will have to be translated into something positive that they *can* do (e.g. 'If you weren't losing your temper, what would you be doing instead?'). This is because it is difficult to detect when something has stopped.
- *Realistic*: when those involved identify impossible goals, such as for their divorced parents to reunite, you can respond to such wishes by asking, 'That means a lot to you because . . . ?'. This allows you then to focus on finding ways to meet the underlying need.

If students answer that they want someone else to change – such as for a teacher to stop getting on their back – this makes them passive and powerless to get change happening.[27] Therefore, you will first acknowledge their frustration and then ask something such as, 'What do you do when they get on your back?' and explore with them whether they can think of a different strategy that might work better for them. You might ask, 'What could you do differently to get your teacher to be nicer to you?'.

Once goals are framed in achievable terms, scaling questions can ask those involved to rate the severity of the current problem on a scale of 1 to 10 (with 1 being the worst it's ever been, and 10 being the day after the miracle), so they can assess how close they already are to achieving their goal. Being concrete, using numbers suits children well.[28] With very young children, you can use gaps between the finger and thumb, versus arms stretched

---

BOX 19.6 **Questions to elicit students' goals**[29]

- What will be the first small sign that things are getting better?
- Once this problem is fixed, what will it look like?
- What do you think your teacher (parents or classmates) will notice first about you once things start improving?
- If, while you were sleeping tonight, a miracle happened and this problem were fixed, what would have changed? Who will be doing what differently?
- If those involved still say that they do not know what they want, you can ask hypothetical questions: 'If you did know . . . If you had to take a guess, what might it be?' or distal questions such as, 'What would your Mum tell me was the most important thing to you?'.
- Pretend that there are two movies of your life, one with the problem as it is now, and one without the problem: What does the second movie look like?
- How would that make a difference to (each person involved)?

BOX 19.7 — **Translating vague goals into specific actions**[30]

Vague goal	Concrete action
I want to be less depressed.	If I were watching a movie of you being less depressed, what would that look like?
I don't want to get detention any more.	What needs to happen for you to get detention less often?
I want to get into less trouble at school.	What will you be doing instead of getting into trouble?
I don't want to fail science.	What can you do to prevent yourself from failing?
I want to stop worrying so much.	What will you be doing when you are worrying less?

BOX 19.8 — **Scaling questions**[31]

- *Scaling*: On a scale of 1 to 10 (with 1 being dismal and 10 ideal), at what number is your life at the moment?
- *Motivation*: How happy are you with that number? (This will tell you how motivated they are to change.)
- *Goal*: What number would you prefer to be at? This is the goal number (x).
- *Hope*: What will life be like when you reach (x)? What will you be doing differently?
- *Examine exceptions*: Have you ever been at ($x + 1$) before? If so, what was happening then?
- *Confidence*: What do you think are the chances that you will reach x (the goal number)? (This allows you to gauge how confident they are about the possibility of change.)
- *Progress*: How will you know that you are making progress? What will be the first sign?
- *Concrete objective*: When this problem is entirely solved, what will be happening that is different from what is happening now?

out widely, or use a picture of a ladder on which they can indicate their rating.

Identify solutions

To get a chronic behaviour to change, we have to change the current solution. Here the reasoning is that if the solution were going to work, it would have by now. Again, trusting young people to know their own minds, we will ask them about solutions that have been tried and which worked, those that have been tried but which failed, and those they or others have considered but rejected.[32]

Pattern interruption

There will be times when you do not have enough information or you lack the time or confidence to reframe the purposes of

BOX 19.9   Using scaling to identify a solution

A student has thrown scissors in class and is sent to the principal. This behaviour, of course, is completely unacceptable because it is dangerous and intimidating. However, rather than asking why the student did it (which guidance already knows anyway: the behaviour was an effort to meet a need), after greeting the student, the principal can ask the following series of questions:

- 'At the time when you threw the scissors, on a scale of 1 to 10, how angry were you?'. (Let's say that the student nominates 9.)
- 'It has taken you 45 seconds to get from your classroom to my office . . . On a scale of 1 to 10, how angry are you now?'. (Let's say that the student nominates 7.)
- 'How did you get from 9 to 7?'

This supplies the principal with three pieces of information. First, the student has the skill to calm down (to go from a rating of 9 to a 7). Second, you do not have to think up a new solution, because the student is already using one. Third, if the student can go from 9 to 7 on the scale, he or she can equally go from 7 to 5, from 5 to 3 and from 3 to 1. Therefore, you do not need to impose a solution, just enquire about what the student needs in order to employ the solution more often so that in future the student's feelings do not escalate into violence.

a student's behaviour. In this case, you can simply take note of the corrective measures that have been attempted so far and, on the grounds that they have not worked (otherwise the problem would have disappeared), do something else.

Remember that a troublesome behaviour persists because it is working – at least in part. On this basis, this method permits the behaviour to continue, while insisting that it be less disruptive to surrounding individuals. The key to this strategy is to identify the chain or sequences of events. Given that a chain is only as strong as its weakest link, one option is to disrupt the sequence or pattern to see if that will change how it is expressed. Possibilities for pattern interruption include:

- changing the location of the behaviour
- changing who is involved

- changing the sequence of the steps involved
- interrupting the sequence in its initial stages ('derailing'). For example, before a child starts to refuse to pack up the equipment, say 'I bet you don't feel like packing up')
- introducing random starting and stopping
- increasing the frequency of the behaviour (but this is not to be used for aggression).

Examine exceptions

No problem occurs all of the time.[33] Therefore, another source of solutions is to examine the times when the problem could have occurred but did not, when it happened less often, or was less intense than usual. These occasions are called

BOX 19.10   **Questions that unlock solutions[34]**

Solution-oriented questions

Finding out what has failed tells you what not to try again, while finding out what has worked even partially gives you a clue about what might work again. It also tells you what strengths those involved have already brought to bear on the problem and hence could use again.

- What ideas do you have about what needs to happen for this to change?
- What's your hunch about how to solve this?
- Everyone has made changes in their lives. How do you usually get change to happen in yours?
- What's one small thing that you did in the past that seemed to help a little?
- What have your tried so far? Did it help? How did it help? Why didn't it help?
- What have you thought about trying?
- Of all the things that you and others have done, what has worked best? What has worked least?
- What have other people said you should try? Of all those ideas, which one do you think has the best chance of working?

Future-oriented questions

These questions ask those involved to picture a time a few months hence when this problem is resolved and, looking back from this mythical future time, to imagine what they did to achieve the improvement.

- How did you solve it?
- What have you been doing differently to achieve this success?
- What have you (or others) been doing that contributed to the improvement?

exceptions. They are solutions that are already in place. They save us from having to invent a new solution, because we can use one that is already activated.

The first step is to identify these exceptions. These might be signalled in everyday statements such as, 'I'm failing in *almost* every class . . . *Hardly anyone* ever talks to me . . . He *usually* picks on me. I'm not the one who starts it'. Or, you can enquire about the exceptions, using questions such as those in Box 19.15.

Identify strengths

In order to identify how students get the exceptions to happen, we need to understand the strengths and resources they bring to bear on the problem. This is the enactment of Principles 5 and 6 (that all individuals are doing *some*thing to keep their problems from getting worse and all environments provide *some* support for them to do so). To identify their strengths, you can ask questions such as those listed in Box 19.16. In listening to their answers,

BOX 19.11   Pattern interruption: Increase the frequency

Referring back to the case of Martin (Box 19.4, page 300) if it had not been possible to deliver the reframe to Martin, or if we did not have all the background information we needed to deduce the purpose of his behaviour, we could instead interrupt the pattern. The sequence is: Martin disrupts, a teacher tries to calm him; if that does not work, his mother is summonsed, and Martin can check that she is okay.

Instead of waiting for an outburst, then, we could *impose* the checking up, by insisting that Martin call his mother at every recess and lunch time, until he realised for himself that this was no longer necessary. This is increasing the frequency of the behaviour. Or we could invite his mother to call into the school on her way past, perhaps when walking the dog. This is random starting and stopping. Or we could give Martin permission to go home every lunch time (and miss out on play time!) to check up on his mother, again until he realised that it was no longer necessary.

BOX 19.12   Pattern interruption: Derailing

Over the course of a week, I observed two year-10 students repeatedly in physically rough (not quite violent) disputes with each other. They would usually desist once I entered the room but it was clearly upsetting for them and disruptive for everyone else. I didn't have enough information to know what was going on and I knew they wouldn't tell me. So, when I walked into the room at the end of lunch time to observe that it was happening again, I told one that I wanted to talk to him after class. Amid protests of why I was picking on him (when they were both involved), I just repeated that I would see him after the lesson.

At the end of the lesson, we moved out to the corridor outside the classroom. I am short. ('Vertically challenged' be damned: I'm just short.) He was 16 and taller than me and was able to laud it over me – so I sat down. Now he felt ridiculous, so had to sit too.

Then I said, 'I've been watching the two of you and it seems to me that you're getting picked on. And I need to ask if there is anything I can do to help you?'. The bluster came out of him instantly. He took pains to assure me that he was fine. After a brief discussion, I concluded, 'Well I'm still concerned. So if I see it happening again, I'll step in to help'. The last thing this young man wanted was some slip of a female standing up for him, so the fighting stopped.

It would not have mattered which one of the pair I had chosen to speak with. If I had spoken instead with the other protagonist, he too would have agreed with me that he was getting picked on. Given that they were both involved, I needed only one of them to make it stop.

BOX 19.13

Pattern interruption: Disrupt the sequence

In one of the child-care centres where I was observing for my doctorate, two boys were continually being sent indoors to the 'thinking chair' (time-out) after getting into a dispute in the playground. They loved outdoor playtime above all else – and yet routinely lost at least 10 minutes of precious outdoor time each day sitting indoors allegedly 'thinking about their behaviour'.

The sequence was that they went outside . . . got into a dispute . . . and were sent inside. After watching this sequence for a few days, I explained the pattern to them and explained that their disputes were costing them 10 minutes of play time each day and then added, 'It's now 10 minutes until we go outside. How about you start your dispute *now* so that you can sit on the chair *now*, instead of later?' Astonished and bemused, they rejected the offer to fight now . . . but neither did they fight once they went outdoors.

BOX 19.14

Identify natural exceptions

In preparation for presenting to the teachers at a school in South Australia, I met with the school counsellor for a briefing so that I made sure to cover the behavioural issues of concern to the group. We talked about a few students and one student in particular, named Amanda, who repeatedly took items of stationery from her classmates. Up to 150 pens, pencils, rulers and erasers were found in her desk whenever a search was mounted.[35]

After our meeting, I went for a walk to clear my head and returned to find the school counsellor and a student helping to set out snacks for the meeting. The counsellor introduced me to her helper: 'Louise, this is Amanda. She's a thief.'[36]

Mortified for Amanda, who did not know that this is the sort of information I am paid to hear, I needed to get her out from under such a pejorative label. I told her that it was good to meet her and that, one thing I knew about young people is that, at the end of the school day they are really hungry. (She agreed.) And here she was, apparently a thief, helping to set out the food for the teachers' meeting. So did this mean that she had some chocolate biscuits in her pocket? Amanda declared that she did not. I feigned surprise. 'Why not?' I asked, 'Don't you like chocolate biscuits?' She assured me that she did like chocolate biscuits – but had not stolen any.

I repeated the questioning about cheese and crackers, and then about the grapes and, for each, Amanda assured me that she had not taken any, despite that fact that she liked them *and* was hungry. I asked how she did that: how did she manage not to steal the food when she was so hungry?

'I just thought about it and decided not to,' she told me.

'Good idea,' I commended. 'Do more of that.'

BOX 19.15

Questions that identify exceptions[37]

- When is the problem absent or less noticeable?
- In which class do you get into least trouble?
- What is your best class?
- What's different about that class compared to your other classes?
- In what ways is that teacher different from your other teachers? What else?
- What difference does that difference make to you?
- At what time in the past week have things been a little better than usual?
- Tell me about a time recently when (the problem) wasn't happening.
- Tell me about a time in the past month when you were above a 3 (reflecting the student's scaling question).
- What's better since last time we talked?

BOX 19.16

Questions that elicit strengths[38]

Once those involved can recount instances when the problem was absent or less severe than usual, you can ask 'positive blaming' questions to help them identify what they did to generate these exceptions.

- How did you do that?
- How did you get that to happen?
- What did you do to pull that off?
- What did you tell yourself that helped you do that?
- What steps did you take leading up to it?
- How did you manage to get your work done in that class?
- How do you resist the urge to muck around?
- Did you know you could do that?
- Is that something different for you?
- Can you tell me about other times you've tried something useful like that?

A second set of follow-up questions implies something about the student's identity:

- What does it tell us about what is important to you in life that you were willing to do that?
- What does this tell you about yourself and your ability to solve this problem?
- What did the problem have you thinking about yourself before? What do you think about yourself now?

you will look out for examples of the following skills:[39]

- *actions* that indicate courage, healthy risk taking (adventurousness)
- *effort* that demonstrates strength, growth, application, impulse control
- *commitments* that show loyalty, dedication, devotion, follow-through, persistence, diligence
- *attitudes* that reflect tolerance, acceptance, flexibility, enthusiasm, confidence, patience
- *social orientation*, including empathy, caring, cooperation, loyalty, independence, compromise, negotiation, listening, assertiveness, problem solving
- *thoughts* that are creative, imaginative, positive, realistic, sensitive, insightful
- *goals* that are healthy, sensible, realistic, strategic or growth producing
- *decisions* based on wise judgment, values, self-awareness, maturity, planfulness.

The decision to focus on aspects other than the problem is not merely to help everyone feel better, but to gather information about children's skills and personal attributes that can become part of the solution. If students are not able to name some strengths or cannot locate exceptions, you can ask what their best friend would tell you about these.

Highlight strengths

We then build these instances of students' successes into positive stories about them that contradict the problematised description of themselves. In addition to discussing this new information directly with them, we can tell their parent or a colleague these positive tales within their hearing (in celebration, not manipulation,

of course). This 'keyhole listening' can make these stories especially newsworthy, because when we overhear something that we think we were not supposed to hear, the information is more meaningful. Your purpose in commenting positively is not to flatter them, but to help them recognise their own successes. Neither is your purpose to gloss over their pain, but to see it as an outcome of the problem.[40]

> Listening for client strengths does not mean ignoring pain or assuming a cheerleading role. Rather, it requires the practitioner to listen to the whole story: the confusion *and* the clarity, the suffering *and* the endurance, the pain *and* the coping, the desperation *and* the desire.[41]

This is powerful, because it implies that you see students as having the capacity to make things happen and gives them hope about their future.[42] Depending on their ages, you might ask the questions in Box 19.16 or, for children who are too young to reflect, you could ask the questions of yourself in an effort to understand what is working.

A particularly inspirational approach is to amass these strengths into a new story about the student. As with externalising the problem, this technique is based on awareness that we all have stories about our lives. These stories are partial in the sense that we do not have enough time to tell all of the events in our lives, so we leave things out. They are also partial in the sense of being biased. When students' behaviour has been difficult for a long time, their identity comes to be defined by 'The Problem'. The image that others have of them (and often the image they hold of themselves) becomes saturated with instances of their problematic behaviour. They come to be defined as being mad, bad or sad, while their many other skills and qualities are often overlooked.[43] In this case, we need to find ways to re-write the 'story' of who they are, drawing on the exceptions that we revealed in Step 1. For example, a student who does not persist at schoolwork may be diligent when practising soccer. This tells us that the student does not need to learn to persist, but instead just needs to transfer that ability from the soccer field to the classroom. We can reflect:

- 'So you're the sort of person who is diligent about doing your best for your team. Not letting your team down must mean a lot to you that you're prepared to practise so hard.'
- 'What other things do you work hard at?'
- 'What helps you to keep at it when you feel like giving up?'
- 'What does it say about you that you're willing to do that?'

Expand on exceptions

Once those involved can identify the exceptions, you can expand on these so that they feel capable of performing the exceptions more often and in more circumstances. There will be four possible scenarios. First, when those involved can identify their successful strategies, you can ask what it would take for them to use these again.

Second, if they doubt their abilities to repeat a success, you can invite them to observe what is different about those times when they do manage to create an exception,[44] or invite them to experiment with ways to get it to happen again.

Third, when students believe that the exceptions are just flukes, you will need to raise their awareness that these are not mere accidents but happen as a result of something they do. To achieve this, you could enquire about their heroes and then ask: 'What do you think (their hero's name) would do if faced with this problem? Would that be something you'd be willing to try?'[46] Alternatively, you could suggest that they pretend that their miracle/solution/goal has been achieved.[47] For example, you could invite students who are often aggressive to pretend that they feel friendly. You can then conspire with them that, each day you

---

BOX 19.17 **Re-writing her- or his-story[45]**

- Pinpoint recent actions that do not fit with the problem version of the student.
- Ask how the student achieved these exceptions.
- Ask about other similar actions.
- Ask about the strengths and resources they used to bring these about.
- Ask whether they want to use those skills again.
- Give the new story (the counterplot) a name.
- Explore its history in their lives.
- Draw connections between the counterplot and current exceptions.

or a colleague have to guess whether they are only pretending to be friendly, or are 'for real'.

Finally, when students are convinced that they have no control over the problem, you can ask them to think about how come it is no worse than it is: what is keeping it from becoming even more serious?[48] Another possibility is to invite them to act as your consultant, asking questions such as, 'When I work with another student with a problem like this, what do you think I should do to help that person?'.[49]

Review progress

In this final step, check that progress is occurring. If there has been an improvement, use 'positive blaming' questions (see Box 19.16) to ask how they got the change to happen and if they want to keep doing what they have been doing to sustain the changes. Alternatively, if there has been no change, this means that people are being too unpredictable and, therefore, should do something unexpected.

One way to reduce the chances of old habits taking hold again is to produce documents about a student's progress. These can be photos of a formerly aggressive student playing happily alongside others, or certificates of achievement, or positive stories about the student. It will be vital, however, that the intent of these is to celebrate and congratulate, rather than to manipulate students into repeating their new behaviours. The documents are to punctuate their achievements, to serve as a concrete reminder to them of what they are achieving. Whereas conversations are ephemeral, documents endure so can reaffirm children's knowledges and successes

at times when they feel discouraged.[50] The documents can be used for the student's personal use, or can be circulated to family members or trusted friends. The audience can even be hypothetical (such as deceased or absent relatives or friends, the child's pet or, for younger children, a stuffed toy or imaginary friend). The main criterion for deciding whether to circulate the documents will be that the students do not see the publicity as an attempt to manipulate them into continuing the improvement, but merely as an invitation to others to share in the celebration of the changes they have made.

Plan for overcoming obstacles to change

A basic principle of the guidance approach is that behaviours persist because they work. Therefore, if we remove a behaviour, we will need to replace it with another strategy for meeting the same need. Otherwise, people will revert to their old ways, because these are their only method for meeting their needs. For example, when young people are unsuccessful in school, chances are that they will be friends with other disenchanted students. If a student suddenly starts to be conscientious, old friends are likely to desert him or her. Meanwhile, a negative reputation might mean that the student is shunned by the more prosocial students. In order to retain old friendships in an effort to avoid loneliness, the student might revert to being unsuccessful.

Therefore, ahead of time, we need a plan for overcoming these types of obstacles that could block change. There may be new or unfamiliar experiences that occur as a result of the change. (Indeed, on the basis of the eighth principle that big changes can grow out of small solutions, we can *expect* other changes to occur.) Planning for obstacles helps us to be realistic about the work that is ahead of us, and prevents us being caught off guard by unforeseen challenges.[51]

Deal with setbacks

If there has been a deterioration in the problem, listen to people's despondency but then ask coping questions as listed in Box 19.18. At the same time, you will have to manage your own despondency by realising that relapses:

- are a way of telling us that some of what we are doing is working and some is not
- are a reminder to keep doing what works
- are ways that the problem tests us to see if we can 'get back on track'
- provide extra information about the tricks and tactics the problem uses to take over our lives.[52]

We can choose to focus on the setback, or to search within it for evidence of a success, however partial: when students have been verbally abusive towards a peer or teacher, they did something to stop themselves lashing out physically as well. In other words, we can highlight the successes and consider the setback to be an interruption to (or a hiccup in) the overall trend of improvement. We can treat relapses as a reminder to resume using the strategies that we originally used to overcome the problem.[53]

Conclusion

In contrast to approaches where the practitioner is the hero while those with problems are regarded as fragile and ineffective, the solution-focused approach chooses to see young people and others involved in school problems as the heroes in their own story, the creators of their own solutions.[54] The approach saves us from searching for causes, on the grounds that many effective solutions are unrelated to their cause: we take painkillers for a headache, even though clearly the headache was not caused by a lack of painkillers. As de Shazer observes:

> we end up searching for explanations believing that without explanation a solution is irrational, not recognizing that the solution itself is its own best explanation.[56]

BOX 19.18   Questions that identify resilience and coping skills[55]

- How have you prevented things from getting worse?
- How come you haven't given up?
- What tells you that there is hope?
- What is it about you that keeps you hanging in there?
- How do you resist the urge to just give up?
- What does your persistence tell you about your faith in yourself?

Distilled down to its simplest notions, solution-focused approaches advise that when present solutions are not working, you either view something differently or do something differently.[57] Viewing differently encompasses noticing non-problems (exceptions), externalising, or reframing problems. Doing something differently obeys the maxims:[58]

> When something is working, *do more of it.* (Do more of the same.)
>
> If something isn't working, stop it. (Do less of the same.)
>
> If something isn't working, do something else. (Do something different.)

Recommended further reading

Berg, I.K. & Steiner, S. (2003). *Children's solution work.* New York: Norton.

De Jong, P. & Berg, I.K. (2013). *Interviewing for solutions.* (4th ed.) Pacific Grove, CA: Brooks/Cole.

Durrant, M. (1995). *Creative strategies for school problems: Solutions for psychologists and teachers.* Epping, NSW: Eastwood Family Therapy Centre/New York: Norton.

Freeman, J., Epston, D. & Lobovits, D. (1997). *Playful approaches to serious problems: Narrative therapy with children and their families.* New York: Norton.

Morgan, A. (Ed.) (1999). *Once upon a time . . . Narrative therapy with children and their families.* Adelaide, SA: Dulwich Centre Publications.

——(2000) *What is narrative therapy?: An easy-to-read introduction.* Adelaide, SA: Dulwich Centre Publications.

Murphy, J.J. (2008). *Solution-focused counseling in schools.* (2nd ed.) Alexandria, VA: American Counseling Association.

Murphy, J.J. & Duncan, B.L. (2007). *Brief intervention for school problems: Outcome-informed strategies.* (2nd ed.) New York: Guilford.

Selekman, M.D. (2010). *Collaborative brief therapy with children.* New York: Guilford.

Sklare, G.B. (2005). *Brief counseling that works: A solution-focused approach for school counselors and administrators.* (2nd ed.) Thousand Oaks, CA: Corwin Press.

Winslade, J. & Monk, G. (2007). *Narrative counseling in schools: Powerful and brief.* (2nd ed.) Thousand Oaks, CA: Corwin Press.

Websites

Brief Therapy Institute of Sydney: www.brieftherapysydney.com.au

Brief Therapy Practice, UK: www.brieftherapy.org.uk

Dulwich Centre, Adelaide, SA: www.dulwichcentre.com.au

CHAPTER 20

Critique of the guidance approach

Any approach to discipline is judged to be a failure not only on the obvious criterion that it fails to establish and affect appropriate standards of behavior, but also if, in establishing such standards, it does so primarily by teaching children to obey rules rather than to make reasoned judgments about what actions are desirable, and about how actually to decide to act in those desirable ways.[1]

I contend that behaviourism is bankrupt. As a philosophy, it fails to question the politics inherent in imposing controls on defenceless people. Behaviourism is, Kohn claims, 'a profoundly conservative doctrine posing as a value-free technique'.[2] As a pedagogy, it says nothing about education other than that teachers must manage classrooms and that schools must ensure that students conform. Its only recommendations for making schools safer is to have safety audits of the school buildings, make students wear school uniforms, develop a school-wide discipline plan, and secure school campuses with fencing and guards.[3] This approach makes control a priority over creating humane environments where young people might want to be.[4] And as a personal ethic, although it claims to be amoral,[5] I believe that it is *im*moral to be *a*moral – that is, to take no moral stand. We have to stand for something: otherwise, we will fall for anything.

Politics

To this and other reviewers[6] the most troubling of the assumptions of controlling discipline is its political stance: that is, its attitude to power differentials between teachers and students. In its resolute focus on minute details, it overlooks the social circumstances of students and, in doing so, mirrors and legitimates the inequalities of society.[7] In contrast, the guidance approach recognises that oppressive social forces, such as poverty and racial or sexual discrimination, marginalise individuals and limit their options. To ensure that discipline does not compound such injustices, guidance believes that it must not be repressive – that is, it cannot aim to correct and suppress troublesome behaviour by forcing students to conform.[8]

Children's rights

Once human needs are accepted in the public realm, they are elevated to the status of rights.[9] These reflect the equal status of individuals: they are not conditional on any characteristic or capacity, including age.[10] Article 12 of the UN Convention on the Rights of the Child specifies that young people have a right to participate in matters that affect them.[11] Although only the US and Somalia have not signed this charter,[12] young people are still treated as the object of adults' actions, rather than being the subjects in their own lives, with the result that they seldom have opportunities to participate in making decisions in schools.[13] Just as the disenfranchisement of women was justified on the basis of their apparent weakness, the supposed fragility and incompetence of children (and, in some folklore, their self-indulgent natures) disqualifies them from exercising agency over their own lives. By taking for granted the teacher's right to impose both the curriculum and rules on young people, behaviourism marginalises students and silences their points of view, resulting in school discipline becoming a matter of doing things *to* students rather than *with* them.[14]

Lack of pedagogical theory

In contrast to the copious research verifying the teaching methods subsumed under the guidance approach (as reviewed here in chapters 11 to 16), pragmatic behaviourists simply define teacher effectiveness in terms of whether teachers' management methods allow them to dominate the classroom.[15] These writers mention nothing about pedagogy, other than that teaching should be highly structured, teachers should be 'with-it' and monitor student engagement and behaviour, and should prevent behaviour problems by teaching students the rules

and consequences for their infractions. This model makes no mention of the needs of students other than their supposed 'need' for limits. Gordon agrees that, of course, children want to know if their behaviour is interfering with someone else but that, once they have this information, they are willing to place 'limits' on their own behaviour in order to consider others.[16]

Noddings says that we must constantly ask ourselves, 'If you are aiming at X, why are you doing Y?'.[17] This question has special relevance to discipline in schools where, if we aim to prepare students for democratic citizenship, we must ask ourselves why are we modelling dictatorships in classrooms? Similarly, if we are aiming at teaching students to think for themselves, why do we force them to do as they are told?[18]

Ethics of disciplinary practices

It is not enough to base recommendations for practice on observations or even research about what works. Cattle prods and tasers would *work*. Not only must practices be effective, they must also be ethical – that is, we must do what is right, just and good, rather than what is merely expedient, convenient or practical.[19]

Quality of life

This principle implies that, when trying to correct disruptive behaviour, any measures used must be in students' own interests. That is, the methods must be aimed at improving the safety or quality of life of young people themselves. Although behaviourists concur with this aim,[20] they assume that being more successful will improve students' quality of life, whereas guidance assumes that a lack of autonomy guarantees a poor quality of life, given that autonomy is a fundamental human need.

Do no harm

A second ethical principle is that we must *do no harm*. Martin and Pear concede that, 'The history of civilisation is a continuous story of the abuse of power'[21] and go on to argue that practitioners' own ethics must protect the less powerful. That is to say, given students' lack of power to advocate on their own behalf, teachers must employ practices that are respectful of and provide security for children and in no way 'degrade, endanger, exploit, intimidate, or harm them psychologically or physically'.[22]

As already mentioned, guidance contends that the narrow behaviourist view of the precursors to behavioural disruptions represents a callous and unethical disregard of the broader social context and the effects that curricular content and teaching methods have on students' behaviour.[23] This unfairness is compounded when disciplinary technologies are imposed in schools on students who are already disadvantaged by their living circumstances. Students with emotional and behavioural disturbances are typically subjected at home to harsh discipline.[24] While 16.5 per cent of the general population endure physical or emotional maltreatment, by school age, perhaps as many as 70 per cent of students experiencing ongoing behavioural problems have suffered abuse or neglect.[25] Rather than receiving support to overcome adversity, however, behaviourism recommends that these students be met with more of the same coercion at school.[26]

Canter's reported defence to such criticisms is that behaviourist programs are harsh only when not grounded in respectful and supportive student–teacher relationships.[27] In contrast, informed by self-determination theory, guidance practitioners contend that controlling discipline, by definition, is disrespectful. The concept of a benevolent dictatorship is an oxymoron.

Inclusion

A third ethical principle is of *inclusion*. This means that we cannot scapegoat students because of their disruptiveness, any more than we would discriminate against them on the basis of their sex, culture or religion. On this criterion, behaviourism fails resoundingly. Across many Western countries, including Britain, the US, Australia and New Zealand, minority cultural students figure disproportionately in the statistics for school suspension and exclusion, and for special education referrals.[28] Even after controlling for the contributing effects of poverty, this still represents excessive disciplinary action directed against minority students.[29] Controlling discipline has failed to question this inequity and instead masquerades as a neutral ('consistent') approach.

After cultural minorities and the impoverished, boys are a third group to be disadvantaged by the power imbalance in schools. There is a well-documented negative perception of boys in schools and higher rates of negative teacher feedback to them.[30] Boys are disproportionately the focus of school disciplinary measures and suspension. Rather than blaming boys' inherent nature for this, schools should honour their biology and adjust teaching so that boys are both more willing and more able to engage. This will involve allowing boys more movement and active participation in classes. Instead, in a tendency that has been termed 'petticoat tyranny' a largely female teaching profession denigrates and attempts to suppress boys' more active nature and, when it cannot, pathologises their behaviour by blaming the children themselves.

As for girls, their lives and needs are often overlooked in educational research and in schools themselves.[31] Perhaps their superior academic performance as a group (relative to boys') is partly why individual girls' behavioural and learning difficulties are so often neglected, both within classrooms and in the official statistics that foster accountability of the education system.[32] For example, because their behaviour is typically less disruptive, girls with learning difficulties such as the attention deficits get overlooked and are less likely than boys to receive remedial support.[33] A second example is that, while one in four students permanently excluded from British schools is female, we know little about the causes of girls' disaffection with school or about the resulting social exclusion that follows school expulsion.[34] Meanwhile, patriarchal values impose a compliance on girls that allows them to do well in their schoolwork, but produces a conventionality that disadvantages them in adult life.[35] Their docility in the classroom can result in a progressive decline in girls' hopes, aspirations, self-esteem and achievements during adolescence and adulthood.[36]

Elements of effectiveness

Pragmatic behaviourists claim that 'everyone knows' that punishments and rewards work, whereas radical behaviourists at least gather data on the effects of their practices, typically counting how often students perform a negative behaviour prior to an intervention, and then demonstrate a decrease in disruptiveness during the intervention. However, to paraphrase Einstein: 'Not everything that can be counted counts, and not everything that counts can be counted'.[37] That is, counting the number of incidents pays no heed to side effects of interventions.

It is clear that there is more to effectiveness than merely ending the immediate disruption or gaining compliance. Instead, to be effective, ultimately, any truly optimal style of discipline should lead to its own demise.[38] That is, students should outgrow the need for adult supervision. For methods to be considered effective in this broader sense, they must achieve the following.[39]

- Disruptions in general need to be prevented from occurring.
- The particular disruption should be less likely to recur in future.
- Young people should learn something positive during the process of correction, such as how to solve disputes or regulate their impulses and emotions – not how to avoid detection, to tell lies to get out of trouble, to deny responsibility, or to blame someone else.
- There must be no unintended emotional side effects for the students whom we discipline, such as feeling intimidated or fearful, or being seen by peers as troublesome and therefore as someone to avoid or victimise.
- Surrounding students must continue to feel safe about how they would be treated if in future they were to make a mistake.

- We have to feel that we are abiding by our principles and doing a good job as teachers.
- Our disciplinary methods must preserve the student–teacher relationship. Students should be equally willing to interact with us after a corrective intervention as they were before, not least because our relationship is the only currency we have for influencing them.
- The methods that we use must in themselves convey our values, such as respect (for both children and adults) and fairness of treatment.
- Students need to develop a healthy attitude to authority. They should not display blind obedience but neither should there be reflexive opposition. Instead, students need a disposition to question the legitimacy of authority.

Although controlling discipline can attest to its ability to achieve (temporary) compliance and thus the cessation of a disruption, it fails to measure these other ancillary outcomes. Evidence for the effects of guidance on these and other aspects follows.

Outcomes of the guidance approach

To my knowledge, the first study of controlling versus democratic leadership was published in 1939.[40] Under controlling discipline, the 10-year-old subjects' hostility towards each other was 30 times more frequent and aggression eight times more common than in a democratically run group.[41] The target was not the autocrat himself, but two group members in turn, enabled by the rigid hierarchical nature

of the group (which sounds eerily like the processes seen in bullying). Under the most repressive leader, the students were apathetic rather than aggressive in the group leader's presence, but were aggressive once the leader left the room, and initially once they were transitioned into a more democratic grouping.[42] Inter-group conflict was also apparent under autocratic leadership.

Schools that have systematically implemented the social-emotional component of the guidance approach have achieved benefits for students' connectedness to school, academic achievement levels and sense of efficacy, and a reduction in behavioural difficulties in adolescents.[43] Teachers feel closer to their students, and the students are more prosocial and assertive, and less anxious.[44] Schools where students feel supported and with clear structures, experience lower rates of bullying and other behavioural problems, with students having higher perceptions of safety.[45] One study found that authoritative schools (broadly speaking, those which use guidance principles) have significantly less student disengagement than schools employing controls.[46] Moreover, punitive schools serving low socioeconomic students have significantly higher dropout rates, whereas wealthier students remain in the school but have high levels of disaffection.[47]

Although not purist guidance approaches, under both the *Consistency management* program[48] and the *Seattle social development intervention*,[49] teachers include students in establishing rules and routines, employ active and cooperative learning strategies, and collaborate with parents. Students in these classes showed greater achievements on national normed tests, perceived their learning environment more positively, were more motivated and engaged, and more bonded to school.[50] In another study, students in classrooms with more positive social climates showed declining anxiety and depressive symptoms over time.[51]

A meta-analytic study found that teachers who were trained in choice theory (which is a contributor to the guidance approach) developed more positive attitudes to school in general and to disciplinary issues in particular. They made fewer referrals for behavioural difficulties – perhaps because fewer problems were actually occurring or because the teachers simply felt better equipped to cope with these themselves.[52] A separate study also achieved fewer disciplinary referrals alongside improvements in teachers' morale.[53]

Pilot projects that, in collaboration with students and parents, introduced no-fault problem solving and consensual decision making with attention to students' social as well as their academic needs resulted in the students' grades rising from the lowest rankings towards the top ranking in their state.[54] In another school implementing this approach, whereas only 42 per cent of students met grade-level academic expectations prior to the commencement of the intervention, four years into it, 98 per cent were proficient at grade level.[55] The achievement gap between Black and White students (this being a US study) closed considerably, almost reaching parity over a five-year period.[56] In another study, teachers who employed guidance and fostered relationships with their students experienced lower rates of defiant behaviour, which was explained by the greater trust that their students held in their teachers.[57]

These students were also more engaged in the learning process.[58]

Observations in classrooms have shown that, when controlling teachers do secure students' compliance, the students commonly display a grudging attitude and resistance.[59] My own research in centre-based child care found that caregivers using controlling discipline experienced far higher rates of behavioural disruptions in their young charges, than did those using the guidance approach. It could not have been that the adults' controlling methods were a response to a higher rate of behavioural problems in the children, because the difference held for two caregivers (one controlling and the other employing guidance) who were team-teaching the same group of children.[60] The conclusion, then, was that (as predicted by Gordon),[61] the children resisted, rebelled and retaliated against controlling forms of discipline. These reactive behavioural difficulties were typically both more serious and more challenging to resolve than had been the original disruption.[62]

Finally, a meta-analysis showed that student-directed interventions achieved both significantly better outcomes than teacher-directed interventions, while also producing superior generalisation of skills.[63] Meanwhile, children dislike highly teacher-directed classrooms.[64]

Researchers also provide support for Gordon's *Teacher effectiveness training*, which they found achieved improved student attitudes to schooling, to themselves and to their teachers plus there were achievement gains for students, with some studies also demonstrating positive benefits for teachers.[65] Research into the effectiveness of the parallel program for parents (*Parent effectiveness training*) is beset by a lack of rigour, although meta-analyses based on well-designed studies found that PET courses were moderately effective in improving parenting attitudes and behaviour and were increasingly effective over time (after cessation of the training course) at improving child behaviour and parent–child interactions.[66] Gains compared with parents who received no training remained after seven years.[67] Parents undertaking a PET course displayed considerable improvements in their use of all three communication skills of listening, assertiveness and conflict resolution; and significant qualitative improvements in their self-reported satisfaction in their parenting and parent–child relationships, including reduced stress and increased family harmony.[68]

The conclusion is clear: the exhaustive body of research cited in chapters 11 to 16 is clear evidence of the effectiveness of guidance practices. These findings can be supplemented by a robust body of research into parenting styles. In excess of 50 years of research has compared controlling discipline with the guidance approach. Of these many studies, *every single one* has shown the guidance approach to produce superior results to controlling discipline, across all domains of children's development.[69] These studies are especially credible because many are longitudinal – that is, they follow parents and their children over many years (in some cases, well into adulthood). Many of these studies have been cross-national,[70] producing consistent findings across cultures, having been tested in the US, South America (Colombia), Asia (Bangladesh, China and India), South Africa,

the Middle East (Palestine), and Europe (Bosnia and Germany).[71]

Research findings that students benefit from the same kinds of relationships with teachers as with parents[72] indicate that this parenting literature is relevant to the debate about discipline in schools. This research has demonstrated that, of all the influences on children's outcomes, adults' sensitivity and responsiveness are the most powerful.[73]

Behavioural outcomes

Parents who employ a controlling style of discipline that lacks warmth fail to teach their children self-regulatory skills and prosocial means of solving problems. In comparison, young people whose parents use the guidance approach are better able to regulate their own behaviour and accordingly have fewer behavioural problems in school, with children in the most disadvantaged circumstances benefitting the most from nurturing parenting.[74]

Oppositional behaviour. Controlling discipline results in increasing defiance and uncooperativeness over time, particularly for children with early high rates of behavioural problems.[75] Young people who comply with prohibitions simply out of fear of reprisals do not develop self-regulatory skills and therefore continue to require adults to oversee their conduct.[76] Other than for fearful children (who comply compulsively because they cannot risk parental rejection), repeated experience with having to surrender their own interests in the service of arbitrary compliance increases children's oppositional tendencies and hostility towards and conflicts with parents.[77] Frustration of their need for autonomy incites increased defiance.[78]

Fearless children in particular become uncooperative in the face of controlling parenting, presumably because it damages their desire to please their parents – and these spirited children are bold enough to risk disapproval by behaving defiantly.[79]

In contrast, mothers' responsiveness can cause angry infants to cooperate and render ordinarily non-conformist children as cooperative as their more typically well-behaved counterparts.[80] Parents who are sensitive and responsive to their children and who provide support, structure and emotional warmth (that is, parents who use guidance) tend to produce children who are increasingly cooperative, self-controlled and autonomous and decreasingly antisocial over time.[81]

Delinquency. For both girls and boys, parenting that lacks warmth and is coercive or neglectful contributes to the *initiation* of delinquency because adolescents are unlikely to perceive this disciplinary style as legitimate.[82] (Subsequent association with delinquent peers accounts for its *persistence*.)[83] Strained relationships with their parents cause young people to be more susceptible to peer pressure – to use drugs, for example.[84]

Parental monitoring does prevent violent delinquency and other antisocial behaviours.[85] However, intrusive levels of surveillance and control are associated with high rates of externalising behavioural problems in young people.[86] The guidance approach is associated with low rates and cessation of delinquency because adolescents view their parents' leadership as legitimate and spontaneously inform parents about their school life, friends and activities away from home.[87]

Moral reasoning

Advocates of the guidance approach believe that *why* young people behave as they do is as important as *what* they do. Moral reasoning is the ability to balance the interests of all those involved, rather than focusing solely on self-interest.[88]

Although authoritarian discipline can achieve child compliance in the short term, it is less likely that children reared under rewards and punishments will internalise adults' values.[89] Young people who are externally regulated feel compelled to behave in particular ways, but they do not accept the imposed values as their own. As a result, they are both less compliant and more negative under supervision and behave morally only when they anticipate receiving rewards or punishment for their actions.[90] In short, controlling discipline is likely to produce low levels of moral reasoning.[91] It will not teach moral behaviour in the long term and may even inhibit it[92] because it does not give young people information or practice at moral reasoning. Instead, young people comply because they are being forced to ('I'm only doing this because s/he made me'). That is, behavioural control achieves only external or introjected levels of moral regulation in which children's and adolescents' behaviour is still driven by the rigid application of rules, rather than by value-driven reasoning.[93]

In contrast, young people who have a warm relationship with their parents and who are granted emotional autonomy are more likely to develop principled moral reasoning.[94] They abide voluntarily by their parents' guidelines because their parents reason and negotiate with them, rather than deliver lectures about their behaviour.[95] Their experience of negotiating their parents' standards – rather than merely obeying them – fosters independence and a willingness to stand up for their values.[96] This is known as committed compliance, which is the first step towards self-regulation and integration of a coherent set of values.[97]

Empathy and altruism. Controlling discipline does not foster compassion, altruism or empathy. Delivering rewards for helping can foster altruism in children when the reward is available but it undermines children's subsequent motivation to be helpful.[98] To guidance practitioners, it is obvious that we cannot teach young people to be humane by using inhumane methods.[99] In comparison, children raised under the guidance approach develop more empathy for and compassion towards others.[100]

Consideration of others. Behavioural control teaches children to focus on their own pleasures and pain, rather than on the effects of their behaviours on other people.[101] In contrast, aware that their parents have their own goals and needs, children raised under the guidance approach are more willing to take their parents' needs into account.[102]

Learning style

Even at low levels, parents' use of achievement-oriented psychological control is damaging to their children's motivation.[103] Intrusive control in the form of authoritarian surveillance by parents of their children's homework and their delivery of rewards for high grades generates in children greater negativity towards and less enjoyment of school, particularly for boys.[104] These findings are paralleled in the early childhood years, where one study found that demanding or didactic parental instruction produced in children poorer task orientation and greater negativity towards schoolwork.[105]

Achievement goals. Parents' conditional positive regard for their children causes children to feel anxious about and internally compelled to meet parental expectations; this reflects a performance orientation to achievement (see chapter 16) where children are focused on grades rather than on gaining new competencies.[106] These students are also more dependent on teacher approval.[107] In contrast, parents' support for their sons' and daughters' autonomy generates a mastery orientation to learning, where motivation is intrinsic rather than driven by a quest to outdo others in an effort to assuage doubts about their worth.[108]

Intrinsic motivation. The administration of rewards for high grades produces students who are extrinsically motivated, dependent on external sources for academic guidance, and lacking initiative and persistence.[109] In contrast, those whose autonomy needs are met at home and school show increased intrinsic motivation and interest in schoolwork and a preference for challenge.[110] This trend persists throughout the school years and even into university, when young people reared under the guidance approach score highest on all indicators of academic engagement.[111] The same is true of teachers: when they support young people's autonomy, students engage with tasks more and feel better about themselves as learners.[112]

Educational outcomes

Parents' support of children's self-regulation and a lack of behavioural and psychological controls are the most influential aspects of parenting with respect to academic outcomes.[113] Across cultures, academic achievement is negatively related to controlling parental discipline.[114] Young people in economic hardship particularly benefit academically when parents employ the guidance approach; the same is true in schools, where the students who most benefit from a warm relationship with their teachers are those at risk of school failure. For them a high-quality relationship compensates for a lack of educational resources within the home.[115]

Academic achievement. Supportive parenting leads to improved academic performance in children, particularly in disadvantaged neighbourhoods.[116] In early childhood, guiding discipline and parents' responsiveness to their children's interests during play improves the children's school readiness.[117] In contrast, the negative learning styles just mentioned that are engendered by controlling discipline lead to declining academic and social performances and reduced creativity.[118]

Verbal abilities. Because parents using controlling discipline engage in fewer language-rich interactions with their children – both overall and during disciplinary encounters – their children develop significantly poorer language comprehension skills compared with those whose parents use reasoning and negotiation to discipline.[119]

Literacy skills. While the literacy skills of children whose mothers have little education are typically behind their peers', when these mothers are responsively involved in their children's schooling, the gaps in both the children's skills and their self-appraisals dissipate.[120]

Executive function skills. Infants whose parents support their autonomy develop stronger working memory and executive functioning skills that contribute to improved self-regulation.[121]

Extra-curricular activities. Young people benefit when their parents facilitate and support their recreational endeavours but, when parents pressure or control their children's sporting engagement, the children become less motivated, more anxious, enjoy the activities less, develop less proficiency and are more likely to cease participating.[122]

Emotional development

Children and adolescents whose parents use guidance have a healthier emotional adjustment overall, with guidance contributing to declining emotional difficulties in young people over time.[123] Under the guidance approach, adolescents acquire greater psychosocial maturity; this, in turn, persuades their parents to grant them further increments of independence and, more importantly, greater volitional control over their lives.[124] Autonomy supportive parenting is probably the mechanism for improved academic self-esteem and declining behavioural difficulties in adolescents whose parents use guidance, whereas emotional and somatic problems increase significantly for those raised by controlling parents.[125]

Negative emotionality. Emotionally, compared with children whose parents use the guidance approach, children of controlling parents are more angry, negative, withdrawn, depressed, anxious, unhappy, and hostile when frustrated.[126] Children who are irritable, emotional or reactive benefit *most* from warm and responsive parenting.[127]

Self-regulation. Controlling parents' conditional positive regard for their children contributes to the children's inability to regulate negative emotion, while parental use of negative regard (such as withdrawal of love when children fail to please) leads to dysregulated anger and fear.[128] Parents' dismissal of their children's feelings or harsh responses to children's negative emotions leads in the children to poorer emotional knowledge, increased emotional arousal, and weaker emotional and behavioural self-regulation. In turn, this produces an escalation of these feelings, both in terms of the intensity and frequency of outbursts.[129]

Across the age range from toddlerhood to adolescence, when parents use guidance their sons and daughters are better able to regulate their emotions and, in turn, control their own behaviour.[130] Mothers' soothing of infants and acceptance of toddlers' feelings teaches them emotional self-regulation skills that they are then able to employ independently at a later age.[131] Even easily distressed or irritable infants can be soothed by sensitive and responsive parenting and thereby learn to regulate their emotions, such that they become more sociable and positive than infants who were initially more settled.[132] Similarly, students in behaviourally supportive classrooms are more likely to learn behavioural self-regulation.[133]

Suppression of emotion. When parents control their children's emotional expression, the children learn to suppress emotions such as sadness, anger and fear.[134] Girls in particular have been shown to be especially vulnerable to emotional constriction when their parents censor their expression of negative emotions.[135] In contrast, parental autonomy support is associated with young people's ability to integrate their emotions and exercise choice over their expression.[136] The receipt of support when they are distressed gives children an understanding of their own emotions and allows them to experience empathy,[137] which is the necessary precursor to being able to extend empathy to others.

Emotional problems. A combination of psychological and behavioural control is linked with increasing internalising (emotional) difficulties in children.[138] The mechanism appears to be anxiety over contingent parental approval.[139] Fearful children are the most disadvantaged, presumably because they become anxious about the potential for parental rejection.[140] Children of controlling parents are also lonelier and more depressed.[141] In contrast, those raised under guidance are less vulnerable to depression and more resilient in adversity.[142]

Anxiety. Children and adolescents whose parents use guidance tend to be self-confident, with minimal anxiety about failing.[143] In classrooms, evaluative social feedback about their performance has been found to exacerbate students' anxiety to do well, increasing the risk that their emotions will sabotage their performance.[144]

Stress. Children of controlling parents are more emotionally reactive to family adversity, while students in controlling classrooms display twice as much stress as those in more accepting climates, with disadvantaged children (who may have higher life–stress levels overall) being particularly vulnerable.[145]

Locus of causality. Particularly when parents use psychological control, adolescents of controlling parents have an external locus of causality and a less well-formulated sense of identity.[146] In contrast, young people whose parents use guidance have high self-efficacy.[147]

Self-esteem. Particularly when authoritarian parents employ psychological control, both genders – but girls especially – have lower self-esteem as a result of their limited input into decisions affecting them, circumscribed power and reduced sense of personal worth.[148] Their self-esteem is dependent on meeting others' expectations.[149] In one study, 84 per cent of those with low self-esteem had two controlling parents, whereas 89 per cent of the high self-esteem group had parents who used guidance.[150] The guidance approach in general and, specifically, parents' acceptance of their children's emotions through life communicate to the children that they are valued, and hence contribute to children's higher self-esteem and lower risk of depression.[151]

Perfectionism. Self-referenced perfectionism is acquired when parents' love is not conditional on their children's attainments. These families tend to be cohesive, nurturing and supportive of young people's autonomy.[152] In contrast, the more dysfunctional form, socially prescribed perfectionism, is learned when parents' approval of their children is contingent on their achievements, when controlling parents demand rather than encourage high standards and when parents react by inducing guilt or withdrawing their love when the children perform below expectations.[153]

Social outcomes

Sensitive parenting is the most significant predictor of children's social functioning across all settings and throughout the early childhood and school years.[154] Dysregulated emotional interactions between parents and preschool children are associated with children's social problems into the early school years, whereas children's warm connectedness to or engagement with their guiding parents extends into more positive peer relationships and connection to their communities.[155] Guidance imparts to young people a disposition of 'social trust', which is the basis for interacting positively with others.[156] Accordingly, young people whose parents use guidance tend to be socially outgoing, generous, less competitive and less aggressive towards others.[157]

Aggression. Children's lack of emotional knowledge when raised under controlling discipline contributes to future propensities for aggression.[158] Controlling interactions with parents can cause children to develop negative expectations of peers and, in turn, to engage with them in antisocial or less competent ways, including both physical and relational aggression.[159] Across cultures, children who are physically disciplined have been found to develop higher rates of aggression than those not spanked and, in turn, to experience higher rates of peer victimisation.[160]

Girls' use of relational aggression at age 10 has been associated with hostile and ineffective parenting and a lack of parental support during their toddler years.[161] Even children in disadvantaged families (who on average have elevated levels of aggression compared with middle-class children) display persistent problems only in the face of insensitive, unresponsive and harsh parenting.[162] The same is true of emotionally supportive teaching, which has been found to be vital for these disadvantaged children's ongoing behavioural trajectories.[163]

Bullying. An intervention teaching parenting skills to parents of seven- to nine-year-olds resulted in a reduction in relational bullying into mid-adolescence. The effect was attributed to a reduction in the parents' coercive discipline.[164] As well as coercive discipline affecting perpetration rates, it also causes victims to be less willing to report maltreatment to adults because they do not trust that the adults will act to protect them.[165] As is true for parents, teachers' willingness to take students' perspective has been found to result in the students' adoption of prosocial values and, in turn, a reduction in bullying.[166]

Social skills. Children of controlling parents use fewer constructive strategies and resolution techniques in conflicts with peers, probably because they have not learned these in their interactions with their parents and have not had practice at taking others' perspective.[167] Thus, behaviourally controlling discipline produces children who are more disruptive in the playground and less prosocial in their peer interactions, with the result that they are less well liked by peers.[168]

In comparison, guidance gives children experience of and teaches them the skills for social competence, such as managing their emotions,[169] power sharing, influencing and being influenced by others, making suggestions, negotiation, compromise, collaboration, intimacy and positive emotion. Children whose parents consider their needs during parent–child conflicts later use reasoning and compromise to resolve conflicts with their peers.[170]

Social withdrawal. An alternative pattern is that psychologically controlling parenting can produce passive social behaviours such as withdrawal, leaving children vulnerable to both loneliness and to being bullied.[171]

Affiliation with deviant peers. Controlling relationships with parents can cause young people to become excessively and prematurely independent of their parents and therefore more oriented towards their peers.[172] Given the lack of warmth in their relationship, young people will fail to disclose to their parents their activities and whereabouts.[173] Children raised by parents who use guidance are less likely to choose deviant peers as friends[174] or to engage in delinquent behaviour in order to be popular within their group.

Assertiveness. Toddlers raised under the guidance approach display more appropriate self-assertion – that is, assertiveness – which does not escalate into defiance or oppositional behaviour.[175] Support from parents also allows young females in particular to retain their voice and to be assertive within their relationships.[176]

Competitive relationships. Parents' conditional approval of their children can give rise to excessive sibling rivalry, in which the children try to compete for their parents' affections. In schools, teacher-directed instruction tends to create a competitive social hierarchy, whereas being in a child-centred setting teaches children empathy and increases peer acceptance.[177]

Parent–child relationships

At young ages, infants whose parents control their emotional expressiveness are less connected to and have less secure relationships with their parents.[178] Although young people may do as they are told, they become estranged from, resentful of and hostile towards their controlling parents, rejecting both them and their values.[179] While children's anger at the restrictions on their autonomy protects them from some of the adverse effects of psychological control,[180] it damages the parent–child relationship. Their parents' willingness to cause them pain will decrease the children's desire to relate to their parents or care how they feel.[181] In turn, a lack of concern for parental approval leaves parents with little influence over the behaviour of their sons and daughters.

In contrast, guidance improves young people's connectedness to or engagement with their parents.[182] Adolescents who feel that their parents give them enough freedom feel close to their parents and respect their wishes.[183] When their parents impose few controls on them, their sons and daughters are more willing to cooperate, enjoy interacting with their parents, and are less negative.[184] They voluntarily discuss with their parents their school-based activities, their friends and their activities outside of home.[185]

Resistance to abandoning controlling discipline

The research reviewed here has been accumulating for over 50 years and is impressive in its unanimity and rigour. Its conclusions are clear: compared with guidance, controlling discipline is less effective and more harmful in important ways. Despite this, many teachers who believe in the guidance approach find nevertheless that they impose controlling discipline on students.[186] Of the reasons given in chapter 2 for teachers' choice of discipline style, I want here to highlight two: a fundamental distrust of human nature, and a lack of exposure to alternatives to authoritarian controls.

Handed down through countless centuries, the view that humans are bad by nature causes us to regard children's views and opinions as irrelevant at best or, worse still, purely self-serving.[187] Moralistic thinking causes us to assert that, even when very young children make mistakes, justice demands that there must be retribution; otherwise, children will never overcome their evil tendencies.

Second, controlling discipline is the only style that is familiar to most teachers because their parents raised them that way and the approach is not supplanted during teacher training by information about alternative methods. The combination of a negative view of children's nature and a lack of experience with alternatives to controlling discipline is manifested in *either-or* thinking which proclaims that *either* we impose our will on children *or* they will run amok. This dichotomy causes adults to fear being too permissive in the false belief (dating back to the Victorian era) that meeting children's needs will somehow 'spoil' them.

Eclecticism

Tentative about the unfamiliar guidance approach, many people ask if they can use *some* of its ideas, while still reserving the right to use coercive discipline for the big issues[188] (in the false belief that nothing else would work). However, in light of the fact that no studies find that controlling discipline produces superior outcomes to guidance, why would you choose to use controls at all? Not only are the methods inferior, but the use of coercion will undo the benefits of guidance. Just as you cannot be a little bit pregnant, neither can you be a little bit authentic.

A more detailed answer has to do with eclecticism, which is the merging of various approaches. This comes in three forms. The most basic is atheoretical eclecticism. This merges ideas but without a coherent theory base, resulting in using practices whose only justification is that they 'seemed like a good idea at the time'. Atheoretical eclecticism will not help teachers to solve novel problems, because they do not understand the rationale for their practices. Corey contends that this type of eclecticism is merely a justification for picking and choosing ideas that support our preconceived notions and biases.[189]

The next form, technical eclecticism, utilises one organising theory but borrows in some supplementary methods, which may or may not be compatible with the core theory. The result is that practices can contradict and undermine each other.

The third and highest form of eclecticism is synthetic. This is the synthesis or integration of congruent approaches, resulting in a more complex and comprehensive blend than any of the original components alone. This is the accomplishment of the guidance approach: its philosophy and practices form a coherent whole whose integrity produces clear understandings of student behaviours and whose methods represent a comprehensive response to nurturing and supporting considerate behaviour.

Conclusion

Guidance believes that 'There is no right way to do the wrong thing'.[190] Discussions about which behaviourist method works best, in which circumstances, can give the appearance of a lively debate[191] but the suppositions behind controlling discipline are seldom questioned. In challenging the paradigm of behaviourism, guidance contends that rewards and punishments do not teach young people the skills they need in order to behave well: they do not teach self-regulation, flexibility, adaptability, problem solving, listening, or empathy for others.[192] As well as failing to teach vital skills, we must also scrutinise the secondary effects of controlling discipline on students' sense of themselves as worthy, responsible, capable learners who can solve problems and exercise self-control.[193] Teachers must also examine their impact on the school climate. Behaviourism has no answer to these questions.

Recommended further reading

Grolnick, W.S. 2003 *The psychology of parental control: How well-meant parenting backfires.* Mahwah, NJ: Lawrence Erlbaum.

Kohn, A. (1996). *Beyond discipline: From compliance to community.* Alexandria, VA: Association for Supervision and Curriculum Development.

——(1999). *Punished by rewards: The trouble with gold stars, incentive plans, A's, praise and other bribes.* (2nd ed.) Boston, MA: Houghton Mifflin.

——(2000). *What to look for in a classroom . . . and other essays.* San Francisco, CA: Jossey-Bass.

——(2004). *What does it mean to be well educated?* Boston, MA: Beacon.

——(2011). *Feel-bad education: And other contrarian essays on children and schooling.* Boston, MA: Beacon.

PART FOUR

Applications

CHAPTER 21

Attention deficits

One of the core reasons for overdiagnosing ADHD
is that it appears to offer an individual solution
couched in the language of 'disease and healing' for
what are in reality complex social problems . . . Once
the problem is located in the child, the field of
intervention narrows, since the aim is to dispose of
the problem rather than to understand it.[1]

In a survey of teachers in 21 countries spanning 30,000 students, the most common student behavioural problems reported were inattentiveness and aggression, with emotional difficulties also being frequent concerns for both teachers and parents.[2] Although aggression seems the most serious of these problems, inattentiveness and hyperactivity have more influence on whether students will complete high school.[3]

Two forms of inattentiveness generate problems for teachers: students who are disruptive but still achieve well, and students with attention difficulties and low overall ability that lead, in turn, to both behavioural disruptiveness and low academic achievement.[4] The first group – who have been labelled as 'bright but bored' – tend to be more able than their peers and are disruptive for entertainment. The second group may or may not qualify for a formal diagnosis of an attention deficit disorder, but their risk for school failure requires primarily a proactive educational intervention, supplemented by behavioural responses.

Definition

The attention deficit disorders are a heterogeneous cluster of developmentally extreme symptoms that persist throughout childhood and adolescence and, to a lesser extent, into adulthood. Having said this, many aspects of this definition need elaboration: *heterogeneous* means that various individuals will have differing constellations of symptoms and those symptoms will change over time and will have different implications through the life span;[5] *developmentally extreme* means that, while many of the behaviours themselves are normal, their frequency or intensity is not; and *persistence* means that whereas children typically mature out of less severe versions of these behaviours, when they occur to the level that warrants a diagnosis, the symptoms typically persist even in adulthood.

Officially, there are three types of attention deficits: ADD involves inattentiveness only; ADHD combines inattentiveness and hyperactivity; and a 'predominantly hyperactive' label is reserved for children whose attention skills are intact (although in practice this diagnosis is uncommon).[6] Both terms are replacement labels for a condition that was first identified in 1902 as a 'lapse in volitional control' and which subsequently has variously been called minimal brain dysfunction, hyperkinesis and hyperactivity.[7] The criteria for diagnosis are listed in Box 21.1. To be diagnosed, the listed symptoms must:[8]

- have been present prior to 12 years of age
- manifest to a degree that is maladaptive in that the symptoms interfere with the child's social, emotional and academic functioning
- be inconsistent with the child's developmental level
- continue for at least six months and (ideally) for longer in preschool-aged children

- be present in at least two settings (such as home, school and with friends)
- not be the result of other conditions, such as resistance, a lack of understanding, or another disorder such as anxiety disorder or schizophrenia.

This represents the US definition, as outlined in the DSM-5 (Diagnostic and Statistical Manual of Diseases, fifth edition). In contrast, the British employ the ICD-10 (International Classification of Diseases, tenth edition), which highlights overactivity and inattention, whereas the US definition adds impulsivity. For this reason, the US definition includes more children in the category of ADHD. It also includes children whose behaviours occur at home *or* at school (termed 'situational' hyperactivity) whereas the British definition accepts only pervasive symptoms – that is, symptoms that occur in both contexts.[9] Pervasive hyperactivity is much less common than situational hyperactivity, is normally associated with lower measured IQ, clumsiness and language delay, and has a poorer prognosis than situational hyperactivity.[10]

BOX 21.1   Diagnostic criteria for attention deficit disorders[11]

Attention-deficit/hyperactivity disorder
A persistent pattern of inattention and/or hyperactivity-impulsivity that interferes with functioning or development, as characterised by inattention and/or hyperactivity and impulsivity.

Inattention
Six (or more) of the following symptoms have persisted for at least six months to a degree that is inconsistent with developmental level and that negatively impacts directly on social and academic/occupational activities. Note: the symptoms are not solely a manifestation of oppositional behaviour, defiance, hostility, or failure to understand tasks or instructions. For older adolescents and adults (age 17 and older), at least five symptoms are required.

- Often fails to give close attention to details or makes careless mistakes in schoolwork (e.g. overlooks or misses details).
- Often has difficulty sustaining attention in tasks or play activities (e.g. has difficulty remaining focused during lectures, conversations, or lengthy reading).
- Often seems not to listen when spoken to directly (e.g. mind seems elsewhere, even in the absence of any obvious distraction).
- Often does not follow through on instructions or fails to finish schoolwork or chores (e.g. starts tasks but quickly loses focus and is easily sidetracked).
- Often has difficulty organising tasks and activities (e.g. difficulties managing sequential tasks; difficulties keeping materials and belongings in order; messy, disorganised work; has poor time management.
- Often avoids, dislikes or is reluctant to engage in tasks that require sustained mental effort (e.g. schoolwork or homework.
- Often loses things necessary for tasks or activities (e.g. school materials, pencils, books, tools, wallets, keys, paperwork, eyeglasses, mobile telephones).
- Is often easily distracted by extraneous stimuli (for older adolescents and adults, may include unrelated thoughts).
- Is often forgetful in daily activities (e.g. doing chores, running errands).

Hyperactivity and impulsivity

Six or more of the following symptoms have persisted for at least six months to a degree that is inconsistent with developmental level and that negatively impacts directly on social and academic/ occupational activities. Note: the symptoms are not solely a manifestation of oppositional behaviour, defiance, hostility, or failure to understand tasks or instructions. For older adolescents and adults (age 17 and older), at least five symptoms are required.

- Often fidgets with or taps hands or feet or squirms in seat.
- Often leaves seat in situations when remaining seated is expected (e.g. leaves his or her place in the classroom, or in other situations that require remaining in place).
- Often runs about or climbs in situations where it is inappropriate. (Note: in adolescents or adults, may be limited to feeling restless.)
- Often unable to play or engage in leisure activities quietly.
- Is often 'on the go', acting as if 'driven by a motor' (e.g. is unable to be or uncomfortable being still for extended time; may be experienced by others as being restless and difficult to keep up with).
- Often talks excessively.
- Often blurts out an answer before a question has been completed (e.g. completes people's sentences; cannot wait for a turn in conversation).
- Often has difficulty waiting for his or her turn (e.g. while waiting in line).
- Often interrupts or intrudes on others (e.g. butts into conversations, games, or activities; may start using other people's things without asking or receiving permission; for adolescents and adults, may intrude into or take over what others are doing).

Reprinted by permission of the APA (American Psychiatric Association).

Nature of the attention deficit disorders

Despite the longevity of the conditions, some writers claim that ADD and ADHD do not exist at all and that the labels are simply a form of oppression in which those with power (namely, parents, teachers and doctors) try to enforce child compliance and, when they cannot, will do so chemically.[12] Jacobs is not alone in arguing that it is not children's noncompliance which is the problem, but society's intolerance of diversity.[13]

However, most assert that these conditions are not behavioural, but instead represent a cluster of disabling and distressing learning impairments from which children deserve some relief.[14] Affected children typically have low school achievement, reading impairments and lowered scores on IQ tests, with 15 to 25 per cent recording IQ scores below 85[15] (when the average score is 100 and a score of 85 equates to a percentile ranking of 16).

The core symptoms are deficiencies in executive control. Over half of affected children also have accompanying externalising problems, particularly aggression and oppositionality (but not spite), and an additional one-third experience internalising problems such as anxiety and depression.[16] The attention deficits represent cognitive *deficits*, whereas these associated problems are characterised by *distortions* to thinking, and it may be that deficits are less easy to ameliorate than distortions.[17]

Despite 20 years between editions of the DSM, the new diagnostic criteria have been barely changed from the earlier edition. In my view, this represents a lost opportunity to have the criteria reflect these learning difficulties, which are more salient but require more thorough assessment than do the children's outward behaviours.

Executive function impairments

Extensive research is concluding that the learning difficulties underpinning ADD or ADHD are deficits in the brain's executive functions.[18] These are the metacognitive processes that direct our thinking. It is like the conductor in an orchestra. Deficits in these processes lead to:

- poor control and regulation of thinking and problem solving
- lack of self-awareness
- poor planning: that is selecting, supplying and evaluating solutions according to their anticipated outcomes[19]
- poor judgment and organisational skills
- lack of reflection
- coordination difficulties (probably from involvement of the basal ganglia and cerebellum).

Extending the orchestra analogy, for affected children, the orchestra (the brain) is playing, but the conductor has left the room. As a result, affected children know what to do, but cannot do it – that is, they do not lack knowledge, but have difficulties with performance.[20] Accordingly, they employ unsuccessful study skills; this in turn, limits their achievement in reading in particular and academic skills in general.[21] Students with behavioural difficulties accompanying their attention deficits appear to have poorer executive skills than those with an attention deficit alone.[22]

Language impairments

In expression, children with ADD and ADHD have problems organising and monitoring their conversation, making it difficult for listeners to follow their train of thought; in comprehension, they have problems organising a sequence of ideas and checking their information recall.[23] In short, they both are misunderstood by listeners and misunderstand speakers.[24]

To overcome the disorganisation of their thinking, these children talk out loud to themselves more than usual.[25] This can lead to constant reminders to be quiet. When their hyperactivity is in verbal rather than in motor skills, the children are insatiable: once they get an idea, they go on and on about it.[26]

Attention skills

As mentioned in chapter 1, attention skills comprise alertness, focus, selective attention, alternating attention, divided (or parallel) attention, and attention span. While the diagnostic criteria reflect mainly attention span and alertness (hyperactivity), over-alertness alone should not signify an attention deficit, if all other forms of attention are fine.

The children's attention deficits are seen in the form of motor, verbal and passive off-task behaviours.[27] These children are 2.5 times more likely to be disengaged than unaffected students which, naturally, detracts from their academic achievements.[28] They are less able to divide their attention between aspects of the task, while classroom activities that require passive engagement (such as listening to teacher-led instruction) are the most problematic for affected students.[29]

Self-regulation

Impulse control is the ability to delay responding and to inhibit behaviour,

particularly when one does not feel like doing so.[30] Individuals who act impulsively, by definition, are behaving in unthinking ways that fail to take account of others' needs.[31] While a certain level of spontaneity is necessary and can even be helpful when tasks call for speedy responses, impulsivity becomes dysfunctional when children cannot adjust their behaviour to the circumstances.[32] The children will produce the first behaviour they think of, rather than scanning a broad range of possible responses.

Second, students with attention deficits have difficulty regulating the intensity and duration of their emotional reactions (especially anger); when combined with impaired regulation of impulses, this leads to behavioural difficulties including proactive aggression.[33] The speed and intensity of their emotional reactions can be startling.[34] Parents often describe them as 'going from zero to 100 in microseconds'; I refer to these children as having the temperaments of car alarms. This produces a cascading effect, whereby poor self-regulation leads to emotional problems including low self-efficacy, depression and anxiety[35] which, in turn, cause social isolation that, in its turn, then produces emotional problems.

Children who are impulsive are attracted to short-term payoffs or immediate rewards, rather than being able to delay gratification.[36] In combination with their poor planning skills, this means that they have trouble working towards long-term goals.[37]

Emotional difficulties

Students with attention deficits have been found to have deficient understanding of their own and others' emotions, and deficient ability to communicate or express their feelings.[38] They have an academic or theoretical understanding of emotions but are less able to cope with their feelings of frustration, anxiety, sadness and anger.[39] They have exaggerated arousal responses when under threat or provocation, which suggests problems with the regulation of cortisol.[40] Given that cortisol crosses the blood-brain barrier, it directly affects executive function.[41] Once roused, affected children are more likely to display verbal or physical reactive aggression.[42]

Although rates vary across studies, as many as one-third of affected children have accompanying anxiety or depression.[43] They also have low self-efficacy and difficulty with mood repair, and hence may ruminate when sad and hold a grudge when aggrieved.[44] While these emotional difficulties may be caused by the children's problems with emotional self-regulation,[45] they are almost certainly also a result of their social difficulties.

Learning impairments

Although most writers say that the attention deficits are due to performance difficulties rather than skill deficits, this is not the case for around 34 per cent of students, who do have an accompanying learning disability, as identified from a discrepancy between their IQ scores and their academic achievements.[46] They tend to have lower verbal than performance IQs.[47] Affected domains are particularly reading and language skills, mathematics and written language.[48]

Attention difficulties (but not hyperactivity) also lead to reading impairments for around 20 to 30 per cent of children.[49] Subsequently, their reading failure leads to progressive declines in attention skills and academic attainment.[50] Even those who do not qualify for a diagnosis but who have some features of ADD have significantly lower academic achievement throughout their schooling.[51] The link between inattentiveness and reading difficulties is partly because these students miss out on early instruction, but in large part is due to the reduced support that distractible students receive in class.[52]

Working memory impairments

Affected children cannot retain a long sequence of steps in their working memory and thus have to get started prematurely. They take less time to plan ahead before initiating a response and, because they respond too quickly, they are often inaccurate.[53] Their inability to sustain a planful approach to tasks is manifested in impulsive behaviour. These impairments of working memory may be more detrimental to academic achievement than impulsivity.[54]

Social impairments

The children's poor emotional self-regulation appears to underpin their social dysfunction.[55] They also lack self-awareness, having inflated evaluations of their social performance and thus not moderating their actions in response to others' negative feedback.[56] This produces socially intrusive and disruptive behaviours that generate such significant social problems for them that these really should be included in the criteria for diagnosis.[57]

Their social problems exceed those of children with pure behavioural difficulties alone, and generate significant difficulties establishing and maintaining friendships.[58]

Their social difficulties are more extreme when they have accompanying high rates of aggression, when they have the same social biases as other aggressive students (see chapter 22). These include a hostile attribution bias, positive attitudes towards aggression, the generation of aggressive solutions to conflict,[59] and the anticipation that responding aggressively will be effective at achieving their goals and at gaining them social approval.

Having ADHD makes it more likely that males will perpetrate bullying and, for females, more likely that they will be its victims.[60] Presumably the underlying skill deficits for perpetrators are impulsivity, self-regulation difficulties, lack of empathy and aggressive responses to threat.[61] In contrast, becoming a victim seems to be related to children's feelings of inadequacy and low self-efficacy that arise from chronic school failure, which emotional vulnerabilities target them for persecution.[62] It could also be that the non-normative gender behaviour of affected girls increases their chances of social rejection.[63]

As well as impairment of everyday social interaction, parents report that affected children have less involvement in sports, leisure activities and social organisations such as clubs and teams, and that they have fewer friends.[64]

Behavioural difficulties

Although the attention deficit disorders are often assumed to be a behavioural problem, they are in fact a learning disability. Nevertheless, behavioural or conduct problems are found in 40 to 60 per cent of children with ADHD.[65] These span argumentativeness, aggression and oppositional behaviour, with a tenfold elevation of physical aggression and a threefold increase in verbal aggression in males with ADHD (but not ADD).[66] These behavioural problems tend to increase over the early school years but, nevertheless, are considered a byproduct rather than a defining feature of the attention deficits: they reflect the children's poor planning and self-regulation skills.[67] Again, affected children typically know how to act appropriately, but cannot stop long enough to allow this knowledge to influence their behaviour. They are not behaving with any deliberate malice but cannot inhibit responses to competing stimuli, delay gratification, or adjust their behaviour to the circumstances.[68]

Deficiencies in adaptive skills

Because of affected children's lack of organisation, coordination and cooperation, parents tend to perform chores and self-care tasks for them, and parents report that children with ADHD need closer supervision than would be expected for their age. This places great demands on parents and leads to repeated conflict between parents and children.[69]

Motor skills

In terms of motor activity, unlike normally boisterous activity, ADHD activity levels are excessive, task irrelevant, developmentally inappropriate, and pervasive across settings.[70] In short, children with ADHD fail to regulate their motor activity to suit the context. Their additional movement is particularly apparent when they are engaged in passive, teacher-led instruction, on verbal tasks and those calling on executive skills.[71]

Health

The children's impulsiveness also results in a high rate of injuries, both accidental and arising from child abuse. They also have elevated rates of health problems such as incoordination, sleep disturbances (affecting 86 per cent of those not on medication), middle ear and upper respiratory infections, asthma, and allergies.[72] Some of these health outcomes may be related to maternal smoking during pregnancy.[73]

Gender differences

Girls with the disorder have fewer symptoms than do affected boys.[74] These girls tend to be physically aggressive at the same rate as unaffected girls but to have treble the rate of verbal aggression compared with unaffected girls and double the rate of unaffected boys (although its absolute occurrence is still low).[75] Nevertheless, their violation of gender norms means that affected girls are outliers (and often outcasts) compared with other girls. At the same time, however, they do not stand out as obviously within a mixed-gender group, and therefore tend to have less access than boys to remedial support.[76]

Problems with the diagnosis

There are many problems with conferring an accurate diagnosis of attention deficit disorder. The first of these is that the diagnostic criteria are vague, qualified by the word 'often' (e.g. 'often fails to give close attention to details'), with no objective criteria to determine how much is 'often'.[77] In other words, in the absence of any definitive test (say, of prefrontal lobe functioning), the diagnosis is behavioural. However, behaviour problems are in the eye of the beholder – that is, their assessment is highly subjective.

Second, in the early childhood years in particular, it is difficult to distinguish normal childhood exuberance from ADHD, making accurate diagnosis difficult. Diagnosis on the basis of observations is further complicated by the fact that the children's behaviour varies according to the circumstances. This requires that assessment be conducted in different locations.[78]

Third, the criteria assume that expectations are realistic (e.g. 'often leaves seat in situations when remaining seated is expected'). By situating the diagnosis within the child, there is inadequate attention paid to the demands imposed by the context.

Fourth, the criteria overlook more salient features of the condition, principally the associated learning difficulties.

Fifth, a vital inadequacy of diagnostic practice is insufficient assessment to allow diagnosticians to distinguish the attention deficits from other conditions. In particular, attention deficits can be a feature of many other conditions, including:

- central auditory processing difficulties
- language impairments
- sensory integration difficulties
- conceptual learning style (see chapter 16)
- giftedness
- low motivation
- over-alertness arising from health problems.

Finally, the diagnosis is descriptive, rather than explanatory. With explanatory diagnoses, the diagnosis explains the symptoms. In this case, the sequence of enquiry is sequential:

'Why does this child have learning difficulties?'

'Because she has Down syndrome.'

'How do you know that she has Down syndrome?'

'Because chromosome 21 has fractured.'

In contrast, descriptive diagnoses are simply shorthand for a list of symptoms, but do not imply any understanding of cause. The attention deficit diagnosis is a prime example. For this class of diagnosis, the sequence of enquiry is circular:

'Why can't this child pay attention?'

'Because he has an attention deficit disorder.'

'How do you know that he has an attention deficit disorder?'

'Because he can't pay attention.'

Hence, adding the word *disorder* to the term *attention deficit* gives the diagnosis more authority than it deserves.

Prevalence

Although pure ADD is more common than its hyperactive counterpart, in the US, ADHD provides the largest single source of referrals to child mental health centres.[79] In Australasia and the US, around 2 per cent of preschool-aged children have ADHD, rising to 3 to 5 per cent during the school years, once children's attention difficulties become apparent in the more structured school setting.[80] The broader American definition and higher incidence of the condition may reflect the fact that ADHD attracts US federal funding for educational support; therefore, as many children as possible are being diagnosed so that they can receive this support.[81] This could mean that children in the US are over-diagnosed, but could equally mean that children elsewhere are under-diagnosed.[82]

Most children show their first signs of hyperactivity at between three and four

---

BOX 21.2   Prevalence rates across cultures[83]

	Overall	Boys	Girls
Australia	3–5 per cent		
Brazil	6 per cent		
Canada		9 per cent	3.3 per cent
China		6–9 per cent	
Colombia		19.8 per cent	12.3 per cent
Germany	4–10 per cent		
Japan	8 per cent		
Netherlands	1–2 per cent		
New Zealand	2–6 per cent		
United States	3–5 per cent		

years of age. Nevertheless, the condition tends not to be identified until school age, in response to the children's difficulties with sustaining attention. By the school years, ADD is more prevalent than ADHD but is referred to specialists less often because, while debilitating in terms of learning, it is less disruptive.[84]

As with most learning disabilities, more boys than girls are identified, with little variation across socioeconomic groups,[85] although children from middle-class families may be rated more poorly by their teachers because of being compared to a more capable peer group.[86]

There is widespread concern that ADHD in particular is over-diagnosed. This does happen, but under-diagnosis is also a concern, especially among girls. Girls tend to cluster on the inattentive dimension of ADD whereas boys tend to cluster on the impulsive–hyperactive dimension.[87] Within a mixed-sex group, girls may stand out less, when among their same-sexed peers they can be quite disadvantaged.[88]

This raises the dilemma of whether to identify girls using the normal list of ADHD symptoms – in which case girls are under-identified – or to classify girls according to how much they differ from their sex peers – in which case, girls who are functioning reasonably well might nevertheless be labelled as having ADHD.

Prognosis

In clinical studies, a significant number of children – as many as two-thirds – who are diagnosed with ADHD do not display the symptoms a year later.[89] However, parents seldom rush for a diagnosis; this means that, by the time children are diagnosed,

they will already have had the symptoms for a year and therefore are likely to maintain these.

For those who still have ADHD a year after diagnosis, the symptoms do typically improve during the first year or two of school, after which inattentiveness remains stable, while hyperactivity and impulsive behaviours slowly improve.[90] From middle childhood, the condition remains relatively stable into adolescence, with students with ADD experiencing ongoing academic (particularly literacy) difficulties and those who have ADHD continuing to experience academic plus behavioural problems.[91]

Perhaps only one in four no longer displays ongoing problems into adolescence.[92] However, while it can appear that children have outgrown the condition because their overt agitation improves, their inner restlessness often remains into adulthood.

Most adults make better adjustments to their workplace than they did to school, although many experience relationship and emotional difficulties into adult life.[93] It may be these issues – rather than their attention difficulties as such – which are responsible for the maladjustment of those adults who continue to be affected.

Those with the most favourable adjustment in adulthood have at least average intelligence and language skills, are able to develop and maintain friendships during childhood, are emotionally stable, are not aggressive, and have well-adjusted parents with low levels of family stress.[94] The severity of inattentive or hyperactive symptoms in childhood appears not to make them any more prone to antisocial behaviour in adolescence and adulthood, unless they were also aggressive and oppositional in their early years and experienced socio-economic disadvantage.[95]

Causes

Inattentiveness and impulsivity–hyper-activity are thought to result from immaturity in how the frontal parts of the brain function. This area of the brain is responsible for planning and impulse control. Early signs of attention difficulties and impairment in self-regulation appear well before any behavioural difficulties emerge,[96] which indicates that there is a genuine neuro-developmental impairment underlying the conditions. However, it is fair to say that we still know little about the cause of these impairments.

Genetics

There is a high genetic component to these conditions, with genetics implicated in up to 80 per cent of cases.[97] Three genes governing dopamine levels in the prefrontal cortex and basal ganglia have been identified through molecular genetic studies.[98] Children of parents with ADHD have a greater than 50 per cent chance of also having the condition; siblings are 5 to 7 times more likely to have it if a brother or sister is affected (with concordance rates of around 32 per cent); identical twins have concordance rates of between 55 and 92 per cent.[99] Both ADHD and reading diffi-culties appear to have a common genetic cause.[100]

Prenatal environment

Whatever the genetic component, genes do not act alone: 'Genes load the gun and the environment pulls the trigger'.[101] Maternal diet during pregnancy can alter the baby's genetic makeup, affecting which genes are activated.[102]

Mothers' health during pregnancy is implicated, although most risk factors experienced during pregnancy are still present after the birth, in which case the effects might be due to lifestyle rather than to the pregnancy itself.[103] Maternal stress during pregnancy slightly elevates the risk of attention deficits in the baby, perhaps by priming the baby to be sensitised to cortisol. Meanwhile smoking in the first half of pregnancy increases the risk by 2.7 times.[104] Cigarette smoke deprives the fetus's brain of nutrients and oxygen[105] while nicotine alters the fetus's serotonin production and brain cell growth.[106] It also may increase the concen-trations of dopamine and norepinephrine (noradrenaline) in the brain centres that react to stress.[107]

Prenatal exposure to cocaine has subtle effects on infants' visual memory and perceptual skills that are detectable from infancy, while selective attention, concentration, memory and regulation of emotion (e.g. when frustrated) seem most affected.[108] These difficulties can be disrup-tive from an early age, but may not produce a functional impairment until the school years, when children are expected to be able to control their emotions and atten-tion processes.[109] Other risk factors are premature birth and/or low birth weight (below 2500 grams); brain infections; and inborn errors in metabolism.[110]

Parenting quality

Given the highly genetic nature of the attention deficit disorders, many parents will themselves have similar difficulties. Accordingly, mothers of affected children are less warm and positive with their children.[111] Maternal hostility and negativity could prove to be the link between maternal smoking with their children's ADHD in that women with higher levels of hostility are more likely to smoke; their hostile parenting induces stress in their children, who are then primed to react hotly when provoked.[112] Maternal warmth has also been linked to children's task persistence, with mothers' warm, supportive feedback to their children producing improvements in their children's ability to persist over time.[113]

Physical health

My working hypothesis is that the brain malfunction seen in the attention deficits can arise in genetically vulnerable individuals whose body is assaulted on many fronts. Being so aerobically active, brain tissue is especially susceptible to becoming oxidised by trauma, allergies and intolerances, infections, chemical exposure, or prolonged exposure to cortisol and adrenaline.[114] Children are particularly vulnerable to oxidative stress because their brains have limited antioxidant capacity,[115] while during pregnancy and the neonatal period in particular, their blood-brain barrier is less functional. Similarly, the cerebellum (at the back of the brain, just above the spine and responsible for motor control) is still organising at a cellular level at birth. This makes it most susceptible to insult during the first few months of life.[116]

Poor digestion, particularly of protein. Proteins provide the amino acids necessary to manufacture neurotransmitters, in which case improper digestion of protein can lead to amino acid deficiencies. In turn, this will cause a deficiency of vital neurotransmitters, affecting cognition and behaviour.[117] Protein also slows the absorption of carbohydrates, thus levelling out sugar levels in both the blood and brain.[118]

A deficiency of probiotic flora in the gut will affect brain function directly by impairing absorption of essential fatty acids and certain amino acids that are vital for brain function.[119] Meanwhile, candida organisms convert dietary glucose into ethanol and acetaldehyde which (among other things) affect cognitive function including self-control, speech and motor coordination.[120] The toxins produced by opportunistic gut flora, including histamine and piperidine, are known to produce behavioural and emotional difficulties in particular.[121]

Nutrient deficiencies. As illustrated in Figure 11.1 (see page 165), many vitamins and minerals are needed to convert amino acids into vital neurotransmitters. Common deficiencies affecting the irritability of the nervous system are calcium and magnesium; those important for energy supply to the brain (and all cells) include chromium, iron, manganese, phosphorus and potassium.[122] Zinc is particularly vital for emotional wellbeing and cognitive function through its role in the conversion of amino acids into melatonin (the sleep hormone) and serotonin (the neurotransmitter mainly responsible for mood).[123]

A key nutritional deficiency in any neurological condition is the essential fatty acid, DHA, which is vital for the health of neurones that produce dopamine (particularly in the pre-frontal lobes) and for signal transmission between neurones.[124]

Infections. Receptors for the immune system are found in the brain.[125] Therefore, any pathogen affecting the immune system can also affect the brain once the blood-brain barrier is compromised. As detailed in chapter 1, the most suspect viruses are the herpes family (*herpes simplex* or 'cold sores', *herpes zoster* or chicken pox, Epstein-Barr virus and CMV). In my experience, children whose mothers have a history of cold sores commonly have early neurological issues, such as attention deficits, brain fog, chronic fatigue, and emotional meltdowns. Epstein-Barr virus (glandular fever) is a particular concern because preliminary evidence is that it can inflame the blood-brain barrier and, hence, aid the admission of pathogens into the brain.[126]

A second common culprit is *influenza* during the second trimester of pregnancy, although the cause appears not to be the flu virus itself, but the antibodies produced by the mother that somehow alter fetal brain development. Specifically, dopamine and glutamine receptors are implicated.[127]

Third, *streptococci* infections seem to affect the nervous system.[128] An earlier onset of and more frequent ear infections (commonly but not always caused by *strep* infections) have been associated with hyperactivity later in life.[129]

Toxins. Genetic differences may account for a hundred-fold difference among individuals in their capacity to excrete toxic metals.[130] Children are particularly susceptible to metal toxicity, because their detoxification systems are still immature; because (weight for weight) they eat and

drink around seven times more than an adult and have a less varied diet; they breathe more air than adults per kilogram of body weight and therefore inhale more airborne toxins; and their exposure to toxins is greater because they are closer to carpets and other surfaces that outgas chemicals.[131] The main metals that are toxic to the brain and implicated in the attention deficits are aluminium, mercury and lead.[132] Children's intestines absorb any lead that they ingest five times more readily than do adults' and children's developing brains are particularly susceptible to this neurotoxin.[133]

Allergies and intolerances. Children with attention deficits have elevated rates of asthma and allergies.[134] As is the case for any neurological condition, a gluten allergy is highly suspect. After the digestive system, the nervous system is the most affected by celiac disease (a sensitivity to gluten), with neurological symptoms possible even without gastrointestinal symptoms.[135] Cultures which do not consume grains have no schizophrenia until wheat is introduced into their diet,[136] suggesting that the peptides resulting from the maldigestion of gluten can affect brain function if the peptides get into circulation and if inflammation of the blood-brain barrier permits their entry into nervous system tissue.

Endocrine disruption. With respect to the attention deficits, the most vital endocrine (or hormonal) systems involve insulin and adrenaline metabolism. Of all the organs, the brain depends on sugar the most for its functioning. This means that low blood sugar levels (hypoglycaemia) are a particular problem for children aged under 10 years because their brains use between 40 and 50 per cent of available blood glucose, which is twice as much as adults' brains use.[137] Low blood sugars can cause the pre-frontal lobes of the brain to be deprived of sufficient fuel to function; accordingly, hypoglycaemia has been found to be the underlying cause of one-third of cases of attention deficit disorder.[138]

Hypoglycaemia is most likely in children who have a family member with diabetes, who crave carbohydrates, who have a magnesium deficiency,[139] or whose symptoms appear around two hours after their last meal. It is also especially likely in children taking amphetamine medication for their condition, because this suppresses appetite, with the result that the children eat only once the medication has worn off – namely, at dinner time. Food deprivation by day will not help their concentration. Meanwhile, low blood sugar levels cause the release of adrenaline to alert us that we need to eat. Repeated episodes of hypoglycaemia (or chronic life stress) will lead to chronic release of this stress hormone and its partner, cortisol. This can leave the children in constant fight-flight mode, making them vulnerable to emotional meltdowns when hungry or when they experience provocation.

Assessment

To achieve an accurate diagnosis, children with suspected attention deficits need assessment from a range of professionals and from their parents, and in a variety of settings.

Information from parents and teachers

Parents' reports are a particularly good indicator of a child's difficulties,[140] despite a common myth that many parents overstate their child's problems in order to receive medication. (This can happen, but is rare.) Adult ratings identify more boys than girls, while the child's negative behaviours can bias reports of teachers in particular.[141]

Behavioural observations

Despite the fact that the conditions are intellectual, students' behaviours as listed in Box 21.1 will be the first signal of underlying cognitive impairments. Direct observation of the student in natural settings – looking for both primary and secondary symptoms – is the most valid means of identifying ADHD.[142] In contrast, observation in a clinic setting is likely to lead to false negatives because children seldom misbehave in clinicians' offices.[143] Direct observation – rather than rating scales – is recommended for the identification of girls.[144]

Disruptive behaviours are most noticeable when the children are tired; are expected to concentrate for long periods; are in a group rather than one-to-one setting; when the activity is tedious or repetitive; and when movement is restricted.[145] The children have most trouble when having to plan and monitor their behaviour independently, compared with having an adult supervise them.[146]

Developmental assessments

The attention deficit disorders are essentially a learning disability and, therefore, assessment needs to focus mainly on how the conditions affect the children's learning skills. To achieve this, the children will need specialist assessments and, where relevant, remediation from a range of practitioners:

- a child psychologist, whose developmental assessment will be able to rule in or out various explanations for the child's learning issues

- a special education assessment of the children's reading, spelling, writing and maths skills
- an audiologist for a hearing assessment for any children with speech or language delays or impairments
- a speech pathologist for children with speech or language delays or impairments
- a behavioural optometrist to assess the vision skills of children with reading or writing difficulties and eye–hand or eye–foot coordination difficulties
- an occupational therapist for children with sensory integration difficulties, fine hand skill delays, eye–hand coordination difficulties or handwriting problems
- a paediatric physiotherapist, osteopath or chiropractor for children with motor delays, postural problems, coordination difficulties, poor balance or persistent toe walking.

A core purpose of these tests is to ensure that children are not diagnosed with an attention deficit when instead they have other conditions with different treatment priorities. Interpretation of these assessments will be based both on the findings themselves and by comparing these to observations of the child's conduct. The aim of this comparison will be to determine whether there is a significant discrepancy between the children's measured intellectual abilities and their ability to apply their intelligence in their daily lives.[147]

Medical assessments

One of the main barriers to a diagnosis of ADD and ADHD is that parents seldom request medical assessments.[148] Such assessments will be useful to gain an understanding of any associated health conditions and to exclude other potential health problems that could account for the children's behaviours and developmental skills.[149]

Blood tests will be inadequate measures of many mineral deficiencies because, for example, most of the body's calcium and magnesium is not in the blood but in bone and other tissue, and hence a deficiency will seldom be evident in the blood. Another example is that an iron deficiency can lead to fatigue for years before a deficiency shows in a blood test. Stool samples of bowel microbes only show what microbes are being shed, not necessarily the full range of those living on the gut wall,[150] while hair, urine and blood tests for metal toxicity only show what the body is excreting, rather than what load it may be carrying.[151]

Similarly, conventional blood tests for food allergies have many false negative results, because these identify antibodies produced by B cells (immunoglobulins), but only around 10 per cent of food reactions fit this classic allergic picture; instead, an intolerant reaction is largely due to the release of histamine being triggered by T cells, which is undetectable by blood tests.[152]

Interventions

The attention deficits are complex conditions with many elements; accordingly, they will need a multidimensional intervention. Referring back to Figure 10.3 on the causes of behavioural difficulties (see page 148), and working from the outer circle inwards, what we know about the conditions implies the following interventions:

- Teachers will need to use guidance methods to respond to disruptive behaviours, on the grounds that controlling discipline will provoke reactive behavioural problems.

- Reduce external demands at school (and support parents at home) to reduce the external demands on students, at the same time as increasing supports for meeting those demands. These will encompass instructional and emotional support especially, including support for their relationships with peers.
- Teach children the skills that are deficient: principally self-regulation skills and executive skills.
- Assist their physical wellbeing.

The aim of these measures is to enhance students' engagement by making it *easier* for them to pay attention and to act thoughtfully, and helping students to be more *willing* to cooperate and apply themselves.

Behavioural supports

All students, but in particular those whose attention deficit is accompanied by aggression and oppositionality, need behavioural support that includes the removal of all forms of coercion: rewards or punishments. Because children with ADHD lack self-control, adults' temptation is to try to control their behaviour externally by using star charts, time-out, loss of privileges, and other controlling discipline methods. There are three problems with this approach.

First, these approaches – if they worked – would only teach children to do as they are told, whereas the children need to learn to regulate their own behaviour. Controlling discipline cannot teach children the emotional regulation skills that

they most lack.[153] If adults manage their behaviour for them, the children will never learn how to do it for themselves. Although their condition means that learning this will take longer, that fact does not absolve us of the responsibility for teaching it, any more than a complaint that children with dyslexia take longer to learn to read, means that we don't have to teach them.

Second, controlling discipline does not work. One study found that an extensive behaviourist treatment of children with attention deficits produced some improvements in their functioning within the classroom, but no measurable improvement at home or on any test of academic skills.[154] In contrast, guidance was shown to improve children's social skillfulness and to reduce antisocial and defiant behaviour.[155] Improved parenting produced complete normalisation of the children's disruptive behaviour at school and vast improvements in their social skills.[156]

Finally, coercive discipline not only fails to improve the children's attention skills, but also exacerbates their behavioural problems.[157] It gives rise to resistance, rebellion and retaliation, particularly in spirited children (those for whom autonomy is the main source of their self-esteem).[158]

The guidance approach starts with the assumption that children do well when they can.[159] If they are not doing well, this is because they cannot – not because they are *trying* to be disruptive. That is, the children do not need incentives (rewards and punishments) to motivate them to behave well: they are already doing the best they can. If my working hypothesis of an underlying physical problem is correct, affected students simply cannot calm their nervous system by willpower alone, any more than they could calm an irritated appendix by effort of will.

In short, guidance recognises that students with attention deficits have a genuine learning disability. If we imposed punishment for acting impulsively, we would be punishing them for having a disability – yet we would never punish a student with a vision impairment for being unable to see. Therefore, we will use acknowledgment in place of rewards for achievement and behaviour (see chapter 12) and, in the case of disruptions, employ communication skills to resolve the problem (see chapter 17). In crises, we will use time in and time away to support the children's self-regulation, rather than punishing them for lacking these skills.

Adjust educational demands

There is a mismatch between affected students' academic enabling skills (attention, persistence, planning, motivation, engagement) and the demands of the setting. While it can be useful to minimise distractions,[160] it is now recognised that students with ADHD distract not because they cannot resist the attraction of competing stimuli, but because they have a low investment in the activity.[161] Therefore, we need to provide structural, emotional and instructional support to make it easier for them to engage.

Structural support

Children can be more productive in settings that are well organised, with clear procedures and predictable schedules. Allocating affected children two desks can give them a legitimate reason to move from one to the next (while briefly giving their neighbours a reprieve from their distracting influence), or providing a water dispenser at the back of the room can give a reason to move, while also ensuring that dehydration does not contribute to brain malfunction.

At times when children are required to sit still and listen, those who are overly alert will be able to achieve this only by repeatedly telling themselves to keep still. However, with this constant stream of self-talk going on, they will be unable to hear their teacher. To overcome this, you can give them a fidget item (such as a stress ball or wad of Blu-Tack) during passive activities, so that the brain automatically engages mechanisms for regulating their movement.[162]

For students for whom low blood sugar levels are suspected, I recommend that they be allowed to graze throughout the day, with healthy snacks available at their desk. It also pays to ensure that they can have a more substantial meal (comprising a minimum of 50 per cent protein) every 90 minutes to ward off critically low blood sugar levels and executive function collapses.

Emotional support

Building a positive relationship with children with attention deficits is particularly vital, as the children's actions tend to alienate the adults and children around them. Both parents and teachers are more negative in interacting with hyperactive children because the children's constellation of difficulties generate stress and, in the case of parents, many will themselves have elevated rates of symptoms and, correspondingly, shorter fuses when parenting.[163] Thus, the conditions contribute to adults' negative disciplinary styles – as evidenced by the fact that adults become more positive when the children's behaviour improves, (perhaps in response to medication).[164]

improves, (perhaps in response to medication).[164] This rejection and isolation, in turn, are likely to exacerbate students' learning and behavioural difficulties, and signal to onlooking classmates that they can exclude the affected child. Therefore, teachers need to build a warm, supportive relationship with students with attention deficits.

You will be able to improve the students' self-esteem by delivering acknowledgment rather than praise and by focusing your feedback not on outcomes, but on effort. One study found that children with attention deficits persisted as long and were as accurate on tasks as unaffected children, but did not complete as many items.[165] Affected students are slowed down in their task completion by difficulties with attentional control but also with slow mood repair if they believe that they are failing.[166] Hence, feedback needs to focus on process and not product and to highlight the strategies they use, not the outcome.

Teacher feedback must also reflect the quality, rather than the quantity of their work output.[167] This will also have the benefit of ensuring that ability is not the salient feature of the classroom which, in turn, avoids generating a hierarchy of status based on ability, thus relegating these students to the bottom rung in status.

Instructional support

Adjustments to content. Affected students will need remediation of any reading difficulties. This tutoring will need to be sustained, at least over two academic years, because research has found that short-term interventions are not sufficient to promote reading comprehension.[168] Improvements in their reading skills have been found to improve the students' social skills as well,[169]

perhaps because they feel more efficacious in general.

Second, if students have an early history of repeated ear infections (chronic otitis media), even once their hearing has been corrected, they can have residual deficits in language processing, enduring phonological awareness problems that affect their reading, and may not acquire a habit of attending to spoken language.[170] Therefore, they may need speech therapy. Meanwhile, measures to quieten noise within the classroom can assist children with hearing difficulties to attend to spoken language.

Third, on their own, metacognitive interventions to teach self-instruction, problem solving, error coping and social skills cannot reverse the cognitive deficiencies characteristic of the attention deficits, but as part of a multi-faceted intervention, can reduce academic failure.[171] Instruction can focus on any of the skills listed in Box 16.6 (see page 256) assessed to be problematic for individual students. Students whose behaviour is impulsive will particularly need to practise how to achieve their goals within social settings at the same time as maintaining positive relationships with others.[172] For this, a range of skills is needed, including anger management, accurate interpretation of others' actions, and social problem-solving skills. The main way to teach these social skills, however, will be in conversation with you and with the class when problems arise[173] (see chapter 17).

Adjustments to teaching and learning processes. Students with attention deficits have an active learning style: they need to talk, question, debate and challenge.[174] Teachers will need to target tasks at each student's developmental level, vary the activities, explain to a student with ADHD how a task is relevant, repeat instructions more often than is usually necessary, and closely supervise transition times. Teachers need also to provide and withdraw instructional support as students require it[175] and to capitalise on – rather than try to suppress – the children's spontaneous self-instructions.

One immediate intervention is to never give these (or any) students compulsory homework: they have been failing all day and they (and their families) do not need to confront further failure in the evenings. They will also be more than usually fatigued by the extra effort needed by day to stay focused.

Keep in mind that children naturally congregate in groups whose size numbers one more than the children's birthdays and, therefore, asking any child – let alone one with attentional or behavioural difficulties – to sit in a group of 15 or 20 children is a recipe for inattentiveness. To prevent these children's nervous system becoming too aroused during group activities, they need to sit on the outer fringes of the group or, in line-ups, they need to stand at either end of the group so they are not unexpectedly jostled. (There is very little justification for insisting that young children line up anyway, so that practice could be abandoned altogether.)

Parent support

Parents whose children have attention deficits and highly disruptive behaviours experience high levels of stress.[176] Compounding this, those parents who share their children's condition will have difficulties structuring everyday family life. Therefore, you might be able to recommend support for parents from community agencies, while your own nonjudgmental attitude will assist them to have high self-efficacy about their ability to improve their child's behaviour. Even minimal support to reduce parental discord can result in more durable improvements in children's behaviours than does teaching parenting skills alone.[177]

Emotional self-regulation

Lapses of self-control are inevitable, given that these define the attention deficits. Therefore, students will need permission to have time away to soothe themselves when stressed and time in (support from teachers) – which, depending on their age, may just be the receipt of empathy.

Reveal solutions

To counterbalance the focus on their problems, students will need ample opportunities to demonstrate their strengths.[178] Externalising the problem can be a useful tool because students' condition has often come to define their whole selves and, being seen to be a part of them, it is simultaneously defined as uncontrollable (see chapter 19).

Physical treatments

Orthodox medicine offers little other than medication. Some enlightened medical practitioners and naturopaths advise nutrient supplementation, but doses are difficult to get right and synthetic supplements may not be readily absorbed by these children – and, indeed can add to their toxicity. I have, however, been noting considerable benefits in affected children from a biophysical (in contrast to biochemical) treatment known as bioresonance. (See my website for more information.)

That leaves medication. Quite by accident, stimulants were discovered in 1937 to help ADHD, but they did not come into more common use until the late 1950s.[179] For children aged over five years and those with moderate to severe symptoms, medication still appears to have more benefits than any other form of treatment, although its superiority over other treatments lessens over time.[180]

The classes of drugs usually employed include the following.[181]

- Amphetamines: methylphenidate (Ritalin), dextroamphetamine (Dexedrine) and mixed amphetamine salts (Adderall). These work by enhancing dopamine and norepinephrine transmission in the brain. While around 70 per cent of those who are accurately diagnosed respond to an amphetamine, the debate continues about which children benefit most from this medication, and at which doses.
- Sustained-release versions of these include Concerta and other long-acting forms whose proportions of immediate versus delayed doses vary between brands. Daytrana is a methylphenidate patch, with the dose continuous while the patch is worn. Sustained-release medications are designed to minimise side-effects and, being a once-daily dose, also avert both the detrimental effects of missed doses and the social stigma for students of having to take medication at school. However, their therapeutic effects are more variable.
- Atomoxetine (Strattera) is a non-stimulant that makes available more norepinephrine (also known as noradrenaline). Appetite suppression, mood lability, sedation and rare reversible liver damage have been noted.
- Anti-depressants can be used to target the depressive symptoms but are less successful with the attention deficit symptoms.

Methylphenidate begins working within 30 to 45 minutes after oral ingestion, peaking in its therapeutic impact within two to four hours and dissipating within three to seven hours.[182] As children grow older, their optimal dose of methylphenidate tends not to increase in direct proportion to their increased weight.[183]

Benefits of medication

Methylphenidate (Ritalin) is not usually recommended for children aged under six, because there might be more negative side effects and fewer benefits in young children.[184] After this age, the benefits are similar for children and adolescents.[185]

There is some preliminary evidence that inattentiveness responds better to medication than do the hyperactive–impulsive symptoms.[186] Medication markedly improves most core symptoms, and both peer interactions and peer status improve, while 75 per cent of appropriately medicated children show additional improvements in academic engagement and productivity, attention span, reading comprehension and complex problem solving.[187] The majority of young people report that medication helps them to get along better with peers and their parents.[188]

Medication does not completely ameliorate the children's restlessness, impatience, talkativeness or inattention or improve their educational outcomes, while the secondary problems such as academic functioning, social skills and aggression seem even less amenable to medication.[189] A few studies have even found that children taking Ritalin are *more* reactively aggressive than when not on medication.[190]

Medication produces no permanent improvements in symptoms or full normalisation of behaviours; the side effects can be prohibitive; and the effects appear to wane after the initial gains.[191] This last is partly because, once regular practitioners are overseeing the medication regime (in contrast to researchers), the regime is less appropriately tailored to each child. Finally, methylphenidate depletes magnesium stores[192] and can stress children's already compromised detoxification capacities, particularly the liver. Given the limitations in outcomes, even when children are medicated, additional interventions remain necessary.[193]

Side effects

Almost 40 per cent of children using amphetamines experience troubling side effects. Most of these respond to a change of medication or an adjustment of dose, although in one large study, 3.6 per cent of children demonstrated side effects that were serious enough to cause the medication to be stopped.[194]

The most common side effects are worsened insomnia and appetite suppression. The resulting decrease in the child's growth can make the medication unsuitable for many children, especially if they were slightly built to begin with. In addition, daytime fasting while the medication is in the system will contribute to hypoglycaemia and thereby reduce the fuel available for brain function. Other side effects include lethargy, fatigue, emotional dulling,

nausea, tremors and tics, particularly at higher doses.[195] A resulting slight elevation of blood pressure can lead to headaches but otherwise is mostly asymptomatic.[196]

As the medication leaves their system, some children's symptoms get worse than they were without any medication at all, although the severity of this rebound effect varies considerably for different children and can improve with a different dosage regime.[197]

There is no doubt that medication is wrongly prescribed. One study found that half of all participants who were on medication for an attention deficit did not have the condition; conversely, however, only 12 to 25 per cent of children with the condition are placed on medication.[198] On the few occasions when I have recommended it to parents, this is always because the students' self-esteem is suffering from failing academically and socially, and the medication is instigated to give everyone a breather and on the understanding that it is a stop-gap measure until other treatments take effect. The decision to use medication, then, will depend on:[199]

- the severity of the condition
- whether other methods have been tried and have failed
- the child's age
- the child's and family's attitude to medication
- the ability of parents and teachers to supervise a medication regime adequately.

Conclusion

If the brain were simple to understand, we would be too simple to understand it.

Accordingly, our knowledge of how the brain functions – or *mal*functions in the case of attention difficulties – is still incomplete. Nevertheless, we cannot wait to act until we have accumulated all the answers because the students in front of us need our help now. The educational adjustments suggested here are intended to make it easier for affected children to engage with learning; at the same time, our emotional support must help them be more willing to do so by enhancing the children's relationships with adults.

Some criticise guidance methods for adjusting demands and supports for students with attention deficits on the grounds that this is unfair. However, equity does not mean giving everyone the same resources, but giving everyone the resources that meet his or her needs.

Recommended further reading

Bock, K. & Stauth, C. (2008). *Healing the new childhood epidemics: Autism, ADHD, asthma, and allergies.* New York: Ballantine.

Campbell-McBride, N. (2010). *Gut and psychology syndrome.* Cambridge, UK: Medinform.

Green, C. & Chee, K. (2001). *Understanding ADHD: Attention-deficit hyperactivity disorder in children.* (3rd ed.) Sydney: Doubleday.

Lyon, M.R. (2000). *Healing the hyperactive brain: Through the new science of functional medicine.* Calgary, AB: Focused Publishing.

Websites

GAPS diet www.gapsdiet.com

Louise Porter www.louiseporter.com.au

CHAPTER 22

Resolving aggression and bullying

A well-designed program of prosocial instruction
will include training in cooperative conflict resolution
and in methods of achieving one's goals that do not
require the use of force or manipulation.[1]

After attention difficulties and their resulting disruptions, the second class of difficulties that challenge teachers is student aggression.[2] Like other social skills, aggression can be a positive skill when used in self-defence or to suppress serious transgressions by others.[3] However, when used to dominate and hurt others, it is detrimental to the perpetrator, to the victim, to the group and to the adults who are obliged to intervene.

Types of aggression

Aggression is an intent to inflict harm on another. As described in chapter 1, aggression can be a retaliation against some real or imagined provocation or threat and arises from feelings of anger or frustration (reactive aggression); or proactive, when perpetrators are not angry but are using aggression strategically to secure resources or social dominance.[4] Therefore, when reprimanded, these perpetrators lack remorse because the hurt that they caused was intentional.

Bullying is a specific form of aggression in which individuals oppress others who are typically younger or weaker than themselves in gratuitous, unjustified, deliberate and repeated attempts to dominate and inflict hurt.[5] Although most bullying is proactive, it can be reactive to a real or imagined injustice supposedly inflicted by the target, such as in revenge for aggression, for gossiping or for poaching friends.[6] It is distinguished from simple proactive aggression by its repeated and targeted nature: victims perceive it as intentional targeting of them personally, which they see as a sustained threat over which they have little personal control.[7]

A second distinction is that, with aggression, when perpetrators realise that their victim is hurt, they pull back; whereas with bullying, perpetrators crank it up another gear – because hurting their victim is their intention. (This is why teaching young victims to tell the perpetrator, 'Stop it. That hurt my feelings' is so ineffective – because hurting the other's feelings was the goal.)

Bullying

Bullying is so widespread that, 'No study of social behaviour in any school anywhere in the world has shown an absence of bullying'.[8] Firm rates of bullying are difficult to establish, although estimates tend to settle on up to 10 per cent being victims, 13 per cent being perpetrators and 6 per cent being both, with this last group of aggressive victims declining in number from middle to late primary school.[9] The consensus is that almost one in five school students is subjected to bullying at least once a week and over half experience it during their school lives, with one-third saying that it makes them feel unsafe at school.[10]

Most bullying takes place in the playground, with one-third occurring on the way to and from school, although this usually involves those who are bullied in school as well.[11] A considerable amount also happens in the classroom.[12]

When all forms are considered, both girls and boys report being bullied more in coeducational than in single-sex schools, with girls in coeducational settings also being sexually harassed more than in single-sex schools.[13] Victimisation also occurs more often in classes with a preponderance of boys.[14]

Trends

Prior to the school years, young children can be relationally aggressive but do not yet have the planning skills to bully systematically.[15] After this age, children are less likely to be perpetrators or victims of physical aggression, but more likely to be perpetrators and targets of verbal and relational bullying.[16] This is partly because children's social and verbal skills become more sophisticated with age and partly because physical aggression gets them into increasing trouble with peers and adults.[17]

A longitudinal study found that, while 65 per cent of children use relational aggression infrequently throughout childhood, around 35 per cent increase their use of it as they age.[18] Although physical means decline with age, the tendency to use relational bullying is a fairly stable characteristic across time, with half of childhood bullies persisting with this behaviour into adolescence.[19] Boys of all ages are more likely than girls to be both perpetrators and victims of physical aggression and bullying, whereas girls typically employ mainly indirect means.[20]

Aside from individual trends, aggression is more common when a new group forms, while its hierarchy is being established.[21] Subsequently, once individuals' status positions are settled, physical aggression declines while dominant children continue to use verbal aggression to cement their high status.[22] This means that aggression is most common in the first years of primary school and in the year before and the year after the transition to high school.[23] It typically declines thereafter.

Types of bullying

Although early literature focused mainly on physical bullying, recent research has examined its more furtive forms.

Direct attacks

Direct, open or overt bullying comprises *direct physical attacks* such as pushing, shoving, punching, tripping up, damaging the victim's clothing or possessions, and striking with or without weapons; and *direct verbal attacks* such as taunting, name calling or using a person consistently as the butt of jokes.[24] A final form, *extortion* entails the extraction of money or other possessions under threat, or being forced to commit antisocial or illegal acts such as theft or vandalism.

Relational (social) bullying

A form with particular social aims, known as relational bullying, entails threatening to damage a relationship if the target does not do as directed. These methods become increasingly covert and subtle as children mature,[25] and span surreptitious behaviours such as those listed in Box 22.1.

Gossip

Gossiping is more common among girls[26] and, like other forms of verbal aggression, serves to cement the in-group and exclude outsiders. Being in the know also enhances individuals' status.[27] Sometimes gossiping is

---

BOX 22.1   Exclusionary manoeuvres[28]

- ignoring someone briefly or for extended periods
- outright prolonged ostracism
- hiding from, and thus isolating, particular peers
- blocking a child's access to play
- prematurely terminating play once a particular peer joins in
- restricting children's access to other peers or to play equipment
- restricting or threatening to restrict a peer's access to social events, as in, 'You can't come to my birthday party'
- dominating or bossing peers during play
- placing constraints on a friendship: 'You can't be my friend unless . . .'
- gossiping
- telling secrets or circulating shared confidences
- using hurtful nicknames that parody a person's personal characteristics
- manipulating group acceptance by invoking a third party to collude in exclusion, as in, 'We're not playing with her, are we?'
- talking about others behind their backs
- using code names for victims, which they suspect refer to themselves
- spreading malicious rumours
- threatening to expose shared confidences
- leaving anonymous messages in notes, emails, phone or text messages or websites
- displaying public affection such as huddles, loud talk and extravagant greetings with only the 'in' members of a clique
- employing nonverbal signals that are aimed at conveying disgust or anger while asserting one's own power or status.

discreet but at other times it is semi-public, with nearby students hearing and numbers of students laughing and perhaps looking meaningfully at the isolated, unhappy student who is the obvious topic of the conversation.[29] Although detrimental when malicious, gossip may also have some positive benefits, such as confirming group norms, facilitating social bonding, and soliciting social support.[30]

Teasing

Benign teasing combines three elements: *aggressive* verbalisation made *ambiguous* by the qualifier that it is intended to be playful or *humorous*.[31] Most teasing is good natured and is experienced as playful and affiliative, although there is a delicate line between this and nasty teasing that is experienced negatively by recipients.[32] Although teasing depends on the communicator's intent, the perception of teasing is definitely in the eye of the beholder.[33] Individuals interpret the teasing benevolently or negatively depending on their relationship with the teaser, each person's gender, and the topic of the teasing, with references to academic abilities and physical appearance (especially weight) being the least likely to be well received.[34]

Rates of teasing increase dramatically during early adolescence in reflection of young people's increased appreciation of irony and humour.[35] Boys are more likely to tease antisocially than are girls, and tend to use cross-gendered teasing.[36] Individuals with high status are likely to be most humiliated by ridicule or insults and hence most provoked into an aggressive reaction, while those with low social status commonly react aggressively because they lack self-regulation skills to respond otherwise.[37]

Non-verbal bullying

Relational bullying is often accompanied by nonverbal signals that are aimed at conveying disgust or anger while asserting one's own power or status.[38] These include stares, 'bitchy' looks, looking someone up and down in a disparaging manner, rolling the eyes, using a sarcastic tone of voice and tossing the head in 'telegraphic' displays of emotion.[39] These nonverbal means ensure that relational bullying remains covert, allowing perpetrators to disguise their aggressive intentions and give deniability.[40] The bullying has maximum effect on the victim with minimum risk to the perpetrator, as any reaction or report can be met with accusations that the victim is over-reacting, imagining things or is 'paranoid'. Further relational bullying can be inflicted on the victim in retaliation for reporting or for appearing unable to be assertive on his or her own behalf.[41]

Cyber bullying

As distinct from predatory behaviour made possible through electronic communications, cyber bullying involves wilful, deliberate and repeated harassment or threat over the internet.[42] It can entail using text messages, emails or websites (including social media) to defame or threaten the target, circulate rumours, post malicious comments or circulate compromising photos. Other forms involve impersonating someone online to disrupt friendships or get him or her into trouble. Some forms also constitute stalking, which is a crime. Females are more commonly the targets than males.[43]

In many cases, the anonymity of cyber bullies fosters disinhibition[44] (rather similar to our occasionally ungracious behaviour when driving, compared with face-to-face encounters). The invisibility of the victim allows perpetrators to avoid seeing the harm they are doing.[45] Their view of electronic media as entertainment also allows perpetrators to view cyber bullying as a game, which they do 'for fun'.[46] Electronic means are particularly pernicious because in half of all cases, the instigator is anonymous and because the target cannot escape the victimisation.[47] It seems that the majority (94 per cent) of perpetrators who use electronic media to bully also use traditional means as well, while 84 per cent of electronic victims are traditional victims also.[48]

Although schools could argue that they can do nothing about cyber bulling, the school is often where perpetrators meet and select their victims.[49] Therefore, both school policy and interventions need to protect targets on this medium as well as in its face-to-face forms. One rule that schools can institute is the IRL (In Real Life) rule: namely, that you can only do or say on the internet what you could do or say in real life.[50]

Sexual harassment

A final form of bullying is sexual harassment, to which over 80 per cent of females and 50 per cent of males are subjected at school.[51] This behaviour is an expression of hostility towards females because of their gender.[52] It involves sexually toned verbal comments about girls' physical appearance; circulation of rumours affecting their sexual reputation; physical touch; pressure to engage in unwanted sexual behaviour; rape; using acronyms to refer to sexual acts or sex organs; and visual harassment such as using pornography or defacing school posters of females to embarrass or intimidate them.[53] Girls may be required to perform favours (not necessarily sexual) at the threat of having sexual rumours spread about them. All these forms of harassment are pernicious, persistent and often public in nature.[54]

Most perpetrators of such forms of heterosexual harassment are males and use these acts to gain status with their male peers, while regarding their taunts as jokes or as flattering to females. However, their victims find them threatening and nasty, feel helpless and frightened, and may feel obliged to avoid areas in which males congregate.[55] The public nature of this harassment adds to the distress of victims because their humiliation is public, their reputation is damaged (although the perpetrators' is not – go figure!), and it can result in rumours being spread about them.[56] This pattern of belittling girls for being female begins in preschool[57] and persists because teachers either accept it or blame the girls for doing something to provoke it.[58]

A particular class of sexual harassment focuses on the recipient's sexual orientation, targeting gay, lesbian, bisexual and sexually questioning adolescents.[59] These sexual minority adolescents often endure not only interpersonal verbal bullying (with an average of 26 homophobic insults per day in high school) and physical bullying from school peers (and teachers), but also mobbing by unknown assailants and continuous sociocultural heterosexist harassment about their sexual orientation.[60] The combination of a homophobic school climate, low teacher support and elevated levels of victimisation contributes to a hostile learning environment for victims and onlookers alike. But, for its victims in particular, it reduces their sense of safety within school and results in declining academic performance, elevated absenteeism and increased high-risk behaviour.[61] As many as 28 per cent drop out of school as a result of continual attacks, and they are more likely than straight adolescents to attempt suicide, often making multiple attempts.[62] Sexual prejudice repudiates who they are, with the result that victims suffer more compared to those who endure random assaults.[63] Keeping in mind that they too may have been taught to be disgusted by homosexuality before discovering that they themselves were same-sex oriented, they can have deep feelings of worthlessness.

Bullying by and of teachers

Although usually spoken of with reference to peers, it is important to highlight that teachers can also be the perpetrators of bullying in schools.[64] This was discussed in chapter 11. In reverse, we also need to be aware of the bullying of teachers by colleagues or by their students.[65]

Causes of chronic aggression

Given that everyone starts life with the propensity for aggression, those who are most likely to persist in their antisocial behaviour are boys brought up in disadvantaged circumstances.[66] Troubled aggressors and aggressive victims are distinguished by an early pattern of physical abuse, being two to three times more likely than non-aggressive children to have been maltreated, with this figure being five times more likely for aggressive victims.[67] Their parents are typically hostile, coercive

and punitive, with the children being exposed to violence between their parents, which often becomes directed towards themselves.[68] Their home life is likely to be chaotic.[69] They are also more likely to be the victims of crime, sexual assaults, and victimisation by siblings.[70]

Causes of bullying

Young people's use of relational aggression with peers is common when their parents use psychological controls such as love withdrawal or the induction of guilt or shame – that is, when parents themselves model relationally manipulative behaviours or fail to check older siblings' relational aggression towards their younger brothers or sisters.[71] Subsequently, aggression and bullying persist because *they work*. Moreover, they work in social terms.

Social positioning. Relational aggression, in particular, cannot occur unless the perpetrator is embedded in relationships that are hierarchical in nature, in which context bullying is a strategy for establishing power or dominance within groups.[72] In turn, the dominant gain access to resources: in early childhood to toys; by later adolescence, to peer status and to sexual relationships.[73]

Group solidification. Bullying allows perpetrators to manipulate who is 'in' while excluding outsiders. This establishes, maintains and strengthens bonds within the peer group and differentiates it from others.[74]

Friendship. Some students bully in order to win or keep friends, particularly to gain acceptance by antisocial boys.[75]

(This, however, works for antisocial girls, but appears not to lead to acceptance for boys.[76])

Group pressure. Some young people report that they engage in bullying because of group pressure, or because they are fearful of becoming the next target or of being excluded if they do not participate.[77]

Revenge or retaliation. Some bullying is a strategy to get revenge or payback for social aggression such as gossiping, or for the poaching of same-sex friends or boyfriends.[78]

Entertainment. Other reasons that adolescents have given for social bullying include to alleviate boredom or for 'fun'.[79] Sometimes, the reaction of the target is considered amusing, whereas sometimes it is just fun to be haughty and mean[80] (presumably because it defies adult injunctions against such behaviour).

Effects of bullying

Compared to simple aggression, the targeted and unwarranted nature of bullying can lead to ineffectual responses, and sustained sadness and depression in its victims.[81] At the time of direct or covert attacks, victims are likely to feel confusion about why they have been targeted, followed by covering up or denying the reality of their victimisation or, perhaps less adaptively, blaming themselves for it.[82] Subsequently, they may experience reactions such as those listed in Box 22.2. They might seek either to escape by joining other friendship groups; or to retaliate, but this can exacerbate – and be seen to justify – peers' subsequent victimisation of them.[83] In turn, victims'

sensitive demeanour causes others to see them as 'easy marks' and thus they repeat their maltreatment.

Although students typically recover from the emotional effects of shortlived bullying, protracted victimisation can have a persistent social impact characterised by social mistrust and alienation.[84] Some victims report few longlasting effects, whereas others experience ongoing maladjustment, commonly enduring emotional effects characteristic of post-traumatic stress.[85] Boys may recover more readily than girls, whose anxiety, depressive symptoms and low self-esteem can persist even after the bullying has ceased.[86]

It seems that those living in adversity or who are primed by other forms of victimisation (including child abuse) are more likely to experience enduring effects.[87] Other qualities of the targets that affect their adjustment include their self-efficacy for enlisting the support of a friend, the extent to which they ruminate about their victimhood, and whether they receive support from parents, peers and teachers.[88] Hence, the most vulnerable group are aggressive victims, because they are the least able to recruit support.[89]

A profile of participants in aggression and bullying

Figure 22.1 illustrates the actors involved in bullying, with school, group and cultural norms forming the backdrop against which bullying is sanctioned.

Group norms
Aggression is a characteristic of the group, as well as the individual. Group norms

BOX 22.2 — **Effects and signs of victimisation from bullying[90]**

Physical signs
- unexplained physical injuries
- unexplained damage to clothing and property
- disappearance of money
- sleeping difficulties resulting in tiredness at school
- loss of appetite
- being unusually ravenous when they come home from school (having had their lunch or lunch money stolen)

Social signs
- involvement in quarrels or fights in which individuals appear defenceless
- being recipients of constant teasing
- isolation at recess and lunch times
- trying to stay close to adults at recess and lunch times
- seeking to escape by joining other friendship groups
- lacking out-of-school-hours contact with classmates
- receiving few invitations to social gatherings of peers
- elevated levels of aggression
- increased delinquency in adolescence

Emotional signs
- feeling distressed, anxious, subdued, unhappy or tearful but refusing to say what is wrong
- feelings of isolation, unhappiness and loneliness
- changes in mood and behaviour

- explosive anger
- low self-esteem (especially in the social domain)
- impaired self-efficacy
- depressive tendencies and suicidal ideation
- fear of going to school
- avoidance of interactions at the time and subsequently, even into adult life
- requests to leave the school
- feeling intimidated and lacking the confidence to seek social support or to report the abuse to adults
- fear for future relationships

Academic signs
- academic disengagement
- sudden difficulty asking or answering questions in class
- decline in school performance (output) and/ or processes such as concentration
- reduced participation in class activities
- absenteeism, particularly when harassment is prolonged
- leaving school altogether

Health signs
- victims of persistent bullying experience increased health complaints, possibly because stress undermines immune system functioning
- increased alcohol, nicotine and drug use by victims, either to cope with stress or in an effort to gain entry to a delinquent peer group.

FIGURE 22.1   Participants in bullying

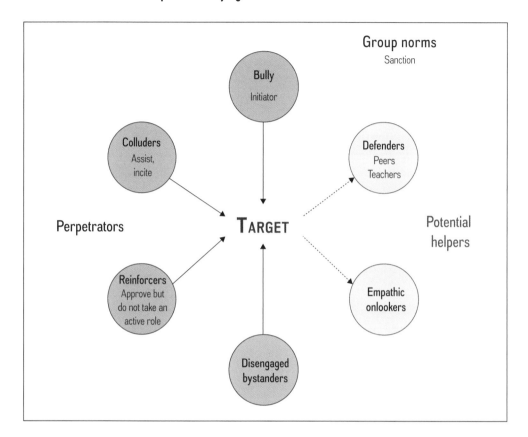

– and, to a lesser extent school norms – govern the acceptability of aggression to the group.[91] Except for physical aggression, over time, group members adopt similar rates of aggression to each other.[92] In groups with high levels of relational aggression, individuals' bullying increases over time.[93] In contrast, when there are high levels of acceptance and friendships, rates of aggression are lower.[94]

The group plays a significant role in supporting aggression and bullying, and in choosing the targets for victimisation.[95] This is demonstrated by the fact that high-status group members are never the target.[96]

Perpetrators

Young children often judge an action to be wrong only if it attracts punishment. Perhaps because they experience controlling discipline only, there is some suggestion that aggressive students are delayed in moving from this sanctions basis to more sophisticated moral reasoning that considers the effects of their actions on others.[97] Alternatively, they might simply have higher levels of moral disengagement, and moral asymmetry whereby is it not acceptable for others to hurt them, but they justify hurting others in various ways, including the following:[98]

- *Moral justification*: the behaviour is justified, say, to defend the honour of the group
- *Euphemistic labelling*: sanitising actions by giving them a positive label
- *Diffusion of responsibility*: the involvement of multiple actors means that each individual can deny a significant role
- *Blaming the victim*: say, for some characteristic or prior behaviour
- *Disregarding or minimising the consequences*: for example, 'I hardly touched her. She bruises easily.'

- *Dehumanisation*: which is commonly used to justify persecution of out-groups such as cultural or sexual minorities
- *Blaming the social life of the school*: this conveys a sense that aggression and bullying are natural and inevitable, or that someone else (teachers or the victim's friends) should do something about it.

Socially skilled perpetrators

The first group of aggressors are those 'tough' boys and dominant girls who, in addition to employing domineering behaviour strategically to gain access to resources and social influence, also display high levels of prosocial behaviour.[99] These individuals are well adjusted emotionally

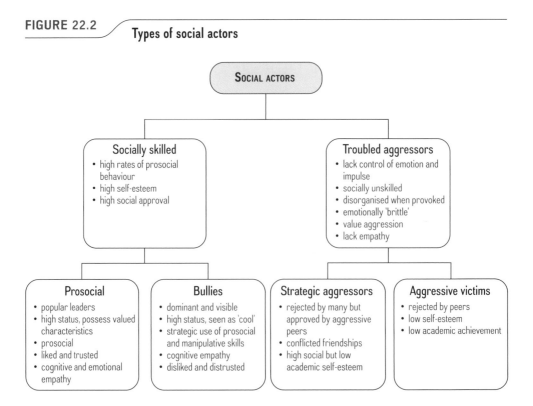

FIGURE 22.2 **Types of social actors**

and have high social self-efficacy.[100] Even from their toddler years, they are more socially active, engaged, outgoing and confident.[101] Their social and cognitive maturity allows them to understand people very well.[102] They have cognitive empathy and hence understand what they are doing, but may lack emotional empathy in that they do not care about the hurt they cause.[103] They enjoy a wide base of peer support both within and beyond their clique, with this broad support giving them the 'social authority' to direct the peer relationships around them.[104] Central to their network, they have prestige, power and high status and are seen as 'cool'.[105] In turn, having high status then adds to their self-efficacy and confidence.[106]

At the same time, they are also disliked for being manipulative.[107] These influential characters are dominant and prominent[108] but are also vulnerable because, if their actions are nasty enough to generate concerted opposition, they can lose support suddenly in a shocking and permanent fall from grace. Hence, they differ from *popular* individuals, who are likeable because they are prosocial and possess characteristics that peers value, such as leadership skills and being attractive, athletic, cooperative, tough, funny and stylish.[109]

Troubled aggressors

The second group of aggressors are the 'troubled' aggressive students who are socially inept and display limited prosocial behaviour. While lacking both cognitive and emotional empathy for victims, the main deficit of troubled aggressors is impulsivity, resulting in acting without considering the effects of their actions.[110] These dysregulated children tend to display behavioural difficulties across settings.[111] Despite their aggressive exterior, they could be described as 'brittle' in the sense that they are easily distressed, are overly sensitive to threat, have low tolerance for frustration, and display poor problem-solving and coping skills, and elevated levels of hostility.[112] In other words, they have emotional or internalising problems as well as their externalising difficulties.[113]

Their social processing errors contribute to the lack of social skilfulness:[114]

- Their goal is competitive and to dominate others: they value aggression, believe it to be a legitimate response; and believe that it will be effective.
- They rely on fewer social cues and are more likely to perceive anger in others where it is not present. Accordingly, they react with aggression that, to outsiders, appears unprovoked.
- They are sensitive to rejection, retaliating against unintended snubs and attributing hostile intent in ambiguous situations.
- They are impulsive, with deficient self-regulation of their behaviour and emotions.
- Their emotions such as anger are easily roused, whereas they have too little fear and empathy to consider the effects of their aggression on others or to anticipate the social rejection that it attracts for themselves, caring only if their actions secure their dominance.
- They fail to heed feedback, overestimating their social competence, while underestimating and failing to take responsibility for their own aggressiveness.

They have low self-efficacy, and therefore they blame others for provoking them.[115] In my experience, these children exaggerate the consequences of affronts to their dignity, employing defeatist thinking which claims that they 'cannot stand' another's behaviour, and therefore they react as if threatened even when little or no threat exists.

Troubled aggressors attract high levels of (often negative) teacher engagement.[116] As a result of their sense of themselves as victims, they perceive their treatment by teachers during disciplinary encounters as unfair. Their negative attitude to institutional authority leads to declining academic engagement.[117]

Some of this group can use aggression strategically (albeit at some cost to their social approval); others are aggressive victims, lashing out in response to the bullying they receive at the same time as acting aggressively against others.

Strategic aggressors. Although their outbursts of aggression are less frequent than bullies' more subtle aggressive acts, nevertheless strategic aggressors are more isolated because their actions are directed against others.[118] They are three to four times more likely to be rejected by their peers, particularly in groups where aggression is uncommon, although in adolescence, they do enjoy a brief period when they are admired and emulated by peers seeking personal autonomy.[119] Their social self-esteem is high because they value dominance, which their aggression helps them achieve (whereas their academic self-esteem is typically lower).[120]

Strategic aggressors tend to have acquaintances rather than friends and few reciprocal friendships.[121] Supportive friendships are associated with declining rates of aggression but these aggressors typically affiliate with similarly disaffected peers, who then reinforce each other's antisocial behaviours, contributing to increasing aggression over time.[122] Although their friends provide them with emotional support, these friendships comprise more hostility and conflict than usual.[123]

Aggressive victims. This small minority of the student population – perhaps just 2 per cent[124] (although probably more at younger ages) – react hotly to being tormented; they become emotionally roused and angry, then vent or lash out aggressively (but ineffectually).[125] Emotionally, they are distressed, anxious and depressed.[126] They become disorganised when provoked, which their peers regard as both age- and situationally inappropriate.[127] Therefore, their peers usually dislike and reject them; and their fiery reactions escalate conflict and increase the likelihood of their becoming victims in future.[128] Their victimhood and rejection, in turn, contribute to loneliness and an escalating trajectory of aggression.[129]

At the same time, they also bully others, particularly physically.[130] They are would-be strategic aggressors, except that their lack of emotional regulation makes them ineffectual at using aggression.[131] Their isolation restricts them to physical forms of aggression because verbal and relational bullying requires peer support, which they lack.[132] Their impulsivity also means that they may be less strategic in selecting their target, thereby guaranteeing that they will often emerge the loser.[133]

Given their history of troubled, rejecting relationships with parents, these students have the lowest self-esteem of all victims.[134] They are the most disadvantaged in school because they do not enjoy the social benefits of being successfully aggressive and 'cool'; they experience the negative effects of being victimised; adults have little sympathy for their plight as victims, believing that they 'bring it on themselves', as a result of which they perceive that their teachers treat them unfairly; and they commonly have low academic achievement.[135]

A profile of targets

Particularly in early childhood, aggressive students initially direct their hostility towards anyone in their vicinity and then hone in on particular targets on the basis of their gratifying response to an initial attack.[136] In other cases, aggressors deliberately target peers because of their personal characteristics:[137]

- *Deviance.* Aggressors may target peers who look different, behave oddly (such as employing ineffective humour), display atypical personality characteristics (being 'nerdy', for example), have a disability, or are seen to be deviant by association (such as having a strange mother, or an unusual religion, culture or country of origin). Nevertheless, these atypical qualities are merely a trojan horse: an excuse for bullying or a justification for it after the fact. Moreover, the group defines which characteristics are seen to be deviant.
- *Isolation.* Individual students' sensitivity, nonaggression, depression and lack of friendships make them low-risk targets in that they are less likely to defend themselves. There is indeed safety in numbers, because social isolation means that there are no defenders available.

However, when friends lack the qualities needed to defend victims, their presence offers minimal protection.

- *Attractive female adolescents* are at 35 per cent elevated risk of victimisation, presumably because they are perceived to be rivals in cross-sex relationships. In contrast, attractive males are at a 25 per cent *reduced* risk of victimisation.

Victimhood is reasonably stable over three to four months,[138] with more prolonged bullying (across three years) experienced by as many as 14 per cent of students and 4 per cent enduring persistent bullying across four years.[139] As already mentioned, victims can respond aggressively themselves, which accounts for 10 per cent of female victims and 20 per cent of male victims.[140] The remainder are either passive or active responders.

Passive victims

Passive victims often feel sad and frightened, as a result of which they submit or withdraw when threatened.[141] Their surrender of contested items and displays of sadness signal capitulation and suffering, and hence reinforce the bully's personal power.[142] Their main coping strategy is to ignore the bullying which, however, tends to perpetuate it.[143] Accordingly, passive victimhood is fairly stable over time.[144]

Nevertheless, their victimisation is not usually a reflection of their social skilfulness. Other than being physically less equipped to fend off attacks, victims differ little from non-victims.[145] Their observed lower self-esteem and loneliness can precede victimisation but is in large part the *result* of the bullying, rather than being its cause.[146] This is verified by the finding that victims' school adjustment is normal prior to the onset of bullying but deteriorates once bullying begins.[147]

Active responders

The main feelings of active responders are fear or embarrassment, which cause them either to tell the perpetrator to stop, or to seek help from peers or teachers.[148] The latter is less common in adolescents, who generally cope alone.[149] Seeking help from friends is usually beneficial, unless their friend is also victimised, in which case conversations about their shared victimhood can add to their personal rumination and feed both young people's disaffection towards school.[150]

Colluders

Present in 80–85 per cent of relational bullying incidents,[151] peers' most common response is to support the aggressor.[152] Colluders encompass *assistants*, who take an active role either under the direction of the instigator or by inciting that person on, while *reinforcers* look on approvingly but do not actively participate.[153] For both, the group setting results in the diffusion of responsibility, which allows them to evade personal awareness of their part in causing the victim's distress.[154] Some colluders hold no personal malice against the victim – and may even feel shame for their actions – but participate in the bullying to avoid becoming victims themselves, or to elevate their own status within the group.[155]

Bystanders

There are two main types of bystanders: the first is disengaged onlookers who consider the aggression to be none of their business. They might assume that the target's friends should assist, whereas they have no obligation to help.[156] A second group comprises around one-third of onlookers who are empathic but nevertheless do nothing to help.[157] They might not know what to do, fear doing the wrong thing, or are fearful of becoming targets themselves.[158] Given the punishing attitudes that groups have to deviance, onlookers also fear being labelled as deviant by association with a stigmatised peer.[159] From the target's perspective, however, their inaction causes bystanders to appear to be colluding with the aggression.[160]

Peer defenders

Peers intervene in just under 20 per cent of incidents, with boys intervening more often than girls simply because they are present more often.[161] Defenders typically seek help, comfort the victim, or use problem-solving skills to resolve the dispute.[162] In around half of instances, if these assertive responses fail, they escalate into aggression.[163]

Unlike most others, defenders have little interest in being dominant.[164] These altruists are high in both cognitive and emotional empathy and are motivated by a desire to relieve another's pain.[165] They have generally been raised by parents who use guidance methods to teach moral reasoning and who demonstrate altruism themselves.[166] However, only those with high status can risk being seen to support low-status victims. Hence, although many feel empathic, few are empowered to help.

Teachers

Teachers who believe that bullying is normative are least likely to intervene and instead expect boys in particular to deal with it on their own (to 'Man up').[167] Whereas 25 to 60 per cent of students believe that their teachers seldom act to protect them, and observations reveal that teachers intervene in only 4 per cent of bullying episodes, between 91 and 97 per cent of teachers report that they take action to deal with aggression and bullying.[168] This discrepancy in perspectives partly reflects the difference between the number of incidents that actually occur, versus the number that teachers witness.

Teachers are more dismissive of relational bullying because there is less evidence of tangible harm to its recipients and tend to minimise those incidents that they do not witness.[169] When they do observe aggression, teachers' actual responses depend on the reputation and popularity of the protagonists and the extent to which teachers identify with their students.[170] Teachers are more likely to intervene in physical aggression compared with the social aggression that might have preceded it and are activated to intervene when they judge an incident to be serious, as measured by the distress of the victim, by parental concern, the duration of the bullying, or the physicality of the attack.[171]

Teachers with a justice orientation typically use behaviourist or rules-sanctions interventions.[172] However, 20 to 40 per cent of students report that interventions such as reprimanding or yelling at students actively exacerbate the problem.[173] (Just 7 per cent of teachers believe that their interventions make matters worse.)[174] In contrast, teachers with a care orientation are more inclined to employ problem solving.[175] This is most likely to resolve the immediate incident and to prevent a recurrence.

The guidance response to bullying

Guidance accepts findings from a considerable and unanimous body of research with parents and in schools that a controlling, hostile and rejecting style of discipline fails to teach young people self-regulatory skills and prosocial means of solving problems, resulting in their escalating and ongoing antisocial behaviour.[176] Therefore, although teachers must protect students, most researchers favour non-punitive (non-behaviourist) approaches to bullying.[177] The reasons for this stance are that those who do not share the school values will not be won over by rules of the 'be nice to each other' variety.[178] Indeed, aggressive students are likely to resist and even be contemptuous of adult-imposed, authoritarian interventions.[179] Moreover, controlling discipline models the 'Might makes right' stance that aggressive students already endorse. Authoritarian interventions would thus not only be ineffective but also hypocritical, as they would simply replicate and reinforce dominance over the vulnerable.

Nevertheless, aggression causes victims, perpetrators and teachers to experience school as an unsafe place.[180] Given their right to safety and need to belong, your priority will be to protect victims from actual harm and from the social isolation that can accompany being a recipient of aggression.[181] You also have an obligation to protect perpetrators from resulting maladjustment and from developing a negative reputation because, once in place, reputations are resistant to change even when students' behaviour improves.[182] Third, it is also vital to protect the group from contagious aggression, which will both intimidate reticent students in particular and exacerbate the aggression of those individuals who are prone to antisocial behaviour. Fourth, you have a right to have fewer conflicts to handle.

The differences in types of aggression (reactive versus proactive), between aggression and bullying, between the various forms of bullying, and between pure versus aggressive victims, all indicate that interventions to reduce bullying need to be specific.[183]

- Bullies need to be deprived of some of the contextual support for their actions by changing the social climate and group norms so that these repudiate bullying.
- Strategic aggressors and aggressive victims can benefit from increased emotional support, social skills training, and methods that reveal solutions (see chapter 19). Abandoning coercion (as described in chapter 18) may be needed.
- Victims will need emotional support at the time and instruction about coping methods. A solution-focused approach and social supports might ease their isolation, making them less ready targets.

School and group climate and norms

Bullying persists because it is embedded in systems (families, classrooms and schools) that inadvertently model, maintain and reinforce domination and intimidation.[184] Two key aspects of schools that allow bullying to occur are status differences between students and teachers and among the various grade levels of the student population, and a school ethos that does not question oppression.[185] In such a climate, there will be too few countervailing forces to dissuade students from using their power in aversive ways against vulnerable peers.

The degree of support from teachers, the school and classroom climate and the authoritarian tone of the school all contribute to the risk that students will be involved in bullying, either as perpetrator or victim.[186] Girls with initial behavioural difficulties can be particularly likely to escalate in aggression when exposed to aggressive peers.[187]

Structural support

The provision of support and structure (in contrast to punishment) accounts for 8 to 50 per cent of the differences between schools in the rates of bullying and aggression.[188]

Supervision. Because most bullying goes on behind teachers' backs, schools would need saturation supervision of all areas to make even a dent in its incidence. Moreover, supervision will not help when harassment is going on in acronyms or in a language that teachers do not speak.[189] And, even if schools could afford the expense, saturation monitoring would generate a siege mentality across the school, which would be detrimental to the school climate.[190] Therefore, although supervision is necessary at reasonable levels, it can never suppress all aggression and bullying.

Structured activities. Enriching playgrounds and offering structured activities at breaks gives students something productive to do.[191] They will then be less likely to become aggressive or manipulate relationships for entertainment (to 'stir things up a little').[192]

Extra-curricular activities. Participating meaningfully in their school, family and community can serve a protective function for bullies and victims, giving them purpose and thereby fostering their resilience.[193] Afterhours activities can also provide victims with a venue for locating a supportive friendship.

Home-group teachers. Having home groups allows students to get to know at least one teacher, to whom they may be willing to report bullying or aggression.[194]

Policies. Having an anti-bullying policy provides a structure for a response by the school once an issue is reported. The policy should make special mention of sexual harassment, and of sexual and cultural minority students who are often targeted for victimisation.

Reporting procedures. Young people seldom report individual incidents to their teachers but, once bullying becomes chronic, are more likely to do so.[195] It will be necessary to clarify with students how and to whom they can report incidents. Given that you will seldom directly witness relational bullying, you will need to be receptive to students' reports, particularly about subtle forms of intimidation such as exclusion and nonverbal manipulation.[196] Where possible, the name of informants should be kept confidential so that they are not targeted in retaliation for reporting.[197]

External support. When responding to bullying, teachers may need support from the principal, colleagues, a school counsellor, outside health professionals or, for criminal assaults, the police. Nevertheless, while victims and their parents have some legal remedies – such as provided by anti-stalking legislation or apprehended violence orders[198] – once they have had to resort to the criminal courts to protect

themselves, it is already too late to prevent harm to victims.

Emotional support

When students believe that their teachers will take action to support them, they are more willing to report incidents.[199] In schools where students perceive a low level of support, boys are five times less likely to report bullying than are girls, whereas in schools with high support, this disparity narrows to half that.[200] When students believe that their teachers care about them, they are more willing to report incidents to the teachers, confident that the teachers will take action to protect them.[201]

Acceptance. Given that aggression is less common within stable, cooperative groups, it will be important to foster cohesion within the peer group in general.[202] Also, because children's aggression typically alienates their parents and teachers (thereby contributing to its persistence),[203] you will need to build a warm relationship with perpetrators. In turn, your acceptance will foster more tolerance from peers.[204] As for victims, high peer *and* teacher support provides the most effective protection against negative outcomes from being bullied.[205]

Prosocial opportunities to lead. While insisting that aggressive students control their impulse to boss others around, it can also be useful to give them prosocial opportunities to lead and exercise autonomy, so they are less invested in exerting control antisocially.

Time in and *time away.* When students have become overwhelmed by their feelings, you can empathise with them (*time in*) or invite them to withdraw to do something relaxing until they are back in command of themselves (*time away* – see chapter 18).

Foster victims' self-efficacy. Students with a performance orientation to learning carry this into their social relationships. When victimised, they will endeavour to prove their worth, either by retaliating (which can either be planful or an involuntary response arising from poor self-regulation), or by withdrawing helplessly in an effort to save face.[206] Those with a performance-avoidant orientation – in which the social goal is avoid embarrassment or negative appraisals by others – are more likely to pacify aggressors, disengage, or ignore the attacks. These responses work if students are targeted only occasionally, but are less successful with managing chronic victimisation.[207]

In contrast, those with a mastery orientation have high self-efficacy and their self-worth is less reliant on others' approval.[208] Therefore, they will strive to improve their relationships and will regulate their emotions. Interventions with targets of bullying, then, should focus on shifting their priorities from proving themselves to their peers, towards bolstering their self-efficacy and self-regulation skills.[209]

Mentors. Troubled aggressors and all three types of victims (aggressive, passive and active) could benefit from access to mentors and to peer buddies who can provide them with company and also model or teach more constructive social skills.

Support groups. School-based support groups can also be beneficial.[210] When, for example, sexual minority students can form alliances with other gay students, they can be as well adjusted as heterosexual youth.[211]

Be alert for signs of child abuse. High levels of aggression are a common result of child abuse.[212] Therefore, reflect on whether aggressive students are displaying other signs of abuse (as listed in Box 1.2 on page 19) and, where indicated, report your concerns to the relevant child welfare authorities.

Family support. Schools may be able to reduce the stress load on perpetrators by supporting their families.[213] It may be possible to put parents in touch with parent education courses or welfare agencies that can provide formal support, or to hold parent gatherings at school where they can be supported within the parent group.

Behavioural support

Behavioural support is any action intended at the time of an incident to support victims. The most successful of these help victims to help themselves.[214]

Direct intervention. At younger ages (below nine years), and for individual rather than gang bullying, simply telling the bully to stop can be effective.[215] For students aged over nine, various approaches have been recommended. These include Pikas's method of shared concern employed for gang bullying, the no-blame approach, restorative responses and counselling of victims and their parents.[216] The steps involved in these methods differ slightly but, in essence, they aim to repair relationships by listening to victims and dispassionately conveying their feelings to perpetrators and any colluders, either individually or as a group. This explains that victims are in a bad situation, without accusing perpetrators or asking them to admit guilt. Pikas also aims to support collaborators so that they do not need to fear retribution or to worry that they will become the next victim. Thus empowered and with their empathy aroused, you invite perpetrators to suggest ways they could help improve the victims' circumstances and ask for a commitment to these measures. In follow-up meetings you would check that these are working. Perhaps even less confronting to perpetrators is the solution-focused approach described in chapter 19 and outlined in Box 22.5.

Peer mediation. In high school, peer mediation may be more successful than interventions by teachers, particularly given adolescents' belief that teachers should stay out of their conflicts.[217] However, the selection, training and supervision of mediators must be handled sensitively so that mediators are not exploited or undermined when antisocial peers denigrate them for colluding with the 'establishment'.[218] In addition to the time and costs involved, key problems are the under-use of mediators by students, despite the typical judgments by those who use it that it is helpful.[219] Peer mediation may also be less successful with severe bullying.[220]

Separate the bully and victim. Separating perpetrator and target can be highly effective because it leads to fewer opportunities for repeat attacks and also avoids attacks in retribution for disclosing the bullying.[221] An 'invisibility' strategy whereby victims temporarily avoid those areas where most bullying occurs can be useful until the problem is resolved.[222]

Consider suspending recalcitrant aggressors. Given the serious effects of severe bullying (as listed in Box 22.2), the physical and psychological health of victims must take precedence over perpetrators' rights. Therefore, in those rare cases where perpetrators have had every chance to cease their harassment but have been unwilling to do so, in order to support their victim, the perpetrator will need to be suspended from school. When you suspend perpetrators, justice demands that you recommend alternative placements and, in the meantime, provide a home-based curriculum. While some authors understandably repudiate excluding students on the grounds that it contradicts inclusive practice,[223] suspension can be a positive force that impels the parents of perpetrators to instigate problem solving. It is also preferable to obliging victims to change schools, which seems unfair given that they are not at fault and therefore should not be the ones to have their education disrupted.

Instructional support

When teachers use communication skills and support students' autonomy in everyday teaching and during commonplace disagreements among students, students internalise prosocial values and, accordingly, bully less.[224] In addition, instructional support will supply mostly long-term solutions.

Professional development and parent information sessions can convey information that disputes myths about bullying and empowers adults to respond effectively.[225]

Anti-bullying curricula. Although their success is limited and adolescents are generally contemptuous of efforts to include anti-bullying curricula at their level, younger students can be receptive to these curricula, perhaps because both bully and victim roles are not yet stable.[226] Primary teachers could include anti-bullying themes within regular subject areas, in class meetings, or within their pastoral care program. While it is difficult to dissuade the use of aggression when it secures status for its user, awareness raising can mobilise bystanders to give less assistance to bullies and instead to defend victims.[227]

The Olweus Bullying Prevention Program has achieved a 25 to 50 per cent reduction across schools.[228] Such resounding results have not been replicated elsewhere, however, with the level of staff commitment on an ongoing basis likely a decisive factor.[229] Some interventions have modestly reduced aggression and bullying in early to middle primary school;[230] one primary school program achieved a reduction of 20 per cent in victimisation and lesser reductions in social isolation.[231] Another seemed only to prevent a normative escalation in bullying,[232] while other programs have been found to improve students' social competence and problem solving, self-esteem and peer acceptance, and teachers' efficacy for intervening.[233]

Helping skills. Onlookers could benefit from training in conflict resolution skills that they could employ during an incident, but will also need reminders to seek adult help if intervening could inflame the situation or further endanger the victim or themselves.[234]

Social skills training. Given that victims seldom lack social skills, programs to teach these have done little to improve victims' social status (or victimhood) or their skill levels, although global self-esteem has shown some improvement.[235] In contrast, troubled aggressors might benefit from training in skills such as emotion regulation in general and anger management in particular, problem-solving skills and social skills. Although some training programs show minimal results, others have been moderately effective with this proscribed subset of perpetrators, particularly when the courses teach actual behaviours rather than trying to change students' thought patterns (such as attribution bias).[236]

Some packaged programs for which the research evidence is promising include *The incredible years,*[237] *Coping power*[238] the P.E.A.C.E. program,[239] and *Behaviour recovery.*[240] These curricular programs are directed at all students in a class and have the advantage of not requiring teachers to possess therapeutic skills. At the same time, however, most students receiving the training may not need or benefit from it. But the alternative of offering social skills training in pull-out programs where disaffected students congregate together can have detrimental effects. In one study, the older, more delinquent group members monopolised most attention within the group, probably adding to their cool status and thereby increasing the chances that others would copy their antisocial behaviour.[241]

Assess and remediate aggressive students' learning difficulties. As many as two-thirds of reactively aggressive students have learning impairments; cognitive processing problems such as attention and concentration difficulties, impulsivity and problem-solving deficits; and language difficulties, including auditory working memory impairments.[242] Although any of these can result in both poor school achievement and a limited repertoire for solving social dilemmas, impulsivity is the strongest predictor of engaging in bullying.[243] Therefore, their academic and self-regulation skills will need assessment and remediation where indicated.

Similarly, if victimisation has gone undetected for some time, victims may also need educational interventions to reverse the academic disengagement and declining performance that has resulted from their prolonged isolation.[244]

Training in countering skills for victims. Practical advice is designed to help students respond appropriately during an incident and enfranchise them to resist future harassment.[245] In the junior primary years, the most successful strategy is to enlist the support of a friend; by late primary school, conflict resolution skills, assertiveness in the form of 'brave talk' and responding humorously to teasing (see Box 22.3) can all be successful.[246] One measure *not* to recommend to victims is to ignore the bullying, because doing so leads to its escalation, with the target also interpreting this advice as a lack of support.[247]

Solutions

Counselling. Counselling of perpetrators can be effective, producing reductions in their aggression, although their reputation

---

BOX 22.3 **Retorts for teasing**[248]

Nonchalance or indifference
- Look the teaser in the eye with a bored expression.
- Walk away slowly.
- 'Whatever.'
- 'Yeah, yeah, I've heard that before. Let me know when you've got something new to say.'
- 'So, what's your point?'
- 'Tell me when you get to the funny part.'
- 'Good thing you laughed – because no one else thought it was funny.'

Disgust
- 'Get a life.'
- 'Tell someone who cares.'
- Roll your eyes.

Humour
- 'Thank you for noticing.'
- 'That's just a lucky guess.'
- 'Yes, I'm very proud of that.'

Assertiveness
- 'Cut it out.'
- 'Stop that. I don't like it.'

However, assertiveness is best used only when friends are present for backup and if there is some degree of friendship with the teaser; otherwise, assertiveness can sound like over-sensitivity and could incite the teaser to persist.

Responses that never work
- 'You hurt my feelings.'
- 'I'm telling on you.'
- 'You're going to get into trouble.'
- 'That's not nice.'

BOX 22.4   **Some bullying-prevention curricula**[249]

Early childhood friendship project[250]
Targets: 3- to 5-year-olds
Skills: friendship-making skills, relational aggression
Outcomes: decreases in physical and relational aggression and victimisation, with an increase in prosocial behaviours such as inclusion
Comment: This program for young children could be supplemented with a parent education component.

I Can Problem Solve (ICPS)[251]
Targets: 6- to 8-year-olds
Skills: problem solving
Outcomes: increases in prosocial behaviour, with lesser reductions in overt aggression and relational bullying, particularly for the two-year (in contrast with the one-year) program
Comment: The program is very long (83 sessions).

You can do it! and Program Achieve[252]
Targets: 4- to 16-year-olds
Skills: teaches five 'habits of mind": Confidence (accepting myself, taking risks, being independent); Persistence; Organisation (setting goals and planning my time); Getting along (being tolerant of others, thinking first, playing by the rules, and social responsibility); and Emotional resilience
Outcomes: increases in class attendance, effort and achievement and positive interactions between students
Comment: This is a six-volume social-emotional curriculum of personal development activities designed to be taught by teachers or mental health professionals.

Walk away, Ignore, Talk, Seek help (WITS)[253]
Targets: primary (elementary) school students
Skills: social skills
Outcomes: Reduced relational and physical victimisation, increased social competence
Comment: The program includes community members in delivering lessons. The website has extensive curricular resources.[254]

Making Choices: social problem-solving skills for children (MC)[255]
Targets: primary (elementary) school children with behavioural problems
Skills: social skills
Outcomes: enhanced social competence, emotional regulation and concentration, reduced aggression
Comment: The program includes an add-on program, the Strong families program, which involves five evening information sessions for parents. Program elements are tailored to the cultural backgrounds of the children and families.

Friend to Friend (F2F)[256]

Targets: 8 to 10-year-old African-American relationally aggressive girls

Skills: relational and physical aggression, social problem-solving skills, attribution training, anger management, prosocial behaviours

Outcomes: large decreases in relational aggression, more moderate decreases in physical aggression, hostile attributions, and loneliness

Comment: Although this program is culture-specific, there will be adaptations that can be made for other minority groups elsewhere.

Second Step: A Violence Prevention Curriculum[257]

Targets: Early childhood to grade 8

Skills: Attitudes towards aggression, empathy and social problem-solving

Outcomes: student attitudes to aggression improved and observers recorded a decline in playground bullying with lesser changes in aggression, although students reported no differences in victimisation[258]

Comment: Training materials are readily available.[259]

Social Aggression Prevention Program[260]

Targets: girls in grades 4 to 6

Skills: empathy and social problem-solving, prosocial skills and relational aggression

Outcomes: Students' social problem-solving skills improved, with a slight improvement in empathy and a decline in relational aggression. Those participants with the greatest social problems at the outset improved the most.

Comment: This program is relatively brief (10 sessions).[261]

Creating A Safe School (CASS)[262]

Targets: grade 6

Skills: relational aggression

Outcomes: Students' awareness was raised because after the program their reports of relational aggression increased. Those with high initial levels of relational aggression showed decreases.

Comment: This program appears to be accessible only through direct staff training.

Steps to respect[263]

Targets: Primary (elementary) school.

Skills: Relational aggression, gossip, social exclusion

Outcomes: Reductions in gossip were substantial. Those who endorsed retaliation as a justification for aggression showed declines. Victimisation rates did not decline unless target had support from friends.

Comment: This program involves 11 lessons on helping students identify bullying, and training in empathy, assertiveness, conflict resolution and friendship skills.

is harder to shift.[264] In the longer term, some entrenched targets of bullying can benefit from counselling, as those who are emotionally sensitive are at some elevated risk of persistent victimisation.[265] Solution-focused conversations with victims could highlight their role in generating exceptions and emphasise the resiliency skills that they already employ.

Reveal solutions. Students with a reputation for being aggressive can come to be defined by it. The methods of looking for exceptions, rewriting their story, reframing and externalising the problematic behaviour can all be used to help them turn around a negative reputation (see chapter 19).

Abandon coercion. When the other measures described here are not helping chronic aggression to remit, you could employ the *Abandon coercion* method described in chapter 18, observing the cautions for its use given it that chapter.

Question the goals of proactive aggressors. Proactive aggressors have adequate emotional self-control, but fail to discipline their impulses. With these students, the hurdle you must overcome is that they value aggression because it gains them status. In light of the fact reported earlier that this dominance comes at the cost of peer acceptance, you can raise doubts in younger students about their goal by asking: 'I am wondering: Do you want to have friends, or do you want to be boss?'. If they say that they want friends, you can ask how they think their behaviour is working for them. To help them answer this, you might invite them to reflect on their peers' verbal and nonverbal feedback to them.

If instead they tell you that they want to be boss, you can ask what being the boss makes them believe about themselves. If they respond, for example, that having power makes them feel good about themselves, you can feign puzzlement when you enquire (with the exact wording adjusted in accord with students' ages):

- Where did you get that idea?
- What makes you think that you're not already a good person, whether you are the boss or not?

BOX 22.5   A solution-focused approach to bullying[266]

Statement of the problem
In an interview with the victim, open up discussion by stating that you, another teacher, or the student's parent is worried about him or her. You can follow this up with the question, 'Are we right to be worried about you?'.

Having received assent that the worry is justified, you will need to state that answers to the next three questions will not get anyone into trouble. These questions are:

- 'Who do you find difficult to deal with at the moment?' Do not ask what the named students are doing, because this can make the conversation deteriorate into problem-saturated talk.
- 'Who else is around when (the named peer) is being difficult?' This allows you to identify bystanders who could be recruited to help.
- 'Who are your friends?' or, for those who are now completely isolated from their

peer group, 'Who would you like to be your friend?'.

Recruit the support group

Meet as a group with the perpetrators, onlookers and potential or actual friends named by the victim. Begin by telling them that the victim has been unhappy at school lately and that you have chosen to talk with them because you know they can help the victim. Do not mention bullying or talk about aggressive incidents, because this could degenerate into accusations of fault and blame. Instead, discuss with them times when they have been unhappy at school, and express empathy that it is not easy to be so. Then ask for their suggestions of what can be done to help the focus student. As they raise suggestions, you can compliment promising ideas while checking that they are realistic: 'That's a good idea. Would that be difficult or easy for you to do?'. When in reply students volunteer that it would not be difficult, you can thank them for their kindness. While not asking them to be friends with the focus student or demanding a commitment to carrying out the suggestions, you can end this session with a comment that you think their plan will work to make the victim happier at school.

Review

A week later, meet with the victim to hear what has been better over the past week and ask how he or she managed to make that happen (e.g. responding to or trusting the friendlier overtures of the former bullies). Also contact the student's parents for their feedback about his or her progress.

Next, meet again with the support group and ask what each member has done over the previous week to make the focus student happier at school. There is no need to refer back to their original suggestions, because it does not matter if they employed those particular strategies, only that they did something to make the situation improve for the victim. Congratulate them personally and as a group for a job well done and ask if they would like to continue for another week.

Conduct one more review and, if no further problems surface, cease the intervention.

Comment

The advantages of this method are that the bullies are not confronted, which might activate denials and counter-accusations. Neither are the perpetrators punished, which prevents their retaliating against the victim for disclosing the bullying. It also applies to aggressive victims, because culpability is not an issue.[267] Most parties are relieved not to have to discuss the actual bullying behaviour but to focus instead on finding a solution. Once that is achieved, the details of who did what to whom become irrelevant anyway.

- 'How many people do you have to boss around before you will have enough proof that you are okay: this peer, the whole class, the whole school, the whole city, everyone in the country ... or *all the world*? How likely is that?'

Supporting parents of victims

Parents of victims want to see action. Although their first reaction might be to ask how you have punished perpetrators, you can assure them that research shows

BOX 22.6 Advice for parents of victims[268]

- Accept that social problems are inevitable, normal but nevertheless painful (without necessarily being traumatic).
- Reflect children's hurt without feeling the need to 'fix' it.
- Trust your child's resilience.
- Trust friendship: it cycles between aggression and affection.
- Do not 'interview for pain' at the end of each school day, to discover the hurts that children have suffered during the day.
- Ask children: 'Do I need to be worried?' Do not intervene if they answer 'No' but reserve the right to do so if your concerns escalate.
- Adult solutions interfere with children's learning to work things out themselves. Therefore, intervene only in emergencies.

that this only exacerbates aggression. You can explain that you are looking for a solution, rather than to punish the culprit. Box 22.6 lists some suggestions for parents to support their son or daughter.

You could encourage parents to provide opportunities for their child to socialise with peers outside of school hours. Cementing friendships will alleviate victims' isolation and make aggression less likely because children are less hostile towards others whom they know well,[269] and may provide opportunities for the two sets of parents to support each other.

Collaborating with parents of perpetrators

In my 30 years of psychology practice, I have never yet met a physically well child from a well-resourced, well-functioning family who was displaying repeated aggression. In my experience, troubled and isolated children have troubled and isolated families.[270] That is, chronic aggression in children can be a sign of stress in a family. Moreover, children's aggression is likely to be most severe at home,[271] thereby adding to parents' stress. Meanwhile, their child's aggressive behaviour often exacerbates parents' isolation, with not only their child being shunned by peers but the parents also being spurned by other parents. Therefore, you will need to take active steps to include the parents of aggressors within the wider parent group.

Parents of aggressors need to be told about their child's behaviour, without their son or daughter being condemned and without themselves being criticised. To avoid angry parents punishing their children at home, it will be crucial to communicate that this is a school-based problem, which the school intends to solve. In those rare cases where you suspect that the parents might severely punish the child, it could be necessary to provide limited specifics about the incident.

Like their children, parents often view relational aggression as both more normative and benign than physical aggression,[272] which may reduce their commitment to intervening. Some of their reluctance can be that, although their child is the perpetrator in the current instance, in the past the roles of the protagonists were reversed, in which case parents might feel that their child's behaviour is justified.[273] Alternatively, perpetrators are unlikely to volunteer information to their parents about their transgressions, in which case your report may be the first the parents have heard of the incident. If parents become defensive, listen without agreeing with them, giving a rationale for why the school is concerned, and then move on to find a solution.[274]

Solution-focused interventions with parents of perpetrators can be useful, particularly if they attempt to 'gang up' with parents of other perpetrators to ostracise the victim or the victim's parents;[275] if parents of aggressive victims overlook their child's culpability in the bullying and claim victim status only; or if parents of victims either feel powerless to help their child or intend to confront the bullies or their parents themselves, thus potentially inflaming the situation. The strength of the solution-focused approach is that it does not require both sets of parents to agree on the facts about incidents or to apportion blame, but merely to acknowledge that victims are having a difficult time.

Conclusion

The most successful way to prevent bullying and aggression is to be supremely effective at responding to incidents, thus avoiding a repetition.[276] However, to achieve this, our focus cannot just be on the individuals involved: we cannot change individuals' behaviour without changing the context that incites and supports their actions. This will require changing the school climate, such that the presence of hierarchical relationships does not promote differential power between students. We will also need to ensure that discriminatory treatment of students does not heighten the salience of racial, ability or other differences and thereby generate differences in status between students that the dominant can then exploit.

Recommended further reading

McGrath, H. & Noble, T. (Eds.) (2006). *Bullying solutions: Evidence-based approaches to bullying in Australian schools.* Sydney: Pearson Longman.

O'Moore, M. & Minton, S.J. (2004). *Dealing with bullying in schools: A training manual for teachers, parents and other professionals.* London: Paul Chapman.

Rigby, K. (1996). *Bullying in schools: And what to do about it.* Melbourne: ACER.

——(2003). *Stop the bullying: A handbook for schools.* (2nd ed.) Melbourne: ACER.

Slee, P.T. (2001). *The P.E.A.C.E. pack: A program for reducing bullying in our schools.* (3rd ed.) Adelaide, SA: Flinders University.

For early childhood teachers

Sprung, B., Froschl, M. & Hinitz, B. (2005). *The anti-bullying and teasing book for preschool classrooms.* Beltsville, MD: Gryphon House.

For parents

Coloroso, B. (2008). *The bully, the bullied, and the bystander.* (2nd ed.) New York: HarperCollins.

Dellasega, C. & Nixon, C. (2003). *Girl wars: Twelve strategies that will end female bullying.* New York: Fireside.

Elman, N.M. & Kennedy-Moore, E. (2003). *The unwritten rules of friendship.* New York: Little Brown.

Haber, J. (2007). *Bullyproof your child for life.* New York: Perigee.

Thompson, M., Cohen, L.J. & Grace, C.O'N. (2002). *Mom, they're teasing me: Helping your child solve social problems.* New York: Ballantine.

Thompson, M. & Grace, C.O'N. (2001). *Best friends, worst enemies.* New York: Ballantine.

Wiseman, R. (2002). *Queen bees and wannabes: Helping your daughter survive cliques, gossip, boyfriends and other realities of adolescence.* London: Piatkus.

Websites

Child and Adolescent Psychological and Educational Resources (CAPER): www.caper.com.au

Cyber safety: www.i-safe.org

Ken Rigby's site: www.education.unisa.edu.au/bullying

National Coalition Against Bullying: www.ncab.org.au

PART FIVE

Beyond the classroom

CHAPTER 23

Collaborating with parents

> When a teacher talks to parents about their children, he [or she] inevitably intrudes on family dreams . . . What the teacher says about the child touches on deep feelings and hidden fantasies. A concerned teacher is aware of the impact of his [or her] words. He [or she] consciously avoids comments that may casually kill dreams.[1]

When the term *parent* is used in this chapter, it is meant to encompass any caregivers who are significant in the lives of young people, regardless of whether these adults are the children's biological parents. In many families, grandparents or other extended family members have a crucial role either as an elder or as a major or supplementary care provider for a child.

A rationale for parent involvement

Parents who have high aspirations and are active supporters of their children's education tend to have children who are academically successful, hold positive attitudes towards school and are well adjusted emotionally and socially.[2] Meanwhile, the decline in the quality of students' relationships with their teachers over the school years is slowed when parents and teachers are in regular contact with each other.[3] These academic gains are usually the principal reason for collaborating with parents. However, in terms of the topic of this book, a second rationale is that, when students have behavioural or educational problems, parents are a prime source of information about how those problems can be solved. Collaboration allows parents to be your informants and consultants.

These advantages aside, my rationale for collaborating with parents is that they employ teachers to educate their children; therefore, you are accountable to them for your execution of this task. It is your job to collaborate with your employers. Not only is that common courtesy, but it reflects the true lines of accountability.

Styles of interaction between teachers and parents

Part of the complexity in teachers' relationships with parents arises because teachers are supposed to remain professional on the one hand (which is equated with being distant), at the same time as being caring.[4]

However, as defined in chapter 16, caring means caring *about* rather than caring *for* (in an affectionate sense), while professional relationships do not require distance: they require respect. Instead, parent–teacher relationships have historically been hierarchical, with interactions between them being a vehicle for advancing teachers' agenda and priorities.[5] This stance of professional dominance is a liability when teachers need to recruit parents' support about their son's or daughter's behavioural difficulties in schools.

Professional-driven interactions

The first style of parent–teacher relationships is characterised by teacher dominance. These relationships are not occurring on neutral terrain, but are sites of power.[6] When professionals drive relationships with parents, it is assumed that they are exclusively qualified to apply a specialised body of knowledge, and that this is the only information relevant to the issue at hand.[7] They are the ones to assess students' needs, interpret these to parents in a one-way flow of communication, and formulate a program – with parents expected either to defer to teachers' diagnoses and comply with their recommendations, or clear the scene to allow the professionals to get on with their job. Parents must either passively accept teachers' advice, or go elsewhere.[8]

This expert body of knowledge is a source of what has been termed *normalisation power*, in which teachers uphold a norm for how parents should behave towards themselves and in support of their children, and then judge parents critically if they fall short of this ideal.[9] From their elevated position, professionals often regard parents as the source of their children's problems, particularly when the family is disadvantaged socially or has a structure other than the idealised nuclear family.[10] This deficit orientation criticises parents and leaves teachers feeling increasingly pessimistic about their ability to counteract family 'inadequacies'.[11] This judgmental attitude can be mutual. Aware that they are being judged and themselves suspicious of teachers, this stance involves parents and teachers in mutual surveillance and suspicion of each other.[12]

This is not a model for the 21st century. Pulling rank makes it difficult for teachers to acquire from parents the information and support that teachers need to resolve children's behavioural difficulties. This sets them up to fail. And this professional-driven stance contravenes both the spirit and provisions of government policies on parent collaboration.

Associative interactions

A second style recognises that parents need schools and that teachers need parents.[13] Therefore, parents are invited into the school, but often only for token activities that do not challenge teachers' domain, such that teachers and parents work in parallel rather than jointly.[14] This stance has been termed 'turfism'.[15] One review found it to be common in schools today, particularly at high-school level.[16] It dictates that parents assist their children with their schoolwork and behaviour, but must not interfere at school by questioning teachers about their curriculum or teaching strategies.[17] This is reflected in an unwritten ethos of, 'No parents past this point'.[18]

In this model, parents are expected to support the school by overseeing homework and following through at home on interventions being applied at school. However, these expectations can be both excessive and unworkable. They are excessive inasmuch as it is not parents' job to act as their children's teachers: parents function best as parents. And the expectations are unworkable, because parents' instructional support is seldom beneficial to children.[19] Finally, when parents cannot conform to these expectations, an adversarial and confrontational relationship is established which leads to either more negative or fewer interactions between teachers and nonconformist parents.[20] The end result is that the parents and students whose educational success most relies on teacher support are the ones who are least likely to receive it.[21]

Collaboration

A third form of the teacher–parent relationship is collaboration. This is an interaction between parties of equal status engaged in shared decision making towards a common goal.[22] Collaboration is a philosophical stance of openness to parents that implies a shared responsibility for the education of their children, although teachers and parents will fulfil differing roles according to their complementary expertise. By harnessing parents' intimate knowledge of their children, teachers gain information that helps them to teach their students, while feeling assured of parents' support for their efforts.

A parent-driven model

In its stance that teachers and parents are full and equal partners, it is my contention that collaboration gives too much power to teachers. A more respectful option is a parent-driven model, which recognises that, more than being mere consumers or even equal participants in a partnership with you, parents are actually your employers. Their function is not to help you teach their children, but the reverse: they employ you to assist them in raising skilled, knowledgeable and well-adjusted children. They hire you for your expertise as an educator, much as they might employ doctors, naturopaths or dentists to support their children's health. Parents pay your salary by way of private school fees or taxes for public education. Therefore, your task is to further their aims for their children. In a parent-driven model, you are accountable to parents: they are not accountable to you.

Using the analogy of taking a road trip, in a parent-driven approach, parents determine the goal, while the teacher holds the map as a guide so that the parents can reach their destination satisfied both by the journey and its outcome.[23] In other words, parents are the ones to steer their children's education and, when searching for solutions to their children's behavioural difficulties, can be our consultants. This liberates teachers from being responsible for fixing problems when they are not privy to the information needed to solve them.

Parents' motivations for involvement

All parents want their children to do well in school, to have friends, and to contribute to their communities in adulthood.[24] Despite this uniformity of aspirations, parents differ in their beliefs about the roles for teachers and parents with respect to education. For example, parents in lower socioeconomic circumstances tend to give schools more autonomy over their children's education than do middle-class parents and may be less proactive than middle-class parents who understand 'the system'.[25] Meanwhile, parents with high self-efficacy will be able to harness the family's internal resources and secure any necessary external support to promote their children's achievements.[26] In contrast, parents with low self-efficacy will doubt their ability to solve their child's problems or to influence his or her educational trajectory, even if they did become involved.[27]

Parents' involvement has two main aspects.[28] The first – support at home – entails conveying to children their parents' values about education, keeping apprised of what is happening for their children at school, being emotionally available for support, and providing intellectually stimulating activities such as reading to them. This emotional or moral support actually has more influence on students' academic outcomes than does parents' direct participation at school,[29] which is the second, more visible form of parental engagement. Direct involvement at school can span passive activities such as being an audience at school performances, volunteering in the classroom or on fundraising activities, communicating with teachers, advocating for their son or daughter at school, and contributing to the governance of the school. Many parents experience a range of practical impediments (such as work commitments or a lack of babysitters) that limit their presence at school, but their absence does not reflect their educational aspirations, emotional investment or personal interest in their children's education.[30]

Everyday measures for engaging with parents

Schools require sustained administrative commitment to establishing proactive relationships with parents.[31] This begins with establishing an inviting school climate or family ethos.[32] Parents' perceptions of the school's receptivity to them is the most crucial factor affecting their attendance at school, having been found in one study to account for slightly over 22 per cent of the differences in parental participation rates between schools.[33]

A second quality that enables interaction with parents is teachers' self-efficacy.[34] This is influential because, although few teachers receive any specific training for collaborating with parents, those who are confident about their expertise as teachers tend to be more open to collaboration – in all likelihood because they feel less threatened about having others scrutinise their work.[35]

You can communicate your openness to parents through verbal or written communications with them, advising them about school events and their child's progress and about your own aims for their children's education. (*Please*, do, however, avoid both the patronising holier-than-thou and the jollier-than-thou tones that signal insincerity and fail to disguise a hierarchical attitude towards parents.) More than this, you can ask parents about their own goals for their son or daughter[36] and, in the case of parents from a culture other than your own, can enquire about their cultural beliefs and practices, both to aid in understanding their child and to include these within your curriculum. Your welcome can

BOX 23.1 Sample statement of welcome to families[37]

Dear parent

Our school is honoured that you have entrusted us with your child's education. While our teachers have considerable knowledge and skills about children and teaching, we are also eager to learn from your expertise and knowledge about your particular child, family and culture. We invite your voice, your perspective and your participation as an advocate for your child and family as well as for our community of students and families. Our school is fortunate to include a diverse group of families, students and staff whose range of life experiences enriches the entire school community and each one of us individually. We believe that every family deserves support in its efforts to raise healthy and skilled children and we work to build and encourage this support among families, school staff and the larger community.

be expressed in an invitation to parents or other community members and cultural elders to attend the school to tutor, mentor, coach, perform, or tell stories that convey their cultural practices.

Your school can also respond to parents' needs by providing information sessions on topics that parents nominate, such as (for parents of young children) normal development or parenting skills and (for parents of adolescents) the admission criteria for tertiary courses and various occupations. Information about extracurricular activities can be useful across all ages.[38]

Within a family-driven model, schools can reach out to parents through practical measures such as establishing a lending library to give disadvantaged parents access to resources that can support their children's literacy skills.[39] Or you could provide a parent lounge or drop-in centre to promote informal contacts between parents, or provide a venue for the delivery of community health services on campus.[40] Meeting parents' needs in these ways is valuable in its own right, while ongoing contact can also form a healthy base for collaborating with parents to resolve their son's or daughter's behavioural difficulties.

Principles of solution-focused parental consultation

Under the parent-driven model adopted by the guidance approach, interactions with parents recognise that parents want the best for their son or daughter (as do you). At the same time, parents may have been co-opted somewhat involuntarily into discussing their child's behaviour with you. While willing to be involved, they would prefer not to have the problem in the first place and will not relish the prospect of yet another encounter with school personnel about their child's behaviour. The fact that previous efforts at solving chronic problems have been unsuccessful means that parents' self-efficacy may have been undermined and they may feel sceptical and lack hope about the chances of success of any new intervention. Furthermore, their child's failure at school may mirror their own unsuccessful school career, in which case they are likely to approach you with suspicion and distrust.

Nevertheless, you both want relief from the problem. With this as your starting point, four principles inform how you engage with parents when their son or daughter is displaying disruptive behaviour at school. First, you must recognise that this is a school-based problem and therefore the school must be the one to solve it, not the parents. Even if parents instigated disciplinary measures at home, these would have little impact on their child's behaviour at school.[41]

Second, your purpose in collaborating is not to have the parents punish their child at home for behavioural incidents at school. You would not punish a child at school for something that happened at home. On rare occasions when you sense that parents might punish their child harshly, you may have to hold back some of the specifics about their child's problems.

The third principle is that all parents from all backgrounds want to be proud of their children.[42] They want to have hope for their children. When collaborating with parents to resolve school-based behavioural difficulties it is your task, therefore, to restore parents' faith in their children.

Finally, it is self-evident that you will be working with parents at times when there is a problem to be solved, rather than when all is going well. At such times of stress, it could be easy to fall into a trap of judging parents or assuming that their personal or parenting deficiencies are the cause of their children's difficulties. However, school pressures on students can stress even a well-functioning family and can add intolerable pressure to one that is already strained. The source of the stress can be beyond the family's influence – as with poverty – or can even be a product of the problem itself. This implies that the final key ingredient of collaborating with parents is to bear in mind that the child (or family) is not the problem: *The problem is the problem.*[43]

Include students

As those most affected by the outcome of any meeting between you and their parents, students have a right to be included in discussions concerning them. More than this, however, young people are the experts on their own problems and can advise adults how to respond. Therefore, they will need to be involved in the process of solution finding. If, however, students would be heavily outnumbered by adults, they can invite a best friend to the meeting for moral support or as their co-adviser to the adults. If the friend cannot attend, or if students decline to invite anyone, you can allocate an empty seat on which you place the friend's name. Participants at the meeting can speak hypothetically to the friend in his or her absence, by posing questions such as, 'I wonder what Shara would say is your best quality?'.

Recruit parents' expertise

Given that parents see their children in a wide variety of contexts and over a longer time period than teachers, that children behave differently at home versus school, and that parents have intimate knowledge of their children's emotional wellbeing, they can be more accurate than teachers at describing their child's characteristic behaviours.[44] This expertise can inform solutions. Using a solution-focused approach (as outlined in chapter 19), the teacher is freed from having to know how

BOX 23.2   **Questions that reveal solutions**[45]

Consultancy questions
These can explicitly capitalise on parents' knowledge:

- Given that you know your child better than anyone else, what suggestions do you have for us to help him/her at school?
- You've spoken to your child's previous teachers about this in the past. What have we all missed so far that could help?
- If I have another student with similar issues in my class in future, what could you tell me about how I might help that child?
- If there was one useful question about your child's behaviour that I could ask, what would that question be?
- (To the student): What are your suggestions of how your parents/teachers could help with this?

Questions to ask when parents are despondent
- What does your worry for your son/daughter tell you about your feelings for him/her?
- What is it about him/her that tells you s/he can do better?
- What is going well for (name the student)?
- What needs to happen to encourage more of that success?

to fix a student's behavioural problem, and instead can adopt a curious stance, asking questions that draw out the student's and parents' own expertise. Some questions that are relevant to consultation with parents are listed in Box 23.2.

Reveal solutions

The steps for revealing solutions are illustrated in Figure 19.1, with questions that elicit this information given in chapter 19. These steps are:

- Clarify the problem, being sure to define it in concrete terms (Box 19.2).
- Identify the goals of parents, students and teachers (Box 19.6).
- Identify solutions (Box 19.10) by noting exceptions (Box 19.15) and identifying

the strengths employed by those involved that enable these exceptions to occur (Box 19.16).
- Review progress.
- Deal with setbacks by noting participants' coping and resilience skills (Box 19.18).

As detailed in chapter 19, the purpose of questioning is to identify exceptions to the problems and discover what those involved did to make these happen. When, however, parents are so paralysed by the problem that they cannot notice exceptions or their role in enabling these, future-oriented questions can help (see Box 19.10, page 307). If even these future-oriented questions do not assist them to identify solutions and to recognise their capacity to generate these, you can externalise the problem, as outlined in chapter 19. This allows the problem to be the villain, rather than the student.

As mentioned in chapter 19, at subsequent meetings you will ask what has changed since the previous meeting. In response, those involved could report that there has been some improvement, no change, a deterioration in the student's behaviour, or different members could have mixed opinions. For each of these four scenarios Selekman advises the following.[46]

- When there have been improvements, highlight these and ask what each person has done to bring them about. You can then all agree to continue using more of these successful strategies.
- When there appears to all those involved to have been no change in the student's behaviour, you could externalise the problem or suggest pattern interruption (see chapter 19). Giving parents the task of observing their child for any signs of non-problematic behaviour can also be a way to help them notice small improvements that they might otherwise overlook in their discouragement.
- When the problem seems worse than before, begin by listening to and empathising with the parents' despondency.[47] Then ask the consultancy questions given in Box 23.2 and, finally, move on to asking coping and resilience questions from Box 19.18 (see page 314). Another possibility is to suggest to parents that, despite not knowing in advance how it might help, they simply do the opposite of what they have been trying so far.[48]
- When progress reports are mixed, with some individuals reporting improvement while others still feeling pessimistic, begin by highlighting the improvements.

This can help sceptics to rise above their pessimism. At the same time, however, acknowledge their caution, agreeing that it is only sensible, given how long they have been battling the problem.

Recommend outside services

A teacher's role is not to support families directly, in which case you can refer parents on to specialist services. In order to do so, you will need to find out about available services, including details of waiting times, costs and contact phone numbers. Your parent group might be a useful resource here by supplying the names of medical and allied health practitioners whom they have found helpful.

Cross-cultural collaboration

The term *culture* encompasses demographic characteristics such as race, gender, country of origin, language and socioeconomic status, as well as less explicit features such as individuals' beliefs, values and attitudes.[49] Or, much more elegantly, culture is 'a system of permissions'.[50] With respect to behaviour in schools, it encompasses the norms and customs of the institution. In these settings, within the dominant culture's frame of reference, a student's behaviour might be interpreted as problematic when it may be appropriate within the child's family culture[51] or be a natural reaction to social disadvantage or disempowerment. Thus, cultural sensitivity applies not only to how we interact with parents to solve a problem, but also to how we frame problems in the first place.

Given that we cannot possibly know the nuances of every culture and, given that there is considerable variation in beliefs and practices within any cultural group, the most useful stance when working with parents from other cultures is the one adopted by the solution-focused approach – that is, a posture of 'not-knowing'.[52] This entails asking parents specifically about their values and preferred practices concerning discipline.[53] This is not to say that we have to accept parents' values (cultural or otherwise) but merely to recognise that parents believe that their perceptions are the proper and logical way to understand and respond to the problem.

When consulting with parents from a culture other than your own, you could invite them to bring along to the meeting a member of their own community or extended family. Or, if you have a teacher on staff from their culture, you could ask if they would like you to invite that person to attend. This has to be their choice entirely because, in some cultures, the presence of an outsider would be experienced as supportive whereas in others it would cause parents to lose face. If no cultural advocate is available or they choose to see you without one, you can check with them in the opening phases of the conversation whether they are willing to discuss their concerns with you, despite your cultural differences.[54]

Accurate communication depends on parents' prowess with English. Without this, you can be denied vital information about their child, while limiting how much information parents can receive from you. Even when parents can use everyday language, they might have difficulty comprehending more technical terms.[55] Therefore, it can be essential to locate a translator for formal conversations or to invite a community volunteer to accompany non-English speaking parents. It is wise to avoid using their son or daughter as a translator because that burdens a child with inappropriate responsibility, while the use of translators who are children or family friends can lead to discomfort when they are privy to information that parents regard as personal.[56]

A solution-focused approach is ideal for working cross-culturally because, in having parents generate their own definitions of problems, determine their own goals and design interventions based on their own past successes, necessarily these will match their perspectives (be these personal, cultural, religious or related to social class). And a distinct advantage of using this approach within the umbrella of guidance is that its goal of teaching considerate behaviour is universal, one that crosses cultures. This congruence with parents' values will contribute to trust and to their openness to working with you to reveal solutions.

Collaborating with families in adversity

A solution-focused approach is the same for families experiencing multiple problems as for those who are more advantaged: find out from parents which problem is their priority and assist them in solving that.[57] This will relieve the most stress and might open the way for spontaneous improvement of other troubling aspects of their lives, or their early success will bolster their self-efficacy for moving on to solve their next problem.

At a deeper level, solution-focused approaches openly acknowledge social forces that oppress cultural minorities, women and those living in poverty, to name but a few. Although you are powerless to control these external factors, you can challenge the message they often convey to parents about their personal worth. The first step will be to acknowledge the special stressors they face in bringing up young people within a subculture of deprivation, violence and (where relevant) racism. You can ask these parents what it is like for them to have to function under oppression: does it cause them to believe that they cannot raise healthy children? Do they feel criticised and believe that they have to be perfect to counter stereotypes about single parents (say), or about members of their culture or religion? How do they manage to raise their children in a loving way in an environment characterised by poverty, prejudice, disadvantage or violence?[58]

More so with this population than with others, you cannot expect parents to follow up at home any school-based interventions. Children's behavioural difficulties render home-based interventions very demanding on any parent,[59] but can add intolerably to the stress of families already functioning under adversity.

Responding to parents' complaints

A prime occasion when you will need to use listening skills is when parents have approached you with a complaint. As consumers of an important – and, in terms of private school fees or tax contributions for public education – an expensive service, parents would be irresponsible if they did not closely question what you offer their child.[60] This means that, regardless of their manner, you need to meet their questions and demands with courtesy. Even 'difficult' parents are not being demanding just to make you jump through hoops: they both need and have a right to ask questions.

Although strong emotions can be intimidating, it will help not to take parents'

behaviour personally, but to remember that it is being triggered by their situation (not by you) and that, from their perspective, they believe that they have a valid reason for their feelings. Mammals are supposed to become feral when their young are under threat. Hence, the vehemence of parents' feelings reflects the size of the perceived threat, while any expression of blame or hopelessness is a sign that they care deeply about their son or daughter. Given that you also want the best for their child, a statement of this, your shared interest, is a good starting point.[61] Also keep in mind that it takes courage for parents to confront you with a complaint and perhaps they have had to stir themselves up to summon the nerve. On that basis, you will need to listen, acknowledge their frustration or anger, and reflect what they are saying.

Nevertheless, if they become belligerent, abusive or otherwise disrespectful, offensive or overpowering you will need them to moderate how they are talking to you. It might help to direct them to what they want to accomplish.[62] For example: 'I accept that you are angry that Simon was sent out of class. Perhaps we can focus on what you would like to see happen next time so that his behaviour doesn't hurt others but he still feels that he has been listened to?'. It is crucial that you do not get hooked into placating or appeasing parents, because that would demean either yourself or whoever handled the incident.[63]

A method called negative assertion can be useful, as long as it is genuinely meant. In this approach, after listening to parents' first complaint, you ask them to tell you more about it, until you have explored all you can about that particular issue. You then ask what else is a concern for them . . . and then what else, until finally they have exhausted their head of steam and are now willing to move on to the next step of working with you to find a solution.

Sometimes, inevitably, your time will be limited. When anxious about an impending commitment, your response is likely to be less than ideal. In that case, it will help to advise the parents of your time constraints at the outset and suggest that all you can do now is schedule another meeting. A second occasion that might put you under pressure is when parents confront you with a grievance without prior warning. In that event, it can be useful to impose a postponement deliberately to give yourself time to evaluate their complaint. A delay will also give them time to calm down. No one can listen to even the most reasonable explanation while he or she is angry. Therefore, take the information, offer to think about it or to gather more facts from those involved, and then commit to getting back to them for a follow-up conversation. If this does not satisfy them, you can invite them to speak with the principal. Even if, like you, the principal cannot resolve the issue immediately, nevertheless being granted access to someone in authority can assure the parents that you are taking the matter seriously.

In most instances, listening to the need behind parents' manner will effectively avoid a confrontation. However, for those rare instances when that does not work, your school will require a policy for protecting staff from intimidation by angry parents. This might include procedures for withdrawing to a safe location and for requesting backup from a colleague or even from the police or security personnel.

In the long term, it will be helpful to inform parents of a procedure for expressing complaints. This will specify that, in the first instance, they make an appointment to meet with the teacher involved, rather than speaking first with the principal. To go to superiors before giving those involved a chance to explain or respond is disrespectful and will make them defensive.[64]

Conclusion

Under a professional-driven model, teachers believe that parental questioning of their judgment undermines them in much the same way that they consider challenges from students to be insubordinate. However, to my mind professionalism is not only knowing what to do, but also knowing why. In that case, being able to explain to inquiring parents the rationale for practices only cements one's authority.

Students' behavioural and academic difficulties will not disappear with a single intervention but can be resolved only through ongoing supportive interaction between teachers and parents.[65] A parent-driven stance and solution-focused approach liberate you from having to generate solutions to problems about which you have inadequate information, while also honouring the expertise of students and their parents. This is more than a case of two heads being better than one: it's that *individuals know more about themselves than outsiders ever will.*

Recommended further reading

Bolton, R. (1993). *People skills.* Sydney: Simon & Schuster.
Porter, L. (2008). *Teacher-parent collaboration: From early childhood to adolescence.* Melbourne: ACER.
Rosenberg, M.B. (2003). *Nonviolent communication: A language of life.* (2nd ed.). Encinitas, CA: Puddle Dancer Press.

CHAPTER 24

Supporting teachers

The teachers of our children deserve the same quality of treatment that we expect them to offer our children.[1]

Children – particularly the very young – are highly sensitive to the morale of the people around them.[2] Therefore, providing teachers with conducive working conditions helps not only them, but directly affects their students' wellbeing.[3] A supportive work environment also enables teachers to care about their students, to be less distant and less controlling.[4]

Primary teachers' prime motivation for teaching and the satisfaction that they gain from it are largely fed by their relationships with students, while secondary teachers gain considerable satisfaction from facilitating breakthroughs in their students.[5] Yet teacher closeness with students declines from the first year of schooling.[6] This largely results from the anonymity of large schools and the limited contact time or 'fragmented interactions' students have with their many specialist teachers at high school level.[7] The bureaucratic and compartmentalised structure of high school also makes close relationships with students difficult, as does a curriculum devoid of personal meaning for the students, in which they invest little emotional commitment.

Both students and teachers are harmed by the emotional aridity of schools. As is true for their students, secondary teachers feel unknown by their students in any deep sense, with the high school classroom lacking emotional intensity.[8] High school teachers report being regarded as a functionary by their students, which entails not appreciating others on the basis of personal knowledge of them but instead pigeonholing them on the basis of a stereotype.[9]

Teacher commitment

Teacher commitment to teaching predicts attrition, turnover, absenteeism, teaching performance, burnout, and attitudes to students.[10] Commitment encompasses four aspects: commitment to the profession, to the school as an organisation, to the students, and to the academic goals of the school.[11] Commitment to teaching is strong when the school values the social and emotional wellbeing of both students and teachers, with vibrant collaboration among colleagues enhancing teachers' commitment to the school.[12]

Nine out of 10 teachers claim that the motivating force behind their commitment to teaching is passion, or a strong valuing of teaching.[13] Harmonious passion emanates from integrating the activity into one's identity and results in increased job satisfaction, whereas its detrimental version is an obsessive passion in which their work occupies a disproportionate role in their lives.[14] Although both entice student learning, they have opposite implications for teacher wellbeing.[15]

Teacher self-efficacy

There is a strong link between teachers' self-efficacy and job satisfaction, burnout, student outcomes and teachers' ability to manage conflict with students.[16] Professional self-efficacy is a belief in teachers that they *can* make a difference in students' lives, which precedes the intention to do so.[17] It has two aspects: a generalised belief that teaching can have an impact in students' lives, and teachers' beliefs that they themselves can influence student outcomes.[18] This second aspect has six elements:[19]

- *instructional self-efficacy*: confidence that they can design and deliver activities and assessments that will facilitate student learning
- *adapting teaching* to students' individual needs
- *student engagement*: teachers' belief that they can secure and retain students' engagement, investment and motivation in learning
- *classroom management*: teachers' belief that they can maintain an orderly classroom

- *work circumstances*: their ability to recruit support from colleagues and parents
- *coping with change and challenges.*

Preschool and primary teachers report higher self-efficacy than secondary school teachers, with the latter expressing less confidence in their ability to engage students meaningfully in learning.[20] Teachers' self-efficacy tends to increase in their first years of teaching as they develop their skills and to stabilise subsequently.[21] Those who remain in the profession tend to be characterised by higher self-efficacy than those who eventually leave.[22]

Teachers with high self-efficacy not only become less stressed but, when faced with challenges, take action to resolve the problems rather than avoiding them, venting emotion inappropriately or using emotion-focused coping methods (such as alcohol or drug taking).[23] Willing to take personal responsibility and confident of their ability to generate solutions rather than feeling helpless, teachers with high self-efficacy employ win–win conflict solving strategies in response to disruptions.[24]

In terms of instruction, they exhibit high levels of planning and organisation, are open to new ideas, are willing to implement an array of teaching methods, are open to experiment with new approaches, and to implement a varied program and modify tasks to attract students' engagement and make them achievable by students.[25] These teachers are also more likely to retain students with learning or behavioural difficulties within their class rather than referring them for special services, because they believe that they can cater for the students' additional needs.[26] Socially, they can foster students' independence and prosocial behaviours, and forge more positive relationships with students.[27] Teachers with high self-efficacy create a classroom climate that expects and supports high achievement and maintains student engagement.[28] In turn, their successful use of all of these strategies confirms their sense of themselves as effective teachers.

In contrast, teachers with low professional efficacy are more likely to become overwhelmed by teaching, stressed by student disruptiveness,[29] and more concerned with conveying the curriculum and promoting order than with meeting students' needs. They have poorer rapport with their students and are more critical of students' errors, and more preoccupied with their own personal deficiencies.[30] They commonly experience conflict in their relationships with students who have behavioural difficulties and who appear to be challenging their authority. This conflict can cause the teachers to feel helpless and, although they are likely still to feel positively about these students, like everyone else, they dislike feeling helpless.[31]

Teachers with high workloads report greater self-efficacy,[32] which may seem odd when high workloads lead to stress, and stress is related to low self-efficacy. However, having seen this phenomenon in human services, I suspect that the explanation is that the better teachers are given the most demanding students and higher workload. This can work in the short-term but, without support, burnout is a real risk.

Teacher attributions

As described in chapter 2, teachers' implicit theories about the causes of students' behavioural problems govern how they respond.

Teachers who blame students themselves or their home life see these causes as being outside of teachers' control and become fatalistic about the power of teaching to improve student skills. In turn, they are less likely to expend the effort needed to ensure student success, thus depressing student outcomes, which confirms their low expectations.[33] Instead, guidance believes that adjustments to teaching and learning content and processes make significant differences to student outcomes.

With respect to responding to disruptive behaviour, teachers with an external locus of causality who blame students or their parents for behavioural difficulties in the classroom will engage in fallacious thinking whose sequence is:

- It's their fault.
- My job will not be tolerable until they stop it.
- Therefore, I have to make them stop it.

This will lead to unproductive, authoritarian – even autocratic – behaviour management strategies. The ineffectiveness of these methods can further undermine teachers' self-efficacy, leading to feelings of inadequacy.[34]

Collective efficacy

In order for teachers to feel personally able to make a difference in students' lives, the faculty of the school must have a shared or collective sense of efficacy.[35] This is grounded in frequent interactions and joint decision making in schools that gives all individuals a sense that, as a whole, the school has the capacity to operate collectively to achieve its mission.[36] Collective efficacy reflects teachers' shared perceptions of their ability to respond adequately to their student population, given the constraints under which they are functioning, and the resources and expertise available to them.[37]

As well as instructional and engagement efficacy that it shares with personal self-efficacy, collective efficacy includes being able to withstand external influences.[38] It can be impaired when the school leadership must choose between its visions of reform and external accountability to politicians, bureaucrats or the parent body.[39]

A sense of collective efficacy contributes to a school's prestige and is a potent source of teachers' job satisfaction.[40] It requires strong leadership from the principal and a well-qualified teaching team who individually and collectively fulfil their role obligations.[41] A strong sense of collective efficacy emboldens teachers to accept challenging goals and to expend effort and persist in achieving them.[42] This is likely to produce better outcomes for students which, in turn, strengthens the faculty's efficacy.[43] Indeed, collective efficacy has more of an effect on students' academic outcomes than does the socioeconomic status or other demographic features of the student population.[44] In one study, collective efficacy was found to explain just over half of the difference between schools in students' mathematics attainment, and over two-thirds of between-school differences in students' reading abilities.[45] Collective efficacy also reduces the number of suspensions within schools because, when teachers collectively believe that they can be effective in their responses to students' disruptive behaviour, they have less need to use the more extreme measures of suspension or expulsion.[46]

Teacher autonomy

By its nature, teaching accords teachers with considerable professional discretion about how to run their classrooms and to teach curricula. However, this autonomy needs to extend to contributing to organisational decisions within the school.[47] A lack of autonomy at this level contributes to conflict with the school administration. If teachers are compelled to enact decisions to which they did not contribute, they typically resent feeling pressured and apply the decision inconsistently, with those teachers who are committed in turn resenting this.[48]

Leadership

Effective leadership sets the tone for the entire school, contributing significantly to teachers' commitment to the mission of the school, to teaching, to partnerships with parents and to the establishment and maintenance of collective efficacy.[49] Leadership is a process of influencing the thoughts and actions of others.[50] In addition to influencing individual teachers, the principal also must steer the school culture (or 'the way we do things around here'). To that end, school principals need to be able to:[51]

- enthuse teachers to share a common vision of their purpose by guiding them to enunciate an inspirational but achievable vision with clear goals and objectives: in short, the principal must be 'the keeper of the dream'
- invite teachers to challenge their beliefs and scrutinise practice in light of their values and research about effectiveness

- support teachers to cope with the ambiguity that reflection can engender
- maintain open communication that does not demand closure or conformity
- create networks of conversation
- support teachers' ideas for innovation
- establish a respectful collegial culture that effectively manages conflict
- nurture collaborative decision-making processes, in which the principal is not the central problem solver, or imposes decisions from above only in extreme circumstances
- trust staff members' decision making and creativity so that their professional autonomy can blossom into taking increased ownership of their work
- respond to students' and parents' changing needs
- respond to external demands and, in reverse, represent the school vision to external stakeholders
- motivate and manage change.

The most effective leaders are proactive rather than reactive.[52] They can balance the need for task attainment with a concern for the individuals who make that happen.[53] Just as is the case with students, democratic leaders of adults do not dominate or exercise power over others but instead act with them, gaining moral authority from their expertise. Their competence earns team members' respect and loyalty and increases the team members' willingness to follow their leader's direction. At a more prosaic level, leadership also involves efficient administration to ensure that bureaucratic functions do not impair teachers' day-to-day work and that resources are secured to enable the school to function.[54]

Collegial support

Teachers at all levels express appreciation for working with colleagues and being in a supportive school climate.[55] A community of professionals can reinforce and augment the talents and insights of individual teachers. Support from colleagues is powerful in refreshing teachers and preventing stress, and is a promising way to prevent teachers from leaving the profession.[56] Respect throughout the staff hierarchy becomes a feature of teachers' relationships with students.[57] And, support for stressed teachers protects their students from negative teacher behaviours that arise from emotional exhaustion.

A successful school culture offers the following forms of support to teachers:[58]

- openness about disciplinary challenges
- willingness by staff to give time to each other to help solve behavioural difficulties
- strong relationships with the principal
- opportunities for teachers to contribute to decisions
- respectful relationships among the various levels of staff within the school
- recognition of colleagues' efforts and achievements.

Primary or proactive measures include mentoring novice teachers.[59] Principals' interest and presence in classrooms is also crucial for communicating to teachers that their efforts are valued.[60]

The next (secondary) tier of collegial support can be provided in the immediate aftermath of a disciplinary incident, of which there are three phases: release, reflect and rebuild.[61] During the immediate aftermath of a stressful incident, teachers need to release some emotional energy, with the opportunity to vent to colleagues being a useful part of this; next, they will need to talk through the incident in order to reflect on what happened and why; finally, in the rebuilding phase, there is a need to develop a plan for dealing in future with similar incidents, based on a judgment about what helped or did not in the present case.[62]

Tertiary collegial support measures can include problem solving in a one-to-one relationship to help a troubled colleague to analyse a problem, set goals and develop a plan to solve the problem, or collective problem solving with a group of teachers.[63] To develop a single, coherent plan, Roffey recommends routine 'cause for concern' meetings where all teachers involved with given students can discuss the issues that concern them and how these might be solved.[64]

A last form of tertiary support is the provision of emergency time away for teachers, which can entail taking over their class on the pretence that they must 'retrieve a message' from the front office, or temporarily finding an external task for a troublesome student while his or her teacher regains control of the class.

One specific case for collegial support is the bullying or harassment of teachers, to which inexperienced teachers may be particularly vulnerable.[65] As is true for student victims, bullying of teachers needs a rapid response, which will be enabled when they feel confident of collegial support rather than feeling that they risk criticism for being victimised.[66]

Professional development

Teachers who have more extensive training and child-focused beliefs tend to be less restrictive or controlling with students and to provide more instructional and structural support.[67] They can attain this training prior to entry to the profession or from inservice professional development. The latter can renew teachers' enthusiasm for their work, improve their confidence in their abilities, and allow them to continue to grow professionally.[68] Its most important outcome is to facilitate teachers' reflection on their practices, questioning their underlying values, beliefs and assumptions which otherwise might be taken for granted.[69]

Professional development opportunities need to reflect the varied needs of teachers depending on their length of experience.[70] New initiates into teaching will be trying to define themselves as teachers and will be unable to take on new projects, for example, whereas experienced teachers might be ready for new challenges and may be seeking to diversify and experiment in an effort to breathe new life into a job that otherwise might have come to feel stale to them.[71]

Sustaining the impetus to achieve lasting change is more likely when staff development is ongoing, involves the whole school faculty and relates to the core vision of the school.[72] It is unlikely that one-off seminars will be adequate.[73] This is because most seminars work on the assumption that changing attitudes and knowledge will lead to a change in teachers' practices, whereas the reverse is more likely.[74] (Insight usually follows rather than causes behavioural change: otherwise smokers would all quit.) Ongoing education can allow teachers to change their practices, following which the 'Aha' phenomenon will trigger a change in beliefs.[75]

BOX 24.1   **Features of schools that foster teacher satisfaction**[76]

Manageable demands
- role clarity
- reasonable workload and physical demands
- avoidance of overload (e.g. by providing breaks)
- provision of planning time

Teachers' personal resources
- high self-efficacy
- avoidance of perfectionism, over-striving or over-commitment
- recognition of one's own skills
- high levels of training
- reflection on practice

School culture
- collective efficacy
- efficient administration and management so that staff can perform their duties unencumbered by bureaucratic duties
- effective leadership
- good working conditions: reasonable pay, adequate staffing levels, opportunities for advancement, job security
- supervision and mentoring
- trusting relationships with colleagues, parents and students
- a sense of professionalism and respect conveyed to teachers
- teacher control (decision latitude) over their work
- clear policies and procedures (e.g. for responding to behavioural disruptions)
- flexibility to enable teachers to attend to personal or family responsibilities
- flexibility to allow teachers to implement programs for students
- opportunities for professional development

Securing the services of outside experts can be expensive but also worthwhile because all the staff hear the same information and they can process it together as a team. Another approach is to send a small group or an individual to a particular staff development event, with the expectation that attendees subsequently offer staff training to those who did not attend. A disadvantage of this approach is that some can resent being incited by a peer to change their practices,[77] although these individuals may not be any more open to outside experts either.

Occupational stress

The sheer complexity of working with groups of children is an everyday challenge. The work is multi-dimensional, which is to say that many different people with different interests and abilities are sharing the same space; many things are happening simultaneously; and events can unfold rapidly and unpredictably, demanding immediate responses.[78] Meanwhile, all of teachers' responses are public, being witnessed by students and, occasionally, by colleagues and visitors to the classroom.

Despite this complexity, stress is not inevitable. As illustrated in Figure 24.1, stress arises when we believe that work demands exceed the available resources to support our coping.[79] These work demands can encompass administrative and bureaucratic tasks; an excessive workload; time constraints or inadequate time for planning and preparation; student disruptiveness; a lack of control over working conditions; a negative school climate; and high levels of organisational stress.[80] Other sources include conflict with parents and feeling obliged to teach in ways that violate one's principles.[81] This can arise when using pre-packaged curricular materials, for example, or in team teaching, when colleagues must coordinate with and adjust to each other.[82]

Perhaps surprisingly, structural features of schools have little impact on teacher stress. School size; level (primary or secondary); or sector (public, private or parochial); urban versus rural; and the socioeconomic status of the student population seem not to affect teachers' stress levels – unless these elements are allowed to impair collective efficacy.[83] Large class sizes have been thought to contribute to teacher stress via

the additional workload. However, the link is not as straightforward as might be imagined. As in many human services, the most competent staff are typically allocated the largest and most complex caseload.[84] The exceptional skills of the most able teachers mean that their larger groups do not necessarily result in declining quality or in added stress to the teachers themselves. While this is a testament to their skills, it nevertheless runs the risk of eventual overload.

New teachers and females experience higher stress levels than males, partly because of higher professional workloads, women's extra non-work duties, and because in high school they can find male adolescents physically intimidating.[85] While low in absolute incidence, feeling physically insecure at school and being the recipient of verbal abuse by students can also impair teachers' wellbeing and can lead to dissatisfaction, absenteeism and attrition.[86] With respect to this last outcome, US statistics tell us that half of all teachers leave the profession within their first five years, and 7 per cent leave the school sector annually.[87] A massive 30 per cent of early childhood teachers depart the sector every year.[88] This has numerous detrimental effects: disrupting students and unsettling remaining staff members, and introducing new teachers who must be inducted into the school culture.

Meanwhile, for teachers who remain in the profession, stress has an impact on themselves, their students, and the whole school.[89] Teachers who are exhausted are less capable of creating positive environments for students and may even model negative behaviours such as emotional venting.[90] Burnout is the result of prolonged stress, characterised by emotional exhaustion, depersonalisation and reduced effectiveness.[91] Emotional exhaustion speaks for itself, while depersonalisation refers to adopting negative, callous and detached attitudes to others, in this case, to students.[92] Cynicism about teaching in general can also abound.[93]

Resilience is the opposite of stress. Although usually attributed to the personal coping skills of individuals, of more significance are the proximal supports that surround them.[94] Resilience is associated with high job satisfaction and high self-efficacy, plus an ability to distance oneself from work and to cope with failure.[95] Teachers who are engaged but resilient employ the most effective teaching methods, whereas those who are engaged but who cannot distance themselves from work demands are most vulnerable to stress.[96]

Collaboration and consultation

Teachers can gain support with challenging student behaviours through collaboration and consultation with external consultants or with specialist colleagues such as

FIGURE 24.1 **Contributors to occupational stress**

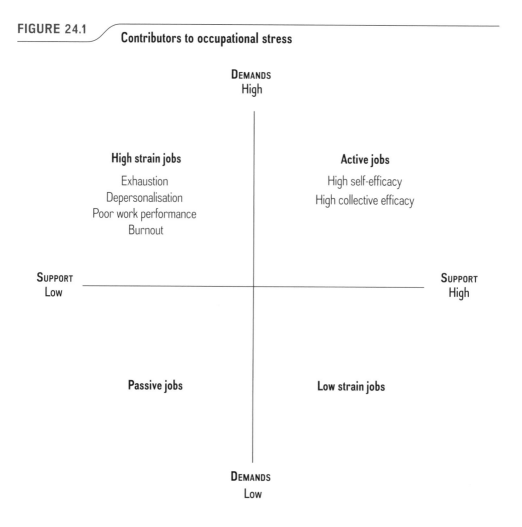

the school counsellor or special educator. This can help generate new solutions to chronic difficulties. Successful collaboration involves having mutual goals, sharing problem solving and decision making, and valuing each party's expertise.[97]

In teachers' interactions with consultants, the parent-driven style (described in chapter 23) instead becomes teacher-driven. That is to say, the classroom teacher employs the consultant for his or her specialist knowledge and, therefore, is the one who drives their interaction. The consultant is accountable to the teacher and responsible for suggesting appropriate and feasible solutions,[98] which requires familiarity with the teacher's setting and its constraints. For their part, teachers will also be responsible for generating potential solutions, but they have the ultimate authority to determine which are practicable in their classrooms. They are also expected to be open to being innovative and incorporating adjustments to their practices. This is more likely when they are extremely knowledgeable about curriculum and pedagogy, are student-centred in their teaching, and able to reflect on whether their teaching is achieving their goals for students' engagement and outcomes.[99]

The typical expectation of consultants in schools is that they adopt a clinical style of assessment to diagnose a cause for students' difficulties in order to generate a prescription detailing what teachers and parents can do about it.[100] However, this can degenerate into the administration of increasingly detailed assessments to discover more and more obscure names for conditions that ultimately prove to be untreatable. Meanwhile, teachers are frustrated by the delay in gaining the support and advice they need. Furthermore, this approach represents a top-down rather than collaborative style that violates the basic tenets of the teacher-driven approach. It fails to respect the wisdom and expertise of teachers, while confirming students' deficits and negative reputation which, in turn, invites feelings of hopelessness.

Instead, solution-oriented case conferences will not yield a 'laundry list' of what is going wrong, but will examine exceptions to the problem and what occasions those.[101] Useful questions that consultants can ask teachers, parents or students include, 'When faced with this kind of behaviour before, what did you do that worked? . . . What effects did you notice? . . . How do you explain those? . . . How could you do that again?'.[102]

Meetings with consultants can follow the same format as used with the students themselves.[103] That is, they will describe and redefine the problem, formulate goals, discuss present interventions and identify which of these have worked by highlighting exceptions and noting the skills employed by those involved to bring these exceptions about, and then plan to do more of what is working.

On a scale of 1 to 10, each person in attendance can rate the behavioural problem before, during and after the planned intervention. The different ratings by various stakeholders and by the same person over time help identify what contributes to the higher ratings, can clarify what goal is realistic ('What rating would you settle for?') and, later, can document progress.[104]

The first meeting can close on the following questions:[105]

- How close are we to making a plan?
- What else do we need to consider?
- What would it take to put these ideas into action?

- If you were to do this as an experiment, what would you do?

In the period between consultations, teachers can experiment with new ways of responding to the disruptive behaviour and notice exceptions, observing what they and the student are doing differently when these occur. Guided by the acronym EARS, subsequent consultations will *e*licit the exceptions, *a*mplify changes, *r*einforce these (without using rewards but instead employing authentic feedback) and *s*tart on the next problem, if necessary.[106]

When using consultants, it pays for everyone to be clear who the client is. For special educators or schools psychologists who are employed by and work in the school, the school is often the client. They may not be able to advocate for students' needs without jeopardising their relationships with teachers. In contrast, the client of outside consultants is more likely to be the student (particularly when being paid by that child's parents). This difference can make a difference.

Conclusion

The structures of a school can be defined, charted and changed intentionally so that they foster community; however, the culture or norms of a school are less tangible and, therefore, more difficult to change.[107] In an unsupportive setting, teachers' child-focused beliefs can dissipate in the face of contextual constraints that limit the support available to them, with the result that they become less effective, less satisfied with their work and, in turn, more likely to leave their job or the profession altogether.[108] When they are obliged to act in ways that violate their principles,[109] *that* – not the number of hours they put in – is *hard work*.

In contrast, teachers whose environment meets their basic needs for safety and whose social, educational and spiritual needs are met through their work are likely to be happy, stable employees who offer students a high quality of teaching.[110] When teachers are treated with respect and valued for their contributions, they are likely to treat students similarly, relate to them with interest and warmth, guide rather than control them, respond to them individually rather than as a group, and facilitate their active learning. In turn, in a context of a supportive school community, students similarly develop a supportive peer culture.[111]

CHAPTER 25

Formulating policy about student behaviour

As long as the management of students' challenging behaviours focuses solely on correction techniques, teachers will continue to experience failure and frustration. Teachers should spend as much time developing positive, proactive behavior management plans as they spend developing instructional lesson plans.[1]

In the opening paragraph of this book, I invited you to contemplate how you would design schools if you did not know what your role would be within them. When we write policy, we are in effect documenting our answers to that question. In this chapter, therefore, I take you through the steps needed to formulate your answer.

In general, policies are statements about what services you will offer and how you will deliver them. It expresses how school members are expected to behave towards each other so that they can work productively together.[2] Nevertheless, it is important to keep in mind that students do not behave well because of a school's discipline policy: they behave well because they *can*.[3] Therefore, the policy is not an enforcement tool but a means of communicating the school's mission. It enshrines a strategic vision for the school that embodies capable leadership and attendance to the needs of students, teachers and parents. To that end, the principal needs to have cultivated a shared vision of what the school can accomplish, be supportive of innovation, and espouse a culture of questioning everyday practice.[4]

Although formulating policy is time consuming, the process has many benefits including the following.[5]

- A policy can provide a means for all members of the school community to communicate and embrace a shared purpose.
- It offers students, teachers and parents safeguards and clear expectations of their roles, rights and responsibilities.
- The process of formulating policy allows teachers to plan how to respond to disruptiveness rather than having to make hasty reactive decisions.

- A policy can be the basis for staff development.
- It clarifies for teachers how to recruit support to deal with demanding behaviours.
- A policy can provide an orienting framework for inexperienced, temporary or new teachers to the school. At the same time, it must still allow teachers some autonomy, as befits their professionalism.

For these benefits to eventuate, you cannot simply import the policy of a sister school or merely revamp an old policy document: it is the process of discussing and understanding nuance, not the final document, that is the potent aspect of policy formulation.

The planning process

To generate the energy for writing new policy, there needs to be dissatisfaction with present practices.[6] Before you can proceed with formulating any changes, however, decisions will have to be made about who will steer the process, whether staff will need some professional development to inform their options, how and whom you will consult, and time lines for doing all this (see Figure 25.1).

Typically an action group or steering committee will be appointed to lead the process. This group should include teachers who have credibility and can occupy leadership roles, as well as parent representatives. The committee must also span grade levels and include general and special education teachers or other specialist personnel.[7] Naturally, the people most affected by the policy will be students

themselves and therefore they need to be active participants, both because there is a moral obligation to consult them and also because doing so improves policy effectiveness.[8]

An initial step for the steering committee will be to collate the present policy and other policies that affect it, such as directives of the school's governing bodies. Then, committee members will gather resources they need to inform their options (such as texts on teaching and behaviour management) or source some professional development training on the topic. The next step will be to scrutinise the school's data about behavioural problems and to survey the opinions of students, parents and teachers about current practices. Given that some behavioural problems such as bullying are covert, it can be useful to gather data from students and parents about the frequency of bullying and the effectiveness of current measures for responding to it.[9]

This information will then be presented back to the wider staff group who, over a series of meetings, will discuss each of the elements of policy: philosophy, goals and preventive and interventive practices. The action group will collate the group's decisions in the form of a draft document for subsequent discussion and ultimate ratification by all stakeholders.

Wide consultation with teachers, students and parents throughout this process will ensure that they do not feel that the policy has been imposed on them from above. Their inclusion will in turn increase the chances that they will both understand and support the policy and its procedures. At the same time, it must be acknowledged that this represents a considerable investment of time, which might require restructuring of key individuals' teaching loads, the provision of assistants, or the streamlining of course offerings so that the task of policy development is not just another duty that adds to teachers' already considerable workload.[10]

Power relations

King and colleagues remind us that constructing a policy that achieves broad support necessarily requires that governance be shared within the school.[11] When power is consolidated within a few power holders, the school may be cohesive but participation will be limited. Other models whereby subgroups coalesce but communicate poorly with each other, or when individuals have their own disparate goals, will result in a proliferation of programs and ideas that lack a common vision. Instead, shared power enables equal access and voice for all members of the school community in the service of focusing on issues relevant to the collective good.[12] Principals will still need to reserve the right of veto, but this should be used sparingly lest teachers feel manipulated.

Participatory decision making

Teachers can find it easier to dismantle present approaches than to specify what will replace them.[13] This task of specifying new policy can ignite conflict, power struggles and personality clashes that can only be overcome through constructive debate and participatory decision making. Lencioni proposes that this requires a strong team, which is characterised by five features (as listed in Box 25.1): the

FIGURE 25.1   Steps for formulating policy

DECISION
Teachers decide to review the present policy.

STEERING GROUP APPOINTED
A steering group is appointed to develop new policy recommendations.

DATA GATHERING
The steering group gathers data about types and rates of disciplinary problems and teachers', parents' and students' opinions about ethics and effectiveness of current practices.

WRITING
The steering group incorporates findings and its recommendations into a draft policy and presents this for broad discussion.

RATIFICATION
In consultation with teachers, parents and students, the draft is adjusted and then ratified.

IMPLEMENTATION
New procedures are implemented on a trial basis.

EVALUATION
Quantitative and qualitative data are amassed to gauge the effectiveness of the new practices.

first is *trust*.[14] This is the faith that one's colleagues' intentions are good. People will trust their colleagues when they are permitted to make mistakes, express their weaknesses and ask for support when they need it – without their worth being questioned or their vulnerabilities being used against them. This is established when the principal is willing to identify his or her own weaknesses and does not punish teachers for their mistakes.

The benefit of developing trust is that morale is improved and staff turnover reduced. In Lencioni's model, it also paves the way for the other four features necessary for effective teamwork. The first of these is that, once members do not have to be concerned about protecting themselves, they will be able to risk engaging in open, constructive *debates* over ideologies. It is only when people do not trust each other that they fear conflict. In that setting, an artificial harmony is preserved because people speak politically – that is, they choose their words based on how they want others to react – rather than expressing what they truly think. The result of a lack of open debate can be gossip and back biting, which covert methods both add to tensions and fail to resolve the issues.

To achieve open debate, the principal must ensure that discussions are restricted to concepts and ideas, and do not instead stray into personal attacks. The leader must also objectively 'mine' for conflict that is hidden beneath differences of opinion, so that these can be aired and resolved. This is in contrast to suppressing or prematurely ending a conflict in the misguided desire to protect individuals. All the while, all members must keep in mind that their only purpose is to achieve the best possible decision.

Without robust debate, there will be a lack of *commitment* to and failure to buy into the group's decisions because, as Lencioni puts it, people have to weigh in before they can buy in. Although unanimity of support is unlikely in any diverse group, teams that trust in each other's good intentions will be able to engage in lively ideological debates and, rather than achieve consensus, will nevertheless achieve commitment to the final decision as long as individuals believe that they have been heard and their opinions have been considered. Without robust debate, the result can be decision paralysis because the group realises it cannot please everyone and therefore defers decisions until it can arrive at consensus; or else a decision is expressed so ambiguously that individuals will enact it in different ways; or a decision is imposed from the top, which individuals then resist or sabotage.

Fourth, team members need to be *accountable* for achieving the group's vision. This relies on commitment; otherwise, individual teachers can avoid accountability by saying they never agreed to the plan in the first place.

With each member of the school accountable for achieving the school vision, the last quality of an effective team will be achieved: that is, *attention to results*. This means caring more about the collective goals than about personal advancement or simply being part of a powerful subgroup.[15] In schools driven by a guidance philosophy, accountability will be about more than student results on national tests or the number of disciplinary referrals, but instead will focus on indices of student engagement, enthusiasm about learning, mastery of meaningful knowledge and skills, and personal and social satisfaction with school.

It will be important that policy statements are clear and that individuals are able to tolerate uncertainty about whether the group decision will prove to be correct. Groups can increase members' tolerance for uncertainty by outlining the worst-case outcome of the decision, which can reassure those who are hesitant that an incorrect decision is survivable.[16] This will help create and sustain the momentum for implementation.

Components of policy

Discipline is a process for helping students to learn and to gain personal skills: it is

---

BOX 25.1   **The five characteristics of effective teams**[17]

Characteristic	Evidence of its presence	Signs of its absence	Principal's role
Trust	Admission of mistakes and weaknesses. High morale. Low staff turnover.	Politics. Tension. Artificial harmony. Gossip, back-stabbing.	Demonstrate vulnerability. Support innovation. Guide others how to reverse or learn from mistakes.
Debate	Passionate expression of opinions. Constructive debate. Clear decisions.	Fear of conflict. Ambiguous decisions. Lack of decisions. Imposed decisions.	Encourage healthy debate. Identify underlying differences of opinion.
Commitment	Buy-in to group decisions. Tolerance of uncertainty.	Lack of follow-through. Sabotage.	Not to seek consensus. Push the group to achieve closure around issues.
Accountability	Clear deadlines, roles and responsibilities. Minimal bureaucracy around performance management.	Acceptance of low standards of performance.	Oversee regular progress reviews. Give feedback. Publicise goals to other stakeholders.
Attention to results	Passionate pursuit of the school's vision.	Clamouring for status for oneself or one's subgroup.	Objective pursuit of outcomes.

not an end in itself. Moreover, it is more effective and humane to prevent behavioural problems than to respond to them. Therefore, a policy about student behaviour must include far more than a direct focus on intervening with disruptions. The model presented in Figure 25.2 details the core components that your policy will comprise.

Mandate

Your policy will need to situate itself within its legal obligations and the strictures of the school's governing body. This might also include a brief statement about behaviours (such as the use of illicit drugs and stalking) that are illegal in the community and, therefore, are illegal on school grounds also.

Statement of beliefs

Teachers' beliefs drive both why and how they teach. Your statements in this section will need to make explicit your beliefs about:

- purposes of education: economic, competitive mobility, equity, or personal development
- purposes of discipline: conformity to external controls, internalised control, or considerateness
- beliefs about students: their nature, skilfulness and worth
- beliefs about the causes of behavioural problems in schools: external consequences, or internal needs
- locus of causality and locus of volition
- adults' role: authority figure, or leader.

It is paramount that your philosophy statement be consistent with your recommended practices. Sometimes, schools espouse a personal development purpose of education and a guidance philosophy, but then in their practices section detail authoritarian interventions.[18] To avoid this, once subsequent sections of your policy are written, you will need to compare them with your philosophy statement to ensure that the two align.

Values

For the school to unite under a policy and to function as a community, teachers will need to discuss their values with respect to students and their ability to learn; their priorities for the use of resources; and the relative roles of the principal, teachers, parents and students in school governance.[19] The likelihood that new practices will be implemented depends on the extent to which teachers believe that these fit with their values.[20] Shared values 'find expression in practices';[21] therefore although teachers cannot be required to reach consensus on their personal values, the community will need to find a way to enact their professional values so that practices are coherent. In this way, individuality and professional discretion are embedded within community.[22]

Goals

Goals need to be specific. You should avoid 'motherhood' statements such as, 'We strive for excellence'. Given that no school has ever proclaimed to strive for mediocrity, this statement is meaningless. It may be an attractive motto for public relations purposes but it cannot be operationalised: that is, it does not imply what staff, students or parents will actually *do*.

The main focus of your educational goals is what you want your students to achieve as members of the classroom and

FIGURE 25.2   **Components of policy**

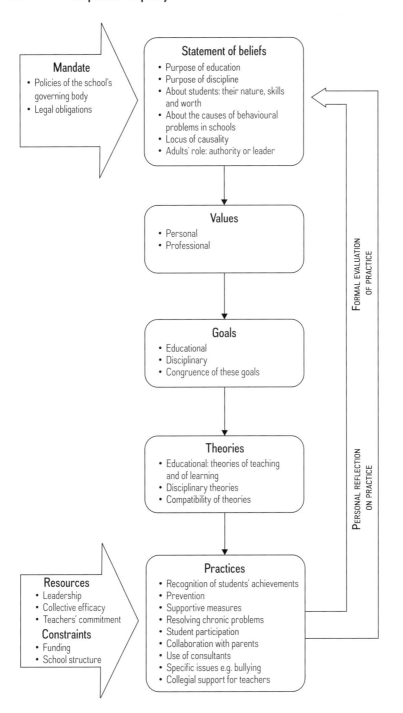

of the wider society.[23] One way to identify these goals is to ask the 'miracle question' which requires teachers to imagine how their class and school would be operating after a miracle occurred and all its present challenges were eliminated: what would endure in their place?[24] What would teachers be doing differently? What would students be doing? These post-miracle qualities and the small signs of progress towards them are your goals.

If your goals include the acquisition of skills in addition to academic achievement, you will need to decide whether a focus on students' personal needs is an end in itself, or is merely instrumental in that it will facilitate student engagement in learning. Such goals might include:

- provision of a safe physical and caring emotional environment that supports and protects the rights of all students to learn and grow personally and safeguards the rights of teachers to teach
- facilitation of students' success by providing a meaningful curriculum
- recognition of students' achievements: this will require a judgment about the debate on intrinsic versus external reinforcement (acknowledgment versus rewards)
- student participation in all aspects of school life
- collaborating with parents.

Your second cluster of goals will be disciplinary. In general, your overall aim will probably be to create a well-ordered environment in which teachers can teach and students can learn. The specifics, however, must answer whether you believe you can achieve that through controlling methods that secure compliance versus the guidance approach that aims for considerate behaviour.

Theories

The next section of your policy will have three parts.

- *Educational theory.* This section will detail your theory about teaching and learning, selecting from a teacher-directed or a constructivist model.
- *Theory of discipline.* You will need to choose between controlling discipline and guidance. It will also be useful in this section to define behavioural 'problems', differentiating between those behaviours that you regard as disciplinary and those which are educational issues.
- *Compatibility.* First, these two theories must be compatible with each other. Second, they must be compatible with your beliefs, goals and values. Third, you will need to scrutinise them for compatibility with the edicts of your governing body. For example, if you are obliged to impose compulsory testing on students and if this is incompatible with your theories, you will need to address how to adjust the testing processes so that they are a better fit with your philosophy and theory.

This section of your document will need to be guided by research evidence and to represent a synthesis of compatible ideas in contrast to an atheoretically eclectic blend.

Practices

Next, in wide consultation across the school community, you will need to detail some efficient, self-sustaining procedures for achieving your goals.

Recognition of students' achievements. You will need to choose between rewards such as praise, grades, school awards and activity reinforcers versus authentic feedback and assessment.

Prevention. The next section will focus on how you can organise your school and classrooms to meet students' needs and prevent disruptions, for example:

- structural support: size of classes, resources for playtimes and breaks, timing of breaks
- emotional support: measures to enhance the school and class climate, class meetings, looping, peer mediation, mentoring schemes, student support groups, peer support systems, pastoral care programs
- instructional support: your policy for providing for students' educational needs and about the impostion of homework.

Supportive measures to meet the needs of students who are struggling to be successful and to behave considerately. These include targeted structural, emotional, instructional (especially remediation of literacy difficulties) and behavioural support. These were detailed here in chapters 7 (for controlling measures) and 18 (for guidance solutions).

Measures to solve chronic problems, as detailed here in chapters 8 (for controlling measures) and 19 (for guidance solutions).

Student participation. This section will detail ways for students to participate in organisational and procedural decision making, both within their classrooms and in the school. It will also specify students' rights and responsibilities, particularly their right to due process in the case of disciplinary actions.[25]

Collaboration with parents. The policy will need to enunciate systematic procedures for routine communications with parents, for the provision of any services to parents, and for eliciting parents' advice and support with academic and behavioural issues when these arise (see chapter 23).

Use of consultants. This section will specify procedures for securing the services of consultants and a list of agencies that can support needy students and families.

Specific issues. The discipline policy will also need to cover specific issues such as:

- sexual harassment of students and teachers
- bullying by and of students and teachers
- child protection and abuse (given that maltreatment is linked to many emotional and behavioural problems, particularly aggression)
- the particular needs of girls and of boys, as indicated by the preponderance of boys as recipients of disciplinary measures.

Collegial support for teachers. Your policy needs to describe the structure that enables staff to support each other and empower their problem solving.[26] This support needs to be both long term and an immediate response to an incident (see chapter 24).

Inventory of resources and constraints

Your recommended practices will have to be realistic. To that end, you will need to conduct an audit to determine

BOX 25.2   **Tip for maintaining guidance values within an authoritarian school policy**

> When the school espouses an authoritarian discipline policy but you believe in the guidance approach, you can still commit to abiding by the policy and to apply its sanctions whenever the students in your class behave inappropriately. However, all the students in your class behave as expected for their age. Therefore, you will not need to invoke the sanctions enshrined in the official policy.

if the necessary resources and supports are available to implement your recommended practices. You will need to plan how to surmount constraints such as a non-conducive physical environment, large school size or the socioeconomic disadvantage of the student population, for example. Given their larger size and fragmented structure, high schools may have more organisational constraints than primary schools.[27] For example, specialised discipline subgroups can develop their own norms and values separate from the larger school community because size and a complex structure makes it difficult to integrate them into the larger whole.[28]

Implementation

Once a policy direction has been settled, implementation will need to be true to it. It will be easier to achieve this when the recommended practices are clear and practical. Programs are more likely to be implemented with fidelity when they have principal support, when teachers receive high-quality training and when the practices are efficient and can be incorporated into regular practices, rather than adding to teachers' existing workloads.[29] Innovations must be user-friendly.[30]

In a climate of low morale and efficacy, resistance to the policy can be overcome by agreeing in the first instance to implement it on a trial basis only. (I recommend a minimum of three months.) In this way, objections are not being discounted but the initial success of the measures during the trial period may improve teachers' efficacy and motivate continued implementation.

There will also need to be some tolerance for teachers to modify the practices at their professional discretion. Although the usual assumption is that this impairs the quality or fidelity of a program, adjustments that can be soundly justified and which fit within a teacher's belief system may well be more effective than purist applications.[31] Nevertheless, the school leadership will need to decide how much slippage is reasonable.

Personal reflection and evaluation

The final section of your policy will detail how the school faculty and principal in particular can mentor individual teachers to promote personal reflection on practices. Second, it will need to specify when and by whom the procedures are to be formally evaluated. The effectiveness of practices might be evaluated on the basis of:

- tallying the number of times that particular interventions have been invoked (e.g. numbers of referrals to

the principal, peer mediation sessions, time-outs or detentions)
- direct observations of classrooms by consultants (which may be prohibitive)
- questionnaires or interviews of teachers, students and parents about their satisfaction with the school's disciplinary methods
- teacher focus groups or surveys to assess teacher morale, stress levels or perceived levels of work satisfaction.

Such data need to be interpreted in light of the school's special circumstances, however. For example, with highly mobile student populations, there might be little change in the actual number of disruptions or disciplinary referrals, which could either mean that the practices are ineffective or that they are being invoked most with new initiates to the school.[32] Or the total number of interventions might decrease overall, but the same students are referred repeatedly, or the same teachers are the source of most referrals, signifying that for these individuals at least, something is not working.

Negative answers to the following questions posed to school staff, parents and students will indicate a need to change practices.[33]

- Are the practices enshrined in the policy consistent with your philosophy and theory?
- Are the procedures being enacted as originally conceived? Do the recommendations reflect actual practice or are they a 'wish list'?

- Are the outcomes congruent with what you set out to accomplish – that is, your original goals?
- Are there other, important, unanticipated outcomes (positive or negative) of the procedures?
- Are there students for whom the procedures are more or less successful than others?
- Are there teachers for whom the procedures are more or less successful than others?
- Are there behaviours for which the procedures are more or less successful than others?
- What additional resources (including materials and personnel) are necessary to make the policy more effective? Are these available?

As well as assessing these outcomes, you will need to evaluate the efficiency of inputs – the resources being used, teachers' time and the involvement of parents.[34] Although such evaluation may seem burdensome, it can be professionally fulfilling to be able to demonstrate to yourself – if to no one else – that what you are doing is effective.

Conclusion

The policy that you arrive at will need to be adjusted in response to changes in the school community brought about by staff turnover, the enrolment of new students[35] and external social or political changes. Above all, it has to be a living document: one that is relevant, owned, communicated, practised and regularly reflected upon.[36]

References

Abbott, R.D., O'Donnell, J., Hawkins, J.D., Hill, K.G., Kosterman, R. & Catalano, R.F. (1998). Changing teaching practices to promote achievement and bonding to school. *American Journal of Orthopsychiatry, 68* (4), 542–552.

Abbott-Shim, M., Lambert, R. & McCarty, F. (2000). Structural model of Head Start classroom quality. *Early Childhood Research Quarterly, 15* (1), 115–134.

Aber, J.L. & Ellwood, D.T. (2001). Thinking about children in time. In B. Bradbury, S.P. Jenkins and J. Micklewright (Eds.) *The dynamics of child poverty in industrialised countries.* Cambridge, UK: Cambridge University Press, 281–300.

Abikoff, H. & Klein, R.G. (1992). Attention-deficit hyperactivity and conduct disorder: Comorbidity and implications for treatment. *Journal of Consulting and Clinical Psychology, 60* (6), 881–892.

Abikoff, H.B., Jensen, P.S., Arnold, L.L.E., Hoza, B., Hechtman, L., Pollack, S., Martin, D., Alvir, J., March, J.S., Hinshaw, S., Vitiello, B., Newcorn, J., Greiner, A., Cantwell, D.P., Conners, C.K., Elliott, G., Greenhill, L.L., Kraemer, H., Pelham, W.E. Jr. Severe, J.B., Swanson, J.M., Wells, K. & Wigal, T. (2002). Observed classroom behavior of children with ADHD: Relationship to gender and comorbidity. *Journal of Abnormal Child Psychology, 30* (4), 349–359.

Abou-ezzeddine, T., Schwartz, D., Chang, L., Lee-Shin, Y., Farver, J. & Xu, Y. (2007). Positive peer relationships and risk of victimization in Chinese and South Korean children's peer groups. *Social Development, 16* (1), 106–126.

Acee, T.W., Kim, H., Kim, H.J., Kim, J.-I., Chu, H.-N.R., Kim, M., Cho, Y., Wicker, F.W. & The Boredom Research Group (2010). Academic boredom in under-and over-challenging situations. *Contemporary Educational Psychology, 35* (1), 17–27.

Ackerman, B.P., Brown, E.D., D'Eramo, K.S. & Izard, C.E. (2002). Maternal relationship instability and the school behavior of children from disadvantaged families. *Developmental Psychology, 38* (5), 694–704.

Ackerman, B.P., Brown, E.D. & Izard, C.E. (2004). The relations between persistent poverty and contextual risk and children's behavior in elementary school. *Developmental Psychology, 40* (3), 367–377.

Adams, C.M. & Forsyth, P.B. (2009). The nature and function of trust in schools. *Journal of School Leadership, 19* (2), 126–152.

Adams, J.B. (2010). Chelation: Removal of toxic metals. In K. Siri & T. Lyons (Eds.) *Cutting-edge therapies for autism 2010-2011.* New York: Skyhorse, 74–78.

Adams, J.F. (2001). Impact of parent training on family functioning. *Child and Family Behavior Therapy, 23* (1), 29–42.

Adams, J.B., Johansen, L.J., Powell, L.D., Quig, D. & Rubin, R.A. (2011). Gastrointestinal flora and gastrointestinal status in children with autism – comparisons to typical children and correlation with autism severity. *Gastroenterology, 11.* Retrieved 16/06/2011 from http://www.biomedcentral.com/1471-230X/11/22.

Afifi, T.O., Brownridge, D.A., Cox, B.J. & Sareen, J. (2006). Physical punishment, childhood abuse and psychiatric disorders. *Child Abuse and Neglect, 30* (10), 1093–1103.

Aguilar, B., Sroufe, A., Egeland, B. & Carlson, E. (2000). Distinguishing the early-onset/persistent and adolescent-onset antisocial behavior types: From birth to 16 years. *Development and Psychopathology, 12* (2), 109–132.

Ahearn, W.H., Kerwin, M.E., Eicher, P.S. & Lukens, C.T. (2001). An ABAC comparison of two intensive interventions for food refusal. *Behavior Modification, 25* (3), 385–405.

Akom, A.A. (2001). Racial profiling at school: The politics of race and discipline at Berkeley High. In W. Ayes, B. Dohrn & R. Ayers (Eds.) *Zero tolerance: Resisting the drive for punishment in our schools.* New York: The New Press, 51–63.

Albert, L. (2003). *Cooperative discipline: Teacher's handbook.* Circle Pines, MN: AGS Publishing.

Alberto, P.A. & Troutman, A.C. (2013). *Applied behavior analysis for teachers.* (9th ed.) Boston, MA: Pearson.

Albrecht, S.F. & Braaten, S. (2008). Strength-based assessment of behavior competencies to distinguish students referred for disciplinary intervention from nonreferred peers. *Psychology in the Schools, 45* (2), 91–103.

Albrecht, S.F., Johns, B.H., Mounsteven, J. & Olorunda, O. (2009). Working conditioins as risk or resiliency factors for teachers of students with emotional and behavioral disabilities. *Psychology in the Schools, 46* (10), 1006–1022.

Alder, N. (2002). Interpretation of the meaning of care: Creating caring relationships in urban middle school classrooms. *Urban Education, 37* (2), 241–266.

Algozzine, B. & Kay, P. (Eds.) (2002). *Preventing problem behaviors: A handbook of successful prevention strategies.* Thousand Oaks, CA: Corwin Press.

Algozzine, B., Wang, C. & Violette, A.S. (2011). Reexamining the relationship between academic achievement and social behavior. *Journal of Positive Behavior Interventions, 13* (1), 3–16.

Algozzine, B. & White, R. (2002). Preventing problem behaviors using schoolwide discipline. In B. Algozzine and P. Kay (Eds.) *Preventing problem behaviors: A handbook of successful prevention strategies.* Thousand Oaks, CA: Corwin Press, 85–103.

Alink, L.R.A., Mesman, J., Koot, H.M., van Zeijl, J., Stolk, M.N., Juffer, F., Bakermans-Kranenburg, M.J. & van IJzedoorn, M.H. (2006). The early childhood aggression curve: Development of physical aggression in 10- to 50-month old children. *Child Development, 77* (4), 954–966.

Alink, L.R.A., Mesman, J., van Zeijl, J., Stolk, M.N., Juffer, F., Bakermans-Kranenburg, M.J., van IJzedoorn, M.H. & Koot, H.M. (2008). Maternal sensitivity moderates the relation between negative discipline and aggression in early childhood. *Social Development, 18* (1), 99–120.

Allen, J. (1995). Friends, fairness, fun, and the freedom to choose: Hearing student voices. *Journal of Curriculum and Supervision, 10* (4), 286–301.

Allen, L.B., McHugh, R.K. & Barlow, D.H. (2008). Emotional disorders: A unified protocol. In D.H. Barlow (Ed.) *Clinical handbook of psychological disorders: A step-by-step treatment manual.* (4th ed.) New York: Guilford, 216–249.

Amabile, T.M. (1990). Within you, without you: The social psychology of creativity, and beyond. In M. Runco and R.S. Albert (Eds.) *Theories of creativity.* Claremont, CA: Pitzer College, 61–91.

Amabile, T.M. & Gitomer, J. (1984). Children's artistic creativity: Effects of choice in task materials. *Personality and Social Psychology Bulletin, 10* (2), 209–215.

Amato-Zech, N.A., Hoff, K.E. & Doepke, K.J. (2006). Increasing on-task behavior in the classroom: Extension of self-monitoring strategies. *Psychology in the Schools, 43* (2), 211–221.

American Psychiatric Association (2013). *Desk reference to the diagnostic criteria from DSM-5* Washington, DC: American Psychiatric Publishing.

Ames, C. (1978). Children's achievement attributions and self-reinforcement: Effects of self-concept and competitive reward structure. *Journal of Educational Psychology, 70* (3), 345–355.

Ames, C. (1981). Competitive versus cooperative reward structures: The influence of individual and group performance factors on achievement attributions and affect. *American Educational Research Journal, 18* (3), 273–287.

——(1992). Classrooms: Goals, structures, and student motivation. *Journal of Educational Psychology, 84* (3), 261–271.

Ames, C. & Ames, R. (1981). Competitive versus individualistic goal structures: The salience of past performance information for causal attributions and affect. *Journal of Educational Psychology, 73* (3), 411–418.

Ames, C. & Felker, D.W. (1979). An examination of children's attributions and achievement-related evaluations in comparative, cooperative, and individualistic reward structures. *Journal of Educational Psychology, 71* (4), 413–420.

Anastopoulos, A.D. & Barkley, R.A. (1992). Attention deficit-hyperactivity disorder. In C.E. Walker and M.C. Roberts (Eds.) *Handbook of clinical child psychology.* (2nd ed.) New York: John Wiley and Sons, 413–430.

Anda, R.F., Felitti, V.J., Bremner, J.D., Walker, J.D., Whitfield, C., Perry, B.D., Dube, S.R. & Giles, W.H. (2006). The enduring effects of abuse and related adverse experiences in childhood: A convergence of evidence from neurobiology and epidemiology. *European Archives of Psychiatry and Clinical Neuroscience, 256* (3), 174–186.

Anderson, J.C., Funk, J.B., Elliott, R. & Smith, P.H. (2003). Parental support and pressure and children's extracurricular activities: Relationships with amount of involvement and affective experience of participation. *Journal of Applied Developmental Psychology, 24* (2), 241–257.

Anderson, M. (1992). *Intelligence and development: A cognitive theory.* Oxford, UK: Blackwell.

Angleitner, A. & Ostendorf, F. (1994). Temperament and the big five factors of personality. In C.F. Halvorson Jr, G.A. Kohnstamm & R.P. Martin (Eds.) *The developing structure of temperament and personality from infancy to adulthood.* Hillsdale, NJ: Lawrence Erlbaum, 69–90.

Antil, L.R., Jenkins, J.R., Wayne, S.K. & Vadasy, P.F. (1998). Cooperative learning: Prevalence, conceptualizations, and the relation between research and practice. *American Educational Research Journal, 35* (3), 419–454.

Appleton, J.J., Christenson, S.L. & Furlong, M.J. (2008). Student engagement with school: Critical conceptual and methodological issues of the construct. *Psychology in the Schools, 45* (5), 369–386.

Armstrong, M. & Thorsborne, M. (2006). Restorative responses to bullying. In H. McGrath and T. Noble (Eds.) *Bullying solutions: Evidence-based approaches to bullying in Australian schools.* Sydney: Pearson Longman, 175–188.

Arnett, J. (1989). Caregivers in day care centers: Does training matter? *Journal of Applied Developmental Psychology, 10* (4), 541–552.

Arnold, D.H. (1997). Co-occurrence of externalizing behavior problems and emergent academic difficulties in young high-risk boys: A preliminary evaluation of patterns and mechanisms. *Journal of Applied Developmental Psychology, 18* (3), 317–330.

Arnold, D.H., McWilliams, L. & Arnold, E.H. (1998). Teacher discipline and child misbehavior in day care: Untangling causality with correlational data. *Developmental Psychology, 34* (2), 276–287.

Arnold, L.E. (1996). Sex differences in ADHD: Conference summary. *Journal of Abnormal Child Psychology, 24* (5), 555–569.

Arnold, M.E. & Hughes, J.N. (1999). First do no harm: Adverse effects of grouping deviant youth for skills training. *Journal of School Psychology, 37* (1), 99–115.

Arsenio, W.F. & Lemerise, E.A. (2001). Varieties of childhood bullying: Values, emotion processes, and social competence. *Social Development, 10* (1), 59–73.

Arthur, M., Gordon, C. & Butterfield, N. (2003). *Classroom management: Creating positive learning environments.* Melbourne: Thomson.

Ascherio, A. & Munger, K.L. (2007). Environmental risk factors for multiple sclerosis. Part I: The role of infection. *Annals of Neurology, 61* (4), 288–299.

Asher, S.R. (1983). Social competence and peer status: Recent advances and future directions. *Child Development, 54* (6), 1427–1434.

Asher, S.R., Hymel, S. & Renshaw, P.D. (1984). Loneliness in children. *Child Development, 55* (4), 1456–1464.

Asher, S.R. & Paquette, J.A. (2003). Loneliness and peer relations in childhood. *Current Directions in Psychological Science, 12* (3), 75–78.

Asher, S.R. & Parker, J.G. (1989). Significance of peer relationship problems in childhood. In B.H. Schneider, G. Attili, J. Nadel and R.P. Weissberg (Eds.) *Social competence in developmental perspective.* Dordrecht: Kluwer Academic Publishers, 5–23.

Asher, S.R. & Renshaw, P.D. (1981). Children without friends: Social knowledge and social skill training. In S.R. Asher and J.M. Gottman (Eds.) *The development of children's friendships.* Cambridge, UK: Cambridge University Press, 273–296.

Ashman, A. & Conway, R.N.F. (1989). *Cognitive strategies for special education.* London: Routledge.

Ashton, J. & Bailey, J. (2004). Slipping through the policy cracks: Children with chronic illness in early childhood settings. *Australian Journal of Early Childhood, 29* (1), 50–58.

Åslund, C., Starrin, B., Leppert, J. & Nilsson, K.W. (2009). Social status and shaming experience related to adolescent overt aggression at school. *Aggressive Behavior, 35* (1), 1–13.

Assor, A., Kaplan, H. & Roth, G. (2002). Choice is good, but relevance is excellent: Autonomy-enhancing and suppressing teacher behaviours predicting students' engagement in schoolwork. *British Journal of Educational Psychology, 72* (2), 261–278.

Assor, A., Roth, G. & Deci, E.L. (2004). The emotional costs of parents' conditional regard: A self-determination theory analysis. *Journal of Personality, 72* (1), 47–88.

Assor, A. & Tal, K. (2012). When parents' affection depends on child's achievement: Parental conditional positive regard, self-aggrandizement, shame and coping in adolescents. *Journal of Adolescence, 35* (2), 249–260.

Atkins, M.S., McKay, M.M., Frazier, S.L., Jakobsons, L.J., Arvanitis, P., Cunningham, T., Brown, C. & Lambrecht. L. (2002). Suspensions and detentions in an urban, low-income school: Punishment or reward? *Journal of Abnormal Child Psychology, 30* (4), 361–371.

Atwater, J.B. & Morris, E.K. (1988). Teachers' instructions and children's compliance in preschool classrooms: A descriptive analysis. *Journal of Applied Behavior Analysis, 21* (2), 157–167.

Aucoin, K.J., Frick, P.J. & Bodin, S.D. (2006). Corporal punishment and child adjustment. *Journal of Applied Developmental Psychology, 27* (6), 527–541.

Auerbach, S. (2007). From moral supporters to struggling advocates: Reconceptualizing parent roles in education through the experience of working-class families of color. *Urban Education, 42* (3), 250–283.

Aunola, K. & Nurmi, J.-E. (2004). Maternal affection moderates the impact of psychological control on a child's mathematical performance. *Developmental Psychology, 40* (6), 965–978.

——(2005). The role of parenting styles in children's problem behavior. *Child Development, 76* (6), 1144–1159.

Austin, J.L. & Bevan, D. (2011). Using differential reinforcement of low rates to reduce children's requests for teacher attention. *Journal of Applied Behavior Analysis, 44* (3), 451–461.

Australian Early Childhood Association. (1991). Australian Early Childhood Association code of ethics. *Australian Journal of Early Childhood, 16* (1), 3–6.

Awong, T., Grusec, J.E. & Sorenson, A. (2008). Respect-based control and anger as determinants of children's socio-emotional development. *Social Development, 17* (4), 941–959.

Axelrod, S. (1977). *Behavior modification for the classroom teacher.* New York: McGraw Hill.

Ayers, W., Ayers, R. & Dohrn, B. (2001). Introduction: Resisting zero tolerance. In W. Ayes, B. Dohrn & R. Ayers (Eds.) *Zero tolerance: Resisting the drive for punishment in our schools.* New York: The New Press, xi–xvi.

Baccini, D., Affuso, G. & Trotta, T. (2008). Temperament, ADHD and peer relations among schoolchildren: The mediating role of bullying. *Aggressive Behavior, 34* (5), 447–459.

Bailey, D.B. Jr (2002). Are critical periods critical for early childhood education?: The role of timing in early childhood pedagogy. *Early Childhood Research Quarterly, 17* (3), 281–294.

Bailey, J.S. (1991). Marketing behavior analysis requires different talk. *Journal of Applied Behavior Analysis, 24* (3), 445–448.

——(1992). Gentle teaching: Trying to win friends and influence people with euphemism, metaphor, smoke, and mirrors. *Journal of Applied Behavior Analysis, 25* (4), 879–883.

Baillargeon, R.H., Normand, C.L., Séguin, J.R., Zoccolillo, M., Japel, C., Pérusse, D., Wu, H.-X., Boivin, M. & Tremblay, R.E. (2007a). The evolution of problem and social competence behaviors during toddlerhood: A prospective

population-based cohort survey. *Infant Mental Health Journal, 28* (1), 12–38.

Baillargeon, R.H., Zoccolillo, M., Keenan, K., Côté, S., Pérusse, D., Wu, H.-X., Boivin, M. & Tremblay, R.E. (2007b). Gender differences in physical aggression: A prospective population-based survey of children before and after 2 years of age. *Developmental Psychology, 43* (1), 13–26.

Baker, J.A. (2006). Contributions of teacher-child relationships to positive school adjustment during elementary school. *Journal of School Psychology, 44* (3), 211–229.

Baker, J.A., Grant, S. & Morlock, L. (2008). The teacher-student relationship as a developmental context for children with internalizing and externalizing behavior problems. *School Psychology Quarterly, 23* (1), 3–15.

Baker-Sennett, J., Matusov, E. & Rogoff, B. (2008). Children's planning of classroom plays with adult or child direction. *Social Development, 17* (4), 998–1018.

Balch, P.A. (2006). *Prescription for nutritional healing.* (4th ed.) New York: Avery Trade.

Baldwin, M.W. & Sinclair, L. (1996). Self esteem and 'If . . . Then' contingencies of interpersonal acceptance. *Journal of Personality and Social Psychology, 71* (6), 1130–1141.

Balson, M. (1992). *Understanding classroom behaviour.* (3rd ed.) Melbourne: ACER.

——(1994). *Becoming better parents.* (4th ed.) Melbourne: ACER.

Bambara, L.M., Nonnemacher, S. & Kern, L. (2009). Sustaining school-based individualized positive behavior support: Perceived barriers and enablers. *Journal of Positive Behavior Interventions, 11* (3), 161–176.

Bandura, A. (1986). *Social foundations of thought and action.* Englewood Cliffs, NJ: Prentice Hall.

——(1993). Perceived self-efficacy in cognitive development and functioning. *Educational Psychologist, 28* (2), 117–148.

——(2001). Social cognitive theory: An agentic perspective. *Annual Review of Psychology, 52,* 1–26.

Banerjee, T.D., Middleton, F., Faraone, S.V. (2007). Environmental risk factors for attention-deficit hyperactivity disorder. *Acta Paediatrica, 96* (9), 1269–1274.

Banks, R. (2005). Solution-focused group therapy. In T.S. Nelson (Ed.) *Education and training in solution-focused brief therapy.* New York: Haworth Press, 17–21.

Bao, X.-H. & Lam, S.-F. (2008). Who makes the choice?: Rethinking the role of autonomy and relatedness in Chinese children's motivation. *Child Development, 79* (2), 269–283.

Barber, B.K., Stolz, H.E., Olsen, J.A., Collins, W.A. & Burchinal, M. (2005). Parental support, psychological control, and behavioral control: Assessing relevance across time, culture, and method. *Monographs of the Society for Research in Child Development, 70* (4), i–147.

Barber, B.K., Xia, M., Olsen, J.A., McNeely, C.A. & Bose, K. (2012). Feeling disrespected by parents: Refining the measurement and understanding of psychological control. *Journal of Adolescence, 35* (2), 273–287.

Barchia, K. & Bussey, K. (2010). The psychological impact of peer victimization: Exploring social-cognitive mediators of depression. *Journal of Adolescence, 33* (5), 615–623.

Barker, E.D., Vitaro, F., Lacourse, E., Fontaine, N.M.G., Carbonneau, R. & Tremblay, R.E. (2010). Testing the developmental distinctiveness of male proactive and reactive aggression with a nested longitudinal experimental intervention. *Aggressive Behavior, 36* (2), 127–140.

Barkley, R.A. (1988). Attention deficit disorder with hyperactivity. In E.J. Mash and L.G. Terdal (Eds.) *Behavioral assessment of childhood disorders.* (2nd ed.) New York: Guilford, 69–104.

Barkley, R.A., Fischer, M., Smallish, L. & Fletcher, K. (2004). Young adult follow-up of hyperactive children: Antisocial activities and drug use. *Journal of Child Psychology and Psychiatry, 45* (2), 195–211.

Barkley, R.A., Shelton, T.L., Crosswait, C., Moorehouse, M., Fletcher, K., Barrett, S., Jenkins, L. & Metevia, L. (2000). Multi-method psycho-educational intervention for preschool children with disruptive behavior: Preliminary results at post-treatment. *Journal of Child Psychology and Psychiatry, 41* (3), 319–332.

Barnett, M.A. & Bryan, J.H. (1974). Effects of competition with outcome feedback on children's helping behavior. *Developmental Psychology, 10* (6), 838–842.

Barnett, M.A., Burns, S.R., Sanborn, F.W., Bartel, J.S. & Wilds, S.J. (2004). Antisocial and prosocial teasing among children: Perceptions and individual differences. *Social Development, 13* (2), 292–310.

Barr, C.E., Mednick, S.A. & Munk-Jorgensen, P. (1990). Exposure to influenza epidemics during gestation and adult schizophrenia: A 40-year study. *Archives of General Psychiatry, 47* (9), 869–874.

Barry, T.D., Thompson, A., Barry, C.T., Lochman, J.E., Adler, K. & Hill, K. (2007). The importance of narcissism in predicting proactive and reactive aggression in moderately to highly aggressive children. *Aggressive Behavior, 33* (3), 185–197.

Bates, L., Luster, T. & Vandenbelt, M. (2003). Factors related to social competence in elementary school among children of adolescent mothers. *Social Development, 12* (1), 107–124.

Batson, C.D., Coke, J.S., Janoski, M.L. & Hanson, M. (1978). Buying kindness: Effect of an extrinsic incentive for helping on perceived altruism. *Personality and Social Psychology Bulletin, 4* (1), 86–91.

Battistich, V., Solomon, D., Kim, D., Watson, M. & Schaps, E. (1995). Schools as communities, poverty levels of student populations, and students' attitudes, motives, and performance: A multilevel analysis. *American Educational Research Journal, 32* (3), 627–658.

Battistich, V., Schaps, E. & Wilson, N. (2004). Effects of an elementary school intervention on students' 'connectedness' to school and social adjustment during middle school. *Journal of Primary Prevention, 24* (3), 243–262.

Battistich, V., Solomon, D., Watson, M. & Schaps, E. (1997). Caring school communities. *Educational Psychologist, 32* (3), 137–151.

Baum, W. (2011). What is radical behaviorism?: A review of Jay Moore's Conceptual foundations of radical behaviorism. *Journal of the Experimental Analysis of Behavior, 95* (1), 119–126.

Baumeister, R.F., Campbell, J.D., Krueger, J.I. & Vohs, K.D. (2003). Does high self-esteem cause better performance, interpersonal success, happiness, or healthier lifestyles? *Psychological Science in the Public Interest, 4* (1), 1–44.

Baumeister, R.F., Heatherton, T.F. & Tice, D.M. (1993). When ego threats lead to self-regulation failure: Negative consequences of high self-esteem. *Journal of Personality and Social Psychology, 64* (1), 141–156.

Baumeister, R.F. & Leary, M.F. (1995). The need to belong: Desire for interpersonal attachments as a fundamental human motivation. *Psychological Bulletin, 117* (3), 497–529.

Baumeister, R.F., Smart, L. & Boden, J.M. (1996). Relation of threatened egotism to violence and aggression: The dark side of high self-esteem. *Psychological Review, 103* (1), 5–33.

Baumrind, D. (1967). Child care practices anteceding three patterns of preschool behavior. *Genetic Psychology Monographs, 75,* 43–88.

——(1971a). Current patterns of parental authority. *Developmental Psychology Monographs, 4* (1), 1–98.

——(1971b). Harmonious parents and their preschool children. *Developmental Psychology, 4* (1), 99–102.

——(1991). Effective parenting during the early adolescent

transition. In P.A. Cowan and M. Hetherington (Eds.) *Advances in family research series: Family transitions.* Hillsdale, NJ: Lawrence Erlbaum, 111–163.

Baumrind, D., Larzelere, R.E. & Cowan, P.A. (2002). Ordinary physical punishment: It is harmful? Comment on Gershoff (2002). *Psychological Bulletin, 128* (4), 580–589.

Bean, R.A., Bush, K.R., McKenry, P.C. & Wilson, S.M. (2003). The impact of parental support, behavioral control, and psychological control on the academic achievement and self-esteem of African American and European American adolescents. *Journal of Adolescent Research, 18* (5), 523–541.

Beane, J.A. (1991). Sorting out the self-esteem controversy. *Educational Leadership, 49* (1), 25–30.

Beets, M.W., Flay, B.R., Vuchinich, S., Acock, A.C., Li, K.-K. & Allred, C. (2008). School climate and teachers' beliefs and attitudes associated with implementation of the positive action program: A diffusion of innovations model. *Prevention Science, 9* (4), 264–275.

Beishuizen, J.J., Hof, E., van Putten, C.M., Bouwmeester, S. & Asscher, J.J. (2001). Students' and teachers' cognitions about good teachers. *British Journal of Educational Psychology, 71* (2), 185–201.

Belsky, J., Hsieh, K.-H. & Crnic, K. (1998). Mothering, fathering, and infant negativity as antecedents of boys' externalizing problems and inhibition at age 3 years: Differential susceptibility to rearing experience? *Development and Psychopathology, 10* (2), 301–319.

Ben-Shahar, T. (2007). *Happier.* Boston, MA: McGraw Hill.

Benasich, A.A., Curtiss, S. & Tallal, P. (1993). Language, learning, and behavioral disturbances in childhood: A longitudinal perspective. *Journal of the American Academy of Child and Adolescent Psychiatry, 32* (3), 585–594.

Benbenishty, R., Zeira, A. & Astor, R.A. (2002a). Children's reports of emotional, physical and sexual maltreatment by educational staff in Israel. *Child Abuse and Neglect, 26* (8), 763–782.

Benbenishty, R., Zeira, A., Astor, R.A. & Khoury-Kassabri, M. (2002b). Maltreatment of primary school students by educational staff in Israel. *Child Abuse and Neglect, 26* (12), 1291–1309.

Benes, K.M. & Kramer, J.J. (1989). The behavioral tradition in schools (and miles to go before we sleep). In J.N. Hughes and R.J. Hall (Eds.) *Cognitive-behavioral psychology in the schools.* New York: Guilford, 15–36.

Bennett, D.S., Bendersky, M. & Lewis, M. (2002). Children's intellectual and emotional-behavioral adjustment at 4 years as a function of cocaine exposure, maternal characteristics, and environmental risk. *Developmental Psychology, 38* (5), 648–658.

Benson, M.J. & Buehler, C. (2012). Family process and peer deviance influences on adolescent aggression: Longitudinal effects across early and middle adolescence. *Child Development, 83* (4), 1213–1228.

Berg, I.K. & Steiner, S. (2003). *Children's solution work.* New York: Norton.

Berk, L.E. & Landau, S. (1993). Private speech of learning disabled and normally achieving children in classroom academic and laboratory contexts. *Child Development, 64* (2), 556–571.

Berk, L.E. & Potts, M.K. (1991). Development and functional significance of private speech among attention-deficit hyperactivity disordered and normal boys. *Journal of Abnormal Child Psychology, 19* (3), 357–377.

Berkel, C., Mauricio, A.M., Schoenfelder, E. & Sandler, I.N. (2011). Putting the pieces together: An integrated model of program implementation. *Prevention Science, 12* (1), 23–33.

Berlin, L.J., Appleyard, K. & Dodge, K.A. (2011). Intergenerational continuity in child maltreatment:

Mediating mechanisms and implications for prevention. *Child Development, 82* (1), 162–176.

Berlin, L.J. & Cassidy, J. (2003). Mothers' self-reported control of their preschool children's emotional expressiveness: A longitudinal study of associations with infant-mother attachment and children's emotion regulation. *Social Development, 12* (4), 477–495.

Bernard, M.E. (2006). It's time we teach social-emotional competence as well as we teach academic competence. *Reading and Writing Quarterly, 22* (2), 103–119.

Berndt, T.J. (2004). Children's friendships: Shifts over a half-century in perspectives on their development and effects. *Merrill-Palmer Quarterly, 50* (3), 206–223.

Berndt, T.J. & Miller, K.E. (1990). Expectancies, values, and achievement in junior high school. *Journal of Educational Psychology, 82* (2), 319–326.

Bernier, A., Carlson, S.M. & Whipple, N. (2010). From external regulation to self-regulation: Early parenting precursors of young children's executive functioning. *Child Development, 81* (1), 326–339.

Bertolino, B. & Schultheis, G. (2002). *The therapist's notebook for families: Solution-oriented exercies for working with parents, children, and adolescents.* New York: Haworth.

Bessell, A.G. (2001). Children surviving cancer: Psychosocial adjustment, quality of life, and school experiences. *Exceptional Children, 67* (3), 345–359.

Bibou-Nakou, I., Kiosseoglou, G. & Stogiannidou, A. (2000). Elementary teachers' perceptions regarding school behavior problems: Implications for school psychological services. *Psychology in the Schools, 37* (2), 123–134.

Bigler, R.S. (1999). The use of multicultural curricula and materials to counter racism. *Journal of Social Issues, 55* (4), 687–705.

Billman, J. (1995). Child care program directors: What skills do they need?: Results of a statewide survey. *Early Childhood Education Journal, 23* (2), 63–70.

Binder, L.M., Dixon, M.R. & Ghezzi, P.M. (2000). A procedure to teach self-control to children with attention deficit hyperactivity disorder. *Journal of Applied Behavior Analysis, 33* (2), 233–237.

Birch, L.L., Johnson, S.L. & Fisher, J.A. (1995). Children's eating: The development of food-acceptance patterns. *Young Children, 50* (2), 71–78.

Birch, L.L., Martin, D.W. & Rotter, J. (1984). Eating as the 'means' activity in a contingency: Effects on young children's food preference. *Child Development, 55* (2), 431–419.

Birch, S.H. & Ladd, G.W. (1997). The teacher-child relationship and children's early school adjustment. *Journal of School Psychology, 35* (1), 61–79.

——(1998). Children's interpersonal behaviors and the teacher-child relationship. *Developmental Psychology, 34* (5), 934–946.

Birchwood, J. & Daley, Đ. (2012). Brief report: The impact of attention deficit hyperactivity disorder (ADHD) symptoms on academic performance of an adolescent community sample. *Journal of Adolescence, 35* (1), 225–231.

Birkeland, M.S., Melkevik, O., Holsen, I. & Wold, B. (2012). Trajectories of global self-esteem development during adolescence. *Journal of Adolescence, 35* (1), 43–54.

Black, A.E. & Deci, E.L. (2000). The effects of instructors' autonomy support and students' autonomous motivation on learning organic chemistry: A self-determination theory perspective. *Science Education, 84* (6), 740–756.

Blair, C., Granger, D. & Razza, R.P. (2005). Cortisol reactivity is positively related to executive function in preschool children attending Head Start. *Child Development, 76* (3), 554–567.

Blankemeyer, M., Flannery, D.J. & Vazsonyi, A.T. (2002). The role of aggression and social competence in children's

perceptions of the child-teacher relationship. *Psychology in the Schools, 39* (3), 293–304.

Blatchford, P., Baines, E., Kutnick, P. & Martin, C. (2001). Classroom contexts: Connections between class size and within class grouping. *British Journal of Educational Psychology, 71* (2), 283–302.

Bleiberg, K.L. & Markowitz, J.C. (2008). Interpersonal psychotherapy for depression. In D.H. Barlow (Ed.) *Clinical handbook of psychological disorders: A step-by-step treatment manual.* (4th ed.) New York: Guilford, 306–327.

Bloomquist, M.L., August, G.J., Cohen, C., Doyle, A. & Everhart, K. (1997). Social problem solving in hyperactive-aggressive children: How and what they think in conditions of automatic and controlled processing. *Journal of Clinical Child Psychology, 26* (2), 172–180.

Blum, N.J. & Mercugliano, M. (1997). Attention-deficit/hyperactivity disorder. In M.L. Batshaw (Ed.) *Children with disabilities.* (4th ed.) Sydney: MacLennan & Petty, 449–470.

Bock, K. & Stauth, C. (2008). *Healing the new childhood epidemics: Autism, ADHD, asthma, and allergies.* New York: Ballantine.

Bogat, G.A., DeJonghe, E., Levendosky, A.A., Davidson, W.S. & von Eye, A. (2006). Trauma symptoms among infants exposed to intimate partner violence. *Child Abuse and Neglect, 30* (2), 109–125.

Bolger, K.E. & Patterson, C.J. (2001). Developmental pathways from child maltreatment to peer rejection. *Child Development, 72* (2), 549–568.

Bolton, R. (1987). *People skills.* Sydney: Simon and Schuster.

Bondy, E., Ross, D.D., Gallingane, C. & Hambacher, E. (2007). Creating environments of success and resilience: Culturally responsive classroom management and more. *Urban Education, 42* (4), 326–348.

Bong, M. & Skaalvik, E.M. (2003). Academic self-concept and self-efficacy: How different are they really? *Educational Psychology Review, 15* (1), 1–40.

Bonner, B.L., Kaufman, K.L., Harbeck, C. & Brassard, M.R. (1992). Child maltreatment. In C.E. Walker and M.C. Roberts (Eds.) *Handbook of clinical child psychology.* (2nd ed.) New York: John Wiley and Sons, 967–1008.

Bontempo, D.E. & D'Augelli, A.R. (2002). Effects of at-school victimization and sexual orientation on lesbian, gay, or bisexual youths' health risk behavior. *Journal of Adolescent Health, 30* (5), 364–374.

Booth, C.L., Rose-Krasnor, L., McKinnon, J. & Rubin, K.H. (1994). Predicting social adjustment in middle childhood: The role of preschool attachment security and maternal style. *Social Development, 3* (3), 189–204.

Borba, M. (2005). *Nobody likes me, everybody hates me: The top 25 friendship problems and how to solve them.* San Francisco, CA: Jossey-Bass.

Borland, J.H. (1986). A note on the existence of certain divergent-production abilities. *Journal for the Education of the Gifted, 9* (4), 239–251.

——(2003). Evaluating gifted programs: A broader perspective. In N. Colangelo and G.A. Davis (Eds.) *Handbook of gifted education.* (3rd ed.) Boston, MA: Allyn & Bacon, 293–307.

Boulard, A., Quertemont, E., Gauthier, J.-M. & Born, M. (2012). Social context in school: Its relation to adolescents' depressive mood. *Journal of Adolescence, 35* (1), 143–152.

Boulton, M.J. (1994). Understanding and preventing bullying in the junior school playground. In P.K. Smith and S. Sharp (Eds.) *School bullying: Insights and perspectives.* London: Routledge, 132–159.

——(1997). Teachers' views on bullying: Definitions, attitudes and ability to cope. *British Journal of Educational Psychology, 67* (2), 223–233.

Bourre, J.M., Pascal, G., Durand, G., Masson, M., Dumont, O. &

Piciotti, M. (1984). Alterations in the fatty acid composition of rat brain cells (neurons, astrocytes, and oligodendrocytes) and of subcellular fractions (myelin and synaptosomes) induced by a diet devoid of n-3 fatty acids. *Journal of Neurochemistry, 43* (2), 342–348.

Bowles, S. & Gintis, H. (2011a). *Schooling in capitalist America: Educational reform and the contradictions of economic life.* (2nd ed.) Chicago, IL: Haymarket.

——(2011b). *A cooperative species: Human reciprocity and its evolution.* Princeton, NJ: Princeton University Press.

Boyle, D. & Hassett-Walker, C. (2008). Reducing overt and relational aggression among young children: The results from a two-year outcome evaluation. *Journal of School Violence, 7* (1), 27–42.

Boyle, M.H., Georgiades, K., Racine, Y. & Mustard, C. (2007). Neighborhood and family influences on educational attainment: Results from the Ontario child health study follow-up 2001. *Child Development, 78* (1), 168–189.

Bracken, B.A., Bunch, S., Keith, T.Z. & Keith, P.B. (2000). Child and adolescent multidimensional self-concept: A five-instrument factor analysis. *Psychology in the Schools, 37* (6), 483–493.

Brackett, M.A., Palomera, R., Mojsa-Kaja, J., Reyes, M.G. & Salovey, P. (2010). Emotion-regulation ability, burnout, and job satisfaction among British secondary-school teachers. *Psychology in the Schools, 47* (4), 406–416.

Bradshaw, C.P., Mitchell, M.M. & Leaf, P.J. (2010). Examining the effects of schoolwide positive behavioral interventions and supports on student outcomes: Results from a randomized controlled effectiveness trial on elementary schools. *Journal of Positive Behavior Interventions, 12* (3), 133–148.

Bradshaw, C.P., Sawyer, A.L., O'Brennan, L.M. (2007). Bullying and peer victimization at school: Perceptual differences between students and school staff. *School Psychology Review, 36* (3), 361–382.

Brady, K. & Woolfson, L. (2008). What teacher factors influence their attributions for children's difficulties in learning? *British Journal of Educational Psychology, 78* (4), 527–544.

Brand, S., Felner, R.D., Seitsinger, A., Burns, A. & Bolton, N. (2008). A large scale study of the assessment of the social environment of middle and secondary schools: The validity and utility of teachers' ratings of school climate, cultural pluralism, and safety problems for understanding school effects and school improvement. *Journal of School Psychology, 46* (5), 507–535.

Brendgen, M., Dionne, G., Girard, A., Boivin, M., Vitaro, F. & Pérusse, D. (2005). Examining genetic and environmental effects on social aggression: A study of 6-year-old twins. *Child Development, 76* (4), 930–946.

Brendgen, M., Vitaro, F. & Bukowski, W.M. (2000). Stability and variability of adolescents' affiliations with delinquent friends: Predictors and consequences. *Social Development, 9* (2), 205–225.

Brendgen, M., Wanner, B. & Vitaro, F. (2006). Verbal abuse by the teacher and child adjustment from kindergarten through grade 6. *Pediatrics, 117* (5), 1585–1598.

Brendgen, M., Wanner, B., Vitaro, F., Bukowski, W.M. & Tremblay, R.E. (2007). Verbal abuse by the teacher during childhood and academic, behavioral, and emotional adjustment in young adulthood. *Journal of Educational Psychology, 99* (1), 26–38.

Brenner, V. & Fox, R.A. (1999). An empirically derived classification of parenting practices. *Journal of Genetic Psychology, 160* (3), 343–356.

Brier, N. (1995). Predicting antisocial behaviour in youngsters displaying poor academic achievement: A review of risk factors. *Developmental and Behavioral Pediatrics, 16* (4), 271–276.

Briere, D.E. III & Simonsen, B. (2011). Self-monitoring interventions for at-risk middle school students: The importance of considering function. *Behavioral Disorders, 36* (2), 129–140.

Briesch, A.M. & Chafouleas, S.M. (2009). Review and analysis of literature on self-management interventions to promote appropriate classroom behaviors (1988–2008). *School Psychology Quarterly, 24* (2), 106–118.

Briggs, F. (1993). *Why my child?: Supporting the families of victims of child sexual abuse.* Sydney: Allen & Unwin.

Briggs, F. & McVeity, M. (2000). *Teaching children to protect themselves.* Sydney: Allen & Unwin.

Brody, G.H. & Shaffer, D.R. (1982). Contributions of parents and peers to children's moral socialization. *Developmental Review, 2* (1), 31–75.

Broidy, L.M., Nagin, D.S., Tremblay, R.E., Bates, J.E., Brame, B., Dodge, K.A., Fergusson, D., Horwood, J.L., Loeber, R., Laird, R., Lynam, D.R., Moffitt, T.E., Pettit, G.S. & Vitaro, F. (2003). Developmental trajectories of childhood disruptive behaviors and adolescent delinquency: A six-site, cross-national study. *Developmental Psychology, 39* (2), 222–245.

Broinowski, I. & Dau, E. (2004). *Managing children's services.* Melbourne: Tertiary Press.

Bromberg, D.S. & Johnson, B.T. (2001). Sexual interest in children, child sexual abuse, and psychological sequelae for children. *Psychology in the Schools, 38* (4), 343–355.

Bronson, P. & Merryman, A. (2009). *Nurture shock: New thinking about children.* New York: Twelve.

Brophy, J. (1981). Teacher praise: A functional analysis. *Review of Educational Research, 51* (1), 5–32.

——(1983a). Research on the self-fulfilling prophecy and teacher expectations. *Journal of Educational Psychology, 75* (5), 631–661.

——(1983b). Classroom organization and management. *The Elementary School Journal, 83* (4), 264–285.

——(1985). Classroom management as instruction: Socializing self-guidance in students. *Theory into Practice, 24* (4), 233–240.

Brophy, J. & Good, T.L. (1970). Teachers' communication of differential expectations for children's classroom performance: Some behavioral data. *Journal of Educational Psychology, 61* (5), 365–374.

Brophy, J. & McCaslin, M. (1992). Teachers' reports of how they perceive and cope with problem students. *The Elementary School Journal, 93* (1), 3–68.

Brown, A.S. & Susser, E.S. (2008). Prenatal nutritional deficiency and risk of adult schizophrenia. *Schizophrenia Bulletin, 34* (6), 1054–1063.

Brown, A.S., van Os, J., Driessens, C., Hoek, H.W. & Susser, E.S. (2000). Further evidence of relation between prenatal famine and major affective disorder. *American Journal of Psychiatry, 157* (2), 190–195.

Brown, B. (2008). *I thought it was just me (but it isn't).* New York: Gotham.

——(2010). *The gifts of imperfection.* Center City, MN: Hazelden

——(2012). *Daring greatly.* New York: Gotham.

Brown, D.F. (2004). Urban teachers' professed classroom management strategies: Reflections of culturally responsive teaching. *Urban Education, 39* (3), 266–289.

Brown, J.V., Bakeman, R., Coles, C.D., Platzman, K.A. & Lynch, M.E. (2004). Prenatal cocaine exposure: A comparison of 2-year-old children in parental and nonparental care. *Child Development, 74* (4), 1282–1295.

Brownell, C.A., Ramani, G.B. & Zerwas, S. (2006). Becoming a social partner with peers: Cooperation and social understanding in one- and two-year-olds. *Child Development, 77* (4), 803–821.

Bruess, C. & Richardson, G. (1989). *Decisions for health.* (2nd ed.) Dubuque, IO: Brown.

Bryant, B.K. (1977). The effects of the interpersonal context of evaluation on self- and other-enhancement behavior. *Child Development, 48* (3), 885–892.

Bryant, D., Vizzard, L.H., Willoughby, M. & Kupersmidt, J. (1999). A review of interventions for preschoolers with aggressive and disruptive behavior. *Early Education and Development, 10* (1), 47–68.

Bryson, K. (2004). *Don't be nice, be real: Balancing passion for self with compassion for others.* Santa Rosa, CA: Elite Books.

Bub, K.L., McCartney, K. & Willett, J.B. (2007). Behavior problem trajectories and first-grade cognitive ability and achievement skills: A latent growth curve analysis. *Journal of Educational Psychology, 99* (3), 653–670.

Buchanan, C.M., Eccles, J.S. & Becker, J.B. (1992). Are adolescents the victims of raging hormones: Evidence for activational effects of hormones on moods and behavior at adolescence. *Psychological Bulletin, 111* (1), 62–107.

Buchs, C., Gilles, I., Dutrévis, M. & Butera, F. (2011). Pressure to cooperate: Is positive reward interdependence really needed in cooperative learning? *British Journal of Educational Psychology, 81* (1), 135–146.

Buckingham, D. (2000). *After the death of childhood: Growing up in the age of electronic media.* Cambridge, UK: Polity Press.

Buckley, S.D. & Newchok, D.K. (2005). An evaluation of simultaneous presentation and differential reinforcement with response cost to reduce packing. *Journal of Applied Behavior Analysis, 38* (3), 405–409.

Bugental, D.B. & Happaney, K. (2004). Predicting infant maltreatment in low-income families: The interactive effects of maternal attributions and child status at birth. *Developmental Psychology, 40* (2), 234–243.

Bugental, D.B., Lyon, J.E., Krantz, J. & Cortez, V. (1997). Who's the boss?: Differential accessibility of dominance ideation in parent-child relationships. *Journal of Personality and Social Psychology, 72* (6), 1297–1309.

Bugental, D.B., Martorell, G.A. & Barraza, V. (2003). The hormonal costs of subtle forms of infant maltreatment. *Hormones and Behavior, 43* (1), 237–244.

Buhs, E.S. & Ladd, G.W. (2001). Peer rejection as an antecedent of young children's social adjustment: An examination of mediating processes. *Developmental Psychology, 37* (4), 550–560.

Buhs, E.S., Ladd, G.W. & Herald, S.L. (2006). Peer exclusion and victimization: Processes that mediate the relation between peer group rejection and children's classroom engagement and achievement? *Journal of Educational Psychology, 98* (1), 1–13.

Bukowski, W.M. (2003). What does it mean to say that aggressive children are competent or incompetent? *Merrill-Palmer Quarterly, 49* (3), 390–400.

Bukowski, W.M. & Sippola, L.K. (2001). Groups, individuals, and victimization: A view of the peer system. In J. Juvonen and S. Graham (Eds.) *Peer harassment in school: The plight of the vulnerable and victimized.* New York: Guilford, 355–377.

Burack, J.A., Flanagan, T., Peled, T., Sutton, H.M., Zygmuntowicz, C. & Manly, J.T. (2006). Social perspective-taking skills in maltreated children and adolescents. *Developmental Psychology, 42* (2), 207–217.

Burchinal, M.R. & Cryer, D. (2003). Diversity, child care quality, and developmental outcomes. *Early Childhood Research Quarterly, 18* (4), 401–426.

Burchinal, M.R., Howes, C. & Kontos, S. (2002). Structural predictors of child care quality in child care homes. *Early Childhood Research Quarterly, 17* (1), 87–105.

Burchinal, M.R., Roberts, J.E., Riggins, R. Jr, Zeisel, S.A., Neebe, E. & Bryant, D. (2000). Relating quality of center-based child care to early cognitive and language development longitudinally. *Child Development, 71* (2), 339–357.

Burden, R.L. & Fraser, B.J. (1993). Classroom environment assessments. *Psychology in the Schools, 30* (3), 232–240.

Burgess, K.B., Wojslawowicz, J.C., Rubin, K.H., Rose-Krasnor, L., Booth-LaForce, C. (2006). Social information processing and coping strategies of shy/withdrawn and aggressive children: Does friendship matter? *Child Development, 77* (2), 371–383.

Buri, J.R., Louiselle, P.A., Misukanis, T.M. & Mueller, R.A. (1988). Effects of parental authoritarianism and authoritativeness on self-esteem. *Personality and Social Psychology Bulletin, 14* (2), 271–282.

Burns, A. & Goodnow, J. (1985). *Children and families in Australia.* (2nd ed.) Sydney: Allen & Unwin.

Burns, R.B. (1982). *Self-concept development and education.* London: Holt, Rhinehart and Winston.

Burt, S.A., Mikolajewski, A.J. & Larson, C.L. (2009). Do aggression and rule-breaking have different interpersonal correlates?: A study of antisocial subtypes, negative affect, and hostile perceptions of others. *Aggressive Behavior, 35* (6), 453–461.

Burton, L., Westen, D. & Kowalski, R. (2009). *Psychology.* (2nd Aust. & NZ ed.) Milton, Qld: Wiley.

Busseri, M.A., Willoughby, T., Chalmers, H. & Bogaert, A.R. (2006). Same-sex attraction and successful adolescent development. *Journal of Youth and Adolescence, 35* (4), 563–575.

Bussey, K. (1999). Children's categorization and evaluation of different types of lies and truths. *Child Development, 70* (6), 1338–1347.

Butler, R. & Nisan, M. (1986). Effects of no feedback, task-related comments, and grades on intrinsic motivation and performance. *Journal of Educational Psychology, 78* (3), 210–216.

Butler-Por, N. (1993). Underachieving gifted students. In K.A. Heller, F.J. Mönks and A.H. Passow (Eds.) *International handbook of research and development of giftedness and talent.* Oxford, UK: Pergamon, 649–668.

Buyse, E., Verschueren, K., Doumen, S., Van Damme, J. & Maes, F. (2008). Classroom problem behavior and teacher-child relationships in kindergarten: The moderating role of classroom climate. *Journal of School Psychology, 46* (4), 367–391.

Cabot, S. (2001). *Can't lose weight?: You could have Syndrome X.* Sydney: Health Books Australia.

——(2004). *Magnesium: The miracle mineral.* Camden, NSW: WHAS.

Cabot, S. & Jasinska, M. (2011). *Infertility: The hidden causes.* Camden, NSW: WHAS.

Cabrera, N.J., Fagan, J., Wight, V. & Schadler, C. (2011). Influence of mother, father, and child risk on parenting and children's cognitive and social behaviors. *Child Development, 82* (6), 1985–2005.

Cacioppo, J.T., Hawkley, L.C. & Berntson, G.G. (2003). The anatomy of loneliness. *Current Directions in Psychological Science, 12* (3), 71–74.

Cadima, J., Leal, T. & Burchinal, M. (2010). The quality of teacher-student interactions: Associations with first graders' academic and behavioral outcomes. *Journal of School Psychology, 48* (6), 457–482.

Calkins, S.D., Gill, K.L., Johnson, M.C. & Smith, C.L. (1999). Emotional reactivity and emotional regulation strategies as predictors of social behavior with peers during toddlerhood. *Social Development, 8* (3), 310–334.

Calkins, S.D. & Johnson, M.C. (1998). Toddler regulation of distress to frustrating events: Temperamental and maternal correlates. *Infant Behavior and Development, 21* (3), 379–395.

Cameron, C.E., Connor, C.M. & Morrison, F.J. (2005). Effects of variation in teacher organization on classroom functioning. *Journal of School Psychology, 43* (1), 61–85.

Cameron, J. (2001). Negative effects of reward on intrinsic motivation – a limited phenomenon: Comment on Deci, Koestner, and Ryan (2001). *Review of Educational Research, 71* (1), 29–42.

Cameron, J. & Pierce, W.D. (1994). Reinforcement, reward, and intrinsic motivation: A meta-analysis. *Review of Educational Research, 64* (3), 363–423.

——(1996). The debate about rewards and intrinsic motivation: Protests and accusations do not alter the results. *Review of Educational Research, 66* (1), 39–51.

Camodeca, M. & Goossens, F.A. (2005). Aggression, social cognitions, anger and sadness in bullies and victims. *Journal of Child Psychology and Psychiatry, 46* (2), 186–197.

Camodeca, M., Goossens, F.A., Terwogt, M.M. & Schuengel, C. (2002). Bullying and victimization among school-age children: Stability and links to proactive and reactive aggression. *Social Development, 11* (3), 332–345.

Campbell, S.B. (1995). Behavior problems in preschool children: A review of recent research. *Journal of Child Psychology and Psychiatry, 36* (1), 113–149.

Campbell, S.B. & Ewing, L.J. (1990). Follow-up of hard-to-manage preschoolers: Adjustment at age 9 and predictors of continuing symptoms. *Journal of Child Psychology and Psychiatry, 31* (6), 871–889.

Campbell, S.B., March, C.L., Pierce, E.W., Ewing, L.J. & Szumowski, E.K. (1991a). Hard-to-manage preschool boys: Family context and the stability of externalizing behavior. *Journal of Abnormal Child Psychology, 19* (3), 301–318.

Campbell, S.B., Pierce, E.W., March, C.L. & Ewing, L.J. (1991b). Noncompliant behavior, overactivity, and family stress as predictors of negative maternal control with preschool children. *Development and Psychopathology, 3* (2), 175–190.

Campbell, S.B., Pierce, E.W., Moore, G., Marakovitz, S. & Newby, K. (1996). Boys' externalizing problems at elementary school age: Pathways from early behavior problems, maternal control, and family stress. *Development and Psychopathology, 8* (4), 701–719.

Campbell, S.B., Shaw, D.S. & Gilliom, M. (2000). Early externalizing behavior problems: Toddlers and preschoolers at risk for later maladjustment. *Development and Psychopathology, 12* (3), 467–488.

Campbell, S.B., Spieker, S., Burchinal, M., Poe, M.D. & The NICHD Early Child Care Research Network (2006). Trajectories of aggression from toddlerhood to age 9 predict academic and social functioning through age 12. *Journal of Child Psychology and Psychiatry, 47* (8), 791–800.

Campbell-McBride, N. (2010). *Gut and psychology syndrome.* Cambridge, UK: Medinform.

Cangelosi, J.S. (2004). *Classroom management strategies: Gaining and maintaining students' cooperation.* (5th ed.) New York: Wiley.

Canter, L. (2010). *Assertive discipline: Positive behavior management for today's classroom.* (4th ed.) Bloomington, IN: Solution Tree Press.

Canter, L. & Canter, M. (2001). *Assertive discipline: Positive behavior management for today's classroom.* Los Angeles, CA: Canter and Associates.

Cappella, E. & Weinstein, R. (2006). The prevention of social aggression among girls. *Social Development, 15* (3), 434–462.

Caprara, G.V., Barbaranelli, C., Borgogni, L. & Steca, P. (2003). Efficacy beliefs as determinants of teachers' job satisfaction. *Journal of Educational Psychology, 95* (4), 821–832.

Caprara, G.V., Barbaranelli, C., Steca, P. & Malone, P.S. (2006). Teachers' self-efficacy beliefs as determinants of job satisfaction and students' academic achievement: A study at the school level. *Journal of School Psychology, 44* (6), 473–490.

Caravita, S.C.S., Di Blasio, P. & Salmivalli, C. (2009). Unique and interactive effects of empathy and social status on involvement in bullying. *Social Development, 18* (1), 140–163.

Carbonneau, N., Vallerand, R.J., Fernet, C. & Guay, F. (2008). The role of passion for teaching in intrapersonal and interpersonal outcomes. *Journal of Educational Psychology, 100* (4), 977–987.

Card, N.A. & Little, T.D. (2006). Proactive and reactive aggression in childhood and adolescence: A meta-analysis of differential relations with psychosocial adjustment. *International Journal of Behavioral Development, 30* (5), 466–480.

Carey, M. & Russell, S. (2003). Re-authoring: Some answers to commonly asked questions. *The International Journal of Narrative Therapy and Community Work, 2003* (3), 60–71.

Caron, A., Weiss, B., Harris, V. & Catron, T. (2006). Parenting behavior and child psychopathology: Specificity, task dependency, and interactive relations. *Journal of Clinical Child and Adolescent Psychology, 35* (1), 34–45.

Carr, E.G. (1997). Invited commentary: The evolution of applied behavior analysis into positive behavior support. *Journal of the Association for Persons with Severe Handicaps, 22* (4), 208–209.

Carrey, N.J., Butter, H.J., Persinger, M.A. & Bialik, R.J. (1995). Physiological and cognitive correlates of child abuse. *Journal of the American Academy of Child and Adolescent Psychiatry, 34* (8), 1067–1075.

Carter, J.F. (1993). Self management: Education's ultimate goal. *Teaching Exceptional Children, 25* (3), 28–32.

Carver, P.R., Egan, S.K. & Perry, D.G. (2004). Children who question their heterosexuality. *Developmental Psychology, 40* (1), 43–53.

Casas, J.F., Weigel, S.M., Crick, N.R., Ostrov, J.M., Woods, K.E., Yeh, E.A.J. & Huddleston-Casas, C.A. (2006). Early parenting and children's relational and physical aggression in the preschool and home contexts. *Journal of Applied Developmental Psychology, 27* (3), 209–227.

Cashwell, T.H., Skinner, C.H. & Smith, E.S. (2001). Increasing second-grade students' reports of peers' prosocial behavior via direct instruction, group reinforcement, and progress feedback: A replication and extension. *Education and Treatment of Children, 24* (2), 161–175.

Castro, C.C., Bryant, D.M., Peisner-Feinberg, E.S. & Skinner, M.L. (2004). Parent involvement in Head Start programs: The role of parent, teacher and classroom characteristics. *Early Childhood Research Quarterly, 19* (3), 413–430.

Cattley, G. (2004). The impact of teacher-parent-peer support on students' well-being and adjustment to the middle years of schooling. *International Journal of Adolescence and Youth, 11* (4), 269–282.

Cedar, R.B. & Levant, R.F. (1990). A meta-analysis of the effects of Parent Effectiveness Training. *American Journal of Family Therapy, 18* (4), 373–384.

Cefai, C. (2012). Resilience-enhancing classrooms for children with social, emotional, and behavioural difficulties. In T. Cole, H. Daniels & J. Visser (Eds.) *The Routledge international companion to emotional and behavioural difficulties.* London: Routledge, 184–192.

Champion, K., Vernberg, E. & Shipman, K. (2003). Nonbully victims of bullies: Aggression, social skills, and friendship characteristics. *Journal of Applied Developmental Psychology, 24* (5), 535–551.

Chan, L.K.S. (1988). The perceived competence of intellectually talented students. *Gifted Child Quarterly, 32* (3), 310–314.

——(1996). Motivational orientations and metacognitive

abilities of intellectually gifted students. *Gifted Child Quarterly, 40* (4), 184-194.

Chang, L. (2003). Variable effects of children's aggression, social withdrawal, and prosocial leadership as functions of teacher beliefs and behaviors. *Child Development, 74* (2), 535-548.

——(2004). The role of classroom norms in contextualizing the relations of children's social behaviors to peer acceptance. *Developmental Psychology, 40* (5), 691-702.

Chao, R.K. & Aque, C. (2009). Interpretations of parental control by Asian immigrant and European American youth. *Journal of Family Psychology, 23* (3), 342-354.

Chapman, M. & Zahn-Waxler, C. (1982). Young children's compliance and noncompliance to parental discipline in a natural setting. *International Journal of Behavioral Development, 5* (1), 81-94.

Chapman, R.L., Buckley, L., Sheehan, M.C., Shochet, I.M. & Romaniuk, M. (2011). The impact of school connectedness on violent behavior, transport risk-taking behavior, and associated injuries in adolescence. *Journal of School Psychology, 49* (4), 399-410.

Charles, C.M. & Senter, G.W. (2005). *Building classroom discipline.* (8th ed.) Boston, MA: Pearson Allyn & Bacon.

Charles, C.M., Senter, G.W. & Charles, M. (2014). *Building classroom discipline.* (11th ed.). Boston, MA: Pearson.

Chauhan, A. & Chauhan, V. (2006). Oxidative stress in autism. *Pathophysiology, 13* (3), 171-181.

Chen, X., Dong, Q. & Zhou, H. (1997). Authoritative and authoritarian parenting practices and social and school performance in Chinese children. *International Journal of Behavioral Development, 21* (4), 855-873.

Chen, X., Wang, L. & Cao, R. (2011). Shyness-sensitivity and unsociability in rural Chinese children: Relations with social, school, and psychological adjustment. *Child Development, 82* (5), 1531-1543.

Cheng, H., Dunn, J., O'Connor, T.G., Golding, J. & the ALSPAC Study Team (2006). Factors moderating children's adjustment to parental separation: Findings from a community study in England. *Journal of Abnormal Child Psychology, 34* (2), 230-241.

Cheng, P.-W. (1993). Metacognition and giftedness: The state of the relationship. *Gifted Child Quarterly, 37* (3), 105-112.

Cheng, R.W.-Y., Lam, S.-F. & Chan, J.C.-Y. (2008). When high achievers and low achievers work in the same group: The roles of group heterogeneity and processes in project-based learning. *British Journal of Educational Psychology, 78* (2), 205-221.

Cheung, C.S.-S. & Pomerantz, E.M. (2012). Why does parents' involvement enhance children's achievement?: The role of parent-oriented motivation. *Journal of Educational Psychology, 104* (3), 820-832.

Chien, N.C., Howes, C., Burchinal, M., Pianta, R.C., Ritchie, S., Bryant, D.M., Clifford, R.M., Early, D.M. & Barbarin, O.A. (2010). Children's classroom engagement and school readiness gains in prekindergarten. *Child Development, 81* (5), 1534-1549.

Childs, G. & McKay, M. (2001). Boys starting school disadvantaged: Implications from teachers' ratings of behaviour and achievement in the first two years. *British Journal of Educational Psychology, 71* (2), 303-314.

Chirkov, V., Ryan, R.M., Kim, Y. & Kaplan, U. (2003). Differentiating autonomy from individualism and independence: A self-determination theory perspective on internalization of cultural orientations and well-being. *Journal of Personality and Social Psychology, 84* (1), 97-110.

Chiu, L.H. & Tulley, M. (1997). Student preferences of teacher discipline styles. *Journal of Instructional Psychology, 24* (3), 168-175.

Christenson, S.L. (2004). The family-school partnership: An opportunity to promote the learning competence of all students. *School Psychology Review, 33* (1), 83-104.

Chronis, A.M., Lahey, B.B., Pelham, W.E. Jr, Williams, S.H., Baumann, B.L., Kipp, H., Jones, H.A. & Rathouz, P.J. (2007). Maternal depression and early positive parenting predict future conduct problems in children with attention-deficit/hyperactivity disorder. *Developmental Psychology, 43* (1), 70-82.

Chronis-Tuscano, A., Raggi, V.L., Clarke, T.L., Rooney, M.E., Diaz, Y. & Pian, J. (2008). Associations between maternal attention-deficit/hyperactivity disorder symptoms and parenting. *Journal of Abnormal Child Psychology, 36* (8), 1237-1250.

Ciani, K.D., Sheldon, K.M., Hilpert, J.C. & Easter, M.A. (2011). Antecedents and trajectories of achievement goals: A self-determination theory perspective. *British Journal of Educational Psychology, 81* (2), 223-243.

Cillessen, A.H.N. & Mayeux, L. (2004). From censure to reinforcement: Developmental changes in the association between aggression and social status. *Child Development, 75* (1), 147-163.

Claes, M., Perchec, C., Miranda, D., Benoit, A., Bariaud, F., Lanz, M., Marta, E. & Lacourse, E. (2011). Adolescents' perceptions of parental practices: A cross-national comparison of Canada, France, and Italy. *Journal of Adolescence, 34* (2), 225-238.

Claes, M. & Simard, R. (1992). Friendship characteristics of delinquent adolescents. *International Journal of Adolescence and Youth, 3* (3-4), 287-301.

Clark, C., Prior, M. & Kinsella, G. (2002). The relationship between executive function abilities, adaptive behaviour, and academic achievement in children with externalizing behaviour problems. *Journal of Child Psychology and Psychiatry, 43* (6), 785-796.

Clark, J. (2004). Against the corporal punishment of children. *Cambridge Journal of Education, 34* (3), 363-371.

Clark, K.E. & Ladd, G.W. (2000). Connectedness and autonomy support in parent-child relationships: Links to children's socioemotional orientation and peer relationships. *Developmental Psychology, 36* (4), 485-498.

Clarke-Stewart, K.A., Vandell, D.L., Burchinal, M., O'Brien, M. & McCartney, K. (2002). Do regulable features of child-care homes affect children's development? *Early Childhood Research Quarterly, 17* (1), 52-86.

Clausen, J. (1988). Chromium induced clinical improvement in symptomatic hypoglycemia. *Biological Trace Element Research, 17* (1), 229-236.

Clay, D.L., Cortina, S., Harper, D.C., Cocco, K.M. & Drotar, D. (2004). Schoolteachers' experiences with childhood chronic illness. *Children's Health Care, 33* (3), 227-239.

Clayton, L.O. (1985). The impact upon child-rearing attitudes, of parental views of the nature of humankind. *Journal of Psychology and Christianity, 4* (3), 49-55.

Cleary, T.J. & Zimmerman, B.J. (2004). Self-regulation empowerment program: A school-based program to enhance self-regulated and self-motivated cycles of student learning. *Psychology in the Schools, 41* (5), 537-550.

Clickenbeard, P.R. (2012). Motivation and gifted students: Implications for theory and research. *Psychology in the Schools, 49* (7), 622-630.

Cohen, E.G. (1994). Restructuring the classroom: Conditions for productive small groups. *Review of Educational Research, 64* (1), 1-35.

Coie, J.D., Cillessen, A.H.N., Dodge, K.A., Hubbard, J.A., Schwartz, D., Lemerise, E.A. & Bateman, H. (1999). It takes two to fight: A test of relational factors and a method for assessing aggressive dyads. *Developmental Psychology, 35* (5), 1179–1188.

Colangelo, N. (2003). Counseling gifted students. In N. Colangelo and G.A. Davis (Eds.) *Handbook of gifted education.* (3rd ed.) Boston, MA: Allyn & Bacon, 373–387.

Colangelo, N. & Davis, G.A. (Eds.) (2003). *Handbook of gifted education.* (3rd ed.) Boston, MA: Allyn & Bacon.

Colder, C.R., Lochman, J.E. & Wells, K.C. (1997). The moderating effects of children's fear and activity level on relations between parenting practices and childhood symptomatology. *Journal of Abnormal Child Psychology, 25* (3), 251–263.

Colder, C.R., Mott, J.A. & Berman, A.S. (2002). The interactive effects of infant activity level and fear on growth trajectories or early childhood behavior problems. *Development and Psychopathology, 14* (1), 1–23.

Coldwell, J., Pike, A. & Dunn, J. (2006). Household chaos – links with parenting and child behaviour. *Journal of Child Psychology and Psychiatry, 47* (11), 1116–1122.

Cole, D.A., Maxwell, S.E., Martin, J.M., Peeke, L.G., Seroczynski, A.D., Tram, J.M., Hoffman, K.B., Ruiz, M.D., Jacquez, F. & Maschman, T. (2001). The development of multiple domains of child and adolescent self-concept: A cohort sequential longitudinal design. *Child Development, 72* (6), 1723–1746.

Cole, P.M., Dennis, T.A., Smith-Simon, K.E. & Cohen, L.H. (2009). Preschoolers' emotion regulation strategy understanding: Relations with emotion socialization and child self-regulation. *Social Development, 18* (2), 324–352.

Coleman, J.M. & Fults, B.A. (1982). Self-concept and the gifted classroom: The role of social comparison. *Gifted Child Quarterly, 26* (3), 116–120.

Coleman, L.J. & Cross, T.L. (1988). Is being gifted a social handicap? *Journal for the Education of the Gifted, 11* (4), 41–56.

Collie, R.J., Shapka, J.D. & Perry, N.E. (2011). Predicting teacher commitment: The impact of school climate and social-emotional learning. *Psychology in the Schools, 48* (10), 1034–1048.

Collison, D.R. & Hall, T. (1989). *Why do I feel so awful?* Melbourne: Angus & Robertson.

Colman, R.A., Hardy, S.A., Albert, M., Raffaelli, M. & Crockett, L. (2006). Early predictors of self-regulation in middle childhood. *Infant and Child Development, 15* (4), 421–437.

Combs-Ronto, L.A., Olson, S.L., Lunkenheimer, E.S. & Sameroff, A.J. (2009). Interactions between maternal parenting and children's early disruptive behavior: Bidirectional associations across the transition from preschool to school entry. *Journal of Abnormal Child Psychology, 37* (8), 1151–1163.

Comer, J.P. (2005). Child and adolescent development: The crucial missing focus in school reform. *Phi Delta Kappan, 86* (10), 757–763.

Compas, B.E. (1987). Coping with stress during childhood and adolescence. *Psychological Bulletin, 101* (3), 393–403.

Conger, K.J., Conger, R.D. & Scaramella, L.V. (1997). Parents, siblings, psychological control, and adolescent adjustment. *Journal of Adolescent Research, 12* (1), 113–138.

Connell, S., Sanders, M.R., & Markie-Dadds, C. (1997). Self-directed behavioral family intervention for parents of oppositional children in rural and remote areas. *Behavior Modification, 21* (4), 379–408.

Conners-Burrow, N.A., Johnson, D.L., Whiteside-Mansell, L., McKelvey, L. & Gargus, R.A. (2009). Adults matter: Protecting children from negative impacts of bullying. *Psychology in the Schools, 46* (7), 593–604.

Conrad, P. (2006). *Identifying hyperactive children: The medicalization of deviant behavior.* (exp. ed.) Aldershot, UK: Ashgate.

Conroy, M., Sutherland, K., Haydon, T., Stormont, M. & Harmon, J. (2009). Preventing and ameliorating young children's chronic problem behaviors: An ecological classroom-based approach. *Psychology in the Schools, 46* (1), 3–17.

Conyers, C., Miltenberger, R., Maki, A., Barenz, R., Jurgens, M., Sailer, A., Haugen, M. & Kopp, B. (2004). A comparison of response cost and differential reinforcement of other behavior to reduce disruptive behavior in a preschool classroom. *Journal of Applied Behavior Analysis, 37* (3), 411–415.

Cook, C.R., Crews, S.D., Wright, D.B., Mayer, G.R., Gale, B., Kraemer, B. & Gresham, F.M. (2007). Establishing and evaluating the substantive adequacy of positive behavior support plans. *Journal of Behavioral Education, 16* (3), 191–206.

Coolahan, K., McWayne, C., Fantuzzo, J. & Grim, S. (2002). Validation of a multidimensional assessment of parenting styles for low-income African-American families with preschool children. *Early Childhood Research Quarterly, 17* (3), 356–373.

Cooper, H., Lindsay, J.J., Nye, B. & Greathouse, S. (1998). Relationships among attitudes about homework, amount of homework assigned and completed, and student achievement. *Journal of Educational Psychology, 90* (1), 70–83.

Cooper, H., Robinson, J.C & Patall, E.A. (2006). Does homework improve academic achievement?: A synthesis of research, 1987–2003. *Review of Educational Research, 76* (1), 1–62.

Cooper, L.J., Wacker, D.P., McComas, J.J., Brown, K., Peck, S.M., Richman, D., Drew, J., Frischmeyer, P. & Millard, T. (1995). Use of component analyses to identify active variables in treatment packages for children with feeding disorders. *Journal of Applied Behavior Analysis, 28* (2), 139–153.

Coots, J.J. (1998). Family resources and parent participation in schooling activities for their children with developmental delays. *The Journal of Special Education, 31* (4), 498–520.

Coplan, R.J., Girardi, A., Findlay, L.C. & Frohlick, S.L. (2007). Understanding solitude: Young children's attitudes and response toward hypothetical socially withdrawn peers. *Social Development, 16* (3), 390–409.

Coplan, R.J. & Prakash, K. (2003). Spending time with teacher: Characteristics of preschoolers who frequently elicit versus initiate interactions with teachers. *Early Childhood Research Quarterly, 18* (1), 143–158.

Coplan, R.J., Prakash, K., O'Neil, K. & Armer, M. (2004). Do you 'want' to play?: Distinguishing between conflicted shyness and social disinterest in early childhood. *Developmental Psychology, 40* (2), 244–258.

Cordova, D.I. & Lepper, M.R. (1996). Intrinsic motivation and the process of learning: Beneficial effects of contextualization, personalization, and choice. *Journal of Educational Psychology, 88* (4), 715–730.

Corey, G. (1996). *Theory and practice of counseling and psychotherapy.* (5th ed.) Monterey, CA: Brooks/Cole.

Cornell, D.G. & Mayer, M.J. (2010). Why do school order and safety matter? *Educational Researcher, 39* (1), 7–15.

Cornell, D.G. & Sheras, P.L. (1998). Common errors in school crisis response: Learning from our mistakes. *Psychology in the Schools, 35* (3), 297–307.

Corno, L. (1992). Encouraging students to take responsibility for learning and performance. *The Elementary School Journal, 93* (1), 69–83.

——(1996). Homework is a complicated thing. *Educational Researcher, 25* (8), 27–30.

Costenbader, V. & Markson, S. (1998). School suspension: A study with secondary school students. *Journal of School Psychology, 36* (1), 59–82.

Côté, S.M., Vaillancourt, T., Barker, E.D., Nagin, D. & Tremblay, R.E. (2007). The joint development of physical and indirect aggression: Predictors of continuity and change during childhood. *Development and Psychopathology, 19* (1), 37–55.

Côté, S.M., Vaillancourt, T., LeBlanc, J.C., Nagin, D.S. & Tremblay, R.E. (2006). The development of physical aggression from toddlerhood to pre-adolescence: A nation wide longitudinal study of Canadian children. *Journal of Abnormal Child Psychology, 34* (1), 68–82.

Cothran, D.J. & Ennis, C.D. (1997). Students' and teachers' perceptions of conflict and power. *Teaching and Teacher Education, 13* (5), 541–553.

Cotler, S. & Palmer, R.J. (1971). Social reinforcement, individual difference factors, and the reading performance of elementary school children. *Journal of Personality and Social Psychology, 18* (1), 97–104.

Covaleskie, J.F. (1992). Discipline and morality: Beyond rules and consequences. *The Educational Forum, 56* (2), 173–183.

Covington, M.V. & Müeller, K.J. (2001). Intrinsic versus extrinsic motivation: An approach/avoidance reformulation. *Educational Psychology Review, 13* (2), 157–176.

Cowie, H. (2000). Bystanding or standing by: Gender issues in coping with bullying in English schools. *Aggressive Behavior, 26* (1), 85–97.

Cowie, H. & Olafsson, R. (2000). The role of peer support in helping victims of bullying in a school with high levels of aggression. *School Psychology International, 21* (1), 79–95.

Cowin, M., Freeman, L., Farmer, A., James, M., Drent, A. & Arthur, R. (1990). *Positive school discipline: A practical guide to developing policy.* (rev. ed.) Boronia. Victoria: Narbethong Publications.

Coyne, S.M., Archer, J. & Eslea, M. (2006). 'We're not friends anymore! Unless . . .': The frequency and harmfulness of indirect, relational, and social aggression. *Aggressive Behavior, 32* (4), 294–307.

Craig, W.M., Pepler, D. & Atlas, R. (2000). Observations of bullying in the playground and in the classroom. *School Psychology International, 21* (1), 22–36.

Craig, W.M., Vitaro, F., Gagnon, C. & Tremblay, R.E. (2002). The road to gang membership: Characteristics of male gang and nongang members from ages 10 to 14. *Social Development, 11* (1), 53–68.

Craske, M.G. & Barlow, D.H. (2008). Panic disorder and agoraphobia. In D.H. Barlow (Ed.) *Clinical handbook of psychological disorders: A step-by-step treatment manual.* (4th ed.) New York: Guilford, 1–64.

Craven, R.G. & Marsh, H.W. (1997). Threats to gifted and talented students' self-concepts in the big pond: Research results and educational implications. *The Australasian Journal of Gifted Education, 6* (2), 7–17.

Crick, N.R., Casas, J.F. & Ku, H.-C. (1999). Relational and physical forms of peer victimization in preschool. *Developmental Psychology, 35* (2), 376–385.

Crick, N.R. & Dodge, K.A. (1994). A review and reformulation of social information-processing mechanisms in children's social adjustment. *Psychological Bulletin, 115* (1), 74–101.

Crick, N.R. & Grotpeter, J.K. (1995). Relational aggression, gender, and social-psychological adjustment. *Child Development, 66* (3), 710–722.

Crick, N.R., Grotpeter, J.K. & Bigbee, M.A. (2002). Relationally and physically aggressive children's intent attributions and feelings of distress for relational and instrumental peer provocations. *Child Development, 73* (4), 1134–1142.

Crick, N.R., Nelson, D.A., Morales, J.R., Cullerton-Sen, C., Casas, J.F. & Hickman, S.E. (2001). Relational victimization in childhood and adolescence: I hurt you through the grapevine. In J. Juvonen and S. Graham (Eds.) *Peer harassment in school: The plight of the vulnerable and victimized.* New York: Guilford, 196–214.

Crick, N.R., Ostrov, J.M., Burr, J.E., Cullerton-Sen, C., Jansen-Yeh, E. & Ralston, P. (2006a). A longitudinal study of relational and physical aggression in preschool. *Journal of Applied Developmental Psychology, 27* (3), 254–268.

Crick, N.R., Ostrov, J.M. & Werner. N.E. (2006b). A longitudinal study of relational aggression, physical aggression, and children's social-psychological adjustment. *Journal of Abnormal Child Psychology, 34* (2), 131–142.

Criss, M.M., Pettit, G.S., Bates, J.E., Dodge, K.A. & Lapp, A.L. (2002). Family adversity, positive peer relationships, and children's externalizing behavior: A longitudinal perspective on risk and resilience. *Child Development, 73* (4), 1220–1237.

Criss, M.M., Shaw, D.S. & Ingoldsby, E.M. (2003). Mother-son positive synchrony in middle childhood: Relation to antisocial behavior. *Social Development, 12* (3), 379–400.

Criss, M.M., Shaw, D.S., Moilanen, K.L., Hitchings, J.E. & Ingoldsby, E.M. (2009). Family, neighborhood, and peer characteristics as predictors of child adjustment: A longitudinal analysis of additive and mediation models. *Social Development, 18* (3), 511–535.

Crockenberg, S.B., Bryant, B.K. & Wilce, L.S. (1976). The effects of cooperatively and competitively structured learning environments on inter- and intrapersonal behavior. *Child Development, 47* (2), 386–396.

Crockenberg, S. & Litman, C. (1990). Autonomy as competence in 2-year-olds: Maternal correlates of child defiance, compliance, and self-assertion. *Developmental Psychology, 26* (6), 961–971.

Crocker, J. (2002). The costs of seeking self-esteem. *Journal of Social Issues, 58* (3), 597–615.

Crocker, J., & Park, L.E. (2003). Seeking self-esteem: Construction, maintenance, and protection of self-worth. In M. Leary & J. Tangney (Eds.) *Handbook of self and identity.* New York: Guilford Press, 291–313.

Crocker, J. & Wolfe, C.T. (2001). Contingencies of self-worth. *Psychological Review, 108* (3), 593–623.

Cropley, A.J. (2000). Defining and measuring creativity: Are creativity tests worth using? *Roeper Review, 23* (2), 72–79.

Cropper, C. (1998). Is competition an effective classroom tool for the gifted student? *Gifted Child Today, 21* (3), 28–31.

Crosby, J.W., Oehler, J. & Capaccioli, K. (2010). The relationship between peer victimization and post-traumatic stress symptomatology in a rural sample. *Psychology in the Schools, 47* (3), 297–310.

Cross, T.L., Coleman, L.J. & Stewart, R.A. (1992). The social cognition of gifted adolescents: An exploration of the stigma of giftedness paradigm. *Roeper Review, 16* (1), 37–40.

Crothers, L.M., Kehle, T.J., Bray, M.A. & Theodore, L.A. (2009). Correlates and suspected causes of obesity in children. *Psychology in the Schools, 46* (8), 787–796.

Csikszentmihalyi, M. (1990). *Flow: The psychology of optimal experience.* New York: Harper Perennial.

Csikszentmihalyi, M. & Wolfe, R. (2000). New conceptions and research approaches for creativity: Implications of a systems perspective for creativity in education. In K.A. Heller, F.J. Mönks, R.J. Sternberg & R.F. Subotnik (Eds.) *International handbook of giftedness and talent.* (2nd ed.) Oxford, UK: Elsevier, 81–93.

Cumberland-Li, A., Eisenberg, N. & Reiser, M. (2004). Relations of young children's agreeableness and resiliency to effortful control and impulsivity. *Social Development, 13* (2), 193–212.

Cummings, E.M. (1998). Stress and coping approaches and research: The impact of marital conflict on children. In B.B.R. Rossman and M.S. Rosenberg (Eds.) *Multiple victimization of children: Conceptual, developmental, research, and treatment issues.* New York: Haworth Press, 31–50.

Cummings, E.M., Goeke-Morey, M.C. & Papp, L.M. (2003).

Children's responses to everyday marital conflict tactics in the home. *Child Development, 74* (6), 1918–1929.

Cummings, E.M., Schermerhorn, A.C., Davies, P.T., Goeke-Morey, M.C. & Cummings, J.S. (2006). Interparental discord and child adjustment: Prospective investigations of emotional security as an explanatory mechanism. *Child Development, 77* (1), 132–152.

Cunningham, M., Corprew, J.S. III & Becker, J.E. (2009). Associations of future expectations, negative friends, and academic achievement in high-achieving African American adolescents. *Urban Education, 44* (3), 280–296.

Cunningham, M.M. & Wodrich, D.L. (2006). The effect of sharing health information on teachers' production of classroom accommodations. *Psychology in the Schools, 43* (5), 553–564.

Curbow, B., Spratt, K., Ungaretti, A., McDonnell, K. & Breckler, S. (2000). Development of the child care worker job stress inventory. *Early Childhood Research Quarterly, 15* (4), 515–536.

Curby, T.W., Rimm-Kaufman, S.E. & Ponitz, C.C. (2009). Teacher-child interactions and children's achievement trajectories across kindergarten and first grade. *Journal of Educational Psychology, 101* (4), 912–925.

Curwin, R.L. & Mendler, A.N. (1988). Packaged discipline programs: Let the buyer beware. *Educational Leadership, 46* (2), 68–71.

Cushing, L.S. & Kennedy, G.H. (1997). Academic effects of providing peer support in general education classrooms on students without disabilities. *Journal of Applied Behavior Analysis, 30* (1), 139–151.

D'Onofrio, B.M., Turkheimer, E., Emery, R.E., Maes, H.H., Silberg, J. & Eaves, L.J. (2007). A children of twins study of parental divorce and offspring psychopathology. *Journal of Child Psychology and Psychiatry, 48* (7), 667–675.

Dahl, R.E. (1999). The consequences of insufficient sleep for adolescents: Links between sleep and emotional regulation. *Phi Delta Kappan, 80* (5), 354–359.

Dahlberg, G., Moss, P. & Pence, A. (1999). *Beyond quality in early childhood education and care: Postmodern perspectives.* London: Routledge Falmer.

Dallaire, D.H. & Weinraub, M. (2005). The stability of parenting behaviors over the first 6 years of life. *Early Childhood Research Quarterly, 20* (2), 201–219.

Damon, W. & Phelps, E. (1989). Critical distinctions among three approaches to peer education. *International Journal of Educational Research, 13* (1), 9–19.

Daniels, D.H. & Shumow, L. (2003). Child development and classroom teaching: A review of the literature and implications for educating teachers. *Journal of Applied Developmental Psychology, 23* (5), 495–526.

Daniels, L.M., Stupnisky, R.H., Pekrun, R., Haynes, T.L., Perry, R.P. & Newall, N.E. (2009). A longitudinal analysis of achievement goals: From affective antecedents to emotional effects and achievement outcomes. *Journal of Educational Psychology, 101* (4), 948–963.

Danielsen, A.G., Wiium, N., Wilhelmsen, B.U. & Wold, B. (2010). Perceived support provided by teachers and classmates and students' self-reported academic initiative. *Journal of School Psychology, 48* (3), 247–267.

Darwich, L., Hymel, S. & Waterhouse, T. (2012). School avoidance and substance use among lesbian, gay, bisexual, and questioning youths: The impact of peer victimization and adult support. *Journal of Educational Psychology, 104* (2), 381–392.

Daschmann, E.C., Goetz, T. & Stupnisky, R.H. (2011). Testing the predictors of boredom at school: Development and validation of the precursors to boredom scales. *British Journal of Educational Psychology, 81* (3), 421–440.

Daunic, A.P., Smith, S.W., Garvan, C.W., Barber, B.R., Becker, M.K., Peters, C.D., Taylor, G.G., Van Loan, C.L. Li, W. & Naranjo, A.H. (2012). Reducing developmental risk for emotional/behavioral problems: A randomized controlled trial examining the Tools for Getting Along curriculum. *Journal of School Psychology, 50* (2), 149–166.

Davidov, M. & Grusec, J.E. (2006). Untangling the links of parental responsiveness to distress and warmth to child outcomes. *Child Development, 77* (1), 44–58.

Davidson, A.J., Gest, S.D. & Welsh, J.A. (2010). Relatedness with teachers and peers during early adolescence: An integrated variable-oriented and person-oriented approach. *Journal of School Psychology, 48* (6), 483–510.

Davidson, L.M. & Demaray, M.K. (2007). Social support as a moderator between victimization and internalizing-externalizing distress from bullying. *School Psychology Review, 36* (3), 383–405.

Davidson, P.W. & Myers, G.J. (2007). Environmental toxins. In M.L. Batshaw, L. Pellegrino & N.J. Roizen (Eds.) *Children with disabilities.* (6th ed.) Sydney: Elsevier, 63–72.

Davies, J.D. (2005). Voices from the margins: The perceptions of pupils with emotional and behavioural difficulties about their educational experiences. In P. Clough, P. Garner, J.T. Pardeck & F. Yuen (Eds.) *Handbook of emotional and behavioural difficulties.* London: SAGE, 299–316.

Davis, E.L. (2006). *Lessons for tomorrow: Bringing America's schools back from the brink.* Northport, MI: Orgone Press.

Davis, G.A. (2003). Identifying creative students, teaching for creative growth. In N. Colangelo & G.A. Davis (Eds.) *Handbook of gifted education.* (3rd ed.) Boston, MA: Allyn & Bacon, 311–324.

Davis, G.A. & Rimm, S.B. (2004). *Education of the gifted and talented.* (5th ed.) Boston, MA: Pearson Allyn & Bacon.

Davis, T.E. & Osborn, C.J. (2000). *The solution-focused school counselor: Shaping professional practice.* New York: Brunner-Routledge.

de Castro, B.O., Veerman, J.W., Koops, W., Bosch, J.D. & Monshouwer, H.J. (2002). Hostile attribution of intent and aggressive behavior: A meta-analysis. *Child Development, 73* (3), 916–934.

De Cremer, D. & Tyler, T.R. (2007). The effects of trust in authority and procedural fairness on cooperation. *Journal of Applied Psychology, 92* (3), 639–649.

De Jong, P. & Berg, I.K. (2002). *Interviewing for solutions.* (2nd ed.) Pacific Grove, CA: Brooks/Cole Thomson.

de Shazer, S. (1988). *Clues: Investigating solutions in brief therapy.* New York: Norton.

de Shazer, S., Berg, I.K., Lipchik, E., Nunnally, E., Molnar, A., Gingerich, W. & Weiner-Davis, M. (1986). Brief therapy: Focused solution development. *Family Process, 25* (2), 207–222.

de Shazer, S., Dolan, Y., Korman, H., Trepper, T., McCollum, E. & Berg, I.K. (2007). *More than miracles: The state of the art of solution-focused brief therapy.* New York: Haworth.

De Wit, D.J., Karioja, K., Rye, B.J. & Shain, M. (2011). Perceptions of declining classmate and teacher support following the transition to high school: Potential correlates of increasing student mental health difficulties. *Psychology in the Schools, 48* (6), 556–572.

Dearing, E. (2004). The developmental implications of restrictive and supportive parenting across neighborhoods and ethnicities: Exceptions are the rule. *Journal of Applied Developmental Psychology, 25* (5), 555–575.

Dearing, E., Kreider, H., Simpkins, S. & Weiss, H.B. (2006a). Family involvement in school and low-income children's literacy: Associations between and within families. *Journal of Educational Psychology, 98* (4), 653–664.

Dearing, E., McCartney, K. & Taylor, B.A. (2006b). Within-child associations between family income and externalizing and internalizing problems. *Developmental Psychology, 42* (2), 237–252.

Deater-Deckard, K. (2001). Annotation: Recent research examining the role of peer relationships in the development of psychopathology. *Journal of Child Psychology and Psychiatry, 42* (5), 565–579.

Deater-Deckard, K. & Dodge, K.A. (1997). Externalizing behavior problems and discipline revisited: Nonlinear effects and variation by culture, context, and gender. *Psychological Inquiry, 8* (3), 161–175.

Deater-Deckard, K., Dodge, K.A., Bates, J.E. & Pettit, G.S. (1996). Physical discipline among African American and European American mothers: Links to children's externalizing behaviors. *Developmental Psychology, 32* (6), 1065–1072.

Deater-Deckard, K., Petrill, S.A., Thompson, L.A. & DeThorne, L.S. (2006). A longitudinal behavioral genetic analysis of task persistence. *Development Science, 9* (5), 498–504.

Debnam, K.J., Pas, E.T. & Bradshaw, C.P. (2012). Secondary and tertiary support systems in schools implementing school-wide positive behavioral interventions and supports: A preliminary descriptive analysis. *Journal of Positive Behavior Interventions, 14* (3), 142–152.

Deci, E.L. (1971). Effects of externally mediated rewards on intrinsic motivation. *Journal of Personality and Social Psychology, 18* (1), 105–115.

——(1972). Intrinsic motivation, extrinsic reinforcement, and equity. *Journal of Personality and Social Psychology, 22* (1), 113–120.

Deci, E.L., Eghrari, H., Patrick, B.C. & Leone, D.R. (1994). Facilitating internalization: The self-determination theory perspective. *Journal of Personality, 62* (1), 119–142.

Deci, E.L., Koestner, R. & Ryan, R.M. (1999a). A meta-analytic review of experiments examining the effects of extrinsic rewards on intrinsic motivation. *Psychological Bulletin, 125* (6), 627–668.

——(1999b). The undermining effect is a reality after all – extrinsic rewards, task interest, and self-determination: Reply to Eisenberger, Pierce, and Cameron (1999) and Lepper, Henderlong, and Gingras (1999). *Psychological Bulletin, 125* (6), 692–700.

——(2001). Extrinsic rewards and intrinsic motivation in education: Reconsidered once again. *Review of Educational Research, 71* (1), 1–27.

Deci, E.L. & Ryan, R.M. (1987). The support of autonomy and the control of behavior. *Journal of Personality and Social Psychology, 53* (6), 1024–1037.

——(2000). The 'what' and 'why' of goal pursuits: Human needs and the self-determination of behavior. *Psychological Inquiry, 11* (4), 227–268.

Deci, E.L., Schwartz, A.J., Sheinman, L. & Ryan, R.M. (1981). An instrument to assess adults' orientations toward control versus autonomy with children: Reflections on intrinsic motivation and perceived competence. *Journal of Educational Psychology, 73* (5), 642–650.

Deci, E.L., Vallerand, R.J., Pelletier, L.G. & Ryan, R.M. (1991). Motivation and education: The self-determination perspective. *Educational Psychologist, 26* (3 & 4), 325–346.

Decker, D.M., Dona, D.P. & Christenson, S.L. (2007). Behaviorally at-risk African American students: The importance of student-teacher relationships for student outcomes. *Journal of School Psychology, 45* (1), 83–109.

DeGarmo, D.S. (2010). Coercive and prosocial fathering, antisocial personality, and growth in children's postdivorce noncompliance. *Child Development, 81* (2), 503–516.

Dekovic, M., Janssens, J.M.A.M. & Van As, N.M.C. (2003). Family predictors of antisocial behavior in adolescence. *Family Process, 42* (2), 223–235.

DeLeel, M.L., Hughes, T.L., Miller, J.A., Hipwell, A. & Theodore, L.A. (2009). Prevalence of eating disturbance and body image dissatisfaction in young girls: An examination of the variance across racial and socioeconomic groups. *Psychology in the Schools, 46* (8), 767–775.

Delfabbro, P., Winefield, T., Trainor, S., Dollard, M., Anderson, S., Metzer, J. & Hammarstrom, A. (2006). Peer and teacher bullying/victimization of South Australian secondary students: Prevalence and psychosocial profiles. *British Journal of Educational Psychology, 76* (1), 71–90.

Dellasega, C. & Nixon, C. (2003). *Girl wars: Twelve strategies that will end female bullying.* New York: Fireside.

Demaray, M.K. & Jenkins, L.N. (2011). Relations among academic enablers and academic achievement in children with and without high levels of parent-rated symptoms of inattention, impulsivity, and hyperactivity. *Psychology in the Schools, 48* (6), 573–586.

Demaray, M.K. & Malecki, C.K. (2002). The relationship between perceived social support and maladjustment for students at risk. *Psychology in the Schools, 39* (3), 305–316.

——(2003a). Perceptions of the frequency and importance of social support by students classified as victims, bullies, and bully/victims in an urban middle school. *School Psychology Review, 32* (3), 471–489.

——(2003b). Importance ratings of socially supportive behaviors by children and adolescents. *School Psychology Review, 32* (1), 108–131.

Demaray, M.K., Malecki, C.K., Davidson, L.M., Hodgson, K.K. & Rebus, J. (2005). The relationship between social support and student adjustment: A longitudinal analysis. *Psychology in the Schools, 42* (7), 691–706.

Dempsey, A.G. & Storch, E.A. (2008). Relational victimization: The association between recalled adolescent social experiences and emotional adjustment in early adulthood. *Psychology in the Schools, 45* (4), 310–322.

Den Brok, P., Tartwijk, J., Wubbels, T. & Veldman, I. (2010). The differential effect of the teacher-student interpersonal relationship on student outcomes for students with different ethnic backgrounds. *British Journal of Educational Psychology, 80* (2), 199–221.

Denham, S.A., Caverly, S., Schmidt, M., Blair, K., DeMulder, E., Caal, S., Hamada, H. & Mason, T. (2002). Preschool understanding of emotions: Contributions to classroom anger and aggression. *Journal of Child Psychology and Psychiatry, 43* (7), 901–916.

Denham, S.A., Mitchell-Copeland, J., Strandberg, K., Auerbach, S. & Blair, K. (1997). Parental contributions to preschoolers' emotional competence: Direct and indirect effects. *Motivation and Emotion, 21* (1), 65–86.

Denham, S.A., Workman, E., Cole, P.M., Weissbrod, C., Kendziora, K.T. & Zahn-Waxler, C. (2000). Prediction of externalizing behavior problems from early to middle childhood: The role of parental socialization and emotion expression. *Development and Psychopathology, 12* (1), 23–45.

DeRosier, M.E. & Mercer, S.H. (2009). Perceived behavioral atypicality as a predictor of social rejection and peer victimization: Implications for emotional adjustment and academic achievement. *Psychology in the Schools, 46* (4), 375–387.

Derman-Sparks, L. & the A.B.C. Task Force (1989). *Anti-bias curriculum: Tools for empowering young children.* Washington, DC: National Association for the Education of Young Children.

Deslandes, R., Royer, E., Turcotte, D. & Bertrand, R. (1997). School achievement at secondary level: Influence of parenting style and parent involvement in schooling. *McGill Journal of Education, 32* (3), 191–207.

DesRosiers, F., Vrsalovic, W.T., Knauf, D.E., Vargas, M. & Busch-Rossnagel, N.A. (1999). Assessing the multiple dimensions of the self-concept of young children: A focus on Latinos. *Merrill-Palmer Quarterly, 45* (4), 543–566.

Dettmers, S., Trautwein, U., Lüdtke, O., Kunter, M. & Baumert, J. (2010). Homework works if homework quality is high: Using multilevel modeling to predict the development of achievement in mathematics. *Journal of Educational Psychology, 102* (2), 467–482.

Deutsch, M. (1979). Education and distributive justice: Some reflections on grading systems. *American Psychologist, 34* (5), 391–401.

Dev, P.C. (1997). Intrinsic motivation and academic achievement: What does their relationship imply for the classroom teacher? *Remedial and Special Education, 18* (1), 12–19.

Dewey, J. (1916/1944). *Democracy and education.* New York: Free Press.

Diamantopoulou, S., Rydell, A.-M. & Henricsson, L. (2008). Can both low and high self-esteem be related to aggression in children? *Social Development, 17* (3), 682–698.

Diaz, R.M. & Berk, L.E. (1995). A Vygotskian critique of self-instructional training. *Development and Psychopathology, 7* (2), 369–392.

DiCintio, M.J. & Gee, S. (1999). Control is the key: Unlocking the motivation of at-risk students. *Psychology in the Schools, 36* (3), 231–237.

Dickman, S.J. (1990). Functional and dysfunctional impulsivity: Personality and cognitive correlates. *Journal of Personality and Social Psychology, 58* (1), 95–102.

Diener, E. & Diener, M. (1995). Cross-cultural correlates of life satisfaction and self-esteem. *Journal of Personality and Social Psychology, 68* (4), 653–663.

Diener, M.L., Nievar, M.A. & Wright, C. (2003). Attachment security among mothers and their young children living in poverty: Associations with maternal, child, and contextual factors. *Merrill-Palmer Quarterly, 49* (2), 154–182.

Dinkmeyer, D. & McKay, G. (1989). *Systematic training for effective parenting.* (3rd ed.) Circle Pines, MN: American Guidance Service.

Dinkmeyer, D., McKay, G. & Dinkmeyer, D. (1980). *Systematic training for effective teaching.* Circle Pines, MN: American Guidance Service.

Dinkmeyer, D. Sr, McKay, G.D., Dinkmeyer, J.S., Dinkmeyer, D. Jr, McKay, J.L. (1997). *Parenting young children: Systematic training for effective parenting (STEP) of children under six.* Circle Pines, MN: American Guidance Service.

Dionne, G., Tremblay, R., Boivin, M., Laplante, D. & Pérusse, D. (2003). Physical aggression and expressive vocabulary in 19-month-old twins. *Developmental Psychology, 39* (2), 261–273.

DiPrima, A.J., Ashby, J.S., Gnilka, P.B. & Noble, C.L. (2011). Family relationships and perfectionism in middle school students. *Psychology in the Schools, 48* (8), 815–827.

Diseth, Å. & Kobbeltvedt, T. (2010). A mediation analysis of achievement motives, goals, learning strategies, and academic achievement. *British Journal of Educational Psychology, 80* (4), 671–687.

Dishion, T.J., McCord, J. & Poulin, F. (1999). When interventions harm: Peer groups and problem behavior. *American Psychologist, 54* (9), 755–764.

Dishion, T.J. & McMahon, R.J. (1998). Parental monitoring and the prevention of child and adolescent problem behavior: A conceptual and empirical formulation. *Clinical Child and Family Psychology Review, 1* (1), 61–75.

Dix, T., Ruble, D.N. & Zambarano, R.J. (1989). Mothers' implicit theories of discipline: Child effects, parent effects, and the attribution process. *Child Development, 60* (6), 1373–1391.

Dixon, F.A. (1998). Social and academic self-concepts of gifted adolescents. *Journal for the Education of the Gifted, 22* (1), 80–94.

Dixon, L., Hamilton-Giachritsis, C. & Browne, K. (2005). Attributions and behaviours of parents abused as children: A mediational analysis of the intergenerational continuity of child maltreatment (Part II). *Journal of Child Psychology and Psychiatry, 46* (1), 58–68.

Dixon, M.R., Hayes, L.J., Binder, L.M., Manthey, S., Sigman, C. & Zdanowski, D.M. (1998). Using a self-control training procedure to increase appropriate behavior. *Journal of Applied Behavior Analysis, 31* (2), 203–209.

Doane, K.B. (1996). Careen and Lamar elementary schools. In F.M. Newmann (Ed.) *Authentic achievement: Restructuring schools for intellectual quality.* San Francisco, CA: Jossey-Bass, 77–103.

Dobson, J. (1970). *Dare to discipline.* Toronto: Bantam.

——(1992). *The new dare to discipline.* Wheaton, IL: Tyndale House.

Dockett, S., Mason, T. & Perry, B. (2006). Successful transition to school for Australian Aboriginal children. *Childhood Education, 82* (3), 139–144.

Docking, J. (1982). The impact of control and management styles on young children in the early years of schooling. *Early Child Development and Care, 8,* 239–252.

Doctoroff, G.L., Greer, J.A. & Arnold, D.H. (2006). The relationship between social behavior and emergent literacy among preschool boys and girls. *Journal of Applied Developmental Psychology, 27* (1), 1–13.

Doctoroff, S. (2001). Adapting the physical environment to meet the needs of *all* young children for play. *Early Childhood Education Journal, 29* (2), 105–109.

Dodge, K.A. (1983). Behavioral antecedents of peer social status. *Child Development, 54* (6), 1386–1399.

Dodge, K.A., Bates, J.E. & Pettit, G.S. (1990). Mechanisms in the cycle of violence. *Science, 250* (4988), 1678–1683.

Dodge, K.A. & Coie, J.D. (1987). Social-information-processing factors in reactive and proactive aggression in children's peer groups. *Journal of Personality and Social Psychology, 53* (6), 1146–1158.

Dodge, K.A. & Crick, N.R. (1990). Social information-processing bases of aggressive behavior in children. *Personality and Social Psychology Bulletin, 16* (1), 8–22.

Dodge, K.A., Laird, R., Lochman, J.E., Zelli, A. & the Conduct Problems Prevention Research Group. (2002). Multidimensioinal latent-construct analysis of children's social information processing patterns: Correlations with aggressive behavior problems. *Psychological Assessment, 14* (1), 60–73.

Dodge, K.A., Lansford, J.E., Burks, V.S., Bates, J.E., Pettit, G.S., Fontaine, R. & Price, J.M. (2003). Peer rejection and social information-processing factors in the development of aggressive behavior problems in children. *Child Development, 74* (2), 374–393.

Dodge, K.A., Lochman, J.E., Harnish, J.D., Bates, J.E. & Pettit, G.S. (1997). Reactive and proactive aggression in school children and psychiatrically chronically assaultive youth. *Journal of Abnormal Psychology, 106* (1), 37–51.

Dodge, K.A., Pettit, G.S. & Bates, J.E. (1994). Socialization mediators of the relation between socioeconomic status and child conduct problems. *Child Development, 65* (2), 649–665.

Doherty-Derkowski, G. (1995). *Quality matters: Excellence in early childhood programs.* Don Mills, Ontario: Addison Wesley.

Doll, B. & Lyon, M.A. (1998). Risk and resilience: Implications for the delivery of educational and mental health services in schools. *School Psychology Review, 27* (3), 348–363.

Donaldson, J.M. & Vollmer, T.R. (2011). An evaluation and comparison of time-out procedures with and without release contingencies. *Journal of Applied Behavior Analysis, 44* (4), 693–705.

Donaldson, J.M., Vollmer, T.R., Krous, T., Downs, S. & Berard, K.P. (2011). An evaluation of the good behavior game in kindergarten classrooms. *Journal of Applied Behavior Analysis, 44* (3), 605–609.

Donohue, K.M., Perry, K.E. & Weinstein, R.S. (2003). Teachers' classroom practices and children's rejection by their peers. *Journal of Applied Developmental Psychology, 24* (1), 91–118.

Donovan, W.L., Leavitt, L.A. & Walsh, R.O. (2000). Maternal illusory control predicts socialization strategies and toddler compliance. *Developmental Psychology, 36* (3), 402–411.

Dornbusch, S.M., Ritter, P.L., Liederman, P.H., Roberts, D.F. & Fraleigh, M.J. (1987). The relation of parenting style to adolescent school performance. *Child Development, 58* (5), 1244–1257.

Dower, N. (1997). Human rights and international relations. *The International Journal of Human Rights, 1* (1), 86–111.

Downer, J.T. & Pianta, R.C. (2006). Academic and cognitive functioning in first grade: Associations with earlier home and child care predictors and with concurrent home and classroom experiences. *School Psychology Review, 35* (1), 11–30.

Downer, J.T., Rimm-Kaufman, S.E. & Pianta, R.C. (2007). How do classroom conditions and children's risk for school problems contribute to children's behavioral engagement in learning? *School Psychology Review, 36* (3), 413–432.

Downey, G., Lebolt, A., Rincón, C. & Freitas, A.L. (1998). Rejection sensitivity and children's interpersonal difficulties. *Child Development, 69* (4), 1074–1091.

Doyle, R. (2003). Developing the nurturing school: Spreading nurture groups and principles into mainstream classrooms. *Emotional and Behavioural Difficulties, 8* (4), 252–266.

Doyle, W. (1986). Classroom organization and management. In M.C. Wittrock (Ed.) *Handbook of research on teaching.* (3rd ed.) New York: Macmillan, 392–431.

Dreikurs, R. & Cassel, P. (1990). *Discipline without tears.* (2nd ed.) New York: Dutton.

Drifte, C. (2004). *Encouraging positive behaviour in the early years: A practical guide.* London: Paul Chapman.

Drouet, D. (1993). Adolescent female bullying and sexual harassment. In D. Tattum (Ed.) *Understanding and managing bullying.* Oxford, UK: Heinemann Educational, 173–188.

Dubanoski, R.A., Inaba, M. & Gerkewicz, K. (1983). Corporal punishment in schools: Myths, problems and alternatives. *Child Abuse and Neglect, 7* (7), 271–278.

Duchesne, S. & Ratelle, C. (2010). Parental behaviors and adolescents' achievement goals at the beginning of middle school: Emotional problems as potential mediators. *Journal of Educational Psychology, 102* (2), 497–507.

Duda, M.A., Dunlap, G., Fox, L., Lentini, R. & Clarke, S. (2004). An experimental evaluation of positive behavior support in a community preschool program. *Topics in Early Childhood Special Education, 24* (3), 143–155.

Duffy, A.L. & Nesdale, D. (2009). Peer groups, social identity, and children's bullying behavior. *Social Development, 18* (1), 1221–139.

Duncan, G.J. & Brooks-Gunn, J. (2000). Family poverty, welfare reform, and child development. *Child Development, 71* (1), 188–196.

Dunlap, G., dePerczel, M., Clarke, S., Wilson, D., Wrights, S., White, R. & Gomez, A. (1994). Choice making to promote adaptive behavior for students with emotional and behavioral challenges. *Journal of Applied Behavior Analysis, 27* (3), 505–518.

Dunn, J. & Cutting, A.L. (1999). Understanding others, and individual differences in friendship interactions in young children. *Social Development, 8* (2), 201–219.

Dunst, C.J. (2002). Family-centered practices: Birth through high schools. *The Journal of Special Education, 36* (3), 139–147.

Duong, M.T., Schwartz, D., Chang, L., Kelly, B.M. & Tom, S.R. (2009). Associations between maternal physical discipline and peer victimization among Hong Kong Chinese children: The moderating role of child aggression. *Journal of Abnormal Child Psychology, 37* (7), 957–966.

DuPaul, G.J., Ervin, R.A., Hook, C.L. & McGoey, K.E. (1998). Peer tutoring for children with attention deficit hyperactivity disorder: Effects on classroom behavior and academic performance. *Journal of Applied Behavior Analysis, 31* (4), 579–592.

Durrant, J. & Ensom, R. (2012). Physical punishment of children: Lessons from 20 years of research. *Canadian Medical Association Journal, 184* (12), 1371–1377.

Durrant, M. (1995). *Creative strategies for school problems.* Epping, NSW: Eastwood Family Therapy Centre/New York: Norton.

Dweck, C.S. (1986). Motivational processes affecting learning. *American Psychologist, 41* (10), 1040–1048.

——(2008). Brainology: Transforming students' motivation to learn. *Independent School, 67* (2), 110–119.

Dweck, C.S. & Leggett, E.L. (1988). A social-cognitive approach to motivation and personality. *Psychological Review, 95* (2), 256–273.

Dwyer, K.P., Osher, D. & Hoffman, C.C. (2000). Creating responsive schools: Contextualizing early warning, timely response. *Exceptional Children, 66* (3), 347–365.

Eamon, M.K. (2001). Antecedents and socioemotional consequences of physical punishment on children in two-parent families. *Child Abuse and Neglect, 6* (6), 787–802.

Eccles, J.S., Buchanan, C.M., Flanagan, C., Fuligni, A., Midgley, C. & Yee, D. (1991). Control versus autonomy during early adolescence. *Journal of Social Issues, 47* (4), 53–68.

Eccles, J.S., Midgley, C., Wigfield, A., Buchanan, C.M., Reuman, D., Flanagan, C. & Mac Iver, D. (1993). Development during adolescence: The impact of stage-environment fit on young adolescents' experiences in schools and in families. *American Psychologist, 48* (2), 90–101.

Eckert, T.L., Ardoin, S.P., Daly, E.J. III & Martens, B.K. (2002). Improving oral reading fluency: A brief experimental analysis of combining an antecedent intervention with consequences. *Journal of Applied Behavior Analysis, 35* (3), 271–281.

Edwards, C.H. & Surma, M. (1980). The relationship between type of teacher reinforcement and student inquiry behavior in science. *Journal of Research in Science Teaching. 17* (4), 337–341.

Edwards, C.H. & Watts, V. (2008). *Classroom discipline and management.* (2nd Aust. ed.) Milton, Qld: Wiley.

Egan, S.K., Monson, T.C. & Perry, D.G. (1998). Social-cognitive influences on change in aggression over time. *Developmental Psychology, 34* (5), 996–1006.

Egan, S.K. & Perry, D.G. (1998). Does low self-regard invite victimization? *Developmental Psychology, 34* (2), 299–309.

Eisenberg, N. (2001). The core and correlates of affective social competence. *Social Development, 10* (1), 119–124.

Eisenberg, N., Champion, C. & Ma, Y. (2004b). Emotion-related regulation: An emerging construct. *Merrill-Palmer Quarterly, 50* (3), 236–259.

Eisenberg, N., Cumberland, A., Spinrad, T.L., Fabes, R.A.,

Shepard, S.A., Reiser, M., Murphy, B.C., Losoya, S.H. & Guthrie, I.K. (2001). The relations of regulation and emotionality to children's externalizing and internalizing problem behavior. *Child Development, 72* (4), 1112–1134.

Eisenberg, N., Fabes, R.A., Guthrie, I.K. & Reiser, M. (2000a). Dispositional emotionality and regulation: Their role in predicting quality of social functioning. *Journal of Personality and Social Psychology, 78* (1), 136–157.

Eisenberg, N., Fabes, R.A., Shepard, S.A., Guthrie, I.K., Murphy, B.C. & Reiser, M. (1999). Parental reactions to children's negative emotions: Longitudinal relations to quality of children's social functioning. *Child Development, 70* (2), 513–534.

Eisenberg, N., Fabes, R.A., Shepard, S.A., Murphy, B.C., Guthrie, I.K., Jones, S., Friedman, J., Poulin, R. & Maszk, P. (1997a). Contemporaneous and longitudinal prediction of children's social functioning from regulation and emotionality. *Child Development, 68* (4), 642–664.

Eisenberg, N., Guthrie, I.K., Fabes, R.A., Reiser, M., Murphy, B.C., Holgren, R., Maszk, P. & Losoya, S. (1997b). The relations of regulation and emotionality to resiliency and competent social functioning in elementary school children. *Child Development, 68* (2), 295–311.

Eisenberg, N., Lennon, R. & Roth, K. (1983). Prosocial development: A longitudinal study. *Developmental Psychology, 19* (6), 846–855.

Eisenberg, N., Sadovsky, A., Spinrad, T.L., Fabes, R.A., Losoya, S.H., Valiente, C., Reiser, M., Cumberland, A. & Shepard, S.A. (2005a). The relations of problem behavior status to children's negative emotionality, effortful control, and impulsivity: Concurrent relations and prediction of change. *Developmental Psychology, 41* (1), 193–211.

Eisenberg, N., Shepard, S.A., Fabes, R.A., Murphy, B.C. & Guthrie (1998). Shyness and children's emotionality, regulation, and coping: Contemporaneous, longitudinal, and across-context relations. *Child Development, 69* (3), 767–790.

Eisenberg, N., Spinrad, T.L., Fabes, R.A., Reiser, M., Cumberland, A., Shepard, S.A., Valiente, C., Losoya, S.H., Guthrie, I.K. & Thompson, M. (2004a). The relations of effortful control and impulsivity to children's resiliency and adjustment. *Child Development, 75* (1), 25–46.

Eisenberg, N., Zhou, Q., Spinrad, T.L., Valiente, C., Fabes, R.A. & Liew, J. (2005b). Relations among positive parenting, children's effortful control, and externalizing problems: A three-wave longitudinal study. *Child Development, 76* (5), 1055–1071.

Eisenberger, R. & Armeli, S. (1997). Can salient reward increase creative performance without reducing intrinsic creative interest? *Journal of Personality and Social Psychology, 72* (3), 652–663.

Eisenberger, R., Pierce, W.D. & Cameron, J. (1999). Effects of reward on intrinsic motivation: Comment on Deci, Koestner, and Ryan (1999). *Psychological Bulletin, 125* (6), 677–691.

El-Sheikh, M., Buckhalt, J., Mize, J. & Acebo, C. (2006). Marital conflict and disruption of children's sleep. *Child Development, 77* (1), 31–43.

El-Sheikh, M. & Harger, J. (2001). Appraisals of marital conflict and children's adjustment, health, and physiological reactivity. *Developmental Psychology, 37* (6), 875–885.

Eliot, M., Cornell, D., Gregory, A. & Fan, X. (2010). Supportive school climate and student willingness to seek help for bullying and threats of violence. *Journal of School Psychology, 48* (6), 533–553.

Ellingson, S.A., Miltenberger, R.G., Stricker, J., Galensky, T.L. & Garlinghouse, M. (2000). Functional assessment and intervention for challenging behaviors in the classroom by general education teachers. *Journal of Positive Behavior Interventions, 2* (2), 85–97.

Elliot, A.J. & McGregor, H.A. (2001). A 2 x 2 achievement goal framework. *Journal of Personality and Social Psychology, 80* (3), 501–519.

Elliot, A.J. & Murayama, K. (2008). On the measurement of achievement goals: Critique, illustration and application. *Journal of Educational Psychology, 100* (3), 613–628.

Elliot, A.J. & Thrash, T.M. (2004). The intergenerational transmission of fear of failure. *Personality and Social Psychology Bulletin, 30* (8), 957–971.

Elliott, E.S. & Dweck, C.S. (1988). Goals: An approach to motivation and achievement. *Journal of Personality and Social Psychology, 54* (1), 5–12.

Elliott, R. (2003). Sharing care and education: Parents' perspectives. *Australian Journal of Early Childhood, 28* (4), 14–21.

Ellis, A. (1962). *Reason and emotion in psychotherapy.* Secaucus, NJ: Lyle Stuart.

——(2005). Rational emotive behavior therapy. In R.J. Corsini and D. Wedding (Eds.) *Current psychotherapies.* (7th ed.) Belmont, CA: Thomson Brooks/Cole, 166–201.

Ellis, A.A. & Shute, R. (2007). Teacher responses to bullying in relation to moral orientation and seriousness of bullying. *British Journal of Educational Psychology, 77* (3), 649–663.

Ellis, J. & Magee, S.K. (1999). Determination of environmental correlates of disruptive classroom behavior: Integration of functional analysis into public school assessment process. *Education and Treatment of Children, 22* (3), 291–316.

Ellis, M.L., Weiss, B. & Lochman, J.E. (2009). Executive functions in children: Associations with aggressive behavior and appraisal processing. *Journal of Abnormal Child Psychology, 37* (7), 945–956.

Elman, N.M. & Kennedy-Moore, E. (2003). *The unwritten rules of friendship.* New York: Little Brown.

Elmore, G.M. & Huebner, E.S. (2010). Adolescents' satisfaction with school experiences: Relationships with demographics, attachment relationships, and school engagement behavior. *Psychology in the Schools, 47* (6), 525–537.

Emmer, E.T. & Aussiker, A. (1990). School and classroom discipline programs: How well do they work?. In O. Moles (Ed.) *Student discipline strategies: Research and practice.* Albany, NY: State University of New York Press, 129–166.

Emmer, E.T. & Evertson, C.M. (2009). *Classroom management for middle and high school teachers.* (8th ed.) Upper Saddle River, NJ: Pearson.

Emmer, E.T., Evertson, C.M. & Anderson, L.M. (1980). Effective classroom management at the beginning of the school year. *The Elementary School Journal, 80* (5), 219–231.

Emmer, E.T., Evertson, C.M. & Worsham, M.E. (2006). *Classroom management for middle and high school teachers.* (7th ed.) Boston, MA: Pearson Allyn & Bacon.

Englund, M.M., Luckner, A.E., Whaley, G.J.L. & Egeland, B. (2004). Children's achievement in early elementary school: Longitudinal effects of parental involvement, expectations, and quality of assistance. *Journal of Educational Psychology, 96* (4), 723–730.

Erath, S.A., Flanagan, K.S. & Bierman, K.L. (2008). Early adolescent social adjustment: Associations with friendship and peer victimization. *Social Development, 17* (4), 853–870.

Ervin, R.A., Ehrhardt, K.E. & Poling, A. (2001a). Functional assessment: Old wine in new bottles. *School Psychology Review, 30* (2), 173–179.

Ervin, R.A, Radford, P.M., Bertsch, K., Piper, A.L., Ehrhardt, K.E. & Poling, A. (2001b). A descriptive analysis and critique of the empirical literature on school-based functional assessment. *School Psychology Review, 30* (2), 193–210.

Ervin, R.A., Schaughency, E., Matthews, A., Goodman, S.D. &

McGlinchey, M.T. (2007). Primary and secondary prevention of behavior difficulties: Developing a data-informed problem-solving model to guide decision making at a school-wide level. *Psychology in the Schools, 44* (1), 7–18.

Espelage, D.L., Aragon, S.R., Birkett, M. & Koenig, B.W. (2008). Homophobic teasing, psychological outcomes, and sexual orientation among high school students: What influence do parents and schools have? *School Psychology Review, 37* (2), 202–216.

Espelage, D.L. & Swearer, S.M. (2003). Research on school bullying and victimization: What have we learned and where do we go from here?. *School Psychology Review, 32* (3), 365–383.

Espinoza, G. & Juvonen, J. (2011). Perceptions of the school social context across the transition to middle school: Heightened sensitivity among Latino students?. *Journal of Educational Psychology, 103* (3), 749–658.

Esposito, C. (1999). Learning in urban blight: School climate and its effect on the school performance of urban, minority, low-income children. *School Psychology Review, 28* (3), 365–377.

Essa, E.L. & Murray, C.I. (1999). Sexual play: When should you be concerned?. *Childhood Education, 75* (4), 231–234.

Estell, D.B., Farmer, T.W., Pearl, R., Van Acker, R. & Rodkin, P.C. (2008). Social status and aggressive and disruptive behavior in girls: Individual, group, and classroom influences. *Journal of School Psychology, 46* (2), 193–212.

Evans, G.W. & English, K. (2002). The environment of poverty: Multiple stressor exposure, psychophysiological stress, and socioemotional adjustment. *Child Development, 73* (4), 1238–1248.

Evans, G.W., Maxwell, L.E. & Hart, B. (1999). Parental language and verbal responsiveness to children in crowded homes. *Developmental Psychology, 35* (4), 1020–1023.

Everatt, J. & Reid, G. (2009). Dyslexia: An overview of recent research. In G. Reid (Ed.) *The Routledge companion to dyslexia*. London: Routledge, 3–21.

Evertson, C.M., Emmer, E.T. & Worsham, M.E. (2003). *Classroom management for elementary teachers*. (6th ed.) Boston, MA: Pearson Allyn and Bacon.

Faber, A., Mazlish, E., Nyberg, L. & Templeton, R.A. (1995). *How to talk so kids can learn at home and in school*. New York: Fireside.

Fabes, R.A., Fultz, J., Eisenberg, N., May-Plumlee, T. & Christopher, F.S. (1989). Effects of rewards on children's prosocial motivation: A socialization study. *Developmental Psychology, 25* (4), 509–515.

Fabes, R.A., Leonard, S.A., Kupanoff, K. & Martin, C.L. (2001). Parental coping with children's negative emotions: Relations with children's emotional and social responding. *Child Development, 72* (3), 907–920.

Fairburn, C.G., Cooper, Z., Shafran, R. & Wilson, G.T. (2008). Eating disorders: A transdiagnostic protocol. In D.H. Barlow (Ed.) *Clinical handbook of psychological disorders: A step-by-step treatment manual*. (4th ed.) New York: Guilford, 578–614.

Fairchild, L. & Erwin, W.M. (1977). Physical punishment by parent figures as a model of aggressive behavior in children. *Journal of Genetic Psychology, 130* (2), 279–284.

Fall, A.-M., & Roberts, G. (2012). High school dropouts: Interactions between social context, self-perceptions, school engagement, and student dropout. *Journal of Adolescence, 35* (4), 787–798.

Fan, X. (2001). Parental involvement and students' academic achievement: A growth modeling analysis. *The Journal of Experimental Education, 70* (1), 27–61.

Fan, X. & Chen, M. (2001). Parental involvement and students'

academic achievement: A meta-analysis. *Educational Psychology Review, 13* (1), 1–22.

Fantuzzo, J.W. & Polite, K. (1990). School-based, behavioral self-management: A review and analysis, *School Psychology Quarterly, 5* (3), 180–198.

Fantuzzo, J.W., Polite, K., Cook, D.M. & Quinn, G. (1988). An evaluation of the effectiveness of teacher- versus student-management classroom interventions. *Psychology in the Schools, 25* (2), 154–163.

Fantuzzo, J.W., Rohrbeck, C.A. & Azar, S.T. (1987). A component analysis of behavioral self-management interventions with elementary school students. *Child and Family Behavior Therapy, 9* (1–2), 33–43.

Farmer, T.W., Estell, D.B., Bishop, J.L., O'Neal, K.K. & Cairns, B.D. (2003). Rejected bullies or popular leaders?: The social relations of aggressive subtypes of rural African American early adolescents. *Developmental Psychology, 39* (6), 992–1004.

Farmer, T.W. & Xie, H. (2007). Aggresion and school social dynamics: The good, the bad, and the ordinary. *Journal of School Psychology, 45* (5), 461–478.

Farrell, A.D., Henry, D.B., Mays, S.A. & Schoeny, M.E. (2011). Parents as moderators of the impact of school norms and peer influences on aggression in middle school students. *Child Development, 82* (1), 146–161.

Farrell, A.D., Sullivan, T.N., Kliewer, W., Allison, K.W., Erwin, E.H., Meyer, A.L. & Esposito, L. (2006). Peer and school problems in the lives of urban adolescents: Frequency, difficulty, and relation to adjustment. *Journal of School Psychology, 44* (3), 169–190.

Farrell, A.D. & White, K.S. (1998). Parental influences and drug use among urban adolescents: Family structure and parent-adolescent relationship as protective factors. *Journal of Consulting and Clinical Psychology, 66* (2), 248–258.

Farrington, D.P., Ttofi, M.M. & Coid, J.W. (2009). Development of adolescence-limited, late-onset, and persistent offenders from age 8 to 48. *Aggressive Behavior, 35* (2), 150–163.

Farver, J.M. (1996). Aggressive behavior in preschoolers' social networks: Do birds of a feather flock together? *Early Childhood Research Quarterly, 11* (3), 333–350.

Fatouros, C. (1986). Early identification of gifted children is crucial . . . but how should we go about it?. *Gifted Education International, 4* (1), 24–28.

Feagans, L.V., Kipp, E. & Blood, I. (1994). The effects of otitis media on the attention skills of day-care-attending toddlers. *Developmental Psychology, 30* (5), 701–708.

Feindler, E.L. (1991). Cognitive strategies in anger control interventions for children and adolescents. In P.C. Kendall (Ed.) *Child and adolescent therapy: Cognitive-behavioral procedures*. New York: Guilford, 66–97.

Feindler, E.L. & Engel, E.C. (2011). Assessment and intervention for adolescents with anger and aggression difficulties in school settings. *Psychology in the Schools, 48* (3), 243–253.

Feinstein, L. & Symons, J. (1999). Attainment in secondary school. *Oxford Economic Papers, 51* (2), 300–321.

Feiring, C., Taska, L. & Lewis, M. (2002). Adjustment following sexual abuse discovery: The role of shame and attributional style. *Developmental Psychology, 38* (1), 79–92.

Feldhusen, J.F., Dai, D.Y. & Clinkenbeard, P.R. (2000). Dimensions of competitive and cooperative learning among gifted learners. *Journal for the Education of the Gifted, 23*. (3), 328–342.

Feldman, R. & Klein, P.S. (2003). Toddlers' self-regulated compliance to mothers, caregivers, and fathers: Implications for theories of socialization. *Developmental Psychology, 39* (4), 680–692.

Fergusson, D.M., Horwood, L.J. & Ridder, E.M. (2005). Show me the child at seven: The consequences of conduct problems in childhood for psychosocial functioning in adulthood. *Journal of Child Psychology and Psychiatry, 46* (8), 837–849.

Fergusson, D.M. & Lynskey, M.T. (1997). Physical punishment/maltreatment during childhood and adjustment in young adulthood. *Child Abuse and Neglect, 21* (7), 617–630.

Fergusson, D., Swain-Campbell, N. & Horwood, J. (2004). How does childhood economic disadvantage lead to crime?. *Journal of Child Psychology and Psychiatry, 45* (5), 956–966.

Field, E. & Carroll, P. (2006). Effective ways to work with parents. In H. McGrath and T. Noble (Eds.) *Bullying solutions: Evidence-based approaches to bullying in Australian schools.* Sydney: Pearson Longman, 209–225.

Field, T., Diego, M., Hernandez-Reif, M., Schanberg, S. & Kuhn, C. (2003). Depressed mothers who are 'good interaction' partners versus those who are withdrawn or intrusive. *Infant Behavior and Development, 26* (2), 238–252.

Fields, M. & Boesser, C. (2002). *Constructive guidance and discipline.* (3rd ed.) Upper Saddle River, NJ: Merrill Prentice Hall.

Fiese, B.H., Everhart, R.S. & Wildenger, L. (2009). Wheezing, sleeping, and worrying: The hidden risks of asthma and obesity in school-age children. *Psychology in the Schools, 46* (8), 728–738.

Fine, S.E., Trentacosta, C.J., Izard, C.E., Mostow, A.J. & Campbell, J.L. (2004). Anger perception, caregivers' use of physical discipline, and aggression in children at risk. *Social Development, 13* (2), 213–228.

Fineran, S. (2001). Peer sexual harassment in high school. *Journal of School Social Work, 11* (2), 50–69.

Finn, J.D., Pannozzo, G.F.M. & Achilles, C.M. (2003). The 'why's' of class size: Student behavior in small classes. *Review of Educational Research, 73* (3), 321–368.

Fisch, R. & Schlanger, K. (1999). *Brief therapy with intimidating cases: Changing the unchangeable.* San Francisco, CA: Jossey-Bass.

Fisch, R., Weakland, J.H. & Segal, L. (1982). *The tactics of change: Doing therapy briefly.* San Francisco, CA: Jossey-Bass.

Fischer, M., Barkley, R.A., Edelbrock, C.S. & Smallish, L. (1990). The adolescent outcome of hyperactive children diagnosed by research criteria: II. Academic, attentional and neurological status. *Journal of Consulting and Clinical Psychology, 58* (5), 580–588.

Fischer, M., Barkley, R.A., Fletcher, K.E. & Smallish, L. (1993). The adolescent outcome of hyperactive children: Predictors of psychiatric, academic, social and emotional adjustment. *Journal of the American Academy of Child and Adolescent Psychiatry, 32* (2), 324–332.

Fisher, H.L., Moffitt, T.E., Houts, R.M., Belsky, D.W. & Arseneault, L. (2012). Bullying victimization and risk of self harm in early adolescence: Longitudinal cohort study. *British Medical Journal, 344.* http://www.bmj.com/content/344/bmj.e2683.

Fisher, W.W., O'Connor, J.T., Kurtz, P.F., DeLeon, I.G. & Gotjen, D.L. (2000b). The effects of noncontingent delivery of high- and low-preference stimuli on attention-maintained destructive behavior. *Journal of Applied Behavior Analysis, 33* (1), 79–83.

Fisher, W.W., Thompson, R.H., Hagopian, L.P., Bowman, L.G. & Krug, A. (2000a). Facilitating tolerance of delayed reinforcement during functional communication training. *Behavior Modification, 24* (1), 3–29.

Flaspohler, P.D., Elfstrom, J.L., Vanderzee, K.L., Sink, H.E. & Birchmeier, Z. (2009). Stand by me: The effects of peer and teacher support in mitigating the impact of bullying on quality of life. *Psychology in the Schools, 46* (7), 636–649.

Fletcher, A.C. & Shaw, R.A. (2000). Sex differences in associations between parental behaviors and characteristics

of adolescent social integration. *Social Development, 9* (2), 133–148.

Flink, C., Boggiano, A.K. & Barrett, M. (1990). Controlling teaching strategies: Undermining children's self-determination and performance. *Journal of Personality and Social Psychology, 59* (5), 915–926.

Flook, L., Repetti, R.L. & Ullman, J.B. (2005). Classroom social experiences as predictors of academic performance. *Developmental Psychology, 41* (2), 319–327.

Flores, E., Cicchetti, D. & Rogosch, F.A. (2005). Predictors of resilience in maltreated and nonmaltreated Latino children. *Developmental Psychology, 41* (2), 338–351.

Flouri, E. (2006). Parental interest in children's education, children's self-esteem and locus of control, and later educational attainment: Twenty-six year follow-up of the 1970 British birth cohort. *British Journal of Educational Psychology, 76* (1), 51–55.

Flouri, E., Buchanan, A. & Bream, V. (2002). Adolescents' perceptions of their fathers' involvement: Significance to school attitudes. *Psychology in the Schools, 39* (5), 575–582.

Flynn, C.P. (1994). Regional differences in attitudes towards corporal punishment. *Journal of Marriage and the Family, 56* (2), 314–324.

Ford, D.Y. (2003). Equity and excellence: Culturally diverse students in gifted education. In N. Colangelo and G.A. Davis (Eds.) *Handbook of gifted education.* (3rd ed.) Boston, MA: Allyn & Bacon, 506–520.

Ford, D.Y. & Harris, J.J. III (2000). A framework for infusing multicultural curriculum into gifted education. *Roeper Review, 23* (1), 4–10.

Ford, D.Y., Howard, T.C., Harris, J.J. III & Tyson, C.A. (2000). Creating culturally responsive classrooms for gifted African American students. *Journal for the Education of the Gifted, 23* (4), 397–427.

Ford, D.Y. & Trotman, M.F. (2001). Teachers of gifted students: Suggested multicultural characteristics and competencies. *Roeper Review, 23* (4), 235–239.

Ford, M.A. (1989). Students' perceptions of affective issues impacting the social emotional development and school performance of gifted/talented youngsters. *Roeper Review, 11* (3), 131–134.

Forman, S.G. & Barakat, N.M. (2011). Cognitive-behavioral therapy in the schools: Bringing research to practice through effective implementation. *Psychology in the Schools, 48* (3), 283–296.

Fox, A.M. & Rieder, M.J. (1993). Risks and benefits of drugs used in the management of the hyperactive child. *Drug Safety, 9* (1), 38–50.

Fox, C.L. & Boulton, M.J. (2003). Evaluating the effectiveness of a social skills training (SST) programme for victims of bullying. *Educational Research, 45* (3), 231–247.

——(2006). Friendship as a moderator of the relationship between social skills problems and peer victimization. *Aggressive Behavior, 32* (2), 110–121.

Fox, H. (2003). Using therapeutic documents: A review. *The International Journal of Narrative Therapy and Community Work, 2003* (4), 26–36.

Fox, J.K., Halpern, L.F., Ryan, J.L. & Lowe, K.A. (2010). Stressful life events and the tripartite model: Relations to anxiety and depression in adolescent females. *Journal of Adolescence, 33* (1), 43–54.

Foxx, R. M. (1982). *Decreasing behaviors of persons with severe retardation and autism.* Champaign, IL: Research Press.

Fraga, C.G., Oteiza, P.I., Golub, M.S., Gershwin, M.E. & Keen, C.L. (1990). Effects of aluminum on brain lipid peroxidation. *Toxicology Letters, 51* (2), 213–219.

Frankel, F. & Myatt, R. (1996). Self-esteem, social competence and psychopathology in boys without friends. *Personality and Individual Differences, 20* (3), 401–407.

Franklin, M.E. & Foa, E.B. (2008). Obsessive-compulsive disorder. In D.H. Barlow (Ed.) *Clinical handbook of psychological disorders: A step-by-step treatment manual.* (4th ed.) New York: Guilford, 164–215.

Fraser, M.W., Day, S.H., Galinsky, M.J., Hodges, V.G. & Smokowski, P.R. (2004). Conduct problems and peer rejection in childhood: A randomized trial of the Making Choices and Strong Families programs. *Research on Social Work Practice, 14* (5), 313–324.

Fraser, S. & Gestwicki, C. (2002). *Authentic childhood: Exploring Reggio Emilia in the classroom.* Albany, NY: Delmar.

Freedman, J.L., Cunningham, J.A. & Krismer, K. (1992). Inferred values and the reverse-incentive effect in induced compliance. *Journal of Personality and Social Psychology, 62* (3), 357–368.

Freeman, J. (1996). *Highly able girls and boys.* London: Department for Education and Employment.

Freeman, J., Epston, D. & Lobovits, D. (1997). *Playful approaches to serious problems: Narrative therapy with children and their families.* New York: Norton.

Freiberg, H.J., Stein, T.A. & Huang, S. (1995). Effects of a classroom management interventon on student achievement in inner-city elementary schools. *Educational Research and Evaluation, 1* (1), 36–66.

French, D.C., Jansen, E.A., Riansari, M. & Setiono, K. (2003). Friendships of Indonesian children: Adjustment of children who differ in friendship presence and similarity between mutual friends. *Social Development, 12* (4), 605–621.

Frenzel, A.C., Pekrun, R. & Goetz, T. (2007). Perceived learning environment and students' emotional experiences: A multilevel analysis of mathematics classrooms. *Learning and Instruction, 17* (5), 478–493.

Frey, B.B., Schmitt, V.L. & Allen, J.P. (2012). Defining authentic classroom assessment. *Practical Assessment, Research and Evaluation, 17* (2), 1–18.

Frey, K.S., Hirschstein, M.K., Edstrom, L.V., Snell, J.L. (2009). Observed reductions in school bullying, nonbullying aggression, and destructive bystander behavior: A longitudinal evaluation. *Journal of Educational Psychology, 101* (2), 466–481.

Frias-Armenta, M. (2002). Long-term effects of child punishment on Mexican women: A structural model. *Child Abuse and Neglect, 26* (4), 371–386.

Frick, P.J., Cornell, A.H., Bodin, S.D., Dane, H.E., Barry, C.T. & Loney, B.R. (2003). Callous-unemotional traits and developmental pathways to severe conduct problems. *Developmental Psychology, 39* (2), 246–260.

Frick, P.J., Stickle, T.R., Dandreaux, D.M., Farrell, J.M. & Kimonis, E.R. (2005). Callous-unemotional traits in predicting the severity and stability of conduct problems and delinquency. *Journal of Abnormal Child Psychology, 33* (4), 471–487.

Friedman, I.A. (2003). Self-efficacy and burnout in teaching: The importance of interpersonal-relations efficacy. *Social Psychology of Education, 6* (3), 191–215.

Friedman-Weieneth, J.L., Harvey, E.A., Youngwirth, S.D. & Goldstein, L.H. (2007). The relation between 3-year-old children's skills and their hyperactivity, inattention, and aggression. *Journal of Educational Psychology, 99* (3), 671–681.

Friend, M. & Cook, L. (2007). *Interactions: Collaboration skills for school professionals.* (5th ed.) Boston, MA: Pearson Allyn & Bacon.

Frith, U. (2004). Emanuel Miller lecture: Confusions and controversies about Asperger syndrome. *Journal of Child Psychology and Psychiatry, 45* (4), 672–686.

Fritz, J.N., Iwata, B.A., Rolider, N.U., Camp, E.M. & Neidert, P.L. (2012). Analysis of self-recording in self-management interventions for stereotypy. *Journal of Applied Behavior Analysis, 45* (1), 55–68.

Frodi, A., Bridges, L. & Grolnick, W. (1985). Correlates of mastery-related behavior: A short-term longitudinal study of infants in their second year. *Child Development, 56* (5), 1291–1298.

Fudge, D.L., Skinner, C.H., Williams, J.L., Cowden, D., Clark, J. & Bliss, S.L. (2008). Increasing on-task behavior in every student in a second-grade classroom during transitions: Validating the color wheel system. *Journal of School Psychology, 46* (5), 575–592.

Fujiura, G.T. & Yamaki, K. (2000). Trends in demography of childhood poverty and disability. *Exceptional Children, 66* (2), 187–199.

Fuller, A. (2006). A resilience-based approach to helping victims of bullying and their families. In H. McGrath and T. Noble (Eds.) *Bullying solutions: Evidence-based approaches to bullying in Australian schools.* Sydney: Pearson Longman, 161–173.

Fuller-Rowell, T.E. & Doan, S.N. (2010). The social costs of academic success across ethnic groups. *Child Development, 81* (6), 1696–1713.

Furlong, M.J. & Christenson, S.L. (2008). Engaging students at school and with learning: A relevant construct for *all* students. *Psychology in the Schools, 45* (5), 365–368.

Furnham, A. & Cheng, H. (2000). Lay theories of happiness. *Journal of Happiness Studies, 1* (2), 227–246.

Furrer, C. & Skinner, E. (2003). Sense of relatedness as a factor in children's academic engagement and performance. *Journal of Educational Psychology, 95* (1), 148–162.

Fylling, I. & Sandvin, J.T. (1999). The role of parents in special education: The notion of partnership revised. *European Journal of Special Needs Education, 14* (2), 144–157.

Gable, R.A., Hendrickson, J.M. & Van Acker, R. (2001). Maintaining the integrity of FBA-based interventions in schools. *Education and Treatment of Children, 24* (3), 248–260.

Gabriele, A.J. (2007). The influence of achievement goals on the constructive activity of low achievers during collaborative problem solving. *British Journal of Educational Psychology, 77* (1), 121–141.

Gadbois, S.A. & Sturgeon, R.D. (2010). Academic self-handicapping: Relationships with learning specific and general self-perceptions and academic performance over time. *British Journal of Educational Psychology, 81* (2), 207–222.

Galand, B., Lecocq, C. & Philippot, P. (2007). School violence and teacher professional disengagement. *British Journal of Educational Psychology, 77* (2), 465–477.

Gamman, R. (2003). Sharing the load, supporting the staff: Collaborative management of difficult behaviour in primary schools. *Emotional and Behavioural Difficulties, 8* (3), 217–229.

Garber, J., Robinson, N.S. & Valentiner, D. (1997). The relation between parenting and adolescent depression: Self-worth as a mediator. *Journal of Adolescent Research, 12* (1), 12–33.

Garcia, D.C. (2004). Exploring connections between the construct of teacher efficacy and family involvement practices: Implications for urban teacher preparation. *Urban Education, 39* (3), 290–315.

Gardner, H. (1983). *Frames of mind: The theory of multiple intelligences.* New York: Basic Books.

——(1999). *Intelligence reframed: Multiple intelligences for the 21st Century.* New York: Basic Books.

Garner, P.W. & Spears, F.M. (2000). Emotion regulation in low-income preschoolers. *Social Development, 9* (2), 246–264.

Garofalo, R., Wolf, C., Wissow, L.S., Woods, E.R. & Goodman, E. (1999). Sexual orientation and risk of suicide attempts among a representative sample of youth. *Archives of Pediatrics and Adolescent Medicine, 153* (5), 487-493

Gartrell, D. (1987). Assertive discipline: Unhealthy for children and other living things. *Young Children, 42 (2),* 10-11.

——(2003). *A guidance approach for the encouraging classroom.* (3rd ed.) New York: Delmar.

Gartstein, M.A. & Fagot, B.I. (2003). Parental depression, parenting and family adjustment, and child effortful control: Explaining externalizing behaviors for preschool children. *Journal of Applied Developmental Psychology, 24* (2), 143-177.

Garza, R. (2009). Latino and White high school students' perceptions of caring behaviors: Are we culturally responsive to our students?. *Urban Education, 44* (3), 297-321.

Gaylord-Harden, N.K. (2008). The influence of student perceptions of parenting and coping on achievement and classroom behavior among African American children. *Psychology in the Schools, 45* (8), 763-777.

Gazelle, H. & Ladd, G.W. (2003). Anxious solitude and peer exclusion: A diathesis-stress model of internalizing trajectories in childhood. *Child Development, 74* (1), 257-278.

Geake, J. (2008). Neuromythologies in education. *Educational Research, 50* (2), 123-133.

Gecas, V. (1982). The self-concept. *Annual Review of Sociology, 8,* 1-33.

Gehlbach, H., Brinkworth, M.E. & Harris, A.D. (2012). Changes in teacher-student relationships. *British Journal of Educational Psychology, 82* (4), 690-704.

George, C. & Main, M. (1979). Social interactions of young abused children: Approach, avoidance, and aggression. *Child Development, 50* (2), 306-318.

George, M.P., White, G.P. & Schlaffer, J.J. (2007). Implementing school-wide behavior change: Lessons from the field. *Psychology in the Schools, 44* (1), 41-51.

Gerris, J.R.M., Dekovic, M. & Janssens, J.M.A.M. (1997). The relationship between social class and childrearing behaviors: Parents' perspective taking and value orientations. *Journal of Marriage and the Family, 59* (4), 834-847.

Gershoff, E.T. (2002). Corporal punishment by parents and associated child behaviors and experiences: A meta-analytic and theoretical review. *Psychological Bulletin, 128* (4), 539-579.

Gershoff, E.T., Aber, J.L., Raver, C.C. & Lennon, M.C. (2007). Income is not enough: Incorporating material hardship into models of income associations with parenting and child development. *Child Development, 78* (1), 70-95.

Gershoff, E.T., Grogan-Kaylor, A., Lansford, J.E., Chang, L., Zelli, A. Deater-Deckard, K. & Dodge, K.A. (2010). Parent discipline practices in an international sample: Associations with child behaviors and moderation by perceived normativeness. *Child Development, 81* (2), 497-502.

Gershoff, E.T., Lansford, J.E., Sexton, H.R., Davis-Kean, P. & Sameroff, A.J. (2012). Longitudinal links between spanking and children's externalizing behaviors in a national sample of White, Black, Hispanic, and Asian American families. *Child Development, 83* (3), 838-843.

Gesser, R.M. & Koo, S.C. (1996). Oral inoculation with herpes simplex virus type 1 infects enteric neurons and mucosal nerve fibers within the gastrointestinal tract in mice. *Journal of Virology, 70* (6), 4097-4102.

Gest, S.D., Freeman, N.R., Domitrovich, C.E. & Welsh, J.A. (2004). Shared book reading and children's language comprehension skills: The moderating role of parental discipline practices. *Early Childhood Research Quarterly, 19* (2), 319-336.

Ghazvini, A.S. & Readdick, C.A. (1994). Parent-caregiver communication and quality of care in diverse child care settings. *Early Childhood Research Quarterly, 9* (2), 207-222.

Giannopulu, I., Escolano, S., Cusin, F., Citeau, H. & Dellatolas, G. (2008). Teachers' reporting of behavioural problems and cognitive-academic performances in children aged 5-7 years. *British Journal of Educational Psychology, 78* (1), 127-147.

Gibbs, S. & Powell, B. (2011). Teacher efficacy and pupil behaviour: The structure of teachers' individual and collective beliefs and their relationship with numbers of pupils excluded from school. *British Journal of Educational Psychology, 82* (4), 564-584.

Gilding, M. (1997). *Australian families: A comparative perspective.* South Melbourne: Longman.

Giles-Sims, J., Straus, M.A. & Sugarman, D.B. (1995). Child, maternal, and family characteristics associated with spanking. *Family Relations, 44* (2), 170-176.

Gillies, R.M. (2000). The maintenance of cooperative and helping behaviours in cooperative groups. *British Journal of Educational Psychology, 70* (1), 97-111.

——(2006). Teachers' and students' verbal behaviours during cooperative and small-group learning. *British Journal of Educational Psychology, 76* (2), 271-287.

Gillies, R.M. & Ashman, A.F. (1998). Behavior and interactions of children in cooperative groups in lower and middle elementary grades. *Journal of Educational Psychology, 90* (4), 746-757.

Gilliom, M. & Shaw, D.S. (2004). Codevelopment of externalizing and internalizing problems in early childhood. *Development and Psychopathology, 16* (2), 313-333.

Gilliom, M., Shaw, D.S., Beck, J.E., Schonberg, M.A. & Lukon, J.L. (2002). Anger regulation in disadvantaged preschool boys: Strategies, antecedents, and the development of self-control. *Developmental Psychology, 38* (2), 222-235.

Gillison, F., Standage, M. & Skevington, S. (2008). Changes in quality of life and psychological need satisfaction following the transition to secondary school. *British Journal of Educational Psychology, 78* (1), 149-162.

Gilman, R. & Anderman, E.M. (2006). The relationship between relative levels of motivation and intrapersonal, interpersonal, and academic functioning among older adolescents. *Journal of School Psychology, 44* (5), 375-391.

Gilman, R. & Ashby, J.S. (2003). Multidimensional perfectionism in a sample of middle school students: An exploratory investigation. *Psychology in the Schools, 40* (6), 677-689.

Gini, G. (2006). Social cognition and moral cognitive in bullying: What's wrong?. *Aggressive Behavior, 32* (6), 528-539.

Gini, G., Albiero, P., Benelli, B. & Altoè, G. (2007). Does empathy predict adolescents' bullying and defending behavior?. *Aggressive Behavior, 33* (5), 467-476.

Ginott, H.G. (1969). *Between parent and child.* London: Crosby Lockwood Staples.

——(1972). *Teacher and child.* New York: Macmillan.

Ginott, H.G., Ginott, A. & Goddard, H.W. (2003). *Between parent and child.* (2nd ed.) New York: Three Rivers Press.

Ginsberg, G.S. & Bronstein, P. (1993). Family factors related to children's intrinsic/extrinsic motivational orientation and academic performance. *Child Development, 64* (5), 1461-1474.

Ginsberg-Block, M.D., Rohrbeck, C.A. & Fantuzzo, J.W. (2006). A meta-analytic review of social, self-concept, and behavioral outcomes of peer-assisted learning. *Journal of Educational Psychology, 98* (4), 732–749.

Gladwell, M. (2008). *Outliers: The story of success.* London, UK: Allen Lane.

Glanzman, M. & Blum, N. (2007). Attention deficits and hyperactivity. In M.L. Batshaw, L. Pellegrino & N.J. Roizen (Eds.) *Children with disabilities.* (6th ed.) Sydney: Elsevier, 349–369.

Glaser, D. (2000). Child abuse and neglect and the brain – A review. *Journal of Child Psychology and Psychiatry, 41* (1), 97–116.

Glasser, W. (1969). *Schools without failure.* New York: Harper and Row.

——(1985). Discipline has never been the problem and it isn't the problem now. *Theory into Practice, 24* (4), 241–246.

——(1988). *Choice theory in the classroom.* (rev. ed.) New York: HarperCollins.

——(1992a). *The quality school: Managing students without coercion.* (2nd ed.) New York: Harper and Row.

——(1992b). The quality school curriculum. *Phi Delta Kappan, 73* (9), 690–694.

——(1998a). *The quality school: Managing students without coercion.* (rev. ed.) New York: Harper Perennial.

——(1998b). *The quality school teacher.* (rev. ed.) New York: HarperCollins.

——(1998c). *Choice theory: A new psychology of personal freedom.* New York: HarperCollins.

Gmitrova, V. & Gmitrov, J. (2003). The impact of teacher-directed and child-directed pretend play on cognitive competence in kindergarten children. *Early Childhood Education Journal, 30* (4), 241–246.

Goddard, R.D., Hoy, W.K. & Hoy, A.W. (2000). Collective teacher efficacy: Its meaning, measure, and impact on student achievement. *American Educational Research Journal, 37* (2), 479–507.

Goetz, T., Frenzel, A.C., Pekrun, R., Hall, N.C. & Lüdtke, O. (2007). Between- and within-domain relations of students' academic emotions. *Journal of Educational Psychology, 99* (4), 715–733.

Gohm, C.L., Humphreys, L.G. & Yao, G. (1998). Underachievement among spatially gifted students. *American Educational Research Journal, 35* (3), 515–531.

Golberg, M.E., Olweus, D. & Endresen, I.M. (2007). Bullies and victims at school: Are they the same pupils?. *British Journal of Educational Psychology, 77* (2), 441–464.

Goldstein, M. & Goldstein, S. (1995). Medications and behavior in the classroom. In S. Goldstein (Ed.) *Understanding and managing children's classroom behavior.* New York: John Wiley and Sons, 181–219.

Goldstein, M. & Heaven, P.C.L. (2000). Perceptions of the family, delinquency, and emotional adjustment among youth. *Personality and Individual Differences, 29* (6), 1169–1178.

Goldstein, S. (1995). Attention deficit hyperactivity disorder. In S. Goldstein (Ed.) *Understanding and managing children's classroom behavior.* New York: John Wiley and Sons, 56–78.

Goldstein, S. & Naglieri, J.A. (2008). The school neuropsychology of ADHD: Theory, assessment, and intervention. *Psychology in the Schools, 45* (9), 859–874.

Goleman, D. (1994). *Emotional intelligence.* New York: Bantam Books.

Golombok, S., Perry, B., Burston, A., Murray, C., Mooney-Somers, J., Stevens, M. & Golding, J. (2003). Children with lesbian parents: A community study. *Developmental Psychology, 39* (1), 20–33.

Gonzalez, J.E., Nelson, J.R., Gutkin, T.B., Saunders, A., Galloway, A. & Shwery, C.S. (2004). Rational emotive therapy with children and adolescents: A meta-analysis. *Journal of Emotional and Behavioral Disorders, 12* (4), 222–235.

Gonzalez-DeHass, A.R., Willems, P.P. & Holbein, M.F.D. (2005). Examining the relationship between parental involvement and student motivation. *Educational Psychology Review, 17* (2), 99–123.

Good, T.L. & Brophy, J.E. (2008). *Looking in classrooms.* (10th ed.) Boston, MA: Pearson.

Goodenow, C. (1993). Classroom belonging among early adolescent students: Relationships to motivation and achievement. *Journal of Early Adolescence, 13* (1), 21–43.

Goodenow, C., Szalacha, L. & Westheimer, K. (2006). School support groups, other school factors and the safety of sexual minority adolescents. *Psychology in the Schools, 43* (5), 573–589.

Goodwin, R.D., Fergusson, D.M. & Horwood, L.J. (2004). Early anxious/withdrawn behaviours predict later internalising disorders. *Journal of Child Psychology and Psychiatry, 45* (4), 874–883.

Gordon, G.L. (1999). Teacher talent and urban schools. *Phi Delta Kappan, 81* (4), 304–307.

Gordon, T. (1970). *Parent effectiveness training.* New York: Plume.

——(1974). *Teacher effectiveness training.* New York: Peter H. Wyden.

——(1991). *Teaching children self-discipline at home and at school.* Sydney: Random House.

——(1997). *Parent effectiveness traning workbook: Revised Australian edition.* Solana Beach, CA: Gordon Training International.

——(2000). *Parent effectiveness training.* (2nd ed.) New York: Three Rivers Press.

Gottfried, A.E., Fleming, J.S. & Gottfried, A.W. (1994). Role of parental motivational practices in children's academic intrinsic motivation and achievement. *Journal of Educational Psychology, 86* (1), 104–113.

Gowen, J.W. & Nebrig, J.B. (2002). *Enhancing early emotional development: Guiding parents of young children.* Baltimore, MD: Paul H. Brookes.

Graham, S., Bellmore, A.D. & Mize, J. (2006). Peer victimization, aggression, and their co-occurrence in middle school: Pathways to adjustment problems. *Journal of Abnormal Child Psychology, 34* (3), 363–378.

Granic, I. & Patterson, G.R. (2006). Toward a comprehensive model of antisocial development: A dynamic systems approach. *Psychological Review, 113* (1), 101–131.

Graue, M.E. & Walsh, D.J. (1998). *Studying children in context: Theories, methods and ethics.* Thousand Oaks, CA: SAGE.

Gray, M.R. & Steinberg, L. (1999). Unpacking authoritative parenting: Reassessing a multidimensional construct. *Journal of Marriage and the Family, 61* (3), 574–587.

Graziano, P.A., Reavis, R.D., Keane, S.P. & Calkins, S.D. (2007). The role of emotion regulation in children's early academic success. *Journal of School Psychology, 45* (1), 3–19.

Green, C. & Chee, K. (2001). *Understanding ADHD: Attention-deficit hyperactivity disorder in children.* (3rd ed.) Sydney: Doubleday.

Green, J., Liem, G.A.D., Martin, A.J., Colmar, S., Marsh, H.W. & McInerney, D. (2012). Academic motivation, self-concept, engagement, and performance in high school: Key processes from a longitudinal perspective. *Journal of Adolescence, 35* (5), 1111–1122.

Greene, R.W. (2008). *Lost at school.* New York: Scribner.

——(2010). *The explosive child.* New York: Harper.

Greene, R.W., Biederman, J., Faraone, S.V., Sienna, M. & Garcia-Jetton, J. (1997). Adolescent outcome of boys with attention-deficit/hyperactivity disorder and social disability: Results from a 4-year longitudinal follow-up. *Journal of Consulting and Clinical Psychology, 65* (5), 758–767.

Greenman, J. & Stonehouse, A. (2007). *Prime times: A handbook for excellence in infant and toddler programs.* (2nd ed.) St Paul, MN: Redleaf Press.

Gregory, A., Cornell, D., Fan, X., Sheras, P., Shih, T.-H. & Huang, F. (2010). Authoritative school discipline: High school practices associated with lower bullying and victimization. *Journal of Educational Psychology, 102* (2), 483–496.

Gregory, A. & Rimm-Kaufman, S. (2008). Positive mother-child interactions in kindergarten: Predictors of school success in high school. *School Psychology Review, 37* (4), 499–515.

Gregory, A. & Ripski, M.B. (2008). Adolescent trust in teachers: Implications for behavior in the high school classroom. *School Psychology Review, 37* (3), 337–353.

Gregory, A., Skiba, R.J. & Noguera, P.A. (2010). The achievement gap and the discipline gap: Two sides of the same coin?. *Educational Researcher, 39* (1), 59–68.

Gregory, A. & Weinstein, R.S. (2004). Connection and regulation at home and in school: Predicting growth in achievement for adolescents. *Journal of Adolescent Research, 19* (4), 405–427.

——(2008). The discipline gap and African Americans: Defiance or cooperation in the high school classroom. *Journal of School Psychology, 46* (4), 455–475.

Gregory, A.M. & Sadeh, A. (2012). Sleep, emotional and behavioral difficulties in children and adolescents. *Sleep Medicine Reviews, 16* (2), 129–136.

Gren-Landell, M., Aho, N., Andersson, G. & Svedin, C.G. (2011). Social anxiety disorder and victimization in a community sample of adolescents. *Journal of Adolescence, 34* (3), 569–577.

Gresham, F.M., Cohen, S., Gansle, K.A., Noell, G.H. & Rosenblum, S. (1993). Treatment integrity of school-based behavioral intervention studies: 1980–1990. *School Psychology Review, 22* (2), 254–272.

Gresham, F.M., McIntyre, L.L., Olson-Tinker, H., Dolstra, L., McLaughlin, V. & Van. M. (2004). Relevance of functional behavioral assessment research for school-based interventions and positive behavior support. *Research in Developmental Disabilities, 25* (1), 19–37.

Gresham, F.M., Watson, T.S. & Skinner, C.H. (2001). Functional behavioral assessment: Principles, procedures, and future directions. *School Psychology Review, 30* (2), 156–172.

Greven, P. (1990). *Spare the child: The religious roots of punishment and the psychological impact of physical abuse.* New York: Vintage.

Griffith, J., Steptoe, A. & Cropley, M. (1999). An investigation of coping strategies associated with job stress in teachers. *British Journal of Educational Psychology, 69* (4), 517–531.

Griggs, M.S., Gagnon, S.G., Huelsman, T.J., Kidder-Ashley, P. & Ballard, M. (2009). Student-teacher relationships matter: Moderating influences between temperament and preschool social competence. *Psychology in the Schools, 46* (6), 553–567.

Grille, R. (2005). *Parenting for a peaceful world.* Alexandria, NSW: Longueville Media.

Grogan-Kaylor, A. (2005). Corporal punishment and the growth trajectory of children's antisocial behavior. *Child Maltreatment, 10* (3), 283–292.

Grolnick, W.S. (2003). *The psychology of parental control: How well-meant parenting backfires.* Mahwah, NJ: Lawrence Erlbaum.

Grolnick, W.S., Benjet, C., Kurowski, C.O. & Apostoleris, N.H. (1997). Predictors of parent involvement in children's schooling. *Journal of Educational Psychology, 89* (3), 538–548.

Grolnick, W.S., Bridges, L.J. & Connell, J.P. (1996). Emotion regulation in two-year-olds: Strategies and emotional expression in four contexts. *Child Development, 67* (3), 928–941.

Grolnick, W.S., Frodi, A. & Bridges, L.J. (1984). Maternal control

style and the mastery motivation of one-year-olds. *Infant Mental Health Journal, 5,* 72–82.

Grolnick, W.S., Gurland, S.T., DeCourcey, W. & Jacob, K. (2002). Antecedents and consequences of mothers' autonomy support: An experimental investigation. *Developmental Psychology, 38* (1), 143–155.

Grolnick, W.S. & Pomerantz, E.M. (2009). Issues and challenges in studying parental control: Toward a new conceptualization. *Child Development Perspectives, 3* (3), 165–170.

Grolnick, W.S. & Ryan, R.M. (1987). Autonomy in children's learning: An experimental and individual difference investigation. *Journal of Personality and Social Psychology, 52* (5), 890–898.

——(1989). Parent styles associated with children's self-regulation and competence in school. *Journal of Educational Psychology, 81* (2), 143–154.

Groot, A.S., de Sonneville, L.M.J., Stins, J.F. & Boomsma, D.I. (2004). Familial influences on sustained attention and inhibition in preschoolers. *Journal of Child Psychology and Psychiatry, 45* (2), 306–314.

Gross, M.U.M. (1997). How ability grouping turns big fish into little fish - or does it?: Of optical illusions and optimal environments. *The Australasian Journal of Gifted Education, 6* (2), 18–30.

——(2004). *Exceptionally gifted children.* (2nd ed.) Routledge Falmer: London.

Grossman, D.C., Neckerman, H.J., Koepsell, T.D., Liu, P.-Y., Asher, K.N., Beland, K., Frey, K. & Rivara, F.P. (1997). Effectiveness of a violence prevention curriculum among children in elementary school: A randomized controlled trial. *Journal of the American Medical Association, 277* (20), 1605–1611.

Grusec, J.E. & Goodnow, J.J. (1994). Impact of parental discipline methods on the child's internalization of values: A reconceptualization of current points of view. *Developmental Psychology, 30* (1), 4–19.

Grusec, J.E. & Mammone, N. (1995). Features and sources of parents' attributions about themselves and their children. In N. Eisenberg (Ed.) *Review of Personality and Social Psychology: Social Development, (15).* Thousand Oaks, CA: SAGE, 49–73.

Grych, J.H., Jouriles, E.N., Swank, P.R., McDonald, R. & Norwood, W.D. (2000). Patterns of adjustment among children of battered women. *Journal of Consulting and Clinical Psychology, 68* (1), 84–94.

Guerin, D.W. & Gottfried, A.W. (1994). Temperamental consequences of infant difficultness. *Infant Behavior and Development, 17* (4), 413–421.

Gump, P.V. (1990). A short history of the Midwest Psychological Field Station. *Environment and Behavior, 22* (4), 436–457.

Gunnoe, M.L. & Mariner, C.L. (1997). Toward a developmental-contextual model of the effects of parental spanking on children's aggression. *Archives of Pediatric and Adolescent Medicine, 151* (8), 768–775.

Gutin, B. (2011). Diet vs exercise for the prevention of pediatric obesity: The role of exercise. *International Journal of Obesity, 35* (1), 29–32.

Hadjivassiliou, M., Grünewald, R.A., Lawden, M., Davies-Jones, G.A.B., Powell, T. & Smith, C.M.L. (2001). Headache and CNS white matter abnormalities associated with gluten sensitivity. *Neurology, 56* (3), 385–388.

Haensly, P.A. & Reynolds, C.R. (1989). Creativity and intelligence. In J.A. Glover, R.R. Ronning and C.R. Reynolds (Eds.) *Handbook of creativity.* New York: Plenum Press, 111–132.

Hagerman, R.J. & Falkenstein, A.R. (1987). Association between recurrent otitis media in infancy and later hyperactivity. *Clinical Pediatrics, 26* (5), 253–257.

Haines, D.B. & McKeachie, W.J. (1987). Cooperative versus competitive discussion methods in teaching introductory psychology. *Journal of Educational Psychology, 58* (6), 386–390.

Halberstadt, A.G., Denham, S.A. & Dunsmore, J.C. (2001). Affective social competence. *Social Development, 10* (1), 79–119.

Haley, J. (1980). *Leaving home: The therapy of disturbed young people.* San Francisco, CA: Jossey-Bass.

Hallahan, D.P. & Kauffman, J.M. (2003). *Exceptional learners: Introduction to special education.* (9th ed.) Boston, MA: Allyn & Bacon.

——(2006). *Exceptional learners: Introduction to special education.* (10th ed.) Boston, MA: Pearson Allyn & Bacon.

Halle, T.G., Kurtz-Costes, B. & Mahoney, J.L. (1997). Family influences on school achievement in low-income, African American children. *Journal of Educational Psychology, 89* (3), 527–537.

Halpern, L.F. (2004). The relations of coping and family environment to preschoolers' problem behavior. *Journal of Applied Developmental Psychology, 25* (4), 399–421.

Hamre, P.K. & Pianta, R.C. (2001). Early teacher-child relationships and the trajectory of children's school outcomes through eighth grade. *Child Development, 72* (2), 625–638.

——(2005). Can instructional and emotional support in the first-grade classroom make a difference for children at risk of school failure? *Child Development, 76* (5), 949–967.

Han, K-S. & Marvin, C. (2002). Multiple creativities: Investigating domain-specificity of creativity in young children. *Gifted Child Quarterly, 46* (2), 98–109.

Handler, M.W., Rey, J., Connell, J., Thier, K., Feinberg, A. & Putnam, R. (2007). Practical considerations in creating school-wide positive behavior support in public schools. *Psychology in the Schools, 44* (1), 29–39.

Hanish, L.D. & Guerra, N.G. (2000). Predictors of peer victimization among urban youth. *Social Development, 9* (4), 521–543.

——(2004). Aggressive victims, passive victims, and bullies: Developmental continuity or developmental change? *Merrill-Palmer Quarterly, 50* (1), 17–38.

Hanish, L.D., Martin, C.L., Fabes, R.A., Leonard, S. & Herzog, M. (2005a). Exposure to externalizing peers in early childhood: Homophily and peer contagion processes. *Journal of Abnormal Child Psychology, 33* (3), 267–281.

Hanish, L.D., Ryan, P., Martin, C.L. & Fabes, R.A. (2005b). The social context of young children's peer victimization. *Social Development, 14* (1), 2–19.

Hansen, A.L. (2007). School-based support for GLBT students: A review of three levels of research. *Psychology in the Schools, 44* (8), 839–848.

Hansen, M., Janssen, I., Schiff, A., Zee, P.C. & Dubocovich, M.L. (2005). The impact of school daily schedule on adolescent sleep. *Pediatrics, 115* (6), 1555–1561.

Hanson, M.J., Wolfberg, P., Zercher, C., Morgan, M., Gutlerrez, S., Barnwell, D. & Beckman, P. (1998). The culture of inclusion: Recognizing diversity at multiple levels. *Early Childhood Research Quarterly, 13* (1), 185–209.

Harachi, T.W., Fleming, C.B., White, H.R., Ensminger, M.E., Abbott, R.D., Catalano, R.F. & Haggerty, K.P. (2006). Aggressive behavior among girls and boys during middle childhood: Predictors and sequelae of trajectory group membership. *Aggressive Behavior, 32* (4), 279–293.

Harackiewicz, J.M., Barron, K.E., Pintrich, P.R., Elliot, A.J. & Thrash, T.M. (2002). Revision of achievement goal theory: Necessary and illuminating. *Journal of Educational Psychology, 94* (3), 638–645.

Hardre, P.L. & Reeve, J. (2003). A motivational model of rural students' intentions to persist in, versus drop out of, high school. *Journal of Educational Psychology, 95* (2), 347–356.

Harel-Fisch, Y., Walsh, S.D., Fogel-Grinvald, H., Amitai, G., Pickett, W., Molcho, M., Due, P., de Matos, M.G., Craig, W., Members of the HBSC Violence and Injury Prevention Focus Group. (2011). Negative school perceptions and involvement in school bullying: A universal relationship across 40 countries. *Journal of Adolescence, 34* (4), 639–652.

Hargreaves, A. (2000). Mixed emotions: Teachers' perceptions of their interactions with students. *Teaching and Teacher Education, 16* (8), 811–826.

Harker, M. (2001). How to build solutions at meetings. In Y. Ajmal and I. Rees (Eds.) *Solutions in schools.* London: BT Press, 30–44.

Harmon, D. (2002). They won't teach me: The voices of gifted African American inner-city students. *Roeper Review, 24* (2), 68–75.

Harris, M.B. (2000). Correlates and characteristics of boredom proneness and boredom. *Journal of Applied Social Psychology, 30* (3), 576–598.

Harris, R. (2007). *The happiness trap: Stop struggling, start living.* Wollombi, NSW: Exisle.

Harrison, J. (2004). *Understanding children: Foundations for quality.* (3rd ed.) Melbourne: ACER.

Harrist, A.W., Zaia, A.E., Bates, J.E., Dodge, K.A. & Pettit, G.S. (1997). Subtypes of social withdrawal in early childhood: Sociometric status and social-cognitive differences across four years. *Child Development, 68* (2), 278–294.

Hart, C.H., Burts, D.C., Durland, M.A., Charlesworth, R., DeWolf, M. & Fleege, P.O. (1998). Stress behaviors and activity type participation of preschoolers in more and less developmentally appropriate classrooms: SES and sex differences. *Journal of Research in Childhood Education, 12* (2), 176–196.

Hart, C.H., DeWolf, D.M. & Burts, D.C. (1992a). Linkages among preschoolers' playground behavior, outcome expectations, and parental disciplinary strategies. *Early Education and Development, 3* (4), 265–283.

Hart, C.H., DeWolf, D.M., Wozniak, P. & Burts, D.C. (1992b). Maternal and paternal disciplinary styles: Relations with preschoolers' playground behavioral orientations and peer status. *Child Development, 63* (4), 879–892.

Hart, E.L., Lahey, B.B., Loeber, R., Applegate, B. & Frick, P.J. (1995). Developmental change in attention-deficit hyperactivity in boys: A four-year longitudinal study. *Journal of Abnormal Child Psychology, 23* (6), 729–749.

Hart, S. & Hodson, V.K. (2004). *The compassionate classroom: Relationship based teaching and learning.* Encinitas, CA: Puddle Dancer Press.

——(2006). *Respectful parents; respectful kids: 7 keys to turn family conflict into co-operation.* Encinitas, CA: Puddle Dancer Press.

Harter, S. (1978). Pleasure derived from challenge and the effects of receiving grades on children's difficulty level choices. *Child Development, 49* (3), 788–799.

——(1998). The effects of child abuse on the self-esteem. In B.B.R. Rossman & M.S. Rosenberg (Eds.) *Multiple victimization of children: Conceptual, developmental, research and treatment issues.* New York: Haworth Press, 147–169.

Harter, S., Waters, P. & Whitesell, N.R. (1997). Lack of voice as a manifestation of false self behavior among adolescents: The school setting as a stage upon which the drama of authenticity is enacted. *Educational Psychologist, 32* (3), 153–173.

Harter, S., & Whitesell, N.R. (2003). Beyond the debate: Why some adolescents report stable self-worth over time and situation, whereas others report changes in self-worth. *Journal of Personality, 71* (6), 1027–1058.

Hartup, W.W. (1979). Peer relations and social competence. In M.W. Kent and J.E. Rolf (Eds.) *Social competence in children*. Hanover, NH: University Press of New England, 150–170.

Hartup, W.W. (1989). Social relationships and their developmental significance. *American Psychologist, 44* (2), 120–126.

——(1996). The company they keep: Friendships and their developmental significance. *Child Development, 67* (1), 1–13.

Hartup, W.W. & Moore, S.G. (1990). Early peer relations: Developmental significance and prognostic implications. *Early Childhood Research Quarterly, 5* (1), 1–17.

Hastings, P.D., Fortier, I., Utendale, W.T., Simard, L.R. & Robaey, P. (2009). Adrenocortical functioning in boys with attention-deficit/hyperactivity disorder: Examining subtypes of ADHD and associated comorbid conditions. *Journal of Abnormal Child Psychology, 37* (4), 565–578.

Hastings, P.D. & Grusec, J.E. (1997). Conflict outcomes as a function of parental accuracy in perceiving child cognitions and affect. *Social Development, 6* (1), 76–90.

Hastings, P.D. & Rubin, K.H. (1999). Predicting mothers' beliefs about preschool-aged children's social behavior: Evidence for maternal attitudes moderating child effects. *Child Development, 70* (3), 722–741.

Hastings, P.D., Zahn-Waxler, C., Robinson, J., Usher, B. & Bridges, D. (2000). The development of concern for others in children with behavior problems. *Developmental Psychology, 36* (5), 531–546.

Haveman, R. & Wolfe, B. (1995). The determinants of children's attainments: A review of methods and findings. *Journal of Economic Literature, 33* (4), 1829–1878.

Hawkins, D.L., Pepler, D.J. & Craig, W.M. (2001). Naturalistic observations of peer interventions in bullying. *Social Development, 10* (4), 512–527.

Hawkins, J.D., Guo, J., Hill, K.G., Battin-Pearson, S. & Abbott, R.D. (2001). Long-term effects of the Seattle Social Development Intervention on school bonding trajectories. *Applied Developmental Science, 5* (4), 225–236.

Hawley, P.H. & Little, T.D. (1999). On winning some and losing some: A social relations approach to social dominance in toddlers. *Merrill-Palmer Quarterly, 45* (2), 185–214.

Hay, D.F., Nash, A. & Pedersen, J. (1981). Responses of six-month-olds to the distress of their peers. *Child Development, 52* (3), 1071–1075.

Hay, D.F., Payne, A. & Chadwick, A. (2004). Peer relations in childhood. *Journal of Child Psychology and Psychiatry, 45* (1), 84–108.

Haynes-Seman, C. & Baumgarten, D. (1998). The victimization of young children. In B.B.R. Rossman and M.S. Rosenberg (Eds.) *Multiple victimization of children: Conceptual, developmental, research, and treatment issues*. New York: Haworth Press, 67–86.

Heatherton, T.F. & Vohs, K.D. (2000). Interpersonal evaluations following threats to self: Role of self-esteem. *Journal of Personality and Social Psychology, 78* (4), 725–736.

Heck, A., Collins, J. & Peterson, L. (2001). Decreasing children's risk taking on the playground. *Journal of Applied Behavior Analysis, 34* (3), 349–352.

Henderson, H.A., Marshall, P.J., Fox, N.A. & Rubin, K.H. (2004). Psychophysiological and behavioral evidence for varying forms and functions of nonsocial behavior in preschoolers. *Child Development, 75* (1), 251–263.

Henington, C., Hughes, J.N., Cavell, T.A. & Thompson, B. (1998). The role of relational aggression in identifying aggressive boys and girls. *Journal of School Psychology, 36* (4), 457–477.

Hennessey, B.A. & Amabile, T.M. (1998). Reward, intrinsic motivation, and creativity. *American Psychologist, 53* (6), 674–675.

Henning-Stout, M. (1998). Assessing the behavior of girls: What we see and what we miss. *Journal of School Psychoogy, 36* (4), 433–455.

Henning-Stout, M., James, S. & Macintosh, S. (2000). Reducing harassment of lesbian, gay, bisexual, transgender, and questioning youth in schools. *School Psychology Review, 29* (2), 180–191.

Henricsson, L. & Rydell, A.-M. (2004). Elementary school children with behavior problems: Teacher-child relations and self-perception: A prospective study. *Merrill-Palmer Quarterly, 50* (2), 111–138.

Henry, D.B., Farrell, A.D., Schoeny, M.E., Tolan, P.H. & Dymnicki, A.B. (2011). Influence of school-level variables on aggression and associated attitudes of middle school students. *Journal of School Psychology, 49* (5), 481–503.

Herrera, C. & Dunn, J. (1997). Early experiences with family conflict: Implications for arguments with a close friend. *Developmental Psychology, 33* (5), 869–881.

Hess, L.L. (1994). Life, liberty and the pursuit of perfection. *Gifted Child Today, 17* (3), 28–31.

Hickey, D.T. (1997). Motivation and contemporary socio-constructivist instructional perspectives. *Educational Psychologist, 32* (3), 175–193.

Hidi, S. & Renninger, K.A. (2006). The four-phase model of interest development. *Educational Psychologist, 41* (2), 111–127.

Hill, A.B. & Perkins, R.E. (1985). Towards a model of boredom. *British Journal of Psychology, 76* (2), 235–240.

Hill, A.L., Degnan, K.A., Calkins, S.D. & Keane, S.P. (2006). Profiles of externalizing behavior problems for boys and girls across preschool: The roles of emotion regulation and inattention. *Developmental Psychology, 42* (5), 913–928.

Hill, L.G. & Werner, N.E. (2006). Affiliative motivation, school attachment, and aggression in school. *Psychology in the Schools, 43* (2), 231–246.

Hill, M.S. & Jenkins, S.P. (2001). Poverty among British children: Chronic or transitory? In B. Bradbury, S.P. Jenkins and J. Micklewright (Eds.) *The dynamics of child poverty in industrialised countries*. Cambridge, UK: Cambridge University Press, 174–195.

Hill, N.E., Castellino, D.R., Lansford, J.E., Nowlin, P., Dodge, K.A., Bates, J.E. & Pettit, G.S. (2004). Parent academic involvement as related to school behavior, achievement and aspirations: Demographic variations across adolescence. *Child Development, 75* (5), 1491–1509.

Hill, N.E. & Taylor, L.C. (2004). Parental school involvement and children's academic achievement: Pragmatics and issues. *Current Directions in Psychological Science, 13* (4), 161–164.

Hill, S. & Hill, T. (1990). *The collaborative classroom: A guide to cooperative learning*. Melbourne: Eleanor Curtin.

Hilliard, A.G. (1985). What is quality care? In B.M. Caldwell and A.G. Hilliard III (Eds.) *What is quality care?* Washington, DC: National Association for the Education of Young Children, 17–32.

Hilton, G. & Hilton, A. (2010). Higher order thinking. In D. Prendergast and N. Bahr (Eds.) *Teaching middle years: Rethinking curriculum, pedagogy and assessment*. (2nd ed.) Sydney: Allen & Unwin.

Hirsch, B.J. & DuBois, D.L. (1991). Self-esteem in early adolescence: The identification and prediction of contrasting longitudinal trajectories. *Journal of Youth and Adolescence, 20* (1), 53–72.

Ho, E.S.-C. & Willms, J.D. (1996). Effects of parental involvement on eight-grade achievement. *Sociology of Education, 69* (2), 126–141.

Hodges, E.V.E., Boivin, M., Vitaro, F. & Bukowski, W.M. (1999). The power of friendship: Protection against an escalating cycle of peer victimization. *Developmental Psychology, 35* (1), 94–101.

Hodges, E.V.E., Malone, M.J. & Perry, D.G. (1997). Individual risk and social risk as interacting determinants of victimization in the peer group. *Developmental Psychology, 33* (6), 1032–1039.

Hodges, E.V.E. & Perry, D.G. (1999). Personal and interpersonal antecedents and consequences of victimization by peers. *Journal of Personality and Social Pyschology, 76* (4), 677–685.

Hoeve, M., Dubas, J.S., Eichelsheim, V.I., van der Laan, P.H., Smeenk, W. & Gerris, J.R.M. (2009). The relationship between parenting and delinquency: A meta-analysis. *Journal of Abnormal Child Psychology, 37* (6), 749–775.

Hoff, K.E., Reese-Weber, M., Schneider, W.J. & Stagg, J.W. (2009). The association between high status positions and aggressive behavior in early adolescence. *Journal of School Psychology, 47* (6), 395–426.

Hoffman, M.L. (1960). Power assertion by the parent and its impact on the child. *Child Development, 31,* 129–143.

——(1981). Is altruism part of human nature?. *Journal of Personality and Social Psychology, 40* (1), 121–137.

Hoffman, M.L. & Saltzstein. H.D. (1967). Parent discipline and the child's moral development. *Journal of Personality and Social Psychology, 5* (1), 45–57.

Hoffman-Plotkin, D. & Twentyman, C.T. (1984). A multimodal assessment of behavioral and cognitive deficits in abused and neglected preschoolers. *Child Development, 55* (3), 794–802.

Hoge, R.D. & Renzulli, J.S. (1993). Exploring the link between giftedness and self-concept. *Review of Educational Research, 63* (4), 449–465.

Hoge, R.D. & McSheffrey, R. (1991). An investigation of self-concept in gifted children. *Exceptional Children, 57* (3), 238–245.

Hoglund, W.L.G., Lalonde, C.E. & Leadbeater, B.J. (2008). Social-cognitive competence, peer rejection and neglect, and behavioral and emotional problems in middle childhood. *Social Development, 17* (3), 528–553.

Holden, G.W. (2002). Perspectives on the effects of corporal punishment: Comment on Gershoff (2002). *Psychological Bulletin, 128* (4), 590–595.

Holland, P. (2004). *Picturing childhood: The myth of the child in popular imagery.* London: I.B. Tauris.

Holt, M.K., Kinkelhor, D. & Kantor, G.K. (2007). Hidden forms of victimization in elementary students involved in bullying. *School Psychology Review, 36* (3), 345–360.

Hong, J.S., Espelage, D.L. & Kral, M.J. (2011). Understanding suicide among sexual minority youth in America: An ecological systems analysis. *Journal of Adolescence, 34* (5), 885–894.

Hong, S. & Ho, H.-Z. (2005). Direct and indirect longitudinal effects of parental involvement on student achievement: Second-order latent growth modeling across ethnic groups. *Journal of Educational Psychology, 97* (1), 32–42.

Honig, A.S. & Wittmer, D.S. (1996). Helping children become more prosocial: Ideas for classrooms, families, schools and communities. *Young Children, 51* (2), 62–70.

Hooper, S.R. & Edmondson, R. (1998). Assessment of young children: Standards, stages and approaches. In W. Umansky and S.R. Hooper (Eds.) *Young children with special needs.* (3rd ed.) Upper Saddle River, NJ: Merrill, 340–371.

Hope, T.L. & Bierman, K.L. (1998). Patterns of home and school behavior problems in rural and urban settings. *Journal of School Psychology, 36* (1), 45–58.

Horner, S.B., Fireman, G.D. & Wang, E.W. (2010). The relation of student behavior, peer status, race, and gender to decisions about school discipline using CHAID decision trees and regression modeling. *Journal of School Psychology, 48* (2), 135–161.

Horner, R.H., Sugain, G., Smolkowski, K., Eber, L., Nakasato, J.,

Todd, A.W & Esperanza, J. (2009). A randomized, wait-list controlled effectiveness trial assessing school-wide positive behavior support in elementary schools. *Journal of Positive Behavior Interventions, 11* (3), 133–144.

Howes, C. (1983). Caregiver behavior in center and family day care. *Journal of Applied Developmental Psychology, 4* (1), 99–107.

——(1997). Children's experiences in center-based child care as a function of teacher background and adult:child ratio. *Merrill-Palmer Quarterly, 43* (3), 404–425.

——(2000). Social-emotional classroom climate in child care, child-teacher relationships and children's second grade peer relations. *Social Development, 9* (2), 191–204.

Howes, C., James, J. & Ritchie, S. (2003). Pathways to effective teaching. *Early Childhood Research Quarterly, 18* (1), 104–120.

Hoza, B., Waschbusch, D.A., Pelham, W.E., Molina, B.S.G. & Milich, R. (2000). Attention-deficit/hyperactivity disordered and control boys' responses to social success and failure. *Child Development, 71* (2), 432–446.

Hubbard, J.A. (2001). Emotion expression processes in children's peer interaction: The role of peer rejection, aggression, and gender. *Child Development, 72* (5), 1426–1438.

Huberman, M. (1989). The professional life cycle of teachers. *Teachers College Record, 91* (1), 31–57.

Hudley, C., Britsch, B., Wakefield, W.D., Smith, T., Demorat, M. & Cho, S.-J. (1998). An attribution retraining program to reduce aggression in elementary school students. *Psychology in the Schools, 35* (3), 271–282.

Huesmann, L.R., Dubow, E.F. & Boxer, P. (2009). Continuity of aggression from childhood to early adulthood as a predictor of life outcomes: Implications for the adolescent-limited and life-course-persistent models. *Aggressive Behavior, 35* (2), 136–149.

Huffman, L.R. & Speer, P.W. (2000). Academic performance among at-risk children: The role of developmentally appropriate practices. *Early Childhood Research Quarterly, 15* (2), 167–184.

Hughes, C., Cutting, A.L. & Dunn, J. (2001). Acting nasty in the face of failure?: Longitudinal observations of 'hard-to-manage' children playing a rigged competitive game with a friend. *Journal of Abnormal Child Psychology, 29* (5), 405–416.

Hughes, J.N., Cavell, T.A. & Willson, V. (2001). Further support for the developmental significance of the quality of the teacher-student relationship. *Journal of School Psychology, 39* (4), 289–301.

Hughes, J.N. & Kwok, O.-M. (2007). Influence of student-teacher and parent-teacher relationships on lower achieving readers' engagement and achievement in the primary grades. *Journal of Educational Psychology, 99* (1), 39–51.

Hughes, J.N., Wu, W. & West, S.G. (2011). Teacher performance goal practices and elementary students' behavioral engagement: A developmental perspective. *Journal of School Psychology, 49* (1), 1–23.

Hunter, S.C. & Boyle, J.M.E. (2004). Appraisal and coping strategy use in victims of school bullying. *British Journal of Educational Psychology, 74* (1), 83–107.

Hunter, S.C., Boyle, J.M.E. & Warden, D. (2007). Perceptions and correlates of peer-victimization and bullying. *British Journal of Educational Psychology, 77* (4), 797–810.

Huntley, J. (1999). A narrative approach to working with students who have 'learning difficulties'. In A. Morgan (Ed.) *Once upon a time . . . Narrative therapy with children and their families.* Adelaide, SA: Dulwich Centre Publications, 35–49.

Huston-Stein, A., Friedrich-Cofer, L. & Susman, E.J. (1977). The relation of classroom structure to social behavior, imaginative play, and self-regulation in economically disadvantaged children. *Child Development, 48* (3), 908–916.

Hyman, I.A. (1995). Corporal punishment, psychological maltreatment, violence, and punitiveness in America: Research, advocacy, and public policy. *Applied and Preventive Psychology, 4* (2), 113–130.

Hyman, I.A. & Perone, D.C. (1998). The other side of school violence: Educator policies and practices that may contribute to student misbehavior. *Journal of School Psychology, 36* (1), 7–27.

Hyman, I.A. & Snook, P.A. (2000). Dangerous schools and what you can do about them. *Phi Delta Kappan 81* (7), 489–501.

Hymel, S., Rubin, K.H., Rowden, L. & LeMare, L. (1990). Children's peer relationships: longitudinal prediction of internalizing and externalizing problems in middle to late childhood. *Child Development, 61* (6), 2004–2021.

Ingersoll, R.M. (1996). Teachers' decision-making power and school conflict. *Sociology of Education, 69* (2), 159–176.

Ingoldsby, E.M., Shaw, D.S., Winslow, E., Schonberg, M., Gilliom, M. & Criss, M.M. (2006). Neighborhood disadvantage, parent-child conflict, neighborhood peer relationships, and early antisocial behavior problem trajectories. *Journal of Abnormal Child Psychology, 34* (3), 303–319.

Irvin, M.J. (2012). Role of student engagement in the resilience of African American adolescents from low-income rural communities. *Psychology in the Schools, 49* (2), 176–193.

Ispa, J.M., Fine, M.A., Halgunseth, L.C., Harper, S., Robinson, J., Boyce, L., Brooks-Gunn, J. & Brady-Smith, C. (2004). Maternal intrusiveness, maternal warmth, and mother-toddler relationship outcomes: Variations across low-income ethnic and acculturation groups. *Child Development, 75* (6), 1613–1631.

Iwata, B.A., Pace, G.M., Cowdery, G.E. & Miltenberger, R.G. (1994). What makes extinction work: An analysis of procedural form and function. *Journal of Applied Behavior Analysis 27* (1), 131–144.

Izzo, C.V., Weissberg, R.P., Kasprow, W.J. & Fendrich, M. (1999). A longitudinal assessment of teacher perceptions of parent involvement in children's education and school performance. *American Journal of Community Psychology, 27* (6), 817–839.

Jack, S.L., Shores, R.E., Denny, R.K., Gunter, P.L., DeBriere, T. & DaPaepe, P. (1996). An analysis of the relationship of teachers' reported use of classroom management strategies on types of classroom interactions. *Journal of Behavioral Education, 6* (1), 67–87.

Jacobs, B. (2005). The myth of ADHD: Psychiatric oppression of children. In J. Bessant, R. Hill and R. Watts (Eds.) *Violations of trust: How social and welfare institutions fail children and young people.* Hampshire, UK: Ashgate, 133–146.

Jaffee, S.R., Moffitt, T.E., Caspi, A. & Taylor, A. (2003). Life with (or without) father: The benefits of living with two biological parents depend on the father's antisocial behavior. *Child Development, 74* (1), 109–126.

Jakubowski, P. (1977). Self-assertion training procedures for women. In E. Rowling and D. Carter (Eds.) *Psychotherapy for women.* Springfield, IL: Charles C. Thomas.

Jakubowski, P. & Lange, A. (1978). *The assertive option: Your rights and responsibilities.* Champaign, IL: Research Press.

James, R. & Owens, L.D. (2004). Peer victimization and conflict resolution among adolescent girls in a single-sex South Australian school. *International Education Journal, 5* (1), 37–49.

——(2005). 'They turned around like I wasn't there': An analysis of teenage girls' letters about their peer conflicts. *School Psychology International, 26* (1), 71–88.

Jan, J. (2010). Melatonin therapy for sleep disorders. In K. Siri & T. Lyons (Eds.) *Cutting-edge therapies for autism 2010-2011.* New York: Skyhorse, 221–226.

Jang, H. (2008). Supporting students' motivation, engagement, and learning during an uninteresting activity. *Journal of Educational Psychology, 100* (4), 798–811.

Jang, H., Reeve, J. & Deci, E.L. (2010). Engaging students in learning activities: It is not autonomy support or structure, but autonomy support and structure. *Journal of Educational Psychology, 102* (3), 588–600.

Jang, H., Reeve, J., Ryan, R.M. & Kim, A. (2009). Can self-determination theory explain what underlies the productive, satisfying learning experiences of collectivistically oriented Korean students?. *Journal of Educational Psychology, 101* (3), 644–661.

Jenkins, J.R., Antil, L.R., Wayne, S.K. & Vadasy, P.F. (2003). How cooperative learning works for special education and remedial students. *Exceptional Children, 69* (3), 279–292.

Jesberger, J.A. & Richardson, J.S. (1991). Oxygen free radicals and brain dysfunction. *International Journal of Neuroscience, 57* (1), 1–17.

Jeynes, W.H. (2007). The relationship between parental involvement and urban secondary school student academic achievement: A meta-analysis. *Urban Education, 42* (1), 82–110.

Jodl, K.M., Michael, A., Malanchuk, O., Eccles, J.S. & Sameroff, A. (2001). Parents' roles in shaping early adolescents' occupational aspirations. *Child Development, 72* (4), 1247–1265.

Johnny, L. (2006). Reconceptualising childhood: Children's rights and youth participation in schools. *International Education Journal, 7* (1), 17–25.

Johnson, B., Whitington, V. & Oswald, M. (1994). Teachers' views on school discipline: A theoretical framework. *Cambridge Journal of Education, 24* (2), 261–276.

Johnson, B.M., Miltenberger, R.G., Egemo-Helm, K., Jostad, C.M., Flessner, C. & Gatheridge, B. (2005). Evaluation of behavioral skills training for teaching abduction-prevention skills to young children. *Journal of Applied Behavior Analysis, 38* (1), 67–78.

Johnson, C., Ironsmith, M., Snow, C.W. & Poteat, G.M. (2000). Peer acceptance and social adjustment in preschool and kindergarten. *Early Childhood Education Journal, 27* (4), 207–212.

Johnson, D.W. & Johnson, R.T. (1974). Instructional goal structure: Cooperative, competitive, or individualistic. *American Educational Research Journal, 44* (2), 213–240.

Johnson, D.W. & Johnson, R.T. (1981). Effects of cooperative and individualistic learning experiences on interethnic interaction. *Journal of Educational Psychology, 73* (3), 444–449.

——(1989). Social skills for successful group work. *Educational Leadership, 47* (4), 29–33.

——(1991). *Learning together and alone.* (3rd ed.) Boston, MA: Allyn & Bacon.

Johnson, D.W., Johnson, R.T. & Maruyama, G. (1983). Interdependence and interpersonal attraction among heterogeneous and homogeneous individuals: A theoretical formulation and a meta-analysis of the research. *Review of Educational Research, 53* (1), 5–54.

Johnson, D.W., Johnson, R.T. & Scott, L. (1978). The effects of cooperative and individualized instruction on student attitudes and achievement. *Journal of Social Psychology, 104* (2), 207–216.

Johnston, J.M. (1972). Punishment of human behavior. *American Psychologist, 27* (11), 1033–1054.

Jolliffe, D. & Farrington, D.P. (2006). Examining the relationship between low empathy and bullying. *Aggressive Behavior, 32* (6), 540–550.

——(2011). Is low empathy related to bullying after controlling for individual and social background variables?. *Journal of Adolescence, 34* (1), 59–71.

Jones, D.C., Newman, J.B. & Bautista, S. (2005). A three-factor model of teasing: The influence of friendship, gender, and topic on expected emotional reactions to teasing during early adolescence. *Social Development, 14* (3), 421–439.

Jones, K.M., Young, M.M. & Friman, P.C. (2000). Increasing peer praise of socially rejected delinquent youth: Effects on cooperation and acceptance. *School Psychology Quarterly, 15* (1), 30–39.

Jones, S.M. & Dindia, K. (2004). A meta-analytic perspective on sex equity in the classroom. *Review of Educational Research, 74* (4), 443–471.

Jones, V.F. & Jones, L.S. (2013). *Comprehensive classroom management: Creating communities of support and solving problems.* (10th ed.) Boston, MA: Pearson.

Jordon, K.M., Vaughan, J.S. & Woodworth, K.J. (1997). I will survive: Lesbian, gay, and bisexual youths' experience of high school. *Journal of Gay and Lesbian Social Services, 7* (4), 17–33.

Joussemet, M., Vitaro, F., Barker, E.D., Côté, S., Nagin, D.S., Zoccolillo, M. & Tremblay, R.E. (2008). Controlling parenting and physical aggression during elementary school. *Child Development, 79* (2), 411–425.

Jules, V. (1991). Interaction dynamics of cooperative learning groups in Trinidad's secondary schools. *Adolescence, 26* (104), 931–949.

Jules, V. & Kutnick, P. (1997). Student perceptions of a good teacher: The gender perspective. *British Journal of Educational Psychology, 67* (4), 497–511.

Juvonen, J., Nishina, A. & Graham, S. (2000). Peer harassment, psychological adjustment, and school functioning in early adolescence. *Journal of Educational Psychology, 92* (2), 349–359.

Kaffenberger, C.J. (2006). School reentry for students with a chronic illness: A role for professional school counselors. *Professional School Counseling, 9* (3), 223–230.

Kagan, S.L. & Knight, G.P. (1979). Cooperation-competition and self-esteem: A case of cultural relativism. *Journal of Cross-Cultural Psychology, 10* (4), 457–467.

Kahng, S.W., Boscoe, J.H. & Byrne, S. (2003). The use of an escape contingency and a token economy to increase food acceptance. *Journal of Applied Behavior Analysis, 36* (3), 349–353.

Kaiser, A.P., Hancock, T.B., Cai, X., Foster, E.M. & Hester, P.P. (2000). Parent-reported behavioral problems and language delays in boys and girls enrolled in Head Start classrooms. *Behavioral Disorders, 26* (1), 26–41.

Kakihara, F. & Tilton-Weaver, L. (2009). Adolescents' interpretations of parental control: Differentiated by domain and types of control. *Child Development, 80* (6), 1722–1738.

Kaler, S.R. & Kopp, C.B. (1990). Compliance and comprehension in very young toddlers. *Child Development, 61* (6), 1997–2003.

Kamins, M.L. & Dweck, C.S. (1999). Person versus process praise and criticism: Implications for contingent self-worth and coping. *Developmental Psychology, 35* (3), 835–847.

Kamps, D.M. (2002). Preventing problems by improving behavior. In B. Algozzine and P. Kay (Eds.) *Preventing problem behaviors: A handbook of successful prevention strategies.* Thousand Oaks, CA: Corwin Press, 11–36.

Kant, I. (1785/1996). Groundwork of the metaphysics of morals.

In M.J. Gregor (Ed.) *Practical philosophy.* Cambridge, UK: Cambridge University Press, 49–93.

Kaplan, A., Gheen, M. & Midgley, C. (2002). Classroom goal structure and student disruptive behaviour. *British Journal of Educational Psychology, 72* (2), 191–211.

Kaplan, C. (1992). Teachers' punishment histories and their selection of disciplinary strategies. *Contemporary Educational Psychologist, 17* (3), 258–265.

Kaplan, J.S. & Carter, J. (1995). *Beyond behavior modification: A cognitive-behavioral approach to behavior management in the school.* (3rd ed.) Austin, TX: Pro-Ed.

Karatekin, C. (2004). A test of integrity of the components of Baddeley's model of working memory in attention-deficit/ hyperactivity disorder (ADHD). *Journal of Child Psychology and Psychiatry, 45* (5), 912–926.

Kasser, T. & Ryan, R.M. (1996). Further examining the American dream: Differential correlates of intrinsic and extrinsic goals. *Personality and Social Psychology Bulletin, 22* (3), 280–287.

Kats-Gold, I. & Priel, B. (2009). Emotion, understanding, and social skills among boys at risk of attention deficit hyperactivity disorder. *Psychology in the Schools, 46* (7), 658–678.

Katsurada, E. & Sugawara, A.I. (1998). The relationship between hostile attributional bias and aggressive behavior in preschoolers. *Early Childhood Research Quarterly, 13* (4), 623–636.

Katz, L.F., Hessler, D.M. & Annest, A. (2007). Domestic violence, emotional competence, and child adjustment. *Social Development, 16* (3), 513–538.

Katz, L.F. & Woodin, E.M. (2002). Hostility, hostile detachment, and conflict engagement in marriages: Effects on child and family functioning. *Child Development, 73* (2), 636–652.

Katz, L.G. (1995). *Talks with teachers of young children.* Norwood, NJ: Ablex.

Kaufmann, D., Gesten, E., Santa Lucia, R.C., Salcedo, O., Rendina-Gobioff, G. & Gadd, R. (2000). The relationship between parenting style and children's adjustment: The parents' perspective. *Journal of Child and Family Studies, 9* (2), 231–245.

Kaukiainen, A., Björkqvist, K., Lagerspetz, K., Österman, K., Salmivalli, C., Rothberg, S. & Ahlbom, A. (1999). The relationship between social intelligence, empathy, and three types of aggression. *Aggressive Behavior, 25* (2), 81–89.

Kavussanu, M. & Harnisch, D.L. (2000). Self-esteem in children: Do goal orientations matter?. *British Journal of Educational Psychology, 70* (2), 229–242.

Kazdin, A.E. (1997). Parent management training: Evidence, outcomes, and issues. *Journal of the American Academy of Child and Adolescent Psychiatry, 36* (10), 1349–1356.

Kazdin, A.E. & Benjet, C. (2003). Spanking children: Evidence and issues. *Current Directions in Psychological Science, 12* (3), 99–103.

Kazdin, A.E. & Weisz, J.R. (1998). Identifying and developing empirically supported child and adolescent treatments. *Journal of Consulting and Clinical Psychology, 66* (1), 19–36.

Kearney, A.J. (2008). *Understanding applied behaviour analysis: An introduction to ABA for parents, teachers, and other professionals.* London: Jessica Kingsley.

Keiley, M.K., Bates, J.E., Dodge, K.E. & Pettit, G.S. (2000). A cross-domain growth analysis: Externalizing and internalizing behaviors during eight years of childhood. *Journal of Abnormal Child Psychology, 28* (2), 161–179.

Kellam, S.G., Ling, X., Merisca, R., Brown, C.H. & Ialongo, N. (1998). The effect of level of aggression in the first grade classroom on the course and malleability of aggressive behavior into middle school. *Development and Psychopathology, 10* (2), 165–185.

Kelley, H.H. & Stahelski, A.J. (1970). Social interaction basis of cooperators' and competitors' beliefs about others. *Journal of Personality and Social Psychology, 16* (1), 66–91.

Kelley, M.E., Piazza, C.C., Fisher, W.W. & Oberdorff, A.J. (2003). Acquisition of cup drinking using previously refused foods as positive and negative reinforcement. *Journal of Applied Behavior Analysis, 36* (1), 89–93.

Kelly, B. (1996). The ecology of peer relations. *Early Child Development and Care, 115* (1), 99–114.

Kelly, K.R. & Moon, S.M. (1998). Personal and social talents. *Phi Delta Kappan, 79* (10), 743–746.

Kelly, M.S., Kim, J.S. & Franklin, C. (2008). *Solution-focused brief therapy in schools: A 360-degree view of research and practice.* New York: Oxford University Press.

Kelso, J. & Stewart, M.A. (1986). Factors which predict the persistence of aggressive conduct disorder. *Journal of Child Psychology and Psychiatry, 27* (1), 77–86.

Kemple, K.M. (1991). Preschool children's peer acceptance and social interaction. *Young Children, 46* (5), 47–54.

Kendall, P.C. & Panichelli-Mindel, S.M. (1995). Cognitive-behavioral treatments. *Journal of Abnormal Child Psychology, 23* (1), 107–124.

Kendrick, K., Jutengren, G. & Stattin, H. (2012). The protective role of supportive friends against bullying perpetration and victimization. *Journal of Adolescence, 35* (4), 1069–1080.

Kennedy, C.H. (2000). When reinforcers for problem behavior are not readily apparent: Extending functional assessment to complex behavior problems. *Journal of Positive Behavior Interventions, 2* (4), 195–201.

Kern, L. & Clemens, N.H. (2007). Antecedent strategies to promote appropriate classroom behavior. *Psychology in the Schools, 44* (1), 65–75.

Kern, L., Hilt-Panahon, A. & Sokol, N.G. (2009). Further examining the triangle tip: Improving support for students with emotional and behavioral needs. *Psychology in the Schools, 46* (1), 18–32.

Kern, L. & Manz, P. (2004). A look at current validity issues of school-wide behavior support. *Behavior Disorders, 30* (1), 47–59.

Kernis, M.H. (2003). Toward a conceptualization of optimal self-esteem. *Psychological Inquiry, 14* (1), 1–26.

Kernis, M.H., Brown, A.C. & Brody, G.H. (2000). Fragile self-esteem in children and its associations with perceived patterns of parent-child communication. *Journal of Personality, 68* (2), 225–252.

Kernis, M.H., Grannemann, B.D. & Barclay, L.C. (1989). Stability and level of self-esteem as predictors of anger arousal and hostility. *Journal of Personality and Social Psychology, 56* (6), 1013–1022.

Kerr, B.A. (1996). *Smart girls two: A new psychology of girls, women and giftedness.* Melbourne: Hawker Brownlow Education.

—(1997). Developing talents in girls and young women. In N. Colangelo and G.A. Davis (Eds.) *Handbook of gifted education.* (2nd ed.) Boston, MA: Allyn & Bacon, 483–497.

Kerr, B., Colangelo, N. & Gaeth, J. (1988). Gifted adolescents' attitudes towards their giftedness. *Gifted Child Quarterly, 32* (2), 245–247.

Kerr, M.M. & Nelson, C.M. (2010). *Strategies for addressing behavior problems in the classroom.* (6th ed.) Boston, MA: Pearson.

Kerr, M. & Stattin, H. (2000). What parents know, how they know it, and several forms of adolescent adjustment: Further support for a reinterpretation of monitoring. *Developmental Psychology, 36* (3), 366–380.

Kerr, M., Stattin, H. & Özdemir, M. (2012). Perceived parenting style and adolescent adjustment: Revisiting directions of effects and the role of parental knowledge. *Developmental Psychology, 48* (6), 1540–1553.

Kerwin, M.E., Ahearn, W.H., Eichers, P.S. & Burd, D.M. (1995). The costs of eating: A behavioral economic analysis of food refusal. *Journal of Applied Behavior Analysis, 28* (3), 245–260.

Keyser, J. (2006). *From parents to partners: Building a family-centered early childhood program.* St Paul, MN: Redleaf Press.

Khoury-Kassabri, M., Astor, R.A. & Benbenishty, R. (2008). Student victimization by school staff in the context of an Israeli national school safety campaign. *Aggressive Behavior, 34* (1), 1–8.

Kiesner, J., Maass, A., Cadinu, M. & Vallese, I. (2003). Risk factors for ethnic prejudice during early adolescence. *Social Development, 12* (2), 288–308.

Kilderry, A. (2004). Critical pedagogy: A useful framework for thinking about early childhood curriculum. *Australian Journal of Early Childhood, 29* (4), 33–37.

Kilgore, K., Snyder, J. & Lentz, C. (2000). The contribution of parental discipline, parenting monitoring, and school risk to early-onset conduct problems in African-American boys and girls. *Developmental Psychology, 36* (6), 835–845.

Kim, J. & Cicchetti, D. (2004). A longitudinal study of child maltreatment, mother-child relationship quality and maladjustment: The role of self-esteem and social competence. *Journal of Abnormal Child Psychology, 32* (4), 341–354.

Kim, J. & Cicchetti, D. (2006). Longitudinal trajectories of self-system processes and depressive symptoms among maltreated and nonmaltreated children. *Child Development, 77* (3), 624–639.

Kim, J.E., Hetherington, E.M. & Reiss, D. (1999). Associations among family relationships, antisocial peers, and adolescents' externalizing behaviors: Gender and family type differences. *Child Development, 70* (5), 1209–1230.

King, K., Gurian, M. & Stevens, K. (2010). Gender-friendly schools. *Educational Leadership, 68* (3), 38–42.

King, L.A. (1996). Who is regulating what and why?: Motivational context of self-regulation. *Psychological Inquiry, 7* (1), 57–60.

King, M.B., Louis, K.S., Marks, H.M. & Peterson, K.D. (1996). Participatory decision making. In F.M. Newmann (Ed.) *Authentic achievement: Restructuring schools for intellectual quality.* San Francisco, CA: Jossey-Bass, 245–263.

King, S., Waschbusch, D.A., Pelham, W.E. Jr, Frankland, B.W., Andrade, B.F., Jacques, S. & Corkum, P.V. (2009). Social information processing in elementary-school aged children with ADHD: Medication effects and comparisons with typical children. *Journal of Abnormal Child Psychology, 37* (8), 579–589.

Kingston, L. & Prior, M. (1995). The development of patterns of stable, transient, and school-age onset aggressive behavior in children. *Journal of the American Academy of Child and Adolescent Psychiatry, 34* (3), 348–358.

Kins, E., Soenens, B. & Beyers, W. (2012). Parental psychological control and dysfunctional separation-individuation: A tale of two different dynamics. *Journal of Adolescence, 35* (5), 1099–1109.

Kitzmann, K.M. (2000). Effects of marital conflict on subsequent triadic family interactions and parenting. *Developmental Psychology, 36* (1), 3–13.

Klassen, R.M. & Chiu, M.M. (2010). Effects on teachers' self-efficacy and job satisfaction: Teacher, gender, years of experience, and job stress. *Journal of Educational Psychology, 102* (3), 741–756.

Klein, J. & Cornell, D. (2010). Is the link between large high schools and student victimization an illusion? *Journal of Educational Psychology, 102* (4), 933–946.

Klimes-Dougan, B. & Kistner, J. (1990). Physically abused preschoolers' responses to peers' distress. *Developmental Psychology, 26* (4), 599–602.

Kline, B.E. & Short, E.B. (1991). Changes in emotional resilience: Gifted adolescent females. *Roeper Review, 13* (3), 118–121.

Klusmann, U., Kunter, M., Trautwein, U., Lüdtke, O. & Baumert, J. (2008). Teachers' occupational well-being and quality of instruction: The important role of self-regulatory patterns. *Journal of Educational Psychology, 100* (3), 702–715.

Knecht, A., Snijders, T.A.B., Baerveldt, C. & Raub, W. (2010). Friendship and delinquency: Selection and influence processes in early adolescence. *Social Development, 19* (3), 494–514.

Knight, B.A. (1995). The influence of locus of control on gifted and talented students. *Gifted Education International, 11* (1), 31–33.

Knight, T. (1991). Democratic schooling: Basis for a school code of behaviour. In M.N. Lovegrove and R. Lewis (Eds.) *Classroom discipline.* Melbourne: Longman Cheshire, 117–144.

Knutson, J.F., DeGarmo, D.S. & Reid, J.B. (2004). Social disadvantage and neglectful parenting as precursors to the development of antisocial and aggressive child behavior: Testing a theoretical model. *Aggressive Behavior, 30* (3), 187–205.

Koch, E.J. (2006). Examining the role of self-esteem in psychological functioning and well-being. In M.H. Kernis (Ed.) *Self-esteem: Issues and answers: A sourcebook of current perspectives.* New York: Psychology Press, 260–266.

Kochanska, G. (1995). Children's temperament, mothers' discipline, and security of attachment: Multiple pathways to emerging internalization. *Child Development, 66* (3), 597–615.

——(1997). Mutually responsive orientation between mothers and their young children: Implications for early socialization. *Child Development, 68* (1), 94–112.

——(2002a). Committed compliance, moral self, and internalization: A mediational model. *Developmental Psychology, 38* (3), 339–351.

——(2002b). Mutually responsive orientation between mothers and their young children: A context for the early development of conscience. *Current Directions in Psychological Science, 11* (6), 191–195.

Kochanska, G. & Aksan, N. (1995). Mother-child mutually positive affect, the quality of child compliance to requests and prohibitions, and maternal control as correlates of early internalization. *Child Development, 66* (1), 236–254.

——(2004). Conscience in childhood: Past, present and future. *Merrill-Palmer Quarterly, 50* (3), 299–310.

Kochanska, G., Aksan, N. & Carlson, J.J. (2005a). Temperament, relationships, and young children's receptive cooperation with their parents. *Developmental Psychology, 41* (4), 648–660.

Kochanska, G., Aksan, N. & Joy, M.E. (2007). Children's fearfulness as a moderator of parenting in early socialization: Two longitudinal studies. *Developmental Psychology, 43* (1), 222–237.

Kochanska, G., Aksan, N. & Nichols, K.E. (2003). Maternal power assertion in discipline and moral discourse contexts: Commonalities, differences, and implications for children's moral conduct and cognition. *Developmental Psychology, 39* (6), 949–963.

Kochanska, G., Coy, K.C. & Murray, K.T. (2001). The development of self-regulation in the first four years of life. *Child Development, 72* (4), 1091–1111.

Kochanska, G., Forman, D.R., Aksan, N. & Dunbar, S.B. (2005b). Pathways to conscience: Early mother-child mutually responsive orientation and children's moral emotion,

conduct, and cognition. *Journal of Child Psychology and Psychiatry, 46* (1), 19–34.

Kochanska, G., Forman, D.R. & Coy, K.C. (1999). Implications of the mother-child relationship in infancy for socialization in the second year of life. *Infant Behavior and Development, 22* (2), 249–265.

Kochanska, G., Murray, K.T. & Harlan, E.T. (2000). Effortful control in early childhood: Continuity and change, antecedents, and implications for social development. *Developmental Psychology, 36* (2), 220–232.

Kochenderfer, B.J. & Ladd, G.W. (1996). Peer victimization: Cause or consequence of school maladjustment? *Child Development, 67* (4), 1305–1317.

Kochenderfer-Ladd, B. (2004). Peer victimization: The role of emotions in adaptive and maladaptive coping. *Social Development, 13* (3), 329–349.

Kochenderfer-Ladd, B. & Ladd, G.W. (2001). Variations in peer victimization: Relations to children's maladjustment. In J. Juvonen and S. Graham (Eds.) *Peer harassment in school: The plight of the vulnerable and victimized.* New York: Guilford, 25–48.

Kochenderfer-Ladd, B. & Pelletier, M.E. (2008). Teachers' views and beliefs about bullying: Influences on classroom management strategies and students' coping with peer victimization. *Journal of School Psychology, 46* (4), 431–453.

Kochenderfer-Ladd, B. & Wardrop, J.L. (2001). Chronicity and instability of children's peer victimization experiences as predictors of loneliness and social satisfaction trajectories. *Child Development, 72* (1), 134–151.

Koegel, L.K., Koegel, R.L., Frea, W.D. & Fredeen, R.M. (2001). Identifying early intervention targets for children with autism in inclusive school settings. *Behavior Modification, 25* (5), 745–761.

Koenig, A.L., Cicchetti, D. & Rogosch, F.A. (2000). Child compliance/noncompliance and maternal contributors to internalization in maltreating and nonmaltreating dyads. *Child Development, 71* (4), 1018–1032.

——(2004). Moral development: The association between maltreatment and young children's prosocial behaviors and moral transgressions. *Social Development, 13* (1), 87–106.

Koestner, R., Ryan, R.M., Bernieri, F. & Holt, K. (1984). Setting limits on children's behavior: The differential effects of controlling vs. informational styles on intrinsic motivation and creativity. *Journal of Personality, 52* (3), 233–248.

Koh, K. & Luke, A. (2009). Authentic and conventional assessment in Singapore schools: An empirical study of teacher assignments and student work. *Assessment in Education: Principles, policy and practice, 16* (3), 291–318.

Koh, K.H., Tan, C. & Ng, P.T. (2012). Creating thinking schools through authentic assessment: The case in Singapore. *Educational Assessment, Evaluation and Accountability, 24* (2), 135–149.

Kohler, F.W. & Strain, P.S. (1993). The early childhood social skills program. *Teaching Exceptional Children, 25* (2), 41–42.

Kohn, A. (1991). Don't spoil the promise of cooperative learning: Response to Slavin. *Educational Leadership, 48* (5), 93–94.

——(1992). *No contest: The case against competition.* (rev. ed.) Boston, MA: Houghton Mifflin.

——(1994). Bribes for behaving: Why behaviorism doesn't help children become good people. *The NAMTA Journal, 19* (2), 71–94.

——(1996a). *Beyond discipline: From compliance to community.* Alexandria, VA: Association for Supervision and Curriculum Development.

——(1996b). By all available means: Cameron and Pierce's defense of extrinsic motivators. *Review of Educational Research, 66* (1), 1–4.

——(1998). *What to look for in a classroom . . . and other essays.* San Francisco, CA: Jossey-Bass.

——(1999a). *Punished by rewards: The trouble with gold stars. incentive plans, As, praise and other bribes.* (2nd ed.) Boston, MA: Houghton Mifflin.

——(1999b). *The schools our children deserve: Moving beyond traditional classrooms and 'tougher standards'.* Boston, MA: Houghton Mifflin.

——(2004). *What does it mean to be well educated?.* Boston, MA: Beacon Press.

——(2005). *Unconditional parenting: Moving from rewards and punishments to love and reason.* New York: Atria Books.

——(2006). *The homework myth: Why our kids get too much of a bad thing.* Cambridge, MA: Da Capo Press.

——(2011). *Feel-bad education: And other contrarian essays on children and schooling.* Boston, MA: Beacon.

Kokkinos, C.M. (2007). Job stressors, personality and burnout in primary school teachers. *British Journal of Educational Psychology, 77* (1), 229–244.

Kokkinos, C.M. & Panayiotou, G. (2004). Predicting bullying and victimization among early adolescents: Associations with disruptive behavior disorders. *Aggressive Behavior, 30* (6), 520–533.

Kokkinos, C.M., Panayiotou, G. & Davazoglou, A.M. (2005). Correlates of teacher appraisals of student behaviors. *Psychology in the Schools, 42* (1), 79–89.

Kokko, K. & Pulkkinen, L. (2005). Stability of aggressive behavior from childhood to middle age in women and men. *Aggressive Behavior, 31* (5), 485–497.

Kolko, D.J., Brent, D.A., Baugher, M., Bridge, J. & Birmaher, B. (2000). Cognitive and family therapies for adolescent depression: Treatment specificity, mediation, and moderation. *Journal of Consulting and Clinical Psychology, 68* (4), 603–614.

Kopp, C.B. (1982). Antecedents of self-regulation: A developmental perspective. *Developmental Psychology, 18* (2), 199–214.

Kotzman, A. (1989). *Listen to me; listen to you.* Melbourne: Penguin Books.

Kounin, J.S. (1970). *Discipline and group management in classrooms.* New York: Holt, Rinehart and Winston.

Kouzma, N.M. & Kennedy, G.A. (2002). Homework, stress, and mood disturbance in senior high school students. *Psychological Reports, 91* (1), 193–198.

Kowalski, K. (1990). The girl with the know-how: Finding solutions to a school problem. *Family Therapy Case Studies, 5* (1), 3–14.

Kral, R. & Kowalski, K. (1989). After the miracle: The second stage in solution focused brief therapy. *Journal of Strategic and Systemic Therapies, 8* (2), 73–76.

Krätzig, G.P. & Arbuthnott, K.D. (2006). Perceptual learning style and learning proficiency: A test of the hypothesis. *Journal of Educational Psychology, 98* (1), 238–246.

Kraus, A.J., Hanley, G.P., Cesana, L.L., Eisenberg, D. & Jarvie, A.C. (2012). An evaluation of strengthening precursors to increase preschooler compliance. *Journal of Applied Behavior Analysis, 45* (1), 131–136.

Krebs, L.L. (1986). Current research on theoretically based parenting programs. *Individual Psychology, 42* (3), 375–387.

Krueger, R.F., Caspi, A., Moffitt, T.E., White, J. & Stouthamer-Loeber, M. (1996). Delay of gratification, psychopathology and personality: Is low self-control specific to externalizing problems?. *Journal of Personality, 64* (1), 107–129.

Krugman, R.D. & Krugman, M.K. (1984). Emotional abuse in the classroom: The pediatrician's role in diagnosis and treatment. *American Journal of Diseases of Children, 138* (3), 284–286.

Kucera, M. & Sullivan, A.L. (2011). The educational

implications of Type 1 diabetes mellitus: A review of research and recommendations for school psychological practice. *Psychology in the Schools, 48* (6), 587–603.

Kuczynski, L (1983). Reasoning, prohibitions, and motivations for compliance. *Developmental Psychology, 19* (1), 126–134.

——(1984). Socialization goals and mother-child interaction: Strategies for long-term and short-term compliance. *Developmental Psychology, 20* (6), 1061–1073.

Kuczynski, L. & Kochanska, G. (1990). Development of children's noncompliance strategies from toddlerhood to age 5. *Developmental Psychology, 26* (3), 398–408.

——(1999). Development of children's noncompliance strategies from toddlerhood to age 5. *Developmental Psychology, 26* (3), 398–408.

Kupersmidt, J.B., DeRosier, M.E. & Patterson, C.P. (1995). Similarity as the basis for children's friendships: The roles of sociometric status, aggressive and withdrawn behavior, academic achievement and demographic characteristics. *Journal of Social and Personal Relationships, 12* (3), 439–452.

Kuppens, S., Grietens, H., Onghena, P., Michiels, S. & Subramanian, S.V. (2008). Individual and classroom variables associated with relational aggression in elementary-school aged children: A multilevel analysis. *Journal of School Psychology, 46* (6), 639–660.

Kurtz, P.F., Chin, M.D., Huete, J.M., Tarbox, R.S.F., O'Connor, J.T., Paclawskyj, T.R. & Rush, K.S. (2003). Functional analysis and treatment of self-injurious behavior in young children: A summary of 30 cases. *Journal of Applied Behavior Analysis, 36* (2), 205–219.

Kutsick, K.A., Gutkin, T.B. & Witt, J.C. (1991). The impact of treatment development process, intervention type, and problem severity on treatment acceptability as judged by classroom teachers. *Psychology in the Schools, 28* (4), 325–331.

Kwon, K., Kim, E. & Sheridan, S. (2012). Behavioral competence and academic functioning among early elementary children with externalizing problems. *School Psychology Review, 41* (2), 123–140.

l'Allemand-Jander, D. (2010). Clinical diagnosis of metabolic and cardiovascular risks in overweight children: Early development of chronic disease in the obese child. *International Journal of Obesity, 34* (Supp. 2), S32–S36,

Labaree, D.F. (1997). Public goods, private goods: The American struggle over educational goals. *American Educational Research Journal, 34* (1), 39–81.

Ladd, G.W. (1985). Documenting the effects of social skill training with children: Process and outcome assessment. In B.H. Schneider, K.H. Rubin and J.E. Ledingham (Eds.) *Children's peer relations: Issues in assessment and intervention.* New York: Springer-Verlag, 243–269.

——(1990). Having friends, keeping friends, making friends, and being liked by peers in the classroom: Predictors of children's early school adjustment?. *Child Development, 61* (4), 1081–1100.

——(2006). Peer rejection, aggressive or withdrawn behavior, and psychological maladjustment from ages 5 to 12: An examination of four predictive models. *Child Development, 77* (4), 822–846.

Ladd, G.W. & Burgess, K.B. (1999). Charting the relationship trajectories of aggressive, withdrawn, and aggressive/withdrawn children during early grade school. *Child Development, 70* (4), 910–929.

——(2001). Do relational and protective factors moderate the linkages between childhood aggression and early psychological adjustment?. *Child Development, 72* (5), 1579–1601.

Ladd, G.W. & Kochenderfer-Ladd, B. (1998). Parenting behaviors and parent-child relationships: Correlates of peer victimization in kindergarten?. *Developmental Psychology, 34* (6), 1450-1458.

Ladd, G.W., Kochenderfer-Ladd, B.J. & Coleman, C.C. (1996). Friendship quality as a predictor of young children's early school adjustment. *Child Development, 67* (3), 1103-1118.

Ladd, G.W., Kochenderfer-Ladd, B.J., Eggum, N.D., Kochel, K.P. & McConnell, E.M. (2011). Characterizing and comparing the friendships of anxious-solitary and unsociable preadolescents. *Child Development, 82* (5), 1434-1453.

Ladd, G.W. & Troop-Gordon, W. (2003). The role of chronic peer difficulties in the development of children's psychological adjustment problems. *Child Development, 74* (5), 1344-1367.

Ladson-Billings, G. (1995). Toward a theory of culturally relevant pedagogy. *American Educational Research Journal, 32* (3), 465-491.

——(2001). America still eats her young. In W. Ayes, B. Dohrn & R. Ayers (Eds.) *Zero tolerance: Resisting the drive for punishment in our schools*. New York: The New Press, 77–88.

LaFontana, K.M. & Cillessen, A.H.N. (2002). Children's perceptions of popular and unpopular peers: A multimethod assessment. *Developmental Psychology, 38* (5), 635-647.

Lagacé-Séguin, D.G. & Coplan, R.J. (2005). Maternal emotional styles and child social adjustment: Assessment, correlates, outcomes and goodness of fit in early childhood. *Social Development, 14* (4), 613-636.

Lahey, B.B., Van Hulle, C.A., Keenan, K., Rathouz, P.J., D'Onofrio, B.M., Rodgers, J.L. & Waldman, I.D. (2008). Temperament and parenting during the first year of life predict future child conduct problems. *Journal of Abnormal Child Psychology, 36* (8), 1139-1158.

Laible, D.J. & Thompson, R. (2002). Mother-toddler conflict in the toddler years: Lessons in emotion, morality, and relationships. *Child Development, 73* (4), 1187-1203.

Laird, R.D., Jordan, K.Y., Dodge, K.A., Pettit, G.S. & Bates, J.E. (2001). Peer rejection in childhood, involvement with antisocial peers in early adolescence, and the development of externalizing behavior problems. *Development and Psychopathology, 13* (2), 337-354.

Lamarche, V., Brendgen, M., Moivin, M., Vitaro, F. Pérusse, D. & Dionne, G. (2006). Do friendships and sibling relationships provide protection against peer victimization in a similar way? *Social Development, 15* (3), 373-393.

Lambert, B. (1990). Hyperactivity: A review of research. *Australian Journal of Early Childhood, 15* (2), 43-48.

——(1994). Beating burnout: A multi-dimensional perspective. *AECA Resource Book Series, 1* (2). Watson, ACT: Australian Early Childhood Association.

Lambert, R.G., McCarthy, C., O'Donnell, M. & Wang, C. (2009). Measuring elementary teacher stress and coping in the classroom: Validity evidence for the Classroom Appraisal of Resources and Demands. *Psychology in the Schools, 46* (10), 973-988.

Lamborn, S.D., Mounts, N.S., Steinberg, L. & Dornbusch, S.M. (1991). Patterns of competence and adjustment among adolescents from authoritative, authoritarian, indulgent, and neglectful families. *Child Development, 62* (5), 1049-1065.

Landis, C.A. (2011). Sleep, pain, fibromyalgia, and chronic fatigue syndrome. *Handbook of Clinical Neurology, 98,* 613-637.

Lansford, J.E., Dodge, K.A., Malone, P.S., Bacchini, D., Zelli, A., Chaudhary, N., Manke, B., Chang, L., Oburu, P., Palmérus, K., Pastorelli, C., Bombi, A.S., Tapanya, S., Deater-Deckard, K. & Quinn, N. (2005). Physical discipline and children's

adjustment: Cultural normativeness as a moderator. *Child Development, 76* (6), 1234-1246.

Lantz, S. (2009). *Chemical free kids*. Buddina, Qld: Joshua Books.

Lanzetta, J.T. & Englis, B.G. (1989). Expectations of cooperation and competition and their effects on observers' vicarious emotional responses. *Journal of Personality and Social Psychology, 56* (4), 543-554.

Larrivee, B. (2005). *Authentic classroom management: Creating a learning community and building reflective practice.* (2nd ed.) Boston, MA: Pearson Allyn & Bacon.

Larson, R.W. & Richards, M.H. (1991). Boredom in the middle school years: Blaming school versus blaming students. *American Journal of Education, 99* (4), 418-443.

Larzelere, R.E. (1986). Moderate spanking: Model or deterrent of children's aggression in the family?. *Journal of Family Violence, 1* (1), 27-36.

——(2000). Child outcomes of nonabusive and customary physical punishment by parents: An updated literature review. *Clinical Child and Family Psychology Review, 3* (4), 199-221.

Lasky, S. (2000). The cultural and emotional politics of teacher-parent interactions. *Teaching and Teacher Education, 16* (8), 843-860.

Lassen, S.R., Steele, M.M. & Sailor, W. (2006). The relationship of school-wide positive behavior support to academic achievement in an urban middle school. *Psychology in the Schools, 43* (6), 701-712.

Last, B.F., Stam, H., Onland-van Nieuwenhuizen, A.-M. & Grootenhuis, M.A. (2007). Positive effects of a psycho-educational group intervention for children with chronic disease: First results. *Patient Education and Counseling, 65* (1), 101-112.

Lau, S. & Nie, Y. (2008). Interplay between personal goals and classroom goal structures in predicting student outcomes: A multilevel analysis of person-context interactions. *Journal of Educational Psychology, 100* (1), 15-29.

Lavigne, J.V., Gibbons, R.D., Christoffel, K.K., Arend, R., Rosenbaum, D., Binns, H., Dawson, N., Sobel, H. & Isaacs, C. (1996). Prevalence rates and correlates of psychiatric disorders among preschool children. *Journal of the American Academy of Child and Adolescent Psychiatry, 35* (2), 204-214.

Lavoie, F., Hébert, M., Tremblay, R., Vitaro, F., Vézina, L. & McDuff, P. (2002). History of family dysfunction and perpetration of dating violence by adolescent boys: A longitudinal study. *Journal of Adolescent Health, 30* (5), 375-383.

Lavoie, M.-E., Rabasa-Lhoret, R., Doucet, E., Mignault, D., Messier, L., Bastard, J.-P. & Faraj, M. (2010). Association between physical activity energy expenditure and inflammatory markers in sedentary overweight and obese women. *International Journal of Obesity, 34* (9), 1387-1395.

Laws, C. & Davies, B. (2000). Poststructuralist theory in practice: Working with 'behaviourally disturbed' children. *Qualitative Studies in Education, 13* (3), 205-221.

Lazarides, L. (2010). *A textbook of modern naturopathy*. London: Health-Diets.net.

Le Messurier, M. (2004). *Cognitive behavioural training: A how-to guide for successful behaviour*. Melbourne: Hawker Brownlow.

LeCompte, M. (1978). Learning to work: The hidden curriculum of the classroom. *Anthropology and Education Quarterly, 9* (1), 22-37.

Leadbeater, B.J., Boone, E.M., Sangster, N.A. & Mathieson, L.C. (2006). Sex differences in the personal costs and benefits of relational and physical aggression in high school. *Aggressive Behavior, 32* (4), 409-419.

Leadbeater, B., Hoglund, W. & Woods, T. (2003). Changing

contexts?: The effects of a primary prevention program on classroom levels of peer relational and physical victimization. *Journal of Community Psychology, 31* (4), 397–418.

Leary, A. & Katz, L.F. (2005). Observations of aggressive children during peer provocation and with a best friend. *Developmental Psychology, 41* (1), 124–134.

Lee, K.-H., Baillargeon, R.H., Vermunt, J.K., Wu, H.-X. & Tremblay, R.E. (2007). Age differences in the prevalence of physical aggression among 5–11-year-old Canadian boys and girls. *Aggressive Behavior, 33* (1), 26–37.

Lee, N. (2001). *Childhood and society: Growing up in an age of uncertainty.* Buckingham, UK: Open University Press.

Leenaars, L.S., Dane, A.V. & Marini, Z.A. (2008). Evolutionary perspective on indirect victimization in adolescence: The role of attractiveness, dating and sexual behavior. *Aggressive Behavior, 34* (4), 404–415.

Leff, S.S., Gullan, R.L., Paskewich, B.S., Abdul-Kabir, S., Jawad, A.F., Grossman, M., Munro, M.A. & Power, T.J. (2009). An initial evaluation of a culturally adapted social problem-solving and relational aggression prevention program for urban African-American relationally aggressive girls. *Journal of Prevention and Intervention in the Community, 37* (4), 260–274.

Leff, S.S., Power, T.J., Costigan, T.E. & Manz, P.H. (2003). Assessing the climate of the playground and lunchroom: Implications for bullying prevention programming. *School Psychology Review, 32* (3), 418–430.

Leff, S.S., Power, T.J., Manz, P.H., Costigan, T.E. & Nabors, L.A. (2001). School-based aggression prevention programs for young children: Current status and implications for violence prevention. *School Psychology Review, 30* (3), 344–362.

Leff, S.S., Waasdorp, T.E. & Crick, N.R. (2010). A review of existing relational aggression programs: Strengths, limitations, and future directions. *School Psychology Review, 39* (4), 508–535.

Lemola, S., Schwarz, B. & Siffert, A. (2012). Interparental conflict and early adolescents' aggression: Is regular sleep a vulnerability factor? *Journal of Adolescence, 35* (1), 97–105.

Lencioni, P. (2002). *The five dysfunctions of a team: A leadership fable.* San Francisco, CA: Jossey-Bass.

Leondari, A. & Gonida, E. (2007). Predicting academic self-handicapping in different age groups: The role of personal achievement and social goals. *British Journal of Educational Psychology, 77* (3), 595–611.

Lepper, M.R. & Greene, D. (1975). Turning play into work: Effects of adult surveillance and extrinsic rewards on children's intrinsic motivation. *Journal of Personality and Social Psychology, 31* (3), 479–486.

Lepper, M.R., Sagotsky, G., Dafoe, J.L. & Greene, D. (1982). Consequences of superfluous social constraints: Effects on young children's social inferences and subsequent intrinsic interest. *Journal of Personality and Social Psychology, 42* (1), 51–65.

Lerman, D.C. & Iwata, B.A. (1996). Developing a technology for the use of operant extinction in clinical settings: An examination of basic and applied research. *Journal of Applied Behavior Analysis, 29* (3), 345–382.

Lerman, D.C., Iwata, B.A., Shore, B.A. & Kahng, S.W. (1996). Responding maintained by intermittent reinforcement: Implications for the use of extinction with problem behavior in clinical settings. *Journal of Applied Behavior Analysis, 29* (2), 153–171.

Lerman, D.C., Iwata, B.A. & Wallace, M.D. (1999). Side effects of extinction: Prevalence of bursting and aggression during the treatment of self-injurious behavior. *Journal of Applied Behavior Analysis, 32* (1), 1–8.

Lerman, D.C. & Vorndran, C.M. (2002). On the status of knowledge for using punishment: Implications for treating behavior disorders. *Journal of Applied Behavior Analysis, 35* (4), 431–464.

Letcher, P., Smart, D., Sanson, A. & Toumbourou, J.W. (2009). Psychosocial precursors and correlates of differing internalizing trajectories from 3 to 15 years. *Social Development, 18* (3), 618–646.

Letcher, P., Toumbourou, J., Sanson, A., Prior, M., Smart, D. & Oberklaid, F. (2004). Parenting style as a moderator of the effect of temperament on adolescent externalising and internalising behaviour problems. *The Australian Educational and Developmental Psychologist, 20* (1), 5–34.

Letzring, T.D., Block, J. & Funder, D.C. (2005). Ego-control and ego-resiliency: Generalization of self-report scales based on personality descriptions from acquaintances, clinicians, and the self. *Journal of Research in Personality, 39* (4), 395–422.

Leung, C., Sanders, M.R., Leung, S., Mak, R. & Lau, J. (2003). An outcome evaluation of the implementation of the Triple P-Positive Parenting Program in Hong Kong. *Family Process, 42* (4), 531–544.

Leung, K., Lau, S. & Lam, W.-L. (1998). Parenting styles and academic achievement: A cross-cultural study. *Merrill-Palmer Quarterly, 44* (2), 157–172.

Leung, P.W.L. & Kwan, K.S.F. (1998). Parenting styles, motivational orientations, and self-perceived academic competence: A mediational model. *Merrill-Palmer Quarterly, 44* (1), 1–19.

Levant, R.F. (1983). Client-centered skills-training programs for the family: A review of the literature. *The Counseling Psychologist, 11* (3), 29–46.

Levin, L. & Carr, E.G. (2001). Food selectivity and problem behavior in children with developmental disabilities: Analysis and intervention. *Behavior Modification, 25* (3), 443–470.

Levine, E.S. & Anshel, D.J. (2011). 'Nothing works'!: A case study using cognitive-behavioral interventions to engage parents, educators and children in the management of attention-deficit/hyperactivity disorder. *Psychology in the Schools, 48* (3), 297–306.

Levy, F. (1993). Side effects of stimulant use. *Journal of Paediatrics and Child Health, 29* (4), 250–254.

Levy, S.R. (1999). Reducing prejudice: Lessons from social-cognitive factors underlying perceiver differences in prejudice. *Journal of Social Issues, 55* (4), 745–765.

Lewin, K., Lippitt, R. & White, R.K. (1939). Patterns of aggressive behavior in experimentally created social climates. *Journal of Social Psychology, 10* (2), 271–299.

Lewis, C.C. (1981). The effects of parental firm control: A reinterpretation of findings. *Psychological Bulletin, 90* (3), 547–563.

Lewis, R. (1997). *The discipline dilemma: Control, management, influence.* (2nd ed.) Melbourne: ACER.

——(2001). Classroom discipline and student responsibility: The students' view. *Teaching and Teacher Education, 17* (3), 307–319.

Lewis, R.B. & Doorlag, D.H. (2003). *Teaching special education students in general education.* (6th ed.) Upper Saddle River, NJ: Prentice Hall.

Lewis, R. & Frydenberg, E. (2002). Concomitants of failure to cope: What we should teach adolescents about coping. *British Journal of Educational Psychology, 72* (3), 419–431.

Lewis, T.J., Powers, L.J., Kelk, M.J. & Newcomer, L.L. (2002). Reducing problem behaviors on the playground: An investigation of the application of schoolwide positive behavior supports. *Psychology in the Schools, 39* (2), 181–190.

Lewis, T.J. & Sugai, G. (1999). Effective behavior support:

A systems approach to proactive schoolwide management. *Focus on Exceptional Children, 31* (6), 1–24.

Lewis, T.J., Sugai, G. & Colvin, G. (1998). Reducing problem behavior through a school-wide system of effective behavioral support: Investigation of a school-wide social skills training program and contextual interventions. *School Psychology Review, 27* (3), 446–459.

Liljeberg, J.F., Eklund, J.M., Fritz, M.V. & Klinteberg, B.A. (2011). Poor school bonding and delinquency over time: Bidirectional effects and sex differences. *Journal of Adolescence, 34* (1), 1–9.

Lindberg, J.A., Kelley, D.A. & Swick, A.M. (2005). *Common-sense classroom management for middle and high school teachers.* Thousand Oaks, CA: Corwin.

Lindsay, G. & Dockrell, J. (2000). The behaviour and self-esteem of children with specific speech and language difficulties. *British Journal of Educational Psychology, 70* (4), 583–601.

Lindsay, G., Dockrell, J.E. & Strand, S. (2007). Longitudinal patterns of behaviour problems in children with specific speech and language difficulties: Child and contextual factors. *British Journal of Educational Psychology, 77* (4), 811–828.

Linnet, K.M., Dalsgaard, S., Obel, C., Wisborg, K., Henriksen, T.B., Rodriguez, A., Kotimaa, A., Moilanen, I., Thomsen, P.H., Olsen, J. & Jarvelin, M.-R. (2003). Maternal lifestyle factors in pregnancy risk of attention deficit hyperactivity disorder and associated behaviors: Review of the current evidence. *American Journal of Psychiatry, 160* (6), 1028–1040.

Lipscomb, S.T., Level, L.D., Harold, G.T., Neiderhiser, J.M., Shaw, D.S., Ge, X. & Reiss, D. (2011). Trajectories of parenting and child negative emotionality during infancy and toddlerhood: A longitudinal analysis. *Child Development, 82* (5), 1661–1675.

Little, C.A. (2012). Curriculum motivation for gifted students. *Psychology in the Schools, 49* (7), 695–705.

Little, E. (2003). *Kids behaving badly: Teacher strategies for classroom behaviour problems.* Sydney: Pearson Prentice Hall.

Little, T.D., Brauner, J., Jones, S.M., Nock, M.K. & Hawley, P.H. (2003). Rethinking aggression: A typological examination of the functions of aggression. *Merrill-Palmer Quarterly, 49* (3), 343–369.

Lochman, J.E., Powell, N.R., Whidby, J.M. & FitzGerald, D.P. (2012). Aggression in children. In P.C. Kendall (Ed.) *Child and adolescent therapy: Cognitive-behavioral procedures.* (4th ed.) New York: Guilford, 27–60.

Lochman, J.E. & Wells, K.C. (2004). The Coping Power program for preadolescent boys and their parents: Outcome effects at the 1-year follow-up. *Journal of Consulting and Clinical Psychology, 72* (4), 571–578.

LoCicero, K.A. & Ashby, J.S. (2000). Multidimensional perfectionism in middle school age gifted students: A comparison to peers from the general cohort. *Roeper Review, 22* (3), 182–185.

Loeb, R.C. & Jay, G. (1987). Self-concept in gifted children: Differential impact in boys and girls. *Gifted Child Quarterly, 31* (1), 9–14.

Loeber, R. & Hay, D. (1997). Key issues in the development of aggression and violence from childhood to early adulthood. *Annual Review of Psychology, 48,* 371–410.

Lomas, J. Stough, C., Hansen, K. & Downey, L.A. (2012). Brief report: Emotional intelligence, victimization and bullying in adolescents. *Journal of Adolescence, 35* (1), 207–211.

Londerville, S. & Main, M. (1981). Security of attachment, compliance, and maternal training methods in the second year of life. *Developmental Psychology, 17* (3), 289–299.

Long, J.D. & Pellegrini, A.D. (2003). Studying change in dominance and bullying with linear mixed models. *School Psychology Review, 32* (3), 401–417.

Long, J.F., Monoi, S., Harper, B., Knoblauch, D. & Murphy, P.K. (2007). Academic motivation and achievement among urban adolescents. *Urban Education, 42* (3), 196–222.

Lonigan, C.J., Bloomfield, B.G., Anthony, J.L., Bacon, K.D., Phillips, B.M. & Samwel, C.S. (1999). Relations among emergent literacy skills, behavior problems, and social competence in preschool children from low- and middle-income backgrounds. *Topics in Early Childhood Special Education, 19* (1), 40–53.

López, E.E., Olaizola, J.H., Ferrer, B.M. & Ochoa, G.M. (2006). Aggressive and nonaggressive rejected students: An analysis of their differences. *Psychology in the Schools, 43* (3), 387–400.

Lösel, F. & Beelmann, A. (2003). Effects of child skills training in preventing antisocial behavior: A systematic review of randomized evaluations. *Annals of the American Academy of Political and Social Science, 587,* 84–109.

Loughran, J. (2010). *What expert teachers do: Enhancing professional knowledge for classroom practice.* Sydney: Allen & Unwin.

Louis, K.S., Kruse, S.D. & Marks, H.M. (1996). Schoolwide professional community. In F.M. Newmann (Ed.) *Authentic achievement: Restructuring schools for intellectual quality.* San Francisco, CA: Jossey-Bass, 179–203.

Loukas, A. (2009). Examining temporal associations between perceived maternal psychological control and early adolescent internalizing problems. *Journal of Abnormal Child Psychology, 37* (8), 1113–1122.

Loukas, A. & Murphy, J.L. (2007). Middle school student perceptions of school climate: Examining protective functions on subsequent adjustment problems. *Journal of School Psychology, 45* (3), 293–309.

Loukas, A., Paulos, S.K. & Robinson, S. (2005). Early adolescent social and overt aggression: Examining the roles of social anxiety and maternal psychological control. *Journal of Youth and Adolescence, 34* (4), 335–345.

Lovejoy, M.C., Graczyk, P.A., O'Hare, E. & Neuman, G. (2000). Maternal depression and parenting behavior: A meta-analytic review. *Clinical Psychology Review, 20* (5), 561–592.

Loveland, J.M., Lounsbury, J.W. & Welsh, D. (2007). The validity of physical aggression in predicting adolescent academic performance. *British Journal of Educational Psychology, 77* (1), 167–176.

Low, S., Frey, K.S. & Brockman, C.J. (2010). Gossip on the playground: Changes associated with universal intervention, retaliation beliefs, and supportive friends. *School Psychology Review, 39* (4), 536–551.

Lubbers, M.J., Van Der Werf, M.P.C., Snijders, T.A.B., Creemers, B.P.M. & Kuyper, H. (2006). The impact of peer relations on academic progress in junior high. *Journal of School Psychology, 44* (6), 491–512.

Luepker, R.V. (1999). How physically active are American children and what can we do about it?. *International Journal of Obesity, 23* (Supp. 2), S12–S17.

Luiselli, J.K., Putnam, R.F., Handler, M.W. & Feinberg, A.B. (2005). Whole-school positive behaviour support: Effects on student discipline problems and academic performance. *Educational Psychology, 25* (2–3), 183–198.

Lundy, B.L., Jones, N.A., Field, T., Nearing, G., Davalos, M., Pietro, P.A., Schanberg, S. & Kuhn, C. (1999). Prenatal depression effects on neonates. *Infant Behavior and Development, 22* (1), 119–129.

Luster, T., Rhoades, K. & Haas, B. (1989). The relation between parental values and parenting behavior: A test of the Kohn hypothesis. *Journal of Marriage and the Family, 51* (1), 139–147.

Luthar, S.S., Cicchetti, D. & Becker, B. (2000). The construct of resilience: A critical evaluation and guidelines for future work. *Child Development, 71* (3), 543–562.

Lutz, M.N., Fantuzzo, J. & McDermott, P. (2002). Multidimensional assessment of emotional and behavioral adjustment problems of low-income preschool children: Development and initial validation. *Early Childhood Research Quarterly, 17* (3), 338–355.

Lynch, E.W. & Hanson, M.J. (1996). Ensuring cultural competence in assessment. In M. McLean, D.B. Bailey Jr and M. Wolery (Eds.) *Assessing infants and preschoolers with special needs.* (2nd ed.) Englewood Cliffs, NJ: Merrill, 69–95.

Lyon, M.R. (2000). *Healing the hyperactive brain: Through the new science of functional medicine.* Calgary, AB: Focused Publishing.

Lytton, H. (1990). Child and parent effects in boys' conduct disorder: A reinterpretation. *Developmental Psychology, 26* (5), 683–697.

——(1997). Physical punishment is a problem, whether conduct disorder is endogenous or not. *Psychological Inquiry, 8* (3), 211–214.

Lyytikäinen, P., Lallukka, T., Laheima, E. & Rahkonen, O. (2011). Sleep problems and major weight gain: A follow-up study. *International Journal of Obesity, 35* (1), 109–114.

Maag, J.W. (2001). Rewarded by punishment: Reflections on the disuse of positive reinforcement in schools. *Exceptional Children, 67* (2), 173–186.

Maag, J.W., Reid, R. & DiGangi, S.A. (1993). Differential effects of self-monitoring attention, accuracy and productivity. *Journal of Applied Behavior Analysis, 26* (3), 329–344.

MacCallum, F. & Golombok, S. (2004). Children raised in fatherless families from infancy: A follow-up of children of lesbian and single heterosexual mothers at early adolescence. *Journal of Child Psychology and Psychiatry, 45* (8), 1407–1419.

Maccoby, E.E. & Lewis, C.C. (2003). Less day care or different day care? *Child Development, 74* (4), 1069–1075.

Maccoby, E.E. & Martin, J.A. (1983). Socialization in the context of the family: Parent-child interaction. In P.H. Mussen and E.M. Hetherington (Eds). *Handbook of child psychology vol. IV: Socialization, personality and social development.* (4th ed.) New York: Wiley, 1–101.

Mace, F.C. & Wacker, D.P. (1994). Toward greater integration of basic and applied behavioral research: An introduction. *Journal of Applied Behavior Analysis, 27* (4), 569–574.

Macgillivray, I.K. (2000). Educational equity for gay, lesbian, isexual, transgendered, and queer/questioning students: The demands of democracy and social justice for America's schools. *Education and Urban Society, 32* (3), 303–323.

Macht, J. & Zirpoli, T. (2012). Functional and curriculum-based assessment. In T.J. Zirpoli (Ed.) *Behavior management: Positive applications for teachers.* (6th ed.) Boston, MA: Pearson, 231–253.

Mackarness, R. (1990). *Not all in the mind.* London: Thorsons.

MacKinnon-Lewis, C., Rabiner, D. & Starnes, R. (1999). Predicting boys' social acceptance and aggression: The role of mother-child interactions and boys' beliefs about peers. *Developmental Psychology, 35* (3), 632–639.

MacMillan, H.E., Boyle, M.H., Wong, M.Y.-Y., Duku, E.K., Fleming, J.E. & Walsh, C.A. (1999). Slapping and spanking in childhood and its association with lifetime prevalence of psychiatric disorders in a general population sample. *Canadian Medical Association Journal, 161* (7), 805–809.

Macmillan, R., McMorris, B.J. & Kruttschnitt, C. (2004). Linked lives: Stability and change in maternal circumstances and trajectories of antisocial behavior in children. *Child Development, 75* (1), 205–230.

Madsen, M.C. (1971). Developmental and cross-cultural differences in the cooperative and competitive behavior of young children. *Journal of Cross-Cultural Psychology, 2* (4), 365–371.

Magee, L. & Hale, L. (2012). Longitudinal associations between sleep duration and subsequent weight gain: A systematic review. *Sleep Medicine Reviews, 16* (3), 231–241.

Maggin, D.M., Chafouleas, S.M., Goddard, K.M. & Johnson, A.H. (2011). A systematic evaluation of token economies as a classroom management tool for students with challenging behavior. *Journal of School Psychology, 49* (5), 529–554.

Mahady Wilton, M.M., Craig, W.M. & Pepler, D.J. (2000). Emotional regulation and display in classroom victims of bullying: Characteristic expressions of affect, coping styles and relevant contextual factors. *Social Development, 9* (2), 226–245.

Maker, C.J. & Schiever, S.W. (1989). Purpose and organization of the volume. In C.J. Maker and S.W. Schiever (Eds.) *Critical issues in gifted education: Defensible programs for cultural and ethnic minorities.* Austin, TX: Pro-Ed, xv–xix.

Mäki, M, & Collin, P. (1997). Coeliac disease. *The Lancet, 349* (9067), 1755–1759.

Maldonado-Carreño, C. & Vortruba-Drzal, E. (2011). Teacher-child relationships and the development of academic and behavioral skills during elementary school: A within- and between-child analysis. *Child Development, 82* (2), 601–616.

Malin, M. (1990). The visibility and invisibility of Aboriginal students in an urban classroom. *Australian Journal of Education, 34* (3), 312–329.

Malinsky, K.P. (1997). Learning to be invisible: Female sexual minority students in America's public high schools. *Journal of Gay and Lesbian Social Services, 7* (4), 35–50.

Mallick, B.N. & Singh, A. (2011). REM sleep loss increases brain excitability: Role of noradrenalin and its mechanism of action. *Sleep Medicine Reviews, 15* (3), 165–178.

Malti, T., Gasser, L. & Buchmann, M. (2009). Aggressive and prosocial children's emotion attributions and moral reasoning. *Aggressive Behavior, 35* (1), 90–102.

Manke, M.P. (1997). *Classroom power relations: Understanding student-teacher interaction.* Mahwah, NJ: Lawrence Erlbaum.

Mapp, S.C. (2006). The effects of sexual abuse as a child on the risk of mothers physically abusing their children: A path analysis using systems theory. *Child Abuse and Neglect, 30* (11), 1293–1310.

Marchand, J.F., Schedler, S. & Wagstaff, D.A. (2004). The role of parents' attachment orientations, depressive symptoms, and conflict behaviors in children's externalizing and internalizing behavior problems. *Early Childhood Research Quarterly, 19* (3), 449–462.

Marchant, G.J., Paulson, S.E. & Rothlisberg, B.A. (2001). Relations of middle school students' perceptions of family and school contexts with academic achievement. *Psychology in the Schools, 38* (6), 505–519.

Marchant, M., Young, K.R. & West, R.P. (2004). The effects of parental teaching on compliance behavior of children. *Psychology in the Schools, 41* (3), 337–350.

Marcon, R.A. (1999). Positive relationships between parent school involvement and public school inner-city preschoolers' development and academic progress. *School Psychology Review, 28* (3), 395–412.

Marini, Z.A., Dane, A.V., Bosacki, S.L. & YLC-CURA. (2006). Direct and indirect bully-victims: Differential psychosocial risk factors associated with adolescents involved in bullying and victimization. *Aggressive Behavior, 32* (6), 551–569.

Marks, H.M., Doane, K.B. & Secada, W.G. (1996a). Support for student achievement. In F.M. Newmann (Ed.) *Authentic achievement: Restructuring schools for intellectual quality.* San Francisco, CA: Jossey-Bass, 209–227.

Marks, H.M., Newmann, F.M. & Gamoran, A. (1996b). Does authentic pedagogy increase student achievement?. In F.M. Newmann (Ed.) *Authentic achievement: Restructuring schools for intellectual quality.* San Francisco, CA: Jossey-Bass, 49–73.

Marsh, H.W., Chessor, D., Craven, R. & Roche, L. (1995). The effects of gifted and talented programs on academic self-concept: The big fish strikes again. *American Educational Research Journal, 32* (2), 285–319.

Marsh, H.W. & Craven, R.G. (1998). The big fish little pond effect, optimal illusions, and misinterpretations: A response to Gross (1997). *The Australasian Journal of Gifted Education, 7* (1), 6–15.

Marsh, H.W. & Martin, A.J. (2010). Academic self-concept and academic achievement: Relations and causal ordering. *British Journal of Educational Psychology, 81* (1), 59–77.

Marsh, H.W., Parada, R.H., Craven, R.G. & Finger, L. (2004). In the looking glass: A reciprocal effects model elucidating the complex nature of bullying, psychological determinants, and the central role of self-concept. In C.E. Sanders and G.D. Phye (Eds.) *Bullying: Implications for the classroom.* San Diego, CA: Elsevier, 63–109.

Martel, M.M. & Nigg, J.T. (2006). Child ADHD and personality/temperament traits of reactive and effortful control, resiliency, and emotionality. *Journal of Child Psychology and Psychiatry, 47* (11), 1175–1183.

Martin, A.J., Linfoot, K. & Stephenson, J. (1999). How teachers respond to concerns about misbehavior in their classroom. *Psychology in the Schools, 36* (4), 347–358.

Martin, G. & Pear, J. (2011). *Behavior modification: What it is and how to do it.* (9th ed.) Boston, MA: Pearson.

Martin-Storey, A. & Crosnoe, R. (2012). Sexual minority status, peer harassment, and adolescent depression. *Journal of Adolescence, 35* (4), 1001–1011.

Martino, S.C., Ellickson, P.L., Klein, D.J., McCaffrey, D. & Edelen, M.O. (2008). Multiple trajectories of physical aggression among adolescent boys and girls. *Aggressive Behavior, 34* (1), 61–75.

Mashburn, A.J., Pianta, R.C., Barbarin, O.A., Bryant, D., Hamre, B.K., Downer, J.T., Burchinal, M., Early, D.M. & Howes, C. (2008). Measures of classroom quality in prekindergarten and children's development of academic, language, and social skills. *Child Development, 79* (3), 732–749.

Maslow, A.H. (1968). *Toward a psychology of being.* (2nd ed.) Princeton, NJ: Van Nostrand.

Mason, C.A., Cauce, A.M., Gonzales, N. & Hiraga, Y. (1996). Neither too sweet nor too sour: Problem peers, maternal control, and problem behavior in African American adolescents. *Child Development, 67* (5), 2115–2130.

Mason, K.L. (2008). Cyberbullying: A preliminary assessment for school personnel. *Psychology in the Schools, 45* (4), 323–348.

Mathieson, K. & Price, M. (2002). *Better behaviour in classrooms: A framework for inclusive behaviour management.* London: Routledge/Falmer.

Matjasko, J.L. (2011). How effective are severe disciplinary policies?: School policies and offending from adolescence to young adulthood. *Journal of School Psychology, 49* (5), 555–572.

Matricciani, L., Olds, T. & Petkov, J. (2012). Secular trends in the sleep time of school-aged children. *Sleep Medicine Reviews, 16* (3), 223–230.

Mattanah, J.F. (2001). Parental psychological autonomy and children's academic competence and behavioral adjustment in late childhood: More than just limit-setting and warmth. *Merrill-Palmer Quarterly, 47* (3), 355–376.

Maughan, A. & Cicchetti, D. (2002). Impact of child maltreatment and interadult violence on children's emotion regulation and socioemotional adjustment. *Child Development, 73* (5), 1525–1542.

Mayall, B. (2002). *Towards a sociology of childhood: Thinking from children's lives.* Buckingham, UK: Open University Press.

Mayer, M.J. & Leone, P.E. (1999). A structural analysis of school violence and disruption: Implications for creating safer schools. *Education and Treatment of Children, 22* (3), 333–356.

Mayeux, L. & Cillessen, A.H.N. (2008). It's not just being popular, it's knowing it too: The role of self-perceptions of status in the associations between peer status and aggression. *Social Development, 17* (4), 871–888.

McAuliffe, M.D., Hubbard, J.A. & Romano, L.J. (2009). The role of teacher cognition and behavior in children's peer relations. *Journal of Abnormal Child Psychology, 37* (5), 665–677.

McBride, B.A., Schoppe-Sullivan, S.J. & Ho, M.-H. (2005). The mediating role of fathers' school involvement on student achievement. *Journal of Applied Developmental Psychology, 26* (2), 201–216.

McCart, M.R., Priester, P.E., Davies, W.H. & Azen, R. (2006). Differential effectiveness of behavioral parent-training and cognitive-behavioral therapy for antisocial youth: A meta-analysis. *Journal of Abnormal Child Psychology, 34* (4), 527–543.

McCarthy, M. (1987). Chronic illness and hospitalization. In J.T. Neisworth and S.J. Bagnato (Eds.) *The young exceptional child: Early development and education.* New York: Macmillan, 231–259.

McCaslin, M. & Good, T.L. (1992). Compliant cognition: The misalliance of management and instructional goals in current school reform. *Educational Researcher, 21* (3), 4–17.

McClintock, C.G. (1974). Development of social motives in Anglo-American and Mexican-American children. *Journal of Personality and Social Psychology, 29* (3), 348–354.

McClun, L.A. & Merrell, K.A. (1998). Relationship of perceived parenting styles, locus of control orientation, and self-concept among junior high age students. *Psychology in the Schools, 35* (4), 381–390.

McConaughy, S.H. & Leone, P.E. (2002). Measuring the success of prevention programs. In B. Algozzine and P. Kay (Eds.) *Preventing problem behaviors: A handbook of successful prevention strategies.* Thousand Oaks, CA: Corwin Press, 183–219.

McConaughy, S.H., Volpe, R.J., Antshel, K.M., Gordon, M. & Eiraldi, R.B. (2011). Academic and social impairments of elementary school children with attention deficit hyperactivity disorder. *School Psychology Review, 40* (2), 200–225.

McConville, D.W. & Cornell, D.G. (2003). Aggressive attitudes predict aggressive behavior in middle school students. *Journal of Emotional and Behavioral Disorders, 11* (3), 179–187.

McCord, J. (1991). Questioning the value of punishment. *Social Problems, 38* (2), 167–179.

——(1997). On discipline. *Psychological Inquiry, 8* (3), 215–217.

McDonnell, A.P. (1993). Ethical considerations in teaching compliance to individuals with mental retardation. *Education and Training in Mental Retardation, 28* (1), 3–12.

McDowell, D.J., Parke, R.D. & Wang, S.J. (2003). Differences between mothers' and fathers' advice-giving style and content: Relations with social competence and psychological functioning in middle childhood. *Merrill-Palmer Quarterly, 49* (1), 55–76.

McEachern, A.G., Aluede, O. & Kenny, M.C. (2008). Emotional abuse in the classroom: Implications and interventions for counselors. *Journal of Counseling and Development, 86* (1), 3-10.

McEvoy, A. & Welker, R. (2000). Antisocial behavior, academic failure, and school climate: A critical review. *Journal of Emotional and Behavioral Disorders, 8* (3), 130-140.

McFadyen-Ketchum, S.A., Bates, J.E., Dodge, K.A. & Pettit, G.S. (1996). Patterns of change in early childhood aggressive-disruptive behavior: Gender differences in predictions from early coercive and affectionate mother-child interactions. *Child Development, 67* (5), 2417-2433.

McFarlane, A.H., Bellissimo, A., Norman, G.R. & Lange, P. (1994). Adolescent depression in a school-based community sample: Preliminary findings on contributing social factors. *Journal of Youth and Adolescence, 23* (6), 601-620.

McGee, R., Partridge, F., Williams, S. & Silva, P.A. (1991). A twelve-year follow-up of preschool hyperactive children. *Journal of the American Academy of Child and Adolescent Psychiatry, 30* (2), 224-232.

McGee, R., Prior, M., Williams, S., Smart, D. & Sanson. A. (2002). The long-term significance of teacher-rated hyperactivity and reading ability in childhood: Findings from two longitudinal studies. *Journal of Child Psychology and Psychiatry, 43* (8), 1004-1017.

McGlone, C. (2001). Wrapping new narratives in golden paper: Solution-focused work with pupils, teachers and parents in mainstream primary schools. In Y. Ajmal and I. Rees (Eds.) *Solutions in schools.* London: BT Press, 122-134.

McGowan, P.O., Sasaki, A., D'Alessio, A.C., Dymov, S., Labonté, B., Szyf, M., Turecki, G. & Meaney, M.J. (2009). Epigenetic regulation of the glucocorticoid receptor in human brain associates with childhood abuse. *Nature Neuroscience, 12* (3), 342-348.

McGrath, H. & Stanley, M. (2006). A comparison of two non-punitive approaches to bullying. In H. McGrath and T. Noble (Eds.) *Bullying solutions: Evidence-based approaches to bullying in Australian schools.* Sydney: Pearson Longman, 189-208.

McGrath, J., Brown, A. & St Clair, D. (2011). Prevention and schizophrenia: The role of dietary factors. *Schizophrenia Bulletin, 37* (2), 272-283.

McGroder, S.M. (2000). Parenting among low-income, African American single mothers with preschool-age children: Patterns, predictors, and developmental correlates. *Child Development, 71* (3), 752-771.

McIntosh, K., Filter, K.J., Bennett, J.L., Ryan, C. & Sugai, G. (2010). Principles of sustainable prevention: Designing scale-up of school-wide positive behavior support to promote durable systems. *Psychology in the Schools, 47* (1), 5-21.

McIntosh, K., Sadler, C. & Brown, J.A. (2012). Kindergarten reading skill level and change as risk factors for chronic problem behavior. *Journal of Positive Behavior Interventions, 14* (1), 17-28.

McIntyre, T. (1996). Does the way we teach create behavior disorders in culturally different students? *Education and Treatment of Children, 19* (3), 354-371.

McKay, M., Forsyth, J.P. & Eifert, G.H. (2010). *Your life on purpose: How to find what matters and create the life you want.* Oakland, CA: New Harbinger.

McKerchar, P.M. & Thompson, R.H. (2004). A descriptive analysis of potential reinforcement contingencies in the preschool classroom. *Journal of Applied Behavior Analysis, 37* (4), 431-444.

McKissock, C., Hawkins, R.O., Lentz, F.E., Hailley, J. & McGuire, S. (2010). Randomizing multiple contingency components to decrease disruptive behaviors and increase student engagement in an urban second-grade classroom. *Psychology in the Schools, 47* (9), 944-959.

McLaughlin, H.J. (1991). Reconciling care and control: Authority in classroom relationships. *Journal of Teacher Education, 42* (3), 182-195.

McLeod, J.D., Kruttschnitt, C. & Dornfeld, M. (1994). Does parenting explain the effects of structural conditions on children's antisocial behavior?: A comparison of Blacks and Whites. *Social Forces, 73* (2), 575-604.

McMillan, D.W. & Chavis, D.M. (1986). Sense of community: A definition and theory. *Journal of Community Psychology, 14* (1), 6-23.

McNeely, C.A., Nonnemaker, J.M. & Blum, R.W. (2002). Promoting school connectedness: Evidence from the National Longitudinal Study of Adolescent Health. *Journal of School Health, 72* (4), 138-146.

McQueeny, T., Schweinsburg, B.C., Schweinsburg, A.D., Jacobus, J., Bava, S., Frank, L.R. & Tapert, S.F. (2009). Altered white matter integrity in adolescent binge drinkers. *Alcoholism: Clinical and Experimental Research, 33* (7), 1278-1285.

McWayne, C., Hampton, V., Fantuzzo, J., Cohen, H.L. & Sekino, Y. (2004). A multivariate examination of parent involvement and the social and academic competencies of urban kindergarten children. *Psychology in the Schools, 41* (3), 363-377.

Meehan, B.T., Hughes, J.N. & Cavell, T.A. (2003). Teacher-student relationships as compensatory resources for aggressive children. *Child Development, 74* (4), 1145-1157.

Meichenbaum, D. (1977). *Cognitive behavior modification: An integrative approach.* New York: Plenum Press.

Menesini, E., Codecasa, E., Benelli, B. & Cowie, H. (2003a). Enhancing children's responsibility to take action against bullying: Evaluation of a befriending intervention in Italian middle schools. *Aggressive Behavior, 29* (1), 1-14.

Menesini, E., Sanchez, V., Fonzi, A., Ortega, R., Costabile, A. & Lo Feudo, G. (2003b). Moral emotions and bullying: A cross-national comparison of differences between bullies, victims and outsiders. *Aggressive Behavior, 29* (6), 515-530.

Mercer, S.H. & DeRosier, M.E. (2008). Teacher preference, peer rejection, and student aggression: A prospective study of transactional influence and independent contributions to emotional adjustment and grades. *Journal of School Psychology, 46* (6), 661-685.

——(2010). A prospective investigation of teacher preference and children's perceptions of the student-teacher relationship. *Psychology in the Schools, 47* (2), 184-192.

Mercer, S.H., McMillen, J.S. & DeRosier, M.E. (2009). Predicting change in children's aggression and victimization using classroom-level descriptive norms of aggression and pro-social behavior. *Journal of School Psychology, 47* (4), 267-289.

Merrell, K.W., Gueldner, B.A., Ross, S.W. & Isava, D.M. (2008). How effective are school bullying intervention programs?: A meta-analysis of intervention research. *School Psychology Quarterly, 23* (1), 26-42.

Merritt, E.G., Wanless, S.B., Rimm-Kauffman, S.E., Cameron, C. & Peugh, J.L. (2012). The contribution of teachers' emotional support to children's social behaviors and self-regulatory skills in first grade. *School Psychology Review, 41* (2), 141-159.

Mesman, J., Stoel, R., Bakermans-Kranenburg, M.J., van IJzendoorn, M.H., Juffer, F., Koot, H.M. & Alink, L.R.A. (2009). Predicting growth curves of early childhood externalizing problems: Differential susceptibility of children with difficult temperament. *Journal of Abnormal Child Psychology, 37* (5), 625-636.

Metzner, J.L. & Ryan, G.D. (1995). Sexual abuse perpetration. In G.P. Sholevar (Ed.) *Conduct disorders in children and adolescents.* Washington, DC: American Psychiatric Press, 119-142.

Meyer, D.K. & Turner, J.C. (2006). Re-conceptualizing emotion and motivation to learn in classroom contexts. *Educational Psychology Review, 18* (4), 377–390.

Meyer, L.H., McClure, J., Walkley, F., Weir, K.F. & McKenzie, L. (2009). Secondary student motivation orientations and standards-based achievement outcomes. *British Journal of Educational Psychology, 79* (2), 273–293.

Meyers, S.A. (1999). Mothering in context: Ecological determinants of parent behavior. *Merrill-Palmer Quarterly, 45* (2), 332–357.

Michalik, N.M., Eisenberg, N., Spindrad, T.L., Ladd, B., Thompson, M. & Valiente, C. (2007). Longitudinal relations among parental emotional expressivity and sympathy and prosocial behavior in adolescence. *Social Development, 16* (2), 286–309.

Miedel, W.T. & Reynolds, A.J. (1999). Parent involvement in early intervention for disadvantaged children: Does it matter?. *Journal of School Psychology, 37* (4), 379–402.

Mikami, A.Y., Griggs, M.S., Reuland, M.M. & Gregory, A. (2012). Teacher practices as predictors of children's classroom social preference. *Journal of School Psychology, 50* (1), 95–111.

Mikkelsen, E.J. (1997). Responding to allegations of sexual abuse in child care and early childhood education programs. *Young Children, 52* (3), 47–51.

Mikulas, W.L. & Vodanovich, S.J. (1993). The essence of boredom. *The Psychological Record, 43* (1), 3–12.

Milgram, N. & Toubiana, Y. (1999). Academic anxiety, academic procrastination, and parents involvement in students and their parents. *British Journal of Educational Psychology, 69* (3), 345–361.

Milgram, S. (1963). Behavioral study of obedience. *Journal of Abnormal and Social Psychology, 67* (4), 371–378.

Mill, D. & Romano-White, D. (1999). Correlates of affectionate and angry behavior in child care educators of preschool-aged children. *Early Childhood Research Quarterly, 14* (2), 155–178.

Mill, J.S. (1859/1978). *On liberty.* Indianapolis, IN: Hackett.

Miller, A. (1987). *For your own good: The roots of violence in child-rearing.* London: Virago Press.

——(2003). *Teachers, parents and classroom behaviour: A psychosocial approach.* Maidenhead, UK: Open University Press.

Miller, A., Ferguson, E. & Byrne, I. (2000). Pupils' causal attributions for difficult classroom behaviour. *British Journal of Educational Psychology, 70* (1), 85–96.

Miller, A., Ferguson, E. & Moore, E. (2002). Parents' and pupils' causal attributions for difficult classroom behaviour. *British Journal of Educational Psychology, 72* (1), 27–40.

Miller, A.G. & Thomas, R. (1972). Cooperation and competition among Blackfoot Indian and urban Canadian children. *Child Development, 43* (3), 1104–1110.

Miller, D., Topping, K. & Thurston, A. (2010). Peer tutoring in reading: The effects of role and organization on two dimensions of self-esteem. *British Journal of Educational Psychology, 80* (3), 417–433.

Miller, G.E., Brehm, K. & Whitehouse, S. (1998). Reconceptualizing school-based prevention for antisocial behavior within a resiliency framework. *School Psychology Review, 27* (3), 364–379.

Miller, J.L., Vaillancourt, T. & Boyle, M.H. (2008). Examining the heterotypic continuity of aggression using teacher reports: Results from a national Canadian study. *Social Development, 18* (1), 164–180.

Miller, L.K. (1991). Avoiding the countercontrol of applied behavior analysis. *Journal of Applied Behavior Analysis, 24* (4), 645–647.

Miller, M. (1991). Self-assessment as a specific strategy for teaching the gifted learning disabled. *Journal for the Education of the Gifted, 14* (2), 178–188.

Miller, M. & Hinshaw, S.P. (2012). Attention-deficit/hyperactivity disorder. In P.C. Kendall (Ed.) *Child and adolescent therapy: Cognitive-behavioral procedures.* (4th ed.) New York: Guilford, 61–91.

Miller, R.C. & Berman, J.S. (1983). The efficacy of cognitive behavior therapies: A quantitative review of the research evidence. *Psychological Bulletin, 94* (1), 39–53.

Miller, S., Loeber, R. & Hipwell, A. (2009). Peer deviance, parenting and disruptive behavior among young girls. *Journal of Abnormal Child Psychology, 37* (2), 139–152.

Miller-Lewis, L.R., Baghurst, P.A., Sawyer, M.G., Prior, M.R., Clark, J.J., Arney, F.M. & Carbone, J.A. (2006). Early childhood externalizing behaviour problems: Child, parenting, and family-related predictors over time. *Journal of Abnormal Child Psychology, 34* (6), 891–906.

Mintz, J. (2003). *No homework and recess all day: How to have freedom and democracy in education.* New York: Bravura.

Miranda, A. & Presentación, M.J. (2000). Efficacy of cognitive-behavioral therapy in the treatment of children with ADHD, with and without aggressiveness. *Psychology in the Schools, 37* (2), 169–182.

Miserandino, M. (1996). Children who do well in school: Individual differences in perceived competence and autonomy in above-average children. *Journal of Educational Psychology, 88* (2), 203–214.

Mitchell, M. (1993). Situational interest: Its multifaceted structure in the secondary school mathematics classroom. *Journal of Educational Psychology, 85* (3), 424–436.

Moe, V. & Smith, L. (2003). The relation of prenatal substance exposure and infant recognition memory to later cognitive competence. *Infant Behavior and Development, 26* (1), 87–99.

Moffitt, T.E. (1993a). Adolescence-limited and life-course-persistent antisocial behavior: A developmental taxonomy. *Psychological Review, 100* (4), 674–701.

——(1993b). The neuropsychology of conduct disorder. *Development and Psychopathology, 5* (1–2), 135–151.

Moilanen, K.L., Shaw, D.S., Dishion, T.J., Gardner, F., & Wilson, M. (2010). Predictors of longitudinal growth in inhibitory control in early childhood, *Social Development, 19* (2), 326–347.

Moline, S. & Frankenberger, W. (2001). Use of stimulant medication for treatment of attention-deficit/hyperactivity disorder: A survey of middle and high school students' attitudes. *Psychology in the Schools, 38* (6), 569–584.

Möller, J. (2005). Paradoxical effects of praise and criticism: Social, dimensional and temporal comparisons. *British Journal of Educational Psychology, 75* (2), 275–295.

Molnar, A. & de Shazer, S. (1987). Solution-focused therapy: Toward the identification of therapeutic tasks. *Journal of Marital and Family Therapy, 13* (4), 349–358.

Molnar, A. & Lindquist, B. (1989). *Changing problem behavior in schools.* San Francisco, CA: Jossey-Bass.

Montgomery, B. (1982). *Coping with stress.* Melbourne: Pitman.

Montgomery, H. (2003). Childhood in time and place. In M. Woodhead and H. Montgomery (Eds.) *Understanding childhood: An interdisciplinary approach.* Milton Keynes, UK: Open University Press, 45–83.

Monuteaux, M.C., Blacker, D., Biederman, J., Fitzmaurice, G. & Buka, S.L. (2006). Maternal smoking during pregnancy and offspring overt and covert conduct problems: A longitudinal study. *Journal of Child Psychology and Psychiatry, 47* (9), 883–890.

Moon, S.M., Swift, M. & Shallenberger, A. (2002). Perceptions of a self-contained class for fourth- and fifth-grade students with high to extreme levels of intellectual giftedness. *Gifted Child Quarterly, 46* (1), 64–79.

Moorman, E.A. & Pomerantz, E.M. (2008). The role of mothers' control in children's mastery orientation: A time frame analysis. *Journal of Family Psychology, 22* (5), 734–741.

Morgan, A. (Ed.) (1999). *Once upon a time . . . Narrative therapy with children and their families*. Adelaide, SA: Dulwich Centre Publications.

——(2000). *What is narrative therapy?: An easy-to-read introduction*. Adelaide, SA: Dulwich Centre Publications.

Morgan, H. (1996). An analysis of Gardner's theory of multiple intelligences. *Roeper Review, 18* (4), 263–269.

Morgan, M. (1983). Decrements in intrinsic motivation among rewarded and observer subjects. *Child Development, 54* (3), 636–644.

Morris, A.S., Silk, J.S., Steinberg, L., Myers, S.S. & Robinson, L.R. (2007). The role of the family context in the development of emotion regulation. *Social Development, 16* (2), 361–388.

Morris-Rothschild, B.K. & Brassard, M.R. (2006). Teachers' conflict management styles: The role of attachment styles and classroom management efficacy. *Journal of School Psychology, 44* (2), 105–121.

Morrison, G.M., Anthony, S., Storino, M. & Dillon, C. (2001). An examination of the disciplinary histories and individual educational characteristics of students who participate in an in-school suspension program. *Education and Treatment of Children, 24* (3), 276–293.

Morrison, G.M. & D'Incau, B. (1997). The web of zero-tolerance: Characteristics of students who are recommended for expulsion from school. *Education and Treatment of Children, 20* (3), 316–335.

Morrison, G.M., Robertson, L. & Harding, M. (1998). Resilience factors that support the classroom functioning of acting out and aggressive students. *Psychology in the Schools, 35* (3), 217–227.

Morrison, J.Q. & Jones, K.M. (2007). The effects of positive peer reporting as a class-wide positive behavior support. *Journal of Behavioral Education, 16* (2), 111–124.

Mortensen, P.B., Nørgaard-Pedersen, B., Waltoft, B.L., Sørensen, T.L., Hougaard, D., Torrey, E.F. & Yolken, R.H. (2007). Toxoplasma gondii as a risk factor for early-onset schizophrenia: Analysis of filter paper blood samples taken at birth. *Biological Psychiatry, 61* (5), 688–693.

Mortimore, P. & Sammons, P. (1987). New evidence on effective elementary schools. *Educational Leadership, 45* (1), 4–8.

Mortimore, P., Sammons, P., Stoll, L., Ecob, R. & Lewis, D. (1988). The effects of school membership on pupils' outcomes. *Research Papers in Education, 3* (1), 3–26.

Moss, H.B. (2008). Special section: Alcohol and adolescent brain development. *Alcoholism: Clinical and Experimental Research, 32* (3), 427–429.

Motivala, S.J., Sarfatti, A., Olmos, L. & Irwin, M.R. (2005). Inflammatory markers and sleep disturbance in major depression. *Psychosomatic Medicine, 67* (2), 187–194.

Mruk, C.J. (2006a). Defining self-esteem: An often overlooked issue with crucial implications. In M.H. Kernis (Ed.) *Self-esteem: Issues and answers: A sourcebook of current perspectives*. New York: Psychology Press, 10–15.

——(2006b). *Self-esteem research, theory, and practice*. (3rd ed.) New York: Springer.

Mueller, C.M. & Dweck, C.S. (1998). Praise for intelligence can undermine children's motivation and performance. *Journal of Personality and Social Psychology, 75* (1), 33–52.

Mueller, M.M., Nkosi, A. & Hine, J.F. (2011). Functional analysis in public schools: A summary of 90 functional analyses. *Journal of Applied Behavior Analysis, 44* (4), 807–818.

Mueller, M.M., Sterling-Turner, H.E. & Scattone, D. (2001). Functional assessment of hand flapping in a general education classroom. *Journal of Applied Behavior Analysis, 34* (2), 233–236.

Mukherjee, S., Lightfoot, J. & Sloper, P. (2000). The inclusion of pupils with a chronic health condition in mainstream school: What does it mean for teachers?. *Educational Research, 42* (1), 59–72.

Mullen, P.E., Martin, J.L., Anderson, J.C., Romans, S.E. & Herbison, G.P. (1996). The long-term impact of the physical, emotional, and sexual abuse of children: A community study. *Child Abuse and Neglect, 20* (1), 7–21.

Mullender, A., Hague, G., Imam, U., Kelly, L., Malos, E. & Regan, L. (2002). *Children's perspectives on domestic violence*. London: SAGE Publications.

Muller, C., Katz, S.B. & Dance, L.J. (1999). Investing in teaching and learning: Dynamics of the teacher-student relationship from each actor's perspective. *Urban Education, 34* (3), 292–337.

Mulvaney, M.K. & Mebert, C.J. (2007). Parental corporal punishment predicts behavior problems in early childhood. *Journal of Family Psychology, 21* (3), 389–397.

Munroe, R.L. & Munroe, R.H. (1977). Cooperation and competition among East African and American children. *Journal of Social Psychology, 101* (1), 145–146.

Murdock, T.B. & Bolch, M.B. (2005). Risk and protective factors for poor school adjustment in lesbian, gay, and bisexual (LGB) high school youth: Variable and person-centered analyses. *Psychology in the Schools, 42* (2), 159–172.

Murphy, B.C., Shepard, S. & Eisenberg, N. & Fabes, R.A. (2004). Concurrent and across time prediction of young adolescents' social functioning: The role of emotionality and regulation. *Social Development, 13* (1), 56–86.

Murphy, J.J. (1994). Brief therapy for school problems. *School Psychology International, 15* (2), 115–131.

——(2006). *Solution-focused counseling in middle and high schools*. Upper Saddle River, NJ: Pearson Merrill Prentice Hall.

——(2008). *Solution-focused counseling in schools*. (2nd ed.) Alexandria,VA: American Counseling Association.

Murphy, J.J. & Duncan, B.L. (1997). *Brief intervention for school problems: Collaborating for practical solutions*. New York: Guilford.

——(2007). *Brief intervention for school problems: Outcome-informed strategies*. (2nd ed.) New York: Guilford.

Murphy, K.A., Theodore, L.A., Aloiso, D., Alric-Edwards, J.M. & Hughes, T.L. (2007). Interdependent group contingency and mystery motivators to reduce preschool disruptive behavior. *Psychology in the Schools, 44* (1), 53–63.

Murray, C. & Greenberg, M.T. (2000). Children's relationships with teachers and bonds with school: An investigation of patterns and correlates in middle childhood. *Journal of School Psychology, 38* (5), 423–445.

Murray, C., Waas, G.A. & Murray, K.M. (2008). Child race and gender as moderators of the association between teacher-child relationships and school adjustment. *Psychology in the Schools, 45* (6), 562–578.

Murray, M. & Lyon, M. (2006). *Beat diabetes naturally*. New York: Rodale.

Murray, R.M., Jones, P., O'Callaghan, E., Takei, N. & Sham, P. (1992). Genes, viruses and neurodevelopmental schizophrenia. *Journal of Psychiatric Research, 26* (4), 225–235.

Murray, S.L., Rose, P., Bellavia, G.M., Holmes, J.G. & Kusche, A.G. (2002). When rejection stings: How self-esteem constrains relationship-enhancement processes. *Journal of Personality and Social Psychology, 83* (3), 556–572.

Murray-Close, D., Crick, N.R. & Galotti, K.M. (2006). Children's moral reasoning regarding physical and relational aggression. *Social Development, 15* (3), 345–372.

Murray-Close, D., Ostrov, J.M. & Crick, N.R. (2007). A short-term longitudinal study of growth of relational aggression during middle childhood: Associations with gender, friendship intimacy, and internalizing problems. *Development and Psychopathology, 19* (1), 187–203.

Murrell, S.A., Meeks, S. & Walker, J. (1991). Protective functions of health and self-esteem against depression in older adults facing illness or bereavement. *Psychology and Aging, 6* (3), 352–360.

Musher-Eizenman, D.R., Boxer, P., Danner, S., Dubow, E.F., Goldstein, S.E. & Heretick, D.M.L. (2004). Social-cognitive mediators of the relation of environmental and emotion regulation factors to children's aggression. *Aggressive Behavior, 30* (5), 389–408.

Musser, E.H., Bray, M.A., Kehle, T.J. & Jenson, W.R. (2001). Reducing disruptive behaviors in students with serious emotional disturbance. *School Psychology Review, 30* (2), 294–304.

Myers, C.L. & Holland, K.L. (2000). Classroom behavioral interventions: Do teachers consider the function of the behavior?. *Psychology in the Schools, 37* (3), 271–280.

Myers, D.G. (2005). *Social psychology.* (8th ed.) Boston, MA: McGraw-Hill.

Mynard, H., Joseph, S. & Alexander, J. (2000). Peer-victimisation and post-traumatic stress in adolescents. *Personality and Individual Differences, 29* (5), 815–821.

Nabors, L.A., Little, S.G., Akin-Little, A. & Iobst, E.A. (2008). Teacher knowledge of and confidence in meeting the needs of children with chronic medical conditions: Pediatric psychology's contribution to education. *Psychology in the Schools, 45* (3), 217–226.

Nagel, M.C. (2012). *In the beginning: The brain, early development and learning.* Melbourne: ACER.

Nagin, D. & Tremblay, R.E. (1999). Trajectories of boys' physical aggression, opposition, and hyperactivity on the path to physically violent and nonviolent juvenile delinquency. *Child Development, 70* (5), 1181–1196.

Naglieri, J.A. & Kaufman, J.C. (2001). Understanding intelligence, giftedness and creativity using the PASS theory. *Roeper Review, 23* (3), 151–156.

Nakamoto, J. & Schwartz, D. (2009). Is peer victimization associated with academic achievement?: A meta-analytic review. *Social Development, 19* (2), 221–242.

Nansel, T.R., Overpeck, M., Pilla, R.S., Ruan, W.J., Simons-Morton, B. & Scheidt, P. (2001). Bullying behaviors among US youth: Prevalence and association with psychosocial adjustment. *Journal of the American Medical Association, 285* (16), 2094–2100.

Neef, N.A., Bicard, D.F. & Endo, S. (2001). Assessment of impulsivity and the development of self-control in students with attention deficit hyperactivity disorder. *Journal of Applied Behavior Analysis, 34* (4), 397–408.

Neef, N.A., Mace, F.C. & Shade, D. (1993). Impulsivity in students with serious emotional disturbance: The interactive effects of reinforcer rate, delay, and quality. *Journal of Applied Behavior Analysis, 26* (1), 37–52.

Nelsen, J., Lott, L. & Glenn, H.S. (2000). *Positive discipline in the classroom.* (3rd ed.) Roseville, CA: Prima Publishing.

Nelson, D.A., Hart, C.H., Yang, C., Olson, J.A. & Jin, S. (2006). Aversive parenting in China: Associations with child physical and relational aggression. *Child Development, 77* (3), 554–572.

Nelson, J.D., Gelfand, D.M. & Hartmann, D.P. (1969). Children's aggression following competition and exposure to an aggressive model. *Child Development, 40* (4), 1085–1097.

Nelson, J.J., Rubin, K.H. & Fox, N.A. (2005). Social withdrawal, observed peer acceptance, and the development of self-perceptions in children ages 4 to 7 years. *Early Childhood Research Quarterly, 20* (2), 185–200.

Nelson, J.R. (1996). Designing schools to meet the needs of students who exhibit disruptive behavior. *Journal of Emotional and Behavioral Disorders, 4* (3), 147–161.

——(1998). The effects of teaching school expectations and establishing a consistent consequence on formal office disciplinary actions. *Journal of Emotional and Behavioral Disorders, 6* (3), 153–161.

Nelson, J.R., Benner, G.J., Lane, K. & Smith, B.W. (2004). Academic achievement of K–12 students with emotional and behavioral disorders. *Exceptional Children, 71* (1), 59–73.

Nelson, J.R., Maculan, A., Roberts, M.L. & Ohlund, B.J. (2001). Sources of occupational stress for teachers of students with emotional and behavioral disorders. *Journal of Emotional and Behavioral Disorders, 9* (2), 123–130.

Nelson, J.R. & Roberts, M.L. (2000). Ongoing reciprocal teacher-student interactions involving disruptive behaviors in general education classrooms. *Journal of Emotional and Behavioral Disorders, 8* (1), 27–37.

Nelson, J.R., Roberts, M.L., Mathur, S.R. & Rutherford, R.B. Jr (1999). Has public policy exceeded our knowledge base?: A review of the functional behavioral assessment literature. *Behavioral Disorders, 24* (2), 169–179.

Nelson, J.R., Stage, S., Duppong-Hurley, K., Synhorst, L. & Epstein, M.H. (2007). Risk factors predictive of problem behavior of children at risk for emotional and behavioral disorders. *Exceptional Children, 73* (3), 367–379.

Nelson, W.M. III, Finch, A.J. Jr & Ghee, A.C. (2012). Anger management with children and adolescents: Cognitive-behavioral therapy. In P.C. Kendall (Ed.) *Child and adolescent therapy: Cognitive-behavioral procedures.* (4th ed.) New York: Guilford, 92–139.

Nesbit, W.C. & Philpott, D.F. (2002). Confronting subtle emotional abuse in classrooms. *Guidance and Counselling, 17* (2), 32–38.

Nesdale, D., Durkin, K. Maass, A. & Griffiths, J. (2005). Threat, group identification, and children's ethnic prejudice. *Social Development, 14* (2), 189–205.

Nesdale, D., Durkin, K., Maass, A., Kiesner, J. & Griffiths, J.A. (2008). Effects of group norms on children's intention to bully. *Social Development, 17* (4), 889–907.

Nesdale, D. & Lawson, M.J. (2011). Social groups and children's intergroup attitudes: Can school norms moderate the effects of social group norms? *Child Development, 82* (5), 1594–1606.

Nesdale, D., Milliner, E., Duffy, A. & Griffiths, J.A. (2009). Group membership, group norms, empathy, and young children's intentions to aggress. *Aggressive Behavior, 35* (3), 244–258.

Nesdale, D. & Pickering, K. (2006). Teachers' reactions to children's aggression. *Social Development, 15* (1), 109–127.

Neumeister, K.L.S. (2004a). Understanding the relation between perfectionism and achievement motivation in gifted college students. *Gifted Child Quarterly, 48* (3), 219–231.

——(2004b). Factors influencing the development of perfectionism in gifted college students. *Gifted Child Quarterly, 48* (4), 259–274.

Neumeister, K.L.S. & Finch, H. (2006). Perfectionism in high-ability students: Relational precursors and influences on achievement motivation. *Gifted Child Quarterly, 50* (3), 218–251.

Neumeister, K.L.S., Williams, K.K. & Cross, T.L. (2009). Gifted high-school students' perspectives on the development of perfectionism. *Roeper Review, 31* (4), 198–206.

Neven, R.S., Anderson, V. & Godber, T. (2002). *Rethinking ADHD: Integrated approaches to helping children at school and at home.* Sydney: Allen & Unwin.

Newcomer, L.L. & Lewis, T.J. (2004). Functional behavioral assessment: An investigation of assessment reliability and effectiveness of function-based interventions. *Journal of Emotional and Behavioral Disorders, 12* (3), 168–181.

Newman, R.S. & Murray, B.J. (2005). How students and teachers view the seriousness of peer harassment: When is it appropriate to seek help? *Journal of Educational Psychology, 97* (3), 347–365.

Newmann, F.M. (Ed.) (1996). *Authentic achievement: Restructuring schools for intellectual quality.* San Francisco, CA: Jossey-Bass.

Newmann, F.M., King, M.B. & Secada, W.G. (1996). Intellectual quality. In F.M. Newmann (Ed.) *Authentic achievement: Restructuring schools for intellectual quality.* San Francisco, CA: Jossey-Bass, 161–178.

Newmann, F.M. & Wehlage, G.G. (1993). Five standards of authentic instruction. *Educational Leadership, 50* (7), 8–12.

Nguni, S., Sleegers, P. & Denessen, E. (2006). Transformational and transactional leadership effects on teachers' job satisfaction, organizational commitment, and organizational citizenship behavior in primary schools: The Tanzanian case. *School Effectiveness and School Improvement, 17* (2), 145–177.

NICHD Early Child Care Research Network (1999). Child care and mother-child interaction in the first three years of life. *Developmental Psychology, 35* (6), 1399–1413.

——(2001). Child care and children's peer interaction at 24 and 36 months: The NICHD study of early child care. *Child Development, 72* (5), 1478–1500.

——(2003). Social functioning in first grade: Associations with earlier home and child care predictors and with current classroom experiences. *Child Development, 74* (6), 1639–1662.

——(2004). Affect dysregulation in the mother-child relationship in the toddler years: Antecedents and consequences. *Development and Psychopathology, 16* (1), 43–68.

——(2005). Predicting individual differences in attention, memory, and planning in first graders from experiences at home, child care, and school. *Developmental Psychology, 41* (1), 99–114.

Nichols, M.P. & Schwartz, R.C. (1995). *Family therapy: Concepts and methods.* (3rd ed.) Boston, MA: Allyn & Bacon.

Nichols, P. (2000). Role of cognition and affect in a functional behavioral analysis. *Exceptional Children, 66* (3), 393–402.

Nicholson, A. (2006). Legal perspectives on bullying. In H. McGrath and T. Noble (Eds.) *Bullying solutions: Evidence-based approaches to bullyng in Australian schools.* Sydney: Pearson Longman, 17–45.

Nickerson, A.B. & Martens, M.P. (2008). School violence: Associations with control, security/enforcement, educational/therapeutic approaches, and demographic factors. *School Psychological Review, 37* (2), 228–243.

Niehaus, K., Rudasill, K.M. & Rakes, C.R. (2012). A longitudinal study of school connectedness and academic outcomes across sixth grade. *Journal of School Psychology, 50* (4), 443–460.

Nigg, J.T., Quamma, J.P., Greenberg, M.T. & Kusche, C.A. (1999). A two-year longitudinal study of neuropsychological and cognitive performance in relation to behavioral problems and competencies in elementary school. *Journal of Abnormal Child Psychology, 27* (1), 51–63.

Nipedal, C., Nesdale, D. & Killen, M. (2010). Social group norms, school norms, and children's aggressive intentions. *Aggressive Behavior, 36* (3), 195–204.

Nishina, A. (2004). A theoretical review of bullying: Can it be eliminated? In C.E. Sanders and G.D. Phye (Eds.) *Bullying: Implications for the classroom.* San Diego, CA: Elsevier, 35–62.

Nix, R.L., Pinderhughes, E.E., Dodge, K.A., Bates, J.E., Pettit, G.S. &

McFadyen-Ketchum, S.A. (1999). The relation between mothers' hostile attribution tendencies and children's externalizing behavior problems: The mediating role of mothers' harsh discipline. *Child Development, 70* (4), 896–909.

Nixon, C.L. & Werner, N.E. (2010). Reducing adolescents' involvement with relational aggression: Evaluating the effectiveness of the Creating a Safe School (CASS) intervention. *Psychology in the Schools, 47* (6), 606–620.

Noaghiul, S. & Hibbein, J.R. (2003). Cross-national comparisons of seafood consumption and rates of bipolar disorders. *The American Journal of Psychiatry, 160* (12), 2222–2227.

Noble, K. & Macfarlane, K. (2005). Romance or reality: Examining burnout in early childhood teachers. *Australian Journal of Early Childhood, 30* (3), 53–58.

Noble, T. (2006). Core components of a school-wide safe schools curriculum. In H. McGrath and T. Noble (Eds.) *Bullying solutions: Evidence-based approaches to bullying in Australian schools.* Sydney: Pearson Longman, 67–83.

Noblit, G.W. (1993). Power and caring. *American Educational Research Journal, 30* (1), 23–38.

Noblit, G.W., Rogers, D.L. & McCadden, B.M. (1995). In the meantime: The possibilities of caring. *Phi Delta Kappan, 76* (9), 680–685.

Noddings, N. (2003). *Happiness and education.* Cambridge, UK: Cambridge University Press.

Noguera, P.A. (1995). Preventing and producing violence: A critical analysis of responses to school violence. *Harvard Educational Review, 65* (2), 189–212.

——(2003). Schools, prisons, and social implications of punishment: Rethinking disciplinary practices. *Theory into Practice, 42* (4), 340–350.

Norem-Hebeisen, A.A. & Johnson, D.W. (1981). The relationship between cooperative, competitive, and individualistic attitudes and differentiated aspects of self-esteem. *Journal of Personality, 49* (4), 415–426.

Norris, J.A. (2003). Looking at classroom management through a social and emotional learning lens. *Theory into Practice, 42* (4), 313–318.

Northey, W.F. Jr, Wells, K.C., Silverman, W.K. & Bailey, C.E. (2003). Childhood behavioral and emotional disorders. *Journal of Marital and Family Therapy, 29* (4), 523–545.

Northup, J. & Gulley, V. (2001). Some contributions of functional analysis to the assessment of behaviors associated with attention deficit hyperactivity disorder and the effects of stimulant medication. *School Psychology Review, 30* (2), 227–238.

Nupponen, H. (2006). Leadership concepts and theories: Reflections for practice for early childhood directors. *Australian Journal of Early Childhood, 31* (1), 43–50.

O'Brennan, L.M., Bradshaw, C.P. & Sawyer, A.L. (2009). Examining developmental differences in the social-emotional problems among frequent bullies, victims, and bully/victims. *Psychology in the Schools, 46* (2), 100–115.

O'Brien, E.J., Bartoletti, M., Leitzel, J.D. & O'Brien, J.P. (2006). Global self-esteem: Divergent and convergent validity issues. In M.H. Kernis (Ed.) *Self-esteem: Issues and answers: A sourcebook of current perspectives.* New York: Psychology Press, 26–35.

O'Connor, E. (2010). Teacher-child relationships as dynamic systems. *Journal of School Psychology, 48* (3), 187–218.

O'Connor, E. & McCartney, K. (2006). Testing associations between young children's relationships with mothers and teachers. *Journal of Educational Psychology, 98* (1), 87–98.

O'Connor, T.G. (2002). Annotation: The 'effects' of parenting reconsidered: Findings, challenges, and applications. *Journal of Child Psychology and Psychiatry, 43* (5), 555–572.

O'Leary, K.D. (1972). Behavior modification in the classroom: A rejoinder to Winett and Winkler. *Journal of Applied Behavior Analysis, 5* (4), 505–511.

O'Leary, S.G., Slep, A.M.S. & Reid, M.J. (1999). A longitudinal study of mothers' overreactive discipline and toddlers' externalizing behavior. *Journal of Abnormal Child Psychology, 27* (5), 331–341.

O'Moore, M. & Minton, S.J. (2004). *Dealing with bullying in schools: A training manual for teachers, parents and other professionals.* London: Paul Chapman.

O'Reilly, M.F., Lacey, C. & Lancioni, G.E. (2000). Assessment of the influence of background noise on escape-maintained problem behavior and pain behavior in a child with Williams syndrome. *Journal of Applied Behavior Analysis, 33* (4), 511–514.

Oberski, I., Ford, K., Higgins, S. & Fisher, P. (1999). The importance of relationships in teacher education. *Journal of Education for Teaching, 25* (2), 135–150.

Odom, S.L., McConnell, S.R., McEvoy, M.A., Peterson, C., Ostrosky, M., Chandler, L.K., Spicuzza, R.J., Skellenger, A., Creighton, M. & Favazza, P.C. (1999). Relative effects of interventions supporting the social competence of young children with disabilities. *Topics in Early Childhood Special Education, 19* (2), 75–91.

Offer, D. & Schonert-Reichl, K.A. (1992). Debunking the myths of adolescence: Findings from recent research. *Journal of the American Academy of Child and Adolescent Psychiatry, 31* (6), 1003–1014.

Ohene, S.-A., Ireland, M., McNeely, C. & Borowsky, I.W. (2006). Parental expectations, physical punishment, and violence among adolescents who score positive on a psychosocial screening test in primary care. *Pediatrics, 117* (2), 441–447.

Okagaki, L. & Frensch, P.A. (1998). Parenting and children's school achievement: A multiethnic perspective. *American Educational Research Journal, 35* (1), 123–144.

Olson, S.L., Bates, J.E. & Bayles, K. (1990). Early antecedents of childhood impulsivity: The role of parent-child interaction, cognitive competence, and temperament. *Journal of Abnormal Child Psychology, 18* (3), 317–334.

Olson, S.L., Bates, J.E., Sandy, J.M. & Schilling, E.M. (2002). Early developmental precursors of impulsive and inattentive behavior: From infancy to middle childhood. *Journal of Child Psychology and Psychiatry, 43* (4), 435–447.

Olszewski, P., Kulieke, M.J. & Willis, G. (1987). Changes in the self-perceptions of gifted students who participate in rigorous academic programs. *Journal for the Education of the Gifted, 10* (4), 287–303.

Olthof, T. & Goossens, F.A. (2008). Bullying and the need to belong: Early adolescents' bullying-related behavior and the acceptance they desire and receive from particular classmates. *Social Development, 17* (1), 24–46.

Olthof, T., Goossens, F.A., Vermande, M.M., Aleva, E.A. & van der Meulen, M. (2011). Bullying as strategic behavior: Relations with desired and acquired dominance in the peer group. *Journal of School Psychology, 49* (3), 339–359.

Olweus, D. (1993). *Bullying at school: What we know and what we can do.* Oxford, UK: Blackwell.

——(2001). Peer harassment: A critical analysis and some important issues. In J. Juvonen and S. Graham (Eds.) *Peer harassment in school: The plight of the vulnerable and victimized.* New York: Guilford, 3–20.

Omer, H. (2001). Helping parents deal with children's acute disciplinary problems without escalation: The principle of nonviolent resistance. *Family Process, 40* (1), 53–66.

O'Neill, S. & Stephenson, J. (2009). Teacher involvement in the development of function-based behaviour intervention plans for students with challenging behaviour. *Australasian Journal of Special Education, 33* (1), 6–25.

Op 't Eynde, P. & Turner, J.E. (2006). Focusing on the complexity of emotion issues in academic learning: A dynamical component systems approach. *Educational Psychology Review, 18* (4), 361–376.

Orobio de Castro, B., Veerman, J.W., Koops, W., Bosch, J.D. & Monshouwer, H.J. (2002). Hostile attribution of intent and aggressive behavior: A meta-analysis. *Child Development, 73* (3), 916–934.

Orpinas, P., Horne, A.M. & Staniszewski, D. (2003). School bullying: Changing the problem by changing the school. *School Psychology Review, 32* (3), 431–444.

OSEP Center on Positive Behavioral Interventions and Supports (2000). Applying positive behavior support and functional behavioral assessment in schools. *Journal of Positive Behavior Interventions, 2* (3), 131–143.

Osher, T.W. & Osher, D.M. (2002). The paradigm shift to true collaboration with families. *Journal of Child and Family Studies, 11* (1), 47–60.

Osler, A. & Vincent, K. (2003). *Girls and exclusion: Rethinking the agenda.* London: RoutledgeFalmer.

Osterman, K.F. (2000). Students' need for belonging in the school community. *Review of Educational Research, 70* (3), 323–367.

Ostrov, J.M., Crick, N.R. & Stauffacher, K. (2006). Relational aggression in sibling and peer relationships during early childhood. *Journal of Applied Developmental Psychology, 27* (3), 241–253.

Ostrov, J.M. & Keating, C.F. (2004). Gender differences in preschool aggression during free play and structured interactions: An observational study. *Social Development, 13* (2), 255–277.

Ostrov, J.M., Massetti, G.M., Stauffacher, K., Godleski, S.A., Hart, K.C., Karch, K.M., Mullins, A.D. & Ries, E.E. (2009). An intervention for relational and physical aggression in early childhood: A preliminary study. *Early Childhood Research Quarterly, 24* (1), 15–28.

Ostrov, J.M., Woods, K.E., Jansen, E.A., Casas, J.F. & Crick, N.R. (2004). An observational study of delivered and received aggression, gender, and social-psychological adjustment in preschool: 'This white crayon doesn't work . . .'. *Early Childhood Research Quarterly, 19* (2), 355–371.

Overbeek, G., Zeevalkink, H., Vermulst, A. & Scholte, R.H.J. (2010). Peer victimization, self-esteem, and ego resilience types in adolescents: A prospective analysis of person-context interactions. *Social Development, 19* (2), 270–284.

Overstreet, S., Devine, J., Bevans, K. & Efreom, Y. (2005). Predicting parental involvement in children's schooling within an economically disadvantaged African American sample. *Psychology in the Schools, 42* (1), 101–111.

Owens, E.B. & Shaw, D.S. (2003). Predicting growth curves of externalizing behavior across the preschool years. *Journal of Abnormal Child Psychology, 31* (6), 575–590.

Owens, L. (1997). Teenage girls: Voices of aggression. In *Proceedings of the International School Psychology 20th Annual Colloquium,* Melbourne, July 1997, 219–222.

Owens, L., Daly, A. & Slee, P. (2005a). Sex and age differences in victimisation and conflict resolution among adolescents in a South Australian school. *Aggressive Behavior, 31* (1), 1–12.

Owens, L., Shute, R. & Slee, P. (2000a). 'Guess what I just heard!': Indirect aggression among teenage girls in Australia. *Aggressive Behavior, 26* (1), 67–83.

——(2000b). 'I'm in and you're out . . .': Explanations for teenage girls' indirect aggression. *Psychology, Evolution and Gender, 2* (1), 19–46.

——(2005). 'In the eye of the beholder . . .': Girls', boys' and teachers' perceptions of boys' aggression to girls. *International Education Journal, 5* (5), 142–151.

Owens, L., Slee, P. & Shute, R. (2000c). 'It hurts a hell of a lot . . .':

The effects of indirect aggression on teenage girls. *School Psychology International, 21* (4), 359–376.

——(2001). Victimization among teenage girls: What can be done about indirect harassment? In J. Juvonen and S. Graham (Eds.) *Peer harassment in school: The plight of the vulnerable and victimized.* New York: Guilford, 215–241.

Pagani, L.S., Tremblay, R.E., Nagin, D., Zoccolillo, M., Vitaro, F. & McDuff, P. (2004). Risk factor models for adolescent verbal and physical aggression towards mothers. *International Journal of Behavioral Development, 28* (6), 528–537.

Palagini, L. & Rosenlicht, N. (2011). Sleep, dreaming, and mental health: A review of historical and neurobiological perspectives. *Sleep Medicine Reviews, 15* (3), 179–186.

Palardy, J.M. (1996). Taking another look at behavior modification and assertive discipline. *NASSP Bulletin, 80* (581), 66–70.

Palmer, E.J. & Hollin, C.R. (2001). Sociomoral reasoning, perceptions of parenting and self-reported delinquency in adolescents. *Applied Cognitive Psychology, 15* (1), 85–100.

Papadopoulos, T.C., Panayiotou, G., Spanoudis, G. & Natsopoulos, D. (2005). Evidence of poor planning in children with attention deficits. *Journal of Abnormal Child Psychology, 33* (5), 611–623.

Papero, A.L. (2005). Is early, high-quality daycare an asset for children of low-income, depressed mothers?. *Developmental Review, 25* (2), 181–211.

Pardini, D.A., Barry, T.D., Barth, J.M., Lochman, J.E. & Wells, K.C. (2006). Self-perceived social acceptance and peer social standing in children with aggressive-disruptive behaviors. *Social Development 15* (1), 46–64.

Park, J., Turnbull, A.P. & Turnbull, H.R. III (2002). Impacts of poverty on quality of life in families of children with disabilities. *Exceptional Children, 68* (2), 151–170.

Park, K.L. (2007). Facilitating effective team-based functional behavioral assessments in typical school settings. *Beyond Behavior, 17* (1), 21–31.

Parke, R.D., Coltrane, S., Duffy, S., Buriel, R., Dennis, J., Powers, J., French, S. & Widaman, K.F. (2004). Economic stress, parenting, and child adjustment in Mexican American and European American families. *Child Development, 75* (6), 1632–1656.

Parker, F.L., Boak, A.Y., Griffin, K.W., Ripple, C. & Peay, L. (1999). Parent-child relationship, home learning environment, and school readiness. *School Psychology Review, 28* (3), 413–425.

Parker, J.G. & Asher, S.R. (1987). Peer relations and later personal adjustment: Are low-accepted children at risk? *Psychological Bulletin, 102* (3), 357–389.

——(1993). Friendship and friendship quality in middle childhood: Links with peer group acceptance and feelings of loneliness and social dissatisfaction. *Developmental Psychology, 29* (4), 611–621.

Parker, L.E. & Lepper, M.R. (1992). Effects of fantasy contexts on children's learning and motivation: Making learning more fun. *Journal of Personality and Social Psychology, 62* (4), 625–633.

Parker, W. (1996). Psychological adjustment in mathematically gifted students. *Gifted Child Quarterly, 40* (3), 154–161.

Parker, W. & Adkins, K.K. (1995). Perfectionism and the gifted. *Roeper Review, 17* (3), 173–176.

Parker, W. & Mills, C.J. (1996). The incidence of perfectionism in gifted students. *Gifted Child Quarterly, 40* (4), 194–199.

Parpal, M. & Maccoby, E.E. (1985). Maternal responsiveness and subsequent child compliance. *Child Development, 56* (5), 1326–1334.

Parrott, D.J. & Peterson, J.L. (2008). What motivates hate crimes based on sexual orientation?: Mediating effects of anger on antigay aggression. *Aggressive Behavior, 34* (3), 306–318.

Parry-Cruwys, D.E., Neal, C.M., Ahearn, W.H., Wheeler, E.E., Premchander, R., Loeb, M.B. & Dube, W.V. (2011). Resistance to disruption in a classroom setting. *Journal of Applied Behavior Analysis, 44* (2), 363–367.

Partinen, M. (2011). Epidemiology of sleep disorders. *Handbook of Clinical Neurology, 98,* 275–314.

Pas, E.T., Bradshaw, C.P. & Hershfeldt, P.A. (2012). Teacher- and school-level predictors of teacher efficacy and burnout: Identifying potential areas for support. *Journal of School Psychology, 50* (1), 129–145.

Pas, E.T., Bradshaw, C.P. & Mitchell, M.M. (2011). Examining the validity of office discipline referrals as an indicator of student behavior problems. *Psychology in the Schools, 48* (6), 541–555.

Patall, E.A., Cooper, H. & Wynn, S.R. (2010). The effectiveness and relative importance of choice in the classroom. *Journal of Educational Psychology, 102* (4), 896–915.

Paterson, G. & Sanson, A. (1999). The association of behavioural adjustment to temperament, parenting and family characteristics among 5-year-old children. *Social Development, 8* (3), 293–309.

Patrick, H., Kaplan, A. & Ryan, A.M. (2011). Positive classroom motivational environments: Convergence between mastery goal structure and classroom social climate. *Journal of Educational Psychology, 103* (2), 367–382.

Patrick, H., Ryan, A.M. & Kaplan, A. (2007). Early adolescents' perceptions of the classroom social environment, motivational beliefs, and engagement. *Journal of Educational Psychology, 99* (1), 83–98.

Patterson, G.R., Shaw, D.S., Snyder, J.J. & Yoerger, K. (2005). Changes in maternal ratings of children's overt and covert antisocial behavior. *Aggressive Behavior, 31* (5), 473–484.

Pauletti, R.E., Menon, M., Menon, M. Tobin, D.D. & Perry, D.G. (2012). Narcissism and adjustment in preadolescence. *Child Development, 83* (3), 831–837.

Pauling, L. (1995). Orthomolecular psychiatry: Varying the concentration of substances normally present in the human body to control mental disease. *Journal of Nutritional and Environmental Medicine, 5* (2), 187–199.

Paulson, S.E. (1994). Relations of parenting style and parental involvement with ninth-grade students' achievement. *Journal of Early Adolescence, 14* (2), 250–267.

Paulson, S.E., Marchant, G.J. & Rothlisberg, B.A. (1998). Early adolescents' perceptions of patterns of parenting, teaching, and school atmosphere: Implications for achievement. *Journal of Early Adolescence, 18* (1), 5–26.

Payne, A.A. (2009). Do predictors of the implementation quality of school-based prevention programs differ by program type? *Prevention Science, 10* (2), 151–167.

Payne, A.A. & Eckert, R. (2010). The relative important of provider, program, school, and community predictors of the implementation quality of school-based prevention programs. *Prevention Science, 11* (2), 126–141.

Pears, K.C., Fisher, P.A., Bruce, J., Kim, H.K. & Yoerger, K. (2010). Early elementary school adjustment of maltreated children in foster care: The roles of inhibitory control and caregiver involvement. *Child Development, 81* (5), 1550–1564.

Pedersen, E., Faucher, T.A. & Eaton, W.W. (1978). A new perspective on the effects of first-grade teachers on children's subsequent adult status. *Harvard Educational Review, 48* (1), 1–31.

Peel, L. (2009). Dyslexia and glue ear: A sticky educational problem. In G. Reid (Ed.) *The Routledge companion to dyslexia.* London: Routledge, 33–42.

Peet, M. (2004). International variations in the outcome of schizophrenia and the prevalence of depression in relation to national dietary practices: An ecological analysis. *British Journal of Psychiatry, 184* (5), 404–408.

Pekrun, R. (2006). The control-value theory of achievement emotions: Assumptions, corollaries, and implications for educational research and practice. *Educational Psychology Review, 18* (4), 315–341.

Pekrun, R., Goetz, T., Daniels, L.M., Stupnisky, R.H. & Perry, R.P. (2010). Boredom in achievement settings: Exploring control-value antecedents and performance outcomes of a neglected emotion. *Journal of Educational Psychology, 102* (3), 531–549.

Pellegrini, A.D. (2004). Bullying during the middle school years. In C.E. Sanders and G.D. Phye (Eds.) *Bullying: Implications for the classroom.* San Diego, CA: Elsevier, 177–202.

Pellegrini, A.D., Bartini, M. & Brooks, F. (1999). School bullies, victims, and aggressive victims: Factors relating to group affiliation and victimization in early adolescence. *Journal of Educational Psychology, 91* (2), 216–224.

Pellerin, L.A. (2005). Applying Baumrind's parenting typology to high schools: Toward a middle-range theory of authoritative socialization. *Social Science Research Journal, 34* (2), 283–303.

Penney, S. & Wilgosh, L. (2000). Fostering parent-teacher relationships when children are gifted. *Gifted Education International, 14* (3), 217–229.

Pepler, D.J., Craig, W.M., Connolly, J.A., Yuile, A., McMaster, L. & Jiang, D. (2006). A developmental perspective on bullying. *Aggressive Behavior, 32* (4), 376–384.

Pepler, D.J., Craig, W.M. & Roberts, W.L. (1998). Observations of aggressive and nonaggressive children on the school playground. *Merrill-Palmer Quarterly, 44* (1), 55–76.

Pepler, D., Craig, W., Ziegler, S. & Charach, A. (1993). A school-based anti-bullying intervention: Preliminary evaluation. In D. Tattum (Ed.) *Understanding and managing bullying.* Oxford, UK: Heinemann Educational, 76–91.

Perra, O., Fletcher, A., Bonell, C., Higgins, K. & McCrystal, P. (2012). School-related predictors of smoking, drinking and drug use: Evidence from the Belfast Youth Development Study. *Journal of Adolescence, 35* (2), 315–324.

Perry, D. & Bussey, K. (1984). *Social development.* Englewood Cliffs, NJ: Prentice Hall.

Perry, D.G., Williard, J.C. & Perry, L.C. (1990). Peers' perceptions of the consequences that victimized children provide aggressors. *Child Development, 61* (5), 1310–1325.

Perry, K.E., Donohue, K.M. & Weinstein, R.S. (2007). Teaching practices and the promotion of achievement and adjustment in first grade. *Journal of School Psychology, 45* (3), 269–292.

Perry, L. (1999). Mitakuyu Oyasin – All of my relations: Exploring metaphors of connectedness. In A. Morgan (Ed.) *Once upon a time: Narrative therapy with children and their families.* Adelaide, SA: Dulwich Centre Publications, 125–144.

Pesonen, A.-K., Heinonen, K., Komsi, N., Järvenpää, A.-L. & Strandberg, T. (2008). A transactional model of temperamental development: Evidence of a relationship between child temperament and maternal stress over five years. *Social Development, 17* (2), 326–340.

Peters, E., Riksen-Walraven, M., Cillessen, A.H.N. & de Weerth, C. (2011). Peer rejection and HPA activity in middle childhood: Friendship makes a difference. *Child Development, 82* (6), 1906–1920.

Peterson, C. (2006). *A primer in positive psychology.* Oxford, UK: Oxford University Press.

Peterson, J.L. & Zill, N. (1986). Marital disruption, parent-child relationships, and behavior problems in children. *Journal of Marriage and the Family, 48* (2), 295–307.

Petterson, S.M. & Albers, A.B. (2001). Effects of poverty and maternal depression on early child development. *Child Development, 72* (6), 1794–1813.

Pettit, G.S. & Bates, J.E. (1989). Family interaction patterns and children's behavior problems from infancy to 4 years. *Developmental Psychology, 25* (3), 413–420.

Pettit, G.S., Laird, R.D., Dodge, K.A., Bates, J.E. & Criss, M.M. (2001). Antecedents and behavior-problem outcomes of parental monitoring and psychological control in early adolescence. *Child Development, 72* (2), 583–598.

Phelan, P., Davidson, A.L. & Cao, H.T. (1992). Speaking up: Students' perspectives on school. *Phi Delta Kappan, 73* (9), 695–704.

Phelan, P., Yu, H.C. & Davidson, A.L. (1994). Navigating the psychosocial pressures of adolescence: The voices and experiences of high school youth. *American Educational Research Journal, 31* (2), 415–447.

Phelan, T.W. (2003). *1-2-3-magic: Effective discipline for children 2-12.* (3rd ed.) Glen Ellyn, IL: ParentMagic Inc.

Phillipsen, L.C., Burchinal, M.R., Howes, C. & Cryer, D. (1997). The prediction of process quality from structural features of child care. *Early Childhood Research Quarterly, 12* (3), 281–303.

Philpott, W.H. & Kalita, D.K. (2000). *Brain allergies: The psychonutrient and magnetic connections.* (2nd ed.) Chicago, IL: Keats Publishing.

Phoenix, A. (2002). Working with diverse communities. In S. Roffey (Ed.) *School behaviour and families.* London: David Fulton, 125–139.

Piacentini, J.C., Peris, T.S., March, J.S. & Franklin, M.E. (2012). Obsessive-compulsive disorder. In P.C. Kendall (Ed.) *Child and adolescent therapy: Cognitive-behavioral procedures.* (4th ed.) New York: Guilford, 259–282.

Pianta, R.C. (1999). *Enhancing relationships between children and teachers.* Washington, DC: American Psychological Association.

Pianta, R.C., Howes, C., Burchinal, M., Bryant, D., Clifford, R., Early, D. & Barbarin, O. (2005). Features of pre-kindergarten programs, classrooms, and teachers: Do they predict observed classroom quality and child-teacher interactions?. *Applied Developmental Science, 9* (3), 144–159.

Pianta, R.C., Steinberg, M.S. & Rollins, K.B. (1995). The first two years of school: Teacher-child relationships and deflections in children's classroom adjustment. *Development and Psychopathology, 7* (2), 295–312.

Pianta, R.C. & Stuhlman, M.W. (2004). Teacher-child relationships and children's success in the first years of school. *School Psychology Review, 33* (3), 444–458.

Pianta, R.C. & Walsh, D.J. (1998). Applying the construct of resilience in schools: Cautions from a developmental systems perspective. *School Psychology Review, 27* (3), 407–417.

Piazza, C.C., Adelinis, J.D., Hanley, G.P., Goh, H.-L. & Delia, M.D. (2000). An evaluation of the effects of matched stimuli on behaviors maintained by automatic reinforcement. *Journal of Applied Behavior Analysis, 33* (1), 13–27.

Piazza, C.C., Fisher, W.W., Hanley, G.P., LeBlanc, L.A., Worsdell, A.S., Lindauer, S.E. & Keeney, K.M. (1998). Treatment of pica through multiple analyses of its reinforcing functions. *Journal of Applied Behavior Analysis, 31* (2), 165–189.

Piazza, C.C., Fisher, W.W., Hanley, G.P., Remick, M.L., Contrucci, S.A. & Aitken, T.L. (1997). The use of positive and negative reinforcement in the treatment of escape-maintained destructive behavior. *Journal of Applied Behavior Analysis, 30* (2), 279–298.

Piazza, C.C., Patel, M.R., Gulotta, C.S., Sevin, B.M. & Layer, S.A. (2003). On the relative contributions of positive reinforcement and escape extinction in the treatment of food refusal. *Journal of Applied Behavior Analysis, 36* (3), 309–324.

Piazza, C.C., Roane, H.S., Keeney, K.M., Boney, B.R. & Abt, K.A.

(2002). Varying response effort in the treatment of pica maintained by automatic reinforcement. *Journal of Applied Behavior Analysis, 35* (3), 233–246.

Piekarska, A. (2000). School stress, teachers' abusive behaviors, and children's coping strategies. *Child Abuse and Neglect, 24* (11), 1443–1449.

Pikas, A. (2002). New developments of the shared concern method. *School Psychology International, 23* (3), 307–326.

Pilsner, J.R., Hu, H., Ettinger, A., Sánchez, B.N., Wright, R.O., Cantonwine, D., Lazarus, A., Lamadrid-Figueroa, H., Mercado-García, A., Téllez-Rojo, M.M. & Hernández-Avila, M. (2009). Influence of prenatal lead exposure on genomic methylation of cord blood DNA. *Environmental Health Perspectives, 117* (9), 1466–1471.

Pinderhughes, E.E., Dodge, K.A., Bates, J.E., Pettit, G.S. & Zelli, A. (2000). Discipline responses: Influences of parents' socioeconomic status, ethnicity, beliefs about parenting, stress, and cognitive-emotional processes. *Journal of Family Psychology, 14* (3), 380–400.

Pintrich, P.R. (2000). Multiple goals, multiple pathways: The role of goal orientation in learning and achievement. *Journal of Educational Psychology, 92* (3), 544–555.

——(2003). A motivational science perspective on the role of student motivation in learning and teaching contexts. *Journal of Educational Psychology, 95* (4), 667–686.

Pinxton, M., De Fraine, B., Van Damme, J. & D'Haenens, E. (2010). Causal ordering of academic self-concept and achievement: Effects of type of achievement measure. *British Journal of Educational Psychology, 80* (4), 689–709.

Polivy, J. (1998). The effects of behavioral inhibition: Integrating internal cues, cognition, behavior, and affect. *Psychological Inquiry, 9* (3), 181–204.

Pollak, S.D., Vardi, S., Bechner, A.M.P. & Curtin, J.J. (2005). Physically abused children's regulation of attention in response to hostility. *Child Development, 76* (5), 968–977.

Pomerantz, E.M. & Wang, Q. (2009). The role of parental control in children's development in Western and East Asian countries. *Current Directions in Psychological Science, 18* (5), 285–289.

Pomeroy, E. (1999). The teacher-student relationship in secondary school: Insights from excluded students. *British Journal of Sociology of Education, 20* (4), 465–482.

Ponitz, C.C., Rimm-Kaufman, S.E., Grimm, K.J. & Curby, T.W. (2009). Kindergarten classroom quality, behavioral engagement, and reading achievement. *School Psychology Review, 38* (1), 102–120.

Pope, A.W., McHale, S.M. & Craighead, E.W. (1988). *Self-esteem enhancement with children and adolescents.* New York: Pergamon.

Pope, D.C. (2001). *Doing school: How we are creating a generatioin of stressed out, materialistic, and miseducated students.* New Haven, CT: Yale University Press.

Pornari, C.D. & Wood, J. (2010). Peer and cyber aggression in secondary school students: The role of moral disengagement, hostile attribution bias, and outcome expectancies. *Aggressive Behavior, 36* (2), 81–94.

Porter, L. (1980). An alcohol education program for periodic detainees. Unpublished Master of Arts (Psychology) thesis. Christchurch, NZ: University of Canterbury.

——(1999). Behaviour management practices in child care centres. Unpublished doctoral thesis. Adelaide: University of South Australia.

——(2005). *Gifted young children: A guide for teachers and parents.* (2nd ed.) Sydney: Allen & Unwin; Buckingham, UK: Open University Press.

——(2006). *Children are people too: A parent's guide to young children's behaviour.* (4th ed.) Adelaide, SA: East Street Publications.

——(2008a). *Young children's behaviour: Practical approaches for caregivers and teachers.* (3rd ed.) Sydney: Elsevier/London: SAGE/Baltimore, MD: Brookes.

——(2008b). *Teacher-parent collaboration: Early childhood to adolescence.* Melbourne: ACER.

——(2010). *A guidance approach to discipline: Practitioner workbook.* Brisbane: Small Poppies International.

Porter, L. & McKenzie, S. (2000). *Professional collaboration with parents of children with disabilities.* Sydney: Elsevier; London: Whurr.

Porter, L., Winter-Sellery, K. & Jamieson, C.N. (2008). *Teaching parents a guidance approach: A manual for group leaders.* Adelaide, SA: Small Poppies International.

Poulin, F. & Boivin, M. (2000). The role of proactive and reactive aggression in the formation and development of boys' friendships. *Developmental Psychology, 36* (2), 233–240.

Poulin, F., Dishion, T.J. & Burraston, B. (2001). 3-year iatrogenic effects associated with aggregating high-risk adolescents in cognitive-behavioral preventive interventions. *Applied Developmental Science, 5* (4), 214–224.

Powell, D.R., Son, S.-H., File, N. & San Juan, R.R. (2010). Parent-school relationships and children's academic and social outcomes in public school pre-kindergarten. *Journal of School Psychology, 48* (4), 269–292.

Powell, N.P., Boxmeyer, C.L., Baden, R., Stromeyer, S., Minney, J.A., Mushtaq, A. & Lochman, J.E. (2011). Assessing and treating aggression and conduct problems in schools: Implications from the Coping Power program. *Psychology in the Schools, 48* (3), 233–242.

Power, T.G. & Chapieski, M.L. (1986). Childrearing and impulse control in toddlers: A naturalistic investigation. *Developmental Psychology, 22* (2), 271–275.

Prat-Sala, M. & Redford, P. (2010). The interplay between motivation, self-efficacy, and approaches to studying. *British Journal of Educational Psychology, 80* (2), 283–305.

Preckel, F., Götz, T. & Frenzel, A. (2010). Ability grouping of gifted students: Effects on academic self-concept and boredom. *British Journal of Educational Psychology, 80* (3), 451–472.

Prince, D.L. & Howard, E.M. (2002). Children and their basic needs. *Early Childhood Education Journal, 30* (1), 27–31.

Prinstein, M.J. & Cillessen, A.H.N. (2003). Forms and functions of adolescent peer aggression associated with high peer status. *Merrill-Palmer Quarterly, 49* (3), 310–342.

Prinzie, P., Onghena, P. & Hellinckx, W. (2006). A cohort-sequential multivariate latent growth curve analysis of normative CBCL aggressive and delinquent problem behavior: Associations with harsh discipline and gender. *International Journal of Behavioral Development, 30* (5), 444–459.

Propper, C. & Moore, G.A. (2006). The influence of parenting on infant emotionality: A multi-level psychobiological perspective. *Developmental Review, 26* (4), 427–460.

Puckett, M.B., Aikins, J.W. & Cillessen, A.H.N. (2008). Moderators of the association between relational aggression and perceived popularity. *Aggressive Behavior, 34* (6), 563–576.

Pulkkinen, L. & Hämäläinen, M. (1995). Low self-control as a precursor to crime and accidents in a Finnish longitudinal study. *Criminal Behaviour and Mental Health, 5* (4), 424–438.

Purdie, N., Hattie, J. & Carroll, A. (2002). A review of research on interventions for attention deficit hyperactivity disorder: What works best? *Review of Educational Research, 72* (1), 61–99.

Purdue, N.H., Manzeske, D.P. & Estell, D.B. (2009). Early predictors of school engagement: Exploring the role of peer relationships. *Psychology in the Schools, 46* (10), 1084–1097.

Purkey, S.C. & Smith, M.S. (1983). Effective schools: A review. *The Elementary School Journal, 83* (4), 426–452.

Purvis, K.L. & Tannock, R. (1997). Language abilities in children with attention deficit hyperactivity disorder, reading disabilities, and normal controls. *Journal of Abnormal Child Psychology, 25* (2), 133–144.

Putallaz, M., Costanzo, P.R., Grimes, C.L. & Sherman, D.M. (1998). Intergenerational continuities and their influences on children's social development. *Social Development, 7* (3), 389–427.

Putallaz, M., Grimes, C.L., Foster, K.J., Kupersmidt, J.B., Coie, J.D. & Dearing, K. (2007). Overt and relational aggression and victimization: Multiple perspectives within the school setting. *Journal of School Psychology, 45* (5), 523–547.

Putnam, R.F., Handler, M.W., Ramirez-Platt, C.M. & Luiselli, J.K. (2003). Improving student bus-riding behavior through a whole-school intervention. *Journal of Applied Behavior Analysis, 36* (4), 583–590.

Qi, C.H. & Kaiser, A.P. (2003). Behavior problems of preschool children from low-income families. *Topics in Early Childhood Special Education, 23* (4), 188–216.

Qin, D.B., Rak, E., Rana, M. & Donnellan, M.B. (2012). Parent-child relations and psychological adjustment among high-achieving Chinese and European-American adolescents. *Journal of Adolescence, 35* (4), 863–873.

Qin, L., Pomerantz, E.M. & Wang, Q. (2009). Are gains in decision-making autonomy during early adolescence beneficial for emotional functioning?: The case of the United States and China. *Child Development, 80* (6), 1705–1721.

Quinn, K.P. & Lee, V. (2007). The wraparound approach for students with emotional and behavioral disorders: Opportunities for school psychologists. *Psychology in the Schools, 44* (1), 101–111.

Rabiner, D., Coie, J.D. & The Conduct Problems Prevention Research Group (2000). Early attention problems and children's reading achievement: A longitudinal investigation. *Journal of the American Academy of Child and Adolescent Psychiatry, 39* (7), 859–867.

Rademacher, J.A., Callahan, K. & Pederson-Seelye, V.A. (1998). How do your classroom rules measure up?: Guidelines for developing an effective rule management routine. *Intervention in School and Clinic, 33* (5), 284–289.

Radke-Yarrow, M., Scott, P.M. & Zahn-Waxler, C. (1973). Learning concern for others. *Developmental Psychology, 8* (2), 240–260.

Raffaele, L.M. & Knoff, H.M. (1999). Improving home-school collaboration with disadvantaged families: Organizational principles, perspectives, and approaches. *School Psychology Review, 28* (3), 448–466.

Raggi, V.L. & Chronis, A.M. (2006). Interventions to address the academic impairment of children and adolescents with ADHD. *Clinical Child and Family Psychology Review, 9* (2), 85–110.

Rah, Y. & Parke, R.D. (2008). Pathways between parent-child interactions and peer acceptance: The role of children's social information processing. *Social Development, 17* (2), 341–357.

Raikes, H.A., Robinson, J.L., Bradley, R.H., Raikes, H.H. & Ayoub, C.C. (2007). Developmental trends in self-regulation among low-income toddlers. *Social Development, 16* (1), 128–149.

Ramirez, S.Z., Lepage, K.M., Kratochwill, T.R. & Duffy, J.L. (1998). Multicultural issues in school-based consultation: Conceptual and research considerations. *Journal of School Psychology, 36* (4), 479–509.

Rapport, M.D., Bolden, J., Kofler, M.J., Sarver, D.E., Raiker, J.S., &

Alderson, R.M. (2009). Hyperactivity in boys with attention-deficit/hyperactivity disorder (ADHD): A ubiquitous core symptom or manifestation of working memory deficits? *Journal of Abnormal Child Psychology, 37* (8), 521–534.

Raskauskas, J. & Stoltz, A.D. (2007). Involvement in traditional and electronic bullying among adolescents. *Developmental Psychology, 43* (3), 564–575.

Raskin, N.J. & Rogers, C.R. (2005). Person-centered therapy. In R.J. Corsini and D. Wedding (Eds.) *Current psychotherapies.* (7th ed.) Belmont, CA: Thomson Brooks/Cole, 130–165.

Ratelle, C.F., Guay, F., Larose, S. & Senécal, C. (2004). Family correlates of trajectories of academic motivation during a school transition: A semiparametric group-based approach. *Journal of Educational Psychology, 96* (4), 743–754.

Rathus, S. & Nevid, J. (1989). *Psychology and the challenges of life – Adjustment and growth.* (4th. ed.) New York: Holt, Rinehart and Winston.

Raviv, T., Kessenich, M. & Morrison, F.J. (2004). A mediational model of the association between socioeconomic status and three-year-old language abilities: The role of parenting factors. *Early Childhood Research Quarterly, 19* (4), 528–547.

Rawls, J. (1991). A theory of justice. In J. Arthur and W.H. Shaw (Eds.) *Justice and economic distribution.* (2nd ed.) Englewood Cliffs, NJ: Prentice Hall, 13–39.

Reddy, L.A., Newman, E., De Thomas, C.A. & Chun, V. (2009). Effectiveness of school-based prevention and intervention programs for children and adolescents with emotional disturbance: A meta-analysis. *Journal of School Psychology, 47* (2), 77–99.

Reed, G.K., Piazza, C.C., Patel, M.R., Laver, S.A., Bachmeyer, M.H., Bethke, S.D. & Gutshall, K.A. (2004). On the relative contributions of noncontingent reinforcement and escape extinction in the treatment of food refusal. *Journal of Applied Behavior Analysis, 37* (1), 27–42.

Reese, R.J., Prout, H.T., Zirkelback, E.A., & Anderson, C.R. (2010). Effectiveness of school-based psychotherapy: A meta-analysus of dissertation research. *Psychology in the Schools, 47* (10), 1035–1045.

Reeve, J. & Jang, H. (2006). What teachers say and do to support students' autonomy during a learning activity. *Journal of Educational Psychology, 98* (1), 209–218.

Régner, I., Escribe, C. & Dupeyrat, C. (2007). Evidence of social comparison in mastery goals in natural academic settings. *Journal of Educational Psychology, 99* (3), 575–583.

Reid, R. & Harris, K.R. (1993). Self-monitoring of attention versus self-monitoring of performance: Effects on attention and academic performance. *Exceptional Children, 60* (1), 29–40.

Reid, R. & Maag, J.W. (1998). Functional assessment: A method for developing classroom-based accommodations and interventions for children with ADHD. *Reading and Writing Quarterly, 14* (1), 9–42.

Reinke, W.M. & Herman, K.C. (2002). Creating school environments that deter antisocial behaviors in youth. *Psychology in the Schools, 39* (5), 549–559.

Reinke, W.M., Lewis-Palmer, T. & Merrell, K. (2008). The classroom check up: A classwide teacher consultation model for increasing praise and decreasing disruptive behavior. *School Psychology Review, 37* (3), 315–332.

Reis, S.M. & Callahan, C.M. (1989). Gifted females: They've come a long way – or have they? *Journal for the Education of the Gifted, 12* (2), 99–117.

Reitzug, U.C. (1994). A case study of empowering principal behavior. *American Educational Research Journal, 31* (2), 283–307.

Rekers, G.A. (1984). Ethical issues in child behavioral

assessment. In T.H. Ollendick and M. Hersen (Eds.) *Child behavioral assessment*. New York: Pergamon, 244–262.

Reschly, A.L., Huebner, E.S., Appleton, J.J. & Antaramian, S. (2008). Engagement as flourishing: The contribution of positive emotions and coping to adolescents' engagement at school and with learning. *Psychology in the Schools, 45* (5), 419–431.

Rescorla, L.A., Achenbach, T.M., Ginzburg, S., Ivanova, M., Dumenci, L., Almqvist, F., Bathiche, M., Bilenberg, N., Bird, H., Domuta, A., Erol, N., Fombonne, E., Fonseca, A., Frigerio, A., Kanbayashi, Y., Lambert, M.C., Liu, X., Leung, P., Minaei, A., Roussos, A., Simsek, Z., Weintraub, S., Weisz, J., Wolanczyk, T., Zubrick, S.R., Zukauskiene, R. & Verhulst, F. (2007). Consistency of teacher-reported problems for students in 21 countries. *School Psychology Review, 36* (1), 91–100.

Resnick, M.D., Bearman, P.S., Blum, R.W., Bauman, K.E., Harris, K.M., Jones, J., Tabor, J., Beuhring, T., Sieving, R.E., Shew, M., Ireland, M., Bearinger, L.H. & Udry, J.R. (1997). Protecting adolescents from harm: Findings from the National Longitudinal Study on Adolescent Health. *Journal of the American Medical Association, 278* (10), 823–832.

Rey, R.B., Smith, A.L., Yoon, J., Somers, C., & Barnett, D. (2007). Relationships between teachers and urban African American children. *School Psychology International, 28* (3), 346–364.

Reynolds, B.M. & Repetti, R.L. (2010). Teenage girls' perceptions of the functions of relationally aggressive behaviors. *Psychology in the Schools, 47* (3), 282–296.

Reynolds, L.K. & Kelley, M.L. (1997). The efficacy of a response cost-based treatment package for managing aggressive behavior in preschoolers. *Behavior Modification, 21* (2), 216–230.

Rhodes, J. (1993). The use of solution-focused brief therapy in schools. *Educational Psychology in Practice, 9* (1), 27–34.

Rhodes, S.L. & Ritz, B. (2008). Genetics of iron regulation and the possible role of iron in Parkinson's disease. *Neurobiology of Disease, 32* (2), 183–195.

Rice, K.G., Ashby, J.S. & Preusser, K.J. (1996). Perfectionism, relationships with parents, and self-esteem. *Individual Psychology, 52* (3), 246–260.

Rich, Y. (1990). Ideological impediments to instructional innovation: The case of cooperative learning. *Teaching and Teacher Education, 6* (1), 81–91.

Richards, L.C., Heathfield, L.T. & Jenson, W.R. (2010). A classwide peer-modeling intervention package to increase on-task behavior. *Psychology in the Schools, 47* (6), 551–566.

Richardson Andrews, R.C. (1990). Unification of the findings in schizophrenia by reference to the effects of gestational zinc deficiency. *Medical Hypotheses, 31* (2), 141–153.

Rigby, K. (1993). Countering bullying in schools. *CAFHS Forum, 1* (2), 19–22.

——(1996). *Bullying in schools: And what to do about it.* Melbourne: ACER.

——(1998). Gender and bullying in schools. In P.T. Slee and K. Rigby (Eds.) *Children's peer relations.* London: Routledge, 47–59.

——(1999). Peer victimisation at school and the health of secondary school students. *British Journal of Educational Psychology, 69* (1), 95–104.

——(2001). Health consequences of bullying and its prevention in schools. In J. Juvonen and S. Graham (Eds.) *Peer harassment in school: The plight of the vulnerable and victimized.* New York: Guilford, 310–331.

——(2003). *Stop the bullying: A handbook for schools.* (2nd ed.) Melbourne: ACER.

——(2006a). What international research tells us about bullying. In H. McGrath and T. Noble (Eds.) *Bullying solutions: Evidence-based approaches to bullying in Australian schools.* Sydney: Pearson Longman, 3–15.

——(2006b). An overview of approaches to managing bully/victim problems. In H. McGrath and T. Noble (Eds.) *Bullying solutions: Evidence-based approaches to bullying in Australian schools.* Sydney: Pearson Longman, 149–160.

Rigby, K. & Bagshaw, D. (2003). Prospects of adolescent students collaborating with teachers in addressing issues of bullying and conflict in schools. *Educational Psychology, 23* (5), 535–546.

——(2006). Using educational drama and bystander training to counteract bullying. In H. McGrath and T. Noble (Eds.) *Bullying solutions: Evidence-based approaches to bullying in Australian schools.* Sydney: Pearson Longman, 133–145.

Riley-Tillman, T.C., Chafouleas, S.M. & Briesch, A.M. (2007). A school practitioner's guide to using daily behavior report cards to monitor student behavior. *Psychology in the Schools, 44* (1), 77–89.

Rimm, G.A. (2003). Identifying creative students, teaching for creative growth. In N. Colangelo & G.A. Davis (Eds.) *Handbook of gifted education.* (3rd ed.). Boston, MA: Allyn & Bacon, 311–324.

Rimm-Kaufman, S.E. & Chiu, Y.-J.I. (2007). Promoting social and academic competence in the classroom: An intervention study examining the contribution of the Responsive Classroom approach. *Psychology in the Schools, 44* (4), 397–413.

Rimm-Kaufman, S.E., Curby, T.W., Grimm, K.J., Nathanson, L. & Brock, L.L. (2009). The contribution of children's self-regulation and classroom quality to children's adaptive behaviors in the kindergarten classroom. *Developmental Psychology, 45* (4), 958–972.

Rimm-Kaufman, S.E., Early, D.M., Cox, M.J., Saluja, G., Pianta, R.C., Bradley, R.H. & Payne, C. (2002). Early behavioral attributes and teachers' sensitivity as predictors of competent behavior in the kindergarten classroom. *Journal of Applied Developmental Psychology, 23* (3), 451–470.

Rimm-Kaufman, S.E., Fan, X., Chiu, Y.-J. & You, W. (2007). The contribution of the Responsive Classroom approach on children's academic achievement: Results from a three year longitudinal study. *Journal of School Psychology, 45* (4), 401–421.

Rimm-Kaufman, S.E. & Pianta, R.C. (1999). Patterns of family-school contact in preschool and kindergarten. *School Psychology Review, 28* (3), 426–438.

Rimm-Kaufman, S.E., Pianta, R.C. & Cox, M.J. (2000). Teachers' judgments of problems in the transition to kindergarten. *Early Childhood Research Quarterly, 15* (2), 147–166.

Ripley, K. & Yuill, N. (2005). Patterns of language impairment and behaviours in boys excluded from school. *British Journal of Educational Psychology, 75* (1), 37–50.

Rivers, I. & Noret, N. (2008). Well-being among same-sex- and opposite-sex-attracted youth at school. *School Psychology Review, 37* (2), 174–187.

Rivers, S. (2001). The bullying of sexual minorities at school: Its nature and long-term correlates. *Educational and Child Psychology, 18* (1), 32–46.

Roane, H.S., Fisher, W.W. & Sgro, G.M. (2001). Effects of a fixed-time schedule on aberrant and adaptive behavior. *Journal of Applied Behavior Analysis, 34* (3), 333–336.

Roane, H.S., Kelly, M.L. & Fisher, W.W. (2003). The effects of noncontingent access to food on the rate of object mouthing across three settings. *Journal of Applied Behavior Analysis, 36* (4), 579–582.

Roberts, B.W., Caspi, A. & Moffitt, T.E. (2001). The kids are alright: Growth and stability in personality development from adolescence to adulthood. *Journal of Personality and Social Psychology, 81* (4), 670–683.

Roberts, J.E., Burchinal, M.R., Zeisel, S.A., Neebe, E.C., Hooper, S.R., Roush, J., Bryant, D., Mundy, M. & Henderson, F.W. (1998). Otitis media, the caregiving environment, and language and cognitive outcomes at 2 years. *Pediatrics, 102* (2), 346–353.

Robertson, J.S. (2000). Is attribution training a worthwhile classroom intervention for K–12 students with learning difficulties? *Educational Psychology Review, 12* (1), 111–134.

Robinson, A. (1990). Cooperation or exploitation? The argument against cooperative learning for talented students. *Journal for the Education of the Gifted, 14* (1), 9–27.

Robinson, K. (2011). *Out of our minds: Learning to be creative.* (2nd ed.) Chichester, UK: Capstone.

Robinson, K. & Aronica, L. (2009). *The element: How finding your passion changes everything.* New York: Penguin.

——(2013). *Finding your element: How to discover your talents and passions and transform your life.* New York: Viking.

Robinson, N.M., Lanzi, R.G., Weinberg, R.A., Ramey, S.L. & Ramey, C.T. (2002). Family factors associated with high academic competence in former Head Start children at third grade. *Gifted Child Quarterly, 46* (4), 278–290.

Robinson, R., Roberts, W.L., Strayer, J. & Koopman, R. (2007). Empathy and emotional responsiveness in delinquent and non-delinquent adolescents. *Social Development, 16* (3), 555–579.

Robinson, T.R., Smith, S.W., Miller, M.D. & Brownell, M.T. (1999). Cognitive behavior modification of hyperactivity-impulsivity and aggression: A meta-analysis of school-based studies. *Journal of Educational Psychology, 91* (2), 195–203.

Robinson, W.P. (1975). Boredom at school. *British Journal of Educational Psychology, 45* (2), 141–152.

Robson, S. (1996). The physical environment. In S. Robson and S. Smedley (Eds.) *Education in early childhood: First things first.* London: David Fulton, 153–171.

Rodd, J. (2006). *Leadership in early childhood.* (3rd ed.) Sydney: Allen & Unwin.

Rodkin, P.C., Farmer, T.W., Pearl, R. & Van Acker, R. (2000). Heterogeneity of popular boys: Antisocial and prosocial configurations. *Developmental Psychology, 36* (1), 14–24.

——(2006). They're cool: Social status and peer group supports for aggressive boys and girls. *Social Development, 15* (2), 175–204.

Rodkin, P.C. & Hodges, E.V.E. (2003). Bullies and victims in the peer ecology: Four questions for psychologists and school professionals. *School Psychology Review, 32* (3), 384–400.

Rodriguez, A. & Bohlin, G. (2005). Are maternal smoking and stress during pregnancy related to ADHD symptoms in children?. *Journal of Child Psychology and Psychiatry, 46* (3), 246–254.

Rodriguez, C.M. (2003). Parental discipline and abuse potential affects on child depression, anxiety and attributions. *Journal of Marriage and the Family, 65* (4), 809–817.

Roeser, R.W., Eccles, J.S. & Sameroff, A.J. (1998). Academic and emotional functioning in early adolescence: Longitudinal relations, patterns, and prediction by experience in middle school. *Development and Psychopathology, 10* (2), 321–352.

Roffey, S. (2004). *The new teacher's survival guide to behaviour.* London: Paul Chapman.

Rogers, B. (1989). *Making a discipline plan: Developing classroom management skills.* Melbourne: Nelson.

——(1995). *Behaviour management: A whole-school approach.* Gosford, NSW: Ashton Scholastic.

——(1998). *'You know the fair rule' and much more: Strategies for making the hard job of discipline and behaviour management in school easier.* Melbourne: ACER.

——(2002). *Classroom behaviour: A practical guide to teaching, behaviour management and colleague support.* London: Paul Chapman.

——(2003). *Behaviour recovery: Practical programs for challenging behaviour.* (2nd ed.) Melbourne: ACER.

——(Ed.) (2004). *How to manage children's challenging behaviour.* London: Paul Chapman.

——(2011). *Classroom behaviour: A practical guide to effective teaching, behaviour management and colleague support.* (3rd ed.) Los Angeles, CA: SAGE.

Rogers, C.R. (1951). *Client-centred therapy.* London: Constable.

——(1978). *On personal power.* London: Constable.

Rogers, C.R. & Freiberg, H. (1994). *Freedom to learn.* (3rd ed.) New York: Merrill.

Rogers, D. & Webb, J. (1991). The ethic of caring in teacher education. *Journal of Teacher Education, 42* (3), 173–181.

Rogers, M.R. (1998). The influence of race and consultant verbal behavior on perceptions of consultant competence and multicultural sensitivity. *School Psychology Quarterly, 13* (4), 265–280.

Rogers, N. (1994). Foreword. In C.R. Rogers and H. Freiberg (Eds.) *Freedom to learn.* (3rd ed.) New York: Merrill, iii–vii.

Rogers, W.S. (2003). What is a child? In M. Woodhead and H. Montgomery (Eds.) *Understanding childhood: An interdisciplinary approach.* Milton Keynes, UK: Open University Press, 1–43.

Rogus, J.F. (1985). Promoting self-discipline: A comprehensive approach. *Theory into Practice, 24* (4), 271–276.

Rohner, R.P., Kean, K.J. & Cournoyer, D.E. (1991). Effects of corporal punishment, perceived caretaker warmth, and cultural beliefs on the psychological adjustment of children in St Kitts, West Indies. *Journal of Marriage and the Family, 53* (3), 681–693.

Root, R.W. & Levant, R.F. (1984). An evaluation of Parent Effectiveness Training for rural parents. *Journal of Rural Community Psychology, 5* (2), 45–54.

Romano, E., Tremblay, R.E., Boulerice, B. & Swisher, R. (2005). Multilevel correlates of childhood physical aggression and prosocial behavior. *Journal of Abnormal Child Psychology, 33* (5), 565–578.

Rose, A.J., Swenson, L.P. & Waller, E.M. (2004). Overt and relational aggression and perceived popularity: Developmental differences in concurrent and prospective relations. *Developmental Psychology, 40* (3), 378–387.

Roseman, M.J. (1999). Quality child care: At whose expense? *Early Childhood Education Journal, 27* (1), 5–11.

Rosen, L.H., Underwood, M.K., Beron, K.J., Gentsch, J.K., Wharton, M.E. & Rahdar, A. (2009). Persistent versus periodic experiences of social victimization: Predictors of adjustment. *Journal of Abnormal Child Psychology, 37* (5), 693–704.

Rosenberg, M.B. (2003a). *Nonviolent communication: A language of life.* (2nd ed.) Encinitas, CA: Puddle Dancer Press.

——(2003b). *Getting past the pain between us: Healing and reconciliation without compromise.* Encinitas, CA: Puddle Dancer Press.

——(2005). *The surprising purpose of anger: Beyond anger management: Finding the gift.* Encinitas, CA: Puddle Dancer Press.

Roseth, C.J., Pellegrini, A.D., Bohn, C.M., Van Ryzin, M. & Vance, N. (2007). Preschoolers' aggression, affiliation, and social dominance relationships: An observational, longitudinal study. *Journal of School Psychology, 45* (5), 479–497.

Rosin, P. (1996). The diverse American family. In P. Rosin, A.D. Whitehead, L.I. Tuchman, G.S. Jesien, A.L. Begun and L. Irwin (Eds.) *Partnerships in family-centred care: A guide to collaborative early intervention.* Baltimore, MD: Paul H. Brookes, 3–28.

Ross, J.A. & Gray, P. (2006). Transformational leadership and teacher commitment to organizational values: The mediating effects of collective teacher efficacy. *School Effectiveness and School Improvement, 17* (2), 179–199.

Ross, S.W. & Horner, R.H. (2009). Bully prevention in positive behavior support. *Journal of Applied Behavior Analysis, 42* (4), 747–759.

Rossman, B.B.R., Hughes, H.M. & Hanson, K.L. (1998). The victimization of school-age children. In B.B.R. Rossman and M.S. Rosenberg (Eds.) *Multiple victimization of children: Conceptual, developmental, research, and treatment issues.* New York: Haworth Press, 87–106.

Rossman, B.B.R. & Rosenberg, M.S. (1998).The multiple victimization of children: Incidence and conceptual issues. In B.B.R. Rossman and M.S. Rosenberg (Eds.) *Multiple victimization of children: Conceptual, developmental, research, and treatment issues.* New York: Haworth Press, 1–5.

Roth, G., Assor, A., Niemiec, C.P., Ryan, R.M. & Deci, E.L. (2009). The emotional and academic consequences of parental conditional regard: Comparing conditional positive regard, conditional negative regard, and autonomy support as parenting practices. *Developmental Psychology, 45* (4), 1119–1142.

Roth, R.A., Kanat-Maymon, Y. & Bibi, U. (2011). Prevention of school bullying: The important role of autonomy-supportive teaching and internalization of pro-social values. *British Journal of Educational Psychology, 81* (4), 654–666.

Rothbaum, F., Grauer, A. & Rubin, D.J. (1997). Becoming sexual: Differences between child and adult sexuality. *Young Children, 52* (6), 22–28.

Rothon, C., Head, J., Klineberg, E. & Stansfeld, S. (2011). Can social support protect bullied adolescents from adverse outcomes?: A prospective study on the effects of bullying on the educational achievement and mental health of adolescents at secondary school in East London. *Journal of Adolescence, 34* (3), 579–588.

Rubie-Davies, C.M. (2006). Teacher expectations and student self-perceptions: Exploring relationships. *Psychology in the Schools, 43* (5), 537–552.

——(2010). Teacher expectations and perceptions of student attributes: Is there a relationship?. *British Journal of Educational Psychology, 80* (1), 121–135.

Rubie-Davies, C.M., Flint, A. & McDonald, L.G. (2012). Teacher beliefs, teacher characteristics, and school contextual factors: What are the relationships?. *British Journal of Educational Psychology, 82* (2), 270–288.

Rubin, K.H., Burgess, K.B. & Hastings, P.D. (2002). Stability and social-behavioral consequences of toddlers' inhibited temperament and parenting behaviors. *Child Development, 73* (2), 483–495.

Rubin, K.H., Burgess, K.B., Dwyer, K.M. & Hastings, P.D. (2003). Predicting preschoolers' externalizing behaviors from toddler temperament, conflict, and maternal negativity. *Developmental Psychology, 39* (1), 164–176.

Rubin, Z. (1980). *Children's friendships.* Boston, MA: Harvard University Press.

Rubinstein, R.P. (1977). Changes in self-esteem and anxiety in competitive and noncompetitive camps. *Journal of Social Psychology, 102* (1), 55–57.

Ruck, M.D. & Horn, S.S. (2008). Charting the landscape of children's rights. *Journal of Social Issues, 64,* (4), 685–699.

Ruck, M.D. & Wortley, S. (2002). Racial and ethnic minority high school students' perceptions of school disciplinary practices: A look at some Canadian findings. *Journal of Youth and Adolescence, 31* (3), 185–195.

Rudasill, K.M., Gallagher, K.C. & White, J.M. (2010a). Temperamental attention and activity, classroom emotional support, and academic achievement in third grade. *Journal of School Psychology, 48* (2), 113–134.

Rudasill, K.M., Reio, T.G. Jr., Stipanovic, N. & Taylor, J.E. (2010b). A longitudinal study of student-teacher relationship quality, difficult temperament, and risky behavior from childhood to early adolescence. *Journal of School Psychology, 48* (5), 389–412.

Rudolph, K.D., Abaied, J.L., Flynn, M., Sugimura, N. & Agoston, A.M. (2011). Developing relationships, being cool, and not looking like a loser: Social goal orientation predicts children's responses to peer aggression. *Child Development, 82* (5), 1518–1530.

Rudolph, K.D., Caldwell, M.S. & Conley, C.S. (2005). Need for approval and children's well-being. *Child Development, 76* (2), 309–323.

Rudy, D., Awong, T. & Lambert, M. (2008). Parental psychological control and authoritarianism in Chinese-Canadian and European-Canadian cultural groups: Their meanings and implications for university students' adjustment. *Journal of Comparative Family Studies, 39* (4), 471–490.

Rueger, S.Y., Malecki, C.K. & Demaray, M.K. (2011). Stability of peer victimization in early adolescence: Effects of timing and duration. *Journal of School Psychology 49* (4), 443–464.

Ruff, H.A. & Capozzoli, M.C. (2003). Development of attention and distractability in the first four years of life. *Developmental Psychology, 39* (5), 877–890.

Ruiz-Olvares, R., Pino, M.J. & Herruzo, J. (2010). Reduction of disruptive behaviors using an intervention based on the good behavior game and the say-do-report correspondence. *Psychology in the Schools, 47* (10), 1046–1058.

Rumberger, R.W. (1995). Dropping out of middle school: A multilevel analysis of students and schools. *American Educational Research Journal, 32* (3), 583–625.

Rusby, J.C., Crowley, R., Sprague, J. & Biglan, A. (2011). Observations of the middle school environment: The context for student behavior beyond the classroom. *Psychology in the Schools, 48* (4), 400–415.

Rusby, J.C., Taylor, T.K. & Foster, E.M. (2007). A descriptive study of school discipline referrals in first grade. *Psychology in the Schools, 44* (4), 333–350.

Russell, A., Pettit, G.S. & Mize, J. (1998). Horizontal qualities in parent-child relationships: Parallels with and possible consequences for children's peer relationships. *Developmental Review, 18* (3), 313–352.

Russell, S.T., Seif, H. & Truong, N.L. (2001). School outcomes of sexual minority youth in the United States: Evidence from a national study. *Journal of Adolescence, 24* (1), 111–127.

Rutherford, E. & Mussen, P. (1968). Generosity in nursery school boys. *Child Development, 39* (3), 755–765.

Rutherford, L.E., DuPaul, G.J. & Jitendra, A.K. (2008). Examining the relationship between treatment outcomes for academic achievement and social skills in school-age children with attention-deficit hyperactivity disorder. *Psychology in the Schools, 45* (2), 145–157.

Rutter, M. (1983). School effects on pupil progress: Research findings and policy implications. *Child Development, 54* (1), 1–29.

——(1985). Resilience in the face of adversity: Protective factors and resistance to psychiatric disorder. *British Journal of Psychiatry, 147* (6), 598–611.

——(1999). Resilience concepts and findings: Implications for family therapy. *Journal of Family Therapy, 21* (2), 119–144.

Rutter, M., Graham, P., Chadwick, O.F.D. & Yule, W. (1976). Adolescent turmoil: Fact or fiction?. *Journal of Child Psychology and Psychiatry, 17* (1), 35–56.

Rutter, M. & Maughan, B. (2002). School effectiveness findings 1979–2002. *Journal of School Psychology, 40* (6), 451–475.

Rutters, R., Gerver, W.J., Nieuwenhuizen, A.G., Verhoef, S.P.M. & Westertero-Plantenga, M.S. (2010). Sleep duration and body-weight development during puberty in a Dutch children cohort. *International Journal of Obesity, 34* (10), 1508–1514.

Ryan, A.M. & Patrick, H. (2001). The classroom social environment and changes in adolescents' motivation and engagement during middle school. *American Educational Research Journal, 38* (2), 437–460.

Ryan, C.S., Casas, J.F., Kelly-Vance, L., Ryalls, B.O. & Nero, C. (2010). Parent involvement and views of school success: The role of parents' Latino and White American cultural orientations. *Psychology in the Schools, 47* (4), 391–405.

Ryan, R.M. & Brown, K.W. (2003). Why we don't need self-esteem: On fundamental needs, contingent love, and mindfulness. *Psychological Inquiry 14* (1), 71–76.

Ryan, R.M. & Deci, E.L. (1996). When paradigms clash: Comments on Cameron and Pierce's claim that rewards do not undermine intrinsic motivation. *Review of Educational Research, 66* (1), 33–38.

——(2000a). Self-determination theory and the facilitation of intrinsic motivation, social development, and well-being. *American Psychologist, 55* (1), 68–78.

——(2000b). Intrinsic and extrinsic motivations: Classic definitions and new directions. *Contemporary Educational Psychology, 25* (1), 54–67.

Ryan, R.M. & Stiller, J. (1991). The social contexts of internalization: Parent and teacher influences on autonomy, motivation, and learning. *Advances in Motivation and Achievement, 7,* 115–149.

Ryan, R.M., Stiller, J.D. & Lynch, J.H. (1994). Representations of relationships to teachers, parents, and friends as predictors of academic motivation and self-esteem. *Journal of Early Adolescence, 14* (2), 226–249.

Sabol, T.J. & Pianta, R.C. (2012). Patterns of school readiness forecast achievement and socioemotional development at the end of elementary school. *Child Development, 83* (1), 282–299.

Sagi, A. & Hoffman, M.L. (1976). Empathic distress in the newborn. *Developmental Psychology, 12* (2), 175–176.

Sagotsky, G., Wood-Schneider, M. & Konop, M. (1981). Learning to cooperate: Effects of modeling and direct instruction. *Child Development, 52* (3), 1037–1042.

Salend, S.J. & Taylor, L. (1993). Working with families: A cross-cultural perspective. *Remedial and Special Education, 14* (5), 25–32.

Salmivalli, C. & Helteenvuori, T. (2007). Reactive, but not proactive aggression predicts victimization among boys. *Aggressive Behavior, 33* (3), 198–206.

Salmivalli, C. & Isaacs, J. (2005). Prospective relations among victimization, rejection, friendlessness, and children's self- and peer-perceptions. *Child Development, 76* (6), 1161–1171.

Salmivalli, C. & Kaukiainen, A. (2004). 'Female aggression' revisited: Variable- and person-centered approaches to studying gender differences in different types of aggression. *Aggressive Behavior, 30* (2), 158–163.

Salmivalli, C., Kaukiainen, A., Kaistaniemi, L. & Lagerspetz, K.M.J. (1999). Self-evaluated self-esteem, peer-evaluated self-esteem, and defensive egotism as predictors of adolescents' participation in bullying situations. *Personality and Social Psychology Bulletin, 25* (10), 1268–1278.

Salmivalli, C., Kaukiainen, A. & Lagerspetz, K. (1998). Aggression in the social relations of school-aged girls and boys. In P.T. Slee and K. Rigby (Eds.) *Children's peer relations.* London: Routledge, 60–75.

Salmivalli, C., Ojanen, T., Haanpää, J. & Peets, H. (2005a). 'I'm OK but you're not' and other peer-relational schemas:

Explaining individual differences in children's social goals. *Developmental Psychology, 41* (2), 363–375.

Salmivalli, C., Kaukiainen, A. & Voeten, M. (2005b). Anti-bullying intervention: Implementation and outcome. *British Journal of Educational Psychology, 75* (3), 465–487.

Sameroff, A.J. (1990). Neo-environmental perspectives on developmental theory. In R.M. Hodapp, J.A. Burack and E. Zigler (Eds.) *Issues in the developmental approach to mental retardation.* Cambridge, UK: Cambridge University Press, 93–113.

Samples, F.L. (2004). Evaluating curriculum-based intervention programs: An examination of preschool, primary, and elementary school intervention programs. In C.E. Sanders and G.D. Phye (Eds.) *Bullying: Implications for the classroom.* San Diego, CA: Elsevier, 203–227.

Sanches, C., Gouveia-Pereira, M. & Carugati, F. (2012). Justice judgements, school failure, and adolescent deviant behaviour. *British Journal of Educational Psychology, 82* (4), 606–621.

Sandefur, G.D. & Wells, T. (1999). Does family structure really influence educational attainment?. *Social Science Research, 28* (4), 331–357.

Sanders, M.R. (1999). Triple P – Positive Parenting Program: Towards an empirically validated multilevel parenting and support strategy for the prevention of behaviour and emotional problems in children. *Clinical Child and Family Psychology Review, 2* (2), 71–90.

Sanders, M.R., Marakie-Dadds, C., Tully, L.A. & Bor, W. (2000). The Triple P – Positive Parenting Program: A comparison of enhanced, standard, and self-directed behavioral family intervention for children with early onset conduct problems. *Journal of Consulting and Clinical Psychology, 68* (4), 624–640.

Sanson, A., Hemphill, S.A. & Smart, D. (2004). Connections between temperament and social development: A review. *Social Development, 13* (1), 142–170.

Santor, D.A., Ingram, A. & Kusumakar, V. (2003). Influence of executive functioning difficulties on verbal aggression in adolescents: Moderating effects of winning and losing and increasing and decreasing levels of provocation. *Aggressive Behavior, 29* (6), 475–488.

Sapon-Shevin, M. (1996). Beyond gifted education: Building a shared agenda for school reform. *Journal for the Education of the Gifted, 19* (2), 194–214.

——(1999). *Because we can change the world: A practical guide to building cooperative, inclusive classroom communities.* Boston, MA: Allyn & Bacon.

Sapouna, M., Wolke, D., Vannini, N., Watson, S., Woods, S., Schneider, W., Enz, S. & Aylett, R. (2012). Individual and social network predictors of the short-term stability of bullying victimization in the United Kingdom and Germany. *British Journal of Educational Psychology, 82* (2), 225–240.

Savin-Williams, R.C. (1994). Verbal and physical abuse as stressors in the lives of lesbian, gay male, and bisexual youths: Associations with school problems, running away, substance abuse, prostitution, and suicide. *Journal of Consulting and Clinical Psychology, 62* (2), 261–269.

Sayal, K., Goodman, R. & Ford, T. (2006). Barriers to the identification of children with attention deficit/hyperactivity disorder. *Journal of Child Psychology and Psychiatry, 47* (7), 744–750.

Saylor, S., Sidener, T.M., Reeve, S.A., Fetherston, A., & Prodger, P.R. (2012). Effects of three types of noncontingent auditory stimulation on vocal stereotypy in children with autism. *Journal of Applied Behavior Analysis, 45* (1), 185–190.

Scambler, D.J., Harris, M.J. & Milich, R. (1998). Sticks and stones: Evaluations of responses to childhood teasing. *Social Development, 7* (2), 234–249.

Scaramella, L.V. & Conger, R.D. (2003). Intergenerational continuity of hostile parenting and its consequences: The moderating influence of children's negative emotional reactivity. *Social Development, 12* (3), 420–439.

Scaramella, L.V., Neppl, T.K., Ontai, L.L. & Conger, R.D. (2008). Consequences of socioeconomic disdvantage across three generations: Parenting behavior and child externalizing problems. *Journal of Family Psychology, 22* (5), 725–733.

Schaeffer, C.M., Petras, H., Ialongo, N., Poduska, J. & Kellam, S. (2003). Modeling growth in boys' aggressive behavior across elementary school: Links to later criminal involvement, conduct disorder, and antisocial personality disorder. *Developmental Psychology, 39* (6), 1020–1025.

Schaffer, H.R. (1998). *Making decisions about children: Psychological questions and answers.* (2nd ed.) Oxford, UK: Blackwell.

Schaps, E. & Lewis, C. (1991). Extrinsic rewards are education's past, not its future. *Educational Leadership, 48* (7), 81.

Schechter, M.G. & Bochenek, M. (2008). Working to eliminate human rights abuses of children: A cross-national comparative study. *Human Rights Quarterly, 30* (3), 579–606.

Scheithauer, H., Hayer, T., Petermann, F. & Jugert, G. (2006). Physical, verbal, and relational forms of bullying among German students: Age trends, gender differences, and correlates. *Aggressive Behavior, 32* (3), 261–275.

Schill, M.T., Kratochwill, T.R. & Elliott, S.N. (1998). Functional assessment in behavioral consultation: A treatment utility study. *School Psychology Quarterly, 13* (2), 116–140.

Schloss, P.J. & Smith, M.A. (1998). *Applied behavior analysis in the classroom.* (2nd ed.) Boston, MA: Allyn & Bacon.

Schmitt, D.R. (1981). Performance under cooperation or competition. *The American Behavioral Scientist, 24* (5), 649–679.

Schmuck, R.A. & Schmuck, P.A. (2001). *Group processes in the classroom.* (8th ed.) Boston, MA: McGraw-Hill.

Schneider, B.H., Clegg, M.R., Byrne, B.M., Ledingham, J.E. & Crombie, G. (1989). Social relations of gifted children as a function of age and school program. *Journal of Educational Psychology, 81* (1), 48–56.

Scholte, R.H.J., Engles, R.C.M.E., Overbeek, G., de Kemp, R.A.T. & Haselager, G.J.T. (2007). Stability in bullying and victimization and its association with social adjustment in childhood and adolescence. *Journal of Abnormal Child Psychology, 35* (2), 217–228.

Schraml, K., Perski, A., Grossi, G. & Simonsson-Sarnecki, M. (2011). Stress symptoms among adolescents: The role of subjective psychosocial conditions, lifestyle, and self-esteem. *Journal of Adolescence, 34* (5), 987–996.

Schuetze, P., Lopez, F., Granger, D.A. & Eiden, R.D. (2008). The association between prenatal exposure to cigarettes and cortisol reactivity in 7-month-old infants. *Developmental Psychobiology, 50* (8), 819–834.

Schulting, A.B., Malone, P.S. & Dodge, K.A. (2005). The effect of school-based kindergarten transition policies and practices on child academic outcomes. *Developmental Psychology, 41* (6), 860–871.

Schultz, B.K., Evans, S.W. & Serpell, Z.N. (2009). Preventing failure among middle school students with attention deficit hyperactivity disorder: A survival analysis. *School Psychology Review, 38* (1), 14–27.

Schultz, C.L. (1981). The family and Parent Effectiveness Training. *Australian Journal of Sex, Marriage and Family, 3* (2), 135–142.

Schultz, C.L. & Khan, J.A. (1982). Mother-child interaction behaviour and Parent Effectiveness Training. *Australian Journal of Sex, Marriage and Family, 3* (3), 133–138.

Schultz, C.L. & Nystul, M.S. (1980). Mother-child interaction behavior as an outcome of theoretical models of parent group education. *Journal of Individual Psychology, 36* (1), 3–15.

Schultz, C.L., Nystul, M.S. & Law, H.G. (1980). Attitudinal outcomes of theoretical models of parent group education. *Journal of Individual Psychology, 36* (1), 16–28.

Schultz, D., Izard, C.E. & Ackerman, B. (2000). Children's anger attribution bias: Relations to family environment and social adjustment. *Social Development, 9* (3), 284–301.

Schutz, P.A., Hong, J.Y., Cross, D.I. & Osbon, J.N. (2006). Reflections on investigating emotion in educational activity settings. *Educational Psychology Review, 18* (4), 343–360.

Schwartz, D. (2000). Subtypes of victims and aggressors in children's peer groups. *Journal of Abnormal Child Psychology, 28* (2), 181–192.

Schwartz, D., Dodge, K.A., Pettit, G.S. & Bates, J.E. (1997). The early socialization of aggressive victims of bullying. *Child Development, 68* (4), 665–675.

Schwartz, D., Dodge, K.A., Pettit, G.S., Bates, J.E. & The Conduct Problems Prevention Research Group (2000). Friendship as a moderating factor in the pathway between early harsh home environment and later victimization in the peer group. *Developmental Psychology, 36* (5), 646–662.

Schwartz, D., Gorman, A.H., Nakamoto, J. & Toblin, R.L. (2005). Victimization in the peer group and children's academic functioning. *Journal of Educational Psychology, 97* (3), 425–435.

Schwinger, M. & Stiensmeier-Pelster, J. (2011). Performance-approach and performance-avoidance classroom goals and adoption of personal achievement goals. *British Journal of Educational Psychology, 81* (4), 680–699.

Scime, M. & Norvilitis, J.M. (2006). Task performance and response to frustration in children with attention deficit hyperactivity disorder. *Psychology in the Schools, 43* (3), 377–386.

Scott, S., Spender, Q., Doolan, M., Jacobs, B. & Aspland, H. (2001). Multicentre controlled trial of parenting groups for childhood antisocial behaviour in clinical practice. *British Medical Journal, 323* (7306), 194–197.

Scott, T.M. & Barrett, S.B. (2004). Using staff and student time engaged in disciplinary procedures to evaluate the impact of school-wide PBS. *Journal of Positive Behavior Interventions, 6* (1), 21–27.

Selekman, M.D. (1997). *Solution-focused therapy with children: Harnessing family strengths for systemic change.* New York: Guilford.

Selekman, M.D. (2006). *Working with self-harming adolescents.: A collaborative, strengths-based therapy approach.* New York: Norton.

——(2010). *Collaborative brief therapy with children.* New York: Guilford.

Seligman, M.E.P. (1975). *Helplessness: On depression, development and death.* San Francisco, CA: W.H. Freeman.

——(2002). *Authentic happiness.* New York: Simon & Schuster.

——(2011). *Flourish: A visionary new understanding of happiness and well-being.* New York: Free Press.

Seligman, M.E.P., Reivich, K., Jaycox, L. & Gillham, J. (1995). *The optimistic child.* Sydney: Random House.

Shaklee, B.D. (1992). Identification of young gifted students. *Journal for the Education of the Gifted, 15* (2), 134–144.

Shapiro, E.S. (1984). Self-monitoring procedures. In T.H. Ollendick and M. Hersen (Eds.) *Child behavioral assessment.* New York: Pergamon, 148–165.

Sharkey, J.D., You, S. & Schnoebelen, K. (2008). Relations among school assets, individual resilience, and student engagement for youth grouped by level of family functioning. *Psychology in the Schools, 45* (5), 402–418.

Sharp, S. & Cowie, H. (1994). Empowering pupils to take positive action against bullying. In P.K. Smith and S. Sharp (Eds.) *School bullying: Insights and perspectives.* London: Routledge, 108–131.

Sharp, S. & Thompson, D. (1994). The role of whole-school policies in tackling bullying behaviour in schools. In P.K. Smith and S. Sharp (Eds.) *School bullying: Insights and perspectives.* London: Routledge, 57–83.

Shavelson, R.J., Hubner, J.J. & Stanton, G.C. (1976). Self-concept: Validation of construct interpretations. *Review of Educational Research, 46* (3), 407–441.

Shaw, D.S., Bell, R.Q & Gilliom, M. (2000). A truly early starter model of antisocial behavior revisited. *Clinical Child and Family Psychology Review, 3* (3), 155–172.

Shaw, D.S., Gilliom, M., Ingoldsby, E.M. & Nagin, D.S. (2003). Trajectories leading to school-age conduct problems. *Developmental Psychology, 39* (2), 189–200.

Shaw, D.S., Lacourse, E. & Nagin, D.S. (2005). Developmental trajectories of conduct problems and hyperactivity from ages 2 to 10. *Journal of Child Psychology and Psychiatry, 46* (9), 931–942.

Shaw, D.S., Owens, E.B., Giovannelli, J. & Winslow, E.B. (2001). Infant and toddler pathways leading to early externalizing disorders. *Journal of the American Academy of Child and Adolescent Psychiatry, 40* (1), 36–43.

Shaw, D.S., Owens, E.B., Vondra, J.I., Keenan, K. & Winslow, E.B. (1996). Early risk factors in the development of early disruptive behavior problems. *Development and Psychopathology, 8* (4), 679–699.

Shaw, D.S., Winslow, E.B. & Flanagan, C. (1999). A prospective study of the effects of marital status and family relations on young children's adjustment among African American and European American families. *Child Development, 70* (3), 742–755.

Shechtman, Z. (2000). An innovative intervention for treatment of child and adolescent aggression: An outcome study. *Psychology in the Schools, 37* (2), 157–182.

Sheehan, M.J. & Watson, M.W. (2008). Reciprocal influences between maternal discipline techniques and aggression in children and adolescents. *Aggressive Behavior, 34* (3), 245–255.

Shek, D.T.L. (2007). A longitudinal study of perceived parental psychological control and psychological well-being in Chinese adolescents in Hong Kong. *Journal of Clinical Psychology, 63* (1), 1–22.

Shelton, T.L., Barkley, R.A., Crosswait, C., Moorehouse, M., Fletcher, K., Barrett, S., Jenkins, L. & Metevia, L. (1998). Psychiatric and psychological morbidity as a function of adaptive disability in preschool children with aggressive and hyperactive-impulsive-inattentive behavior. *Journal of Abnormal Child Psychology, 26* (6), 475–494.

Sheridan, J., Dwyer, S.B. & Sanders, M.R. (1997). Parenting and family support for children with ADHD. *Australian Journal of Early Childhood, 22* (4), 15–23.

Sheridan, S.M. (2000). Considerations of multiculturalism and diversity in behavioral consultation with parents and teachers. *School Psychology Review, 29* (3), 344–353.

Sheu, Y.-S., Polcari, A., Anderson, C.M. & Teicher, M.H. (2010). Harsh corporal punishment is associated with increase T2 relaxation time in dopamine-rich regions. *NeuroImage, 51* (2), 412–419.

Shi, L., Sidwell, R.W., & Patterson, P.H. (2003). Maternal influenza infection causes marked behavioral and pharmacological changes in the offspring. *The Journal of Neuroscience, 23* (1), 297–302.

Shields, A., Ryan, R.M. & Cicchetti, D. (2001). Narrative representations of caregivers and emotion dysregulation as predictors of maltreated children's rejection by peers. *Developmental Psychology, 37* (3), 321–337.

Shipman, K.L., Schneider, R., Fitzgerald, M.M., Sims, C., Swisher, L. & Edwards, A. (2007). Maternal emotion socialization in maltreating and non-maltreating families: Implications for children's emotion regulation. *Social Development, 16* (2), 268–285.

Shiu, S. (2001). Issues in the education of students with chronic illness. *International Journal of Disability, Development and Education, 48* (3), 269–281.

Shonk, S.M. & Cicchetti, D. (2001). Maltreatment, competency deficits, and risk for academic and behavioral maladjustment. *Developmental Psychology, 37* (1), 3–17.

Shriver, M.D., Anderson, C.M. & Proctor, B. (2001). Evaluating the validity of functional behaviour assessment. *School Psychology Review, 30* (2), 180–192.

Shumba, A. (2002). The nature, extent and effects of emotional abuse on primary school pupils by teachers in Zimbabwe. *Child Abuse and Neglect, 26* (8), 783–791.

Shumow, L. & Miller, J.D. (2001). Parents' at-home and at-school academic involvement with young adolescents. *Journal of Early Adolescence, 21* (1), 68–91.

Shumow, L., Vandell, D.L. & Posner, J. (1999). Risk and resilience in the urban neighborhood: Predictors of academic performance among low-income elementary school children. *Merrill-Palmer Quarterly, 45* (2), 309–331.

Shute, R., Owens, L. & Slee, P. (2002). 'You just stare at them and give them daggers': Nonverbal expressions of social aggression in teenage girls. *International Journal of Adolescence and Youth, 10* (4), 353–372.

Siegle, D. & Schuler, P.A. (2000). Perfectionism differences in gifted middle school students. *Roeper Review, 23* (1), 39–44.

Sierens, E., Vansteenkiste, M., Goossens, L., Soenens, B. & Dochy, F. (2009). The synergistic relationship of perceived autonomy support and structure in the prediction of self-regulated learning. *British Journal of Educational Psychology, 79* (1), 57–68.

Sijtsema, J.J., Ojanen. T., Veenstra, R., Lindenberg, S., Hawley, P.H. & Little, T.D. (2010). Forms and functions of aggression in adolescent friendship selection and influence: A longitudinal social network analysis. *Social Development, 19* (3), 515–534.

Sijtsema, J.J., Veenstra, R., Lindenberg, S. & Salmivalli, C. (2009). Empirical test of bullies' status goals: Assessing direction goals, aggression, and prestige. *Aggressive Behavior, 35* (1), 57–67.

Silver, R.B., Measelle, J.R., Armstrong, J.M. & Essex, M.J. (2010). The impact of parents, child care providers, teachers, and peers on early externalizing trajectories. *Journal of School Psychology, 48* (6), 555–583.

Silverman, L.K., Chitwood, D.G. & Waters, J.L. (1986). Young gifted children: Can parents identify giftedness? *Topics in Early Childhood Special Education, 6* (1), 23–38.

Simons, R.L., Lin, K.-H., Gordon, L.C., Brody, G.H., Murry, V. & Conger, R.D. (2002). Community differences in the association between parenting practices and child conduct problems. *Journal of Marriage and the Family, 64* (2), 331–345.

Simons, R.L., Whitbeck, L.B., Conger, R.D. & Wu, C.-I. (1991). Intergenerational transmission of harsh parenting. *Developmental Psychology, 27* (1), 159–171.

Simonsen, B. (2010). School-wide positive behavior support. In M.M. Kerr & C.M. Nelson (Eds.) *Strategies for addressing behavior problems in the classroom.* (6th ed.) Boston, MA: Pearson, 36–68.

Simonsen, B., Fairbanks, S., Briesch, A., Myers, D. & Sugai, G. (2008a). Evidence-based practices in classroom management: Considerations for research to practice. *Education and Treatment of Children, 31* (3), 351-380.

Simonsen, B., Sugai, G. & Negron, M. (2008b). Schoolwide positive behavior supports: Primary systems and practices. *Teaching Exceptional Children, 40* (6), 32-40.

Singer, L.T., Eisengart, L.J., Minnes, S., Noland, J., Jey, A., Lane, C. & Min, M.O. (2005). Prenatal cocaine exposure and infant cognition. *Infant Behavior and Development, 28* (4), 431-444.

Singh, K., Bickley, P.G., Trivette, P., Keith, T.Z., Keith, P.B. & Anderson, E. (1995). The effects of four components of parental involvement on eighth-grade student achievement: Structural analysis of NELS-88 data. *School Psychology Review, 24* (2), 299-317.

Siren-Tiusanen, H. & Robinson H.A. (2001). Nap schedules and sleep practices in infant-toddler groups. *Early Childhood Research Quarterly, 16* (4), 453-474.

Sirin, S.R. (2005). Socioeconomic status and academic achievement: A meta-analytic review of research. *Review of Educational Research, 75* (3), 417-453.

Skaalvik, E.M. & Skaalvik, S. (2007). Dimensions of teacher self-efficacy and relations with strain factors, perceived collective teacher efficacy, and teacher burnout. *Journal of Educational Psychology, 99* (3), 611-625.

Skiba, R.J., Horner, R.H., Chung, C.-G., Rausch, M.K., May, S.L. & Tobin, T. (2011). Race is not neutral: A national investigation of African American and Latino disproportionality in school discipline. *School Psychology Review, 40* (1), 85-107.

Skiba, R.J. & Peterson, R.L. (1999). The dark side of zero tolerance: Can punishment lead to safe schools?. *Phi Delta Kappan, 80* (5), 372-376.

——(2000). School discipline at a crossroads: From zero tolerance to early response. *Exceptional Children 66* (3), 335-346.

Skiba, R.J., Peterson, R.L. & Williams, R.L. (1997). Office referrals and suspension: Disciplinary intervention in middle schools. *Education and Treatment of Children, 20* (3), 295-315.

Skinner, B.F. (1989). *Recent issues in the analysis of behavior.* Columbus, OH: Merrill.

Skinner, C.H., Neddenriep, C.E., Robinson, S.L., Ervin, R. & Jones, K. (2002). Altering educational environments through positive peer reporting: Prevention and remediation of social problems associated with behavior disorders. *Psychology in the Schools, 39* (2), 191-202.

Skinner, C.H., Pappas, D.N. & Davis, K.A. (2005). Enhancing academic engagement: Providing opportunities for responding and influencing students to choose to respond. *Psychology in the Schools, 42* (4), 389-403.

Skinner, C.H., Williams, R.L. & Neddenriep, C.E. (2004). Using interdependent group-oriented reinforcement to enhance academic performance in general education classrooms. *School Psychology Review, 33* (3), 384-397.

Skinner, E., Furrer, C., Marchand, G. & Kindermann, T. (2008). Engagement and disaffection in the classroom: Part of a larger motivational dynamic?. *Journal of Educational Psychology, 100* (4), 765-781.

Sklare, G.B. (2005). *Brief counseling that works: A solution-focused approach for school counselors and administrators.* (2nd ed.) Thousand Oaks, CA: Corwin Press.

Slade, E.P. & Wissow, L.S. (2004). Spanking in early childhood and later behavior problems: A prospective study of infants and young toddlers. *Pediatrics, 113* (5), 1321-1330

Slavin, R.E. (1989). Research on cooperative learning: Consensus and controversy. *Educational Leadership, 47* (4), 52-54.

——(1991). Group rewards make groupwork work: Response to Kohn. *Educational Leadership, 48* (5), 889-891.

Slavin, R.E. & Cooper, R. (1999). Improving intergroup relations: Lessons learned from cooperative learning programs. *Journal of Social Issues, 55* (4), 647-663.

Slee, P.T. (1994a). Life at school used to be good: Victimisation and health concerns of secondary school students. *Youth Studies Australia,* 13 (4), 20-23.

——(1994b). Situational and interpersonal correlates of anxiety associated with peer victimisation. *Journal of Child Psychiatry and Human Development, 25* (2), 97-107.

——(1995a). Peer victimisation and its relationship to depression among Australian primary school students. *Journal of Personality and Individual Differences, 18* (1), 57-62.

——(1995b). Bullying: Health concerns of Australian secondary school students. *International Journal of Adolescence and Youth, 5* (4), 215-224.

——(1998). Bullying amongst Australian primary school students: Some barriers to help-seeking and links with sociometric status. In P.T. Slee and K. Rigby (Eds.) *Children's peer relations.* London: Routledge, 205-214.

——(2001). *The PEACE pack: A program for reducing bullying in our schools.* (3rd ed.) Adelaide, SA: Flinders University.

——(2006). The PEACE Pack: A whole-school program for reducing school bullying. In H. McGrath and T. Noble (Eds.) *Bullying solutions: Evidence-based approaches to bullying in Australian schools.* Sydney: Pearson Longman, 85-99.

Slee, P.T. & Rigby, K. (1994). Peer victimisation at school. *Australian Journal of Early Childhood, 19* (1), 3-10.

Slee, R. (1995). *Changing theories and practices of discipline.* London: Falmer.

Sletta, O., Valås, H., Skaalvik, E. & Sebstad, F. (1996). Peer relations, loneliness, and self-perceptions in school-aged children. *British Journal of Educational Psychology, 66* (4), 431-445.

Sloan, J. (1989). Child abuse in schools. *Educational and Child Psychology, 6* (1), 11-14.

Slocum, S.K. & Tiger, J.H. (2011). An assessment of the efficiency of and child preference for forward and backward training. *Journal of Applied Behavior Analysis, 44* (4), 793-805.

Smeekens, S., Riksen-Walraven, J.M. & van Bakel, H.J.A. (2007). Multiple determinants of externalizing behavior in 5-year-olds: A longitudinal model. *Journal of Abnormal Child Psychology, 35* (3), 347-361.

Smerdon, B.A. (2002). Students' perceptions of membership in their high school. *Sociology of Education, 75* (4), 287-305.

Smerechansky-Metzger, J.A. (1995). The quest for multiple intelligences: Using MI theory to create exciting teaching and learning experiences. *Gifted Child Quarterly, 18* (3), 12-15.

Smidt, S. (1998). *Guide to early years practice.* London: Routledge.

Smith, A.B. (1990). Early childhood on the margins. *Australian Journal of Early Childhood, 15* (4), 12-15.

——(2006). The state of research on the effects of physical punishment. *Social Policy Journal of New Zealand, 27,* 114-127.

Smith, C.A. & Farrington, D.P. (2004). Continuities in antisocial behavior and parenting across three generations. *Journal of Child Psychology and Psychiatry, 45* (2), 230-247.

Smith, C.L., Calkins, S.D., Keane, S.P., Anastopoulos, A.D. & Shelton, T.L. (2004). Predicting stability and change in toddler behavior problems: Contributions of maternal behavior and child gender. *Developmental Psychology, 40* (1), 29-42.

Smith, J.D., Schneider, B.H., Smith, P.K. & Ananiadou, K. (2004). The effectiveness of whole-school antibullying programs:

A synthesis of evaluation research. *School Psychology Review,* *33* (4), 547–560.

Smith, P.K. & Ananiadou, K. (2003). The nature of school bullying and the effectiveness of school-based interventions. *Journal of Applied Psychoanalytic Studies, 5* (2), 189–209.

Smith, P.K., Cowie, H. & Sharp, S. (1994). Working directly with pupils involved in bullying situations. In P.K. Smith and S. Sharp (Eds.) *School bullying: Insights and perspectives.* London: Routledge, 193–212.

Smith, P.K., Pepler, D. & Rigby, K. (Eds.) (2004). *Bullying in schools: How successful can interventions be?.* Cambridge, UK: Cambridge University Press.

Smith, P.K. & Sharp, S. (1994). The problem of school bullying. In P.K. Smith and S. Sharp (Eds.) *School bullying: Insights and perspectives.* London: Routledge, 1–19.

Smith, R.L., Rose, A.J. & Schwartz-Mette, R.A. (2010). Relational and overt aggression in childhood and adolescence: Clarifying mean-level gender differences and associations with peer acceptance. *Social Development, 19* (2), 243–269.

Smith, P.K., Talamelli, L., Cowie, H., Naylor, P. & Chauhan, P. (2004). Profiles of non-victims, escaped victims, continuing victims and new victims of school bullying. *British Journal of Educational Psychology, 74* (4), 565–581.

Smith, S.W. & Daunic, A.P. (2002). Using conflict resolution and peer mediation to support positive behavior. In B. Algozzine and P. Kay (Eds.) *Preventing problem behaviors: A handbook of successful prevention strategies.* Thousand Oaks, CA: Corwin Press, 142–161.

——(2004). Research on preventing behavior problems using a cognitive-behavioral intervention: Preliminary findings, challenges, and future directions. *Behavioral Disorders, 30* (1), 72–76.

Smyth, J. (1989). Developing and sustaining critical reflection in teacher education. *Journal of Teacher Education, 40* (2), 2–9.

Snell, E.K., Adam, E.K. & Duncan, G.J. (2007). Sleep and body mass index and overweight status of children and adolescents. *Child Development, 78* (1), 309–323.

Snyder, J., Cramer, A., Afrank, J. & Patterson, G.R. (2005). The contributions of ineffective discipline and parental hostile attributions of child misbehavior to the development of conduct problems at home and school. *Developmental Psychology, 41* (1), 30–41.

Snyder, J., Horsch, E. & Childs, J. (1997). Peer relationships of young children: Affiliative choices and shaping of aggressive behavior. *Journal of Clinical Child Psychology, 26* (2), 145–156.

Snyder, J., Prichard, J., Schrepferman, L., Patrick, M.R. & Stoolmiller, M. (2004). Child impulsiveness-inattention, early peer experiences, and the development of early onset conduct problems. *Journal of Abnormal Child Psychology, 32* (6), 579–594.

Snyder, J., Stoolmiller, M., Wilson, M. & Yamamoto, M. (2003). Child anger regulation, parental responses to children's anger displays, and early child antisocial behavior. *Social Development, 12* (3), 335–360.

Society for Medical Anthropology (2007). The rights of children: Public policy statement. *Medical Anthropology Quarterly, 21* (2), 234–238.

Soden, Z. (2002). Daily living skills. In L. Porter (Ed.) *Educating young children with additional needs.* Sydney: Allen & Unwin, 117–139.

Soenens, B. & Beyers, W. (2012). The cross-cultural significance of control and autonomy in parent-adolescent relationships. *Journal of Adolescence 35* (2), 243–248.

Soenens, B., Elliot, A.J., Goossens, L., Vansteenkiste, M., Luyten, P. & Duriez, B. (2005b). The intergenerational transmission of perfectionism: Parents' psychological control as an intervening variable. *Journal of Family Psychology, 19* (3), 358–366.

Soenens, B., Park, S.-Y., Vansteenkiste, M. & Mouratidis, A. (2012a). Perceived parental psychological control and adolescent depressive experiences: A cross-cultural study with Belgian and South-Korean adolescents. *Journal of Adolescence, 35* (2), 261–272.

Soenens, B., Sierens, E., Vansteenkiste, M., Dochy, F. & Goossens, L. (2012b). Psychologically controlling teaching: Examining outcomes, antecedents, and mediators. *Journal of Educational Psychology, 104* (1), 108–120.

Soenens, B. & Vansteenkiste, M. (2010). A theoretical upgrade of the concept of parental psychological control: Proposing new insights on the basis of self-determination theory. *Developmental Review, 30* (1), 74–99.

Soenens, B., Vansteenkiste, M. & Luyten, P. (2010). Toward a domain-sepcific approach to the study of parental psychological control: Distinguishing between dependency-oriented and achievement-oriented psychological control. *Journal of Personality, 78* (1), 217–256.

Soenens, B., Vansteenkiste, M., Luyten, P., Duriez, B. & Goossens, L. (2005a). Maladaptive perfectionistic self-representations: The meditational link between psychological control and adjustment. *Personality and Individual Differences, 38* (2), 487–498.

Soenens, B., Vansteenkiste, M., Lens, W., Luyckx, K., Goossens, L., Beyers, W. & Ryan, R.M. (2007). Conceptualizing parental autonomy support: Adolescent perceptions of promotion of independence versus promotion of volitional functioning. *Developmental Psychology, 43* (3), 633–646.

Sohr-Preston, S.L. & Scaramella, L.V. (2006). Implications of timing of maternal depressive symptoms for early cognitive and language development. *Clinical Child and Family Psychology Review, 9* (1), 65–83.

Solberg, M.E., Olweus, D. & Endresen, I.M. (2007). Bullies and victims at school: Are they the same pupils? *British Journal of Educational Psychology, 77* (2), 441–464.

Solomon, B.G., Klein, S.A., Hintze, J.M., Cressey, J.M. & Peller, S.L. (2012). A meta-analysis of school-wide positive behavior support: An exploratory study using single-case synthesis. *Psychology in the Schools, 49* (2), 105–121.

Solomon, C.R. & Serres, F. (1999). Effects of parental verbal aggression on children's self-esteem and school marks. *Child Abuse and Neglect, 23* (4), 339–351.

Solomon, D., Watson, M., Battistich, V., Schaps, E. & Delucci, K. (1996). Creating classrooms that students experience as communities. *American Journal of Community Psychology, 24* (6), 719–748.

Somers, C.L., Chiodo, L.M., Yoon, J., Ratner, H., Barton, E. & Delaney-Black, V. (2011). Family disruption and academic functioning in urban, Black youth. *Psychology in the Schools, 48* (4), 357–370.

Somers, J.M., Goldner, E.M., Waraich, P. & Hsu, L. (2006). Prevalence and incidence studies of anxiety disorders: A systematic review of the literature. *Canadian Journal of Psychiatry, 51* (2), 100–113.

Sommer, K.L. & Baumeister, R.F. (2002). Self-evaluation, persistence, and performance following implicit rejection: The role of trait self-esteem. *Personality and Social Psychology Bulletin, 28* (7), 926–938.

Sommerlad, E.A. & Bellingham, W.P. (1972). Cooperation-competition: A comparison of Australian European and Aboriginal school children. *Journal of Cross-Cultural Psychology, 3* (2), 149–157.

Soodak, L.C. & Podell, D.M. (1993). Teacher efficacy and student problem as factors in special education referral. *The Journal of Special Education, 27* (1), 66–81.

Spence, S.H., Najman, J.M., Bor, W., O'Callaghan, M.J. & Williams, G.M. (2002). Maternal anxiety and depression, poverty and marital relationship factors during early childhood as predictors of anxiety and depressive symptoms in adolescence. *Journal of Child Psychology and Psychiatry, 43* (4), 457–469.

Spera, C. (2005). A review of the relationship among parenting practices, parenting styles, and adolescent school achievement. *Educational Psychology Review, 17* (2), 125–146.

Spieker, S.J., Larson, N.C., Lewis, S.M., Keller, T.E. & Gilchrist, L. (1999). Developmental trajectories of disruptive behavior problems in preschool children of adolescent mothers. *Child Development, 70* (2), 443–458.

Spilt, J.L. & Koomen, H.M.Y., (2009). Widening the view on teacher-child relationships: Teachers' narratives concerning disruptive versus nondisruptive children. *School Psychology Review, 38* (1), 86–101.

Spinrad, T.L., Eisenberg, N., Harris, E., Hanish, L., Fabes, R.A., Kupanoff, K., Ringwald, S. & Holmes, J. (2004a). The relation of children's everyday nonsocial peer play behavior to their emotionality, regulation, and social functioning. *Developmental Psychology, 40* (1), 67–80.

Spinrad, T.L., Stifter, C.A., Donelan-McCall, N. & Turner, L. (2004b). Mothers' regulation strategies in response to toddlers' affect: Links to later emotion self-regulation. *Social Development, 13* (11), 40–55.

Spira, E.G. & Fischel, J.E. (2005). The impact of preschool inattention, hyperactivity, and impulsivity on social and academic development: A review. *Journal of Child Psychology and Psychiatry, 46* (7), 755–773.

Spirito, A., Esposito-Smythers, C., Weismoore, J. & Miller, A. (2012). Adolescent suicidal behavior. In P.C. Kendall (Ed.) *Child and adolescent therapy: Cognitive-behavioral procedures.* (4th ed.) New York: Guilford, 234–256.

Spirito, A., Stark, L.J., Grace, N. & Stamoulis, D. (1991). Common problems and coping strategies reported in childhood and early adolescence. *Journal of Youth and Adolescence, 20* (5), 531–544.

Sprague, J. & Walker, H., (2000). Early identification and intervention for youth with antisocial and violent behavior. *Exceptional Children, 66* (3), 367–379.

Squires, G. (2001). Using cognitive-behavioural psychology with groups of pupils to improve self-control of behaviour. *Educational Psychology in Practice: Theory, research and practice in educational psychology, 17* (4), 317–335.

Stage, S.A. & Quiroz, D.R. (1997). A meta-analysis of interventions to decrease disruptive classroom behavior in public education settings. *School Psychology Review, 26* (3), 333–368.

Stanley, G.K. & Baines, L. (2002). Celebrating mediocrity?: How schools shortchange gifted students. *Roeper Review, 25* (1), 11–13.

Stanley, M. & McGrath, H. (2006). Buddy stystems: Peer support in action. In H. McGrath and T. Noble (Eds.) *Bullying solutions: Evidence-based approaches to bullying in Australian schools.* Sydney: Pearson Longman, 101–122.

Stattin, H. & Kerr, M. (2000). Parental monitoring: A reinterpretation. *Child Development, 71* (4), 1072–1085.

Stauffacher, K. & DeHart, G.B. (2006). Crossing social contexts: Relational aggression between siblings and friends during early and middle childhood. *Journal of Applied Developmental Psychology, 27* (3), 228–240.

Stauffer, S., Heath, M.A., Coyne, S.M. & Ferrin, S. (2012). High school teachers' perceptions of cyberbullying prevention and intervention strategies. *Psychology in the Schools, 49* (4), 353–367.

Stayton, C.J., Hogan, R. & Ainsworth, M.D.S. (1971). Infant obedience and maternal behavior: The origins of socialization reconsidered. *Child Development, 42* (4), 1057–1069.

Steelman, L.M., Assel, M.A., Swank, P.R., Smith, K.E. & Landry, S.H. (2002). Early maternal warm responsiveness as a predictor of child social skills: Direct and indirect paths of influence over time. *Journal of Applied Developmental Psychology, 23* (2), 135–156.

Stefanou, C.R., Perencevich, K.C., DiCintio, M. & Turner, J.C. (2004). Supporting autonomy in the classroom: Ways teachers encourage decision making and ownership. *Educational Psychologist, 39* (2), 97–110.

Stein, M.A., Efron, L.A., Schiff, W.B. & Glanzman, M. (2002). Attention deficits and hyperactivity. In M.L. Batshaw (Ed.) *Children with disabilities.* (5th ed.) Sydney: Elsevier/Baltimore. MD: Brookes, 389–416.

Stein, N. (1995). Sexual harassment in school: The public performance of gendered violence. *Harvard Educational Review, 65* (2), 145–162.

Steinberg, L., Elmen, J.D. & Mounts, N.S. (1989). Authoritative parenting, psychosocial maturity, and academic success among adolescents. *Child Development, 60* (6), 1424–1436.

Steinberg, L., Lamborn, S.D., Darling, N., Mounts, N.S. & Dornbusch, S.M. (1994). Over-time changes in adjustment and competence among adolescents from authoritative, authoritarian, indulgent, and neglectful families. *Child Development, 65* (3), 754–770.

Steinberg, L., Lamborn, S.D., Dornbusch, S.M. & Darling, N. (1992). Impact of parenting practices on adolescent achievement: Authoritative parenting, school involvement, and encouragement to succeed. *Child Development, 63* (5), 1266–1281.

Sterling-Turner, H.E., Robinson, S.L. & Wilczynski, S.M. (2001). Functional assessment of distracting and disruptive behaviors in the school setting. *School Psychology Review, 30* (2), 211–226.

Sterling-Turner, H. & Watson, T.S. (1999). Consultant's guide for the use of time-out in the preschool and elementary classroom. *Psychology in the Schools, 36* (2), 135–148.

Sternberg, K.J., Baradaran, L.P., Abbott, C.B., Lamb, M.E. & Guterman, E. (2006a). Type of violence, age, and gender differences in the effects of family violence on children's behavior problems: A mega-analysis. *Developmental Review, 26* (1), 89–112.

Sternberg, K.J., Lamb, M.E., Guterman, E. & Abbott, C.B. (2006b). Effects of early and later family violence on children's behavior problems and depression: A longitudinal, multi-informant perspective. *Child Abuse and Neglect, 30* (3), 283–306.

Sternberg, R.J. (1988). A three-facet model of creativity. In R.J. Sternberg (Ed.) *The nature of creativity.* Cambridge, UK: Cambridge University Press, 125–147.

——(1999). *Cognitive psychology.* (2nd ed.) Fort Worth, TX: Harcourt Brace College.

Sternberg, R.J. & Lubart, T.I. (1991). An investment theory of creativity and its development. *Human Development, 34,* 1–31.

Stevens, V., De Bourdeauhuij, I. & Van Oost, P. (2000). Bullying in Flemish schools: An evaluation of anti-bullying intervention in primary and secondary schools. *British Journal of Educational Psychology, 70* (2), 195–210.

Stewart, S.L. & Rubin, K.H. (1995). The social problem-solving skills of anxious-withdrawn children. *Development and Psychopathology, 7* (2), 323–336.

Stifter, C.A., Spinrad, T.L., Braungart-Rieker, J.M. (1999). Toward a developmental model of child compliance: The role of emotion regulation in infancy. *Child Development, 70* (1), 21–32.

Stipek, D.J., Feiler, R., Byler, P., Ryan, R., Milburn, S. & Salmon,

J.M. (1998). Good beginnings: What difference does the program make in preparing young children for school? *Journal of Applied Developmental Psychology, 19* (1), 41–66.

Stipek, D.J., Feiler, R., Daniels, D. & Milburn, S. (1995). Effects of different instructional approaches on young children's achievement and motivation. *Child Development, 66* (1), 209–223.

Stoiber, K.C. & Gettinger, M. (2011). Functional assessment and positive support strategies for promoting resilience: Effects on teachers and high-risk children. *Psychology in the Schools, 48* (7), 686–706.

Stonehouse, A. (1991). *Our code of ethics at work.* Watson, ACT: Australian Early Childhood Association.

Stormont, M. (2001). Social outcomes of children with AD/HD: Contributing factors and implications for practice. *Psychology in the Schools, 38* (6), 521–531.

——(2002). Externalizing behavior problems in young children: Contributing factors and early intervention. *Psychology in the Schools, 39* (2), 127–138.

Stormont, M., Lewis, T.J. & Beckner, R. (2005). Positive behavior support systems: Applying key features in preschool settings. *Teaching Exceptional Children, 37* (6), 42–49.

Stormshak, E.A., Bierman, K.L., Bruschi, C., Dodge, K.A., Coie, J.D. & The Conduct Problems Prevention Research Group (1999). The relation between behavior problems and peer preference in different classroom contexts. *Child Development, 70* (1), 169–182.

Stormshak, E.A., Bierman, K.L., McMahon, R.J., Lengua, L.J. & The Conduct Problems Prevention Research Group (2000). Parenting practices and child disruptive behavior problems in early elementary school. *Journal of Clinical Child Psychology, 28* (1), 17–29.

Strage, A. & Brandt, T.S. (1999). Authoritative parenting and college students' academic adjustment and success. *Journal of Educational Psychology, 91* (1), 146–156.

Strain, P.S. & Joseph, G.E. (2004). Engaged supervision to support recommended practices for young children with challenging behavior. *Topics in Early Childhood Special Education, 24* (1), 39–50.

Strassberg, Z. & Treboux, D. (2000). Interpretations of child emotion expressioin and coercive parenting among adolescent mothers. *Social Development, 9* (1), 80–95.

Straus, M.A. & Field, C.J. (2003). Psychological aggression by American parents: National data on prevalence, chronicity, and severity. *Journal of Marriage and the Family, 65* (4), 795–808.

Straus, M.A. & Paschall, M.J. (2009). Corporal punishment by mothers and development of children's cognitive ability: A longitudinal study of two nationally representative age cohorts. *Journal of Aggression, Maltreatment and Trauma, 18* (5), 459–483.

Straus, M.A. & Stewart, J.H. (1999). Corporal punishment by American parents: National data on prevalence, chronicity, severity, and duration, in relation to child and family characteristics. *Clinical Child and Family Psychology Review, 2* (2), 55–70.

Straus, M.A., Sugarman, D.B. & Giles-Sims, J. (1997). Spanking by parents and subsequent antisocial behavior of children. *Archives of Pediatrics and Adolescent Medicine, 151* (8), 761–767.

Strayer, J. & Roberts, W. (2004a). Empathy and observed anger and aggression in five-year-olds. *Social Development, 13* (1), 1–13.

——(2004b). Children's anger, emotional expressiveness, and empathy: Relations with parents' empathy, emotional expressiveness, and parenting practices. *Social Development, 13* (2), 229–254

Strein, W., Simonson, T. & Vail, L. (1999). Convergence of views: Self-perceptions of African American and White kindergartners. *Psychology in the Schools, 36* (2), 125–134.

Strong, R., Silver, H.F. & Robinson, A. (1995). What do students want? *Educational Leadership, 53* (1), 8–12.

Stuhlman, M.W. & Pianta, R.C. (2001). Teachers' narratives about their relationships with children: Associations with behavior in classrooms. *School Psychology Review, 31* (2), 148–163.

Sturaro, C., van Lier, P.A.C., Cuijpers, P. & Koot, H.M. (2011). The role of peer relationships in the development of early school-age externalizing problems. *Child Development, 82* (3), 758–765.

Sturge-Apple, M.L., Davies, P.T. & Cummings, E.M. (2006). Impact of hostility and withdrawal in interparental conflict on parental emotional unavailability and children's adjustment difficulties. *Child Development, 77* (6), 1623–1641.

Sugai, G. & Horner, R. (2002). The evolution of discipline practices: School-wide positive behavior supports. *Child and Family Behavior Therapy, 24* (1–2), 23–50.

Sukhodolsky, D.G., Kassinove, H. & Gorman, B.S. (2004). Cognitive-behavioral therapy for anger in children and adolescents: A meta-analysis. *Aggression and Violent Behavior, 9* (3), 247–269.

Suldo, S.M., Friedrich, A.A., White, T., Farmer, J., Minch, D. & Michalowski, J. (2009). Teacher support and adolescents' subjective well-being: A mixed-methods investigation. *School Psychology Review, 38* (1), 67–85.

Sullivan, M.A. & O'Leary, S.G. (1990). Maintenance following reward and cost token programs. *Behavior Therapy, 23* (1), 139–149.

Sullivan, T.N., Farrell, A.D. & Kliewer, W. (2006). Peer victimization in early adolescence: Association between physical and relational victimization and drug use, aggression, and delinquent behaviors among middle school students. *Development and Psychopathology, 18* (1), 119–137.

Sulzer-Azaroff, B. & Mayer, G.R. (1991). *Behavior analysis for lasting change.* Fort Worth, TX: Holt, Rinehart and Winston.

Susser, E.S. & Lin, S.P. (1992). Schizophrenia after prenatal exposure to the Dutch hunger winter of 1944–1945. *Archives of General Psychiatry, 49* (12), 983–988.

Sutherland, K.S., Wehby, J.H. & Copeland, S.R. (2000). Effect of varying rates of behavior-specific praise on the on-task behavior of students with EBD. *Journal of Emotional and Behavioral Disorders, 8* (1), 2–8; 26.

Swaggart, B.L. (1998). Implementing a cognitive behavior management program. *Intervention in School and Clinic, 33* (4), 235–238.

Swanson, B. & Mallinckrodt, B. (2001). Family environment, love withdrawal, childhood sexual abuse, and adult attachment. *Psychotherapy Research, 11* (4), 455–472.

Sweeting, H., Young, R., West, P. & Der, G. (2007). Peer victimization and depression in early-mid adolescence: A longitudinal study. *British Journal of Educational Psychology, 76* (3), 577–594.

Swiatek, M.A. (1995). An empirical investigation of the social coping strategies used by gifted adolescents. *Gifted Child Quarterly, 39* (3), 154–161.

Swick, K.J. (2003). Communication concepts for strengthening family-school-community partnerships. *Early Childhood Education Journal, 30* (4), 275–280.

——(2005). Preventing violence through empathy development in families. *Early Childhood Education Journal, 33* (1), 53–59.

Swiezy, N.B., Matson, J.L. & Box, P. (1992). The good behavior game: A token reinforcement system for preschoolers. *Child and Family Behavior Therapy, 14* (3), 21–32.

Sylva, K. (1994). School influences on children's development.

Journal of Child Psychology and Psychiatry and Related Disciplines, 35 (1), 135–170.

Szewczyk-Sokolowski, M., Bost, K.K. & Wainwright, A.B. (2005). Attachment, temperament, and preschool children's peer acceptance. *Social Development, 14* (3), 379–397.

Tabrizian, I. (2003). *Nutritional medicine: Fact and fiction.* (4th ed.) Perth, WA: Nutrition Review Service Publications.

Tafarodi, R.W., Tam, J. & Milne, A.B. (2001). Selective memory and persistence of paradoxical self-esteem. *Personality and Social Psychology Bulletin, 27* (9), 1179–1189.

Tafarodi, R.W. & Vu, C. (1997). Two-dimensional self-esteem and reactions to success and failure. *Personality and Social Psychology Bulletin, 23* (6), 626–635.

Talwar, V. & Lee, K. (2011). A punitive environment fosters children's dishonesty: A natural experiment. *Child Development, 82* (6), 1751–1758.

Tangney, J.P., Baumeister, R.F. & Boone, A.L. (2004). High self-control predicts good adjustment, less pathology, better grades, and interpersonal success. *Journal of Personality, 72* (2), 271–324.

Tanol, G., Johnson, L., McComas, J. & Cote, E. (2010). Responding to rule violations or rule following: A comparison of two versions of the good behavior game with kindergarten students. *Journal of School Psychology, 48* (5), 337–355.

Tapola, A. & Niemivirta, M. (2008). The role of achievement goal orientations in students' perceptions of and preferences for classroom environment. *British Journal of Educational Psychology, 78* (2), 291–312.

Tapper, K. & Boulton, M.J. (2004). Sex difference in levels of physical, verbal, and indirect aggression amongst primary school children and their associations with beliefs about aggression. *Aggressive Behavior, 30* (2), 123–145.

——(2005). Victim and peer group responses to different forms of aggression among primary school children. *Aggressive Behavior, 31* (3), 238–253.

Tarbox, R.S.F., Wallace, M.D. & Williams, L. (2003). Assessment and treatment of elopement: A replication and extension. *Journal of Applied Behavior Analysis, 36* (2), 239–244.

Tattum, D. (1993a). What is bullying?. In D. Tattum (Ed.) *Understanding and managing bullying.* Oxford, UK: Heinemann Educational, 3–14.

——(1993b). Short, medium and long-term management strategies. In D. Tattum (Ed.) *Understanding and managing bullying.* Oxford, UK: Heinemann Educational, 59–75.

Taylor, C.A. Manganello, J.A., Lee, S.J. & Rice, J.C. (2010). Mothers' spanking of 3-year-old children and subsequent risk of children's aggressive behavior. *Pediatrics, 125* (5), e1057–e1065.

Taylor, G., Lekes, N., Gagnon, H., Kwan, L. & Koestner, R. (2011). Need satisfaction, work-school interference and school dropout: An application of self-determination theory. *British Journal of Educational Psychology, 82* (4), 622–646.

Taylor, L.C., Hinton, I.D. & Wilson, M.N. (1995). Parental influences on academic performance in African-American students. *Journal of Child and Family Studies, 4* (3), 293–302.

Taylor-Greene, S., Brown, D., Nelson, L, Longton, J., Gassman, T., Cohen, J., Swartz, J., Horner, R.H., Sugai, G. & Hall, S. (1997). School-wide behavioral support: Starting the year off right. *Journal of Behavioral Education, 7* (1), 99–112.

Teicher, M.H. (2002). Scars that won't heal: The neurobiology of child abuse. *Scientific American, 286* (3), 68–75.

Teisl, M. & Cicchetti, D. (2008). Physical abuse, cognitive and emotional processes, and aggressive/disruptive behavior problems. *Social Development, 17* (1), 1–23.

Tenenbaum, H.R. & Ruck, M.D. (2007). Are teachers' expectations different for racial minority than for

European American students?: A meta-analysis. *Journal of Educational Psychology, 99* (2), 253–273.

Terranova, A.M., Morris, A.S. & Boxer, P. (2008). Fear reactivity and effortful control in overt and relational bullying: A six-month longitudinal study. *Aggressive Behavior, 34* (1), 104–115.

Terry, A.A. (1998). Teachers as targets of bullying by their pupils: A study to investigate incidence. *British Journal of Educational Psychology, 68* (2), 255–268.

Thomaes, S., Reijntjes, A., de Castro, B.O., Bushman, B.J., Poorthuis, A. & Telch, M.J. (2010). I like me if you like me: On the interpersonal modulation and regulation of preadolescents' state self-esteem. *Child Development, 81* (3), 811–825.

Thomas, C.R. & Gadbois, S.A. (2007). Academic self-handicapping: The role of self-concept clarity and students' learning strategies. *British Journal of Educational Psychology, 77* (1), 101–119.

Thomas, D.E., Bierman, K.L., Powers, C.J. & The Conduct Problems Prevention Research Group. (2011). The influence of classroom aggression and classroom climate on aggressive-disruptive behavior. *Child Development, 82* (3), 751–757.

Thomas, D.E., Bierman, K.L. & The Conduct Problems Prevention Research Group. (2006). The impact of classroom aggression on the development of aggressive behavior problems in children. *Development and Psychopathology, 18* (2), 471–487.

Thomas, D.E., Bierman, K.L., Thompson, C. & Powers, C.J. (2008). Double jeopardy: Child and school characteristics that predict aggressive-disruptive behavior in first grade. *School Psychology Review, 37* (4), 516–532.

Thompson, A., Hollis, C. & Richards, D. (2003). Authoritarian parenting attitudes as a risk for conduct problems: Results from a British national cohort study. *European Child and Adolescent Psychiatry, 12* (2), 84–91.

Thompson, C.L. & Rudolph, L.B. (2000). *Counseling children.* (5th ed.) Belmont, CA: Brooks/Cole.

Thompson, L., Lobb, C., Elling, R., Herman, S., Jurkiewicz, T. & Hulleza, C. (1997). Pathways to family empowerment: Effects of family-centered delivery of early intervention services. *Exceptional Children, 64* (1), 99–113.

Thompson, M., Cohen, L.J. & Grace, C.O'N. (2002). *Mom, they're teasing me: Helping your child solve social problems.* New York: Ballantine.

Thompson, R.A. & Wyatt, J.M. (1999). Current research on child maltreatment: Implications for educators. *Educational Psychology Review, 11* (3), 173–201.

Thornberg, R. (2010). School children's social representations on bullying causes. *Psychology in the Schools, 47* (4), 311–327.

Tidwell, R. (1980). A psycho-educational profile of 1,593 gifted high school students. *Gifted Child Quarterly, 24* (2), 63–68.

Tileston, D.W. (2004). *What every teacher should know about classroom management and discipline.* Thousand Oaks, CA: Corwin Press.

Todd, A.W., Horner, R.H. & Sugai, G. (1999). Self-monitoring and self-recruited praise: Effects on problem behavior, academic engagement, and work completion in a typical classroom. *Journal of Positive Behavior Interventions, 1* (2), 66–76; 122.

Toland, J. & Boyle, C. (2008). Applying cognitive behavioural methods to retrain children's attributions for success and failure in learning. *School Psychology International, 29* (3), 286–302.

Tollefson, N. (2000). Classroom applications of cognitive theories of motivation. *Educational Psychology Review, 12* (1), 63–83.

Tomoda, A., Suzuki, H., Rabi, K., Sheu, Y.-S., Polcari, A. &

Teicher, M.H. (2009). Reduced prefrontal cortical gray matter volume in young adults exposed to harsh corporal punishment. *NeuroImage, 47* (Supp. 2), T66–T71.

Tortora, G.J. & Derrickson, B. (2006). *Principles of anatomy and physiology.* (11th ed.) New York: Wiley.

Trautwein, U. & Lüdtke, O. (2007). Students' self-reported effort and time on homework in six school subjects: Between-students differences and within-student variation. *Journal of Educational Psychology, 99* (2), 432–444.

Trautwein, U., Lüdtke, O., Schnyder, I. & Niggli, A. (2006). Predicting homework effort: Support for a domain-specific, multilevel homework model. *Journal of Educational Psychology, 98* (2), 438–456.

Trautwein, U., Niggli, A., Schnyder, I. & Lüdtke, O. (2009). Between-teacher differences in homework assignments and the development of students' homework effort, homework emotions, and achievement. *Journal of Educational Psychology, 101* (1), 176–189.

Tremblay, R.E. (2004). Decade of behavior distinguished lecture: Development of physical aggression during infancy. *Infant Mental Health Journal, 25* (5), 399–407.

Tremblay, R.E., Nagin, D.S., Séguin, J.R., Zoccolillo, M., Zelazo, P.D., Boivin, M., Pérusse, D. & Japel, C. (2004). Physical aggression during early childhood: Trajectories and predictors. *Pediatrics, 114* (1), e43–e50.

Tremblay, R.E., Pagani-Kurtz, L., Mâsse, L.C., Vitaro, F. & Pihl, R.O. (1995). A bimodal preventive intervention for disruptive kindergarten boys: Its impact through mid-adolescence. *Journal of Consulting and Clinical Psychology, 63* (4), 560–568.

Trentacosta, C.J., Criss, M.M., Shaw, D.S., Lacourse, E., Hyde, L.W. & Dishion, T.J. (2011). Antecedents and outcomes of joint trajectories of mother-son conflict and warmth during middle childhood and adolescence. *Child Development, 82* (5), 1676–1690.

Trickett, P.K. (1998). Multiple maltreatment and the development of self and emotion regulation. In B.B.R. Rossman & M.S. Rosenberg (Eds.). *Multiple victimization of children: Conceptual, developmental, research and treatment issues.* New York: Haworth Press, 171–187.

Trinkner, R., Cohn, E.S., Rebellon, C.J. & Van Grundy, K. (2012). Don't trust anyone over 30: Parental legitimacy as a mediator between parenting style and changes in delinquent behavior over time. *Journal of Adolescence, 35* (1), 119–132.

Trzesniewski, K.H., Donnellan, M.B., Moffitt, T.E., Robins, R.W., Poulton, R. & Caspi, A. (2006a). Low self-esteem during adolescence predicts poor health, criminal behavior, and limited economic prospects during adulthood. *Developmental Psychology, 42* (2), 381–390.

Trzesniewski, K.H., Moffitt, T.E., Caspi, A., Taylor, A. & Maughan, B. (2006b). Revisiting the association between reading achievement and antisocial behavior: New evidence of an environmental explanation from a twin study. *Child Development, 77* (1), 72–88.

Tucker, C.M., Zayco, R.A., Herman, K.C., Reinke, W.M., Trujillo, M., Carraway, K., Wallack, C. & Ivery, P.D. (2002). Teacher and child variables as predictors of academic engagement among low-income African American children. *Psychology in the Schools, 39* (4), 477–488.

Turk, C.L., Heimberg, R.G. & Magee, L. (2008). Social anxiety disorder. In D.H. Barlow (Ed.) *Clinical handbook of psychological disorders: A step-by-step treatment manual.* (4th ed.) New York: Guilford, 123–163.

Turley, R.N.L. (2003). Are children of young mothers disadvantaged because of their mother's age or family background? *Child Development, 74* (2), 465–474.

Turner, H.A. & Muller, P.A. (2004). Long-term effects of child corporal punishment on depressive symptoms in young adults. *Journal of Family Issues, 25* (6), 761–782.

Ullucci, K. (2009). 'This has to be family': Humanizing classroom management in urban schools. *Journal of Classroom Interaction, 44* (1), 13–28.

Underwood, M.K., Beron, K.J. & Rosen, L.H. (2009). Continuity and change in social and physical aggression from middle childhood through early adolescence. *Aggressive Behavior, 35* (5), 357–375.

Unnever, J.D. (2005). Bullies, aggressive victims, and victims: Are they distinct groups? *Aggressive Behavior, 31* (2), 153–171.

Unnever, J.D. & Cornell, D.G. (2004). Middle school victims of bullying: Who reports being bullied? *Aggressive Behavior, 30* (5), 373–388.

Urdan, T. & Mestas, M. (2006). The goals behind performance goals. *Journal of Educational Psychology, 98* (2), 354–365.

Urdan, T. & Schoenfelder, E. (2006). Classroom effects on student motivation: Goal structures, social relationships, and competence beliefs. *Journal of School Psychology, 44* (5), 331–349.

Vaillancourt, T., Brendgen, M., Boivin, M. & Tremblay, R.E. (2003). A longitudinal confirmatory factor analysis of indirect and physical aggression: Evidence of two factors over time? *Child Development, 74* (6), 1628–1638.

Vaillancourt, T. & Hymel, S. (2006). Aggression and social status: The moderating roles of sex and peer-valued characteristics. *Aggressive Behavior, 32* (4), 396–408.

Vaillancourt, T., Miller, J.L., Fagbemi, J. Côté, S. & Tremblay, R.E. (2007). Trajectories and predictors of indirect aggression: Results from a nationally representative longitudinal study of Canadian children aged 2–10. *Aggressive Behavior, 33* (4), 314–326.

Valentine, J.C., DuBois, D.L. & Cooper, H. (2004). The relation between self-beliefs and academic achievement: A meta-analytic review. *Educational Psychologist, 39* (2), 111–133.

Valeski, T.N. & Stipek, D.J. (2001). Young children's feelings about school. *Child Development, 72* (4), 1198–1213.

Valiente, C., Lemery-Chalfant, K. & Reiser, M. (2007). Pathways to problems behaviors: Chaotic homes, parent and child effortful control, and parenting. *Social Development, 16* (2), 249–267.

Valiente, C., Lemery-Chalfant, K. Swanson, J. & Reiser, M. (2008). Prediction of children's academic competence from their effortful control, relationships, and classroom participation. *Journal of Educational Psychology, 100* (1), 67–77.

Vallerand, R.J., Gagné, F., Senécal, C. & Pelletier, L.G. (1994). A comparison of the school intrinsic motivation and perceived competence of gifted and regular students. *Gifted Child Quarterly, 38* (4), 172–175.

Vallerand, R.J., Gauvin, L.I. & Halliwell, W.R. (1986). Negative effects of competition on children's intrinsic motivation. *Journal of Social Psychology, 126* (5), 649–657.

van Boxtel, H.W. & Mönks, F.J. (1992). General, social, and academic self-concepts of gifted adolescents. *Journal of Youth and Adolescence, 21* (2), 169–186.

Van Camp, C.M., Lerman, D.C., Kelley, M.E., Roane, H.S., Contrucci, S.A. & Vorndran, C.M. (2000). Further analysis of idiosyncratic antededent influences during the assessment and treatment of problem behavior. *Journal of Applied Behavior Analysis, 33* (2), 207–221.

Van de Schoot, R., ven der Velden, F., Bloom, J. & Brugman, D. (2010). Can at-risk young adolescents be popular and anti-social? Sociometric status groups, anti-social behaviour, gender and ethnic background. *Journal of Adolescence, 33* (5), 583–592.

van Houten, R., Axelrod, S., Bailey, J.S., Favell, J.E., Foxx, R.M., Iwata, B.A. & Lovaas, O.I. (1988). The right to effective treatment. *Journal of Applied Behavior Analysis, 21* (4), 381–384.

Van IJzendoorn, M.H. (1997). Attachment, emergent morality, and aggression: Toward a developmental socioemotional model of antisocial behaviour. *International Journal of Behavioral Development, 21* (4), 703–727.

van Lier, P.A.C., Wanner, B. & Vitaro, F. (2007). Onset of antisocial behavior, affiliation with deviant friends, and childhood maladjustment: A test of the childhood- and adolescent-onset models. *Development and Psychopathology, 19* (1), 167–185.

van Lier, P.A.C., Vitaro, F., Barker, E.D., Koot, H.M. & Tremblay, R.E. (2009). Developmental links between trajectories of physical violence, vandalism, theft, and alcohol-drug use from childhood to adolescence. *Journal of Abnormal Child Psychology, 37* (4), 481–492.

van Lier, P.A.C., Vitaro, F., Barker, E.D., Brendgen, M., Tremblay, R.E. & Boivin, M. (2012). Peer victimization, poor academic achievement, and the link between childhood externalizing and internalizing problems. *Child Development, 83* (5), 1775–1788.

Van Schoiack-Edstrom, L., Frey, K.S. & Beland, K. (2002). Changing adolescents' attitudes about relational and physical aggression: An early evaluation of a school-based intervention. *School Psychology Review, 31* (2), 201–216.

Vance, J.J. & Richmond, B.O. (1975). Cooperative and competitive behavior as a function of self-esteem. *Psychology in the Schools, 12* (2), 225–229.

Vannest, K.J., Davis, J.L., Davis, C.R., Mason, B.A., & Burke, M.D. (2010). Effective intervention for behavior with a daily behavior report card: A meta-analysis. *School Psychology Review, 39* (4), 654–672.

Vansteenkiste, M., Simons, J., Lens, W., Sheldon, K.M. & Deci, E.L. (2004). Motivating learning, performance, and persistence: The synergistic effects of intrinsic goal contents and autonomy-supportive contexts. *Journal of Personality and Social Psychology, 87* (2), 246–260.

Vansteenkiste, M., Simons, J., Lens, W., Soenens, B. & Matos, L. (2005). Examining the motivational impact of intrinsic versus extrinsic goal framing and autonomy-supportive versus internally controlling communication style on early adolescents' academic achievement. *Child Development, 76* (2), 483–501.

Vansteenkiste, M., Timmermans, T., Lens, W., Soenens, B. & Ven den Broeck, A. (2008). Does extrinsic goal framing enhance extrinsic goal-oriented individuals' learning and performance? An experimental test of the match perspective versus self-determination theory. *Journal of Educational Psychology, 100* (2), 387–397.

Vartuli, S. (1999). How early childhood teacher beliefs vary across grade level. *Early Childhood Research Quarterly, 14* (4), 489–514.

Vaughan, B.S., Roberts, H.J. & Needelman, H. (2009). Current medications for the treatment of attention-deficit hyperactivity disorder. *Psychology in the Schools, 46* (9), 846–856.

Vaughn, B.E., Colvin, T.N., Azria, M.R., Caya, L. & Krzysik, L. (2001). Dyadic analyses of friendship in a sample of preschool-age children attending Head Start: Correspondence between measures and implications for social competence. *Child Development, 72* (3), 862–878.

Vaughn, B.E., Kopp, C.B. & Krakow, J.B. (1984). The emergence and consolidation of self-control from eighteen to thirty months of age: Normative trends and individual differences. *Child Development, 55* (3), 990–1004.

Vaughn, B.E., Kopp, C.B., Krakow, J.B., Johnson, K. & Schwartz,

S.S. (1986). Process analyses of the behavior of very young children in delay tasks. *Developmental Psychology, 22* (6), 752–759.

Vaughn, B.E., Vollenweider, M., Bost, K.K., Azria-Evans, M.R. & Snider, J.B. (2003). Negative interactions and social competence for preschool children in two samples: Reconsidering the interpretation of aggressive behavior for young children. *Merrill-Palmer Quarterly, 49* (3), 245–278.

Vaz, P.C.M., Piazza, C.C., Stewart, V., Volkert, V.M., Groff, R.A. & Patel, M.R. (2012). Using a chaser to decrease packing in children with feeding disorders. *Journal of Applied Behavior Analysis, 45* (1), 97–105.

Veenstra, R., Oldehinkel, A.J., De Winter, A.F., Lindenberg, S. & Ormel, J. (2006). Temperament, environment, and antisocial behavior in a population sample of preadolescent boys and girls. *International Journal of Behavioral Development, 30* (5), 422–432.

Verkuyten, M. (2002). Ethnic attitudes among minority and majority children: The role of ethnic identification, peer group victimization and parents. *Social Development, 11* (4), 558–570.

Vernon-Feagans, L. & Manlove, E.E. (2005). Otitis media, the quality of child care, and the social/communicative behavior of toddlers: A replication and extension. *Early Childhood Research Quarterly, 20* (3), 306–328.

Vialle, W. (1997). Giftedness from a multiple intelligence perspective. In B.A. Knight and S. Bailey (Eds). *Parents as lifelong teachers of the gifted.* Melbourne: Hawker Brownlow Education, 31–42.

Vigil, J.M., Geary, D.C. & Byrd-Craven, J. (2005). A life history assessment of early childhood sexual abuse in women. *Developmental Psychology, 41* (3), 553–561.

Vile Junod, R.E., DuPaul, G.J., Jitendra, A.K., Volpe, R.J. & Cleary, K.S. (2006). Classroom observations of students with and without ADHD: Differences across types of engagement. *Journal of School Psychology, 44* (2), 87–104.

Vitaro, F., Barker, E.D., Boivin, M., Brendgen, M. & Tremblay, R.E. (2006). Do early difficult temperament and harsh parenting differentially predict reactive and proactive aggression? *Journal of Abnormal Child Psychology, 34* (5), 685–695.

Vitaro, F., Brendgen, M., Larose, S. & Tremblay, R.E. (2005). Kindergarten disruptive behaviors, protective factos, and educational achievement by early adulthood. *Journal of Educational Psychology, 97* (4), 617–629.

Vitaro, F., Brendgen, M. & Tremblay, R.E. (2002). Reactively and proactively aggressive children: Antecedent and subsequent characteristics. *Journal of Child Psychology and Psychiatry, 43* (4), 495–505.

Vo, A.K., Sutherland, K.S. & Conroy, M.A. (2012). Best in class: A classroom-based model for ameliorating problem behavior in early childhood settings. *Psychology in the Schools, 49* (5), 402–415.

Vollmer, T.R., Iwata, B.A., Zarcone, J.R., Smith, R.G. & Mazaleski, J.L. (1993). The role of attention in the treatment of attention-maintained self-injurious behavior: Noncontingent reinforcement and differential reinforcement of other behavior. *Journal of Applied Behavior Analysis, 26* (1), 9–21.

Vollmer, T.R., Roane, H.S., Ringdahl, J.E. & Marcus, B.A. (1999). Evaluating treatment challenges with differential reinforcement of alternative behavior. *Journal of Applied Behavior Analysis, 32* (1), 9–23.

Volpe, R.J., DuPaul, G.J., Jitendra, A.K. & Tresco, K.E. (2009). Consultation-based academic interventions for children with attention deficit hyperactivity disorder: Effects on reading and mathematics outcomes at 1-year follow-up. *School Psychology Review, 38* (1), 5–13.

Votruba-Drzal, E. (2006). Economic disparities in middle

childhood development: Does income matter? *Developmental Psychology, 42* (6), 1154–1167.

Vuijk, P., van Lier, P.A.C., Huizink, A.C., Verhulst, F.C. & Crijnen, A.A.M. (2006). Prenatal smoking predicts non-responsiveness to an intervention targeting attention-deficit/hyperactivity symptoms in elementary schoolchildren. *Journal of Child Psychology and Psychiatry, 47* (9), 891–901.

Waasdorp, T.E. & Bradshaw, C.P. (2011). Examining student responses to frequent bullying: A latent class approach. *Journal of Educational Psychology, 103* (2), 336–352.

Wachtel, T. (1997). *Real justice.* Pipersville, PA: The Pipers Press.

Wager, B.R. (1992). No more suspension: Creating a shared ethical culture. *Educational Leadership, 50* (4), 34–37.

Wagner, P. & Gillies, E. (2001). Consultation: A solution-focused approach. In Y. Ajmal and I. Rees (Eds.). *Solutions in schools.* London: BT Press, 147–162.

Wåhlstedt, C., Thorell, L.B. & Bohlin, G. (2009). Heterogeneity in ADHD: Neuropsychological pathways, comorbidity and symptom domains. *Journal of Abnormal Child Psychology, 37* (8), 551–564.

Wakefield, D., Lloyd, A. & Hickie, I. (1990). The chronic fatigue syndrome. *Modern Medicine of Australia, 33,* 16–22.

Wakenshaw, M. (2002). *Caring for your grieving child.* Oakland, CA: New Harbinger.

Walcott, C.M., Upton, A., Bolen, L.M. & Brown, M.B. (2008). Asssociations between peer-perceived status and aggression in young adolescents. *Psychology in the Schools, 45* (6), 550–561.

Waldrip, A.M., Malcolm, K.T. & Jensen-Campbell, L.A. (2008). With a little help from your friends: The importance of high-quality friendships on early adolescent adjustment. *Social Development, 17* (4), 832–852.

Walker, E., Kestler, L., Bollini, A. & Hochman, K.M. (2004). Schizophrenia: Etiology and course. *Annual Review of Psychology, 55,* 401–430.

Walker, J.E., Shea, T.M. & Bauer, A.M. (2004). *Behavior management: A practical approach for educators.* (8th ed.) Upper Saddle River, NJ: Pearson Merrill Prentice Hall.

Walker, J.M.T., Shenker, S.S. & Hoover-Dempsey, K.V. (2010). Why do parents become involved in their children's education?: Implications for school counselors. *Professional School Counseling, 14* (1), 27–41.

Walker, L.J., Hennig, K.H. & Krettenauer, T. (2000). Parent and peer correlates for children's moral reasoning. *Child Development, 71* (4), 1033–1048.

Walker, L.J. & Taylor, J.H. (1991). Family interactions and the development of moral reasoning. *Child Development, 62* (2), 264–283.

Walker, H.M. & Eaton-Walker, J. (2000). Key questions about school safety: Critical issues and recommended solutions. *NASSP Bulletin, 84* (614), 46–55.

Walker, H.M., Hops, H. & Fiegenbaum, E. (1976). Deviant classroom behavior as a function of combinations of social and token reinforcement and cost contingency. *Behavior Therapy, 7* (1), 76–88.

Walker, H.M., Horner, R.H., Sugai, G., Bullis, M., Sprague, J.R., Bricker, D. & Kaufman, M.J. (1996). Integrated approaches to preventing antisocial behavior patterns among school-age children and youth. *Journal of Emotional and Behavioral Disorders, 4* (4), 194–209.

Walker, H.M., Kavanagh, K., Stiller, B., Golly, A., Severson, H.H. & Feil, E.G. (1998). First steps to success: An early intervention approach for preventing school antisocial behavior. *Journal of Emotional and Behavioral Disorders, 6* (2), 66–80.

Wallace, B. (1986). Creativity: Some definitions: The creative personality; the creative process; the creative classroom. *Gifted Education International, 4* (2), 68–73.

Wallace, M.D., Doney, J.K., Mintz-Resudek, C.M. & Tarbox, R.S.F. (2004). Training educators to implement functional analyses. *Journal of Applied Behavior Analysis, 37* (1), 89–92.

Wang, J., Iannotti, R.J. & Luk, J.W. (2012). Patterns of adolescent bullying behaviors: Physical, verbal, exclusion, rumor, and cyber. *Journal of School Psychology, 50* (4), 521–534.

Wang, M.-T. & Eccles, J.S. (2012). Social support matters: Longitudinal effects of social support on three dimensions of school engagement from middle to high school. *Child Development, 83* (3), 877–895.

Wang, Q., Pomerantz, E.M. & Chen, H. (2007). The role of parents' control in early adolescents' psychological functioning: A longitudinal investigation in the United States and China. *Child Development, 78* (5), 1592–1610.

Ware, F. (2006). Warm demander pedagogy: Culturally responsive teaching that supports a culture of achievement for African American students. *Urban Education, 41* (4), 427–456.

Warren, J.S., Bohanon-Edmonson, H.M., Turnbull, A.P., Sailor, W., Wickham, D., Griggs, P. & Beech, S.E. (2006). School-wide positive behavior support: Addressing behavior problems that impede student learning. *Educational Psychology Review, 18* (2), 197–198.

Warring, D., Johnson, D.W., Maruyama, G. & Johnson, R. (1985). Impact of different types of cooperative learning on cross-ethnic and cross-sex relationships. *Journal of Educational Psychology, 77* (1), 53–59.

Waschbusch, D.A., Pelham, W.E. Jr, Jennings, J.R., Greiner, A.R., Tarter, R.E. & Moss, H.B. (2002). Reactive aggression in boys with disruptive behavior disorders: Behavior, physiology, and affect. *Journal of Abnormal Child Psychology, 30* (6), 641–656.

Watamura, S.E., Donzella, B., Alwin, J. & Gunnar, M.R. (2003). Morning-to-afternoon increases in cortisol concentrations for infants and toddlers at child care: Age differences and behavioral correlates. *Child Development, 74* (4), 1006–1020.

Waters, S., Cross, D. & Shaw, T. (2010). Does the nature of schools matter?: An exploration of selected school ecology factors on adolescent perceptions of school connectedness. *British Journal of Educational Psychology, 80* (3), 381–402.

Watson, M., Battistich, V. & Solomon, D. (1997). Enhancing students' social and ethical development in schools: An intervention program and its effects. *International Journal of Educational Research, 27* (7), 571–586.

Watzlawick, P., Weakland, J. & Fisch, R. (1974). *Change: Principles of problem formation and problem resolution.* New York: W.W. Norton.

Webb, N.M. (2009). The teacher's role in promoting collaborative dialogue in the classroom. *British Journal of Educational Psychology, 79* (1), 1–28.

Webster, R.E. (2001). Symptoms and long-term outcomes for children who have been sexually assaulted. *Psychology in the Schools, 38* (6), 533–547.

Wehby, J.H. & Hollahan, M.S. (2000). Effects of high-probability requests on the latency to initiate academic tasks. *Journal of Applied Behavior Analysis, 33* (2), 259–262.

Wehlage, G.G., Newmann, F.M. & Secada, W.G. (1996a). Standards for authentic achievement and pedagogy. In F.M. Newmann (Ed.) *Authentic achievement: Restructuring schools for intellectual quality.* San Francisco, CA: Jossey-Bass, 21–48.

Wehlage, G.G., Osthoff, E. & Porter, A.C. (1996b). Support from external agencies. In F.M. Newmann (Ed.). *Authentic achievement: Restructuring schools for intellectual quality.* San Francisco, CA: Jossey-Bass, 264–285.

Wehmeyer, M.L., Baker, D.J., Blumberg, R. & Harrison, R. (2004). Self-determination and student involvement in functional assessment: Innovative practices. *Journal of Positive Behavior Interventions, 6* (1), 29–35.

Weiner, B. (2000). Interpersonal and intrapersonal theories of motivation from an attributional perspective. *Educational Psychology Review, 22* (1), 1–14.

Weinstein, C.S. (1979). The physical environment of the school. *Review of Educational Research, 49* (4), 577–610.

Weinstein, C.S., Curran, M. & Tomlinson-Clarke, S. (2003). Culturally responsive classroom management: Awareness into action. *Theory into Practice, 42* (4), 269–276.

Weinstein, C.S., Tomlinson-Clarke, S. & Curran, M. (2004). Toward a conception of culturally responsive classroom management. *Journal of Teacher Education, 55* (1), 25–38.

Weinstein, R.S. (1983). Student perceptions of schooling. *The Elementary School Journal, 83* (4), 286–312.

Weiss, B., Dodge, K.A., Bates, J.E. & Pettit, G.S. (1992). Some consequences of early harsh discipline: Child aggression and a maladaptive social information processing style. *Child Development, 63* (6), 1321–1335.

Weiss, L.H. & Schwarz, J.C. (1996). The relationship between parenting types and older adolescents' personality, academic achievement, adjustment, and substance use. *Child Development, 67* (5), 2101–2114.

Welsh, W.N., Greene, J.R. & Jenkins, P.H. (1999). School disorder: The influence of individual, institutional and community factors. *Criminology, 37* (1), 73–115.

Wentzel, K.R. (1994). Family functioning and academic achievement in middle school: A social-emotional perspective. *Journal of Early Adolescence, 14* (2), 268–291.

——(1997). Student motivation in middle school: The role of perceived pedagogical caring. *Journal of Educational Psychology, 89* (3), 411–419.

——(1998). Social relationships and motivation in middle school: The role of parents, teachers, and peers. *Journal of Educational Psychology, 90* (2), 202–209.

——(2000). What is it that I'm trying to achieve?: Classroom goals from a content perspective. *Contemporary Educational Psychology, 25* (1), 105–115.

——(2003). Sociometric status and adjustment in middle school: A longitudinal study. *Journal of Early Adolescence, 23* (1), 5–18.

Wentzel, K.R. & Asher, S.R. (1995). The academic lives of neglected, rejected, popular, and controversial children. *Child Development, 66* (3), 754–763.

Wentzel, K.R. & Caldwell, J. (1997). Friendships, peer acceptance, and group membership: Relations to academic achievement in middle school. *Child Development, 68* (6), 1198–1209.

Wentzel, K.R. & Watkins, D.E. (2002). Peer relationships and collaborative learning as contexts for academic enablers. *School Psychology Review, 31* (3), 366–377.

Wentzel, K.R. & Wigfield, A. (1998). Academic and social motivational influences on students' academic performance. *Educational Psychology Review, 10* (2), 155–175.

Werner, N.E. & Crick, N.R. (2004). Maladaptive peer relationships and the development of relational and physical aggression during middle childhood. *Social Development, 13* (4), 495–514.

Werner, N.E. & Grant, S. (2009). Mothers' cognitions about relational aggression: Associations with discipline responses, children's normative beliefs, and peer competence. *Social Development, 18* (1), 77–98.

Weston, R. (1993). Well-being of young people in different family circumstances. *Family Matters, 36,* 28–30.

Whalen, C.K., Henker, B. & Dotemoto, S. (1981). Teacher response to the methylphenidate (Ritalin) versus placebo status of hyperactive boys in the classroom. *Child Development, 52* (3), 1005–1014.

Whalen, C.K., Henker, B., Jamner, L.D., Ishikawa, S.S., Floro, J.N., Swindle, R., Perwien, A.R. & Johnston, J.A. (2006). Toward mapping daily challenges of living with ADHD: Maternal and child perspectives using electronic diaries. *Journal of Abnormal Child Psychology, 34* (1), 111–126.

Wheeler, J.J. & Richey, D.D. (2005). *Behavior management: Principles and practices of positive behavior support.* Upper Saddle River, NJ: Pearson Merrill Prentice Hall.

White, K.R. (1982). The relation between socioeconomic status and academic achievement. *Psychological Bulletin, 91* (3), 461–481.

White-Smith, K.A. & White, M.A. (2009). High school reform implementation: Principals' perceptions on their leadership role. *Urban Education, 44* (3), 259–279.

Whitebook, M. & Sakai, L. (2003). Turnover begets turnover: An examination of job and occupational stability among child care centre staff. *Early Childhod Research Quarterly, 18* (3), 273–293.

Whitman, T.L., Scherzinger, M.L. & Sommer, K.S. (1991). Cognitive instruction and mental retardation. In P.C. Kendall (Ed.) *Child and adolescent therapy: Cognitive-behavioral procedures.* New York: Guilford, 276–315.

Whitney, I., Rivers, I., Smith, P.K. & Sharp, S. (1994). The Sheffield project: Methodology and findings. In P.K. Smith and S. Sharp (Eds.) *School bullying: Insights and perspectives.* London: Routledge, 20–56.

Wien, C.A. (2004). From policing to participation: Overturning the rules and creating amiable classrooms. *Young Children, 59* (1), 34–40.

Wigfield, A. & Cambria, J. (2010). Students' achievement values, goal orientations, and interest: Definitions, development, and relations to achievement outcomes. *Developmental Review, 30* (1), 1–35.

Wigfield, A. & Eccles, J.S. (2000). Expectancy-value theory of achievement motivation. *Contemporary Educational Psychology, 25* (1), 68–81.

Wilder, D.A., Myers, K., Fischetti, A., Leon, Y., Nicholson, K. & Allison, J. (2012). An analysis of modifications to the three-step guided compliance procedure necessary to achieve compliance among preschool children. *Journal of Applied Behavior Analysis, 45* (1), 121–130.

Wilder, D.A., Saulnier, R., Beavers, G. & Zonneveld, K. (2008). Contingent access to preferred items versus a guided compliance procedure to increase compliance among preschoolers. *Education and Treatment of Children, 31* (3), 297–305.

Wilkins, J.W., Piazza, C.C., Groff, R.A. & Vaz, P.C.M. (2011). Chin prompt plus re-presentation as treatment for expulsion in children with feeding disorders. *Journal of Applied Behavior Analysis, 44* (3), 513–522.

Williams, L.R., Degnan, K.A., Perez-Edgar, K.E., Henderson, H.A., Rubin, K.H., Steinberg, L. & Fox, N.A. (2009). Impact of behavioral inhibition and parenting style on internalizing and externalizing problems from early childhood through adolescence. *Journal of Abnormal Child Psychology, 37* (8), 1063–1075.

Williams, L.R. & Steinberg, L. (2011). Reciprocal relations between parenting and adjustment in a sample of juvenile offenders. *Child Development, 82* (2), 633–645.

Williams, S.T., Conger, K.J. & Blozis, S.A. (2007). The development of interpersonal aggression during adolescence: The importance of parents, siblings, and family economics. *Child Development, 78* (5), 1526–1542.

Williford, A.P., Calkins, S.D. & Keane, S.P. (2007). Predicting change in parenting stress across early childhood: Child and maternal factors. *Journal of Abnormal Child Psychology, 35* (2), 251–263.

Willoughby, M., Kupersmidt, J. & Bryant, D. (2001). Overt and covert dimensions of antisocial behavior in early childhood. *Journal of Abnormal Child Psychology, 29* (3), 177–187.

Wilson, B.J. (2006). The entry behavior of aggressive/rejected children: The contribution of status and temperament. *Social Development, 15* (3), 463–479.

Wilson, F.C. (1982). A look at corporal punishment and some implications of its use. *Child Abuse and Neglect, 6* (2), 155–164.

Wilson, H.K., Pianta, R.C. & Stuhlman, M. (2007). Typical classroom experiences in first grade: The role of classroom climate and functional risk in the development of social competencies. *The Elementary School Journal, 108* (2), 81–96.

Wilson, S.J., Gottfredson, D.C. & Najaka, S.S. (2001). School-based prevention of problem behaviors: A meta-analysis. *Journal of Quantitative Criminology, 17* (3), 247–272.

Wilson, S.J. & Lipsey, M.W. (2007). School-based interventions for aggressive and disruptive behavior: A meta-analysis. *American Journal of Preventive Medicine, 33* (Supp. 2), S130–S143.

Wilson, S.J., Lipsey, M.W. & Derzon, J.H. (2003). The effects of school-based intervention programs on aggressive behavior: A meta-analysis. *Journal of Consulting and Clinical Psychology, 71* (1), 136–149.

Wiltz, N.W. & Klein, E.L. (2001). 'What do you do in child care?': Children's perceptions of high and low quality classrooms. *Early Childhood Research Quarterly, 16* (2), 209–236.

Winett, R.A. & Winkler, R.C. (1972). Current behavior modification in the classroom: Be still, be quiet, be docile. *Journal of Applied Behavior Analysis, 5* (4), 499–504.

Winslade, J. & Monk, G. (1999). *Narrative counseling in schools: Powerful and brief.* Thousand Oaks, CA: Corwin Press.

——(2007). *Narrative counseling in schools: Powerful and brief.* (2nd ed.) Thousand Oaks, CA: Corwin Press.

Winslow, E.B. & Shaw, D.S. (2007). Impact of neighborhood disadvantage on overt behavior problems during early childhood. *Aggressive Behavior, 33* (3), 207–219.

Witvliet, M., Olthof, T., Hoeksma, J.B., Goossens, F.A., Smits, M.S.I. & Koot, H.M. (2010). Peer group affiliation of children: The role of perceived popularity, likeability, and behavioral similarity in bullying. *Social Development, 19* (2), 285–303.

Wodrich, D.L. (1994). *Attention deficit hyperactivity disorder: What every parent wants to know.* Baltimore, MD: Paul H. Brookes.

Wolery, M., Bailey, D.B. & Sugai, G.M. (1988). *Effective teaching: Principles and procedures of applied behavior analysis with exceptional students.* Boston, MA: Allyn & Bacon.

Wolfgang, C.H., Bennett, B.J. & Irvin, J.L. (1999). *Strategies for teaching self-discipline in the middle grades.* Boston, MA: Allyn & Bacon.

Wolters, C.A. & Daugherty, S.G. (2007). Goal structures and teachers' sense of efficacy: Their relation and association to teaching experience and academic level. *Journal of Educational Psychology, 99* (1), 181–193.

Wong, S.M., Leung, A.N. & McBride-Chang, C. (2010). Adolescent filial piety as a moderator between perceived maternal control and mother-adolescent relationship quality in Hong Kong. *Social Development, 19* (1), 187–201.

Wood, C.D (1985). *A study of Parent Effectiveness Training.* Unpublished Diploma in Psychology thesis. Hobart: University of Tasmania.

——(2003). *How we talk to our children: An evaluation of parent effectiveness training for the development of emotional competence.* Unpublished doctoral thesis. Hobart: University of Tasmania.

Wood, C.D. & Davidson, J.A. (1987). PET: An outcome study. *Australian Journal of Sex, Marriage and Family, 8,* 131–141.

——(1993). Conflict resolution in the family: A PET evaluation study. *Australian Psychologist, 28* (2), 100–104.

Wood, K.J. & Care, E. (2002). The relationship between perfectionism and intelligence in a group of adolescents. *The Australasian Journal of Gifted Education, 11* (1), 22–29.

Wood, W.D. III & Baker, J.A. (1999). Preferences for parent education programs among low socioeconomic status, culturally diverse parents. *Psychology in the Schools, 36* (3), 239–247.

Woodward, L.J. & Fergusson, D.M. (1999). Childhood peer relationship problems and psychosocial adjustment in late adolescence. *Journal of Abnormal Child Psychology, 27* (1), 87–104.

Worchel-Prevatt, F.F., Heffer, R.W., Prevatt, B.C., Miner, J., Young-Saleme, T., Horgan, D., Lopez, M.A., Rae, W.A. & Frankel, L. (1998). A school reentry program for chronically ill children. *Journal of School Psychology, 36* (3), 261–279.

Wray-Lake, L. & Flanagan, C.A. (2012). Parenting practices and the development of adolescents' social trust. *Journal of Adolescence, 35* (3), 549–560.

Wright, D.B., Mayer, G.R., Cook, C.R., Crews, S.D., Kraemer, B.R. & Gale, B. (2007). A preliminary study on the effects of training using Behavior Support Plan Quality Evaluation Guide (BSP-QE) to improve positive behavioral support plans. *Education and Treatment of Children, 30* (3), 89–106.

Wright, J. & Cleary, K.S. (2006). Kids in the tutor seat: Building schools' capacity to help struggling readers through a cross-age peer-tutoring program. *Psychology in the Schools, 43* (1), 99–107.

Wright, P.B. & Leroux, J.A. (1997). The self-concept of gifted adolescents in a congregated program. *Gifted Child Quarterly, 41* (3), 83–94.

Wright, S.P., Horn, S.P. & Sanders, W.L. (1997). Teacher and classroom context effects on student achievement: Implications for teacher evaluation. *Journal of Personnel Evaluation in Education, 11* (1), 57–67.

Wyman, P.A., Cowen, E.L., Work, W.C., Hoyt-Meyers, L., Magnus, K.B. & Fagen, D.B. (1999). Caregiving and developmental factors differentiating young at-risk urban children showing resilient versus stress-affected outcomes: A replication and extension. *Child Development, 70* (3), 645–659.

Xie, H., Swift, D.J., Cairns, B.D. & Cairns, R.B. (2002). Aggressive behaviors in social interaction and developmental adaptation: A narrative analysis of interpersonal conflicts during early adolescence. *Social Development, 11* (2), 205–224.

Xu, F., Bao, X., Fu, G., Talwar, V. & Lee, K. (2010). Lying and truth-telling in children: From concept to action. *Child Development, 81* (2), 581–596.

Xu, M.-Q., Sun, W.-S., Liu, B.-X., Feng, G.-Y., Yu, L., Yang, L., He, G., Sham, P., Susser, E., St Clair, D. & He, L. (2009). Prenatal malnutrition and adult schizophrenia: Further evidence from the 1959–1961 Chinese famine. *Schizophrenia Bulletin, 35* (3), 568–576.

Yell, M.L. (2012). Legal considerations for schools. In T.J. Zirpoli (Ed.) *Behavior management: Positive applications for teachers.* (6th ed.) Boston, MA: Pearson, 33–51.

Yell, M.L., Busch, T. & Drasgow, E. (2012). Cognitive behavior modification. In T.J. Zirpoli (Ed.) *Behavior management: Positive applications for teachers.* (6th ed.) Boston, MA: Pearson, 289–324.

Yoon, J.S., Hughes, J.N., Cavell, T.A. & Thompson, B. (2000). Social cognitive differences between aggressive-rejected and aggressive-nonrejected children. *Journal of School Psychology, 38* (6), 551–570.

Young, E.L., Boye, A.E. & Nelson, D.A. (2006). Relational aggression: Understanding, identifying, and responding in schools. *Psychology in the Schools, 43* (3), 297–312.

Young, J.E., Rych, J.L., Weinberger, A.D. & Beck. A.T. (2008). Cognitive therapy for depression. In D.H. Barlow (Ed.) *Clinical handbook of psychological disorders: A step-by-step treatment manual.* (4th ed.) New York: Guilford, 250–305.

Young, S. (2001). Solution focused anti-bullying. In Y. Ajmal and I. Rees (Eds.) *Solutions in schools.* London: BT Press, 86–96.

Young, S., Heptinstall, E., Sonuga-Barke, E.J.S., Chadwick, O. & Taylor, E. (2005). The adolescent outcome of hyperactive girls: Self-report of psychosocial status. *Journal of Child Psychology and Psychiatry, 46* (3), 255–262.

Young, S.K., Fox, N.A. & Zahn-Waxler, C. (1999). The relations between temperament and empathy in 2-year-olds. *Developmental Psychology, 35* (5), 1189–1197.

Youssef, R.M., Attia, M. S.-E.-D. & Kamel, M.I. (1998a). Children experiencing violence I: Parental use of corporal punishment. *Child Abuse and Neglect, 22* (10), 959–973.

——(1998b). Children experiencing violence I: Prevalence and determinants of corporal punishment in schools. *Child Abuse and Neglect, 22* (10), 975–985.

Zahn-Waxler, C. & Radke-Yarrow, M. (1990). The origins of empathic concern. *Motivation and Emotion, 14* (2), 107–130.

Zahn-Waxler, C., Radke-Yarrow, M. & King, R.A. (1979). Child rearing and children's prosocial initiations toward victims of distress. *Child Development, 50* (2), 319–330.

Zakriski, A.L. & Coie, J.D. (1996). A comparison of aggressive-rejected and nonaggressive-rejected children's interpretations of self-directed and other-directed rejection. *Child Development, 67* (3), 1048–1070.

Zanolli, K. & Daggett, J. (1998). The effects of reinforcement rate on the spontaneous social initiations of socially withdrawn preschoolers. *Journal of Applied Behavior Analysis, 31* (1), 117–125.

Zarcone, J.R., Iwata, B.A., Mazaleski, J.L. & Smith, R.G. (1994). Momentum and extinction effects on self-injurious escape behavior and noncompliance. *Journal of Applied Behavior Analysis, 27* (4), 649–658.

Zehr, H. (2002). *The little book of restorative justice.* Intercourse, PA: Good Books.

Zentall, S.S. (1989). Self-control training with hyperactive and impulsive children. In J.N. Hughes and R.J. Hall (Eds.) *Cognitive-behavioral psychology in the schools.* New York: Guilford, 305–346.

Zhou, Q., Eisenberg, N., Losoya, S.H., Fabes, R.A., Reiser, M., Guthrie, I.K., Murphy, B.C., Cumberland, A.J. & Shepard, S.A. (2002). The relations of parental warmth and positive expressiveness to children's empathy-related responding and social functioning: A longitudinal study. *Child Development, 73* (3), 893–915.

Zhou, Q., Hofer, C., Eisenberg, N., Reiser, M., Spinrad, T.L. & Fabes, R.A. (2007). The developmental trajectories of attention focusing, attentional and behavioral persistence, and externalizing problems during school-age years. *Developmental Psychology, 43* (2), 369–385.

Zimmer-Gembeck, M.J., Chipuer, H.M., Hanisch, M., Creed, P.A. & McGregor, L. (2006). Relationships at school and stage-environment fit as resources for adolescent engagement and achievement. *Journal of Adolescence, 29* (6), 911–933.

Zimmerman, B.J. (2000). Self-efficacy: An essential motive to learn. *Contemporary Educational Psychology, 25* (1), 82–91.

Zirkelback, E.A. & Reese, R.J. (2010). A review of psychotherapy outcome research: Considerations for school-based mental health providers. *Psychology in the Schools, 47* (10), 1084–1100.

Zirpoli, T.J. (2012a). Basic concepts of behavior and behavior management. In T.J. Zirpoli (Ed.) *Behavior management: Positive applications for teachers.* (6th ed.) Boston, MA: Pearson, 3–31.

——(2012b). Positive behavioral supports: Reinforcement strategies. In T.J. Zirpoli (Ed.) *Behavior management: Positive applications for teachers.* (6th ed.) Boston, MA: Pearson, 257–287.

——(2012c). Individual strategies for positive behavior supports. In T.J. Zirpoli (Ed.) *Behavior management: Positive applications for teachers.* (6th ed.) Boston, MA: Pearson, 353–385.

Zirpoli, T.J. & Buese, D. (2012). Data collection techniques. In T.J. Zirpoli (Ed.) *Behavior management: Positive applications for teachers.* (6th ed.) Boston, MA: Pearson, 141–179.

Zullig, K.J., Huebner, E.S. & Patton, J.M. (2011). Relationships among school climate domains and school satisfaction. *Psychology in the Schools, 48* (2), 133–145.

Notes

Chapter 1

1 Greene 2008: ix
2 Rawls 1991
3 Letcher et al. 2009; Rescorla et al. 2007
4 Bub et al. 2007
5 Card & Little 2006; Willoughby et al. 2001
6 Campbell 1995; Campbell et al. 2000; Kazdin & Weisz 1998; Lutz et al. 2002
7 Campbell 1995
8 Rescorla et al. 2007; Skiba & Peterson 1999
9 Skiba & Peterson 1999; Skiba et al. 1997
10 Hyman & Perone 1998; Mayer & Leone 1999
11 Vaughn et al. 1984
12 Kochanska et al. 2001
13 Kochanska et al. 2001
14 Lipscomb et al. 2011
15 Eisenberg et al. 1997b; Kaler & Kopp 1990; Kopp 1982; Nigg et al. 1999; Power & Chapieski 1986; Vaughn et al. 1984
16 Kochanska & Aksan 1995; Kochanska et al. 2005a, 2005b; Kuczynski & Kochanska 1990; Londerville & Main 1981; Stifter et al. 1999
17 Atwater & Morris 1988
18 Sternberg 1999
19 Ruff & Capozzoli 2003
20 Zhou et al. 2007
21 Giannopulu et al. 2008
22 Giannopulu et al. 2008; Rudasill et al. 2010a
23 Rudasill et al. 2010a
24 Deater-Deckard et al. 2006; Rimm-Kaufman et al. 2009; Rudasill et al. 2010a
25 Rudasill et al. 2010a
26 Rudasill et al. 2010a
27 Campbell 1995; Colder et al. 2002
28 Hubbard 2001; Prinstein & Cillessen 2003; Vitaro et al. 2006
29 Card & Little 2006: 467
30 Card & Little 2006: 467
31 Vitaro et al. 2002
32 Frick et al. 2003
33 Alink et al. 2006; Baillargeon et al. 2007b; Côté et al. 2006, 2007; Denham et al. 2002; Frick et al. 2003; Hay et al. 2004; Loeber & Hay 1997; Owens & Shaw 2003; Prinzie et al. 2006; Rubin et al. 2003; Schaeffer et al. 2003; Shaw et al. 2003; Vitaro et al. 2006
34 Broidy et al. 2003; Prinzie et al. 2006
35 Baillargeon et al. 2007a, 2007b; Colder et al. 2002; Loeber & Hay 1997

36 Lee et al. 2007: 33
37 Kingston & Prior 1995; Mesman et al. 2009: 633; Underwood et al. 2009
38 McFadyen-Ketchum et al. 1996
39 Côté et al. 2006; Ingoldsby et al. 2006; Kokko & Pulkkinen 2005; Nagin & Tremblay 1999; Patterson et al. 2005; Underwood et al. 2009; Zhou et al. 2007
40 Campbell 1995; Campbell & Ewing 1990; Campbell et al. 2000, 2006
41 Benson & Buehler 2012; Broidy et al. 2003; Campbell et al. 2006; Ingoldsby et al. 2006; Laird et al. 2001; Martino et al. 2008; Underwood et al. 2009; van Lier et al. 2007
42 Kokko & Pulkkinen 2005
43 Kingston & Prior 1995; Kwon et al. 2012; Laird et al. 2001; Nelson et al. 2004; Trzesniewski et al. 2006b; Xie et al. 2002
44 Doctoroff et al. 2006; Harachi et al. 2006; Kingston & Prior 1995; Martino et al. 2008
45 Loveland et al. 2007; Nelson et al. 2004
46 van Lier et al. 2012
47 van Lier et al. 2012; Xie et al. 2002
48 Laird et al. 2001
49 van Lier et al. 2012
50 van Lier et al. 2009
51 Matjasko 2011
52 Benson & Buehler 2012; Miller et al. 2009
53 Matjasko 2011: 557; Moffitt 1993a: 675; Prinzie et al. 2006; van Lier et al. 2009
54 Moffitt 1993:a 676
55 Moffitt 1993a: 679
56 Huesmann et al. 2009; Martino et al. 2008; Moffitt 1993a: 679
57 Moffitt 1993a: 680
58 Farrington et al. 2009: 158; Granic & Patterson 2006; Moffitt 1993a; van Lier et al. 2007
59 Robinson et al. 2007
60 Tremblay et al 1995
61 Frick et al. 2003, 2005; Robinson et al. 2007
62 Moffitt 1993b
63 Laird et al. 2001
64 Benson & Buehler 2012; Brendgen et al. 2000; Craig et al. 2002; Knecht et al. 2010; Miller et al. 2009
65 Dishion et al. 1999; Granic & Patterson 2006
66 Moffitt 1993a: 684
67 Granic & Patterson 2006; Moffitt 1993a: 683;
68 Granic & Patterson 2006; Moffit 1993a
69 Moffitt 1993a: 678 & 685; van Lier et al. 2009
70 van Lier et al. 2009: 489
71 Matjasko 2011: 558

72 Moffitt 1993a: 686
73 Moffitt 1993a: 692
74 Farrington et al. 2009; Granic & Patterson 2006
75 Granic & Patterson 2006
76 Brendgen et al. 2000
77 Moffitt 1993a
78 Bub et al. 2007; Colder et al. 2002: 16; Gilliom & Shaw 2004; Williams et al. 2009
79 Bub et al. 2007; Williams et al. 2009
80 De Wit et al. 2011
81 De Wit et al. 2011
82 Rutter et al. 1976
83 Offer & Schonert-Reichl 1992: 1004, 1007; Rutter et al. 1976
84 Buchanan et al. 1992
85 Allport 1961, in Roberts et al. 2001: 672
86 Buchanan et al. 1992
87 De Wit et al. 2011; Eccles et al. 1993
88 Allen et al. 2008; Eisenberg 2001; Fox et al. 2010
89 Roeser et al. 1998
90 Schrami et al. 2011
91 Schrami et al. 2011: 992
92 De Wit et al. 2011; Schrami et al. 2011: 992
93 Roeser et al 1998
94 Offer & Schonert-Reichl 1992: 1005
95 Somers et al. 2006
96 Northey et al. 2003: 525
97 Northey et al. 2003: 525
98 Legerstee et al. 2011
99 Burton et al. 2009: 621
100 Qin et al. 2012
101 Franklin & Foa 2008: 164; Piacentini et al. 2012: 260
102 Piacentini et al. 2012: 260
103 Piacentini et al. 2012: 260 & 261
104 Craske & Barlow 2008: 1
105 Craske & Barlow 2008: 5
106 Craske & Barlow 2008: 8
107 Craske & Barlow 2008: 9
108 Gren-Landell et al. 2011; Turk et al. 2008: 123
109 Turk et al. 2008: 124
110 Turk et al. 2008: 124
111 Gren-Landell et al. 2011
112 Asher & Paquette 2003
113 Asher & Paquette 2003
114 Cacioppo et al. 2003
115 Asher et al. 1984
116 Asher & Paquette 2003
117 Chen et al. 2011: 1531; Eisenberg et al. 1998, 2001, 2004b; Gilliom & Shaw 2004; Henderson et al. 2004; Stewart & Rubin 1995
118 Ladd et al. 2011; Young et al. 1999
119 Gilliom & Shaw 2004
120 Hawley & Little 1999; Howes 2000
121 Flook et al. 2005; Gazelle & Ladd 2003; Spinrad et al. 2004
122 Chen et al. 2011
123 Chen et al. 2011; Ladd et al. 2011
124 Coplan et al. 2007
125 Coplan et al. 2007; Harrist et al. 1997; Ladd et al. 2011
126 Coplan et al. 2004
127 Coplan et al. 2004
128 Coplan et al. 2004
129 Arnold et al. 1998; Coplan et al. 2007; Dodge 1983; Farver 1996; Harrist et al. 1997; Hartup 1989; Hartup & Moore 1990
130 Dodge 1983; Harrist et al. 1997
131 Odom et al. 1999
132 Harrist et al. 1997

133 Harrist et al. 1997
134 Burton et al. 2009: 615; Patten et al. 2006
135 McFarlane et al. 1994: 616
136 Northey et al. 2003: 525; Young et al. 2008: 253
137 Barchia & Bussey 2010; Bleiberg & Markowitz 2008: 307–308; Burton et al. 2009: 615; Ellis 2005; Gonzalez et al. 2004
138 Fox et al. 2010; McFarlane et al. 1994
139 McFarlane et al. 1994
140 Barchia & Bussey 2010
141 Garber et al. 1997; McFarlane et al. 1994
142 Fairburn et al. 2008: 579 & 583
143 Fairburn et al. 2008: 582
144 Fairburn et al. 2008: 580
145 Fairburn et al. 2008: 580
146 Fairburn et al. 2008: 580
147 DeLeel et al. 2009
148 Harter et al. 1997
149 Tangney et al. 2004
150 Bruess & Richardson 1989: 319
151 Davidson & Myers 2007: 66
152 Moss 2008: 427
153 McQueeney et al. 2009; Moss 2008: 427
154 Moss 2008: 428
155 Collison & Hall 1989: 365; Myers 2005: 384; Porter 1980: 2
156 Fisher et al. 2012; Selekman 2006
157 Selekman 2006
158 Selekman 2006: 18
159 Selekman 2006
160 Cacioppo et al. 2003: 72
161 Cacioppo et al. 2003: 72; Spirito et al. 2012: 234
162 Garofalo et al. 1999: 492
163 Resnick et al. 1997
164 Spirito et al. 2012: 235 & 238
165 Spirito et al. 2012: 235
166 Spirito et al. 2012: 237
167 Garofalo et al. 1999: 490
168 Garofalo et al. 1999: 490; Goodenow et al. 2006
169 Hong et al. 2011: 885
170 Fineran 2001; Henning-Stout et al. 2000
171 Angleitner & Ostendorf 1994: 69; Griggs et al. 2009; Rudasill et al. 2010a; Sanson et al. 2004: 143
172 Wakenshaw 2002
173 Pettit & Bates 1989; Combs-Ronto et al. 2009; Guerin & Gottfried 1994; Lahey et al. 2008. Lytton (1990) draws the same conclusion. However, he attributes children's difficult behaviour at the age of eight years to their difficult temperaments when, by that age, they have already been subjected to parental discipline for many years.
174 Sanson et al. 1991
175 Alink et al. 2008; Campbell 1995; Denham et al. 2000; Hoffman 1960; NICHD Early Child Care Research Network 2004b; Paterson & Sanson 1999; Sanson et al. 2004; Shaw et al. 2001
176 Diener et al. 2003; Grusec & Mammone 1995; Meyers 1999; Scaramella & Conger 2003; Strassberg & Treboux 2000
177 Alink et al. 2008; Calkins et al. 1999; Colder et al. 2002; Colman et al. 2006; Downer & Pianta 2006; Eisenberg et al. 1997a, 2000a, 2005a, 2005b; Kochanska et al. 2001; Krueger et al. 1996; Lengua 2008; Moilanen et al. 2010; Morris et al. 2007; Murphy et al. 2004; NICHD Early Child Care Research Network 2004b; Nigg et al. 1999; Olson et al. 1990; Paterson & Sanson 1999; Raikes et el. 2007; Sanson et al. 2004; Terranova et al. 2008; Tremblay

et al. 2004; Valiente et al. 2007; Veenstra et al. 2006; Williams et al. 2009

178 Alink et al.. 2008; Belsky et al. 1998; Combs-Ronto et al. 2009; Dallaire & Weinraub 2005; Dodge et al. 1994; Donovan et al. 2000; Hastings & Rubin 1999; Hoffman 1960; Joussemet et al. 2008; Kilgore et al. 2000; Nix et al. 1999; O'Leary et al. 1999; C.L. Smith et al. 2004; Snyder et al. 2005
179 Sanson et al. 1991
180 Owens & Shaw 2003
181 Barber et al. 2005: 106; Kerr et al. 2012; Pesonen 2008
182 Benasich et al. 1993; Lindsay et al. 2007
183 Bates et al. 2003; NICHD Early Child Care Research Network 2004b; Sabol & Pianta 2012
184 Algozzine et al. 2011
185 McIntosh et al. 2012; Morrison et al. 2001; Sabol & Pianta 2012
186 McIntosh et al. 2012
187 McIntosh et al. 2012
188 McIntosh et al. 2012; Sabol & Pianta 2012
189 Collison & Hall 1989: 415
190 Blum & Mercugliano 1997
191 Blum & Mercugliano 1997
192 Collison & Hall 1989: 33; Tortora & Derrickson 2006: 820
193 Hadjivassiliou et al. 2001: 385; Mäki & Collin 1997: 1756
194 Mackarness 1990: 103; Philpott & Kalita 2000
195 Lyon 2000: 135; Wakefield et al. 1990: 21
196 Lyon 2000: 135
197 Chauhan & Chauhan 2006: 174
198 Gesser & Koo 1996
199 Barr et al. 1990; Murray et al. 1992
200 Shi et al. 2003: 301
201 Bock & Stauth 2008: 29–30
202 Franklin & Foa 2008: 166
203 Mortensen et al. 2007
204 Mortensen et al. 2007: 691
205 Pauling 1995
206 Brown et al. 2000; Susser & Lin 1992; E. Walker et al. 2004: 409; Xu et al. 2009
207 Brown & Susser 2008; McGrath et al. 2011; Tabrizian 2003: 18 & 112
208 Richardson Andrews 1990
209 Campbell-McBride 2010: 255
210 Lazarides 2010: 87–88; Lyon 2000: 85
211 Noaghiul & Hibbein 2003; Peet 2004
212 Davidson & Myers 2007
213 Lazarides 2010: 190
214 Lazarides 2010: 190
215 Campbell et al. 1996; Coldwell et al. 2006. However, a counter-intuitive finding of Kelso & Stewart (1986) is that children whose mothers married often were at reduced risk of aggressive conduct disorders; the number of marriages signified that the mother had divorced antisocial fathers, which improved outcomes for their sons.
216 Morris et al. 2007
217 Campbell et al. 1996; NICHD Early Child Care Research Network 2004b; Shaw et al. 1996
218 Woodward & Fergusson 1999
219 Field et al. 2003; Leidy et al. 2010; NICHD Early Child Care Research Network 1999
220 Campbell et al. 1996
221 Tremblay et al. 1995: 560
222 Hoeve et al. 2009; Lytton 1990: 693; Owens & Shaw 2003; Pagani et al. 2004; Somers et al. 2011: 366; Tremblay et al. 2004: e47; Trentacosta et al. 2011
223 De Garmo 2010; Jaffee et al. 2003; Kelso & Stewart 1986

224 Cabrera et al. 2011; Chronis et al. 2007; Connell & Goodman 2002; Field et al. 2003; Joussemet et al. 2008; Lovejoy 2000; McGroder 2000; NICHD Early Child Care Research Network 1999; Nelson et al. 2007; Papero 2005; Scaramella et al. 2008; Sohr-Preston & Scaramella 2006; Tremblay et al. 2004; Turley 2003
225 Dodge et al. 1990; Knutson et al. 2004
226 Dodge et al. 1997: 44
227 Dodge et al 1997: 44
228 Robinson et al. 2007
229 Straus & Field 2003
230 Straus & Field 2003: 801
231 Straus & Field 2003: 802
232 Brendgen et al. 2006; Delfabbro et al. 2006
233 Delfabbro et al. 2006
234 Anda et al. 2006: 182; Morris et al. 2007; Pears et al. 2010; Schwartz et al. 1997; Teisl & Cicchetti 2008
235 Pears et al. 2010
236 Afifi et al. 2006; Deater-Deckard & Dodge 1997; Gilding 1997; Kim & Cicchetti 2006; Rossman & Rosenberg 1998; Rossman et al. 1998
237 Ackerman et al. 2002; Cummings 1998; Dearing et al. 2006b; Grych et al. 2000; Katz & Woodin 2002; Katz et al. 2007; Kitzmann 2000; Maughan & Cicchetti 2002; Sternberg et al. 2006a; Sturge-Apple et al. 2006
238 Schwartz et al. 1997
239 Anda et al. 2006; Bolger & Patterson 2001; Bonner et al. 1992; Bromberg & Johnson 2001; Bugental & Happaney 2004; Bugental et al. 2003; Burack et al. 2006; Carrey et al. 1995; Essa & Murray 1999; Feiring et al. 2002; Fergusson & Lynskey 1997; Flores et al. 2005; George & Main 1979; Glaser 2000; Goodwin et al. 2004; Gowen & Nebrig 2002; Haynes-Seman & Baumgarten 1998; Hoffman-Plotkin & Twentyman 1984; Kim & Cicchetti 2004, 2006; Klimes-Dougan & Kistner 1990; Koenig et al. 2000, 2004; Lavoie et al. 2002; Luthar et al. 2000; Maughan & Cicchetti 2002; McGowan et al. 2009; Mullen et al. 1996; Nagel 2012: 4; Pollak et al. 2005; Rothbaum et al. 1997; Sheu et al. 2010; Shields et al. 2001; Shipman et al. 2007; Shonk & Cicchetti 2001; Solomon & Serres 1999; Teicher 2002; Thompson & Wyatt 1999; Tomoda et al. 2009; Trickett 1998; Vigil et al. 2005; Webster 2001; Zahn-Waxler & Radke-Yarrow 1990
240 Aber & Ellwood 2001; Gilding 1997; Hill & Jenkins 2001; Prince & Howard 2002
241 Gershoff et al. 2007
242 Sameroff 1990
243 Scaramella et al. 2008
244 Moilanen et al. 2010; Tremblay et al. 2004; Underwood et al. 2009; Williams et al. 2007
245 Sanson et al. 1991
246 Flouri 2006; Gershoff et al. 2007; Robinson et al. 2002; Romano et al. 2005; Sirin 2005; White 1982
247 Ackerman et al. 2002, 2004; Aguilar et al. 2000; Belsky et al. 1998; Campbell 1995; Campbell & Ewing 1990; Campbell et al. 1991a, 1991b, 2000; Coldwell et al. 2006; Coolahan et al. 2002; Côté et al. 2006; Dearing et al. 2006b; Duncan & Brooks-Gunn 2000; Evans & English 2002; Evans et al. 1999; Fergusson et al. 2004, 2005; Fujiura & Yamaki 2000; Gest et al. 2004; Hill et al. 2006; Kaiser et al. 2000; Macmillan et al. 2004; McGroder 2000; Meyers 1999; Miller-Lewis et al. 2006; NICHD Early Child Care Research Network 2005; O'Leary et al. 1999; Papero 2005; Park et al. 2002; Petterson & Albers 2001; Qi & Kaiser 2003; Raviv et al. 2004; Romano et al. 2005; Rubin et al. 2003; Schaffer 1998; Shaw et al. 1999, 2003; Smith & Farrington 2004; Spence et al. 2002; Sturge-Apple et al.

248 2006; Thompson et al. 2003; Tremblay 2004; Votruba-Drzal 2006
248 Sandefur & Wells 1999; Williford et al. 2007
249 Underwood et al 2009
250 Spence et al. 2002
251 Amato 2000; D'Onofrio et al. 2007; Burns & Goodnow 1985; Dearing et al. 2006b; Haveman & Wolfe 1995; Sandefur & Wells 1999
252 Golombok et al. 2003; MacCallum & Golombok 2004; Weston 1993
253 Amato 2000; Burns & Goodnow 1985
254 Amato 2000; Cheng et al. 2006; D'Onofrio et al. 2007
255 Amato 2000
256 Brody et al. 2001; Claes & Simard 1992; Welsh et al. 1999: 106
257 Brody et al. 2001; Fergusson et al. 2004; Ingoldsby et al. 2006
258 Cunningham et al. 2009; Veenstra et al. 2006; Winslow & Shaw 2007
259 Kim et al. 1999; Pettit et al. 2001; Schaffer 1998; Shumow et al. 1999; Smith & Farrington 2004
260 Fall & Roberts 2012; Resnick et al. 1997; Roeser et al 1998
261 see, e.g. Gillison et al. 2008
262 Bradshaw et al. 2007; Elmore & Huebner 2010; Niehaus et al. 2012; Skinner et al. 2008; Wang & Eccles 2012
263 Wang & Eccles 2012
264 Roeser et al. 1998
265 Roeser et al. 1998; Wang & Eccles 2012; Zimmer-Gembeck et al. 2006
266 Battistich et al. 1997; Marks et al. 1996a; McNeely et al. 2002; Mortimore & Sammons 1987; Osterman 2000; Phelan et al. 1992; Purkey & Smith 1983; Rogus 1985; Rutter 1983; Rutter & Maughan 2002; Schmuck & Schmuck 2001: 69–70; Sprague & Walker 2000; Sylva 1994; Waters et al. 2010
267 Thomas et al. 2008
268 Thomas et al. 2008: 527
269 Mortimore et al. 1988; Rutter 1983; Rutter & Maughan 2002
270 Mortimore & Sammons 1987: 6
271 Marks et al. 1996a: 222
272 Collie et al. 2011: 1035
273 Brown 2012: 174; Stanley & McGrath 2006
274 Abbott et al. 1998; Marks et al. 1996a; McNeely et al. 2002; Smerdon 2002; Waters et al. 2010; Zullig et al. 2011
275 Zullig et al. 2011
276 Solomon et al. 1996
277 Smerdon 2002
278 Brand et al. 2008; Esposito 1999; Hawkins et al. 2001; Niehaus et al. 2012; Purkey & Smith 1983: 444
279 Chapman et al. 2011; Fall & Roberts 2012; Hardre & Reeve 2003; Hawkins et al. 2001; Henry et al. 2011; Hill & Werner 2006; Welsh et al. 1999: 102
280 Welsh et al. 1999: 82
281 Liljeberg et al. 2011
282 Elmore & Huebner 2010
283 Cothran & Ennis 1997; De Cremer & Tyler 2007
284 Cothran & Ennis 1997
285 Cothran & Ennis 1997
286 Rutter 1983; Rutter & Maughan 2002; Sylva 1994
287 Adams & Forsyth 2009
288 Adams & Forsyth 2009: 127
289 Pomeroy 1999
290 Sanches et al. 2012
291 Adams & Forsyth 2009; Roeser et al 1998
292 Farrell et al. 2006
293 Ruck & Wortley 2002
294 Pomeroy 1999
295 Sanches et al. 2012
296 McNeely et al. 2002
297 Battistich et al. 1997; McNeely et al. 2002
298 Klein & Cornell 2010: 941
299 Klein & Cornell 2010
300 Battistich et al. 1995, 1997; Dhami et al. 2005; Klein & Cornell 2010; Leadbeater et al. 2003
301 Battistich et al. 1997
302 Welsh et al. 1999: 107
303 Battistich et al. 1995
304 Welsh et al. 1999: 108
305 Rubie-Davies et al. 2012
306 Rusby et al. 2007
307 Hope & Bierman 1998
308 Gump 1990
309 Farrell et al. 2011; Henry et al. 2011; Mercer et al. 2009
310 Espinoza & Juvonen 2011; Waters et al. 2010
311 Gregory et al. 2010: 492
312 Baker et al. 2008; Buyse et al. 2008; Sylva 1994
313 Gregory & Ripski 2008; Skiba et al. 1997
314 Bondy et al. 2007; Gregory & Weinstein 2008
315 Brophy 1985: 236; Noguera 2003
316 Spilt & Koomen 2009
317 Silver et al. 2010: 574
318 Esposito 1999
319 Baker et al. 2008; O'Connor & McCartney 2006
320 Decker et al. 2007: 103
321 Decker et al. 2007
322 Mercer et al. 2009
323 Thomas et al. 2011
324 Decker et al. 2007; Downer et al. 2007; Mashburn et al. 2008; Powell et al. 2010; Rudasill et al. 2010b; Skinner et al. 2008; Valiente et al. 2008
325 Wang & Eccles 2012
326 Baker et al. 2008; Curby et al. 2009; den Brok et al. 2010; Gregory & Ripski 2008; Gregory & Weinstein 2004; Hamre & Pianta 2001; Kellam et al. 1998; Maldonado-Carreño & Votruba-Drzal 2011; O'Connor 2010; Wright et al. 1997
327 Baker et al. 2008; Hamre & Pianta 2001; Larrivee 2005; Mikami et al. 2012; Pianta 1999; Pianta et al. 1995; Sharkey et al. 2008
328 Baker et al. 2006; Bub et al. 2007; Buyse et al. 2008; Gehlbach et al. 2012; Gregory & Ripski 2008; Griggs et al. 2009; Henry et al. 2011; Kellam et al. 1998; Marchant et al. 2001; Merritt et al. 2012; Murray et al. 2008; Perra et al. 2012; Pianta et al. 1995; Rudasill et al. 2010b; Silver et al. 2010
329 Buyse et al. 2008; Maldonado-Carreño & Votruba-Drzal 2011
330 Buyse et al. 2008; Henricsson & Rydell 2004; O'Connor 2010; O'Connor & McCartney 2006; Rudasill et al. 2010b; Stormont 2002; Strein et al. 1999; Tucker et al. 2002
331 Jack et al. 1996: 80
332 Nelson & Roberts 2000
333 Hamre & Pianta 2001; Mikami et al. 2012
334 Buyse et al. 2008
335 e.g. Brophy 1983b; Cameron et al. 2005; Emmer & Evertson 2009; Good & Brophy 2008; Kounin 1970
336 O'Connor 2010
337 Bondy et al. 2007; Cadmia et al. 2010; Maldonado-Carreño & Votruba-Drzal 2011; Merritt et al. 2012; Rimm-Kaufman et al. 2009; Wilson et al. 2007
338 Wright et al. 1997
339 Downer et al. 2007; Maldonado-Carreño & Votruba-Drzal 2011; Rey et al. 2007; Zimmer-Gembeck et al. 2006
340 Perry et al. 2007; Ponitz et al. 2009

341 Cadima et al. 2010; Curby et al. 2009; Decker et al. 2007; Hughes & Kwok 2007; Pianta et al. 1995; Ponitz et al. 2009; Wright et al. 1997
342 Pedersen et al. 1978. The statistics are impressive: the children's father's occupational status had an effect size of .11 on their ultimate adult occupational status; the number of children in their family had a −.27 effect size; the children's own personal characteristics had an effect of .05; their academic ability had an effect of .30 – and their grade 1 teacher in her own right had an effect of .32, higher even than the children's natural ability (Pedersen et al. 1978: 29).
343 Mashburn et al. 2008; Weinstein 1983
344 Curby et al. 2009; Pianta et al. 1995; Scott et al. 2001; Wright et al. 1997
345 Scott et al. 2001
346 Frenzel et al. 2007; Scott et al. 2001
347 Phelan et al. 1994
348 Phelan et al. 1994: 426–427
349 Taylor et al. 2011: 638
350 Phelan et al. 1994: 429
351 Phelan et al. 1994: 429
352 Legault et al. 2006
353 Mortimore et al. 1988; Rutter & Maughan 2002
354 Mortimore et al. 1988; Osterman 2000; Rutter & Maughan 2002; Sylva 1994
355 McEvoy & Welker 2000; Reinke & Herman 2002; Rutter 1983
356 Pomeroy 1999
357 Garza 2009; Pomeroy 1999
358 Murray et al. 2008
359 Mortimore & Sammons 1987
360 Pedersen et al. 1978

Chapter 2

1 Kohn 1999: 3
2 Bowles & Gintis 2011a; Labaree 1997
3 Kilderry 2004
4 Robinson 2011: 71
5 Labaree 1997; Levin 1998; Robinson 2011: 59
6 Robinson 2011
7 Labaree 1997
8 Gladwell 2008; Labaree 1997: 64
9 Labaree 1997: 55
10 Gross 2004; Stanley & Baines 2002
11 Gladwell 2008: 257
12 Gladwell 2008: 258
13 Dahlberg et al. 1999; Fraser & Gestwicki 2002
14 Noguera 1995
15 Noguera 1995
16 Gartrell 2003
17 Baumrind 1967, 1971a
18 Putallaz et al. 1998; Scaramella & Conger 2003; Simons et al. 1991
19 Baumrind 1971b; Brenner & Fox 1999; Coolahan et al. 2002
20 Maccoby & Martin 1983
21 Williams et al. 2009
22 Brenner & Fox 1999
23 Maccoby & Martin 1983
24 Brier 1995; Dishion & McMahon 1998
25 Weiss & Schwarz 1996
26 Maccoby & Martin 1983
27 Omer 2001: 55
28 Grolnick & Pomerantz 2009: 166
29 Rudy et al. 2008; Soenens & Vansteenkiste 2010: 78 & 80; Soenens et al. 2012a: 261–262
30 Roth et al. 2009
31 Assor & Tal 2012
32 Soenens & Beyers 2012; Soenens et al. 2010, 2012a: 262
33 Grolnick & Pomerantz 2009: 166; Roth et al. 2009
34 Soenens & Beyers 2012; Soenens et al. 2010, 2012a: 262
35 Barber et al. 2012; Loukas 2009: 1113; Soenens & Vansteenkiste 2010
36 Soenens et al. 2010, 2012a: 262
37 Barber et al. 2005; Grolnick & Ryan 1989; Palmer & Hollin 2001; Pomerantz & Wang 2009; Qin et al. 2009; Soenens & Vansteenkiste 2010; Soenens et al. 2010
38 Soenens & Vansteenkiste 2010: 75
39 Awong et al. 2008
40 Alberto & Troutman 2013: 18
41 McGroder 2000
42 Awong et al. 2008; Gregory & Rimm-Kaufman 2008
43 Campbell et al. 2000; McGroder 2000; Mason et al. 1996
44 Grolnick & Pomerantz 2009: 168
45 Awong et al. 2008
46 Gregory & Rimm-Kaufman 2008
47 Mason et al. 1996
48 Gartrell 2003
49 Noblit 1993: 35
50 Rogers & Webb 1991: 174–178
51 Noblit 1993: 35
52 Noblit 1993: 35
53 Grolnick & Pomerantz 2009: 166 & 167
54 Grolnick & Pomerantz 2009: 167
55 Albert 2003; Balson 1992, 1994; Dinkmeyer & McKay 1989; Dinkmeyer et al. 1980, 1997; Dreikurs & Cassel 1990; Harrison 2004
56 Tabrizian 2003: 18 & 112
57 Bourre et al. 1984: 345; Lyon 2000: 85
58 Hadjivassiliou et al. 2001: 385; Mäki & Collin 1997: 1756; Mackarness 1990: 103; Philpott & Kalita 2000
59 Blum & Mercugliano 1997
60 This quote has been variously attributed to philosopher Jeremy Bentham and to comedian Robert Benchley.
61 Rogers, 1989, 1995, 1998, 2002, 2003, 2004, 2011
62 See Charles et al. 2014; Edwards & Watts 2008
63 Greene 2008
64 Alberto & Troutman 2013: 9
65 Kohn 1996a
66 Winslade & Monk 1999
67 Brown 2008: 25
68 Johnson et al. 1994
69 Larrivee 2005; Schmuck & Schmuck 2001
70 Banks 2005: 17
71 Banks 2005: 17
72 Kohn 2005: 125
73 Greene 2008
74 Phelan 2003: 16
75 Canter & Canter 2001: 7
76 Boyson, in Holland 2004: 75. Boyson is a former school principal and one of the architects of Margaret Thatcher's Education policy in the UK.
77 Wolfgang et al. 1999: 173
78 Canter 2010: 5
79 Jacques Barzun, in Wager 1992. (At the time of writing this statement, Wager was a school principal who developed a system of compulsory meetings with students and parents, reward systems and enforced reparations to rescue her school from uproar.)
80 Watzlawick et al. 1974: 33
81 Watzlawick et al. 1974: 33
82 Miller 1987
83 Porter 2006
84 Soenens & Vansteenkiste 2010: 76

85 Greene 2008
86 Greene 2008: 7
87 Kohn 1992: 12
88 Lee 2001; Montgomery 2003
89 Raskin & Rogers 2005
90 Buckingham 2000; Lee 2001
91 Kohn 2011: 10
92 Docking 1982
93 Alberto & Troutman 2013: 25
94 Greene 2008: 10
95 Greene 2008: 10
96 Deci & Ryan 1987
97 Kant 1785/1996
98 Canter 2010
99 Alberto & Troutman 2013
100 Bromberg & Johnson 2001; Metzner & Ryan 1995
101 Briggs & McVeity 2000
102 Briggs & McVeity 2000
103 Kohn 2005; Kuczynski & Kochanska 1999
104 Porter 2006
105 Milgram 1963
106 Snow 1961, in Milgram 1963: 371
107 Dubanoski et al. 1983
108 Canter 2010: 4
109 Kohn 1994
110 Grolnick & Pomerantz 2009
111 Soenens & Vansteenkiste 2010: 79
112 Farrington et al. 2009: 158; Granic & Patterson 2006; van Lier et al. 2007
113 Stattin & Kerr 2000
114 Kerr & Stattin 2000; Stattin & Kerr 2000
115 Cornell & Sheras 1998
116 Lewis 1997
117 Maag 2001
118 Gartrell 2003:134
119 Algozzine & Kay 2002; Kerr & Nelson 2010
120 Lewis et al. 2002
121 McConaughy & Leone 2002
122 Algozzine & Kay 2002
123 Dix et al. 1989; Grusec & Mammone 1995; Pinderhughes et al. 2000
124 Pinderhughes et al. 2000
125 Dix et al. 1989
126 Berlin et al. 2011
127 Pinderhughes et al. 2000
128 Brophy & McCaslin 1992
129 Kuczynski 1984; Luster et al. 1989
130 Deci et al. 1991; Flink et al. 1990
131 Deci et al. 1991
132 Martin et al. 1999
133 Caprara et al. 2003
134 Bugental et al. 1997; Lewis 2001
135 Grusec & Mammone 1995; Lewis 2001
136 Grusec & Mammone 1995
137 Lewis 2001
138 Gerris et al. 1997; Hastings & Grusec 1997
139 Clayton 1985; Flynn 1994
140 Proverbs 22:15, New Revised Standard Version
141 Proverbs 20:30
142 Deuteronomy 20–21
143 Robinson 1628, in Greven 1992: 65
144 Lessin 1979, in Greven 1992: 61
145 Dobson 1970: 16
146 Dobson 1992
147 Dobson 1970: 27
148 Kaplan 1992
149 Kaplan 1992
150 Porter 1999
151 Brophy & McCaslin 1992
152 Brophy & McCaslin 1992; Lewis 1997
153 Bibou-Nakou et al. 2000; Brophy & McCaslin 1992
154 Brophy & McCaslin 1992: 51; Lewis 2001
155 Soenens et al. 2012b: 117
156 Martin & Peer 2011: 385
157 Grille 2005
158 Noguera 1995
159 Croll & Moses 1985, in Miller 2003
160 Buyse et al. 2008
161 Greene 2008: 15; Laws & Davies 2000
162 Henning-Stout 1998; McGlone 2001; Murphy & Duncan 2007
163 Croll & Moses 1985, in Miller 2003. For their part, students and parents blame teacher unfairness and student vulnerability (although parents do also recognise certain disadvantaging home factors) (Miller et al. 2000, 2002). Teacher behaviours blamed by parents and students included favouritism and its opposite – 'picking on' students – rudeness, shouting, not listening to students or noticing their good work, unfairly blaming children and being too soft or too strict. Parents also blame too much homework and a lack of academic help for struggling students.

Chapter 3

1 Nelson 1996: 149
2 Alberto & Troutman 2013: 18
3 Skinner 1989
4 Canter 2010
5 Canter (2010) derides 'so-called experts' who dispute his simplistic system of sanctions, when his own book draws on a total of 26 research-based studies, all of them behaviourist and hence he placed himself in no danger of being contradicted.
6 Gresham et al. 2001
7 Baum 2011
8 Kearney 2008: 20
9 Kearney 2008: 19; Zirpoli 2012a: 12
10 Kearney 2008: 20; Zirpoli 2012a: 13
11 Kerr & Nelson 2010: 72
12 Zirpoli 2012b: 257
13 Zirpoli 2012b: 257
14 Walker et al. 1996: 196
15 McIntosh et al. 2010; Simonsen 2008a
16 OSEP Center on Positive Behavioral Interventions and Supports 2000: 137
17 Simonsen et al. 2008; McIntosh et al. 2010
18 Walker et al. 1996
19 Simonsen 2010: 41
20 Kearney 2008: 59
21 Ervin et al. 2001a; Myers & Holland 2000; Nelson et al. 1999; Northup & Gulley 2001
22 Alberto & Troutman 2013: 191
23 Ervin et al. 2001b; Northup & Gulley 2001; Shriver et al. 2001
24 Gresham et al. 1993
25 Alberto & Troutman 2013: 2
26 Kazdin 1997
27 Alberto & Troutman 2013: 5
28 Alberto & Troutman 2013
29 Alberto & Troutman 2013: 23 & 25
30 Alberto & Troutman 2013: 16
31 Alberto & Troutman 2013: 33
32 Alberto & Troutman 2013: 25
33 Kerr & Nelson 2010
34 Maag 2001

35 Kerr & Nelson 2010: 78
36 McDonnell 1993
37 OSEP Center on Positive Behavioral Interventions and Supports 2000
38 McDonnell 1993
39 McDonnell 1993; Kerr & Nelson 2010
40 Alberto & Troutman 2013: 330; Zirpoli 2012b: 280
41 Alberto & Troutman 2013: 338; Zirpoli 2012b: 281
42 Alberto & Troutman 2013: 329; Kearney 2008; Martin & Pear 2011: 191-202; Schloss & Smith 1998; Zirpoli 2012b
43 Alberto & Troutman 2013: 338
44 Alberto & Troutman 2013: 338
45 Alberto & Troutman 2013: 339
46 Alberto & Troutman 2013: 342; Zirpoli 2012b: 283
47 Foxx 1982
48 Alberto & Troutman 2013: 334; Kearney 2008: 80; Zirpoli 2012b: 283
49 Alberto & Troutman 2013: 335
50 Alberto & Troutman 2013: 347; Zirpoli 2012b: 283
51 Sugai & Horner 2002
52 Sugai & Horner 2002
53 Martin & Pear 2011: 391
54 Alberto & Troutman 2013: 29; OSEP Center on Positive Behavioral Interventions and Supports 2000; Wheeler & Richey 2005
55 Alberto & Troutman 2013; Martin & Pear 2011: 392
56 Alberto & Troutman 2013: 30; Rekers 1984
57 Martin & Pear 2011: 393
58 Rekers 1984
59 Martin & Pear 2011: 393
60 Alberto & Troutman 2013: 31

Chapter 4

1   Skinner et al. 2002: 195
2   McIntosh et al. 2010; Sutherland et al. 2000
3   Sutherland et al. 2000
4   Sutherland et al. 2000: 3
5   Reinke et al. 2008
6   Kearney 2008: 39
7   Kearney 2008: 40
8   Zirpoli 2012a: 26
9   Kearney 2008: 53
10 Kerr & Nelson 2010: 81
11 Kerr & Nelson 2010: 81-82
12 Martin & Pear 2011: 115; Zirpoli 2012a: 20-21
13 Wilder et al. 2008
14 Wilder et al. 2008
15 Axelrod 1977
16 Alberto & Troutman 2013: 311
17 Alberto & Troutman 2013: 309
18 Martin & Pear 2011: 121; Walker et al. 2004;
19 Alberto & Troutman 2013: 324
20 Kearney 2008: 85
21 Alberto & Troutman 2013: 325
22 Alberto & Troutman 2013: 325
23 Martin & Pear 2011: 138
24 Skinner et al. 2005
25 Slocum & Tiger 2011
26 Alberto & Troutman 2013: 319
27 Zirpoli 2012b: 259
28 Alberto & Troutman 2013: 249; Kearney 2008: 41; Zirpoli 2012b: 259
29 Kearney 2008: 43
30 Alberto & Troutman 2013: 252
31 Kamps 2002
32 Kerr & Nelson 2010: 80
33 Alberto & Troutman 2013: 233; Kerr & Nelson 2010: 80

34 Kerr & Nelson 2010: 230
35 Brophy 1981; Sutherland et al. 2000; Zirpoli 2012b: 263
36 Canter 2010: 28; Mathieson & Price 2002; Zirpoli 2012b: 262
37 Alberto & Troutman 2013: 223; Kearney 2008: 68; Kerr & Nelson 2010: 82; Martin & Pear 2011: 35; Zirpoli 2012b: 261
38 Zirpoli 2012b: 262
39 Mathieson & Price 2002
40 Alberto & Troutman 2013: 224; Neef et al. 1993, 2001
41 Alberto & Troutman 2013: 224
42 Alberto & Troutman 2013: 222-3; Zirpoli 2012b: 262
43 Kerr & Nelson 2010: 83
44 Skinner et al. 2005
45 Alberto & Troutman 2013: 222
46 Alberto & Troutman 2013: 229
47 Alberto & Troutman 2013: 225; Kerr & Nelson 2010: 234-240; Maggin et al. 2011; Martin & Pear 2011: 53-54; Reid & Maag 1998; Wolery et al. 1988
48 Alberto & Troutman 2013: 226; Skinner et al. 2004; Walker et al. 2004
49 Zirpoli 2012b: 274 & 276
50 Alberto & Troutman 2013: 229
51 Alberto & Troutman 2013: 230
52 Kamps 2002
53 Piazza et al. 2000
54 Frank-Crawford et al. 2012
55 Kerr & Nelson 2010: 84
56 Alberto & Troutman 2013: 220
57 Alberto & Troutman 2013: 243; Zirpoli 2012b: 266
58 Zirpoli 2012b: 267
59 Parry-Cruwys et al. 2011
60 Alberto & Troutman 2013: 244
61 Wheeler & Richey 2005
62 Kearney 2008: 51
63 Alberto & Troutman 2013: 246; Martin & Pear 2011: 83
64 Kern et al. 2009
65 Alberto & Troutman 2013: 238-9
66 Little 2003
67 Alberto & Troutman 2013: 242; Kerr & Nelson 2010: 244; Reid & Maag 1998
68 Wolfgang et al. 1999
69 Wolery et al. 1988
70 Alberto & Troutman 2013; Kaplan & Carter 1995; Martin & Pear 2011: 34-45 & 57-58; Walker et al. 2004; Wheeler & Richey 2005; Zirpoli 2012b
71 Binder et al. 2000; Neef et al. 1993, 2001
72 Alberto & Troutman 2013: 214
73 Alberto & Troutman 2013: 214; Martin & Pear 2003; Wheeler & Richey 2005
74 Alberto & Troutman 2003: 214
75 Dixon et al. 1998; Zarcone et al. 1994
76 Rusby et al. 2011
77 Bambara et al. 2009; Skinner et al. 2002
78 Conroy et al. 2009: 13

Chapter 5

1   O'Neill et al. 1997: 5, in Macht & Zirpoli 2012: 231
2   McDonnell 1993
3   McDonnell 1993; Kerr & Nelson 2010
4   Alberto & Troutman 2013: 31
5   McIntosh et al. 2010
6   Alberto & Troutman 2103: 259
7   Vollmer et al. 1993
8   Sulzer-Azaroff & Mayer 1991
9   Vollmer et al. 1993

10 Alberto & Troutman 2103: 260–265; Kerr & Nelson 2010: 230–231; Zirpoli 2012c: 357–363
11 Alberto & Troutman 2103: 260
12 Alberto & Troutman 2103: 260–261
13 Sulzer-Azaroff & Mayer 1991
14 Austin & Bevan 2011
15 Kerr & Nelson 2010
16 Alberto & Troutman 2013: 265
17 Alberto & Troutman 2013: 265–266
18 Alberto & Troutman 2013: 265
19 Sulzer-Azaroff & Mayer 1991; Wheeler & Richey 2005
20 Vollmer et al. 1999
21 Walker et al. 2004
22 Martin & Pear 2011: 92
23 Zirpoli 2012c: 259
24 Sulzer-Azaroff & Mayer 1991
25 Alberto & Troutman 2013: 263
26 Martin & Pear 2011: 92
27 Alberto & Troutman 2013: 267
28 Alberto & Troutman 2013: 267
29 The only children with whom I have worked who were hoarders had lost a parent. It seems that this loss (which is significant enough to derail children's emotional development) is so huge that the children store up junk, in case of another privation. As a non-behaviourist, then, I would not attempt to extinguish the behaviour but instead would support the child to grieve.
30 Martin & Pear 2011: 61
31 Iwata et al. 1994; Kearney 2008: 45; Martin & Pear 2011: 64; Zirpoli 2012c: 367
32 Alberto & Troutman 2013: 270
33 Alberto & Troutman 2013: 271
34 Martin & Pear 2011: 65
35 Martin & Pear 2011: 66; Zirpoli 2012c: 368
36 Mace & Wacker 1994; Zarcone et al. 1994
37 Zirpoli 2012c: 366
38 Alberto & Troutman 2013: 271; Kearney 2008: 44; Lerman & Iwata 1996; Lerman et al. 1999; Martin & Pear 2011: 67; Wheeler & Richey 2005; Zirpoli 2012c: 368
39 Alberto & Troutman 2013: 273
40 Alberto & Troutman 2013: 277
41 Kearney 2008: 48; Zirpoli 2012c: 378
42 Zirpoli 2012c: 378
43 Kearney 2008: 88–89
44 Zirpoli 2012c: 370
45 Wheeler & Richey 2005
46 Alberto & Troutman 2013: 278–281; Kerr & Nelson 2010: 87–88; Sterling-Turner & Watson 1999
47 Simonsen et al. 2008a: 365
48 Reid & Maag 1998; Simonsen et al. 2008a: 366
49 Rogers 2002; Sterling-Turner & Watson 1999
50 Alberto & Troutman 2013: 279
51 Zirpoli 2012c: 372–373
52 Sterling-Turner & Watson 1999
53 Kearney 2008: 89
54 Donaldson & Vollmer 2011; Sterling-Turner & Watson 1999
55 Sterling-Turner & Watson 1999
56 Maag 2001; Zirpoli 2012c: 374
57 Zirpoli 2012c: 375
58 Alberto & Troutman 2013: 278–281; Myers & Holland 2000; Newcomer & Lewis 2004; Sterling-Turner & Watson 1999; Wheeler & Richey 2005
59 Kerr & Nelson 2010: 86 & 233
60 Wolery et al. 1988; Zirpoli 2012c: 378
61 Zirpoli 2012c: 379
62 Alberto & Troutman 2013: 288; Zirpoli 2012c: 378
63 Alberto & Troutman 2003: 290; Kerr & Nelson 2010: 88
64 Alberto & Troutman 2003: 290
65 Kerr & Nelson 2010: 89
66 Harrison 2004
67 e.g. Balson 1992; Dinkmeyer & McKay 1989; Dinkmeyer et al. 1980, 1997; Little 2003
68 Nelsen et al. 2000
69 Dreikurs & Cassel 1990
70 Canter 2010: 73
71 Nelsen et al. 2000
72 Nelsen et al. 2000
73 Kohn 1996a: 44
74 Kohn 1994: 77
75 Kohn 1996a: 42
76 Johnston 1972; Lerman & Vorndran 2002; Martin & Pear 2011: 150
77 Johnston 1972; Lerman & Vorndran 2002; Martin & Pear 2011
78 Canter 2010: 34
79 Kearney 2008: 46; Lerman & Vorndran 2002; Martin & Pear 2011: 153; McDonnell 1993; Skiba & Peterson 2000
80 Alberto & Troutman 2013: 286
81 Kearney 2008: 47
82 Kearney 2008: 45 & 47; Martin & Pear 2011: 152
83 Alberto & Troutman 2013: 286; Martin & Pear 2011: 152
84 Alberto & Troutman 2013: 286
85 Skinner et al. 2002
86 Conyers et al. 2004
87 Kearney 2008: 46
88 Alberto & Troutman 2013: 258

Chapter 6

1 Yell 2012: 45
2 Canter 2010: 10
3 Larrivee 2005; Schmuck & Schmuck 2001
4 Canter 2010: 47–55; 16
5 Canter 2010: 16
6 Bailey & Pyles 1989
7 Stormont et al. 2005: 43
8 Walker et al. 1996: 201
9 Conroy et al. 2009: 11; Kern et al. 2009
10 Emmer et al. 1980
11 Jack et al. 1996
12 Kerr & Nelson 2010: 199
13 Canter 2010: 24
14 Lewis & Sugai 1999; Simonsen et al. 2008b: 35; Sugai & Horner 2002
15 Scott et al. 2001
16 Kern et al. 2009
17 Walker et al. 1996: 201
18 Canter 2010: 89–95; Conroy et al. 2009; Kern et al. 2009; Simonsen et al. 2008a: 359
19 Lewis & Sugai 1999: 11
20 Kerr & Nelson 2010: 214; Simonsen et al. 2008a: 359
21 Canter 2010; Gresham et al. 2001; Kamps 2002; Kern & Clemens 2007; Kerr & Nelson 2010; Wheeler & Richey 2005
22 Ervin et al. 2001a; Macht & Zirpoli 2012; Wehmeyer et al. 2004
23 Nelson 1996; Simonsen et al. 2008a: 358
24 Kerr & Nelson 2010: 204
25 Lewis & Sugai 1999
26 Dwyer et al. 2000
27 Canter 2010; Rademacher et al. 1998
28 Little 2003
29 Lassen et al. 2006: 705
30 Simonsen et al. 2008b: 38
31 Sugai & Horner 2002: 32

32 Simonsen et al. 2008a: 358
33 Stormont et al. 2005: 46
34 Wolfgang et al. 1999: 77
35 Zirpoli 2012b: 265
36 Sugai & Horner 2002: 33
37 Fudge et al. 2008
38 Lewis & Sugai 1999
39 Kern & Clemens 2007; Scott et al. 2001
40 Mathieson & Price 2002
41 Stormont et al. 2005: 46
42 Little 2003
43 Canter 2010: 11; Nelson 1996; Simonsen et al. 2008a
44 Canter 2010: 42-44 & 54-55; Emmer & Evertson 2009;
    Kerr & Nelson 2010: 202-203; Lindberg et al. 2005: 48-60
45 Dwyer et al. 2000
46 Kearney 2008: 37
47 Lewis & Sugai 1999: 11
48 Sugai & Horner 2002: 34
49 Canter 2010: 64-65
50 Canter 2010: 26-27
51 Stormont et al. 2005: 46
52 Cashwell et al. 2001
53 Skinner et al. 2002
54 Morrison & Jones 2007; Skinner et al. 2002
55 Skinner et al. 2002
56 Morrison & Jones 2007
57 Jones et al. 2000
58 Tanol et al. 2010
59 Ruiz-Olivares et al. 2010
60 Canter 2010
61 Lewis & Sugai 1999: 6; Sugai & Horner 2002: 33
62 Nelson 1996
63 Lewis & Sugai 1999: 12
64 Conroy et al. 2009; Kerr & Nelson 2010: 208; Lewis &
    Sugai 1999: 10; Sugai & Horner 2002: 35-36
65 Wolfgang et al. 1999
66 Wolfgang et al. 1999
67 Simonsen et al. 2008a: 364
68 Canter 2010: 75
69 Wolfgang et al. 1999
70 See Martin & Pear 2011: 97-110
71 Nelson 1996
72 Lewis & Sugai 1999
73 Canter 2010: 37; George et al. 2007
74 Nelson 1996
75 Nelson 1996: 151
76 Lewis & Sugai 1999: 12
77 Stormont et al. 2005
78 Canter 2010: 36; Wolfgang et al. 1999
79 Lewis & Sugai 1999: 10
80 Canter 2010: 13
81 Morrison & Jones 2007: 111
82 Bailey & Pyles 1989; Morrison & Jones 2007

Chapter 7

1   Simonsen et al. 2008b: 33
2   Sugai & Horner 2002: 37
3   Conroy et al. 2009: 11; Kern & Manz 2004: 48; Kern et al.
    2009; Simonsen et al. 2008b: 33
4   Debnam et al. 2012; Riley-Tillman et al. 2007; Simonsen
    2010: 55
5   Vannest et al. 2010
6   Reid & Maag 1998
7   Alberto & Troutman 2013: 236
8   Zirpoli 2012b: 278
9   Alberto & Troutman 2013: 237
10 Gable et al. 2001

11 Simonsen 2010: 65
12 Cowie & Olafsson 2000
13 James & Owens 2004; Owens et al. 2001; Shute et al. 2002
14 Cowie & Olafsson 2000; Smith & Daunic 2002
15 Bandura 2001: 7
16 Daunic et al. 2012; Yell et al. 2012: 289
17 Alberto & Troutman 2013: 350; Kerr & Nelson 2010: 248
18 Alberto & Troutman 2013: 350; Carter 1993: 28
19 Le Messurier 2004
20 Daunic et al. 2012
21 Fantuzzo & Polite 1990
22 Daunic et al. 2012
23 Fantuzzo & Polite 1990, Fantuzzo et al. 1987, 1988
24 Alberto & Troutman 2013: 353
25 Fantuzzo & Polite 1990: 184
26 Alberto & Troutman 2013: 361; Martin & Pear 2011: 346;
    Meichenbaum 1977; Swaggart 1998; Yell et al. 2012: 303
27 Bandura 2001: 10
28 Swaggart 1998; Yell et al. 2012: 293
29 Briere & Simonsen 2011
30 Bandura 1986; Kaplan & Carter 1995; Maag et al. 1993;
    Reid & Harris 1993
31 Alberto & Troutman 2013: 354; Bandura 1986; Shapiro
    1984; Yell et al. 2012: 294
32 Alberto & Troutman 2013: 357; Kaplan & Carter 1995;
    Whitman et al. 1991; Yell et al. 2012: 294
33 Yell et al. 2012: 295
34 Kaplan & Carter 1995; Whitman et al. 1991; Yell et al.
    2012: 297
35 Alberto & Troutman 2013: 358; Yell et al. 2012: 300-301
36 Todd et al. 1999; Yell et al. 2012: 295
37 Rogers 2003
38 Rogers 2003

Chapter 8

1   Walker et al. 1996: 202
2   Kern et al. 2009
3   Conroy et al. 2009; Lewis & Sugai 1999: 12; Quinn & Lee
    2007; Walker et al. 1996
4   Walker et al. 1996
5   Gable et al. 2001
6   OSEP Center on Positive Behavioral Interventions and
    Supports 2000: 135
7   OSEP Center on Positive Behavioral Interventions and
    Supports 2000: 137
8   Park 2007
9   Alberto & Troutman 2013: 32
10 Zirpoli & Buese 2012: 141
11 Canter 2010
12 Alberto & Troutman 2013: 29; OSEP Center on Positive
    Behavioral Interventions and Supports 2000; Wheeler &
    Richey 2005
13 Kohn 1994: 76; LeCompte 1978; O'Leary 1972; Winett &
    Winkler 1972
14 Kerr & Nelson 2010: 107
15 Zirpoli & Buese 2012: 141-142
16 Zirpoli & Buese 2012: 142
17 Alberto & Troutman 2013: 51; Kearney 2008: 63; Zirpoli
    & Buese 2012: 143
18 Maag 2001
19 Kerr & Nelson 2010: 146
20 Kearney 2008: 63 & 64; Kerr & Nelson 2010: 117
21 Alberto & Troutman 2013: 68-70; Gresham et al. 2001;
    Kerr & Nelson 2010: 145; Rogers 2003; Zirpoli & Buese
    2012: 147-150
22 Zirpoli & Buese 2012: 145
23 Alberto & Troutman 2013: 81

24 Reid & Maag 1998
25 Kerr & Nelson 2010: 152; Zirpoli & Buese 2012: 145
26 Alberto & Troutman 2013: 86
27 Alberto & Troutman 2013: 87; Kerr & Nelson 2010: 153; Martin & Pear 2011: 263; Zirpoli & Buese 2012: 156
28 Alberto & Troutman 2013: 95–96; Kerr & Nelson 2010: 151
29 Gresham et al. 2001; Kern et al. 2009; OSEP Center on Positive Behavioral Interventions and Supports 2000
30 Macht & Zirpoli 2012: 237; Nichols 2000
31 Kerr & Nelson 2010: 120
32 Gresham et al. 2001
33 Bailey & Pyles 1989; Kerr & Nelson 2010: 120; Macht & Zirpoli 2012: 235–236; Reid & Maag 1998; van Houten et al. 1988; Wheeler & Richey 2005
34 Reid & Maag 1998
35 Kearney 2008: 59
36 Kennedy 2000: 196
37 Ervin et al. 2001b; Kerr & Nelson 2010: 122; Northup & Gulley 2001; OSEP Center on Positive Behavioral Interventions and Supports 2000; Shriver et al. 2001
38 Macht & Zirpoli 2012: 233; Reid & Maag 1998
39 Alberto & Troutman 2013: 176; Macht & Zirpoli 2012: 236; Mueller et al. 2011; Nelson 1996: 152
40 Alberto & Troutman 2013: 194; Nichols 2000
41 Martin & Pear 2011: 285
42 Nichols 2000
43 Wheeler & Richey 2005
44 Macht & Zirpoli 2012: 231 & 248
45 Kerr & Nelson 2010: 123
46 Gable et al. 2001
47 Conroy et al. 2009
48 Gable et al. 2001

Chapter 9

1 Murphy & Duncan 1997: 88
2 Alberto & Troutman 2013; Kaplan & Carter 1995
3 Bryant et al. 1999; Marchant et al. 2004
4 e.g. Connell et al. 1997; Kazdin & Weisz 1998; Leung et al. 2003; Sanders 1999; Sanders et al. 2000
5 Simonsen et al. 2008a
6 Richards et al. 2010
7 Cashwell et al. 2001: 172
8 Morrison & Jones 2007: 120 & 122
9 Skinner et al. 2002
10 Vannest et al. 2010
11 Simonsen 2010: 64
12 Vannest et al. 2010
13 Tanol et al. 2010
14 Swieczy et al. 1992
15 Donaldon et al. 2011
16 Sullivan & O'Leary 1990
17 Austin & Bevan 2011
18 Maggin et al. 2011
19 Sullivan & O'Leary 1990
20 Donaldson & Vollmer 2011
21 Simonsen et al. 2008a: 364
22 Briesch & Chafouleas 2009
23 Briesch & Chafouleas 2009; Fatuzzo & Polite 1990; Fantuzzo et al. 1987, 1988
24 Amato-Zech et al. 2006; Briere & Simonsen 2011; Yell et al. 2012
25 Briesch & Chafouleas 2009
26 Smith & Daunic 2004
27 Daunic et al. 2012
28 Camodeca & Goossens 2005; Coie et al. 1999; Egan et al. 1998; Vitaro et al. 2006

29 Northey et al. 2003; Reddy et al. 2009; Reese et al. 2010; Robinson et al. 1999; Squires 2001; Wilson et al. 2001; Zirkelback & Reese 2010
30 Kazdin & Weisz 1998; Kendall & Panichelli-Mindel 1995; Kolko et al. 2000; McCart et al. 2006; Squires 2001
31 Toland & Boyle 2008
32 Levine & Anshel 2011
33 Lösel & Beelmann 2003
34 Miller & Berman 1983; Stage & Quiroz 1997
35 Stage & Quiroz 1997
36 Wilson & Lipsey 2007
37 Alberto & Troutman 2013: 350. Martin & Pear (2011: 351) do some mental gymnastics to conclude that our thinking becomes a conditioned stimulus for our behaviour. In contrast, non-behaviourists are comfortable with saying that, as sentient beings, our thinking directs our behaviour and that both are directed at meeting our needs.
38 Berkel et al. 2011
39 Kern & Manz 2004
40 Bradshaw et al. 2010; McIntosh et al. 2010; Nelson 1996
41 Ervin et al. 2007: 13
42 George et al. 2007: 43
43 George et al. 2007
44 Taylor-Green et al. 1997. You do have to wonder what is going on in these classrooms (a) to have so many infractions occurring and (b) for teachers to be unable to manage these within the classroom.
45 Lewis et al. 1998; Luiselli et al. 2005
46 Nelson et al. 1998
47 Luiselli et al. 2005
48 Scott & Barrett 2004
49 Warren et al. 2006
50 Warren et al. 2006
51 Ervin et al. 2007: 13
52 Walker et al. 1998
53 Tremblay et al. 1995
54 Ross & Horner 2009
55 Wilson et al. 2003
56 Wilson & Lipsey 2007
57 Wilson et al. 2003; Wilson & Lipsey 2007
58 George et al. 2007: 43
59 Vo et al. 2012
60 Kazdin & Weisz 1998; Vannest et al. 2010
61 Kern & Manz 2004: 51
62 Porter 1999
63 Rutter 1983
64 Rutter 1983: 23
65 Ahearn et al. 2001; Buckley & Newchok 2005; Cooper et al. 1995; Fisher et al. 2000b; Fritz et al. 2012; Kahng et al. 2003; Kelley et al. 2003; Kennedy et al. 2000; Kerwin et al. 1995; Kurtz et al. 2003; Levin & Carr 2001; Luiselli 2000; Mueller et al. 2001; O'Reilly et al. 2000; Piazza et al. 1997, 1998, 2002, 2003; Reed et al. 2004; Roane et al. 2001, 2003; Saylor et al. 2012; Van Camp et al. 2000; Vaz et al. 2012; Wilkins et al. 2011; Zanolli & Daggett 1998
66 e.g. Duda et al. 2004; Fritz et al. 2012; Koegel et al. 2001; Kraus et al. 2012; Musser et al. 2001; Wilder et al. 2012
67 Eckert et al. 2002; Heck et al. 2001; Putnam et al. 2003; Reynolds & Kelley 1997; Tarbox et al. 2003; Wehby & Hollahan 2000
68 Carr 1997; Ervin et al. 2001b; Nelson et al. 1999; O'Neill & Stephenson 2009
69 Miller 2003; O'Neill & Stephenson 2009
70 e.g. Amato-Zech et al. 2006; Murphy et al. 2007
71 Alberto & Troutman 2013; Ervin et al. 2001b; Kaplan & Carter 1995; Martin & Pear 2011; Schloss & Smith 1998
72 McIntosh et al. 2010; Nelson 1996; Warren et al. 2006

73   Nelson 1996
74   Horner et al. 2009
75   Solomon et al. 2012
76   Bailey 1992; Miller 1991; Wolery et al. 1988
77   Kutsick et al. 1991
78   Benes & Kramer 1989
79   Kern & Manz 2004
80   Suldo et al. 2009
81   Fantuzzo et al. 1988: 161
82   Chiu & Tulley 1997
83   Battistich et al. 1997: 143
84   Frenzel et al. 2007
85   McNeely et al. 2002
86   Valeski & Stipek 2001
87   Bambara et al. 2009: 172–173
88   Nelson 1996; Stoiber & Gettinger 2011
89   Simonsen et al. 2008b: 34
90   Ervin et al. 2007: 15
91   Lassen et al. 2006
92   Mueller et al. 2011: 812
93   Mueller et al. 2011
94   Schill et al. 1998
95   Schill et al. 1998
96   McKerchar & Thompson 2004
97   Nelson et al. 1999
98   Wehmeyer et al. 2004
99   Fisher et al. 2000a
100   Conyers et al. 2004
101   Bambara et al. 2009: 170
102   Walker et al. 1976
103   Ellis & Magee 1999
104   Gresham et al. 2001
105   Bambara et al. 2009: 170
106   Bradshaw et al. 2010; Vo et al. 2012
107   Ervin et al. 2010
108   McKissock et al. 2010
109   McKissock et al. 2010
110   McKissock et al. 2010
111   McKissock et al. 2010; O'Neill & Stephenson 2009
112   O'Neill & Stephenson 2009
113   Alberto & Troutman 2013; Ellingson et al. 2000; Ervin et al. 2001b; Gresham et al. 2001; Sterling-Turner et al. 2001; van Houten et al. 1988; Wolery et al. 1988
114   Schloss & Smith 1998
115   Wallace et al. 2004
116   Gresham et al. 2004: 26
117   Debnam et al. 2012
118   Cook et al. 2007: 200
119   Wright et al. 2007
120   Bradshaw et al. 2010; Debnam et al. 2012; Kern & Manz 2004
121   George et al. 2007
122   Farmer & Xie 2007
123   Palardy 1996
124   Deci 1971; Deci & Ryan 1987; Deci et al. 1991, 1999a, 2001a; Lepper et al. 1982; Ryan & Deci 1996, 2000
125   McCord 1991
126   Freedman et al. 1992; Lepper et al. 1982; McCord 1991
127   Birch et al. 1995
128   Brophy 1981
129   Brophy 1981; Good & Brophy 2005; Möller 2005; Schmuck & Schmuck 2001
130   Johnston 1972; Lerman & Vorndran 2002
131   Kohn 2005: 63
132   Lerman & Vorndran 2002; Martin & Pear 2011: 153; McDonnell 1993; Skiba & Peterson 2000
133   Greene 2008: 8
134   Greene 2008: 57

135   Skiba & Peterson 1999; Wheeler & Richey 2005
136   Brendgen et al. 2006; Delfabbro et al. 2006
137   Brendgen et al. 2006, 2007; Delfabbro et al. 2006
138   Kohn 2005
139   Elliot & Thrash 2004
140   Chapman & Zahn-Waxler 1982; Elliott & Thrash 2004; Gershoff et al. 2010; Goldstein & Heaven 2000; Hoffman & Saltzstein 1967; Kernis et al. 2000; Kohn 2005; Swanson & Mallinckrodt 2001
141   Costenbader & Markson 1998
142   Noguera 2003
143   Costenbader & Markson 1998: 69; Skiba & Peterson 1999
144   Morrison & D'Incau 1997; Morrison et al. 2001
145   Costenbader & Markson 1998
146   Ladson-Billings 2001:80
147   Crowe 1995, in Walker et al. 1996: 199
148   Costenbader & Markson 1998; Gregory et al. 2010
149   Costenbader & Markson 1998: 75; Noguera 2003
150   Akom 2001: 61; Ayers et al. 2001: xiv
151   Ladson-Billings 2001: 80
152   Skiba et al. 2011
153   Gregory et al. 2010: 62 & 63; Skiba et al. 2011
154   Gregory et al. 2010: 64; Skiba et al. 2011
155   Costenbader & Markson 1998: 70
156   Costenbader & Markson 1998: 70
157   Costenbader & Markson 1998: 76
158   Atkins et al. 2002
159   Costenbader & Markson 1998: 70
160   Gregory et al. 2010
161   Costenbader & Markson 1998: 73; Gregory et al. 2010
162   Skiba & Peterson 2000: 339
163   Morrison et al. 2001
164   Costenbader & Markson 1998: 72
165   Smith 2006: 115; Straus & Paschall 2009: 459; Turner & Muller 2004: 762
166   Straus & Paschall 2009: 475; Turner & Muller 2004: 722
167   Deater-Deckard & Dodge 1997; Giles-Sims et al. 1995; Larzelere 2000; Straus & Stewart 1999; Straus & Paschall 2009
168   Talwar & Lee 2011: 1753
169   Hoffman 1960
170   At the time of writing, the countries where corporal punishment is illegal are: Albania, Austria, Bulgaria, Republic of Congo, Costa Rica, Croatia, Curaçao (part of the Netherlands), Cyprus, Denmark and the Faroe Islands, Finland, Germany, Greece, Hungary, Iceland, Israel, Kenya, Latvia, Liechtenstein, Luxembourg, The Netherlands, New Zealand, Norway, Pitcairn Island, Poland, Portugal, Republic of Moldova, Romania, Republic of South Sudan, Spain, Svalbad (Norway), Sweden, Togo, Tunisia, Ukraine, Uruguay and Venezuela (Source: www.endcorporalpunishment.org; retrieved 14/07/2013)
171   Dixon et al. 2005b; Frias-Armenta 2002; Mapp 2006; Nix et al. 1999; Youssef et al. 1998a
172   Durrant & Ensom 2012; Smith 2006
173   Dixon et al. 2005b; Fine et al. 2004; Frias-Armenta 2002; Gershoff et al. 2010; Gonnoe & Mariner 1997; Hyman 1995; Larzelere 1986; Mapp 2006; Nix et al. 1999; Ohene et al. 2006; Pagani et al. 2004; Sheehan & Watson 2008; Smith 2006; Youssef et al. 1998a
174   Clark 2004; Holden 2002; MacMillan et al. 1999; Rodriguez 2003; Rohner et al. 1991; Smith 2006; Turner & Muller 2004
175   You may be familiar with the grammatical term 'oxymoron' which means an inbuilt contradiction in terms. Some of my favourite examples are smart bombs, Microsoft works, and airline food. In my era as a school

student, I learned as an onlooker that one of the great oxymorons in life was the Sisters of Mercy.

176 Gershoff et al. 2010; Gregory 1995: 461
177 Deater-Deckard et al. 1996; Gershoff et al. 2012; Grogan-Kaylor 2005; Mulvaney & Mebert 2007; Slade & Wissow 2004: 1327; Smith 2006; Taylor et al. 2010
178 Afifi et al. 2006; Aucoin et al. 2006; Colder et al. 1997; Côté et al. 2006; Eamon 2001; Gershoff 2002; Kuczynski & Kochanska 1999; Larzelere 2000; McCord 1997; Nelson et al. 2012; Olson et al. 1990; Palmer & Hollin 2001; Power & Chapieski 1986; Simons et al. 2002; Stormshak et al. 2000; Straus et al. 1997; Weiss et al. 1992
179 Palmer & Hollin 2001
180 Dubanoski et al. 1983; Durrant & Ensom 2012: 1373; Youssef et al. 1998b
181 Straus & Paschall 2009: 476
182 Deater-Deckard et al. 1996; Gunnoe & Mariner 1997; Slade & Wissow 2004
183 Gershoff et al. 2012; Lansford et al. 2005; Mulvaney & Mebert 2007; Rohner et al. 1991
184 Durrant & Ensom 2012; Hyman 1995; Lytton 1997; Simons et al. 2002
185 Bear et al. 2003; Covaleskie 1992; McCaslin & Good 1992; Wien 2004
186 Clark 2004; Durrant & Ensom 2012: 1374; Kazdin & Benjet 2003
187 Fairchild & Erwin 1997; Youssef et al. 1998b
188 Larzelere 1986: 33
189 Dubanoski et al. 1983: 277
190 Clark 2004: 369
191 Durrant & Ensom 2012; Wilson 1982
192 Gregory 1995: 458
193 Smith 2006
194 Dubanoski et al. 1983
195 Hyman 1995: 117
196 Dubanoski et al. 1983
197 Skiba & Peterson 2000
198 Skiba & Peterson 2000
199 Manke 1997; Rutter 1983; Skiba & Peterson 2000
200 Mayer & Leone 1999; Skiba & Peterson 1999, 2000
201 Mayer & Leone 1999; Nickerson & Martens 2008
202 Maag 2001

Chapter 10

1 Noblit et al. 1995: 683
2 Rogers 1942, 1951, 1978; Rogers & Freiberg, 1994
3 Gartrell 2003; Ginott 1969, 1972; Ginott et al. 2003; Glasser 1969, 1988, 1998a, 1998b, 1998c; Gordon 1970, 1974, 2001; Hart & Hodson 2004, 2006; Kohn 1996, 1999, 2000, 2005, 2011; Porter 2006, 2008; Rogers 1942, 1951, 1978; Rogers & Freiberg, 1994
4 Robinson 2011: 66
5 Schaps & Lewis 1991
6 Alder 2002
7 McNeely et al. 2002
8 Davis 2006: 23
9 Blustein 1991, in Garza 2009: 300; Muller et al. 1999; Pomeroy 1999
10 McLaughlin 1991
11 McLaughlin 1991
12 Brown 2004
13 Brown 2004
14 Brown 2004: 270
15 Muller et al. 1999
16 Noddings 2003: 57
17 Baumeister & Leary 1995
18 Maslow 1968
19 Porter 2005, 2006
20 Sommer & Baumeister 2002
21 Baumeister & Leary 1995
22 Solomon et al. 1996; Watson et al. 1997
23 Criss et al. 2002; Dodge et al. 2003; Flook et al. 2005; Fox & Boulton 2006; Gazelle & Ladd 2003; Harel-Fisch et al. 2011; Hymel et al. 1990; Kendrick et al. 2012; Ladd & Burgess 2001; Ladd et al. 1999, 2011; Lubbers et al. 2006; Nelson et al. 2005; Purdue et al. 2009; Rothon et al. 2011; Wang & Eccles 2012
24 Noddings 2003: 127
25 Noddings 2003: 32; 98–100; 116–117
26 Noddings 2003: 121
27 Soenens et al. 2012: 263
28 Kant 1785/1996
29 Seligman 1975
30 Chirkov et al. 2003; Deci & Ryan 2000; Deci et al. 1991, 1999a; Ryan & Deci 2000
31 Gilman & Anderman 2006
32 Gilman & Anderman 2006; Jang et al. 2009, 2010
33 Barber et al. 2005; Grolnick & Ryan 1989; Pomerantz & Wang 2009; Qin et al. 2009; Ryan & Connell 1989; Soenens & Vansteenkiste 2010; Soenens et al. 2010, 2012
34 Bean et al. 2003; Conger et al. 1997; Kakihara & Tilton-Weaver 2009; Loukas et al. 2005; Rudy et al. 2008; Shek 2007; Soenens et al. 2005a, 2005b
35 Bao & Lam 2008; Qin et al. 2009; Rudy et al. 2008; Shek 2007; Soenens & Beyers 2012; Soenens et al. 2012; Wang et al. 2007; Wong et al. 2010
36 Wang et al. 2007: 1606
37 Claes et al. 2011
38 Soenens & Vansteenkiste 2010
39 Mruk 2006a: 12
40 Crocker & Park 2003: 291; Gecas 1982: 21; Mruk 2006b: 90
41 Baumeister et al. 2003; Diener & Diener 1995; Furnham & Cheng 2000; Koch 2006: 261; O'Brien et al. 2006
42 Koch 2006: 260–261
43 Czikszentmihalyi 1990: 12
44 Suldo et al. 2009: 68
45 Suldo et al. 2009
46 Noddings 2003: 88
47 Reschly et al. 2008
48 Brown 2012: 239–240; Seligman 2011: 189
49 Rosenberg 2003b: 14
50 Wachtel 1997; Zehr 2002
51 Rosenberg 2003b: 14
52 Brown 2008: 65
53 Hartling, in Brown 2010: 46
54 Brown 2008: 14
55 Robert Oxton Bolton
56 Sagi & Hoffman 1976; Young et al. 1999; Zahn-Waxler & Radke-Yarrow 1990
57 Young et al. 1999
58 Hay et al. 1981
59 Swick 2005
60 Zahn-Waxler & Radke-Yarrow 1990
61 Phelan 2003: 16
62 Hoffman 1981
63 Radke Yarrow et al. 1973; Swick 2005; Zhou et al. 2002
64 Hoffman 1981: 125
65 Hoffman 1981: 125
66 Bowles & Gintis 2011b; Seligman 2011: 144–145
67 Kelley & Stahelski 1970; Kohn 1992: 30
68 Kelley & Stahelski 1970
69 Bowles & Gintis 2011b; Hart & Hodson 2006; Johnson & Johnson 1974; Kohn 1992: 39; Stayton et al. 1971
70 Zahn-Waxler & Radke-Yarrow 1990

71 Bowles & Gintis 2011b
72 Kohn 1992: 17–39
73 Kohn 1992: 39
74 May & Doob 1937, in Kohn 1992: 24–25
75 Madsen 1971
76 Kagan & Knight 1979; Madsen 1971; McClintock 1974;
    Miller & Thomas 1972; Munroe & Munroe 1977;
    Sommerlad & Bellingham 1972
77 Madsen 1971; Vance & Richmond 1975
78 Sagotsky et al. 1981
79 Stayton et al. 1971
80 Kochanska 1999, 2002a, 2002b; Kochanska & Aksan 2004;
    Kochanska et al. 1999, 2005; Laible & Thompson 2002
81 Hart & Hodson 2006: 17
82 Porter 1999
83 Noblit 1993: 37
84 Kohn 2005: 55
85 Thomas et al. 2008
86 Fisch et al. 1982
87 Ackerman et al. 2002, 2004; Aguilar et al. 2000; Belsky et
    al. 1998; Campbell 1995; Campbell & Ewing 1990;
    Campbell et al. 1991a, 1991b, 2000; Coldwell et al. 2006;
    Coolahan et al. 2002; Côté et al. 2006; Dearing et al.
    2006b; Duncan & Brooks-Gunn 2000; Evans & English
    2002; Evans et al. 1999; Fergusson et al. 2004, 2005;
    Fujiura & Yamaki 2000; Gest et al. 2004; Hill et al. 2006;
    Kaiser et al. 2000; Macmillan et al. 2004; McGroder 2000;
    Meyers 1999; Miller-Lewis et al. 2006; NICHD Early Child
    Care Research Network 2005; O'Leary et al. 1999; Papero
    2005; Park et al. 2002; Petterson & Albers 2001; Qi &
    Kaiser 2003; Raviv et al. 2004; Romano et al. 2005; Rubin
    et al. 2003; Shaw et al. 2003; Schaffer 1998; Shaw et al.
    1999; Smith & Farrington 2004; Spence et al. 2002;
    Sturge-Apple et al. 2006; Thompson et al. 2003; Tremblay
    2004; Votruba-Drzal 2006
88 Graue & Walsh 1998
89 Brier 1995: 273
90 Halberstadt et al. 2001
91 Aguilar et al. 2000; Baumrind 1967, 1971a; Davidov &
    Grusec 2006; Eisenberg et al. 2005; Grusec & Goodnow
    1994; Hoffman & Saltzstein 1967; Ispa et al. 2004;
    Kochanska et al. 2001, 2002a, 2003; Kuczynski 1983,
    1984; Lewis 1981; Maccoby & Martin 1983; Zahn-Waxler
    et al. 1979
92 Kohn 1994: 85
93 Eisenberg et al. 2004b
94 Ryan & Brown 2003: 75
95 Roth et al. 2009: 1121
96 Thompson et al. 2002: 50
97 Roth et al. 2009: 1121
98 Eisenberg et al. 2007b; Letzring et al. 2005; Polivy 1998
99 King 1996; Letzring et al. 2005; Polivy 1998
100 Birch et al. 1984; Brendgen et al. 2005; Casas et al. 2006;
    Deci & Ryan 1987; Deci et al. 1991, 1999a, 2001a; Farson
    1963, in Grolnick 2003; Gordon 1970; Hart & Hodson
    2006: 41; Hennessey & Amabile 1998; Kamins & Dweck
    1999; Kohn 1994, 1996a, 1999a, 2005; Lepper & Greene
    1975; McAuliffe et al. 2009; Morgan 1983; Mueller &
    Dweck 1998; Nelson et al. 2012; Rubinstein 1977; Ryan &
    Deci 1996, 2000a; Vansteenkiste et al. 2008
101 See, e.g. Arthur et al. 2003; Emmer et al. 2006, 2009;
    Evertson et al. 2003
102 Bear et al. 2003; Covaleskie 1992; McCaslin & Good
    1992; Wien 2004
103 Green 2010: 255
104 Goleman 1994
105 Murphy 2006; Winslade & Monk 2007: 11
106 Gordon 1974, 1991, 2000

Chapter 11

1   Sapon-Shevin 1999: 13
2   Cornell & Mayer 2010; Mayer & Leone 1999
3   Noguera 2003
4   Fraser & Gestwicki 2002: 100
5   Weinstein 1979: 582
6   Noddings 2003: 242
7   Fraser & Gestwicki 2002
8   Doctoroff 2001
9   Roberts et al. 1998; Vernon-Feagans & Manlove 2005
10 Weinstein 1979: 598
11 Fraser & Gestwicki 2002; Robson 1996; Smidt 1998
12 Weinstein 1979: 581
13 Feagans et al. 1994
14 Ashton & Bailey 2004; Clay et al. 2004; Kaffenberger
    2006
15 Fiese et al. 2009
16 Mukherjee et al. 2000
17 Some of these strategies were suggested by Gordon 2000:
    160–169
18 Cunningham & Wodrich 2006; Kucera & Sullivan 2011
19 Kaffenberger 2006; Shiu 2001
20 Boyle et al. 2007; Cunningham & Wodrich 2006;
    Kaffenberger 2006
21 Clay et al. 2004; Last et al. 2007; Shiu 2001
22 McCarthy 1987; Watamura et al. 2003
23 Last et al. 2007
24 Clay et al. 2004; Mukherjee et al. 2000; Nabors et al. 2008
25 Mukherjee et al. 2000
26 Nabors et al. 2008
27 Bessell 2001; Worchel-Prevatt et al. 1998
28 Mukherjee et al. 2000
29 Glaser 2000
30 Blum & Mercugliano 1997
31 Blum & Mercugliano 1997
32 Noddings 2003: 90–91
33 Bourre et al. 1984: 345; Lazarides 2010: 87–88
34 Lyon 2000: 85
35 Gesser & Koo 1996
36 Strauss 2002: 244
37 Strauss 2002: 245
38 Tabrizian 2003: 18 & 112
39 Strauss 2002: 245
40 Murray & Lyon 2006: 62
41 Burton et al. 2009: 547 & 548; www.wikipedia.org/wiki/
    Obesity#Effects_on_health. Retrieved 26/03/2011. BMI is
    calculated by dividing one's weight (in kilograms) by one's
    height (in centimetres) squared.
42 Crothers et al. 2009; l'Allemand-Jander 2010
43 Collison & Hall 1989: 443
44 www.uptodate.com/contents/definition-epidemiology-and-
    etiology-of-obesity-in-children-and-
    adolescents?source=search_result&selectedTitle=1%7E150.
    Retrieved 26/03/2011
45 Crothers et al. 2009; Strauss 2002: 247
46 Strauss 2002: 247
47 Crothers et al. 2009: 790
48 Luepker 1999
49 Bruess & Richardson 1989: 161
50 Gutin 2011; Lavoie et al. 2010; Rathus & Nevid 1989:
    260–261
51 Nagel 2012: 184
52 Dahl 1999
53 Mallick & Singh 2011: 168
54 Palagini & Rosenlicht 2011: 182
55 Mallick & Singh 2011: 168 & 171

56 Mallick & Singh 2011: 169
57 Balch 2006: 526; Siren-Tiusanen & Robinson 2001
58 Matricciani et al. 2012
59 Bronson & Merryman 2009: 36
60 Snell et al. 2007
61 Bronson & Merryman 2009: 30
62 Dahl 1999
63 Matricciani et al. 2012
64 Hansen et al. 2005
65 Hansen et al. 2005; Snell et al. 2007
66 Dahl 1999
67 Balch 2006: 525; Magee & Hale 2012; Partinen 2011: 286
68 Gregory & Sadeh 2012; Matricciani et al. 2012
69 Snell et al. 2007
70 Blum & Mercugliano 1997; Bronson & Merryman 2009;
    Dahl 1999; Gregory & Sadeh 2012; Jan 2010; Landis 2011:
    613; Lemola et al. 2012; Lyytikäinen et al. 2011; Magee &
    Hale 2012; Mallick & Singh 2011; Matricciani et al. 2012;
    Motivala et al. 2005; Murray & Lyon 2006; Partinen 2011;
    Rutters et al. 2010; Snell et al. 2007
71 Benbenishty et al. 2002a, 2002b; Brendgen et al. 2006;
    Khoury-Kassabri et al. 2008; Piekarska 2000; Shumba
    2002
72 Hyman 1995: 120
73 Brendgen et al. 2006; Delfabbro et al. 2006; Hyman &
    Perone 1998: 20
74 Delfabbro et al. 2006
75 Brendgen et al. 2006; Delfabbro et al. 2006
76 Nesbit & Philpott 2002: 33
77 Krugman & Krugman 1984; McEachern et al. 2008;
    Nesbit & Philpott 2002; Piekarska 2000
78 Brendgen et al. 2006
79 Hyman 1995: 120; Hyman & Perone 1998: 21; Krugman
    & Krugman 1984
80 Hyman 1995; Krugman & Krugman 1984
81 Krugman & Krugman 1984
82 Piekarska 2000
83 McEachern et al. 2008; Mikkelsen 1997; Sloan 1989
84 e.g. Counsellors or teachers could administer a
    questionnaire such as The My Worst School Experience
    Scale by Hyman et al. (1999): http://portal.wpspublish.
    com/portal/
    page?_pageid=53,70324&_dad=portal&_schema=PORTAL
85 Krugman & Krugman 1984
86 Piekarska 2000
87 Brendgen et al. 2006, 2007; Delfabbro et al. 2006;
    Piekarska 2000
88 Hyman 1995; Hyman & Perone 1998: 20; McEachern et al.
    2008
89 Piekarska 2000
90 Briggs 1993
91 Krugman & Krugman 1984
92 Bussey 1999; Xu et al. 2010
93 Rutter 1999
94 Ackerman et al. 2002, 2004; Aguilar et al. 2000; Belsky et
    al. 1998; Bennett et al. 2002; Bogat et al. 2006; Brown et al.
    2004; Campbell 1995; Campbell & Ewing 1990; Campbell
    et al. 1991a, 1991b, 2000; Chronis et al. 2007; Coldwell et
    al. 2006; Coolahan et al. 2002; Côté et al. 2006; Dearing
    et al. 2006b; Diener et al. 2003; Duncan & Brooks-Gunn
    2000; Evans & English 2002; Evans et al. 1999; Fergusson
    et al. 2004, 2005; Field et al. 2003; Fujiura & Yamaki 2000;
    Gershoff et al. 2007; Gest et al. 2004; Haveman & Wolfe
    1995; Hill et al. 2006; Kaiser et al. 2000; Katz & Woodin
    2002; Kitzmann 2000; Lempers et al. 1989; Macmillan et
    al. 2004; McGroder 2000; Meyers 1999; Miller-Lewis et al.
    2006; Moe & Smith 2003; Mullender et al. 2002; Nelson
    et al. 2007; NICHD Early Child Care Research Network

1999, 2005; Nix et al. 1999; O'Leary et al. 1999; Papero
    2005; Park et al. 2002; Parke et al. 2004; Petterson &
    Albers 2001; Qi & Kaisser 2003; Raviv et al. 2004;
    Romano et al. 2005; Rubin et al. 2003; Shaw et al. 2003;
    Schaffer 1998; Shaw et al. 1999; Shumow et al. 1999;
    Smith & Farrington 2004; Sohr-Preston & Scaramella
    2006; Spence et al. 2002; Steelman et al. 2002; Sternberg
    et al. 2006a; Sturge-Apple et al. 2006; Thompson et al.
    2003; Tremblay 2004; Votruba-Drzal 2006.
95 Chronis et al. 2007; Gartstein & Fagot 2003; Lundy et al.
    1999; Marchand et al. 2004; NICHD Early Child Care
    Research Network 1999; Spence et al. 2002
96 Comer 2005
97 Criss et al. 2002; Rutter 1999
98 Luthar et al. 2000
99 Cummings 1998; Cummings et al. 2003, 2006; El-Sheikh
    & Harger 2001; El-Sheikh et al. 2006; Katz & Woodin
    2002; Maughan & Cicchetti 2002; Peterson & Zill 1986;
    Shaw et al. 1999; Sternberg et al. 2006a, 2006b
100 Hyman & Snook 2000
101 Hyman & Snook 2000
102 Katz 1995
103 Fields & Boesser 2002
104 Ryan & Patrick 2001
105 Haines & McKeachie 1967
106 Frenzel et al. 2007
107 Brown 2008: 23
108 Kelley, in Robinson 2011: 261
109 Noddings 2003: 245
110 Weinstein 1983
111 Noddings 2003: 246
112 Reinke & Herman 2002; Rumberger 1995
113 Doll & Lyon 1998; Rutter 1999
114 Pianta & Walsh 1998
115 Compas 1987; Halpern 2004
116 Spirito et al. 1991
117 Halpern 2004
118 Halpern 2004; Hunter & Boyle 2004; Lewis & Frydenberg
    2002
119 Rutter 1985, 1999
120 Rutter 1999
121 Pianta & Walsh 1998
122 Greene 2008: ix
123 Thompson & Wyatt 1999
124 Campbell & Ewing 1990; Crockenberg & Litman 1990
125 Reinke & Herman 2002
126 Greene 2008: x
127 Winslade & Monk 2007

Chapter 12

1 Noddings 2003: 183
2 Kernis 2003: 3
3 Shavelson et al. 1976
4 Bong & Skaalvik 2003; Cole et al. 2001; Hoge &
   McSheffrey 1991; Pope et al. 1988; van Boxtel & Mönks
   1992
5 Bracken et al. 2000; Burns 1982
6 Kernis 2003: 3
7 Gecas 1982
8 Adapted from Mruk 2006b: 12
9 adapted from Bracken et al. 2000: 484
10 Shavelson et al. 1976; Crocker & Wolfe 2001
11 Porter 2008a: 84
12 Porter 2008a: 84
13 Cole et al. 2001; Crocker & Wolfe 2001
14 Crocker & Wolfe 2001
15 Kernis 2003: 2

16 DesRosiers et al. 1999
17 Thomaes et al. 2010
18 Brown 2012: 169 & 220
19 Baumeister et al. 2003
20 Birkeland et al. 2012: 51; Hirsch & DuBois 1991
21 Baumeister et al. 2003
22 Baumeister et al. 1993; Sommer & Baumeister 2002
23 Baumeister et al. 2003; Birkeland et al. 2012; Diener & Diener 1995; Mruk 2006b: 82; Murrell et al. 1991; Trzesniewski et al. 2006a
24 Kernis et al. 1989
25 Adapted from Mruk 2006b: 150
26 Heatherton & Vohs 2000; Murray et al. 2002
27 Pauletti et al. 2012
28 Pauletti et al. 2012
29 Brown 2012: 22
30 Brown 2012
31 Carrey et al. 1995; Fergusson & Lynskey 1997; Kim & Cicchetti 2004, 2006; Maughan & Cicchetti 2002; Mullen et al. 1996; Solomon & Serres 1999; Webster 2001
32 Baumeister et al. 1996; Frankel & Myatt 1996; Graham et al. 2006; López et al. 2006; Nansel et al. 2001; Salmivalli et al. 2005; Scholte et al. 2007
33 Pauletti et al. 2012
34 Baumeister et al. 1996; Diamantopoulou et al. 2008; Mruk 2006b: 162; Pauletti et al., 2012
35 Tafarodi et al. 2001
36 Hoza et al. 2000
37 Mayeux & Cillessen 2008
38 Assor & Tal 2012: 257; Crocker 2002; Kernis 2003: 9
39 Baumeister et al. 2003
40 Covington & Müeller 2001
41 Assor & Tal 2012: 256; Baumeister et al. 1993; Kernis 2003: 3
42 Feldhusen et al. 2000; Neumeister 2004a, 2004b; Neumeister & Finch 2006
43 Kernis 2003: 12; Kernis et al. 1989; Salmivalli et al. 1999
44 Hess 1994; Parker & Adkins 1995; Parker & Mills 1996
45 Baumeister et al. 1993
46 Gilman & Ashby 2003
47 Rudolph et al. 2005
48 Rudolph et al. 2005
49 Baumeister et al. 2003
50 Harter & Whitesell 2003: 1045
51 Rice et al. 1996; Harter & Whitesell 2003
52 Neumeister 2004b
53 Baldwin & Sinclair 1996: 1138
54 Kernis 2003: 3
55 Mruk 2006b: 68
56 Kernis 2003: 3–4; 9
57 Kernis 2003: 9
58 Kernis 2003: 13
59 Harter & Whitesell 2003: 1045
60 Mruk 2006b: 179
61 Baumeister et al. 1993, 2003; Rogers 1961, in Kernis 2003: 15
62 Mruk 2006b: 179
63 LoCicero & Ashby 2000; Neumeister 2004a ; Parker 1996; Parker & Adkins 1995; Salmivalli et al. 1999; Siegle & Schuler 2000; Wood & Care 2002
64 Gilman & Ashby 2003
65 Baumeister et al. 2003
66 Beane 1991
67 Bong & Skaalvik 2003; Marsh & Martin 2010; Mruk 2006b: 28; Pinxten et al. 2010; Tafarodi & Vu 1997; Valentine et al. 2004
68 Nelsen et al. 2000
69 Beane 1991: 28
70 Frith 2004
71 Swick 2005
72 Deci 1971
73 Deci 1972
74 Butler & Nisan 1986
75 Butler & Nisan 1986; Deci 1972
76 Birch et al. 1984; Deci & Ryan 1987; Deci et al. 1991, 1999a; Farson 1963, in Grolnick 2003; Kamins & Dweck 1999; Lepper & Greene 1975; Morgan 1983; Mueller & Dweck 1998; Rubinstein 1977; Ryan & Deci 1996, 2000a; Vansteenkiste et al. 2008
77 Bong & Skaalvik 2003
78 Porter 2006, 2008a
79 Deci & Ryan 1987; Grolnick 2003
80 Möller 2005
81 Nelsen et al. 2000
82 Porter 2006: 49, 2010: 74; Porter et al. 2008a: 30
83 Ames 1981; Ames & Felker 1979
84 Ames 1981; Ames & Felker 1979
85 Roeser et al 1998
86 Frenzel et al. 2007; Johnson & Johnson 1974
87 Ames 1978; Ames & Ames 1981
88 Ames 1981; Ames & Felker 1979
89 Johnson & Johnson 1974; Robinson 1975: 151
90 Robinson 1975: 151
91 Assor et al. 2004
92 Assor et al. 2004; Kohn 1999b: 30
93 Porter 2010: 75; Porter et al. 2008a: 33
94 Dweck & Leggett 1988; Sylva 1994
95 Brophy 1981; Dev 1997; Kohn 1996b; Porter 2006, 2008a
96 e.g. Cameron & Pierce 1994, 1996; Eisenberger & Armeli 1997
97 Cameron 2001

Chapter 13

1 Schmuck & Schmuck 2001: 115
2 Brand et al. 2008; Patrick et al. 2007
3 Goodenow 1993b; Osterman 2000
4 Burden & Fraser 1993; Finn et al. 2003; Rutter & Maughan 2002
5 McEvoy & Welker 2000
6 Merritt et al. 2012: 147
7 Ryan & Patrick 2001: 438
8 Noddings 2003: 221
9 Cefai 2012
10 Farver 1996
11 Finn et al. 2003; McMillan & Chavis 1980; Schmuck & Schmuck 2001
12 Criss et al. 2002; Dodge et al. 2003; Flook et al. 2005; Gazelle & Ladd 2003; Ladd & Burgess 2001; Ladd et al. 1999
13 Loukas & Murphy 2007
14 De Wit et al. 2011
15 Davidson et al. 2010; Goodenow 1993b; Osterman 2000; Ryan et al. 1994; Tucker et al. 2002; Wentzel 1998
16 Farrell et al. 2006
17 Mercer & DeRosier 2008
18 Doll et al. 2004, in Suldo et al. 2009: 68
19 Allen 1995; Beishuizen et al. 2001; Davies 2005; Jules & Kutnick 1997; Muller et al. 1999; Noguera 1995; Phelan et al. 1992; Schmuck & Schmuck 2001; Wentzel 1997
20 Demaray & Malecki 2002, 2003b; Esposito 1999; Pianta 1999; Pianta & Stuhlman 2004
21 Allen 1995; Beishuizen et al. 2001; Davies 2005; Jules & Kutnick 1997; Merritt et al. 2012; Muller et al. 1999; Noguera 1995; Phelan et al. 1992; Schmuck & Schmuck 2001; Suldo et al. 2009: 68–69; Wentzel 1997

22 Suldo et al. 2009
23 Baker et al. 2008; Larrivee 2005; Pianta 1999
24 Baker 2006; Birch & Ladd 1997; Decker et al. 2007;
   Graziano et al. 2007; Hamre & Pianta 2005; Ladd et al.
   1999; Murray & Greenberg 2000; Pianta & Stuhlman
   2004
25 Ladd & Burgess 2001
26 Rimm-Kaufman et al. 2002
27 Furrer & Skinner 2003
28 Decker et al. 2007; Meehan et al. 2003
29 Mercer & DeRosier 2010
30 Henricsson & Rydell 2004; Stormont 2002; Strein et al.
   1999; Tucker et al. 2002
31 Birch & Ladd 1998; Hamre & Pianta 2005; Henricsson &
   Rydell 2004; Howes 2000; Reinke & Herman 2002
32 Ryan & Patrick 2001: 454
33 Davidson et al. 2010
34 Clark & Ladd 2000; Davidov & Grusec 2006
35 Brown 2012: 231–232
36 Baker et al. 2008; Larrivee 2005; Malin 1990; Pianta 1999
37 Schmuck & Schmuck 2001
38 Chang 2003; Davidson et al. 2010; Hughes et al. 2001;
   McAuliffe et al. 2009; Mikami et al. 2012
39 Chang 2003; Ladd 1990; Osterman 2000; Waldrip et al.
   2008; Wentzel 1998
40 Malin 1990; Schmuck & Schmuck 2001
41 Crick et al. 2006a; Hoglund et al. 2008; Hymel et al. 1990;
   Ladd & Burgess 1999; Laird et al. 2001; van Lier et al.
   2005, 2012; Wentzel 2003
42 Boulard et al. 2012; Buhs & Ladd 2001; De Wit et al.
   2011; Dodge et al. 2003; Flook et al. 2005; Gazelle & Ladd
   2003; Hay et al. 2004; Johnson et al. 2000; Keiley et al.
   2000; Ladd 2006; Ladd & Burgess 2001; Laird et al. 2001;
   Letcher et al. 2009; Overbeek et al. 2010; Spinrad et al.
   2004; Stormshak et al. 1999; Sturaro et al. 2011; Wentzel
   & Caldwell 1997; Werner & Crick 2004
43 Hay et al. 2004; Laird et al. 2001
44 Peters et al. 2011
45 Schmuck & Schmuck 2001
46 Sletta et al. 1996
47 Ladd & Burgess 2001; Ladd & Troop-Gordon 2003; Parker
   & Asher 1987, 1993; Wentzel & Asher 1995; Wentzel &
   Caldwell 1997
48 Berndt 2004; Hartup 1996; Parker & Asher 1993; Waldrip
   et al. 2008
49 Ladd et al. 1996
50 Alder 2002; Brown 2004; Garza 2009; Noguera 1995;
   Pomeroy 1999; Suldo et al. 2009
51 Burgess et al. 2006; Leary & Katz 2005; Vaughn et al.
   2001
52 Champion et al. 2003
53 Ladd et al. 1996
54 Dunn & Cutting 1999; French et al. 2003; Hanish et al.
   2005a; Kupersmidt et al. 1995
55 Asher & Parker 1989; Asher & Renshaw 1981; Demaray
   et al. 2005; French et al. 2003; Hartup 1979; Johnson &
   Johnson 1991; Kemple 1991; Kohler & Strain 1993; Ladd
   et al. 1996; Perry & Bussey 1984; Rubin 1980; Ryan et al.
   1994; Wentzel 1998
56 Kohn 1996a; Solomon et al. 1996
57 Ryan & Patrick 2001: 455
58 Crockenberg et al. 1976; Deutsch 1979
59 Nelson et al. 1969; Ryan & Patrick 2001: 455; Warring et
   al. 1985
60 Kohn 1992: 30
61 Barnett & Bryan 1974; Lanzetta & Englis 1989
62 Deutsch 1979
63 Ames 1981; Bryant 1977
64 Kohn 1992: 26
65 Ames 1981; Bryant 1977
66 Bryant 1977
67 Fuller-Rowell & Doan 2010
68 Fuller-Rowell & Doan 2010
69 Pomeroy 1999
70 Mikami et al. 2012
71 Ford 1989
72 Cropper 1998
73 Battistich et al. 1997; Honig & Wittmer 1996
74 Glasser 1969, 1998a, 1998b
75 Kohn 1996a
76 Nelsen et al. 2000
77 Kohn 1996a
78 Kohn 1996a; Mintz 2003
79 Schmuck & Schmuck 2001
80 Kohn 1996a
81 Pianta et al. 2005; Wright et al. 1997
82 Downer et al. 2007
83 Finn et al. 2003; Rutter 1983; Rutter & Maughan 2002;
   Sylva 1994
84 Finn et al. 2003
85 Blatchford et al. 2001; Finn et al. 2003
86 Finn et al. 2003
87 Eccles et al. 1993
88 Porter 1999
89 Gillies 2006
90 Antil et al. 1998
91 Hertz-Lazarowitz & Shachar 1992: 77, in Gillies 2006: 272
92 Gillies 2006
93 Gillies 2006: 272–273
94 Osterman 2000
95 Cohen 1994; Osterman 2000
96 Jules 1991
97 Wentzel & Watkins 2002
98 Strong et al. 1995
99 Robinson 1990
100 Antil et al. 1998; Deutsch 1979; Gabriele 2007; Jenkins et
   al. 2003; Johnson et al. 1978; Webb 2009
101 Colangelo & Davis 2003; Robinson 1990
102 Cheng et al. 2008; Jenkins et al. 2003; Webb 2009
103 Cheng et al. 2008; Cohen 1994; Hill & Hill 1990; Gillies
   2000; Gillies & Ashman 1998; Johnson & Johnson 1989;
   Johnson et al. 1983; Webb 2009; Wentzel & Watkins 2002
104 Webb 2009
105 Webb 2009
106 Webb 2009: 12
107 Ginsberg-Block et al. 2006; Johnson & Johnson 1989;
   Slavin 1989, 1991
108 Kohn 1991; Sapon-Shevin & Schniedewind 1989
109 Buchs et al. 2011; Cohen 1994
110 Cohen 1994; Schmitt 1981
111 Ginsberg-Block et al. 2006; Slavin 1989
112 Gillies 2006
113 Jenkins et al. 2003; Johnson & Johnson 1981; Johnson et
   al. 1983; Norem-Hebeisen & Johnson 1981; Slavin &
   Cooper 1999; Warring et al. 1985
114 Smerdon 2002
115 Charles & Senter 2005; Pianta 1999
116 Damon & Phelps 1989
117 Cushing & Kennedy 1997; DuPaul et al. 1998; Miller et
   al. 2010; Wright & Cleary 2006
118 Doyle 2003; Stanley & McGrath 2006
119 Russell et al. 2001: 118
120 Carver et al. 2004; Hansen 2007; Malinsky 1997; Rivers
   & Noret 2008
121 Hansen 2007; Martin-Storey & Crosnoe 2012; Savin-
   Williams 1994

122 Busseri et al. 2006
123 Darwich et al. 2012
124 Macgillivray 2000
125 Hansen 2007
126 Jordan 1997
127 Macgillivray 2000: 306
128 Macgillivray 2000
129 Phelan et al. 1994: 437
130 Phelan et al. 1994: 440
131 Phelan et al. 1994: 440; Verkuyten 2002
132 Kiesner et al. 2003; Nesdale et al. 2005b: 192
133 Kiesner et al. 2003; Levy 1999
134 Nesdale et al. 2005b: 200; Verkuyten 2002
135 Nesdale & Lawson 2011
136 Brand et al. 2008
137 Garza 2009
138 Ford & Trotman 2001
139 Ford 2003; Ford & Harris 2000; Ford et al. 2000; Harmon 2002
140 Derman-Sparks & the ABC Task Force 1989; Ford 2003; Ford & Harris 2000; Ford et al. 2000; Ladson-Billings 1995
141 Ladson-Billings 1995; Maker & Schiever 1989
142 Ladson-Billings 1995
143 Dockett et al. 2006; Malin 1990
144 Malin 1990
145 Ullucci 2009; Weinstein et al. 2003
146 Bigler 1999
147 Greene 2008: 189–190
148 Brooks, in Gehlbach et al. 2012

Chapter 14

1 N. Rogers 1994: iv
2 Stefanou et al. 2004: 98
3 Grolnick 2003; Osterman 2000; Ryan & Deci 2000
4 Baumeister et al. 2003
5 Ryan & Stiller 1991:118
6 Grolnick & Ryan 1989; Harter 1978; Miserandino 1996; Ryan & Deci 2000; Vansteenkiste et al. 2005
7 Ciani et al. 2011; Miserandino 1996; Ryan & Stiller 1991; Vansteenkiste et al. 2004
8 Danielsen et al. 2010
9 Hadre & Reeve 2003
10 Miserandino 1996
11 DiCintio & Gee 1999; Ryan & Stiller 1991
12 Soenens et al. 2012
13 Bao & Lam 2008; Black & Deci 2000; Bong & Skaalvik 2003; Cleary & Zimmerman 2004; Deci et al. 1981; Stefanou et al. 2004: 99; Urdan & Schoenfelder 2006; Vansteenkiste et al. 2005
14 Deci et al. 1981, 1991, 1999a, 2001a; Ryan & Deci 1996, 2000
15 Black & Deci 2000
16 Porter 1999
17 Deci & Ryan 1987; Deci et al. 1981; Ryan & Deci 2000b
18 Grolnick & Ryan 1987
19 Ryan & Deci 2000b: 59
20 Grolnick & Ryan 1987
21 Abbott et al. 1998; Smerdon 2002
22 Grolnick & Ryan 1987
23 Kasser & Ryan 1996
24 Kasser & Ryan 1996: 286
25 Ryan & Deci 2000b
26 Deci & Ryan 1987
27 Cheung & Pomerantz 2012
28 Cheung & Pomerantz 2012; Ryan & Deci 2000b
29 Deci & Ryan 1987
30 Deci & Ryan 1987
31 Black & Deci 2000
32 Danielsen et al. 2010
33 Reeve & Jang 2006; Stefanou et al. 2004; Urdan & Schoenfelder 2006
34 Reeve & Jang 2006
35 Wehmeyer et al. 2004; Wheeler & Richey 2005
36 Deci & Ryan 1987
37 Wehmeyer et al. 2004
38 Allen 1995
39 Bao & Lam 2008; Cordova & Lepper 1996; Dunlap et al. 1994
40 Amabile & Gitomer 1984
41 Tileston 2004: 1
42 Bryson 2004: 19; Canter 2010: 73
43 Curwin & Mendler 1989: 83
44 Bryson 2004: 20
45 Ames 1992: 266
46 Assor et al. 2002
47 Kohn 1996a: 78
48 Deci & Ryan 1987; Patall et al. 2010
49 Stefanou et al. 2004
50 Stefanou et al. 2004
51 Stefanou et al. 2004
52 Jang et al. 2010; Sierens et al. 2009
53 DiCintio & Gee 1999: 234
54 Sierens et al. 2009
55 Rutter 1983
56 McMillan & Chavis 1986
57 Bong & Skaalvik 2003
58 Bandura 1993: 138
59 Gecas 1982
60 Knight 1995
61 Bong & Skaalvik 2003
62 Bandura 1993: 144
63 Bandura 1993: 144
64 Bong & Skaalvik 2003
65 Bong & Skaalvik 2003: 32; Urdan & Schoenfelder 2006
66 Patrick et al. 2007
67 Weiner 2000
68 Seligman 1975
69 Robertson 2000
70 Seligman 1995
71 Rogers 2003
72 Tollefson 2000; Weiner 2000
73 Glasser 1985: 244
74 Bandura 1986
75 Skiba et al. 1997
76 Alberto & Troutman 2013; Bailey 1991; Kaplan & Carter 1995
77 Schloss & Smith 1998
78 Kohn 2005: 84
79 Eisenberger et al. 1999
80 Deci et al. 1999b

Chapter 15

1 Robert Byrne, in McKay et al. 2010: 73
2 Mruk 2006b
3 Seligman 2011
4 Csikszentmihalyi 1990: 9
5 Csikszentmihalyi 1990: 223
6 Soenens & Vansteenkiste 2010: 76
7 Ben-Shahar 2007
8 McKay et al. 2010: 90
9 Ben-Shahar 2007
10 Csikszentmihalyi 1990: 216–217
11 Csikszentmihalyi 1990: 217
12 Csikszentmihalyi 1990: 218
13 McKay et al. 2010: 45; Robinson & Aronica 2009

14 Sheldon, in Ben-Shahar 2007: 71
15 McKay et al. 2010: 34–42 & 56
16 Csikszentmihalyi 1990: 46
17 Ben-Shahar 2007
18 Robinson & Aronica 2013: 120; Suldo et al. 2009: 68
19 Brown 2010: 80
20 Noddings 2003: 17
21 Seligman 2002: 9
22 Csikszentmihalyi 1990; Seligman 2002: 116
23 Robinson & Aronica 2009, 2013
24 Glasser 1988: 30; Noddings 2003: 4
25 Robinson & Aronica 2009
26 Robinson & Aronica 2009, 2013
27 Robinson 2011; Robinson & Aronica 2009
28 Robinson & Aronica 2009: 13
29 Robinson 2011; Robinson & Aronica 2013: xii-xiii; Seligman 2011: 79
30 Robinson & Aronica 2009, 2013; Seligman 2002
31 McKay et al. 2010: 104; Robinson 2011; Robinson & Aronica 2009: 46–51
32 Gardner 1983, 1999; Kelly & Moon 1998; Vialle 1997
33 Morgan 1996; Smerechansky-Metzger 1995
34 Geake 2008
35 Robinson & Aronica 2009: 42
36 Csikszentmihalyi & Wolfe 2000: 81; Davis 2003: 311
37 Abridged from Brown 2012: 212
38 Robinson & Aronica 2009: 67 & 77
39 Robinson & Aronica 2009: 57
40 Csikszentmihalyi & Wolfe 2000: 91; Robinson 2011: 47 & 139
41 Robinson 2011: 190
42 Cheng 1993; Csikszentmihalyi & Wolfe 2000; Davis & Rimm 2004; Haensley & Reynolds 1989; Rimm 2003; Robinson 2011; Sternberg 1988; Sternberg & Lubart 1991; Wallace 1986
43 adapted from Parries, in Davis & Rimm 2004: 214
44 Davis & Rimm 2004: 211
45 Richards, in Robinson 2011: 228
46 Brown 2012: 65
47 Davis & Rimm 2004: 208
48 Amabile 1984; Csikszentmihalyi & Wolfe 2000: 86
49 Csikszentmihalyi & Wolfe 2000: 88
50 Han & Marvin 2002
51 Han & Marvin 2002
52 Peterson 2006: 58–59; Seligman 2002: 35 & 39
53 von Oech 1983, in Davis & Rimm 2004: 226
54 Seligman 2002, 2011
55 Seligman 2002: 43
56 Cordova & Lepper 1996; Parker & Lepper 1992
57 Robinson & Aronica 2013: 28
58 Robinson & Aronica 2009, 2013
59 Thurman, in Brown 2010: 115
60 Robinson & Aronica 2009: 186
61 Robinson & Aronica 2009: 179–184. See Robinson & Aronica 2013 for activities that can allow ourselves or others to identify our passions.
62 Robinson & Aronica 2013: 68
63 McKay et al. 2010: 166
64 Seligman 2011: 78
65 Robinson & Aronica 2013: 226
66 McKay et al. 2010: 78–79
67 McKay et al. 2010: 70–85
68 Robinson & Aronica 2009: 139
69 Dewey 1916/1944
70 Robinson & Aronica 2013: 132; Seligman 2011
71 Robinson & Aronica 2009: 96
72 Noddings 2003: 2

Chapter 16

1 Kaplan et al. 2002: 195
2 Glasser 1992b: 694
3 Noddings 2003: 77
4 Robinson 2011: 248
5 Robinson 2011: 251
6 Comer 2005: 762
7 Brown 2004: 276
8 Kohn 1996a
9 Rogers & Freiberg 1994
10 adapted from Davis 2006: 55
11 Bailey 2002
12 Noddings 2003: 86
13 Clinkenbeard 2012; Patrick et al. 2011: 368
14 Baker-Sennett et al. 2008; Donohue et al. 2003; Gmitrova & Gmitrov 2003; Huffman & Speer 2000; Huston-Stein et al. 1977; Kontos et al. 2002; Maccoby & Lewis 2003; NICHD Early Child Care Research Network 2003; Stipek et al. 1998; Wiltz & Klein 2001
15 Roeser et al 1998; Skinner et al. 2008
16 Patrick et al. 2011
17 Wright et al. 1997
18 Brophy 1983; Brophy & Good 1970; Mikami et al. 2012
19 Many gifted learners are aware that, although they themselves value their special skills, many others – including their parents, teachers and peers – do not (Colangelo 2003; Coleman & Cross 1988; Cross et al. 1991, 1992; Kerr et al. 1988; Swiatek 1995; Tidwell 1980; van Boxtel & Mönks 1992).
20 Mikami et al. 2012
21 Brophy & Good 1970
22 Patrick et al. 2011
23 Strong et al. 1995; Jones & Jones 2013: 219
24 Brophy 1983; Tenenbaum & Ruck 2007
25 Brophy 1983: 646
26 Hickey 1997: 188; Ryan & Stiller 1991
27 Chien et al. 2010
28 Schmuck & Schmuck 2001
29 Schmuck & Schmuck 2001
30 Little 2012
31 Seligman 2011: 188
32 Kohn 2011: 2
33 Noddings 2003: 88
34 Newmann & Wehlage 1993: 8; Newmann et al. 1996; Wehlage et al. 1996a: 22 & 25
35 Wehlage et al. 1996a: 33
36 Glasser 1969, 1998b
37 Bruner 1960, in Noddings 2003: 111; Fields & Boesser 2002; Noddings 2003: 112 & 251
38 Glasser 1998a
39 Glasser 1969, 1992b
40 Schwinger & Stiensmeier-Pelster 2011
41 Rubie-Davies et al. 2012
42 Kaplan et al. 2002
43 Patrick et al. 2011
44 Miserandino 1996
45 Hughes et al. 2011: 3
46 Edwards & Surma 1980
47 Wolters & Daugherty 2007
48 Wolters & Daugherty 2007
49 Hughes et al. 2011
50 Lau & Nie 2008
51 DiPrima et al. 2011; Neumeister 2004b
52 Elliot & McGregor 2001; Wigfield & Cambria 2010: 16
53 Roeser et al 1998
54 Vansteenkiste et al. 2008

55 Hughes et al. 2011; Kaplan et al. 2002; Patrick et al. 2011; Roeser et al 1998
56 Hughes et al. 2011; Miserandino 1996
57 Lau & Nie 2008; Wolters & Daugherty 2007
58 Wentzel & Wigfield 1998
59 Muller et al. 1999
60 Rubie-Davies 2010
61 Tenenbaum & Ruck 2007
62 Brophy 1983
63 Brophy 1983; Good & Brophy 2008; Muller et al. 1999; Rubie-Davies 2006
64 Rubie-Davies 2006
65 Good & Brophy 2008
66 Good & Brophy 2008
67 Alder 2002; Ware 2006
68 Brophy 1983: 657
69 Brophy 1983
70 Soenens & Vansteenkiste 2010: 76
71 Banks 2005
72 Meyer & Turner 2006
73 Op 't Eynde & Turner 2006
74 Pintrich 2003
75 Marchant et al. 2001
76 Kohn 1996a
77 Appleton et al. 2008: 379
78 Glasser 1998a
79 Hidi & Renninger 2006: 119
80 Hickey 1997: 181; Wigfield & Cambria 2010: 9
81 Mitchell 1993
82 Hidi & Renninger 2006
83 Hidi & Renninger 2006: 114
84 Mitchell 1993
85 Rogers & Freiberg 1994
86 Hidi & Renninger 2006
87 Dewey 1913, in Mitchell 1993
88 Long et al. 2007
89 Hidi & Renninger 2006: 115
90 Stefanou et al. 2004
91 Long et al. 2007
92 Ware 2006
93 Hidi & Renninger 2006
94 Hidi & Renninger 2006
95 Hidi & Renninger 2006
96 Noddings 2003: 253
97 Noddings 2003: 207
98 Noddings 2003: 207
99 Noddings 2003: 167
100 Berndt & Miller 1990; Deci et al. 1991
101 Tollefson 2000; Weiner 2000
102 Dweck 2008
103 Dweck 2008
104 Dweck 2008; Dweck & Leggett 1988; Kavussanu & Harnisch 2000
105 Porter 2005: 220
106 Dweck 2008
107 Dweck 2008
108 Dweck 2008
109 Weiner 2000
110 Pintrich 2003
111 Zimmerman 2000: 87
112 Zimmerman 2000: 86
113 Zimmerman 2000: 86–87
114 Zimmerman 2000: 88
115 Silverman et al. 1995
116 Chan 1996; DiCintio & Gee 1999; Milgram & Toubiana 1999; Vallerand et al. 1994
117 Deci et al. 1994
118 DiCintio & Gee 1999; Glasser 1998; Tollefson 2000; Wentzel 1997
119 Jones & Jones 2013: 217
120 Berndt & Miller 1990; Deci et al. 1991; Hickey 1997
121 Jones & Jones 2013: 218; Wigfield & Cambria 2010; Wigfield & Eccles 2000
122 Berndt & Miller 1990; Deci et al. 1991
123 Wigfield & Cambria 2010: 27
124 Wigfield & Eccles 2000
125 Wigfield & Eccles 2010: 16
126 Glasser 1992b, 1998b; Jang 2008
127 Wentzel 2000
128 Pintrich 2003
129 Wentzel 2000
130 Wentzel 2000
131 Dweck 1986; Elliott & Dweck 1988
132 Ames 1992
133 Ames 1992; Dweck 1986; Urdan & Schoenfelder 2006
134 Daniels et al. 2009; Dweck 1986; Urdan & Schoenfelder 2006
135 Dweck 1986
136 Neumeister 2004a
137 Régner et al. 2007
138 Urdan & Mestas 2006: 355
139 Urdan & Mestas 2006: 355
140 Elliot & McGregor 2001; Elliott & Murayama 2008: 625; Pintrich 2003
141 Elliot & McGregor 2001
142 LoCicero & Ashby 2000; Parker 1996; Parker & Adkins 1995; Siegle & Schuler 2000; Wood & Care 2002
143 Ames 1992; Patrick et al. 2011
144 Dweck 1986
145 Brown 2008: xxiii & 5
146 Harackiewicz et al. 2002
147 Urdan & Mestas 2006: 362
148 Urdan & Mestas 2006. An opposite motivation is not to excel so that they do not distinguish themselves from the peer group.
149 Vallerand et al. 1986
150 Dweck & Leggett 1988; Kavussanu & Harnisch 2000; Pintrich 2000
151 Dweck 1986; Dweck & Leggett 1988; Sylva 1994
152 Dweck 1986; Kamins & Dweck 1999
153 Chan 1988; Coleman & Fults 1982; Craven & Marsh 1997; Frenzel et al. 2007; Gross 1997; Hoge & Renzulli 1993; Marsh & Craven 1998; Marsh et al. 1995; Moon et al. 2002; Olszewski et al. 1987; Rutter & Maughan 2002; Schneider et al. 1989; Wright & Leroux 1997. Nevertheless, the decline in academic self-esteem is felt only in the initial weeks of placement in the gifted program (Moon et al. 2002; Preckel et al. 2010), remains at higher levels than for non-gifted learners, and is partly offset by a gain in the social self-esteem.
154 Craven & Marsh 1997; Gross 1997
155 Feldhusen et al. 2000; Neumeister 2004a, 2004b; Neumeister & Finch 2006
156 DiPrima et al. 2011
157 Brown 2010: 56
158 Wolters & Daugherty 2007
159 Covington & Müeller 2001
160 Mueller & Dweck 1998
161 Covington & Müeller 2001; Diseth & Kobbeltvedt 2010; Kaplan et al. 2002; Lau & Nie 2008; Leondari & Gonida 2007; Sylva 1994; Thomas & Gadbois 2007
162 Gadbois & Sturgeon 2010; Leondari & Gonida 2007; Thomas & Gadbois 2007
163 Gadbois & Sturgeon 2010
164 Leondari & Gonida 2007

165 Harackiewicz et al. 2002; Régner et al. 2007
166 Schutz et al. 2006: 345
167 Op 't Eynde & Turner 2006
168 Pekrun 2006: 326
169 Pintrich 2003
170 Goetz et al. 2008: 26; Meyer & Turner 2006; Op 't Eynde & Turner 2006
171 Pekrun 2006: 317
172 Pekrun 2006: 317; Wigfield & Cambria 2010: 5
173 Pekrun 2006: 323
174 Pekrun 2006: 326; Pintrich 2003
175 Mikulas & Vodanovich 1993: 4
176 Mikulas & Vodanovich 1993
177 Goetz et al. 2007; Harris 2000; Hill & Perkins 1985; Little 2012; Pekrun et al. 2010
178 Hill & Perkins 1985
179 Acee et al. 2010; Pekrun et al. 2010
180 Pekrun et al. 2010
181 Larson & Richards 1991: 433
182 Pekrun et al. 2010: 536
183 Larson & Richards 1991: 429, 430 & 435; Mikulas & Vodanovich 1993; Robinson 1975
184 Acee et al. 2010; Daschmann et al. 2011; Harris 2000; Little 2012; Pekrun et al. 2010
185 Pekrun et al. 2010
186 Larson & Richards 1991: 438; Robinson 1975
187 Daschmann et al. 2011
188 Csikszentmihalyi 1990; Robinson & Aronica 2009
189 Csikszentmihalyi 1990
190 Csikszentmihalyi 1990: 67
191 Furlong & Christenson 2008
192 Appleton et al. 2008: 379
193 Skinner et al. 2008: 765
194 Irvin 2012
195 Appleton et al. 2008
196 Appleton et al. 2008
197 Daniels et al. 2009
198 Appleton et al. 2008; Green et al. 2012; Hughes et al. 2011
199 Appleton et al. 2008
200 Miserandino 1996; Skinner et al. 2008: 766
201 Appleton et al. 2008
202 Loughran 2010: 28
203 Ames 1992; Diseth & Kobbeltvedt 2010
204 Prat-Sala & Redford 2010: 294 & 300
205 Prat-Sala & Redford 2010: 292
206 Meyer et al. 2009
207 Diseth & Kobbeltvedt 2010
208 Loughran 2010: 28
209 Loughran 2010: 29
210 Prat-Sala & Redford 2010: 288
211 Vansteenkiste et al. 2005
212 Pintrich 2003
213 Wigfield & Cambria 2010: 24
214 Ames 1992; Hickey 1997: 183
215 Deutsch 1979: 393
216 Wentzel & Wigfield 1998
217 Bong & Skaalvik 2003
218 Ames 1992
219 Koh & Luke 2009
220 Koh et al. 2012: 138
221 Koh et al. 2012: 137
222 Kohn 199b: 42
223 Shaklee 1992
224 Fatouros 1986
225 Glasser 1998a
226 Frey et al. 2012
227 Hooper & Edmondson 1998
228 Frey et al. 2012
229 Koh & Luke 2009; Koh et al. 2012; Wehlage et al. 1996a: 23
230 Frey et al. 2012: 14
231 Frey et al. 2012: 14
232 Kohn 1999b: 75
233 Koh & Luke 2009; Kohn 199b: 75; Noddings 2003: 252
234 Roeser et al. 1998: 346; Smerdon 2002
235 Ryan & Stiller 1991
236 Roeser et al. 1998: 346
237 Smerdon 2002
238 Ames 1992; Kohn 1999b: 32
239 Glasser 1992a: 217; Kohn 2004: 78; Pope 2001
240 Pope 2001: 122
241 Phelan et al. 1994: 423
242 Glasser 1992a: 231
243 Glasser 1969: 72
244 Kohn 2011: 2
245 Deutsch 1979; Kohn 1999b: 37-38, 2004: 79
246 Phelan et al. 1994: 424; Pope 2001: 83
247 Deutsch 1979
248 Butler & Nisan 1986: 215
249 Ames 1992
250 Ames 1992; Kohn 1999b
251 Harter 1978; Kohn 2004: 76
252 Pope 2001: 68
253 Deutsch 1979
254 Pope 2001: 154
255 Corno 1992
256 Pope 2001: 169
257 Phelan et al. 1994: 421
258 Butler & Nisan 1986; Daniels et al. 2009
259 Ames 1992
260 Deutsch 1979
261 Butler & Nisan 1986; Tapola & Niemivirta 2008; Urdan & Mestas 2006
262 Deutsch 1979
263 Kohn 2004: 77
264 Pope 2001: 161
265 Deutsch 1979; Kohn 1999b
266 Kohn 2004: 84
267 Glasser 1998a, 1998b
268 Marks et al. 1996b: 50; Wehlage et al. 1996a: 43
269 Marks et al. 1996b: 58. A percentile ranking is a way of expressing how students perform compared to each other. A PR of 30 means that the student did as well as or better than 30 per cent of the population; a ranking of 60 means that the student achieved as well or better than 60 per cent of the cohort.
270 Noddings 2003: 209
271 Porter 2005
272 Robinson & Sloutsky 2004
273 Geake 2008; Krätzig & Arbuthnott 2006
274 McIntyre 1996
275 Gohm et al. 1998
276 King et al. 2010
277 Hilton & Hilton 2010: 240; Wehlage et al. 1996a: 37
278 Rogers & Freiberg 1994
279 Hilton & Hilton 2010: 250; Loughran 2010: 145-146; Wehlage et al. 1996a: 37
280 Noddings 2003: 148
281 Greene 2008
282 Greene 2008: 25
283 Greene: 2008: 288
284 Greene 2008: 28
285 Ashman & Conway 1989; Kaplan & Carter 1995; Yell et al. 2012
286 Cooper et al. 2006; Corno 1996

287 Kouzma & Kennedy 2002
288 Trautwein & Lüdtke 2007
289 Trautwein et al. 2006
290 Cooper et al. 2006: 9
291 Elias et al. 1997, in Norris 2003: 315; Greene: 2008:
     287–288; Halberstadt et al. 2001; Rogers 1951; Rogus
     1985: 271
292 Trautwein et al. 2006
293 Trautwein et al. 2009
294 Cooper et al. 1998, 2006
295 Cooper et al. 2006; Trautwein & Lüdtke 2007
296 Cooper et al. 1998
297 Cooper et al. 1998; Gehlbach et al. 2012
298 Cooper et al. 1998; Kohn 2006: 11; Kouzma & Kennedy
     2002
299 Kouzma & Kennedy 2002
300 Kohn 2006; Kouzma & Kennedy 2002: 197
301 Cooper et al. 2006
302 Trautwein & Lüdtke 2007; Trautwein et al. 2009
303 Sam Sellery, pers. comm.
304 Trautwein & Lüdtke 2007; Trautwein et al. 2009
305 Dettmers et al. 2010; Trautwein et al. 2006
306 Dettmers et al. 2010; Patall et al. 2010; Trautwein et al.
     2006
307 Dettmers et al. 2010; Patall et al. 2010; Trautwein et al.
     2006
308 Kohn 2006: 64
309 Glasser 1998a
310 Noddings 2003: 257
311 Newmann et al. 1996: 161
312 Marks et al. 1996a: 226
313 Glasser 1969, 1998a; Kohn 2006
314 Corno1996
315 McCaslin & Good 1992

Chapter 17

1   Porter & McKenzie 2000: 136
2   Rogers & Freiberg 1994
3   Brown 2012: 234
4   Greene 2008: 54; Gregory & Ripski 2008
5   Baumrind 1971b: 99; Lewis 1981
6   Hargreaves 2000
7   Hargreaves 2000
8   Hargreaves 2000: 823
9   Alder 2002: 245; Noblit et al. 1995: 684
10 Gordon 2000: 54
11 Brenner & Fox 1999; Coolahan et al. 2002; Grolnick 2003;
    Grolnick & Ryan 1989
12 Brown 2010
13 Gordon 1999
14 Glasser 1998b
15 Cate Crombie, pers. comm. 15/06/2013
16 Hargreaves 2000
17 Goleman 1994
18 Eisenberg et al. 2004b
19 Kochanska et al. 2001
20 Gilliom et al. 2002
21 Murphy et al. 1999
22 Eisenberg et al. 2000
23 Harris 2007; McKay et al. 2012: 168
24 Peterson 2006: 58
25 Rosenberg 2005: 11
26 Ellis 1962; Gonzalez et al. 2004
27 Rosenberg 2003a
28 adapted from Hart & Hodson 2006: 135
29 Kotzman 1989: 35
30 Rosenberg 2003b: 8

31 Kohn 2005: 127
32 Bolton 1987: 34–39; Kotzman 1989: 60–66
33 Rosenberg 2003a: 92
34 Hart & Hodson 2006: 107
35 Rosenberg 2003b
36 Rosenberg 2003b: 13
37 Hart & Hodson 2006
38 Cate Crombie, downloaded from www.metacommunicate.
    com 15/06/2013
39 Kotzman 1989: 35
40 Rosenberg 2003b: 8
41 Gordon 1974, 2000
42 Kotzman 1989: 33
43 Kotzman 1989: 80–81
44 Kotzman 1989: 89–90
45 Kohn 2005
46 Bolton 1987: 20–21; Gordon 1974, 2000; Hart & Hodson
    2006; Kernis et al. 2000
47 Kotzman 1989: 127
48 Kotzman 1989: 121
49 Jakubowski 1977
50 Kotzman 1989: 127
51 Jakubowski & Lange 1978: 42–43; Kotzman 1989:
    116–117
52 Gordon 1997: 37
53 Bolton 1987: 173
54 Rosenberg 2003a: 79
55 Hart & Hodson 2004, 2006; Rosenberg 2003a
56 Rosenberg 2003a: 83
57 Baumrind 1971b: 99
58 Greene 2008: 75
59 Gordon 2000: 246
60 Greene 2008: 169
61 adapted from Spirito et al. 2012: 245
62 Gordon 2000: 263; Greene 2008, 2010
63 Greene 2008: 125
64 Greene 2008: 157
65 Gordon 1997: 90
66 Bear et al. 2003; Mayall 2002
67 Hargreaves 2000
68 Hargreaves 2000
69 Gordon 1997: 91–92
70 Gordon 1997: 91
71 Rosenberg 2003a: 144
72 Rosenberg 2005: 12
73 Hart & Hodson 2004: 86
74 Hart & Hodson 2004: 86
75 Rosenberg 2003b: 14
76 Rosenberg 2003b: 14
77 Greene 2008: 58
78 Greene 2008: 94

Chapter 18

1   Faber et al. 1995
2   Porter 2010
3   Murphy 2006
4   Porter 2010: 134
5   Porter 2010: 133
6   Goleman 1994
7   Mill 1859/1978
8   Porter 2010: 21
9   Porter 2010: 135
10 Porter 1999
11 I learned this from Dr Phil McGraw.
12 Omer 2001
13 Gordon 2000: 22

14 Gordon 2000: 23
15 Goleman 1994

Chapter 19

1 Baruch Shalem, in Selekman 2006: 27
2 Murphy 2006
3 Winslade & Monk 2007: 11
4 Banks 2005: 17
5 Selekman 2010
6 Adapted from Kelly et al. 2008: 87; Murphy 2008: 42
7 Winslade & Monk 2007: 2
8 Murphy 2008: 42
9 Murphy & Duncan 2007: 58
10 Murphy & Duncan 2007: 59
11 Bertolino & Schultheis 2002: 49–52
12 Murphy & Duncan 2007: 27
13 Murphy 2008
14 Nichols & Schwartz 1995
15 De Jong & Berg 2002; Molnar & de Shazer 1987; Murphy 1994
16 Haley 1980; Molnar & Lindquist 1989
17 Winslade & Monk 2007: 47
18 Winslade & Monk 2007: 44
19 Huntley 1999
20 Winslade & Monk 2007: 45
21 Winslade & Monk 2007: 7
22 Winslade & Monk 2007: 12
23 Morgan 2000
24 Harris 2007
25 Harris 2007
26 De Jong & Berg 2002; Murphy 2008: 92; Sklare 2005
27 Murphy 2008: 96
28 Berg & Steiner 2003
29 de Shazer 1988; Murphy 2008: 38 & 101; Murphy & Duncan 2007: 21
30 Murphy 2008: 58
31 Kral & Kowalski 1989; Rhodes 1993; Wagner & Gillies 2001
32 Murphy & Duncan 2007
33 Murphy 2008: 41
34 Murphy 2008: 64, 67 & 88; Murphy & Duncan 2007: 23; Selekman 2010: 193
35 I usually find that hoarders have lost a parent at a young age, and are stocking up in case of the next unpredictable privation.
36 You'll be glad to hear she is no longer a school counsellor.
37 Murphy 2008: 104–106
38 Carey & Russell 2003; Selekman 2010: 184
39 De Jong & Berg 2002; Porter 2007: 281; Sklare 2005: 56
40 Winslade & Monk 2007: 42
41 Murphy & Duncan 2007: 34
42 De Jong & Berg 2002
43 Perry 1999
44 de Shazer 1988
45 Winslade & Monk 2007: 61
46 Murphy 2006
47 Durrant 1995
48 Molnar & de Shazer 1987
49 Murphy 2006
50 Fox 2003
51 Sklare 2005
52 Morgan 1999
53 Kowalski 1990
54 Murphy & Duncan 2007
55 Murphy 2008: 108
56 de Shazer 1988: 10
57 Murphy & Duncan 2007

58 de Shazer et al. 1986: 212, de Shazer et al. 2007; Murphy 2008: 40

Chapter 20

1 Covaleskie 1992: 175
2 Kohn 1999: 30
3 Walker & Eaton-Walker 2000
4 Noguera 1995
5 Kaplan & Carter 1995
6 e.g. Gartrell 1987a
7 Akom 2001: 60
8 Winslade & Monk 1999
9 Noddings 2003: 60
10 Dower 1997
11 Johnny 2006: 23
12 Society for Medical Anthropology 2007: 235. Somalia has not signed the Convention on the Rights of the Child because it has no functioning government equipped to sign anything (Ruck & Horn 2008) and the US has not because it would be in violation because of its deployment of child soldiers (aged under 18), imprisonment for life of child criminals and its imposition of the death penalty on criminals who were children at the time of their offence (Schechter & Bochenek 2008; Society for Medical Anthropology 2007: 236).
13 Johnny 2006
14 Johnson et al. 1994; Kohn 1994: 74
15 Kohn 1996a
16 Gordon 2000: 211
17 Noddings 2003: 85
18 McCaslin & Good 1992
19 Katz 1995
20 Alberto & Troutman 2013: 29; OSEP Center on Positive Behavioral Interventions and Supports 2000; Wheeler & Richey 2005
21 Martin & Pear 2011: 385
22 Australian Early Childhood Association 1991: 4
23 Jones & Jones 2013
24 Campbell & Ewing 1990; Crockenberg & Litman 1990
25 Afifi et al. 2006; Thompson & Wyatt 1999
26 Reinke & Herman 2002
27 Charles & Senter 2005; Jones & Jones 2013
28 Albrecht & Braaten 2008; Horner et al. 2010; Osler & Vincent 2003; Pas et al. 2011; Skiba & Peterson 1999; R. Slee 1995
29 Skiba & Peterson 1999
30 Birch & Ladd 1997; Brophy & Good 1970; Childs & McKay 2001; Jones & Dindia 2004; Stuhlman & Pianta 2002
31 Henning-Stout 1998
32 Osler & Vincent 2003; R. Slee 1995
33 Arnold 1996; Hallahan & Kauffman 2003
34 Osler & Vincent 2003
35 Kerr 1996; Kline & Short 1991; Loeb & Jay 1987
36 Butler-Por 1987; Freeman 1996; Kerr 1996, 1997; Reis & Callahan 1989
37 Thompson & Rudolph 2000: 215
38 Maccoby & Martin 1983
39 Porter 2010; Rogers 2002
40 Lewin et al. 1939
41 Lewin et al. 1939: 298
42 Lewin et al. 1939: 298
43 Battistich et al. 2004; Rimm-Kaufman et al. 2007
44 Rimm-Kaufman & Chiu 2007
45 Gregory et al. 2010
46 Pellerin 2005

47 Pellerin 2005
48 Freiberg et al. 1995
49 Hawkins et al. 2001
50 Freiberg et al. 1995; Hawkins et al. 2001
51 Perry et al. 2007
52 Emmer & Aussiker 1990
53 Freiberg et al. 1995
54 Comer 2005
55 Comer 2005
56 Comer 2005
57 Gregory & Ripski 2008
58 Gregory & Ripski 2008
59 Brophy & McCaslin 1992: 14; Kounin 1970
60 Porter 1999
61 Gordon 1970, 1974
62 Porter 1999
63 Fantuzzo et al. 1988
64 Valeski & Stipek 2001
65 Emmer & Aussiker 1990
66 Cedar & Levant 1990; Krebs 1986; Levant 1983; Root & Levant 1984; Schultz 1981; Schultz & Khan 1982; Schultz & Nystul 1980; Schultz et al. 1980
67 Wood & Davidson 1987, 1993
68 Wood 1985, 2003
69 Barber et al. 2005: 17
70 e.g. Gershoff et al. 2010
71 Barber et al. 2005: 63
72 Wentzel 1997
73 Aguilar et al. 2000; Belsky et al. 1998; Campbell 1995; Shaw et al. 2000; Smith & Farrington 2004
74 Brody et al. 2001; Gaylord-Harden 2008; Ryan & Stiller 1991
75 Aguilar et al. 2000; Alink et al. 2008; Campbell & Ewing 1990; Campbell et al. 1996; Coldwell et al. 2006; Combs-Ronto et al. 2009; Côté et al. 2006; Crockenberg & Litman 1990; Denham et al. 2000; Donovan et al. 2000; Fergusson et al. 2005; Hoffman 1960; Joussemet et al. 2008; Loukas et al. 2005; McFadyen-Ketchum et al. 1996; Miller-Lewis et al. 2006; NICHD Early Child Care Research Network 2004b; O'Leary et al. 1999; Prinzie et al. 2006; Romano et al. 2005; Rubin et al. 2003; Scaramella et al. 2008; Shaw et al. 2003; Spieker et al. 1999; Stormshak et al. 2000; Tremblay 2004; Tremblay et al. 2004; Underwood et al. 2009; Veenstra et al. 2006
76 Kochanska et al. 2001, 2003
77 Eccles et al. 1991; Hoffman 1960; Loukas 2009; Williams et al. 2009
78 Hoffman 1960; Veenstra et al. 2006
79 Kochanska 1995; Kochanska et al. 2007
80 Kochanska et al. 2005a; Parpal & Maccoby 1985
81 Aunola & Nurmi 2004; Baumrind 1967, 1971b; Crockenberg & Litman 1990; Denham et al. 2000; Donovan et al. 2000; Feldman & Klein 2003; Gilliom et al. 2002; Hoeve et al. 2009; Kochanska et al. 2005a; Lewis 1981; McLeod et al. 1994; Miller-Lewis et al. 2006; Parpal & Maccoby 1985; Rubin et al. 2003; C.L. Smith et al. 2004; Stayton et al. 1971; Stormshak et al. 2000; Weiss & Schwarz 1996; Zahn-Waxler et al. 1979
82 Brody et al. 2001; Hoeve et al. 2009; Miller et al. 2009; Prinzie et al. 2006; Pulkkinen & Hämäläinen 1995; Trinkner et al. 2012
83 Miller et al. 2009; Prinzie et al. 2006
84 Farrell & White 1998
85 Brody et al. 2001; Criss et al. 2003; Hoeve et al. 2009
86 Stattin & Kerr 2000. An exception to this pattern was that high rates of parental knowledge about their adolescents' activities predicted less delinquency but also

a decline in psychosocial maturity and academic engagement (Williams & Steinberg 2011).
87 Stattin & Kerr 2000; Trinkner et al. 2012; Williams & Steinberg 2011
88 van IJzendoorn 1997: 712–13
89 Kochanska 1997; Sears et al. 1957, in Spera 2005
90 Hoffman & Saltzstein 1967; Kuczynski 1983, 1984
91 Dubanoski et al. 1983; Palmer & Hollin 2001
92 Brody & Shaffer 1982; Hoffman & Saltzstein 1967
93 Assor et al. 2004; Bear et al. 2003; Covaleskie 1992; McCaslin & Good 1992; Wien 2004
94 Eisenberg et al. 1983; van IJzendoorn 1997: 714
95 Hoffman & Saltzstein 1967; Walker et al. 2000; Walker & Taylor 1991
96 Lewis 1981
97 Kochanska 2002a
98 Batson et al. 1978; Fabes et al. 1989
99 Sapon-Shevin 1996: 196
100 Davidov & Grusec 2006; Hastings et al. 2000; Radke Yarrow et al. 1973; Strayer & Roberts 2004b; Zahn-Waxler et al. 1979
101 McCord 1991
102 van IJzendoorn 1997
103 Kins et al. 2012
104 Dornbusch et al. 1987; Eccles et al. 1991; Ginsberg & Bronstein 1993; Gonzalez-DeHass et al. 2005; Gottfried et al. 1994; Grolnick & Ryan 1989; Huffman & Speer 2000; Koestner et al. 1984; Maccoby & Lewis 2003; Maccoby & Martin 1983; Parker et al. 1999; Paulson et al. 1998; Steinberg et al. 1989, 1992, 1994; Stipek et al. 1998
105 Parker et al. 1999
106 Duchesne & Ratelle 2010; Roth et al. 2009
107 Huffman & Speer 2000; Stipek et al. 1995, 1998
108 Baumrind 1991; Duchesne & Ratelle 2010; Frodi et al. 1985; Moorman & Pomerantz 2008; Roth et al. 2009
109 Ginsberg & Bronstein 1993; Gottfried et al. 1994
110 Dornbusch et al. 1987; Duchesne & Ratelle 2010; Eccles et al. 1991; Gonzalez-DeHass et al. 2005; Grolinck & Ryan 1989; Leung & Kwan 1998; Paulson et al. 1998; Steinberg et al. 1989, 1992, 1994
111 Purdue et al. 2009; Strage & Brandt 1999
112 Emmer & Aussiker 1990; Grolnick 2003; Grolnick et al. 2002
113 Bean et al. 2003; Grolnick 2003
114 Leung & Kwan 1998; Leung et al. 1998a; Ryan & Stiller 1991
115 Gaylord-Harden 2008; Gregory & Rimm-Kaufman 2008; Hamre & Pianta 2001
116 Dearing 2004
117 Parker et al. 1999
118 Aunola & Nurmi 2004; Chen et al. 1997; Deslandes et al. 1997; Emmer & Aussiker 1990; Ginsberg & Bronstein 1993; Grolnick 2003; Grolnick & Ryan 1989; Grolnick et al. 2002; Gottfried et al. 1994; Hennessey & Amabile 1998; Hong & Ho 2005; Koestner et al. 1984; Lamborn et al. 1991; Mattanah 200; Singh et al. 1995; Steinberg et al. 1992; Taylor et al. 1995; Weiss & Schwarz 1996
119 Burchinal & Cryer 2003; Gest et al. 2004; Raviv et al. 2004; Steelman et al. 2002
120 Dearing et al. 2006a
121 Bernier et al. 2010
122 Anderson et al. 2003; Jodl et al. 2001
123 Weiss & Schwarz 1996; Williams et al. 2009
124 Dekovic et al. 2003; McClun & Merrell 1998; Soenens et al. 2007; Steinberg et al. 1989, 1992; Wentzel 1994
125 Dekovic et al. 2003; McClun & Merrell 1998; Steinberg et al. 1989, 1992, 1994; Wentzel 1994

126 Baumrind 1967, 1971b; Ispa et al. 2004; Loukas 2009; Snyder et al. 2003; Strayer & Roberts 2004a
127 Belsky et al. 1998; Letcher et al. 2004; Shaw et al. 2000
128 Roth et al 2009
129 Cole et al. 2009; Denham et al. 1997; Eisenberg et al. 1999, 2005; Fabes et al. 2001; Garner & Spears 2000; Grolnick et al. 1996; Kochanska et al. 2005a; Lagacé-Séguin & Coplan 2005; Morris et al. 2007; Rubin et al. 2003; Shipman et al. 2007
130 Aguilar et al. 2000; Calkins & Johnson 1998; Dekovic et al. 2003; Eisenberg et al. 2005; Fabes et al. 2001; Feldman & Klein 2003; Gilliom et al. 2002; Gray & Steinberg 1999; Grolnick et al. 1996; Kochanska et al. 2000, 2005a; McClun & Merrell 1998; Rubin et al. 2003; Steinberg et al. 1989, 1992; Wentzel 1994
131 Spinrad et al. 2004b
132 Belsky et al. 1998; Eisenberg et al. 2005; Propper & Moore 2006
133 Merritt et al. 2012
134 Berlin & Cassidy 2003; Roth et al 2009
135 Denham et al. 1997
136 Roth et al. 2009
137 Denham et al. 1997
138 Caron 2006
139 Campbell & Ewing 1990; Loukas et al. 2005
140 Kochanska et al. 2007; van IJzendoorn 1997
141 Garber et al. 1997; McDowell et al. 2003
142 Criss et al. 2009; Dearing 2004; Garber et al. 1997; Kaufmann et al. 2000; Propper & Moore 2006; Wyman et al. 1999
143 van IJzendoorn 1997
144 Cotler & Palmer 1971
145 Hart et al. 1998; Propper & Moore 2006
146 Aunola & Nurmi 2005; Baumrind 1991
147 Dekovic et al. 2003; Eisenberg et al. 2005; Fabes et al. 2001; Feldman & Klein 2003; Gray & Steinberg 1999; Grolnick et al. 1996; Kochanska et al. 2005a; McClun & Merrell 1998; Rubin et al. 2003; Steinberg et al. 1989, 1992; Wentzel 1994
148 Brown 2012: 227; Buri et al. 1988; Garber et al. 1997; Maccoby & Martin 1983; Rudy et al. 2008
149 Kernis et al. 2000; Kins et al. 2012
150 Buri et al. 1988
151 Assor & Tal 2012; Baumrind 1991; Buri et al. 1988; Eccles et al. 1991; Garber et al. 1997; Kernis et al. 2000
152 DiPrima et al. 2011
153 Neumeister et al. 2009; Rice et al. 1996
154 Bates et al. 2003; National Institute of Child Health and Human Development Early Child Care Research Network 2001a, 2003a, 2003b; Ryan & Stiller 1991; Steelman et al. 2002
155 Criss et al. 2003; Fletcher & Shaw 2000; Hart et al. 1992b; NICHD Early Child Care Research Network 2004b; Russell et al. 1998
156 Szewczyk-Sokolowski 2005; Wray-Lake & Flanagan 2012
157 Baumrind 1967, 1971b, 1991; Ispa et al. 2004; Rutherford & Mussen 1968
158 Denham et al. 2002
159 Booth et al. 1994; Casas et al. 2006; Deater-Deckard & Dodge 1997; Hart et al. 1992a; MacKinnon-Lewis et al. 1999; McDowell et al. 2003; Nelson et al. 2012; O'Connor 2002; Rah & Parke 2008
160 Duong et al. 2009
161 Vaillancourt et al. 2007
162 Ackerman et al. 2002; Aguilar et al. 2000; Campbell 1995; Campbell et al. 1991a, 1991b; Dearing et al. 2006a; Diener et al. 2003; Dodge et al. 1994; McFadyen-Ketchum et al. 1996; NICHD & Human Development Early Child

Care Research Network 2005; Parke et al. 2004; Petterson & Albers 2001; Qi & Kaiser 2003; Sturge-Apple et al. 2006
163 Buyse et al. 2008
164 Barker et al. 2010
165 Unnever & Cornell 2004
166 Roth et al. 2011
167 Hart et al. 1992a; Herrera & Dunn 1997
168 Baumrind 1991; Denham et al. 1997; Hart et al. 1992a; Michalik et al. 2007
169 Szewczyk-Sokolowski 2005
170 Herrera & Dunn 1997
171 Coplan et al. 2004; Ladd & Kochenderfer-Ladd 1998; Rubin et al. 2002
172 Baumrind 1991; Eccles et al. 1991; Kins et al. 2012
173 Stattin & Kerr 2000
174 Brody et al. 2001; Criss et al. 2003
175 Crockenberg & Litman 1990; Donovan et al. 2000; Gilliom et al. 2002; Stormshak et al. 2000
176 Harter et al. 1997
177 Donohue et al. 2003
178 Berlin & Cassidy 2003
179 Assor et al. 2004; Baumrind 1991; Kochanska et al. 2003; Roth et al. 2009
180 Chao & Aque 2009
181 McCord 1991
182 Baumrind 1991; Donovan et al. 2000; Ispa et al. 2004
183 Baumrind 1991; Criss et al. 2003
184 Kochanska 2002a, 2002b; Kochanska & Aksan 2004; Kochanska et al. 1999, 2005a; Kuczynski 1984; Laible & Thompson 2002
185 Stattin & Kerr 2000
186 Lewis 1997
187 Gordon 1991
188 Gordon 2000: 290
189 Corey 1996
190 Calvin Coolidge, in Sapon-Shevin 1996: 196
191 Chomsky 1998, in Kohn 2004: 174
192 Greene 2008: 8
193 Curwin & Mendler 1988

Chapter 21

1 Neven et al. 2002: 49 & 53
2 Rescorla et al. 2007
3 Vitaro et al. 2005
4 Johnson et al. 2005
5 Wåhlstedt et al. 2009
6 American Psychiatric Association 2013: 34
7 Anastopoulos & Barkley 1992; Campbell et al. 2000; Neven et al. 2002: 2
8 American Psychiatric Association 2013: 31–33
9 Levy 1993
10 Levy 1993
11 American Psychiatric Association 2013: 31–33
12 e.g. Jacobs 2005
13 Conrad 2006
14 Karatekin 2004; Olson et al. 2002
15 McConaughy et al. 2011: 218
16 Goldstein & Naglieri 2008: 867; McConaughy et al. 2011: 221; Miller & Hinshaw 2012: 65 & 66
17 Miller & Hinshaw 2012: 69
18 Goldstein & Naglieri 2008: 861
19 Goldstein & Naglieri 2008: 865
20 Goldstein & Naglieri 2008; Purvis & Tannock 1997
21 Demaray & Jenkins 2011
22 Moffitt 1993b: 146
23 Purvis & Tannock 1997

24 Clark et al. 2002
25 Berk & Landau 1993; Berk & Potts 1991; Diaz & Berk 1995; Kopecky et al. 2005
26 Green & Chee 2001
27 Vile Junod et al. 2006
28 Vile Junod et al. 2006: 98
29 Karatekin 2004; Vile Junod et al. 2006: 99
30 Eisenberg et al. 2004b
31 Cumberland-Li et al. 2004
32 Cumberland-Li et al. 2004; Dickman 1990
33 Arsenio & Lemerise 2001; Clark et al. 2002; Eisenberg et al. 2001, 2004a, 2005; Kats-Gold & Priel 2009
34 Goldstein & Naglieri 2008: 863
35 Hoza et al. 2000; Lengua 2003; Miller & Hinshaw 2012; Shelton et al. 1998; Young et al. 2005
36 Goldstein & Naglieri 2008: 863
37 Goldstein & Naglieri 2008: 863
38 Clark et al. 2002; Kats-Gold & Priel 2009
39 Scime & Norvilitis 2006
40 Blair et al. 2005; Hastings et al. 2009; Santor et al. 2003; Waschbusch et al. 2002
41 Blair et al. 2005; Hastings et al. 2009
42 Santor et al. 2003
43 Anastopoulos & Barkley 1992; Hoza et al. 2000; Miller & HInshaw 2012; Shelton et al. 1998; Young et al. 2005
44 Hoza et al. 2000; Miller & HInshaw 2012; Santor et al. 2003; Scime & Norvilitis 2006Shelton et al. 1998; Waschbusch et al. 2002; Young et al. 2005
45 Lengua 2003
46 McConaughy et al. 2011: 219
47 McConaughy et al. 2011: 219
48 McConaughy et al. 2011: 220
49 Clark et al. 2002; Friedman-Weieneth et al. 2007; Lonigan et al. 1999; McGee et al. 2002; Rabiner et al. 2000; Spira & Fischel 2005
50 McGee et al. 2002; Spira & Fischel 2005
51 Birchwood & Daley 2012
52 Valiente et al. 2008: 74
53 Papadopoulos et al. 2005; Zentall 1989
54 Sobol & Pianta 2012:295
55 Clark et al. 2002; Katz-Gold & Priel 2009
56 Hoza et al. 2000
57 Hoza et al. 2000
58 Barkley 1988; Clark et al. 2002; Hoza et al. 2000; Stormont 2001
59 Bloomquist et al. 1997; Ellis et al. 2009
60 Bacchini et al. 2008
61 Bacchini et al. 2008: 455
62 Bacchini et al. 2008: 455
63 Bacchini et al. 2008: 456
64 McConaughy et al. 2011
65 Anastopoulos & Barkley 1992; Miller & Hinshaw 2012: 65
66 Goldstein 1995; Loeber & Hay 1997
67 Ellis et al. 2009; Snyder et al. 2004
68 Goldstein 1995
69 Barkley 1988
70 Anastopoulos & Barkley 1992
71 Rapport et al. 2009
72 Anastopoulos & Barkley 1992; Bock & Stauth 2008: 56; Cabot & Jasinska 2011: 76
73 Rodriguez & Bohlin 2005; Vuijk et al. 2006
74 Abikoff et al. 2002
75 Abikoff et al. 2002: 356
76 Arnold 1996; Hallahan & Kauffman 2006
77 Jacobs 2005
78 Barkley 1988; Miller & Hinshaw 2012
79 Goldstein 1995
80 Lavigne et al. 1996; McGee et al. 1991; Spira & Fischel 2005
81 Levy 1993
82 Hallahan & Kauffman 2006
83 Hallahan & Kauffman 2003: 192
84 Miller & Hinshaw 2012
85 Barkley 1988
86 Barkley 1988; Lonigan et al. 1999
87 Arnold 1996
88 Arnold 1996
89 Hart et al. 1995
90 Hart et al. 1995
91 Barkley 1988; Fischer et al. 1990; McGee et al. 1991, 2002; Spira & Fischel 2005
92 Anastopoulos & Barkley 1992; Goldstein 1995; Hart et al. 1995; McGee et al. 1991
93 Barkley 1988
94 Barkley 1988; Fischer et al. 1990, 1993; Goldstein 1995; Greene et al. 1997; Hart et al. 1995; Shaw et al. 2005; Spira & Fischel 2005
95 Barkley et al. 2004; Broidy et al. 2003; McGee et al. 2002; Nagin & Tremblay 1999
96 Olson et al. 2002
97 Auerbach et al. 2005; Glanzman & Blum 2007; Groot et al. 2004; Miller & Hinshaw 2012; Stein et al. 2002
98 Stein et al. 2002
99 Hallahan & Kauffman 2006; Miller & Hinshaw 2012; Stein et al. 2002
100 Trzesniewski et al. 2006b
101 Bock & Stauth 2008: 56
102 Campbell-McBride 2010: 333
103 Anastopoulos & Barkley 1992; Barkley 1988; Linnet et al. 2003
104 Banerjee et al. 2007: 1271
105 Banerjee et al. 2007: 1271
106 Banerjee et al. 2007: 1271; Monuteaux et al. 2006; Rodriguez & Bohlin 2005; Vuijk et al. 2006
107 Schuetze et al. 2008
108 Brown et al. 2004; Moe & Smith 2003; Singer et al. 2005
109 Bennett et al. 2002
110 Hallahan & Kauffman 2006; Miller & Hinshaw 2012; Stein et al. 2002
111 Chronis-Tuscano et al. 2008
112 Schuetze et al. 2008
113 Deater-Deckard et al. 2006
114 Lyon 2000: 86–87
115 Chauhan & Chauhan 2006: 172
116 Everatt & Reid 2009: 5
117 Lyon 2000: 105
118 Lyon 2000: 104–105
119 Adams et al. 2011: 10; Lyon 2000: 198–199
120 Campbell-McBride 2010: 51–53
121 Campbell-McBride 2010: 43
122 Anderson et al. 1987; Balch 2006; Bock & Stauth 2008: 260; Cabot 2001: 54; Clausen 1988; Lazarides 2010: 85; Lyon 2000: 105–107; Rhodes & Ritz 2008: 186
123 Balch 2006: 67
124 Lazarides 2010: 87–88; Lyon 2000: 85
125 Lyon 2000: 134
126 Ascherio & Munger 2007: 291
127 Shi et al. 2003: 301
128 Bock & Stauth 2008: 29–30
129 Hagerman & Kalkenstein 1987
130 Lyon 2000: 81
131 Lantz 2009: 44–45
132 Chauhan & Chauhan 2006: 175; Fraga et al. 1990; Jesberger & Richardson 1991: 3; Lantz 2009: 44–45;

Lazarides 2010: 191; Lyon 2000: 81; Pilsner et al. 2009: 1466
133 Lyon 2000: 77
134 Anastopoulos & Barkley 1992
135 Hadjivassiliou et al. 2001: 385; Mäki & Collin 1997: 1756
136 Campbell-McBride 2010: 72
137 Glaser 2000
138 Blum & Mercugliano 1997
139 Cabot 2004: 40
140 Barkley 1988
141 Goldstein 1995
142 Barkley 1988; Goldstein 1995
143 Barkley 1988
144 Arnold 1996
145 Anastopoulos & Barkley 1992; Goldstein & Naglieri 2008: 862
146 Clark et al. 2002
147 Shelton et al. 1998
148 Sayal et al. 2006
149 Anastopoulos & Barkley 1992
150 Campbell-McBride 2010: 44
151 Adams 2010: 75
152 Collison & Hall 1989: 42; Jyonouchi 2009; Tortora & Derrickson 2006: 820
153 Casas et al. 2006; Romano et al. 2005; Vitaro et al. 2002, 2006
154 Barkley et al. 2000
155 Miller & Hinshaw 2012
156 Miller & Hinshaw 2012: 73
157 Miller & Hinshaw 2012
158 Campbell 1995; Martel & Nigg 2006; Spira & Fischel 2005
159 Greene 2008
160 Lambert 1990; Raggi & Chronis 2006
161 Goldstein 1995
162 Soden 2002
163 Sheridan et al. 1997; Whalen et al. 2006
164 Whalen et al. 1981; Wodrich 1994
165 Scime & Norvilitis 2006
166 Scime & Norvilitis 2006
167 Scime & Norvilitis 2006
168 Volpe et al. 2009
169 Rutherford et al. 2008
170 Peel 2009: 34 & 35
171 Goldstein & Naglieri 2008: 869; Schultz et al. 2009
172 Green & Rechis 2006; LaFontana & Cillessen 2002
173 Greene 2008
174 Goldstein & Naglieri 2008: 869
175 Diaz & Berk 1995
176 Sheridan et al. 1997; Williford et al. 2007
177 Abikoff & Klein 1992
178 Lewis & Doorlag 2003
179 Neven et al. 2002 :2
180 Miller & Hinshaw 2012: 72
181 Levy 1993; Stein et al. 2002; Vaughan et al. 2009
182 Anastopoulos & Barkley 1992; Barkley 1988; Goldstein & Goldstein 1995; Levy 1993; Vaughan et al. 2009
183 Goldstein & Goldstein 1995
184 Goldstein & Naglieri 2008: 869
185 Goldstein & Goldstein 1995
186 Kopecky et al. 2005
187 Goldstein 1995; Goldstein & Goldstein 1995
188 Moline & Frankenberger 2001; Purdie et al. 2002
189 McConaughy et al. 2011; Miller & Hinshaw 2012; Moline & Frankenberger 2001; Purdie et al. 2002; Raggi & Chronis 2006; Whalen et al. 2006
190 King et al. 2009: 585
191 Anastopoulos & Barkley 1992; Barkley 1988; Fox &

Rieder 1993; Goldstein 1995; Miller & Hinshaw 2012; Neven et al. 2002: 44; Purdie et al. 2002; Vaughan et al. 2009: 853
192 Lyon 2000: 107
193 Vaughan et al. 2009: 853
194 Levy 1993; Vaughan et al. 2009: 847
195 Fox & Rieder 1993; Goldstein & Goldstein 1995; Levy 1993; Moline & Frankenberger 2001; Purdie et al. 2002; Vaughan et al. 2009: 847
196 Levy 1993; Vaughan et al. 2009: 849
197 Goldstein & Goldstein 1995; Vaughan et al. 2009: 849
198 Northey et al. 2003: 526
199 Goldstein & Goldstein 1995

Chapter 22

1 Kohn 1998: 231
2 Rescorla et al. 2007
3 Farmer & Xie 2007
4 Hubbard 2001; Prinstein & Cillessen 2003; Vitaro et al. 2002, 2006
5 Kochenderfer-Ladd & Ladd 2001; Rigby 2006a; Slee 1995a, 1995b; Slee & Rigby 1994; Smith & Sharp 1994
6 Owens et al. 2000b
7 Hunter et al. 2007
8 Noble 2006: 68
9 Espelage & Swearer 2003; Golberg et al. 2007; Nansel et al. 2001; Olweus 1993; Slee & Rigby 1994
10 Delfabbro et al. 2006; Demaray & Malecki 2003a; Pepler et al. 1993; Rigby 1996; Slee 1994b, 1998; Smith & Sharp 1994; Tattum 1993a
11 Boulton 1997; Olweus 1993
12 Bradshaw et al. 2007; Hawkins et al. 2001
13 Rigby 1993, 1998
14 Scheithauer et al. 2006
15 Crick et al. 1999; Porter 1999
16 Coyne et al. 2006; Miller et al. 2008; Olweus 1993; Witvliet et al. 2010
17 Coyne et al. 2006; James & Owens 2004; Leadbeater et al. 2006; Owens et al. 2005a; Vaillancourt et al. 2007
18 Henington et al. 1998; Vaillancourt et al. 2007: 323
19 Camodeca et al. 2002; Crick et al. 2006a; Olweus 1993; Scholte et al. 2007; Vaillancourt et al. 2003
20 Crick et al. 2006a; Harachi et al. 2006; Jolliffe & Farrington 2006; Lee et al. 2007; Loeber & Hay 1997; Loukas et al. 2005; Olthof et al. 2011; Ostrov & Keating 2004; Salmivalli & Kaukiainen 2004; Smith et al. 2010; Tapper & Boulton 2004
21 Roseth et al. 2007
22 Roseth et al. 2007
23 Graham et al. 2006; López et al. 2006; Nansel et al. 2001; Pepler et al. 2006; Scholte et al. 2007
24 O'Moore & Minton 2004
25 Shute et al. 2002
26 Coyne et al. 2006; Low et al. 2010
27 Borba 2005
28 Crick et al. 2001; Deater-Deckard 2001; James & Owens 2005; Olweus 1993; Ostrov et al. 2004; Owens et al. 2000a, 2001; Rigby 1996, 1998; Salmivalli et al. 1998; Shute et al. 2002; Slee 1995b; Smith & Sharp 1994; Tattum 1993a
29 Low et al. 2010
30 Putallaz et al. 2007
31 Scambler et al. 1998: 235
32 Barnett et al. 2004; Scambler et al. 1998
33 Scambler et al. 1998
34 Jones et al. 2005
35 Jones et al. 2005

36 Barnett et al. 2004
37 Åslund et al. 2009
38 Shute et al. 2002
39 Shute et al. 2002
40 James & Owens 2004
41 Newman & Murray 2005; Scholte et al. 2007
42 Mason 2008: 323
43 Pornari & Wood 2010
44 Mason 2008
45 Mason 2008
46 Pornari & Wood 2010
47 Raskauskas & Stoltz 2007; Stauffer et al. 2012: 354
48 Raskauskas & Stoltz 2007; Wang et al. 2012
49 Raskauskas & Stoltz 2007
50 Dellasega & Nixon 2003: 32
51 Stein 1995: 152
52 Eden Prairie School District 1993, in Stein 1995: 153
53 Drouet 1993; Fineran 2001; Owens et al. 2005a
54 Stein 1995: 151
55 Owens et al. 2005a; Stein 1995
56 Stein 1995
57 Harter et al. 1997
58 Stein 1995. It always astonishes me that, when a bank is
     robbed, no one blames the bank for advertising that it has
     money on its premises but, when a female is raped, she is
     to blame for communicating that she is female.
59 Bontempo & D'Augelli 2002; Fineran 2001; Murdock &
     Bolch 2005; Rivers 2001
60 Espelage et al. 2008; Fineran 2001; Henning-Stout et al.
     2000; Jordan et al. 1997; Macgillivray 2000: 306;
     Malinsky 1997; Savin-Williams 1994
61 Bontempo & D'Augelli 2002; Darwich et al. 2012; Fineran
     2001; Jordan 1997; Macgillivray 2000; Murdock & Bolch
     2005
62 Goodenow et al. 2006; Savin-Williams 1994: 264 & 266
63 Parrott & Peterson 2008
64 Rigby 2003
65 Rigby 2003; Terry 1998
66 Belsky et al. 1998; Campbell & Ewing 1990; Côté et al.
     2006; Fergusson et al. 2005; Miller-Lewis et al. 2006;
     O'Leary et al. 1999; Romano et al. 2005; Rubin et al. 2003;
     Shaw et al. 2003; Tremblay 2004
67 Dodge et al. 1997: 44; Schwartz et al. 1997: 672
68 Schwartz et al. 1997
69 Unnever 2005
70 Holt et al. 2007
71 Brendgen et al. 2005; Casas et al. 2006; Nelson et al. 2012;
     Ostrov et al. 2006; Stauffacher & DeHart 2006
72 Long & Pellegrini 2003; Pellegrini 2004; Xie et al. 2002
73 Pellegrini 2004; Reynolds & Repetti 2010; Thornberg
     2010: 316
74 Bukowski 2003; Bukowski & Sippola 2001; McMillan &
     Chavis 1986; Nishina 2004; Owens et al. 2000b
75 Olthof & Goossens 2008; Reynolds & Repetti 2010;
     Thornberg 2010: 316
76 Olthof & Goossens 2008
77 Thornberg 2010
78 Reynolds & Repetti 2010; Xie et al. 2002
79 Owens 1997; Owens et al. 2000b; Reynolds & Repetti
     2010; Thornberg 2010
80 Thornberg 2010
81 Hunter et al. 2007
82 Juvonen et al. 2000; O'Brennan et al. 2009; Owens et al.
     2000c
83 Owens et al. 2000c
84 Juvonen et al. 2000; Kochenderfer-Ladd & Ladd 2001;
     Rosen et al. 2009
85 Crosby et al. 2010; Juvonen et al. 2000;

     Kochenderfer-Ladd & Ladd 2001; Mynard et al. 2000;
     Olweus 2001; Rivers 2001; Smith et al. 2004
86 Kochenderfer-Ladd & Ladd 2001; Rueger et al. 2011
87 Holt et al. 2007; Morrison et al. 1998
88 Barchia & Bussey 2010; Conners-Burrow et al. 2009;
     Davidson & Demaray 2007; Flaspohler et al. 2009
89 Conners-Burrow et al. 2009; Flaspohler et al. 2009
90 Buhs et al. 2006; Dempsey & Storch 2008; Egan & Perry
     1998; Espelage & Swearer 2003; Fekkes et al. 2006; Field
     & Carroll 2006; Graham et al. 2006; Hunter & Boyle
     2004; Juvonen et al. 2000; Kochenderfer-Ladd & Ladd
     2001; Marsh et al. 2004; Martin & Huebner 2007;
     Murray-Close et al. 2007; Mynard et al. 2000; Nansel et
     al. 2001; Olweus 1993; O'Moore & Minton 2004; Owens
     et al. 2000c; Putallaz et al. 2007; Rigby 1996, 1999, 2001,
     2006a; Scholte et al. 2007; Schwartz et al. 2005; Slee
     1995a, 1995b; Slee & Rigby 1994; P.K. Smith et al. 2004;
     Sullivan et al. 2006; Sweeting et al. 2007
91 Chang 2004; Nipedel et al. 2010
92 Sijtsema et al. 2010
93 Kuppens et al. 2008; Nesdale et al. 2008; Olweus 1993;
     Rigby 2006a; Rodkin & Hodges 2003; Thomas et al. 2006
94 Hanish et al. 2005a; Leadbeater et al. 2003; Mercer et al.
     2009
95 Duffy & Nesdale 2009; Hodges et al. 1997
96 Card & Little 2006: 475
97 Malti et al. 2009
98 Arsenio & Lemerise 2001; Gini 2006; Menesini et al.
     2003b; Pornari & Wood 2010: 82; Thornberg 2010
99 Vaughn et al. 2003
100 Espelage & Swearer 2003; Kaukiainen et al 1999;
     Leadbeater et al. 2006; Pelligrini et al. 1999; Puckett et al.
     2008; Putallaz et al. 2007; Rodkin & Hodges 2003;
     Vaughn et al. 2003
101 Hawley & Little 1999
102 Espelage & Swearer 2003; Hawley & Little 1999;
     Kaukiainen et al 1999; Puckett et al. 2008; Vaughn et al.
     2003
103 Jolliffe & Farrington 2006; Lomas et al. 2012; Nesdale et
     al. 2009; Putallaz et al. 2007
104 Caravita et al. 2008; Crick & Grotpeter 1995; Leadbeater
     et al. 2006; Mayeux & Cillessen 2008; Pelligrini et al.
     1999; Putallaz et al. 2007; Rodkin & Hodges 2003;
     Walcott et al. 2008
105 Estell et al. 2008; Hoff et al. 2009; Puckett et al. 2008;
     Rodkin et al. 2006; van de Schoot et al. 2010; Xie et al.
     2002
106 Puckett et al. 2008
107 Cillessen & Mayeux 2004; Estell et al. 2008; Farmer et al.
     2003; LaFontana & Cillessen 2002; Ostrov et al. 2004;
     Prinstein & Cillessen 2003; Rodkin et al. 2000; Rose et al.
     2004; Sijtsema et al. 2009; Smith et al. 2010; Vaillancourt
     & Hymel 2006; Young et al. 2006
108 Estell et al. 2008
109 Estell et al. 2008; Puckett et al. 2008; Vaillancourt &
     Hymel 2006
110 Barry et al. 2007; Bloomquist et al. 1997; Dodge et al.
     1997; Jolliffe & Farrington 2011; Marini et al. 2006;
     McConville & Cornell 2003; Musher-Eizenman et al.
     2004; Nesdale et al. 2009; O'Brennan et al. 2009; Perry et
     al. 1990; Putallaz et al. 2007; Unnever 2005
111 Eisenberg et al. 2006
112 Camodeca & Goossens 2005; Crick et al. 2002; de Castro
     et al. 2002; Little et al. 2003; MacKinnon-Lewis et al.
     1999; Prinstein & Cillessen 2003; Vaughn et al. 2003
113 Card & Little 2006
114 Arsenio & Lemerise 2001; Asher 1983; Bloomquist et al.
     1997; Burt et al. 2009; Champion et al 2003; Crick &

Dodge 1994; Dodge & Coie 1987; Dodge & Crick 1990;
Dodge et al. 1997, 2002; Downey et al. 1998; Feindler
1991; Fine et al. 2004; Frankel & Myatt 1996; Katsurada
& Sugawara 1998; King et al. 2009: 585; Ladd 1985;
Lochman et al. 2012; Marini et al. 2006; McConville &
Cornell 2003; Menesini et al. 2003b; Miller et al. 1998;
Musher-Eizenman et al. 2004; Nelson et al. 2012;
O'Brennan et al. 2009; Orobio de Castro et al. 2002;
Pardini et al. 2006; Perry et al. 1990; Schultz et al. 2000;
Terranova et al. 2008; Wilson 2006; Yoon et al. 2000;
Zakriski & Coie 1996

115 Lochman et al. 2006; Miller et al. 1998; Nelson et al.
2012; Yoon et al. 2000
116 Coplan & Prakash 2003
117 Graham et al. 2006; López et al. 2006
118 Bukowski 2003; Little et al. 2003; Unnever 2005
119 Chang 2004; Dodge et al. 1997: 44; Hay et al. 2004;
Johnson et al. 2000; Moffitt 1993a; Rodkin et al. 2000;
Stormshak et al. 1999
120 Frankel & Myatt 1996; Graham et al. 2006; López et al.
2006; Nansel et al. 2001; Scholte et al. 2007
121 Claes & Simard 1992; Snyder et al. 1997
122 Arnold et al. 1998; Dodge 1983; Farver 1996; Hartup
1989; Hartup & Moore 1990; Hay et al. 2004; Kendrick et
al. 2012; Lamarche et al. 2006; Poulin & Boivin 2000;
Rodkin et al. 2006; Sijtsema et al. 2010; Snyder et al.
1997; Werner & Crick 2004
123 Champion et al. 2003; Claes & Simard 1992; Coie et al.
1999; Hay et al. 2004; Snyder et al. 1997
124 Solberg et al. 2007
125 Kochenderfer-Ladd 2004; Olthof et al. 2011; Schwartz et
al. 1997; Mahady Wilton et al. 2000
126 Schwartz 2000
127 Hubbard 2001; Leary & Katz 2005
128 Flaspohler et al. 2009; Hanish & Guerra 2000; Hodges &
Perry 1999; Hodges et al. 1999; LaFontana & Cillessen
2002; Lamarche et al. 2006; Leadbeater et al. 2006;
Mahady Wilton et al. 2000; O'Brennan et al. 2009;
Prinstein & Cillessen 2003; Salmivalli & Helteenvuori
2007; Schwartz 2000; Unnever 2005
129 Card & Little 2006; Hanish & Guerra 2004; LaFontana &
Cillessen 2002; Prinstein & Cillessen 2003; Unnever 2005
130 Unnever 2005; Waasdorp & Bradshaw 2011
131 Perry et al. 1990; Schwartz 2000
132 Unnever 2005
133 Olthof et al. 2011
134 Kokkinos & Panayiotou 2004
135 Demaray & Malecki 2003a; Graham et al. 2006; Nansel et
al. 2001
136 Hanish et al. 2005b: 13; Perry et al. 1990
137 Abou-ezzeddine et al. 2007; DeRosier & Mercer 2009;
Hodges et al. 1997; Kendrick et al. 2012; Kochenderfer &
Ladd 1996; Leenaars et al. 2008: 410; Olweus 1993; Perry
et al. 1990; Sapouna et al. 2012; Thornberg 2010
138 Sapouna et al. 2012
139 Kochenderfer-Ladd & Wardrop 2001: 146
140 Solberg et al. 2007: 460
141 Kochenderfer-Ladd 2004
142 Mahady Wilton et al. 2000
143 Kochenderfer-Ladd 2004
144 Hanish & Guerra 2004: 33
145 Marsh et al. 2004
146 Kochenderfer & Ladd 1996; Salmivalli & Isaacs 2005;
Scholte et al. 2007; Schwartz et al. 2005
147 Erath et al. 2008; Kochenderfer & Ladd 1996;
Kochenderfer & Wardrop 2001
148 Kochenderfer-Ladd 2004; Waasdorp & Bradshaw 2011
149 Waasdorp & Bradshaw 2011

150 Erath et al. 2008
151 Craig et al. 2000: 29; Hawkins et al. 2001: 513; Xie et al.
2002
152 Tapper & Boulton 2005
153 Olthof et al. 2011
154 Olweus 1993; Pikas 2002
155 James & Owens 2005; Owens et al. 2000b; Rigby 1996
156 Cowie 2000
157 Craig et al. 2000; Olweus 2001
158 Cowie 2000: 86
159 Thornberg 2010: 315
160 Cowie 2000: 86
161 Hawkins et al. 2001
162 Cowie 2000: 87
163 Hawkins et al. 2001: 521
164 Olthof et al. 2011
165 Gini et al. 2007; Hoffman 1981
166 Davidov & Grusec 2006; Maccoby & Martin 1983; Zahn-
Waxler et al. 1979
167 Kochenderfer-Ladd & Pelletier 2008
168 Bradshaw et al. 2007: 375; Olweus 1993; Pepler et al. 1998:
73; Slee 1994a
169 Bradshaw et al. 2007; Young et al. 2006
170 Nesdale & Pickering 2006
171 Ellis & Shute 2007; Xie et al. 2002
172 Ellis & Shute 2007
173 Bradshaw et al. 2007: 375; Rigby & Bagshaw 2003: 539
174 Bradshaw et al. 2007: 375
175 Ellis & Shute 2007
176 Coldwell et al. 2006; Côté et al. 2006; Feldman & Klein
2003; Fergusson et al. 2005; López et al. 2006; Miller-
Lewis et al. 2006; O'Leary et al. 1999; Romano et al. 2005;
Rubin et al. 2003; Rutter 1983; Shaw et al. 2003;
Smeekens et al. 2007; Tremblay 2004; van Lier et al. 2007
177 McGrath & Stanley 2006a
178 see, e.g. Orpinas et al. 2003
179 Rodkin & Hodges 2003
180 O'Brennan et al. 2009
181 Ostrov et al. 2004
182 Crick et al. 2006a, 2006b; Johnson et al. 2000
183 Rigby 2001; Unnever 2005
184 Pepler et al. 1993; Tattum 1993b
185 Nishina 2004; Olweus 1993
186 Harel-Fisch et al. 2011
187 Hanish et al. 2005a
188 Gregory et al. 2010: 492
189 Weinstein et al. 2004
190 McEvoy & Welker 2000
191 Boulton 1994; James & Owens 2005; Leff et al. 2003;
Olweus 1993; Owens et al. 2000b; Whitney et al. 1994
192 Boulton 1994; James & Owens 2005; Leff et al. 2003;
Olweus 1993; Owens et al. 2000b; Whitney et al. 1994
193 Morrison et al. 1998
194 Goodenow et al. 2006
195 Unnever & Cornell 2004
196 Shute et al. 2002
197 Newman & Murray 2005
198 Nicholson 2006
199 Eliot et al. 2010; Unnever & Cornell 2004
200 Eliot et al. 2010: 547
201 Farver 1996
202 Blankemeyer et al. 2002
203 Rodkin & Hodges 2003
204 Flaspohler et al. 2009
205 Eliot et al. 2010; Unnever & Cornell 2004
206 Rudolph et al. 2011
207 Rudolph et al. 2011
208 Rudolph et al. 2011

209 Rudolph et al. 2011: 1527
210 Goodenow et al. 2006
211 Espelage et al. 2008
212 Bolger & Patterson 2001; Teisl & Cicchetti 2007
213 Morrison et al. 1998
214 Rigby 2001
215 Smith et al. 1994
216 Armstrong & Thorsborne 2006; Fuller 2006; McGrath & Stanley 2006a; Pikas 2002
217 James & Owens 2004; Owens et al. 2001; Shute et al. 2002
218 Cowie 2000; Smith & Daunic 2002
219 Cowie 2000
220 Cowie & Olafsson 2000
221 Kochenderfer-Ladd & Pelletier 2008
222 Fuller 2006
223 Strain & Joseph 2004
224 Roth et al. 2011
225 O'Moore & Minton 2004
226 Owens et al. 2000a; Salmivalli et al. 2005; Smith & Ananiadou 2003: 206; Stevens et al. 2000
227 Salmivalli et al. 2005; Vaillancourt & Hymel 2006
228 Mason 2008
229 Smith & Ananiadou 2003
230 see Leff et al. 2001; Samples 2004; P.K. Smith et al. 2004
231 Orpinas et al. 2003
232 Menesini et al. 2003a
233 Cappella & Weinstein 2006; Merrell et al. 2008
234 Rigby & Bagshaw 2006
235 Fox & Boulton 2003
236 Feindler & Engel 2011; Grossman et al. 1997; Hudley et al. 1998; Sukhodolsky et al. 2004
237 www.incredibleyears.com
238 Lochman & Wells 2004; Lochman et al. 2012; Powell et al. 2011; www.copingpower.com
239 Slee 2001, 2006
240 Rogers 2003
241 Dishion et al. 1999; Poulin et al. 2001
242 Dionne et al. 2003; Ripley & Yuill 2005; Schaeffer et al. 2003; Vitaro et al. 2002
243 Jolliffe & Farrington 2011
244 Schwartz et al. 2005
245 Demaray & Malecki 2003a; Fuller 2006
246 Rigby 1996, 2006b; Scambler et al. 1998; Sharp & Cowie 1994
247 Kochenderfer-Ladd & Pelletier 2008
248 adapted from Elman & Kennedy-Moore 2003: 216–217
249 Leff et al. 2010
250 Ostrov et al. 2009
251 Boyle & Hassett-Walker 2008; www.researchpress.com/product/item/4628/
252 Bernard 2006
253 Leadbeater et al. 2003
254 www.witsprogram.ca
255 Fraser et al. 2004
256 Leff et al. 2009
257 Van Schoiack-Edstrom et al. 2002
258 Frey et al. 2009; Grossman et al. 1997
259 www.cfchildren.org
260 Cappella & Weinstein 2006
261 www.cfchildren.org
262 Nixon & Werner 2010; www.orpheliaproject.org
263 Frey et al. 2009; Low et al. 2010
264 Shechtman & Ifargan 2009
265 Sweeting et al. 2007
266 Young 2001
267 Young 2001
268 Thompson et al. 2002
269 Hartup & Moore 1990

270 Hartup & Moore 1990; Kelly 1996
271 Little et al. 2003
272 Murray-Close et al. 2006; Werner & Grant 2009
273 Werner & Grant 2009
274 Mason 2008
275 Field & Carroll 2006
276 Pikas 2002

Chapter 23

1 Ginott 1972: 277–8
2 Demaray & Malecki 2002; Demaray et al. 2005; Deslandes et al. 1997; Englund et al. 2004; Fan 2001; Fan & Chen 2001; Feinstein & Symons 1999; Flouri 2006; Flouri et al. 2002; Gonzalez-DeHass et al. 2005; Hill et al. 2004; Izzo et al. 1999; McBride et al. 2005; McWayne et al. 2004b; Marcon 1999; Miedel & Reynolds 1999; Okagaki & Frensch 1998; Paulson 1994; Ratelle et al. 2004; Shumow et al. 1999. It is unlikely that collaboration itself causes these outcomes, however, it may well be that parents who have the skills to forge good relationships with teachers also have children with a similar skill set.
3 O'Connor 2010
4 Lasky 2000
5 Auerbach 2007; Porter 2008b
6 Auerbach 2007; Lasky 2000
7 Osher & Osher 2002; Thompson et al. 1997
8 Osher & Osher 2002
9 Lasky 2000
10 Fylling & Sandvin 1999
11 Daniels & Shumow 2003
12 Lasky 2000
13 Christenson 2004
14 Elliott 2003
15 Lasky 2000
16 Dunst 2002
17 Daniels & Shumow 2003
18 I have even seen signs saying this in schools.
19 Ginsberg & Bronstein 1993; Gottfried et al. 1994; Parker et al. 1999; Shumow & Miller 2001
20 Rimm-Kaufman & Pianta 1999
21 Hill & Taylor 2004; Rimm-Kaufman et al. 2000; Schulting et al. 2005
22 Friend & Cook 2007
23 Tannen 1996, in Osher & Osher 2002
24 Ryan et al. 2010; Hanson et al. 1998
25 Auerbach 2007; Wood & Baker 1999
26 Thompson et al. 1997
27 Grolnick et al. 1997
28 Fan 2001
29 Auerbach 2007; Ho & Willms 1996; Jeynes 2007
30 Grolnick et al. 1997; Ho & Willms 1996
31 Raffaele & Knoff 1999
32 Christenson 2004; Raffaele & Knoff 1999
33 Christenson 2004; Ho & Willms 1996; Overstreet et al. 2005; Raffaele & Knoff 1999
34 Caprara et al. 2003; Garcia 2004
35 Abbott-Shim et al. 2000; Castro et al. 2004; Ghazvini & Readdick 1994
36 Jones & Jones 2013
37 Keyser 2006: 85–86
38 Walker et al. 2010
39 Halle et al. 1997
40 Raffaele & Knoff 1999
41 Miller 2003
42 Berg & Steiner 2003
43 Winslade & Monk 2007: 2
44 Lindsay & Dockrell 2000

45 Berg & Steiner 2003; Murphy 2006; Selekman 2010: 47
46 Selekman 2010: 183–195
47 Freeman et al. 1997
48 Selekman 1997
49 Sheridan 2000
50 Robinson & Aronica 2009: 148
51 Ramirez et al. 1998
52 Berg & Steiner 2003
53 Phoenix 2000
54 M. Rogers 1998
55 Rosin 1996; Salend & Taylor 1993
56 Lynch & Hanson 1996; Salend & Taylor 1993
57 Fisch & Schlanger 1999
58 De Jong & Berg 2002
59 Coots 1998
60 Greenman & Stonehouse 2007
61 Keyser 2006
62 Jones & Jones 2013
63 Swick 2003
64 Penney & Wilgosh 2000
65 Christenson 2004

Chapter 24

1 Hilliard 1985: 22
2 Smith 1990
3 Doherty-Derkowski 1995; Smith 1990
4 Lambert 1994; Lewis 1997; Mill & Romano-White 1999
5 Hargreaves 2000; Oberski et al. 1999; Pianta 1999
6 Pianta & Stuhlman 2004
7 Cattley 2004
8 Hargreaves 2000
9 Hargreaves 2000
10 Collie et al. 2011
11 Collie et al. 2011
12 Collie et al. 2011
13 Carbonneau et al. 2008: 977 & 984
14 Carbonneau et al. 2008: 978
15 Carbonneau et al. 2008: 984
16 Klassen & Chiu 2010; Morris-Rothschild & Brassard 2006; Skaalvik & Skaalvik 2007
17 Klassen & Chiu 2010
18 Wolters & Daugherty 2007
19 Friedman 2003; Skaalvik & Skaalvik 2007: 620; Wolters & Daugherty 2007
20 Klassen & Chiu 2010; Wolters & Daugherty 2007
21 Klassen & Chiu 2010; Wolters & Daugherty 2007
22 Wolters & Daugherty 2007
23 Friedman 2003; O'Connor 2010
24 Morris-Rothschild & Brassard 2006
25 Bandura 1993; Brady & Woolfson 2008; Caprara et al. 2006; Tollefson 2000; Wolters & Daugherty 2007
26 Soodak & Podell 1993
27 O'Connor 2010
28 Bandura 1993; Brady & Woolfson 2008; Caprara et al. 2006; Tollefson 2000; Wolters & Daugherty 2007
29 Kokkinos et al. 2005; Martin et al. 1999; O'Connor 2010
30 Morris-Rothschild & Brassard 2006: 115; Wolters & Daugherty 2007
31 Spilt & Koomen 2009
32 Klassen & Chiu 2010
33 Tollefson 2000
34 Lambert et al. 2009
35 Gibbs & Powell 2011; Skaalvik & Skaalvik 2007: 621
36 Caprara et al. 2003; Skaalvik & Skaalvik 2007
37 Friedman 2003; Goddard et al. 2000
38 Gibbs & Powell 2011
39 White-Smith & White 2009

40 Caprara et al. 2003
41 Caprara et al. 2003
42 Goddard et al. 2000
43 Goddard et al. 2000
44 Bandura 1993; Goddard et al. 2000
45 Goddard et al. 2000: 500
46 Gibbs & Powell 2011
47 Ingersoll 1996
48 Ingersoll 1996
49 Ross & Gray 2006
50 Reitzug 1994
51 Billman 1995; Broinowski & Dau 2004; King et al. 1996; Louis et al. 1996; Nguni et al. 2006; Nupponen 2006; Reitzug 1994; Rodd 2006; Ross & Gray 2006
52 Nupponen 2006
53 Nupponen 2006; Rodd 2006
54 Bambara et al. 2009: 170
55 Klassen & Chiu 2010
56 Galand et al. 2007
57 Gamman 2003
58 Gamman 2003; Nelson et al. 2001
59 Rogers 2002
60 Gamman 2003
61 Gamman 2003
62 Gamman 2003
63 Rogers 2002
64 Roffey 2004
65 Terry 1998
66 Rogers 2002
67 Abbott-Shim et al. 2000; Arnett 1989; Burchinal et al. 2000, 2002; Clarke-Stewart et al. 2002; Howes 1983, 1997; Howes et al. 2003; Phillipsen et al. 1997
68 Greenman & Stonehouse 2007
69 Roth 1989; Smyth 1989
70 Klassen & Chiu 2010
71 Huberman 1989
72 Wehlage et al. 1996b: 265
73 Forman & Barakat 2011; Wehlage et al. 1996b: 266
74 Rich 1990
75 Rich 1990
76 Curbow et al. 2000; Louis et al. 1996; Noble & Macfarlane 2005
77 Wehlage et al. 1996b: 269
78 Doyle 1986
79 Lambert et al. 2009
80 Albrecht et al. 2009; Friedman 2003; Griffith et al. 1999; Klassen & Chiu 2010; Kokkinos 2007: 239; Lambert et al. 2009; Nelson et al. 2001; Santavirta et al. 2007
81 Skaalvik & Skaalvik 2007: 621
82 Skaalvik & Skaalvik 2007: 621–622
83 Gibbs & Powell 2011; Morris-Rothschild & Brassard 2006
84 Mill & Romano-White 1999
85 Albrecht et al. 2009; Klassen & Chiu 2010
86 Galand et al. 2007; Pas et al. 2012
87 Lambert et al. 2009; Pas et al. 2012
88 Whitebook & Sakai 2003
89 Santavirta et al. 2007
90 Lambert et al. 2009
91 Klusmann et al. 2008: 703; Kokkinos 2009; Skaalvik & Skaalvik 2007
92 Klusmann et al. 2008; Skaalvik & Skaalvik 2007
93 Brackett et al. 2010
94 Brackett et al. 2010
95 Klusmann et al. 2008
96 Klusmann et al. 2008
97 Friend & Cook 2007
98 Friend & Cook 2007
99 Brownell et al. 2006

100 Wagner & Gillies 2001
101 McGlone 2001
102 Wagner & Gillies 2001
103 Harker 2001
104 Harker 2001
105 Wagner & Gillies 2001: 156
106 Wagner & Gillies 2001: 157
107 Newmann 1996: 206
108 Noble & Macfarlane 2005
109 Vartuli 1999
110 Roseman 1999
111 Marks et al. 1996a: 218

Chapter 25

 1 Maag 2001: 182
 2 Cowin et al. 1990
 3 Greene 2008: 172
 4 Beets et al. 2008
 5 Cangelosi 2004; Mathieson & Price 2002; Stonehouse
    1991
 6 Forman & Barakat 2011
 7 Handler et al. 2007
 8 Davies 2005
 9 Noble 2006; Rigby 2001; Rodkin & Hodges 2003
10 Louis et al. 1996: 197
11 King et al. 1996
12 King et al. 1996: 250
13 Doane 1996: 77
14 Lencioni 2002
15 Lencioni 2002: 217
16 Lencioni 2002: 211
17 Lencioni 2002
18 Lewis 1997; R. Slee 1995
19 Louis et al. 1996: 181
20 Forman & Barakat 2011
21 Louis 1996: 181
22 Louis 1996: 184
23 McCaslin & Good 1992
24 Davis & Osborn 2000
25 Knight 1991
26 Gamman 2003
27 Payne 2009; Payne & Eckert 2010
28 Louis et al. 1996: 196
29 McIntosh et al. 2010; Payne 2009
30 Payne & Eckert 2010
31 Berkel et al. 2011
32 McConaughy & Leone 2002
33 Borland 2003; Cowin et al. 1990; Sharp & Thompson
    1994
34 Davis & Rimm 2004
35 Mathieson & Price 2002
36 Drifte 2004; Roffey 2004

Index